Multimedia and resources... ready your 21st century course

INTERACTIVE, MEDIA-ENHANCED LECTURES

PowerLecture™

PowerLecture with JoinIn™ and ExamView®

This one-stop resource makes it easy for you to assemble, edit, and present custom lectures for your course:

- **Interactive Book-Specific PowerPoint Lectures** feature outlines specific to each chapter, as well as photos, figures and tables from each chapter of the textbook.

- **Media-Enhanced PowerPoints** include audio and video clips depicting historic and current events; NEW animated learning modules illustrating key concepts; and tables, statistical charts, and photos. The Media-Enhanced PowerPoints can be used on their own or easily integrated with the Book-Specific PowerPoint Outlines.

- **Animated Learning Modules** illustrate key concepts and include tables, statistical charts and graphs, and photos.

- **Videos** feature dozens of current news stories.

- **Instructor's Manual** includes discussion questions, lecture suggestions, and tips on integrating media into your class.

- **JoinIn™ Student Response System** features book-specific clicker questions that test and track student comprehension to give your classroom immediate interactivity.

◄ OPEN

NEW! The ultimate online and media resources for American government

Simulations

In these realistic scenarios, students assume the roles of vice-president, legislators, jurists, and others related to government.

NewsNow

Featuring a current compilation of weekly news stories from the Associated Press with videos and images, NewsNow brings current events to life. For instructors, NewsNow includes a set of multimedia-rich PowerPoint slides posted each week to the password-protected area of the textbook's Instructor Companion Website. You can use these slides to take a class poll or trigger a lively debate about political events happening right now.

CourseMate also includes

• Learning Objectives

• Critical Thinking Activities

• Video Activities

• Audio Summaries

• Interactive Timelines

• Flashcards

ALSO AVAILABLE

CourseReader: American Government

It's easy to create a customized e-reader for your course! With CourseReader's database of hundreds of documents, readings and videos, instructors can search by criteria or browse the collection, to preview and then select a customized collection to assign their students. The sources are edited to an appropriate length and feature pedagogical support, including a headnote describing the document and critical-thinking and multiple-choice questions to verify that the student has read and understood the selection. Students can take notes, highlight and print content.

CourseMate for American Government

A flexible, online course program that motivates every kind of learner!

 CourseMate offers an extensive variety of rich online learning resources designed to enhance the student experience and to help you assess your students' engagement in your course.

Integrated e-Book
Includes highlighting and search capabilities along with links to simulations, Animated Learning Modules, interactive timelines, video activities, primary source quizzes, tutorial quizzes, and flashcards.

Engagement Tracker
A unique, state-of-the-art instructor tool that enables you to assess student preparation and engagement. Use the tracking tools to see progress for the class as a whole or for individual students. Identify students at risk early in the course.

Animated Learning Modules
Great review tools, these modules cover topics such as The Constitution, Civil Liberties, Political Participation, Interest Groups, Congress, and The Presidency.

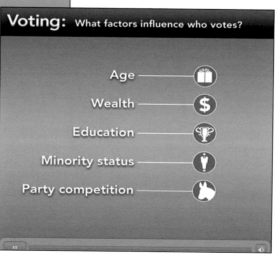

More great resources for your American government course!

WebTutor™ Course Cartridge

Rich with content for your American government course, this Web-based teaching and learning tool includes course management, study/mastery, and communication tools. Use WebTutor™ to provide virtual office hours, post your syllabus, and track student progress with quizzing material. For students, WebTutor offers real-time access to interactive online tutorials and simulations, practice quizzes, and Web links—all correlated to this textbook.

Political Theatre 2.0

Three DVDs show watershed events in American political history, featuring campaign ads, debates and speeches.

- Custom menu allows easy navigation
- Organized chronologically and by theme
- Voiceovers instead of heavy text

The Wadsworth News DVD for American Government 2012

Video supplied by BBC Motion Gallery

One DVD including a variety of two- to four-minute video clips on relevant political issues. Includes:

- The Politics of Health Care Reform
- The Immigration Debate: Undocumented Workers in Arizona
- The Economic Effects of the BP Oil Spill in the Gulf of Mexico
- Tea Party Demonstrators Protest Government Spending and Taxation
- Congresspeople Tweeting to Connect with Constituents

ABC Video: Speeches of President Obama

One DVD includes nine famous speeches by President Obama from 2004 through 2009

- Speeches divided into short segments for easy, time-efficient viewing
- Critical thinking questions and answers for each speech

CourseCare

Our complete post-adoption care program provides expert one-on-one service every step of the way

Available exclusively with Cengage Learning, CourseCare is a revolutionary program that provides you with an unparalleled user experience with our CourseMate products. **Your CourseCare team includes:**

- Digital Solutions Managers who partner with you to understand your unique needs
- TeamUP Service and Training Consultants who work with you, providing online or face-to-face training designed to meet your requirements
- Digital Solutions Coordinators who are your dedicated resources, assuring that your course has a smooth start and stays on target to meet your goals from set-up to student activation, usage reports, and more.

THE SOLUTION

GOVT
Are you in?

CourseMate Engaging. Trackable. Affordable.

CourseMate brings course concepts to life with interactive learning, study, and exam preparation tools that support GOVT3.

FOR INSTRUCTORS:
- First Day of Class Instructions
- Custom options through 4LTR+ Program
- Instructor's Manual
- Test Bank
- PowerPoint Slides
- Tear-out Instructor Prep Cards
- Audio Summaries
- Engagement Tracker

FOR STUDENTS:
- Interactive eBook
- Tutorial Quizzing
- Online Flashcards
- Crossword Puzzles
- PowerPoint Slides
- Videos
- Animated Learning Modules
- Simulations
- Tear-out Student Review Cards
- Web Links
- Audio Summaries

Students sign in at **login.cengagebrain.com**

WADSWORTH
CENGAGE Learning™

GOVT³

Edward Sidlow and **Beth Henschen**

Publisher: Suzanne Jeans

Executive Editor: Carolyn Merrill

Development Editor: Rebecca Green

Associate Development Editor: Kate MacLean

Assistant Editor: Laura Ross

Editorial Assistant: Nina Wasserman

Media Editor: Laura Hildebrand

Senior Marketing Manager: Lydia LeStar

Marketing Communications Manager: Heather Baxley

Marketing Assistant: Josh Hendrick

Content Production Manager: Ann Borman

Print Buyer: Fola Orekoya

Photo Researcher: Anne Sheroff

Copy Editor: Mary Berry

Proofreaders: Judy Kiviat and Loretta Palagi

Indexer: Terry Casey

Art Director: Linda Helcher

Interior Design: Ke Design

Cover Design: Lisa Kuhn

Cover Image Credit: © Getty Images

Compositor: Parkwood Composition

For product information and technology assistance, contact us at **Cengage Learning Academic Resource Center, 1-800-423-0563**

For permission to use material from this text or product, submit all requests online at **www.cengage.com/permissions**
Further permissions questions can be emailed to **permissionrequest@cengage.com**

Library of Congress Control Number: 2010938092

Student Edition ISBN-13: 978-1-111-34247-0
Student Edition ISBN-10: 1-111-34247-4

Instructor's Edition ISBN-13: 978-1-111-34401-6
Instructor's Edition ISBN-10: 1-111-34401-9

Wadsworth Political Science
20 Channel Center
Boston, MA 02210

Cengage Learning products are represented in Canada by Nelson Education, Ltd.

For your course and learning solutions, visit **www.cengage.com.**

Purchase any of our products at your local college store or at our preferred online store at **www.cengagebrain.com.**

Chapter-Opener Photo Credits:
Ch 1: AP Photo/Bradley C Bower.
Ch 2: Steve McAlister/Getty Images.
Ch 3: Robyn Beck/AFP/Getty Images.
Ch 4: Kary Nieuwenhuis/iStockphoto.
Ch 5: Mark Peterson/Redux.
Ch 6: AP Photo/Alastair Grant.
Ch 7: John Moore/Getty Images.
Ch 8: George Frey/Landov.
Ch 9: AP Photo/Morry Gash.
Ch 10: Kevin Lamarque/Reuters/Landov.
Ch 11: Mark Wilson/Getty Images.
Ch 12: Mike Theiler/EPA/Landov.
Ch 13: AP Photo/Manuel Balce Ceneta.
Ch 14: Paul J. Richards/AFP/Getty Images.
Ch 15: Kevin Lamarque/Reuters/Landov.
Ch 16: AP Photo/Andy Wong.

Printed in the United States of America

1 2 3 4 5 6 7 14 13 12 11 10

EDWARD SIDLOW & BETH HENSCHEN

GOVT³

Brief Contents

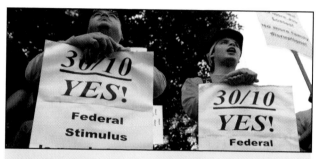

Chapter 3
Federalism 47

2 *Our Liberties and Rights 70*

Chapter 4
Civil Liberties 70

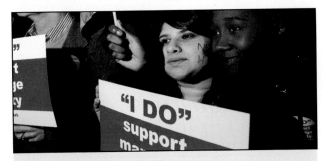

Chapter 5
Civil Rights 93

3 The Politics of Democracy 118

Chapter 6
Interest Groups 118

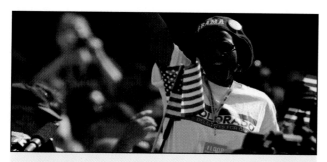

Chapter 7
Political Parties 140

Chapter 8
Public Opinion and Voting 162

Chapter 9
Campaigns and Elections 187

Chapter 10
Politics and the Media 209

4 Institutions 230

Chapter 11
Congress 230

Chapter 12
The Presidency 254

Chapter 13
The Bureaucracy 279

Chapter 14
The Judiciary 302

5 Public Policy 325

Chapter 15
Foreign Policy
Domestic Policy 325

Chapter 16
Foreign Policy 345

Preface

The 2010 congressional elections were expected to be tumultuous and unsettling. They met those expectations, for the Democrats lost a net total of sixty-four seats in the House and six seats in the Senate. Americans—and President Barack Obama among them—find themselves with a divided government. Because the 2010 elections were so important, we have included in this edition a special feature called *Elections 2010*.

Political conflict and divergence of opinion have always characterized our political traditions and way of governing. Nonetheless, our democracy endures, and the U.S. Constitution continues to serve as a model for new democracies around the world. The third edition of GOVT looks at government and politics in this country as a series of conflicts that have led to compromises.

This text was written with today's generation of students in mind. As such, it does the following:

- Provides the historical context for today's most significant political controversies;

- Presents different perspectives on key issues currently being debated;

- Helps students test their beliefs and assumptions and determine their positions on major political issues;

- Assists students in the process of acquiring informed political values and opinions;

- Fully explains major problems facing the American political system; and

- Looks at the global connections between the American political system and the systems of other countries.

New to This Edition

The entire book—including figures, tables, photos, Web sites, and data—has been updated through 2010.

- In Chapter 1, the recent health-care reform is used as an example to illustrate political ideology.

- Chapter 2 contains a new section, *Defining the Executive*, under *Drafting and Ratifying the Constitution*.

- An updated discussion of same-sex marriage and a new section, *Obama and Federalism*, appear in Chapter 3.

- Chapter 4 includes new subsections under *Personal Privacy and National Security: The USA Patriot Act* and *The Civil Liberties Debate*.

- Chapter 5 integrates a new section, *The Feminist Movement*, and includes updated discussions of same-sex marriage and affirmative action.

- Chapter 6 contains a new section *The Constitutional Right to Petition the Government*, a revised look at *Why Interests Groups Form*, and a clarified discussion of the free rider problem. In addition, you will find new sections on rating systems, Astroturf lobbying, *Identity Interest Groups*, and *Ideological Interest Groups*, including a discussion of the Tea Party movement and environmental interest groups.

- Chapter 7 now includes sections called *Triumph of the Jeffersonians*; *Shifting Political Fortunes* (updating the discussion of today's political parties); *Realignment, Dealignment, and Tipping*; *The Parties Return to Their Roots*; and *Duverger's Law*; as well as an expanded discussion of primaries and selecting candidates.

- A new section, *Types of Polls*, and discussion of the accuracy of polling during the 2010 midterm elections appear in Chapter 8.

- Chapter 9 has been thoroughly revised through the 2010 midterm elections and includes new sections: *Primary Voters, Blanket and "Top Two" Primaries*, and *Citizens United v. Federal Election Commission*.

- Chapter 10 integrates new sections *The Media and the First Amendment, The "Wild West" Migrates to Television*, and *Obama's Difficulties*. There is also a new discussion of narrowcasting and an updated section *Political News and Campaigns on the Web*.

- Updates and analysis of the 112th Congress appear in Chapter 11.

- Chapter 12 has been updated throughout to discuss Obama's presidency.

- Chapter 13, on the bureaucracy, has been streamlined, and the revised section *An Expanding Bureaucracy* includes the sections *Expanded Government under President Obama* and *A New Spirit in Congress*.

- Court cases through 2010 and the latest Supreme Court appointments are discussed in Chapter 14.

- Chapter 15 includes an updated and completely revised *Health-Care Policy* section discussing the 2010 legislation, and new sections titled *Nuclear Energy, Offshore Drilling*, and *The BP Oil Spill in the Gulf of Mexico*.

- Chapter 16 includes an updated look at *The War on Terrorism* through 2010—including the troop withdrawal in Iraq and updates on Afghanistan—as well as a new subsection called *Toward New Talks* under *The Israeli-Palestinian Conflict* and an updated discussion of North Korea.

New *Elections 2010* Features

Throughout various chapters, you will find the following *Elections 2010* analyses:

- New Directions for America (Chapter 1)
- Minority Group Members and Women (Chapter 5)
- The Elections and the Parties (Chapter 7)
- Voting by Groups (Chapter 8)
- Campaign Spending (Chapter 9)
- The New Congress (Chapter 11)

New *Our Government Faces a Troubled Economy* Features

The Great Recession officially started in December 2007. Officially, it ended in June 2009, when the economy slowly began to grow again. Even though the Great Recession is technically over, the economy is still extremely troubled. The unemployment rate is above 9.5 percent. Each year the federal government deficit exceeds a trillion dollars. Our new feature for this edition of GOVT is appropriately called *Our Government Faces a Troubled Economy*. Almost every chapter in this edition has this new feature. Here are some examples:

- Printing Money to Fight a Recession (Chapter 2)
- Fighting a Recession with Government Spending (Chapter 3)
- Should We Cut Taxes—and How? (Chapter 11)
- Spending More on Health Care—and Less (Chapter 13)
- Red Ink Forever? (Chapter 15)
- Should We Fight China's Cheap Exports? (Chapter 16)

New *Join the Debate* Features, Too

Most of the popular *Join the Debate* features have been substituted with new debate topics in this edition. Students and instructors will now be able to debate the following:

- Is the Death Penalty a Cruel and Unusual Punishment? (Chapter 2)
- Is Obamacare Constitutional? (Chapter 3)
- Are Admissions to Top Schools Unfair to Asian Americans? (Chapter 5)
- Should D.C. Residents Have a Representative? (Chapter 9)
- Should Judges Be the Ones to Decide Whether Same-Sex Couples Can Marry? (Chapter 14)
- Should Unauthorized Immigrants Be Given a Path to Citizenship? (Chapter 15)

New *America at Odds* Chapter-Opening Features

The majority of chapter-opening *America at Odds* features are new to this edition (and the ones that we have retained have been updated). The new ones include:

- Has Our Government Grown Too Large? (Chapter 1)
- Should the Census Count Be Limited to Citizens? (Chapter 5)
- Is the Republican Party Conservative Enough? (Chapter 7)
- Should Felons Be Allowed to Vote? (Chapter 8)
- Just How Effective Is President Obama? (Chapter 12)
- Do We Send Too Many People to Prison? (Chapter 15)

New *Perception versus Reality* Features

Several of the *Perception versus Reality* features are new to this edition. They include the following:

- Can Congress Really Dig Up Government Corruption? (Chapter 11)
- The Mythical Barack Obama (Chapter 12)
- A United Europe? (Chapter 16)

New *The Rest of the World* Features

Finally, many of *The Rest of the World* features are also new to this edition. They include:

- Fingerprinting 1.1 Billion Citizens of India (Chapter 4)

- Europe's Common Agricultural Policy (Chapter 6)

- Coalition Government in the United Kingdom (Chapter 7)

- Compulsory Voting Elsewhere Improves Voter Turnout (Chapter 9)

- Using Facebook to Organize in Indonesia (Chapter 10)

- The Unusual Role of the French President (Chapter 12)

A Groundbreaking Format

GOVT's daring format has been designed to engage even the most apathetic American government student with its glossy, magazine-style look and dynamic visual appeal. Streamlined, portable, and complete with study resources, this text does more than ever before to accommodate the way students actually use their textbooks. At the same time, our "debate-the-issues" approach effectively involves readers in discussing and debating concepts of American government. **Chapter Review tear-out cards** at the end of the book provide learning objectives with summaries of key concepts, visuals, and key terms for each chapter—making it easier for students to prepare for class and for exams. And because today's students are technologically savvy, we provide **portable study resources in multiple formats** via this text's CourseMate, accessible through CengageBrain. com. Resources there include flashcards, podcasts, chapter reviews, quizzes, and more that students can download whichever way they prefer (cell phone, computer, MP3 files, and so on) in order to study more efficiently. Access to the site is available at no additional cost when packaged with each student text.

Features That Teach

As exciting as the innovative new GOVT format may be, we have not lost sight of the essential goals and challenges of teaching American government. Any American government text must present the basics of the American political process and its institutions, and it must excite and draw the student into the *subject*.

Additionally, we present many of today's controversial political issues in special features. Each of the more than one hundred features contained in the text covers a topic of high interest to students. GOVT includes the following different types of features, in addition to the features outlined earlier:

- *Learning Objectives*—Every chapter-opening page includes a list of three or more Learning Objectives that lets students know what concepts will be covered in the chapter. Each Learning Objective has an identifying number (such as LO1 or LO2). The same number also precedes the major heading of the chapter section in which that topic is presented. This allows students to quickly locate where in the chapter a particular topic is discussed.

- **Chapter-ending** *America at Odds* **feature**—This feature often opens with a general discussion of the historical evolution of the aspect of government addressed in the chapter. When relevant, the founders' views and expectations relating to the topic are set forth and then compared with the actual workings of our political system in that area today. This part of the feature is designed to indicate how American politics and government currently measure up to the expectations of the founders or to those of today's Americans. Following this discussion, we present questions for debate and discussion. Each question briefly outlines two sides of a current political controversy and then asks the student to identify her or his position on the issue. The feature closes with a "Take Action" section that offers tips to students on what they can do to make a difference in an area of interest to them.

- *Politics on the Web*—This section gives selected Web sites that students can access for more information on issues discussed in the chapter.

- *CourseMate*—This section directs students to the text's companion Web site, where they can find additional resources for the chapter.

Versions

- **GOVT 3e, California Version**
  ISBN-10: 1-111-34307-1 | ISBN-13: 978-1-111-34307-1
  Ten additional chapters by Larry Gerston and Terry Christensen cover California politics, including updated content on the current economy.

- **GOVT 3e, Texas Version—Custom Preset**
  ISBN-10: 1-111-77357-2 | ISBN-13: 978-1-111-77357-1
  This custom product includes ten additional chapters on Texas politics.

Supplements

Both instructors and students today expect, and indeed require, a variety of accompanying supplements to teach and learn about American government. GOVT takes the lead in providing the most comprehensive and user-friendly supplements package on the market today.

On **CengageBrain.com** students are able to save up to 60 percent of the cost of their course materials through our full spectrum of options. Students will have the option to rent their textbooks or purchase print textbooks, e-textbooks, or individual e-chapters and audio-books, all at substantial savings over average retail prices. CengageBrain.com also includes access to Cengage Learning's broad range of homework and study tools, including the student resources discussed here. Follow the URL below to access the book-specific resources.

For further information on any of these supplements, contact your Wadsworth, Cengage Learning sales representative.

CourseMate

Go to **cengagebrain.com/shop/ISBN/1111342474** to access your *Political Science CourseMate* resources.

■ **CourseMate**
At the beginning and end of every chapter, you will see the CourseMate icon as a reminder to students to use its wealth of online resources to check their understanding of the chapter and further explore its key concepts.

This media-rich Web site offers a variety of online resources designed to enhance the student learning experience. These resources include video activities, audio summaries, critical-thinking exercises, simulations, animated learning modules, interactive time lines, primary source quizzes, flashcards, learning objectives, glossaries, and crossword puzzles. Chapter resources are correlated to key chapter learning concepts, and users can browse or search for content in a variety of ways.

NewsNow is a new asset available in CourseMate. It is a combination of weekly new stories from the Associated Press and videos and images that bring current events to life for the student. For instructors, NewsNow includes an additional set of multimedia-rich PowerPoint slides posted each week to the password-protected area of the text's instructor companion Web site.

Instructors may use these slides to take a class poll or trigger a lively debate about the events that are shaping the world right now.

The **Engagement Tracker** assesses student preparation and engagement. Use the tracking tools to see progress for the class as a whole or for individual students. Identify students at risk early in the course. Uncover which concepts are most difficult for your class. Monitor time on task. Keep your students engaged.

Coursemate also features an **interactive eBook** that has highlighting and search capabilities, along with links to simulations, animated PowerPoints that illustrate concepts, interactive time lines, video activities, primary source quizzes, and flashcards.

■ **PowerLecture DVD with JoinIn™ and ExamView®**
ISBN-10: 1-111-34252-0 | ISBN-13: 978-1-111-34252-4
This DVD includes two sets of PowerPoint slides—a book-specific and a media-enhanced set; a test bank in both Microsoft Word and ExamView formats; an *Instructor's Manual*; JoinIn "clicker" questions; and a *Resource Integration Guide*.

- **Interactive book-specific PowerPoint® lectures** make it easy for you to assemble, edit, publish, and present book-specific lectures for your course. You will have access to outlines specific to each chapter of the text, as well as photos, figures, and tables found in the text.

- **Media-enhanced PowerPoint slides** can be used on their own or easily integrated with the book-specific PowerPoint outlines. Look for audio and video clips depicting both historic and current-day events; animated learning modules illustrating key concepts; tables, statistical charts, and graphs; and photos from the book. Outside sources also are provided at the appropriate places in the chapter.

- **Test bank in Microsoft® Word and ExamView® computerized testing** offers a large array of well-crafted multiple-choice and essay questions, along with their answers and page references.

- *Instructor's Manual* includes learning objectives, chapter outlines, discussion questions, suggestions for stimulating class activities and projects, tips on integrating media into your class (including step-by-step instructions on how to create your own podcasts), suggested readings and Web resources, and a section specially designed to help teaching assistants and adjunct instructors.

- **JoinIn™ "clicker" questions** test and track student comprehension of key concepts.

- **Resource Integration Guide** outlines the rich collection of resources available to instructors and students within the chapter-by-chapter framework of the book, suggesting how and when each supplement can be used to optimize learning.

■ **American Government CourseReader**
Printed Text + CourseReader Printed Access Card: ISBN-10: 1-111-65357-7 | ISBN-13: 978-1-111-65357-6
This product allows instructors to create a customized reader using a database of hundreds of documents, readings, and videos. Instructors can search by various criteria or browse the collection in order to preview and then select a customized collection to assign to their students. The sources are edited to an appropriate length and include pedagogical support—a headnote describing the document and critical-thinking and multiple-choice questions to verify that the student has read and understood the selection. Students can take notes, highlight, and print content. The CourseReader allows the instructor to select exactly what students will be assigned with an easy-to-use interface and also provides an easily used assessment tool. The sources can be delivered online or in print format.

■ **Instructor Companion Web Site**
The instructor Companion Web site includes the Instructor's Manual; text-specific PowerPoints containing lecture outlines, photos, and figures; and NewsNow PowerPoints.

■ **WebTutor™ on WebCT or Blackboard**
Printed Text + WebCT Printed Access Card: ISBN-10: 1-111-64918-9 | ISBN-13: 978-1-111-64918-0
Printed Text + Blackboard Printed Access Card: ISBN-10: 1-111-64935-9 | ISBN-13: 978-1-111-64935-7
Rich with content for your American government course, this Web-based teaching and learning tool includes course management, study/mastery, and communication tools. Use WebTutor to provide virtual office hours, post your syllabus, and track student progress with WebTutor's quizzing material.

■ **CourseCare**
Available exclusively to Cengage Learning, CourseCare is a revolutionary program designed to provide you and your students an unparalleled user experience with your Cengage Learning digital solution.
CourseCare connects you with a team of training, service, and support experts to help you implement your Cengage Learning Digital Solution. This means real people dedicated to you, your students, and your course from the first day of class through final exams.

■ **Political Theatre 2.0**
ISBN-10: 0-495-79360-4 | ISBN-13: 978-0-495-79360-1
Bring politics home to students with Political Theatre 2.0, which is up-to-date through the 2008 election season. This is the second edition of this three-DVD series and includes real video clips that show American political thought throughout the public sector. Clips include both classic and contemporary political advertisements, speeches, interviews, and more.

■ **JoinIn™ on Turning Point® for Political Theatre**
ISBN-10: 0-495-09550-8 | ISBN-13: 978-0-495-09550-7
For even more interaction, combine Political Theatre with the innovative teaching tool of a classroom response system through JoinIn. Poll your students with questions created for you, or create your own questions.

■ **Wadsworth News Videos for American Government 2012 DVD**
ISBN-10: 1-111-34614-3 | ISBN-13: 978-1-111-34614-0
This collection of three- to six-minute video clips on relevant political issues serves as a great lecture or discussion launcher.

■ **Great Speeches Collection**
Throughout the ages, great orators have stepped up to the podium and used their communication skills to persuade, inform, and inspire their audiences. Studying these speeches can provide tremendous insight into historical, political, and cultural events. The Great Speeches Collection includes the full text of over sixty memorable orations for you to incorporate into your course. Speeches can be collated in a printed reader to supplement your existing course materials or bound into a core textbook.

■ **ABC Video: Speeches by President Barack Obama**
ISBN-10: 1-439-08247-2 | ISBN-13: 9781439082478
This DVD of nine famous speeches by President Barack Obama, from 2004 through his inauguration, includes his speech at the 2004 Democratic National Convention; his 2008 speech on race, "A More Perfect Union"; and his 2009 inaugural address. Speeches are divided into short video segments for easy, time-efficient viewing. This instructor supplement also features critical-thinking questions and answers for each speech, designed to spark classroom discussion.

■ **Election 2010: An American Government Supplement**
Text + Election 2010 supplement: ISBN-10: 1-111-87232-5 | ISBN-13: 978-1-111-87232-8

Written by John Clark and Brian Schaffner, this booklet addresses the 2010 congressional and gubernatorial races, with both real-time analysis and references.

■ **Latino-American Politics Supplement**
Text + Latino-American Politics supplement: ISBN-10: 1-111-87233-3 | ISBN-13: 978-1-111-87233-5 This thirty-two-page supplement uses real examples to detail politics related to Latino Americans.

■ **Instructor's Guide to YouTube for Political Science** Instructors have access to the Instructor's Guide to YouTube, which shows American government instructors where they can look on the Internet to find videos that can be used as learning tools in class. Organized by fifteen topics, the guide follows the sequence of an American government course and includes a Preface with tips on how to use Internet videos in class.

Acknowledgments

A number of political scientists have reviewed GOVT, and we are indebted to them for their thoughtful suggestions on how to create a text that best suits the needs of today's students and faculty.

Anita Anderson
University of Alabama

Kimberly Arvanigian
California State University, Fresno

Yan Bai
Grand Rapids Community College

Janet Barton
Mineral Area College

Catherine Bottrell
Tarrant County College

J. St. Lawrence Brown
Spokane Community College

Michael Ceriello
Clark College

Andrew Civettini
Knox College

Frank DeCaria
West Virginia Northern
Community College

Robert De Luna
St. Philip's College

Henry Esparza
University of Texas at San Antonio
and Northeast Lakeview College

Shawn Fonville
Western Texas College

Barry D. Friedman
North Georgia College &
State University

Michael Gattis
Gulf Coast Community College

Arie Halachmi
Tennessee State University

Jack Hames
Butte College

Jeff Harmon
University of Texas
at San Antonio

David M. Head
John Tyler
Community College

Steve Hoggard
Chowan University

Kristen Huyck
Mt. San Jacinto
Community College,
Mira Costa Community College
and Anthem Online College

Jose Luis Irizarry
St. Francis College

Jean Gabriel Jolivet
Southwestern College

Michael Kanner
University of Colorado

David R. Katz III
Mohawk Valley
Community College

Christine Kelleher
University of Michigan

Sean Kelly
Cal State University
Channel Islands

John Kerr
University of Arkansas

Jeffrey Kraus
Wagner College

Kevin Lasher
Francis Marion University

William Lester
Jacksonville State University

William D. Madlock
University of Memphis

Khalil Marrar
DePaul University and
The University of Chicago

Matthew McNiece
Howard Payne University

Gay Michele
El Centro College

Amy Miller
Western Kentucky University

Eric Miller
Blinn College–Bryan

Kathleen Murnan
Ozarks Technical
Community College

Leah A. Murray
Weber State University

Jalal Nejad
Northwest Vista College

Joseph L. Overton
Kapiolani Community College

James Peterson
Valdosta State University

Daniel Ponder
Drury University

Brett Ramsey
Austin Peay State University

Rob Robinson
University of Alabama–Birmingham

Cy Rosenblatt
University of Mississippi

Robert Sahr
Oregon State University

John Shively
Longview Community College

Susan Siemens
Ozarks Technical
Community College

Frank Signorile
Campbell University

Chris Sixta-Rinehart
Francis Marion University

Robert Sullivan
Dallas Baptist University

Gerald Watkins
West Kentucky Community
and Technical College

Stephen Wiener
UC Santa Barbara

Donald C. Williams
Western New England College

Bruce M. Wilson
University of Central Florida

Robert S. Wood
University of North Dakota

Mary Young
Southwestern Michigan College

Maryann Zihala
Ozarks Technical
Community College

Our styles of teaching and mentoring students were shaped in important ways by our graduate faculty at The Ohio State University. We especially thank Lawrence Baum, Herbert Asher, Elliot Slotnick, and Randall Ripley for lessons well taught. Our colleagues Will McLauchlan (Purdue University) and Barry Pyle (Eastern Michigan University) continue, by their actions, to remind us that the learning environment extends well beyond the classroom. The students we have had the privilege of working with at many fine universities have also taught us a great deal. Of course, we owe an immeasurable debt to our families, whose divergent views on political issues reflect an America at odds.

We thank Jonathan Hulbert, president of Cengage Learning Arts and Sciences, for all of his encouragement and support throughout our work on this project. We were also fortunate to have the editorial advice of Carolyn Merrill, executive editor. We are grateful for the assistance of Rebecca Green, our developmental editor, who supervised all aspects of the text and carefully read the page proofs. We thank Laura Ross, assistant editor, for her coordination of the supplements and related items; Laura Hildebrand and Kate MacLean for their work on the CourseMate; and Nina Wasserman for her editorial assistance. We thank Gregory Scott for his tremendous help in researching the project and for his copyediting and proofreading assistance. We also thank Roxie Lee for her project management and other assistance that ensured a timely and accurate text. The copyediting services of Mary Berry and the proofreading by Judy Kiviat and Lorretta Palagi will not go unnoticed. We are also grateful to Sue Jasin of K&M Consulting.

We are especially indebted to the staff at Parkwood Composition. Their ability to generate the pages for this text quickly and accurately made it possible for us to meet our ambitious schedule. Ann Borman and Ann Sheroff, our cheerful content project managers at Cengage Learning, made sure that all the pieces came together accurately, attractively, and on time. We appreciate the enthusiasm of Lydia LeStar, Heather Baxley, and Josh Hendrick, our hardworking marketing and communications managers and marketing coordinator. We thank Ann Hoffman for her accurate photo research. We would also like to acknowledge Linda Helcher, art director, for her part in producing the most attractive and user-friendly American government text on the market today.

If you or your students have ideas or suggestions, we would like to hear from you. You can e-mail our marketing manager, Lydia, at lydia.lestar@cengage.com, or send us information through Wadsworth, a part of Cengage Learning. Our Web site is **www.cengage.com/political science.**

E.I.S.
B.M.H.

America in the
Twenty-First Century

LEARNING OBJECTIVES

LO1 Explain what is meant by the terms *politics* and *government*.

LO2 Identify the various types of government systems.

LO3 Summarize some of the basic principles of American democracy and the basic American political values.

LO4 Describe how the various topics discussed in this text relate to the "big picture" of American politics and government.

AMERICA AT ODDS

Has Our Government Grown Too Large?

For much of America's history, there was little discussion about whether our government had grown too large. The government, after all, wasn't that big. Since the Great Depression of the 1930s, however, the government has grown by leaps and bounds. Still, only fifteen years ago, President Bill Clinton (1993–2001) pronounced that the "era of big government is over." In fact, the share of U.S. economic activity accounted for by government fell from 1995 through 2000. Today, in contrast, we have seen one of the biggest increases in size of the federal government ever. The value of all federal, state, and local government spending now exceeds 40 percent of the nation's total annual income.

Americans are at odds over the proper size of government. The so-called Tea Party protesters have one basic complaint, expressed in the slogan "Born free, taxed to death." Their opponents, however, believe that the government must be large to address the nation's problems.

Government Must Put On the Golden Straitjacket

Those who oppose the growth of government contend that too much of a good thing can become bad. Every government program to help a specific group starts out with good intentions and certainly does help many people in need of, for example, medical care or better education. The problem is that once government programs are in place, they expand. The result is an "assisted society." Opponents of big government believe that too many people spend too much time seeking government assistance rather than taking care of their problems by themselves or with the help of family and friends.

Conservative economists contend that the growth of government must soon lead to higher taxes. So far, the increases in federal government spending have meant larger budget deficits rather than increased taxes. The government has simply borrowed what it needs. These conservative economists, however, argue that this new government borrowing means that there are fewer funds available for private individuals and businesses to borrow. Moreover, they say, the higher taxes that will eventually be needed will reduce people's incentives to work and to invest, now and in the future. Ultimately, that means less economic growth.

Small May Be Beautiful, but Big Government Is Necessary

Liberal economists believe that these conservative arguments are wrong and that in a recession, government deficits put people back to work. More generally, supporters of an active government say that we have big government for a reason—we are a big country with big problems. Just think of some of them:

- Tens of millions of Americans live below the poverty line.
- Many Americans, especially poor Americans, receive inadequate medical care.
- Unsupervised investment banks created the biggest financial meltdown since the Great Depression.
- Our nation's youth are performing poorly on standardized tests.

How are we to solve these problems and thousands of others? Those who defend government believe that we cannot address these issues by reducing the size of government. If we leave everything to an unregulated, uncontrolled free market, we will have more poor people, more sick people, and more unscrupulous business activities.

Europeans have long understood this. European governments not only have greater control of their economies but also devote more resources to social solidarity. Consequently, they have less income inequality and more fairness. That is where America should be heading.

WHERE DO YOU STAND?

1. Is big government necessary in times of crisis, such as the terrorist attacks of 9/11, the Great Recession that began in December 2007, and the BP oil catastrophe in the Gulf of Mexico? Explain your answer.
2. Would you favor a law that reduced the budget of every federal, state, and local agency by, say, 15 percent? What would be the consequences? Who would gain?

EXPLORE THIS ISSUE ONLINE

- The issue of big government divides conservatives and liberals. One of the most prominent conservative Web sites is www.nationalreview.com, sponsored by the magazine *National Review*. For a top liberal site, consider the Daily Kos at www.dailykos.com.

Introduction

Regardless of how Americans feel about government, one thing is certain: they can't live without it. James Madison (1751–1836) once said, "If men were angels, no government would be necessary." Today, his statement still holds true. People are not perfect. People need an organized form of government and a set of rules by which to live.

Note, though, that even if people were perfect, they would still need to establish rules to guide their behavior. They would somehow have to agree on how to divide up a society's resources, such as its land, among themselves and how to balance individual needs and wants against those of society generally. These perfect people would also have to decide *how* to make these decisions. They would need to create a process for making rules and a form of government to enforce those rules. It is thus not difficult to understand why government is one of humanity's oldest and most universal **institutions.** No society has existed without some form of government. The need for authority and organization will never disappear.

As you will read in this chapter, a number of different systems of government exist in the world today. In the United States, we have a democracy in which decisions about pressing issues ultimately are made by the people's representatives in government. Because people rarely have identical thoughts and feelings about issues, it is not surprising that in any democracy citizens are often at odds over many political and social issues, including the very size of government as discussed in the chapter-opening feature. Throughout this book, you will read about contemporary issues that have brought various groups of Americans into conflict with one another.

Differences in opinion are part and parcel of a democratic government. Ultimately, these differences are resolved, one way or another, through the American political process and our government institutions.

"THE ULTIMATE RULERS

of our democracy are . . . the voters of this country."

~ FRANKLIN D. ROOSEVELT ~
THIRTY-SECOND PRESIDENT
OF THE UNITED STATES
1933–1945

LO1 What Are Politics and Government?

Politics means many things to many people. To some, politics is an expensive and extravagant game played in Washington, D.C., in state capitols, and in city halls, particularly during election time. To others, politics involves all of the tactics and maneuvers carried out by the president and Congress. Most formal definitions of politics, however, begin with the assumption that **social conflict**—disagreements among people in a society over what the society's priorities should be—is inevitable. Conflicts will naturally arise over how the society should use its scarce resources and who should receive various benefits, such as wealth, status, health care, and higher education. Resolving such conflicts is the essence of **politics.** Political scientist Harold Lasswell perhaps said it best

Demonstrators hold signs at a Tea Party rally at Freedom Plaza on tax day in Washington on April 15, 2010.

ROGER L. WOLLENBERG/UPI/LANDOV

institution An ongoing organization that performs certain functions for society.

social conflict Disagreements among people in a society over what the society's priorities should be when distributing scarce resources.

politics The process of resolving conflicts over how society should use its scarce resources and who should receive various benefits, such as public health care and public higher education. According to Harold Lasswell, politics is the process of determining "who gets what, when, and how" in a society.

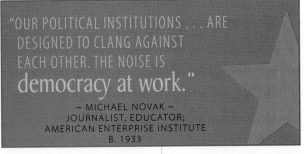

"OUR POLITICAL INSTITUTIONS . . . ARE DESIGNED TO CLANG AGAINST EACH OTHER. THE NOISE IS **democracy at work."**

~ MICHAEL NOVAK ~
JOURNALIST, EDUCATOR;
AMERICAN ENTERPRISE INSTITUTE
B. 1933

when he defined politics as the process of determining "who gets what, when, and how" in a society.[1]

There are also many different notions about the meaning of government. From the perspective of political science, though, **government** can best be defined as the individuals and institutions that make society's rules and that also possess the *power* and *authority* to enforce those rules. Although this definition of government sounds remote and abstract, what the government does is very real indeed. As one scholar put it, "Make no mistake. What Congress does directly and powerfully affects our daily lives."[2] The same can be said for decisions made by state legislators and local government officials, as well as for decisions rendered by the courts—the judicial branch of government.

Of course, a key question remains: How do specific individuals obtain the power and authority to govern? As you will read shortly, the answer to this question varies from one type of political system to another.

To understand what government is, you need to understand what it actually does for people and society. Generally, in any country government serves at least three essential purposes: (1) it resolves conflicts, (2) it provides public services, and (3) it defends the nation and its culture against attacks by other nations.

Resolving Conflicts

Even though people have lived together in groups since the beginning of time, none of these groups has been free of social conflict. As mentioned, disputes over how to distribute a society's resources inevitably arise because valued resources, such as property, are limited, while people's wants are unlimited. To resolve such disputes, people need ways to determine who wins and who loses, and how to get the losers to accept those decisions. Who has the legitimate power—the authority—to make such decisions? This is where government steps in.

Governments decide how conflicts will be resolved so that public order can be maintained. Governments have **power**—the ability to influence the behavior of others. Power is getting someone to do something that he or she would not otherwise do. Power may involve the use of force (often called coercion), persuasion, or rewards. Governments typically also have **authority,** which they can exercise only if their power is legitimate. As used here, the term *authority* means power that is collectively recognized and accepted by society as legally and morally correct. Power and authority are central to a government's ability to resolve conflicts by making and enforcing laws, placing limits on what people can do, and developing court systems to make final decisions.

For example, the judicial branch of government—specifically, the United States Supreme Court—resolved the highly controversial question of whether the Second Amendment to the Constitution grants individuals the right to bear arms. In 2008 and 2010, the Court affirmed that such a right does exist. Because of the Court's stature and authority as a government body, there was little resistance to its decision, even from gun control advocates.

Providing Public Services

Another important purpose of government is to provide **public services**—essential services that many individuals cannot provide for themselves. Governments undertake projects that individuals usually would not or could not carry out on their own, such as building and maintaining roads, providing welfare programs, operating public schools, and preserving national parks. Governments also provide such services as law enforcement, fire protection, and public health and safety programs. As Abraham Lincoln once stated:

> The legitimate object of government is to do for a community of people, whatever they need to have done, but cannot do, *at all,* or cannot, *so well* do, for themselves—in their separate, individual capacities. In all that the people can individually do as well for themselves, government ought not to interfere.[3]

Some public services are provided equally to all citizens of the United States. For example, government services such as national defense and domestic law enforcement allow all citizens, at least in theory, to feel that their lives and property are safe. Laws governing clean air and safe drinking water benefit all Americans. Other services are provided only to citizens who are in need at a particular time, even though they are paid for by all citizens through taxes. Examples of such services include health and welfare benefits, as well as public housing. Laws such as the Americans with Disabilities Act explicitly protect the rights of people with disabilities, although all Americans pay for such protections whether they have disabilities or not.

One of the most crucial public services that the government is expected to provide is protection from hardship caused by economic recessions or depressions. In recent years, this governmental objective has become more important than almost any other, due to the severity of the recession that began in December 2007. We introduce some of the steps the federal government has taken to combat the recession in this chapter's *Our Government Faces a Troubled Economy* feature on the following page. Additional features throughout the book will supply greater detail.

Defending the Nation and Its Culture

Historically, matters of national security and defense have been given high priority by governments and have demanded considerable time, effort, and expense. The U.S. government provides for the common defense and national security with its Army, Navy, Marines, Air Force, and Coast Guard. The departments of State, Defense, and Homeland Security, plus the Central Intelligence Agency, National Security Agency, and other agencies, also contribute to this defense network.

As part of an ongoing policy of national security, many departments and agencies in the federal government are constantly dealing with other nations. The Constitution gives our national government exclusive power over relations with foreign nations. No individual state can negotiate a treaty with a foreign nation.

Of course, in defending the nation against attacks by other nations, a government helps to preserve the nation's culture, as well as its integrity as an independent unit. Failure to defend successfully against foreign attacks may have significant consequences for a nation's culture. For example, consider what happened in Tibet in the 1950s. When that country was taken over by the People's Republic of China, the conquering Chinese set out on a systematic program, the effective

"In all that the people can individually do as well for themselves,
GOVERNMENT OUGHT NOT TO INTERFERE."

~ ABRAHAM LINCOLN ~
SIXTEENTH PRESIDENT OF THE UNITED STATES
1861–1865

result of which was to destroy Tibet's culture.

Since the terrorist attacks on the World Trade Center and the Pentagon in 2001, defending the homeland against future terrorist attacks has become a priority of our government.

Why Politics Matters to You

As the last few pages have shown, the government performs a wide range of functions that are of extreme importance. From the time we are born until the day we die, we constantly interact with various levels of government. Most (although not all) students attend government-run schools. All of us travel on government-owned streets and highways. Many of us serve in the military—a completely government-controlled environment. A few of us get into trouble and meet up with the government's law enforcement system.

All of us pay substantial sums in taxes. Every citizen can expect the government to help with medical and living expenses after reaching the age of sixty-five. As the new health-care reform system kicks in, the government will eventually ensure that the medical needs of all citizens are met, regardless of age or income.

In a representative democracy such as ours, it is politics that controls what the government decides to do. As discussed in this chapter's opening feature, *America at Odds*, the question is, how big should the government be? What combination of taxes and services is best? Should industries such as agriculture and alternative energy be subsidized? When should our leaders use military force against foreign nations or rebellions in foreign countries? How the nation answers these and many other questions will have a major impact on your life—and participation in politics is the only way you can influence what happens.

LO2 *Different Systems of Government*

Through the centuries, the functions of government just discussed have been performed by many different types of government structures. A government's structure is influenced by a number of factors,

OUR GOVERNMENT FACES A
TROUBLED ECONOMY

Making and Fixing an Economic Mess

In recent years, we have witnessed what has been called the Great Recession—the worst economic downturn since the Great Depression of the 1930s. One of the goals of government, as stated in the Preamble to the U.S. Constitution, is "to promote the general Welfare." Maintaining economic prosperity is about as close as you can get to promoting the general welfare.

The Great Depression Was Really Bad

The Great Depression began in 1929. By 1933, the rate of unemployment hit 25 percent, and economic output had dropped by over a third. Republican Herbert Hoover, president until 1933, was voted out of office because the public considered his response to the crisis to be inadequate. The new Democratic president—Franklin D. Roosevelt—undertook a huge number of initiatives, known as the New Deal. Some of these measures helped relieve the suffering of the unemployed and the poor, but they did not pull us out of the Great Depression. That happened later.

Fast-Forward to the Great Recession

From 2002 to 2007, the United States experienced a boom. Credit was easy—Americans with low incomes were able to buy houses with borrowed money at low initial interest rates. But what goes up can come down. The first danger signs appeared in 2006, when housing prices, which had been rising fast, began to fall. By 2007, many people were unable to make payments on their mortgages. Investments based on mortgages lost value. By 2008, major investment firms were failing. On September 15, 2008, Lehman Brothers, a major investment bank, failed. Panic ensued. Banks refused to lend to each other, for fear that they would not get their money back. As the financial markets froze up, our government decided that it had to step in.

Our Modern Government Responds to an Economic Crisis

The government's reaction was far faster than in the 1930s and much more sweeping. Hank Paulson, Treasury secretary under President George W. Bush, obtained $700 billion from Congress for the Troubled Asset Relief Program (TARP), which made large loans to troubled banks—the famous "bank bailout." After Barack Obama became president in 2009, he won from Congress a stimulus package made up of spending increases and tax cuts initially valued at $787 billion.

Ben Bernanke, the head of our central bank—the Federal Reserve, or Fed—also did his part. Bernanke knew that one of the chief causes of the Great Depression was that the Fed let the nation's money supply collapse. This shortage of money choked the life out of the economy. Bernanke once said that he would do anything to prevent another depression, even if it meant shoveling money out of helicopters. This earned him the nickname "Helicopter Ben." After September 2008, Helicopter Ben was true to his word. The Fed loaned out about $1.5 trillion in freshly created money through a dozen new programs.

Were These Responses the Right Way to Go?

The responses were huge, but were they the correct policy? In time, the Great Recession would end. What about the legacy of the government's actions? In 2009, the difference between the federal government's revenues and income—the deficit—jumped by a trillion dollars in one year. By mid-2010, conservative Democrats in Congress, frightened by the deficit, were joining with Republicans to block new spending. Briefly, they even refused to extend unemployment benefits, despite job seekers outnumbering job postings by five to one. One concern was that all the new money might eventually lead to inflation (a sustained rise in prices). There were few signs of such a problem in 2010, though.

You Be the Judge When economic times are tough, how do you react? Does the federal government react differently? Why or why not?

such as a country's history, customs, values, geography, resources, and human experiences and needs. No two nations have exactly the same form of government. Over time, however, political analysts have developed ways to classify different systems of government. One of the most meaningful ways is according to *who* governs. Who has the power to make the rules and laws that all must obey?

Rule by One: Autocracy

In an **autocracy,** the power and authority of the government are in the hands of a single person. At one time, autocracy was a common form of government, and it still exists in some parts of the world. Autocrats usually obtain their power either by inheriting it or by force.

MONARCHY One form of autocracy, known as a **monarchy,** is government by a king, queen, emperor, empress, tsar, or tsarina. In a monarchy, the monarch, who usually acquires power through inheritance, is the highest authority in the government.

Historically, many monarchies were *absolute monarchies,* in which the ruler held complete and unlimited power. Until the eighteenth century, the theory of divine right was widely accepted in Europe. The **divine right theory,** variations of which had existed since ancient times, held that God gave those of royal birth the unlimited right to govern other men and women. In other words, those of royal birth had a "divine right" to rule, and only God could judge them. Thus, all citizens were bound to obey their monarchs, no matter how unfair or unjust they seemed to be. Challenging this power was regarded not only as treason against the government but also as a sin against God.

Most modern monarchies, however, are *constitutional monarchies,* in which the monarch shares governmental power with elected lawmakers. Over time, the monarch's power has come to be limited, or checked, by other government leaders and perhaps by a constitution or a bill of rights. Most constitutional monarchs today serve merely as ceremonial leaders of their nations, as in Spain, Sweden, and the United Kingdom (Britain).

DICTATORSHIP Another form of autocracy is a **dictatorship,** in which a single leader rules, although not typically through inheritance. Dictators gain supreme power by using force, often by overthrowing another dictator or leader. Dictators hold absolute power and are not accountable to anyone else.

A dictatorship can also be *totalitarian,* which means that a leader (or group of leaders) seeks to control almost all aspects of social and economic life. The needs of the nation come before the needs of individuals, and all citizens must work for the common goals established by the government. Examples of this form of government include Adolf Hitler's Nazi regime in Germany from 1933 to 1945, Benito Mussolini's rule in Italy from 1923 to 1943, and Joseph Stalin's dictatorship in the Soviet Union from 1929 to 1953. More contemporary examples of totalitarian dictators include Fidel Castro in Cuba, Kim Jong Il in North Korea, and, until his government was dismantled in 2003, Saddam Hussein in Iraq.

KAL, THE ECONOMIST, LONDON, ENGLAND/CARTOON ARTS INTERNATIONAL/THE NEW YORK TIMES SYNDICATE.

autocracy A form of government in which the power and authority of the government are in the hands of a single person.

monarchy A form of autocracy in which a king, queen, emperor, empress, tsar, or tsarina is the highest authority in the government; monarchs usually obtain their power through inheritance.

divine right theory The theory that a monarch's right to rule was derived directly from God rather than from the consent of the people.

dictatorship A form of government in which absolute power is exercised by a single person who usually has obtained his or her power by the use of force.

democracy A system of government in which the people have ultimate political authority. The word is derived from the Greek *demos* ("the people") and *kratia* ("rule").

direct democracy A system of government in which political decisions are made by the people themselves rather than by elected representatives. This form of government was practiced in some parts of ancient Greece.

representative democracy A form of democracy in which the will of the majority is expressed through smaller groups of individuals elected by the people to act as their representatives.

republic Essentially, a representative democracy in which there is no king or queen and the people are sovereign.

Rule by the Many: Democracy

The most familiar form of government to Americans is **democracy,** in which the supreme political authority rests with the people. The word *democracy* comes from the Greek *demos,* meaning "the people," and *kratia,* meaning "rule." The main idea of democracy is that government exists only by the consent of the people and reflects the will of the majority.

THE ATHENIAN MODEL OF DIRECT DEMOCRACY

Democracy as a form of government began long ago. In its earliest form, democracy was simpler than the system we know today. What we now call **direct democracy** exists when the people participate directly in government decision making. In its purest form, direct democracy was practiced in Athens and other ancient Greek city-states about 2,500 years ago. Every Athenian citizen participated in the governing assembly and voted on all major issues. Although some consider the Athenian form of direct democracy ideal because it demanded a high degree of citizen participation, others point out that most residents in the Athenian city-state (women, foreigners, and slaves) were not deemed to be citizens and thus were not allowed to participate in government.

Clearly, direct democracy is possible only in small communities in which citizens can meet in a chosen place and decide key issues and policies. Nowhere in the world does pure direct democracy exist today. Some New England towns, though, and a few of the smaller political subunits, or cantons, of Switzerland still use a modified form of direct democracy.

REPRESENTATIVE DEMOCRACY Although the founders of the United States were aware of the Athenian model and agreed that government should be based on the consent of the governed, they believed that direct democracy would deteriorate into mob rule. They thought that large groups of people meeting together would ignore

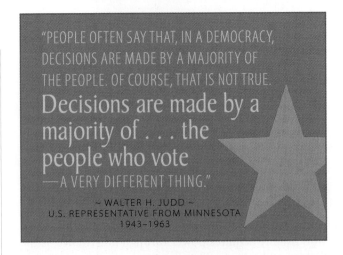

"PEOPLE OFTEN SAY THAT, IN A DEMOCRACY, DECISIONS ARE MADE BY A MAJORITY OF THE PEOPLE. OF COURSE, THAT IS NOT TRUE. Decisions are made by a majority of . . . the people who vote —A VERY DIFFERENT THING."

~ WALTER H. JUDD ~
U.S. REPRESENTATIVE FROM MINNESOTA
1943–1963

the rights and opinions of people in the minority and would make decisions without careful thought. They believed that representative assemblies were superior because they would enable public decisions to be made in a calmer and more deliberate manner.

In a **representative democracy,** the will of the majority is expressed through smaller groups of individuals elected by the people to act as their representatives. These representatives are responsible to the people for their conduct and can be voted out of office. Our founders preferred to use the term **republic,** which means essentially a representative democracy—with one qualification. A republic, by definition, has no king or queen. Rather, the people are sovereign. In contrast, a representative democracy may be headed by a monarch. For example, as Britain evolved into a representative democracy, it retained its monarch as the head of state (but with no real power).

In the modern world, there are basically two forms of representative democracy: presidential and parliamentary. In a *presidential democracy,* the lawmaking and law-enforcing branches of government are separate but equal. For example, in the United States, Congress is charged with the power to make laws, and the president is charged with the power to carry them out. In a *parliamentary democracy,* the lawmaking and law-enforcing branches of government overlap. In Britain, for example, the prime minister and the cabinet are members of the legislature, called Parliament, and are responsible to that body. Parliament thus both enacts the laws and carries them out.

Other Forms of Government

Autocracy and democracy are but two of many forms of government. Traditionally, other types of government have included governments that are ruled "by the few." For example, an aristocracy (from the Greek word *aristos,* or "best") is a government in which a small

These voters are listening to a debate at a town hall meeting in Plainfield, Vermont. Some New England towns use such meetings to engage in a form of direct democracy. Why doesn't the United States as a nation have direct democracy?

privileged class rules. A *plutocracy* is a government in which the wealthy (*ploutos* in Greek means "wealth") exercise ruling power. A *meritocracy* is a government in which the rulers have earned, or merited, the right to govern because of their special skills or talents.

A difficult form of government for Americans to understand is *theocracy*—a term derived from the Greek words meaning "rule by the deity" or "rule by God." In a theocracy, there is no separation of church and state. Rather, the government rules according to religious precepts. In most Muslim countries, government and the Islamic religion are intertwined to a degree that is quite startling to both Europeans and Americans. In Iran, for example, the Holy Koran (or Qur'an), not the national constitution,

serves as the basis for the law. The Koran consists of sacred writings that Muslims believe were revealed to the prophet Muhammad by God. In Iran, the Council of Guardians, an unelected group of religious leaders, ensures that laws and lawmakers conform to their interpretation of the teachings of Islam.

LO3 *American Democracy*

This country, with all its institutions, belongs to the people who inhabit it. Whenever they shall grow weary of the existing government, they can exercise their constitutional right to amend it, or their revolutionary right to dismember or overthrow it.[4]

With these words, Abraham Lincoln underscored the most fundamental concept of American government: that the people, not the government, are ultimately in control.

The British Legacy

In writing the U.S. Constitution, the framers incorporated two basic principles of government that had evolved in England: *limited government* and *representative government*. In a sense, then, the beginnings of our form of government are linked to events that occurred centuries earlier in England. They are also linked to the writings of European philosophers, particularly the English political philosopher John Locke. From these writings, the founders of our nation derived ideas to justify their rebellion against Britain and the establishment of a "government by the people."

LIMITED GOVERNMENT At one time, the English monarch claimed to have virtually unrestricted powers. This changed in 1215, when King John was forced by his nobles to accept the Magna Carta, or Great Charter. This monumental document provided for a trial by a jury of one's peers (equals). It prohibited the taking of a free man's life, liberty, or property except through due process of law. The Magna Carta also forced the king to obtain the nobles' approval of any taxes he imposed on them. Government thus became a contract between the king and his subjects.

The importance of the Magna Carta to England cannot be overemphasized, because it clearly established the principle of **limited government**—a

limited government
A form of government based on the principle that the powers of government should be clearly limited either through a written document or through wide public understanding; characterized by institutional checks to ensure that government serves public rather than private interests.

parliament The name of the national legislative body in countries governed by a parliamentary system, such as Britain and Canada.

bicameral legislature A legislature made up of two chambers, or parts. The United States has a bicameral legislature, composed of the House of Representatives and the Senate.

social contract A voluntary agreement among individuals to create a government and to give that government adequate power to secure the mutual protection and welfare of all individuals.

natural rights Rights that are not bestowed by governments but are inherent within every man, woman, and child by virtue of the fact that he or she is a human being.

government on which strict limits are placed, usually by a constitution. Hence, the Magna Carta signaled the end of the monarch's absolute power. Although many of the rights provided under the original Magna Carta applied only to the nobility, the document formed the basis of the future constitutional government for England and eventually the United States.

The principle of limited government was expanded four hundred years later, in 1628, when King Charles I signed the Petition of Rights. Among other things, this petition prohibited the monarch from imprisoning political critics without a jury trial. Perhaps more important, the petition declared that even the king or queen had to obey the law of the land.

In 1689, the English Parliament (described shortly) passed the English Bill of Rights, which further extended the concept of limited government. This document included several important ideas:

■ The king or queen could not interfere with parliamentary elections.

■ The king or queen had to have Parliament's approval to levy (collect) taxes or to maintain an army.

■ The king or queen had to rule with the consent of the people's representatives in Parliament.

■ The people could not be subjected to cruel or unusual punishment or to excessive fines.

The English colonists in North America were also English citizens, and thus the English Bill of Rights of 1689 applied to them as well. As a result, virtually all of the major concepts in the English Bill of Rights became part of the American system of government.

REPRESENTATIVE GOVERNMENT In a representative government, the people, by whatever means, elect individuals to make governmental decisions for all of the citizens. Usually, these representatives of the people are elected to their offices for specific periods of time. This group of representatives is often referred to as a **parliament,** which is frequently a **bicameral** (two-house) **legislature.** The English Parliament consists of the House of Lords (upper chamber) and the House of Commons (lower chamber). The English form of government provided a model for Americans to follow. Many of the American colonies had bicameral legislatures—as did, eventually, the U.S. Congress that was established by the Constitution.

POLITICAL PHILOSOPHY—SOCIAL CONTRACTS AND NATURAL RIGHTS Our democracy resulted from what can be viewed as a type of **social contract** among early Americans to create and abide by a set of governing rules. Social-contract theory was developed in the seventeenth and eighteenth centuries by such philosophers as John Locke (1632–1704) and Thomas Hobbes (1588–1679) in England and Jean-Jacques Rousseau (1712–1778) in France. According to this theory, individuals voluntarily agree with one another, in a "social contract," to give up some of their freedoms to obtain the benefits of orderly government. The government is given adequate power to secure the mutual protection and welfare of all individuals. Generally, social-contract theory, in one form or another, provides the theoretical underpinnings of most modern democracies, including that of the United States.

Although Hobbes and Rousseau also posited social contracts as the bases of governments, neither theorist was as influential in America as John Locke was. Locke argued that people are born with **natural rights** to life, liberty, and property. He theorized that the purpose of government was to protect those rights. If it did not, it would lose its legitimacy and need not be obeyed. Locke's assumption that people, by nature, are rational and are endowed with certain rights is an essential component of his theory that people can govern themselves. As you will read in Chapter 2, when the American colonists rebelled against British rule, such concepts as "natural rights" and a government based on a "social contract" became important theoretical tools in justifying the rebellion.

Principles of American Democracy

We can say that American democracy is based on five fundamental principles:

■ *Equality in voting.* Citizens need equal opportunities to express their preferences about policies or leaders.

- *Individual freedom.* All individuals must have the greatest amount of freedom possible without interfering with the rights of others.

- *Equal protection of the law.* The law must entitle all persons to equal protection.

- *Majority rule and minority rights.* The majority should rule, while guaranteeing the rights of minorities.

- *Voluntary consent to be governed.* The people who make up a democracy must collectively agree to be governed by the rules laid down by their representatives.

These principles frame many of the political issues that you will read about in this book. They also frequently lie at the heart of America's political conflicts. Does the principle of minority rights mean that minorities should receive preferential treatment in hiring and firing decisions to make up for past mistreatment? Does the principle of individual freedom mean that individuals can express whatever they want on the Internet, including hateful, racist comments? Such conflicts over individual rights and freedoms and over society's priorities are natural and inevitable. Resolving these conflicts is what politics is all about. The key point is that Americans are able to reach acceptable compromises because of their common political heritage.

American Political Values

Historically, as the nations of the world emerged, the boundaries of each nation normally coincided with the boundaries of a population that shared a common ethnic heritage, language, and culture. From its beginnings as a nation, however, America has been defined less by the culture shared by its diverse population than by a set of ideas, or its political culture. A **political culture** can be defined as a patterned set of ideas, values, and ways of thinking about government and politics.

The ideals and standards that constitute American political culture are embodied in the Declaration of Independence, one of the founding documents of this nation, which will be discussed further in Chapter 2 and presented

DIGITAL VISION/GETTY IMAGES

in its entirety in Appendix A. The political values outlined in the Declaration of Independence include natural rights (to life, liberty, and the pursuit of happiness), equality under the law, government by the consent of the governed, and limited government powers. In some ways, the Declaration of Independence defines Americans' sense of right and wrong. It presents a challenge to anyone who might wish to overthrow our democratic processes or deny our citizens their natural rights.

The rights to liberty, equality, and property are fundamental political values shared by most Americans. These values provide a basic framework for American political discourse and debate because they are shared, yet individual Americans often interpret their meanings quite differently. Many of our values are shared by other countries, but in some nations they are rejected.

LIBERTY The term **liberty** refers to a state of being free from external controls or restrictions. In the United States, the Constitution sets forth our *civil liberties* (see Chapter 4), including the freedom to practice whatever religion we choose and to be free from any state-imposed religion. Our liberties also include the freedom to speak freely on any topics and issues. Because people cannot govern themselves unless they are free to voice their opinions, freedom of speech is a basic requirement in a true democracy.

Clearly, though, if we are to live together with others, there have to be some restrictions on individual liberties. If people were allowed to do whatever they wished, without regard for the rights or liberties of others, pandemonium would result. Hence, a more accurate definition of liberty would be as follows: *liberty is the freedom of individuals to believe, act, and express themselves as they choose so long as doing so does not infringe on the rights of other individuals in the society.*

political culture The set of ideas, values, and attitudes about government and the political process held by a community or a nation.

liberty The freedom of individuals to believe, act, and express themselves as they choose so long as doing so does not infringe on the rights of other individuals in the society.

ELECTIONS | 2010

New Directions for America

In the previous election cycle, the American people put in power a Democratic president, a Democratic-controlled Senate, and a Democratic-controlled House of Representatives. Two years later, the mid-term elections seemed to indicate that the American people had changed its collective mind. Of course, in almost every mid-term election, the party in power loses seats, particularly when the economy is bad. What was less predictable was the largest House shakeup of the past half century. Both new and long-time Democrats were swept out of office. In 2010, the Democrats enjoyed a 255 to 180 majority in the House. As of 2011, the Republican majority was 243 to 192. In the Senate, six seats moved from the Democratic side to the Republican side, leaving the Democrats with a slim majority of fifty-three.

Republicans turned out to vote in large numbers. Also, exit polls confirmed that many independents decided to "punish" Democrats—many of whom they had voted for in 2008—because they felt that the Democratic Party had expanded the size of government too much. Finally, a big shakeup took place at the state level. Republicans garnered a total take of more than 680 state legislative seats—possibly a record. Clearly, the next two years in American politics will see a substantial change in direction.

EQUALITY The goal of **equality** has always been a central part of American political culture. Many of the first settlers came to this country to be free of unequal treatment and persecution. They sought the freedom to live and worship as they wanted. They believed that anyone who worked hard could succeed, and America became known as the "land of opportunity." The Declaration of Independence confirmed the importance of equality to early Americans by stating, "We hold these Truths to be self-evident, that all Men are created equal." Because of the goal of equality, the Constitution prohibited the government from granting titles of nobility. Article I, Section 9, of the Constitution states, "No Title of Nobility shall be granted by the United States." (The Constitution did not prohibit slavery, however—see Chapter 2.)

But what, exactly, does equality mean? Does it mean simply political equality—the right to vote and run for political office? Does it mean that individuals should have equal opportunities to develop their talents and skills? What about those who are poor, suffer from disabilities, or are otherwise at a competitive disadvantage? Should it be the government's responsibility to ensure that such individuals also have equal opportunities? Although most Americans believe that all persons should have the opportunity to fulfill their potential, few contend that it is the government's responsibility to totally eliminate the economic and social differences that lead to unequal opportunities. Indeed, some contend that efforts to achieve equality, in the sense of equal treatment for all, are misguided attempts to create an ideal society that can never exist.

> **equality** A concept that holds, at a minimum, that all people are entitled to equal protection under the law.

PROPERTY As noted earlier, the English philosopher John Locke asserted that people are born with "natural" rights and that among these rights are life, liberty, and *property*. The Declaration of Independence makes a similar assertion: people are born with certain "unalienable" rights, including the right to life, liberty, and the pursuit of happiness. For Americans, property and the *pursuit of happiness* are closely related. Americans place a great value on land ownership, on material possessions, and on their businesses. Property gives its owners political power and the liberty to do what they want—within limits.

Private property in America is not limited to personal possessions such as automobiles and houses. Property also consists of assets that can be used to create and sell goods and services, such as factories, farms, and shops. Private ownership of wealth-producing property is at the heart of our capitalist economic

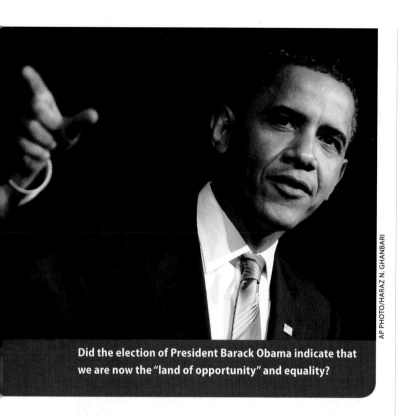

Did the election of President Barack Obama indicate that we are now the "land of opportunity" and equality?

system. **Capitalism** enjoys such widespread support in the United States that we can reasonably call it one of the nation's fundamental political values. In addition to the private ownership of productive property, capitalism is based on *free markets*—markets in which people can freely buy and sell goods, services, and financial investments without undue constraint by the government. Freedom to make binding contracts is another element of the capitalist system. The pre-eminent capitalist institution is the privately owned corporation.

Political Values in a Multicultural Society

From the earliest English and European settlers to the many cultural groups that today call America their home, American society has always been multicultural. Until recently, most Americans viewed the United States as the world's melting pot. They accepted that American society included numerous ethnic and cultural groups, but they expected that the members of these groups would abandon their cultural distinctions and assimilate the language and customs of earlier Americans. One of the outgrowths of the civil rights movement of the 1960s, however, was an emphasis on *multiculturalism,* the belief that the many cultures that

make up American society should remain distinct and be protected—and even encouraged—by our laws.

The ethnic makeup of the United States has changed dramatically in the last two decades and will continue to change (see Figure 1–1 on the following page). Already, non-Hispanic whites are a minority in California. For the nation as a whole, non-Hispanic whites will be in the minority after the year 2050. Some Americans fear that rising numbers of immigrants will threaten traditional American political values and culture. We examine that issue in the feature *Join the Debate: Should We Encourage Immigration?* on page 15.

American Political Ideology

In a general sense, **ideology** refers to a system of political ideas. These ideas typically are rooted in religious or philosophical beliefs about human nature, society, and government. Generally, assumptions as to what the government's role should be in promoting basic values, such as liberty and equality, are important determinants of political ideology.

When it comes to political ideology, Americans tend to fall into two broad political camps: liberals and conservatives. The term *liberal* has been used to refer to someone who advocates change, new philosophies, and new ideas. The term *conservative* has described a person who values past customs and traditions that have proved their value over time. In today's American political arena, however, the terms *liberalism* and *conservatism* have both taken on additional meanings.

LIBERALISM Modern **liberalism** in the United States traces its roots to the administration of Franklin D. Roosevelt (1933–1945). Roosevelt's New Deal programs, launched to counter the effects of the Great Depression, involved the government in the American economic sphere to an extent hitherto unknown. From that time on, the word *liberalism* became associated with the concept of "big government"—that is,

capitalism An economic system based on the private ownership of wealth-producing property, free markets, and freedom of contract. The privately owned corporation is the pre-eminent capitalist institution.

ideology Generally, a system of political ideas that are rooted in religious or philosophical beliefs concerning human nature, society, and government.

liberalism A set of political beliefs that include the advocacy of active government, including government intervention to improve the welfare of individuals and to protect civil rights.

with government intervention to aid economically disadvantaged groups and to promote equality.

Today's liberals continue to believe that the government has a responsibility to undertake social-welfare programs, at the taxpayers' expense, to assist the poor and the disadvantaged. Further, today's liberals believe that the national government should take steps to ensure that our civil rights and liberties are protected and that the government must look out for the interests of the individual against the majority.

The recently enacted health-care system reform can serve as an example of liberal ideals and policies. True, the package included some measures to limit the growth in spending on Medicare, which funds health care for those over the age of sixty-five. (As a result, the reform was unpopular among the elderly.) Most of

> ## "THE THING ABOUT DEMOCRACY,
> beloveds, is that it is not neat, orderly or quiet. It requires a certain relish for confusion."
> ~ MOLLY IVINS ~
> AMERICAN JOURNALIST
> 1944–2007

the moral fervor behind the health-care legislation, however, was based on the liberal, egalitarian belief that every U.S. citizen should have a right to health-care insurance. Liberals believed that it was a scandal that some Americans could not afford insurance coverage and that others were denied coverage at any price. To remedy this situation, liberals were prepared to impose substantial new regulations on the insurance industry, create a new government spending program, and levy a number of new taxes.

Liberals typically believe in the separation of church and state, and generally think that the government should not involve itself in the moral or religious life of the nation. In this area, at least, liberals do not stand for big government, but rather the reverse.

CONSERVATISM Modern **conservatism** in this country can also trace its roots to the Roosevelt administration. Roosevelt gave conservatives a common cause: opposition to the New Deal and to big government. As one author noted, "No factor did more to stimulate

---

Figure 1–1

Distribution of the U.S. Population by Race and Hispanic Origin, 2000 to 2050

After 2050, minorities will constitute a majority of the U.S. population.

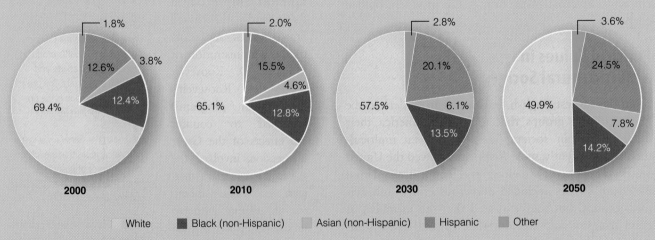

Data for 2010, 2030, and 2050 are projections.

Figures do not necessarily sum to 100%, because of rounding. Hispanics may be of any race. The chart categories "White," "Black," "Asian," and "Other" are limited to non-Hispanics. "Other" consists of the following non-Hispanic groups: "American Indian," "Alaska Native," "Native Hawaiian," "Other Pacific Islander," and "Two or More Races." Sources: U.S. Bureau of the Census and authors' calculations.

JOIN THE DEBATE

Should We Encourage Immigration?

© CLEO PHOTO/ALAMY

Most discussions about immigration focus on what we should do about illegal immigration, a topic we will address later in this text. For now, the question is about immigration in general. America was founded by immigrants, and few restrictions on immigration existed until the twentieth century. Should the federal government change our immigration laws to allow more foreigners to immigrate legally and eventually become citizens of the United States? Or should we reduce immigration because we already have so many immigrants that they threaten to dilute our national character?

What Was Good Once Is Not Good Now

Those who oppose additional immigration admit that we are a nation founded by immigrants. Immigration opponents say, however, that new immigrants resist assimilation into American society and do not acquire core American values such as individualism and self-reliance. These opponents believe that the loyalty of new immigrants—even well-educated ones—to the United States and its core culture is fragile.

Increased legal immigration will bring in more low-skilled, poorly educated residents. That is not going to help our economy. Some second- and third-generation Latinos, for example, have fallen into the underclass culture. If current immigration patterns hold, in the future we will see decline in U.S. literacy and numeracy. If we want to continue to compete in the global economy, we must have an advanced labor force. If we allow some immigration, we should limit it, as much as possible, to professionals and highly skilled tradespeople.

A Nation Founded by Immigrants Needs More of Them

Immigration supporters believe that we benefit when people flow across borders. Indeed, if we made it easier for talented foreigners to move to this country, America would become even richer than it is now. Immigrants fill jobs, but they also create jobs. A quarter of the engineering and technology companies started in the United States from 1995 to 2005 had at least one founder who was foreign-born. The world's brightest brains and cutting-edge innovators come to the United States to study—and often to stay. Foreign students earn 44 percent of U.S. science and engineering doctorates. Yet many of these students are forced to leave the country after graduation because there are not enough visas available for professionals.

Immigration supporters are aware that many immigrants are unskilled. The United States, however, has jobs available at the bottom as well as the top. Even with unemployment at 10 percent in 2009 and 2010, farmers on the West Coast still could not find U.S. citizens willing to pick fruits and vegetables. And as far as assimilation is concerned, studies have shown that the new immigrants assimilate just as quickly as the old ones did.

For Critical Analysis *One interesting statistic is that immigrants from Mexico—legal and illegal—have a substantially larger number of children than Mexicans who remain in their homeland. Why might this be so?*

---

the growth of modern conservatism than the election of Franklin Roosevelt. . . . He is the man conservatives most dislike, for he embodies the big-government ideology they most fear."[5]

As conservative ideology evolved in the latter half of the twentieth century, it incorporated a number of other elements in addition to the emphasis on free enterprise and antipathy toward big government. By the time of Ronald Reagan (1981–1989), conservatives placed a high value on the principles of law and order, states' rights, family values, and individual initiative. Today's conservatives tend to fall into two basic categories: *economic conservatives* (those who seek to minimize government spending and intervention in the economy) and *social conservatives* (those, such as Christian conservatives, who seek to incorporate religious and family values into politics and government).

The health-care reform package was an example of the kind of government program that conservatives typically oppose. Conservatives objected to the additional government spending required by the legislation and to the additional taxes. The new regulations imposed on the insurance industry were, for conservatives, a violation of the free-market principles on which this country was built. Conservatives believe that individuals and families should take responsibility for their own economic circumstances, and if that means that some would go without health-care insurance, so be it.

LIBERALS AND PROGRESSIVES Not all political labels are equally popular, and the term *liberal* has taken a particular beating in the political wars of the last several decades. One result is that most politicians who might have called themselves liberals in the past have abandoned the term and have labeled their philosophy **progressivism** instead. The benefits of the new label are clear. In public opinion polls, voters strongly prefer the term *conservative* to the term *liberal*. In 2009, however, a survey asked Americans to report whether they considered themselves liberal, progressive, conservative, or libertarian. Counting "leaners," the liberals and progressives together were almost as numerous as the conservative/libertarian block.[6]

The term *progressive* dates back to the first years of the twentieth century, when a reforming spirit arose in both major political parties. These "progressives" believed that stronger government was necessary to counterbalance the growing power of large corporations. In the presidential elections of 1912, the two strongest candidates, Theodore Roosevelt and Woodrow Wilson, called themselves progressives, although they disagreed on many issues. Later, the progressive label fell into disuse until it was resurrected in recent years.

The Traditional Political Spectrum

Traditionally, liberalism and conservatism have been regarded as falling within a political spectrum that ranges from the far left to the far right. As Figure 1–2 on the facing page illustrates, there is a close relationship between those holding conservative views and those identifying themselves politically as Republicans. Similarly, in terms of party affiliation and voting, liberals—or progressives—identify with the Democratic Party.

MODERATES People whose views fall in the middle of the traditional political spectrum are generally called **moderates.** Moderates rarely classify themselves as either liberal or conservative, and they may vote for either Republicans or Democrats. Many moderates do not belong to either major political party and often describe themselves as *independent* (see Chapter 7).

THE EXTREME LEFT AND RIGHT On both ends of the spectrum are those who espouse radical views. The **radical left** consists of those who would like major changes in the political order, usually to promote egalitarianism (human equality). Socialists, who have a significant presence in Europe and elsewhere, generally support democracy and work within established political systems to realize their ideals. Communists,

House Speaker Nancy Pelosi signs the revised Health Care and Education Reconciliation Act, the bill that amends the recently enacted health-care law.

AP PHOTO/MANUEL BALCE CENETA

progressivism An alternative, more popular term for the set of political beliefs also known as liberalism.

moderate A person whose views fall in the middle of the political spectrum.

radical left Persons on the extreme left side of the political spectrum, who would like major changes in the political order, usually to promote egalitarianism (human equality).

Figure 1–2

The Traditional Political Spectrum

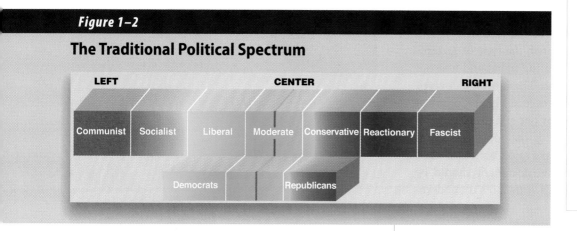

radical right Persons on the extreme right side of the political spectrum. The radical right includes reactionaries (who would like to return to the values and social systems of some previous era) and libertarians (who believe in no regulation of the economy or individual behavior).

ideologue An individual who holds very strong political opinions.

in contrast, have sought to reach their goals through revolutionary violence and totalitarian dictatorships. The political philosopher Karl Marx (1818–1883) is widely considered to be the most important founder of the radical left as it developed in the nineteenth and twentieth centuries.

The **radical right** includes reactionaries, those who wish to turn the clock back to some previous era when, for example, there weren't so many civil rights for the nation's minorities and women. Reactionaries strongly oppose liberal and progressive politics and resist political and social change. Like those on the radical left, members of the radical right may even advocate the use of violence to achieve their goals. This is especially true of fascist movements such as Hitler's Nazi Party. When in power, Fascists have created totalitarian systems based on philosophies of racism or extreme nationalism.

Ideology and Today's Electorate

Those who hold strongly to political ideologies that are well thought out and internally coherent and consistent are called **ideologues.** Ideologues usually fit easily on one side or the other of the political spectrum. Many Americans, though, do not adhere firmly to a particular political ideology. They may not be interested in political issues and may have a mixed set of opinions that do not neatly fit under a liberal or conservative label.

One complication is that many Americans are conservative on economic issues, such as the degree of government intervention in the economy, and at the same time are liberal on social issues, such as abortion. Indeed, the ideology of *libertarianism* favors just this combination. Libertarians oppose government action to regulate the economy, just as they oppose government involvement in issues of private morality. Like the word *liberal,* the term *libertarian* is not particularly popular,

and many people who clearly have libertarian beliefs are unwilling to adopt the label. As you will learn later in this book, however, wealthy Americans often have libertarian attitudes.

Many other voters are liberal on economic issues even as they favor conservative positions on social matters. These people favor government intervention to promote both economic "fairness" *and* moral values. Low-income people frequently are social conservatives and economic progressives. A large number of African Americans and Hispanics fall into this camp. While it is widespread within the electorate, this "anti-libertarian" point of view has no agreed-upon name.

In sum, millions of Americans do not fit neatly into the traditional liberal-conservative spectrum. We illustrate an alternative, two-dimensional political classification in Figure 1–3 on the following page.

LO4 *American Democracy at Work*

Even the most divisive issues can be and are resolved through the political process. How does this process work? Who are the key players? These questions will be answered in the remaining chapters of this book. In the meantime, though, it is helpful to have some kind of a "road map" to guide you through these chapters so that you can see how each topic covered in the text relates to the big picture.

The Big Picture

The U.S. Constitution is the supreme law of the land. It sets forth basic governing rules by which Americans, when they ratified the Constitution, agreed to abide. It is appropriate, then, that we begin this text, following this introductory chapter, with a discussion of how and why the Constitution was created, the type of governing structure it established, and the rights and liberties it guarantees for all Americans. These topics, covered in Chapters 2 through 5, are necessarily the point of departure for any discussion of our system of government. As you will see, some of the most significant political controversies today have to do with how various provisions in this founding document should be applied, more than two hundred years later, to modern-day events and issues.

Who Governs?

Who acquires the power and authority to govern, and how do they obtain that power and authority? Generally, of course, the "winners" in our political system are the successful candidates in elections. But the electoral process is influenced by more than just the issue positions taken by the candidates. As you read Chapters 6 through 10, keep the following questions in mind: How do interest groups influence elections? How essential are political parties to the electoral process? To what extent do public opinion and voting behavior play a role in determining who the winners and losers

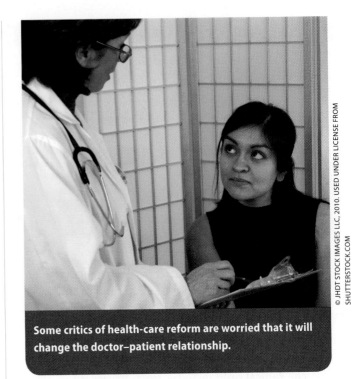

Some critics of health-care reform are worried that it will change the doctor–patient relationship.

will be? Why are political campaigns so expensive, and what are the implications of high campaign costs for our democracy? Finally, what role do the media, including the Internet, play in fashioning the outcomes of campaigns?

Once a winning candidate assumes a political office, that candidate becomes a part of one of the institutions of government. In Chapter 11 and the remaining chapters of this text, we examine these institutions and the process of government decision making. You will learn how those who govern the nation make laws and policies to decide "who gets what, when, and how" in our society. Of course, the topics treated in these chapters are not isolated from the materials covered earlier in the text. For example, when formulating and implementing federal policies, as well as state and local policies, policymakers cannot ignore the wishes of interest groups, particularly those of wealthy groups that can help to fund the policymakers' reelections. And public opinion and the media not only affect election outcomes but also influence which issues will be included on the policymaking agenda.

The political system established by the founders of this nation has endured for more than two hundred years. The challenge facing Americans now is how to make sure that it will continue to endure.

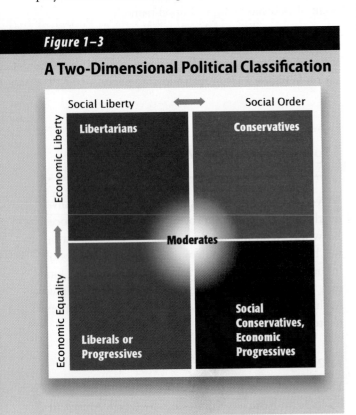

Figure 1–3

A Two-Dimensional Political Classification

Social Liberty ⟷ Social Order

Economic Liberty

Libertarians

Conservatives

Moderates

Economic Equality

Liberals or Progressives

Social Conservatives, Economic Progressives

As you learned in this chapter, Americans are united by a common political culture. At the same time, however, Americans are at odds over how much weight should be given to various fundamental principles. We can summarize these most basic disputes as follows:

- How large should our government be? Should it offer a wide range of services, along with the resulting taxes—or should it provide relatively few services and collect less in taxes?

- Should businesses be strictly regulated to ensure the common good—or should regulation be minimized to promote economic freedom and growth?

- More generally, should we place a greater value on economic liberty and property rights—or on economic egalitarianism and improving the condition of those who are less well-off?

- How active should the government be in promoting moral behavior by Americans? Should the government support traditional values—or place a high value on social liberty?

- Are progressive or liberal policies best for the nation—or does conservatism provide the better answers? Alternatively, is libertarianism the solution—or social conservatism combined with progressive economic policies?

Take Action

Our democratic republic is now more than two hundred years old, and it is easy to assume that it will last forever. It is also easy to forget that the reason we still enjoy the rights and benefits our system provides is that whenever they have been threatened in the past, people spoke out and took action to remove the threat. In the remaining chapters of this book, this *Take Action* section will give examples of how you can take action to make a difference. To function as a free person in our complex society, it is important to know the basic facts about government and politics that are covered in this text. Political science, however, goes well beyond the basics that every citizen ought to know. It is an important field of study in its own right.

Students who major in political science find employment in almost every kind of job imaginable. Naturally, some take employment with government at the federal, state, or local level. Political science is also the most popular major for students who seek to attend law school. Many political science majors also work in law without obtaining a graduate degree—as paralegals, legal assistants, or legal secretaries.

A political science major also can prepare a student for many other jobs. Almost every chapter of this book suggests a possible career. Interest groups? All of them need staff members, and political science can be part of a useful preparation for employment by such groups. Public opinion? Along with statistics, political science is a valuable background for poll takers. The media? Political science makes a good start if you want to go on to study journalism in preparation for a career. Political science can prepare you for jobs in campaign consulting, public relations, or business. Of course, political scientists also teach their subject at the high school and college levels. Regardless of what career they choose, one thing unites all political science majors—they like politics and find it fascinating.

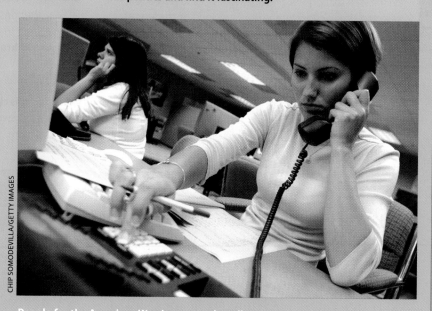

CHIP SOMODEVILLA/GETTY IMAGES

People for the American Way interns make calls to organization members in Louisiana at the organization's "Action Center" in Washington, D.C. Political science majors can start their careers as volunteers.

POLITICS ON THE
WEB

PGIAM/iSTOCKPHOTO

Each chapter of *GOVT* concludes with a list of Internet resources and addresses. Once you are on the Internet, you can use the addresses, or uniform resource locators (URLs), listed in the *Politics on the Web* sections in this book to access the ever-growing number of resources available on the Internet relating to American politics and government.

Internet sites tend to come and go, and there is no guarantee that a site included in a *Politics on the Web* feature will be there by the time this book is in print. We have tried, though, to include sites that have so far proved to be fairly stable. If you do have difficulty reaching a site, do not immediately assume that the site does not exist. First, recheck the URL shown in your browser. Remember, you have to type the URL exactly as written. Uppercase and lowercase are sometimes important. If the URL appears to be keyed in correctly, then try the following technique: delete all of the information after the forward slash mark that is farthest to the right in the address, and press "enter." This may allow you to reach a home page, from which you can link to the topic at issue.

A seemingly infinite number of sites on the Web offer information on American government and politics. A list of even the best sites would fill pages. For reasons of space, in this chapter and in those that follow, the *Politics on the Web* sections will include references to only a few selected sites. Following the links provided by these sites will take you to a host of others. The Web sites listed in the next column all provide excellent points of departure for those who wish to learn more about American government and politics today.

- The U.S. government's "official" Web site offers extensive information on the national government and the services it provides for citizens. To access this site, go to **www.usa.gov**

- ThisNation is a nonpartisan site dealing with current political questions. To access this site, go to **www.thisnation.com**

- To find news on the Web, you can go to the site of any major news organization or even your local newspaper. Links to online newspapers, both within the United States and in other countries, are available at **www.newspapers.com**

- Additionally, CNN's Politics Web site offers a wealth of news, news analysis, polling data, and news articles dating back to 1996. Go to **www.cnn.com/POLITICS**

- The Pew Research Center for the People and the Press offers survey data online on a number of topics relating to American politics and government. The URL for the center's site is **people-press.org**

- Yale University Library, one of the great research institutions, has an excellent collection of sources relating to American politics and government. Go to **www.library.yale.edu/socsci**

CourseMate

Access CourseMate to review and expand on this chapter through quizzes, flashcards, learning objectives, interactive timelines, a crossword puzzle, audio summaries, video, critical-thinking activities, simulations, and more.

The Constitution

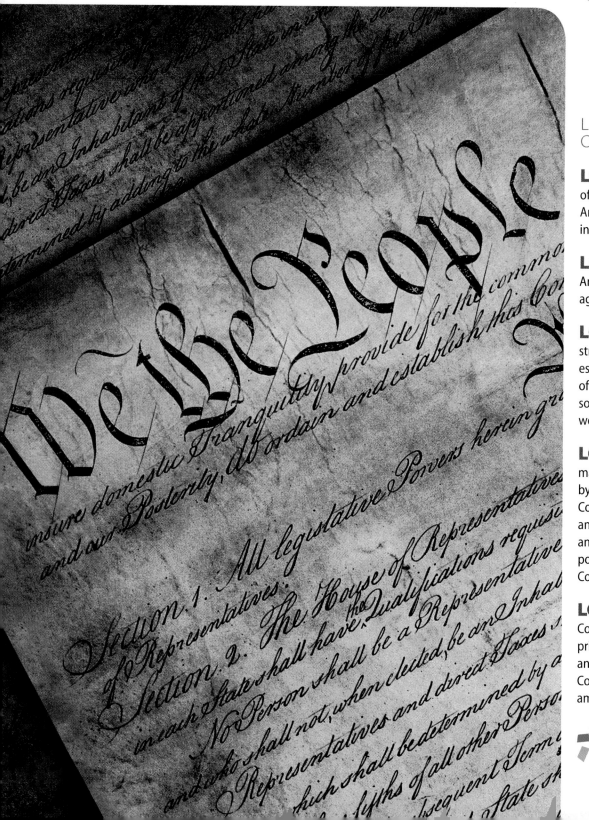

LEARNING OBJECTIVES

LO1 Point out some of the influences on the American political tradition in the colonial years.

LO2 Explain why the American colonies rebelled against Britain.

LO3 Describe the structure of government established by the Articles of Confederation and some of the strengths and weaknesses of the Articles.

LO4 List some of the major compromises made by the delegates at the Constitutional Convention, and discuss the Federalist and Anti-Federalist positions on ratifying the Constitution.

LO5 Summarize the Constitution's major principles of government, and describe how the Constitution can be amended.

CourseMate

AMERICA AT ODDS

Was the Supreme Court Right to Rule That Individuals Have the Right to Bear Arms?

The Second Amendment to the Constitution of the United States says, "A well regulated Militia, being necessary to the security of a free State, the right of the people to keep and bear Arms, shall not be infringed." It seems clear, doesn't it? Actually, it is not clear. Does this amendment allow any individual in the United States to own a gun? Or does it guarantee the right to bear arms only to those who serve in a militia, such as the National Guard?

For decades, those who oppose gun control have argued that the first statement is correct. Gun control advocates have argued that the second statement is what the founders meant. In 1939, a United States Supreme Court decision seemed to suggest that the right to bear arms is constitutionally protected only when individuals function as part of a state militia. In 2008 and 2010, however, the Court found that the right to bear arms was guaranteed to individuals, not just state militias. The 2008 ruling restricted itself to limiting the actions of the federal government, and therefore it was applicable only in jurisdictions such as the District of Columbia. The 2010 ruling applied to state governments as well.[1] Both cases were decided by narrow, five-to-four margins. Americans are at odds over the question of whether the Court made the right decision.

The Supreme Court's Ruling Has Finally Clarified the Issue

Those who oppose gun control legislation strongly approve of the way the Supreme Court has interpreted the Second Amendment. They argue that the "militia" phrase in the Second Amendment is merely a preamble. James Madison, who drafted it, was providing an explanation of why the amendment was desirable, and not placing a limit on its applicability. The federal government cannot prevent individuals from owning guns, and the states should not have that right either. Sixty million Americans own guns. Barely one-third of Americans believe that the way to combat gun violence is through stricter gun laws.

"If guns are made criminal, only criminals will have guns." Studies conducted in cities where concealed weapons are allowed show that there are fewer robberies and murders than in jurisdictions where concealed weapons are *not* allowed. Washington, D.C., which had a total ban on guns, has one of the nation's highest rates of murder, and 80 percent of these murders are committed with firearms.

Without Gun Control, More Americans Will Die Senselessly

When drafted, the Second Amendment was an accommodation to the Anti-Federalists of the time, who believed that "the people in arms" could serve as an effective fighting force. This notion had already been proved wrong in the Revolutionary War. The current Supreme Court rulings on gun control laws can only have a negative effect on the well-being of Americans. Gun rights advocates will use this decision as a legal tool to strike down effective gun control laws nationwide. More than thirty thousand Americans are killed by guns every year. A third of these deaths are instances of murder. The rest are suicides or accidents.

Those in favor of gun control laws will continue to fight for them. They can do so because the Supreme Court decision did allow for certain types of gun restrictions, particularly bans on gun possession by felons and mentally ill individuals. We know that European nations that have banned almost all gun ownership have much lower homicide rates than we do in the United States. Isn't that enough evidence?

WHERE DO YOU STAND?

1. The Supreme Court may have thrown out laws that ban the possession of firearms altogether, but the issue of whether and how guns should be regulated remains open. Should guns be registered, as automobiles are? Should citizens be allowed to carry concealed weapons? In either case, why or why not?
2. Why do you think so many Americans own firearms?

EXPLORE THIS ISSUE ONLINE

Given the heat of the gun control controversy, it's no surprise that you can find many Web sites on either side.

- Web sites that advocate the regulation of firearms are maintained by the Brady Campaign to Prevent Gun Violence at **www.bradycampaign.org** and the Violence Policy Center at **www.vpc.org**.
- Gun rights sites are maintained by the National Rifle Association at **www.nra.org** and the Second Amendment Foundation at **www.saf.org**.

Introduction

Whether Americans as individuals have a constitutional right to own firearms is just one of many debates concerning the government established by the U.S. Constitution. The Constitution, which was written more than two hundred years ago, continues to be the supreme law of the land. Time and again, its provisions have been adapted to the changing needs and conditions of society. The challenge before today's citizens and political leaders is to find a way to apply those provisions to a society and an economy that could not possibly have been anticipated by the founders. Will the Constitution survive this challenge? Most Americans assume that it will—and with good reason: no other written constitution in the world today is as old as the U.S. Constitution. To understand the principles of government set forth in the Constitution, you have to go back to the beginnings of our nation's history.

LO1 The Beginnings of American Government

When the framers of the Constitution met in Philadelphia in 1787, they brought with them some valuable political assets. One asset was their English political heritage (see Chapter 1). Another was the hands-on political experience they had acquired during the colonial era. Their political knowledge and experience enabled them to establish a constitution that could meet not only the needs of their own time but also the needs of generations to come.

The American colonies were settled by individuals from many nations, including France, Germany, Ireland, the Netherlands, Spain, and Sweden. The majority of the colonists, though, came from England and Scotland. The British colonies in North America were established by private individuals and private trading companies and were under the rule of the British Crown. The colonies, which were located along the Atlantic seaboard of today's United States, eventually numbered thirteen.

Although American politics owes much to the English political tradition, the colonists actually derived most of their understanding of social compacts, the rights of the people, limited government, and representative government from their own experiences. Years before Parliament adopted the English Bill of Rights or John Locke wrote his *Two Treatises on Government* (1690), the American colonists were putting the ideas expressed in those documents into practice.

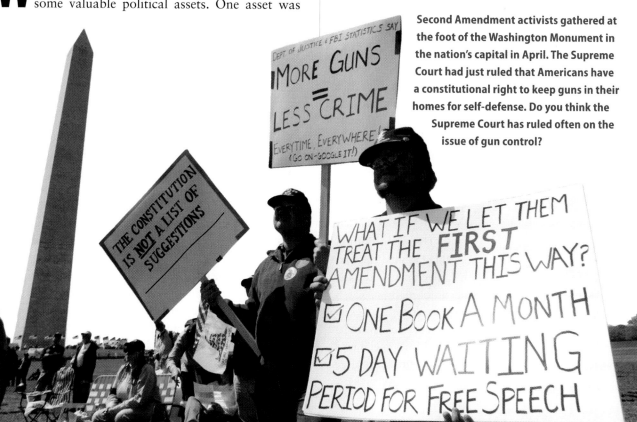

Second Amendment activists gathered at the foot of the Washington Monument in the nation's capital in April. The Supreme Court had just ruled that Americans have a constitutional right to keep guns in their homes for self-defense. Do you think the Supreme Court has ruled often on the issue of gun control?

MARK PETERSON/REDUX

The First English Settlements

The first permanent English settlement in North America was Jamestown, in what is now Virginia.[2] Jamestown was established in 1607 as a trading post of the Virginia Company of London.[3]

The first New England colony was founded by the Plymouth Company in 1620 at Plymouth, Massachusetts. Most of the settlers at Plymouth were Pilgrims, a group of English Protestants who came to the New World on the ship *Mayflower*. Even before the Pilgrims went ashore, they drew up the **Mayflower Compact**, in which they set up a government and promised to obey its laws. The reason for the compact was that the group was outside the jurisdiction of the Virginia Company, which had arranged for them to settle in Virginia, not Massachusetts. Fearing that some of the passengers might decide that they were no longer subject to any rules of civil order, the leaders on board the *Mayflower* agreed that some form of governmental authority was necessary. The Mayflower Compact, which was essentially a social contract, has historical significance because it was the first of a series of similar contracts among the colonists to establish fundamental rules of government.[4]

The Massachusetts Bay Colony was established as another trading outpost in New England in 1630. In 1639, some of the Pilgrims at Plymouth, who felt that they were being persecuted by the Massachusetts Bay Colony, left Plymouth and settled in what is now Connecticut. They developed America's first written constitution, which was called the Fundamental Orders of Connecticut. This document called for the laws to be made by an assembly of elected representatives from each town. The document also provided for the popular election of a governor and judges. Other colonies, in turn, established fundamental governing rules. The Massachusetts Body of Liberties protected individual rights. The Pennsylvania Frame of Government, passed in 1682, and the Pennsylvania Charter of Privileges of 1701 established principles that were later expressed in the U.S. Constitution and **Bill of Rights** (the first ten amendments to the Constitution). By 1732, all thirteen colonies had been established, each with its own political documents and constitution (see Figure 2–1, above right).

Mayflower Compact
A document drawn up by Pilgrim leaders in 1620 on the ship *Mayflower*. The document stated that laws were to be made for the general good of the people.

Bill of Rights The first ten amendments to the U.S. Constitution. They list the freedoms—such as the freedoms of speech, press, and religion—that a citizen enjoys and that cannot be infringed on by the government.

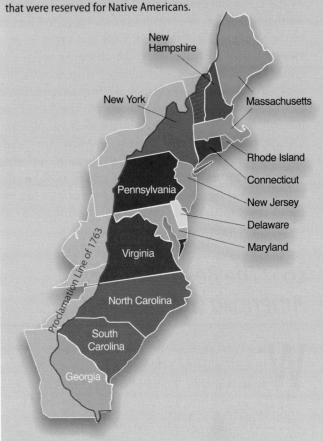

Figure 2–1

The Thirteen Colonies

The thirteen colonies before the American Revolution. The western boundary of the colonies was set by the Proclamation Line of 1763, which banned European settlement in western territories that were reserved for Native Americans.

New Hampshire
New York
Massachusetts
Rhode Island
Connecticut
New Jersey
Delaware
Maryland
Pennsylvania
Virginia
North Carolina
South Carolina
Georgia
Proclamation Line of 1763

Colonial Legislatures

As mentioned, the British colonies in America were all under the rule of the British monarchy. Britain, however, was thousands of miles away—it took two months to sail across the Atlantic. Thus, to a significant extent, colonial legislatures carried on the "nuts and bolts" of colonial government. These legislatures, or *representative assemblies,* consisted of representatives elected by the colonists. The earliest colonial legislature was the Virginia House of Burgesses, established in 1619. By the time of the American Revolution, all of the colonies had representative assemblies, many of which had been in existence for more than a hundred years.

Through their participation in colonial governments, the colonists gained crucial political experience. Colonial leaders became familiar with the practical problems of governing. They learned how to build coalitions among groups with diverse interests and how to make compromises. Indeed, according to Yale University professor Jon Butler, by the time of the American Revolution in 1776, Americans had formed a complex, sophisticated political system. They had also created a wholly new type of society characterized by, among other things, ethnic and religious diversity.[5] Because of their political experiences, the colonists were quickly able to set up their own constitutions and state systems of government—and eventually a new national government—after they declared their independence from Britain in 1776.

LO2 *The Rebellion of the Colonists*

Scholars of the American Revolution point out that by and large, the American colonists did not want to become independent of Britain. For the majority of the colonists, Britain was the homeland, and ties of loyalty to the British monarch were strong. Why, then, did the colonists revolt against Britain and declare their independence? What happened to sever the political, economic, and emotional bonds that tied the colonists to Britain? The answers to these questions lie in a series of events in the mid-1700s that culminated in a change in British policy toward the colonies. Table 2–1 at right shows the chronology of the major political events in early U.S. political history.

One of these events was the Seven Years' War (1756–1763) between Britain and France, which Americans often refer to as the French and Indian War. The British victory in the Seven Years' War permanently altered the relationship between Britain and its American colonies. After successfully ousting the French from North America, the British expanded their authority over the colonies. To pay its war debts and to finance the defense of its expanded North American empire, Britain needed revenues. The British government decided to obtain some of these revenues by imposing taxes on the American colonists and exercising more direct control over colonial trade. At the same time, Americans were beginning to distrust the expanding British presence in the colonies. Having fought alongside British forces, Americans thought that they deserved more credit for the victory. The British, however, attributed the victory solely to their own war effort.

Furthermore, the colonists began to develop a sense of identity separate from the British. Americans were

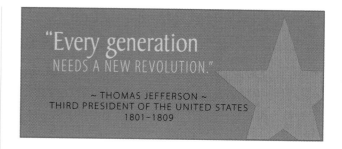

"Every generation
NEEDS A NEW REVOLUTION."

~ THOMAS JEFFERSON ~
THIRD PRESIDENT OF THE UNITED STATES
1801–1809

shocked at the behavior of some of the British soldiers and the cruel punishments meted out to enforce discipline among the British troops. The British, in turn, had little good to say about the colonists alongside whom they had fought. They considered them brutish, uncivilized, and undisciplined. It was during this time that the colonists began to use the word *American* to describe themselves.

Table 2–1
Significant Events in Early U.S. Political History

Year	Event
1607	Jamestown established; Virginia Company lands settlers.
1620	Mayflower Compact signed.
1630	Massachusetts Bay Colony set up.
1639	Fundamental Orders of Connecticut adopted.
1641	Massachusetts Body of Liberties adopted.
1682	Pennsylvania Frame of Government passed.
1701	Pennsylvania Charter of Privileges written.
1732	Last of thirteen colonies established (Georgia).
1756	French and Indian War declared.
1765	Stamp Act; Stamp Act Congress meets.
1773	Boston Tea Party.
1774	First Continental Congress.
1775	Second Continental Congress; Revolutionary War begins.
1776	Declaration of Independence signed.
1777	Articles of Confederation drafted.
1781	Last state signs Articles of Confederation.
1783	"Critical period" in U.S. history begins; weak national government until 1789.
1786	Shays' Rebellion.
1787	Constitutional Convention.
1788	Ratification of Constitution.
1791	Ratification of Bill of Rights.

"Taxation without Representation"

In 1764, in an effort to obtain needed revenues, the British Parliament passed the Sugar Act, which imposed a tax on all sugar imported into the American colonies. Some colonists, particularly in Massachusetts, vigorously opposed this tax and proposed a boycott of certain British imports. This boycott developed into a "nonimportation" movement that soon spread to other colonies.

THE STAMP ACT OF 1765 The following year, in 1765, Parliament passed the Stamp Act, which imposed the first direct tax on the colonists. Under the act, all legal documents and newspapers, as well as certain other items, including playing cards and dice, had to use specially embossed (stamped) paper that was purchased from the government.

The Stamp Act generated even stronger resentment among the colonists than the Sugar Act had aroused. James Otis, Jr., a Massachusetts attorney, declared that there could be "no taxation without representation." The American colonists could not vote in British elections and therefore were not represented in the British Parliament. They viewed Parliament's attempts to tax them as contrary to the principle of representative government. The British saw the matter differently. From the British perspective, it was only fair that the colonists pay taxes to help support the costs incurred by the British government in defending its American territories and maintaining the troops that were permanently stationed in the colonies following the Seven Years' War.

In October 1765, nine of the thirteen colonies sent delegates to the Stamp Act Congress in New York City. The delegates prepared a declaration of rights and grievances, which they sent to King George III. This action marked the first time that a majority of the colonies had joined together to oppose British rule. The British Parliament repealed the Stamp Act.

FURTHER TAXES AND THE COERCIVE ACTS Soon, however, Parliament passed new laws designed to bind the colonies more tightly to the central government in London. Laws that imposed taxes on glass, paint, lead, and many other items were passed in 1767. The colonists protested by boycotting all British goods. In 1773, anger over taxation reached a powerful climax at the Boston Tea Party, in which colonists dressed as Mohawk Indians dumped almost 350 chests of British tea into Boston Harbor as a gesture of tax protest.[6]

First Continental Congress A gathering of delegates from twelve of the thirteen colonies, held in 1774 to protest the Coercive Acts.

The British Parliament was quick to respond to the Tea Party. In 1774, Parliament passed the Coercive Acts (sometimes called the "Intolerable Acts"), which closed Boston Harbor and placed the government of Massachusetts under direct British control.

The Continental Congresses

In response to the "Intolerable Acts," New York, Pennsylvania, and Rhode Island proposed a colonial congress. The Massachusetts House of Representatives requested that all colonies select delegates to send to Philadelphia for such a congress.

THE FIRST CONTINENTAL CONGRESS The **First Continental Congress** met on September 5, 1774, at Carpenter's Hall in Philadelphia. Of the thirteen colonies, only Georgia did not participate. The congress decided that the colonies should send a petition to King George III to explain their grievances, which they did. The congress also passed other resolutions calling for a continued boycott of British goods and requiring each colony to establish an army.

During the Boston Tea Party in 1773, the colonists dumped chests of British tea into Boston Harbor as a gesture of tax protest.

TIME LIFE PICTURES/MANSELL/GETTY IMAGES

To enforce the boycott and other acts of resistance against Britain, the delegates to the First Continental Congress urged that "a committee be chosen in every county, city and town, by those who are qualified to vote for representatives in the legislature, whose business it shall be attentively to observe the conduct of all persons." Over the next several months, all colonial legislatures supported this action. The committees of "safety" or "observation," as they were called, organized militias, held special courts, and suppressed the opinions of those who remained loyal to the British Crown. Committee members spied on neighbors' activities and reported to the press the names of those who violated the boycott against Britain. The names were then printed in the local papers, and the transgressors were harassed and ridiculed in their communities.

THE SECOND CONTINENTAL CONGRESS Almost immediately after receiving the petition from the First Continental Congress, the British government condemned the actions of the congress as open acts of rebellion. Britain responded with even stricter and more repressive measures. On April 19, 1775, British soldiers (Redcoats) fought against colonial citizen soldiers (Minutemen) in the towns of Lexington and Concord in Massachusetts, the first battles of the American Revolution.

Less than a month later, delegates from all thirteen colonies gathered in Pennsylvania for the **Second Continental Congress,** which immediately assumed the powers of a central government. The Second Continental Congress declared that the militiamen who had gathered around Boston were now a full army. It also named George Washington, a delegate to the congress who had some military experience, as its commander in chief.

The delegates to the Second Continental Congress still intended to reach a peaceful settlement with the British Parliament. One declaration stated specifically that "we [the congress] have not raised armies with ambitious designs of separating from Britain, and establishing independent States." The continued attempts to effect a reconciliation with Britain, even after the outbreak of fighting, underscore the colonists' reluctance to sever their relationship with the home country. As one scholar put it, "Of all the world's colonial peoples, none became rebels more reluctantly than did Anglo-Americans in 1776."[7]

"**THE CONSTITUTION**
...is an instrument for the people to restrain the government–lest it come to dominate our lives and interests."

~ PATRICK HENRY ~
AMERICAN STATESMAN AND
OPPONENT OF THE CONSTITUTION
1736–1799

Breaking the Ties: Independence

Public debate about the problems with Britain continued to rage, but the stage had been set for declaring independence. One of the most rousing arguments in favor of independence was presented by Thomas Paine, a former English schoolmaster and corset maker, who wrote a pamphlet called *Common Sense*. In that pamphlet, which was published in Philadelphia in January 1776, Paine addressed the crisis using "simple fact, plain argument, and common sense." He mocked King George III and attacked every argument that favored loyalty to the king. He called the king a "royal brute" and a "hardened, sullen-tempered Pharaoh [Egyptian king in ancient times]."[8]

Paine's writing went beyond a personal attack on the king. He contended that America could survive economically on its own and no longer needed its British connection. He wanted the developing colonies to become a model republic in a world in which other nations were oppressed by strong central governments.

None of Paine's arguments was new. In fact, most of them were commonly heard in tavern debates throughout the land. Instead, it was the pungency and eloquence of Paine's words that made *Common Sense* so effective:

A government of our own is our natural right: and when a man seriously reflects on the precariousness of human affairs, he will become convinced, that it is infinitely wiser and safer, to form a constitution of our own in a cool and deliberate manner, while we have it in our power, than to trust such an interesting event to time and chance.[9]

Many historians regard Paine's *Common Sense* as the single most important publication of the American Revolution. The pamphlet became a best seller; more than 100,000 copies were sold within a few months after its publication.[10] It put independence squarely on the agenda. Above all, *Common Sense* helped sever the remaining ties of loyalty to the British monarch, thus removing the final psychological barrier to independence. Indeed, later John Adams would ask,

What do we mean by the Revolution? The War? That was no part of the Revolution. It was only an effect and consequence of it. The Revolution was in the minds of the people, and this was effected, from 1760 to 1775, in the course of fifteen years before a drop of blood was drawn at Lexington.[11]

Second Continental Congress The congress of the colonies that met in 1775 to assume the powers of a central government and to establish an army.

Thomas Paine (1737–1809). In addition to his successful pamphlet *Common Sense*, Paine also wrote a series of sixteen pamphlets, under the title *The Crisis*, during the American Revolution. He returned to England and, in 1791 and 1792, wrote *The Rights of Man*, in which he defended the French Revolution. Paine returned to the United States in 1802.

TIME LIFE PICTURES/MANSELL/GETTY IMAGES

INDEPENDENCE FROM BRITAIN—THE FIRST STEP

By June 1776, the Second Continental Congress had voted for free trade at all American ports with all countries except Britain. The congress had also suggested that all colonies establish state governments separate from Britain. The colonists realized that a formal separation from Britain was necessary if the new nation was to obtain supplies for its armies and commitments of military aid from foreign governments. On June 7, 1776, the first formal step toward independence was taken when Richard Henry Lee of Virginia placed the following resolution before the congress:

RESOLVED, That these United Colonies are, and of right ought to be, free and independent States, that they are absolved from allegiance to the British Crown, and that all political connection between them and the state of Great Britain is, and ought to be, totally dissolved.

The congress postponed consideration of Lee's resolution until a formal statement of independence could be drafted. On June 11, a "Committee of Five" was appointed to draft a declaration that would present to the world the colonies' case for independence.

THE SIGNIFICANCE OF THE DECLARATION OF INDEPENDENCE

Adopted on July 4, 1776, the Declaration of Independence is one of the world's most famous documents. Like Paine, Thomas Jefferson, who wrote most of the document, elevated the dispute between Britain and the American colonies to a universal level. Jefferson opened the second paragraph of the declaration with the following words, which have since been memorized by countless American schoolchildren and admired the world over:

We hold these Truths to be self-evident, that all Men are created equal, that they are endowed by their Creator with certain unalienable Rights, that among these are Life, Liberty, and the Pursuit of Happiness—That to secure these Rights, Governments are instituted among Men, deriving their just Powers from the Consent of the Governed, that whenever any Form of Government becomes destructive of these Ends, it is the Right of the People to alter or to abolish it, and to institute new Government.

The concepts expressed in the Declaration of Independence clearly reflect Jefferson's familiarity with European political philosophy, particularly the works of John Locke.[12] Locke's philosophy, though it did not cause the American Revolution, provided philosophical underpinnings by which the revolution could be justified.

FROM COLONIES TO STATES

Even before the Declaration of Independence, some of the colonies had transformed themselves into sovereign states with their own permanent governments. In May 1776, the Second Continental Congress had directed each of the colonies to form "such government as shall . . . best be conducive to the happiness and safety of their constituents [those represented by the government]." Before long, all thirteen colonies had created constitutions. Eleven of the colonies had completely new constitutions. The other

The committee chosen to draft a declaration of independence is shown at work in this nineteenth-century engraving. They are, from the left, Benjamin Franklin, Thomas Jefferson, John Adams, Philip Livingston, and Roger Sherman.

LIBRARY OF CONGRESS

two colonies, Rhode Island and Connecticut, made minor modifications to old royal charters. Seven of the new constitutions contained bills of rights that defined the personal liberties of all state citizens. All constitutions called for limited governments.

REPUBLICANISM   Many citizens were fearful of a strong central government because of their recent experiences under the British Crown. They opposed any form of government that resembled monarchy in any way. Consequently, wherever such antiroyalist sentiment was strong, the legislature—composed of elected representatives—became all-powerful. In Pennsylvania and Georgia, for example, **unicameral** (one-chamber) **legislatures** were unchecked by any executive authority. Indeed, this antiroyalist—or *republican*—sentiment was so strong that the executive branch was extremely weak in all thirteen states.

The republican spirit was strong enough to seriously interfere with the ability of the new nation to win the Revolutionary War, for example by failing to adequately supply General Washington's army. Republicans of the Revolutionary Era (not to be confused with supporters of the later Republican Party) were suspicious not only of executive authority in their own states but also of national authority as represented by the Continental Congress. This anti-authoritarian, localist impulse contrasted with the *nationalist* sentiments of many of the nation's founders, especially such leaders as George Washington and Alexander Hamilton. Nationalists favored an effective central authority. Of course, many founders, such as Thomas Jefferson, harbored both republican and nationalist impulses.

Who were the republicans? As with all political movements of the time, the republicans were led by men of "property and standing." Leaders who were strongly republican, however, tended to be less prominent than their nationalist or moderate counterparts. Small farmers may have been the one group that was disproportionately republican. Small farmers, however, were a majority of the voters in every state.

LO3 *The Confederation of States*

Republican sentiments influenced the thinking of the delegates to the Second Continental Congress, who formed a committee to draft a plan of confederation. A **confederation** is a voluntary association of *independent* states (see Chapter 3). The member states

agree to let the central government undertake a limited number of activities, such as forming an army, but do not allow the central government to place many restrictions on the states' own actions. The member states typically can still govern most state affairs as they see fit.

On November 15, 1777, the Second Continental Congress agreed on a draft of the plan, which was finally signed by all thirteen colonies on March 1, 1781. The **Articles of Confederation,** the result of this plan, served as this nation's first national constitution and represented an important step in the creation of our governmental system.[13]

The Articles of Confederation established the Congress of the Confederation as the central governing body. This congress was a unicameral assembly of representatives, or ambassadors, as they were called, from the various states. Although each state could send from two to seven representatives to the congress, each state, no matter what its size, had only one vote. The issue of sovereignty was an important part of the Articles of Confederation:

> Each State retains its sovereignty, freedom, and independence, and every power, jurisdiction, and right, which is not by this Confederation expressly delegated to the United States in Congress assembled.

The structure of government under the Articles of Confederation is shown in Figure 2–2 on the following page.

Powers of the Government of the Confederation

Congress had several powers under the Articles of Confederation, and these enabled the new nation to achieve a number of accomplishments (see Figure 2–3 on page 32). The Northwest Ordinance settled states' claims to many of the western lands and established a basic pattern for the government of new territories. Also, the 1783 peace treaty negotiated with Britain granted to the United States all of the territory from the Atlantic Ocean to the Mississippi River and from the Great Lakes and Canada to what is now northern Florida.

In spite of these accomplishments, the central government created

unicameral legislature
A legislature with only one chamber.

confederation   A league of independent states that are united only for the purpose of achieving common goals.

Articles of Confederation   The nation's first national constitution, which established a national form of government following the American Revolution. The Articles provided for a confederal form of government in which the central government had few powers.

Figure 2–2

American Government under the Articles of Confederation

STATES
★ Retained their independent political authority.
★ Held every power not expressly delegated to Congress.

Each state sent
two to seven representatives.

PRESIDENT
★ Appointed by Congress to preside over meetings.
★ Had no real executive authority.

CIVIL COMMITTEES AND CIVIL OFFICERS
★ Appointed by Congress to manage general affairs under the direction of Congress.

CONGRESS
★ One-house assembly of state representatives, in which each state possessed one vote.
★ Needed the approval of at least nine states to exercise most powers.
★ Needed the consent of all states to amend the Articles.

COMMITTEE OF STATES
★ Consisted of one delegate from each state, appointed by Congress.
★ Authorized to act according to the wishes of Congress while Congress was in recess.

by the Articles of Confederation was quite weak. The Congress of the Confederation had no power to raise revenues for the militia or to force the states to meet military quotas. Essentially, this meant that the new government did not have the power to enforce its laws. Even passing laws was difficult because the Articles of Confederation provided that nine states had to approve any law before it was enacted. Figure 2–4 on page 33 lists these and other powers that the central government lacked under the Articles of Confederation.

Nonetheless, the Articles of Confederation proved to be a good "first draft" for the Constitution, and at least half of the text of the Articles would later appear in the Constitution. The Articles were an unplanned experiment that tested some of the principles of government that had been set forth earlier in the Declaration of Independence. Some argue that without the experience of government under the Articles of Confederation, it would have been difficult, if not impossible, to arrive at the compromises that were necessary to create the Constitution several years later.

A Time of Crisis—The 1780s

The Revolutionary War ended on October 18, 1781. The Treaty of Paris, which confirmed the colonies' independence from Britain, was signed in 1783. Peace with the British may have been won, but peace within the new nation was hard to find. The states bickered among themselves and refused to support the new central government in almost every way. As George Washington stated, "We are one nation today and thirteen tomorrow. Who will treat [with] us on such terms?"

Indeed, the national government, such as it was, did not have the ability to prevent the various states from entering into agreements with foreign powers, despite the danger that such agreements could completely disrupt the confederation, pitting state against state. When Congress proved reluctant to admit Vermont into the Union, Britain began negotiations with influential Vermonters with the aim of annexing the district to Canada. Likewise, the Spanish governor of Louisiana energetically sought to detach Tennessee and the lands south of it from the United States. Several prominent individuals—including Daniel Boone—accepted Spanish gold.

The states also increasingly taxed each other's imports and at times even prevented trade altogether. By 1784, the new nation was suffering from a serious economic depression. States started printing their own money at dizzying rates, which led to inflation. Banks were calling in old loans and refusing to issue new ones. Individuals who could not pay their debts were often thrown into prison.

SHAYS' REBELLION The tempers of indebted farmers in western Massachusetts reached the boiling point in August 1786. Former Revolutionary War captain Daniel Shays, along with approximately two thousand armed farmers, seized county courthouses and disrupted the debtors' trials. Shays and his men then launched an attack on the national government's arsenal in Springfield. **Shays' Rebellion** continued to grow in intensity and lasted into the winter, when it was finally stopped by the Massachusetts volunteer army, paid by Boston merchants.[14]

Similar disruptions occurred throughout most of the New England states and in some other areas as well. The upheavals, and particularly Shays' Rebellion, were an important catalyst for change. The revolts frightened American political and business leaders and caused more and more Americans to realize that a *true* national government had to be created.

THE ANNAPOLIS MEETING The Virginia legislature called for a meeting of representatives from all of the states at Annapolis, Maryland, on September 11, 1786, to consider extending national authority to issues of commerce. Five of the thirteen states sent delegates, two of whom were Alexander Hamilton of New York and James Madison of Virginia. Both of these men favored a strong central government.[15] They persuaded the other delegates to issue a report calling on the states to hold a convention in Philadelphia in May of the following year.

The Congress of the Confederation at first was reluctant to give its approval to the Philadelphia convention. By mid-February 1787, however, seven of the states had named delegates to the Philadelphia meeting. Finally, on February 21, the congress called on the states to send delegates to Philadelphia "for the sole and express purpose of revising the Articles of Confederation." That Philadelphia meeting became the **Constitutional Convention.**

LO4 *Drafting and Ratifying the Constitution*

Although the convention was supposed to start on May 14, 1787, few of the delegates had actually arrived in Philadelphia on that date. The convention formally opened in the East Room of the Pennsylvania State House on May 25, after fifty-five of the seventy-four delegates had arrived.[16] Only Rhode Island, where feelings were strong against creating a more powerful central government, did not send any delegates.

Who Were the Delegates?

Among the delegates to the Constitutional Convention were some of the nation's best-known leaders. George Washington was present, as were Alexander Hamilton,

James Madison, George Mason, Robert Morris, and Benjamin Franklin (who, at eighty-one years old, had to be carried to the convention on a portable chair). Some notable leaders were absent, including Thomas Jefferson and John Adams, who were serving as ambassadors in Europe, and Patrick Henry, who did not attend because he "smelt a rat." (Henry was one of Virginia's most strongly republican leaders.)

For the most part, the delegates were from the best-educated and wealthiest classes. Thirty-three delegates were lawyers, nearly half of the delegates were college graduates, three were physicians, seven were former chief executives of their respective states, six owned large plantations, at least nineteen owned slaves, eight were important business owners, and twenty-one had fought in the Revolutionary War. In other words, the delegates to the convention constituted an elite assembly. No ordinary farmers or merchants were present. Indeed, in his classic work on the Constitution, Charles Beard maintained that the Constitution was produced primarily by wealthy bondholders who had made loans to the government under the Articles and wanted a strong central government that could prevent state governments from repudiating debts.[17] Later historians, however, rejected Beard's thesis, concluding that bondholders played no special role in writing the Constitution.

The Virginia Plan

James Madison had spent months reviewing European political theory before he went to the Philadelphia convention. His Virginia delegation arrived before anybody else, and he immediately put its members to work. On the first day of the convention, Governor Edmund Randolph of Virginia was able to present fifteen resolutions outlining what was to become known as the *Virginia Plan*. This was a masterful political stroke on the part of the Virginia delegation. Its proposals immediately set the agenda for the remainder of the convention.

The fifteen resolutions contained in the Virginia Plan proposed

Shays' Rebellion A rebellion of angry farmers in western Massachusetts in 1786, led by former Revolutionary War captain Daniel Shays. This rebellion and other similar uprisings in the New England states emphasized the need for a true national government.

Constitutional Convention The convention (meeting) of delegates from the states that was held in Philadelphia in 1787 for the purpose of amending the Articles of Confederation. In fact, the delegates wrote a new constitution (the U.S. Constitution) that established a federal form of government to replace the governmental system that had been created by the Articles of Confederation.

Figure 2–3

Powers of the Central Government under the Articles of Confederation

Although the Articles of Confederation were later scrapped, they did allow the early government of the United States to achieve several important goals, including winning the Revolutionary War.

WHAT THE CONGRESS COULD DO	ACCOMPLISHMENT
Congress could establish and control the armed forces, declare war, and make peace.	The United States won the Revolutionary War.
Congress could enter into treaties and alliances.	Congress negotiated a peace treaty with Britain.
Congress could settle disputes among the states under certain circumstances.	Congress passed the Northwest Ordinance, which settled certain states' land claims.
Congress could regulate coinage (but not paper money) and set standards for weights and measures.	Congress carried out these functions, but the inability to regulate paper money proved a major weakness.
Congress could borrow money from the people.	Congress did borrow money, but without the power to tax, it had trouble repaying the loans or obtaining new ones.
Congress could create a postal system, courts to address issues related to ships at sea, and government departments.	Congress created a postal system and departments of foreign affairs, finance, and war.

The smaller states immediately complained because they would have fewer representatives in the legislature. After two weeks of debate, they offered their own plan—the *New Jersey Plan.*

The New Jersey Plan

William Paterson of New Jersey presented an alternative plan favorable to the smaller states. He argued that because each state had an equal vote under the Articles of Confederation, the convention had no power to change this arrangement. The New Jersey Plan proposed the following:

- Congress would be able to regulate trade and impose taxes.
- Each state would have only one vote.
- Acts of Congress would be the supreme law of the land.
- An executive office of more than one person would be elected by Congress.
- The executive office would appoint a national supreme court.

an entirely new national government under a constitution. The plan, which favored large states such as Virginia, called for the following:

- A bicameral legislature. The lower house was to be chosen by the people. The smaller upper house was to be chosen by the elected members of the lower house. The number of representatives would be in proportion to each state's population (the larger states would have more representatives). The legislature could void any state laws.
- A national executive branch, elected by the legislature.
- A national court system, created by the legislature.

Great Compromise A plan for a bicameral legislature in which one chamber would be based on population and the other chamber would represent each state equally. The plan, also known as the Connecticut Compromise, resolved the small-state/large-state controversy.

"The Constitution only gives people the right to **PURSUE HAPPINESS.** You have to catch it yourself."

~ BENJAMIN FRANKLIN ~
AMERICAN STATESMAN AND
SIGNER OF THE CONSTITUTION
1706–1790

The Compromises

Most delegates were unwilling to consider the New Jersey Plan. When the Virginia Plan was brought up again, however, delegates from the smaller states threatened to leave, and the convention was in danger of dissolving. On July 16, Roger Sherman of Connecticut broke the deadlock by proposing a compromise plan. Compromises on other disputed issues followed.

THE GREAT COMPROMISE Roger Sherman's plan, which has become known as the **Great Compromise** (or the Connecticut Compromise), called for a legislature with two houses:

- A lower house (the House of Representatives), in which the number of representatives from each state would be determined by the number of people in that state.

Figure 2–4

Powers That the Central Government Lacked under the Articles of Confederation

The government's lack of certain powers under the Articles of Confederation taught the framers of the Constitution several important lessons, which helped them create a more effective government under that new document.

WHAT THE CONGRESS COULD NOT DO	RESULT
Congress could not force the states to meet military quotas.	The central government could not draft soldiers to form a standing army.
Congress could not regulate commerce between the states or with other nations.	Each state was free to set up its own system of taxes on goods imported from other states. Economic quarrels among the states broke out. There was difficulty in trading with other nations.
Congress could enter into treaties, but could not enforce them.	The states were not forced to respect treaties. Many states entered into treaties independent of Congress.
Congress could not directly tax the people.	The central government had to rely on the states to collect and forward taxes, which the states were reluctant to do. The central government was always short of money.
Congress had no power to enforce its laws.	The central government depended on the states to enforce its laws, which they rarely did.
Any amendment to the Articles required all thirteen states to consent.	In practice, the powers of the central government could not be changed.
There was no national judicial system.	Most disputes among the states could not be settled by the central government.
There was no executive branch.	Coordinating the work of the central government was almost impossible.

three-fifths compromise
A compromise reached during the Constitutional Convention by which three-fifths of all slaves were to be counted for purposes of representation in the House of Representatives.

slavery was legal in parts of the North, most slaves and slave owners lived in the South. Indeed, in the southern states, slaves constituted about 40 percent of the population. Counting the slaves as part of the population would thus greatly increase the number of southern representatives in the House. The delegates from the southern states wanted the slaves to be counted as persons; the delegates from the northern states disagreed. Eventually, the **three-fifths compromise** settled this deadlock: each slave would count as three-fifths of a person in determining representation in Congress. (The three-fifths compromise was eventually overturned in 1868 by the Fourteenth Amendment.)

SLAVE IMPORTATION The three-fifths compromise did not satisfy everyone at the Constitutional Convention. Many delegates wanted slavery to be banned completely in the United States. The delegates compromised on this question by agreeing that Congress could prohibit the importation of slaves into the country beginning in 1808. The issue of slavery itself, however, was never really addressed by the delegates to the Constitutional Convention. As a result, the South won twenty years of unrestricted slave trade and a requirement that escaped slaves who had fled to the northern states be returned to their owners. Domestic slave trading was untouched.

BANNING EXPORT TAXES The South's economic health depended in large part on its exports of agricultural products. The South feared that the northern majority in Congress might pass taxes on these exports. This fear led to yet another compromise: the South agreed

■ An upper house (the Senate), which would have two members from each state; the members would be elected by the state legislatures.

The Great Compromise gave something to both sides: the large states would have more representatives in the House of Representatives than the small states, yet each state would be granted equality in the Senate—because each state, regardless of size, would have two senators. The Great Compromise thus resolved the small-state/large-state controversy.

THE THREE-FIFTHS COMPROMISE A second compromise had to do with how many representatives each state would have in the House of Representatives. Although

The fate of the proposed Constitution was decided in the state ratifying conventions, but it was the subject of intense debates everywhere—in homes, taverns, coffeehouses, and newspapers.

to let Congress have the power to regulate **interstate commerce** as well as commerce with other nations; in exchange, the Constitution guaranteed that no export taxes would ever be imposed on products exported by the states. Today, the United States is one of the few countries that does not tax its exports.

Defining the Executive and the Judiciary

The Great Compromise was reached by mid-July. Still to be determined was the makeup of the executive branch and the judiciary. One of the weaknesses of the Confederation had been the lack of an independent executive authority. The Constitution remedied this problem by creating an independent executive—the president—and by making the president the commander in chief of the army and navy and of the state militias when called into national service. The president was also given extensive appointment powers, although Senate approval was required for certain appointments.

Another problem under the Confederation was the lack of a judiciary that was independent of the state courts. The Constitution established the United States Supreme Court and authorized Congress to establish other "inferior" federal courts.

To protect against possible wrongdoing, the Constitution also provided for a way to remove

interstate commerce
Trade that involves more than one state.

federal officials from office—through the impeachment process. The Constitution provides that a federal official who commits "Treason, Bribery, or other high Crimes and Misdemeanors" may be impeached (accused of, or charged with, wrongdoing) by the House of Representatives and tried by the Senate. If found guilty of the charges by a two-thirds vote in the Senate, the official can be removed from office and prevented from ever assuming another federal government post.

The Final Draft Is Approved

A five-man Committee of Detail handled the executive and judicial issues, plus other remaining work. August 6 presented a rough draft to the convention. On September 8, a committee was named to "revise the stile [style] of, and arrange the Articles which had been agreed to" by the convention. The Committee of Style was headed by Gouverneur Morris of Pennsylvania.[18] On September 17, 1787, the final draft of the Constitution was approved by thirty-nine of the remaining forty-two delegates (some delegates left early).

Looking back on the drafting of the Constitution, an obvious question emerges: Why didn't the founders ban slavery outright? Certainly, as already mentioned, many of the delegates thought that slavery was morally wrong and that the Constitution should ban it entirely. Many Americans have since regarded the framers' failure to deal with the slavery issue as a betrayal of the Declaration of Independence, which proclaimed that "all Men are created equal." Others have pointed out how contradictory it was that the framers of the Constitution complained about being "enslaved" by the British yet ignored the problem of slavery in this country.

A common argument supporting the framers' action (or lack of it) with respect to slavery is that they had no alternative but to ignore the issue. If they had taken a stand on slavery, the Constitution certainly would not have been ratified. Indeed, if the antislavery delegates had insisted on banning slavery, the delegates from the southern states might have walked out of the convention—and there would have been no Constitution to ratify.

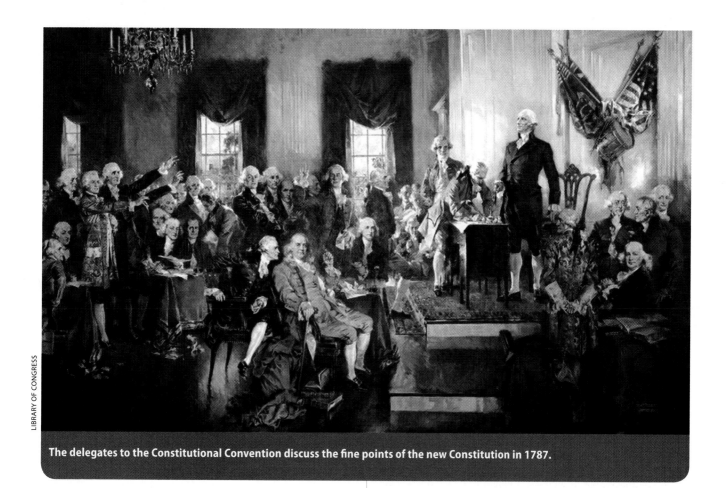

The delegates to the Constitutional Convention discuss the fine points of the new Constitution in 1787.

For another look at this issue, however, see this chapter's *Perception versus Reality* feature on the following page.

The Debate over Ratification

The ratification of the Constitution set off a national debate of unprecedented proportions. The battle was fought chiefly by two opposing groups—the **Federalists** (those who favored a strong central government and the new Constitution) and the **Anti-Federalists** (those who opposed a strong central government and the new Constitution).

In the debate over ratification, the Federalists had several advantages. They assumed a positive name, leaving their opposition with a negative label. (Indeed, the Anti-Federalists could well have called themselves republicans and their opponents nationalists.) The Federalists also had attended the Constitutional Convention and thus were familiar with the arguments both in favor of and against various constitutional provisions.

The Anti-Federalists, in contrast, had no actual knowledge of those discussions because they had not attended the convention. The Federalists also had time, money, and prestige on their side. Their impressive list of political thinkers and writers included Alexander Hamilton, John Jay, and James Madison. The Federalists could communicate with one another more readily because many of them were bankers, lawyers, and merchants who lived in urban areas, where communication was easier. The Federalists organized a quick and effective ratification campaign to elect themselves as delegates to each state's ratifying convention.

THE FEDERALISTS ARGUE FOR RATIFICATION Alexander Hamilton, a leading Federalist, began to answer the Constitution's critics in New York by writing newspaper columns under the pseudonym "Caesar." The Caesar letters appeared to have little effect, so Hamilton switched his pseudonym to "Publius" and enlisted John Jay and James Madison to help him write the papers. In a period of less than a year, these three men wrote a series of eighty-five essays in defense of the Constitution. These essays, which were printed not only in New York newspapers but also in other papers throughout the states, are collectively known as the *Federalist Papers*.

Generally, the papers attempted to allay the fears expressed by the Constitution's critics. One fear was that the rights of those in the minority would not be protected. Another

Federalists A political group, led by Alexander Hamilton and John Adams, that supported the adoption of the Constitution and the creation of a federal form of government.

Anti-Federalists A political group that opposed the adoption of the Constitution because of the document's centralist tendencies and because it did not include a bill of rights.

In the Declaration of Independence, Thomas Jefferson, a Virginia slave owner, pronounced, "all Men are created equal." Jefferson considered slavery a "hideous blot" on America. George Washington, also a southern slave owner, regarded the institution of slavery as "repugnant." Patrick Henry, another southerner, also publicly deplored slavery. Given such views among the leading figures of the era, why didn't the founders stay true to the Declaration of Independence and free the slaves?

The Perception

Most Americans assume that southern economic interests and racism alone led the founders to abandon the principles of equality expressed in the Declaration of Independence. African slaves were the backbone of American agriculture, particularly for tobacco, the most profitable export. Without their slaves, southern plantation owners would not have been able to earn such high profits. Presumably, southerners would not have ratified the Constitution unless it protected the institution of slavery.

The Reality

The third chief justice of the United States Supreme Court, Oliver Ellsworth, declared that "as population increases, poor laborers will be so plenty as to render slaves useless. Slavery in time will not be a speck in our country."[19] He was wrong, of course. But according to Pulitzer Prize–winning historian Gordon S. Wood, Ellsworth's sentiments mirrored those of most prominent leaders in the United States in the years leading up to the creation of our Constitution. Indeed, great thinkers of the time firmly believed that the liberal principles of the Revolution would destroy the institution of slavery.

At the time of the Constitutional Convention, slavery was disappearing in the northern states (it would be eliminated there by 1804). Many founders thought the same thing would happen in the southern states. After all, there were more anti-slavery societies in the South than in the North. The founders also thought that the ending of the international slave trade in 1808 would eventually end slavery in the United States. Consequently, the issue of slavery was taken off the table when the Constitution was created simply because the founders had a mistaken belief about the longevity of the institution. They could not have predicted at the time that growing cotton would give slavery a new lease on life.[20]

Blog On Slavery and the Constitution is just one of many subjects that you can read about in the Legal History Blog at **legalhistoryblog.blogspot.com.** If you type "slavery" into the box at the top left of the screen and press "enter," you will see the postings on this topic.

---

was that a minority might block the passage of measures that the majority felt were in the national interest. Many critics also feared that a republican form of government would not work in a nation the size of the United States. Various groups, or **factions,** would struggle for power, and chaos would result. Madison responded to the latter argument in *Federalist Paper* No. 10 (see Appendix F), which is considered a classic in political theory. Among other things, Madison argued that the nation's size was actually an advantage in controlling factions: in a large nation, there would be so many diverse interests and factions that no one faction would be able to gain control of the government.[21]

faction A group of persons forming a cohesive minority.

tyranny The arbitrary or unrestrained exercise of power by an oppressive individual or government.

THE ANTI-FEDERALISTS' RESPONSE Perhaps the greatest advantage of the Anti-Federalists was that they stood for the status quo. Usually, it is more difficult to institute changes than it is to keep what is already known and understood. Among the Anti-Federalists were such patriots as Patrick Henry and Samuel Adams. Patrick Henry said of the proposed Constitution: "I look upon that paper as the most fatal plan that could possibly be conceived to enslave a free people."

In response to the *Federalist Papers*, the Anti-Federalists published their own essays, using such pseudonyms as "Montezuma" and "Philadelphiensis." They also wrote brilliantly, attacking nearly every clause of the new document. Many Anti-Federalists contended that the Constitution had been written by aristocrats and would lead the nation to aristocratic **tyranny** (the exercise of absolute, unlimited power). Other Anti-

Federalists feared that the Constitution would lead to an overly powerful central government that would limit personal freedom.[22]

The Anti-Federalists strongly argued that the Constitution needed a bill of rights. They warned that without a bill of rights, a strong national government might take away the political rights won during the American Revolution. They demanded that the new Constitution clearly guarantee personal freedoms. The Federalists generally did not think that a bill of rights was all that important. Nevertheless, to gain the necessary support, the Federalists finally promised to add a bill of rights to the Constitution as the first order of business under the new government. This promise turned the tide in favor of the Constitution.

Ratification

The contest for ratification was close in several states, but the Federalists finally won in all of the state conventions. In 1787, Delaware, Pennsylvania, and New Jersey voted to ratify the Constitution, followed by Georgia and Connecticut early in the following year. Even though the Anti-Federalists were perhaps the majority in Massachusetts, a successful political campaign by the Federalists led to ratification by that state on February 6, 1788.

Following Maryland and South Carolina, New Hampshire became the ninth state to ratify the Constitution on June 21, 1788, thus formally putting the Constitution into effect. New York and Virginia had not yet ratified, however, and without them the Constitution would have no true power. That worry was dispelled in the summer of 1788, when both Virginia and New York ratified the new Constitution. North Carolina waited until November 21 of the following year to ratify the Constitution, and Rhode Island did not ratify until May 29, 1790.

LO5 *The Constitution's Major Principles of Government*

The framers of the Constitution were fearful of the powerful British monarchy, against which they had so recently rebelled. At the same time, they wanted a central government strong enough to prevent the kinds of crises that had occurred under the weak central authority of the Articles of Confederation. The principles of government expressed in the Constitution reflect both of these concerns.

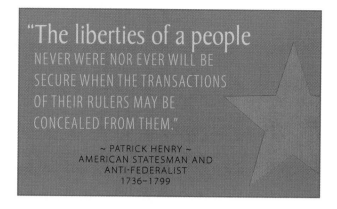

"The liberties of a people NEVER WERE NOR EVER WILL BE SECURE WHEN THE TRANSACTIONS OF THEIR RULERS MAY BE CONCEALED FROM THEM."

~ PATRICK HENRY ~
AMERICAN STATESMAN AND
ANTI-FEDERALIST
1736–1799

Limited Government and Popular Sovereignty

The Constitution incorporated the principle of limited government, which means that government can do only what the people allow it to do through the exercise of a duly developed system of laws. This principle can be found in many parts of the Constitution. For example, while Articles I, II, and III indicate exactly what the national government *can* do, the first nine amendments to the Constitution list the ways in which the government *cannot* limit certain individual freedoms.

Implicitly, the principle of limited government rests on the concept of popular sovereignty. Remember the phrases that frame the Preamble to the Constitution: "We the People of the United States . . . do ordain and establish this Constitution for the United States of America." In other words, it is the people who form the government and decide on the powers that the government can exercise. If the government exercises powers beyond those granted to it by the Constitution, it is acting illegally. The idea that no one, including government officers, is above the law is often called the **rule of law.**

Ultimately, the viability of a democracy rests on the willingness of the people and their leaders to adhere to the rule of law. A nation's written constitution, such as that of Iraq under the dictator Saddam Hussein, may guarantee numerous rights and liberties for its citizens. Yet, unless the government of that nation enforces those rights and liberties, the law does not rule the nation. Rather, the government decides what the rules will be. Consider the situation in Russia today. After the collapse of the Soviet Union, Russia established a federal republic. By all appearances, though, Vladimir Putin, Russia's leader, is not constrained by the principles set forth in Russia's constitution—see this chapter's *The Rest of the World* feature on the following page for details.

> **rule of law** A basic principle of government that requires those who govern to act in accordance with established law.

Russia's Short-Lived Flirtation with Democracy

From the Russian Revolution in 1917 to the end of the Soviet Union in 1991, Russians lived under a Communist dictatorship. For centuries prior to 1917, they had lived under an autocracy headed by a tsar. In short, Russians had no experience with democracy before the fall of the Soviet Union.

A Democracy at Last . . .

On December 25, 1993, the Russian Federation (its formal name) saw its first independent constitution. If you read a translation of that constitution, you would conclude that modern Russia is now a democracy. That conclusion seemed to be true for a number of years because Russians freely voted for members of the Duma (the Russian counterpart of our Congress). They voted overwhelmingly in favor of President Vladimir Putin in 2000, too. Western commentators expressed some concern that Putin was formerly the head of the Soviet Union's brutal secret police. Nevertheless, after meeting Putin, President George W. Bush said, "I looked him in the eyes, and I know I can work with this man."

. . . or Not

Perhaps Putin showed his true colors when he referred to the collapse of the Soviet Union as "the greatest geopolitical catastrophe of the twentieth century." Under Putin, freedom of the press all but disappeared—the state simultaneously shut down independent sources of information and expanded government ownership of the media. A formerly promising independent court system all but vanished. In 2005, the election of regional governors was abolished. Governors are now appointed by the president. Beginning in 2006, Putin's administration instituted electoral reforms so that his political party, United Russia, was guaranteed control of the Duma and the presidency. The government won the right to exclude candidates from party slates and to bar parties from running altogether.

Increasingly, Russian authorities arrested and detained public activists. In the economy, the Russian government gradually took control of all oil, natural gas, and other natural resources. Anyone who did not go along with Putin ended up in prison.

The Russian Public's Reaction

Are Russian citizens worried about this reversion to an undemocratic state? Apparently not, for public opinion polls in Russia have shown that more than 80 percent of the Russian people approve of Putin's "strong leadership."

In March 2008, Putin's second term as president came to an end, and under the constitution he could not immediately run again. Instead, he sponsored the election of Dmitry Medvedev, a supporter, as president. Medvedev named Putin as Russia's prime minister, and events soon proved that Putin still held the real power in the government. Putin has hinted that he may return as president in 2012. Given that in that year the presidential term will expand from four years to six, Putin could remain in power until 2024.

For Critical Analysis *Why do you think so many Russians are unconcerned about the erosion of democracy in their country?*

federal system A form of government that provides for a division of powers between a central government and several regional governments. In the United States, the division of powers between the national government and the states is established by the Constitution.

commerce clause The clause in Article I, Section 8, of the Constitution that gives Congress the power to regulate interstate commerce (commerce involving more than one state).

The Principle of Federalism

The Constitution also incorporated the principle of federalism. In a **federal system** of government, the central (national) government shares sovereign powers with the various state governments. Federalism was the solution to the debate over whether the national government or the states should have ultimate sovereignty.

The Constitution gave the national government significant powers—powers that it had not had under the Articles of Confederation. For example, the Constitution expressly states that the president is the nation's chief executive as well as the commander in chief of the armed forces. The Constitution also declares that the Constitution and the laws created by the national government are supreme—that is, they take precedence over conflicting state laws. Other powers given to the national government include the power to coin money, to levy and collect taxes, and to regulate interstate commerce, a power granted by the **commerce clause.** Finally, the national government was authorized to undertake all laws that are "necessary and proper" for carrying out its expressly delegated powers.

The founders granted the federal government exclusive rights over creating money because in previous years, several states had printed excessive quantities of paper money, thus devaluing the currency. How might the founders react to the way in which today's federal government manages the money supply? Consider that question as you read this chapter's *Our Government Faces a Troubled Economy* feature on the following page.

Because the states feared too much centralized control, the Constitution also allowed for many states' rights. These rights include the power to regulate commerce within state borders and generally the authority to exercise any powers that are not delegated by the Constitution to the central government. (See Chapter 3 for a detailed discussion of federalism.)

Separation of Powers

As James Madison once said, after you have given the government the ability to control its citizens, you have to "oblige it to control itself." To force the government to "control itself" and to prevent the rise of tyranny, Madison devised a scheme, the **Madisonian Model,** in which the powers of the national government were separated into different branches: legislative, executive,

> "The truth is that all men having power **OUGHT TO BE MISTRUSTED."**
> ~ JAMES MADISON ~
> FOURTH PRESIDENT OF THE UNITED STATES
> 1809–1817

and judicial.[23] The legislative branch (Congress) passes laws; the executive branch (the president) administers and enforces the laws; and the judicial branch (the courts) interprets the laws. By separating the powers of government, the framers ensured that no one branch would have enough power to dominate the others. This principle of **separation of powers** is laid out in Articles I, II, and III of the Constitution.

Checks and Balances

A system of **checks and balances** was also devised to ensure that no one group or branch of government can exercise exclusive control. Even though each branch of government is independent of the others, it can also check the actions of the others. Look at Figure 2–5 on page 41, and you can see how this is done. As the figure shows, the president checks Congress by holding a **veto power,** which is the ability to return bills to Congress for reconsideration. Congress, in turn, controls taxes and spending, and the Senate must approve presidential appointments. The judicial branch of government can also check the other branches of government through *judicial review*—the power to rule congressional or presidential actions unconstitutional.[24] In turn, the president and the Senate exercise some control over the judiciary through the president's power to appoint federal judges and the Senate's role in confirming presidential appointments.

Among the other checks and balances built into the American system of government are staggered terms of office. Members of the House of Representatives serve for

Madisonian Model The model of government devised by James Madison, in which the powers of the government are separated into three branches: executive, legislative, and judicial.

separation of powers The principle of dividing governmental powers among the executive, the legislative, and the judicial branches of government.

checks and balances A major principle of American government in which each of the three branches is given the means to check (to restrain or balance) the actions of the others.

veto power A constitutional power that enables the chief executive (president or governor) to reject legislation and return it to the legislature with reasons for the rejection. This prevents or at least delays the bill from becoming law.

James Madison (1751–1836). Madison's contributions at the Constitutional Convention in 1787 earned him the title "Master Builder of the Constitution." As a member of Congress from Virginia, he advocated the Bill of Rights. He was secretary of state under Thomas Jefferson (1801–1809) and became our fourth president in 1809.

LIBRARY OF CONGRESS

OUR GOVERNMENT FACES A TROUBLED ECONOMY

Printing Money to Fight a Recession

The U.S. Constitution in Article I, Section 8, gave Congress the power "To borrow Money on the credit of the United States" and "To coin Money [and] regulate the value thereof." The framers of the Constitution would probably be shocked at what the federal government has done with the supply of money in circulation in this country.

What Is Monetary Policy?

Monetary policy involves changing the amount of money in circulation to affect interest rates, credit markets, the rate of inflation, the rate of economic growth, and the rate of unemployment. Monetary policy is not under the direct control of Congress and the president. Instead, it is determined by the Federal Reserve System (the Fed), an independent agency. The Fed is controlled by a board of seven governors, including the very powerful chairperson, currently Ben Bernanke. The president appoints the members of the board of governors, and the Senate must approve the nominations.

The Fed's Response to the Great Depression

The Fed was created to be the "lender of last resort" for the banking system, a bank that could lend to other banks when no one else would. It turns out that as the Great Depression took hold in the 1930s, the Fed acted in the opposite manner. Indeed, many scholars argue that the Fed was responsible for the severity of the Great Depression because it allowed the money supply in circulation to fall by fully one-third by 1933. The result was a severe contraction in economic activity.

Monetary Policy during the Current Economic Crisis

When the Great Recession began in December 2007, the Fed at first appeared not quite sure what to do. When the crisis became acute in September 2008, the Fed went

AP PHOTO/DOUG MILLS

along with the Bush administration's request to Congress to provide a fund of $700 billion to bail out the banks. In an attempt to restart borrowing and lending, the Fed pushed the interest rate on short-term government debt down almost to zero. When this turned out not to be sufficient, the Fed began doing something it had never done before. It started buying huge quantities of debt directly from the private sector—bonds backed up by mortgages, credit-card debt, and student loans. In effect, if banks were reluctant to lend, the Fed would do the lending itself. This practice has been named "quantitative easing." These purchases have the effect of creating new money and expanding the money supply.

What the Future Holds

Some economists fear that by creating money in this way, the Fed has guaranteed that inflation will be a serious problem when the recession comes to an end. True, for the moment, the newly created money simply replaces funds that are "parked by the curb"—that is, pulled out of action by institutions and investors that are afraid to lend. Sooner or later, though, that sidelined money will be put to work again, and that's when inflation becomes a danger. Will the Fed be able to react quickly enough to prevent a big rise in prices? The historical record is not encouraging.

You Be the Judge Why do you think Congress gave control over monetary policy to an independent body?

Figure 2–5

Checks and Balances among the Branches of Government

CONGRESS
★ Can override presidential vetoes
★ Can impeach and remove the president from office
★ Senate confirms presidential appointments and ratifies treaties

THE PRESIDENT
★ Appoints members of the Supreme Court and other federal courts

EXECUTIVE BRANCH
(enforces laws)
President

THE PRESIDENT
★ Can veto legislation

THE SUPREME COURT
★ Can declare an executive action unconstitutional (judicial review)

LEGISLATIVE BRANCH
(passes laws)
Congress

JUDICIAL BRANCH
(interprets laws)
Supreme Court and other federal courts

CONGRESS
★ Can impeach and remove judges from office

THE SUPREME COURT
★ Can declare a legislative act unconstitutional (judicial review)

two years, members of the Senate for six, and the president for four. Federal court judges are appointed for life but may be impeached and removed from office by Congress for misconduct. Staggered terms and changing government personnel make it difficult for individuals within the government to form controlling factions. The American system of government also includes numerous other checks and balances, many of which you will read about in later chapters of this book. We look next at another obvious check on the powers of government: the Bill of Rights.

The Bill of Rights

To secure the ratification of the Constitution in several important states, the Federalists had to provide assurances that amendments would be passed to protect individual liberties against violations by the national government. At the state ratifying conventions, delegates set forth specific rights that should be protected.

James Madison considered these recommendations as he labored to draft what became the Bill of Rights.

After sorting through more than two hundred state recommendations, Madison came up with sixteen amendments. Congress tightened the language somewhat and eliminated four of the amendments. Of the remaining twelve, two—one dealing with the apportionment of representatives and the other with the compensation of the members of Congress—were not ratified by the states during the ratification process.[25] By 1791, all of the states had ratified the ten amendments that now constitute our Bill of Rights. Table 2–2 on the following page presents the text of the first ten amendments to the Constitution, along with explanatory comments. Note that many phrases in the Bill of Rights are imprecise and call for further judicial interpretation. For example, what exactly did the founders mean by "cruel and unusual punishments" (Eighth Amendment)? We consider that issue in this chapter's *Join the Debate* feature on page 43.

Table 2–2

The Bill of Rights

Amendment I.
Religion, Speech, Press, Assembly, and Petition

Congress shall make no law respecting an establishment of religion, or prohibiting the free exercise thereof; or abridging the freedom of speech, or of the press; or the right of the people peaceably to assemble, and to petition the Government for a redress of grievances.

Congress may not create an official church or enact laws limiting the freedom of religion, speech, the press, assembly, and petition. These guarantees, like the others in the Bill of Rights (the first ten amendments), are not absolute—each may be exercised only with regard to the rights of other persons.

Amendment II.
Militia and the Right to Bear Arms

A well regulated Militia, being necessary to the security of a free State, the right of the people to keep and bear Arms, shall not be infringed.

Each state has the right to maintain a volunteer armed force. Although individuals have the right to bear arms, states and the federal government may regulate the possession and use of firearms by individuals.

Amendment III.
The Quartering of Soldiers

No Soldier shall, in time of peace be quartered in any house, without the consent of the Owner, nor in time of war, but in a manner to be prescribed by law.

Before the Revolutionary War, it had been common British practice to quarter soldiers in colonists' homes. Military troops do not have the power to take over private houses during peacetime.

Amendment IV.
Searches and Seizures

The right of the people to be secure in their persons, houses, papers, and effects, against unreasonable searches and seizures, shall not be violated, and no Warrants shall issue, but upon probable cause, supported by Oath or affirmation, and particularly describing the place to be searched, and the persons or things to be seized.

Here, the word warrant *refers to a document issued by a magistrate or judge indicating the name, address, and possible offense committed. Anyone asking for the warrant, such as a police officer, must be able to convince the magistrate or judge that an offense probably has been committed.*

Amendment V.
Grand Juries, Self-Incrimination, Double Jeopardy, Due Process, and Eminent Domain

No person shall be held to answer for a capital, or otherwise infamous crime, unless on a presentment or indictment of a Grand Jury, except in cases arising in the land or naval forces, or in the Militia, when in actual service in time of War or public danger; nor shall any person be subject for the same offense to be twice put in jeopardy of life or limb; nor shall be compelled in any criminal case to be a witness against himself, nor be deprived of life, liberty, or property, without due process of law; nor shall private property be taken for public use, without just compensation.

There are two types of juries. A grand jury considers physical evidence and the testimony of witnesses and decides whether there is sufficient reason to bring a case to trial. A petit jury hears the case at trial and decides it. "For the same offense to be twice put in jeopardy

of life or limb" means to be tried twice for the same crime. A person may not be tried for the same crime twice or forced to give evidence against herself or himself. No person's right to life, liberty, or property may be taken away except by lawful means, called the due process of law. Private property taken for public purposes must be paid for by the government.

Amendment VI.
Criminal Court Procedures

In all criminal prosecutions, the accused shall enjoy the right to a speedy and public trial, by an impartial jury of the State and district wherein the crime shall have been committed, which district shall have been previously ascertained by law, and to be informed of the nature and cause of the accusation; to be confronted with the witnesses against him; to have compulsory process for obtaining witnesses in his favor, and to have the Assistance of Counsel for his defence.

Any person accused of a crime has the right to a fair and public trial by a jury in the state in which the crime took place. The charges against that person must be so indicated. Any accused person has the right to a lawyer to defend him or her and to question those who testify against him or her, as well as the right to call people to speak in his or her favor at trial.

Amendment VII.
Trial by Jury in Civil Cases

In Suits at common law, where the value in controversy shall exceed twenty dollars, the right of trial by jury shall be preserved, and no fact tried by a jury, shall be otherwise re-examined in any Court of the United States, than according to the rules of the common law.

A jury trial may be requested by either party in a dispute in any case involving more than $20. If both parties agree to a trial by a judge without a jury, the right to a jury trial may be put aside.

Amendment VIII.
Bail, Cruel and Unusual Punishment

Excessive bail shall not be required, nor excessive fines imposed, nor cruel and unusual punishments inflicted.

Bail is that amount of money that a person accused of a crime may be required to deposit with the court as a guarantee that she or he will appear in court when requested. The amount of bail required or the fine imposed as punishment for a crime must be reasonable compared with the seriousness of the crime involved. Any punishment judged to be too harsh or too severe for a crime shall be prohibited.

Amendment IX.
The Rights Retained by the People

The enumeration in the Constitution, of certain rights, shall not be construed to deny or disparage others retained by the people.

Many civil rights that are not explicitly enumerated in the Constitution are still held by the people.

Amendment X.
Reserved Powers of the States

The powers not delegated to the United States by the Constitution, nor prohibited by it to the States, are reserved to the States respectively, or to the people.

Those powers not delegated by the Constitution to the federal government or expressly denied to the states belong to the states and to the people. This clause in essence allows the states to pass laws under their "police powers."

Is the Death Penalty a Cruel and Unusual Punishment?

AP PHOTO/PAT SULLIVAN

The Eighth Amendment to the U.S. Constitution explicitly states that the government cannot inflict "cruel and unusual punishments." It is also true that criminals have been executed since the earliest days of the republic.

Even before there were prisons in America, we had the death penalty, also called "capital punishment." In 1608, a man named George Kendall was executed by a firing squad in Virginia on charges of spying for Spain. Since Kendall's time, more than 18,000 Americans have been executed as punishment for their crimes. In addition to murder, a variety of other crimes have been punished by death in this country. In the 1700s, citizens were executed for robbery, forgery, and illegally cutting down trees.

No state executes people for such crimes today. In our modern world, though, is the death penalty itself cruel and unusual, and therefore a violation of the Eighth Amendment?

An Eye for an Eye Makes the Whole World Blind

Some argue that the death penalty is inappropriate even for someone who has committed murder. Violence and death may always be with us, but the law should not encourage violent sentiments. Already in 1764, the Italian jurist Cesare Beccaria asserted that "the death penalty cannot be useful, because of the example of barbarity it gives men."

As United States Supreme Court justice Arthur J. Goldberg once wrote, "The deliberate institutionalized taking of human life by the state is the greatest conceivable degradation of the dignity of a human personality." Face it—capital punishment is barbaric whether it is carried out by a firing squad, an electric chair, a gas chamber, lethal injection, or hanging. Nations other than the United States that permit capital punishment are not ones that we would seek to emulate: they include China, Iran, North Korea, and Saudi Arabia. Almost all of our allies have abolished the practice.

There Is Nothing Cruel and Unusual about Executing a Murderer

Strangely enough, some who are against capital punishment have argued that life in prison without parole is even crueler than death. Prisoners are confined in an environment of violence where they are treated like animals, and the suffering goes on for decades. If you think about it, this is an argument that the death sentence can be merciful. In any event, capital punishment is not cruel and unusual as meant by the Eighth Amendment. Indeed, the current method of execution used in most states— lethal injection—appears quite civilized compared with methods of execution used in England back in the 1700s, which included drawing and quartering and burning at the stake. Practices such as these are what the founders sought to ban.

For Critical Analysis *Can there be a humane method of extinguishing someone's life? Why or why not?*

Amending the Constitution

Since the Constitution was written, more than eleven thousand amendments have been introduced in Congress. Nonetheless, in the years since the ratification of the Bill of Rights, the first ten amendments to the Constitution, only seventeen proposed amendments have actually survived the amendment process and become a part of our Constitution. It is often contended that members of Congress use the amendment process simply as a political ploy. By proposing an amendment, a member of Congress can show her or his position on an issue, knowing that the odds *against* the amendment's being adopted are high.

One of the reasons there are so few amendments is that the framers, in Article V, made the formal amendment process difficult (although it was easier than it had been under the Articles of Confederation, as just discussed). There are two ways to propose an amendment and two ways to ratify one. As a result, there are four possible ways for an amendment to be added to the Constitution.

METHODS OF PROPOSING AN AMENDMENT The two methods of proposing an amendment are as follows:

1. A two-thirds vote in the Senate and in the House of Representatives is required. All of the twenty-seven existing amendments have been proposed in this way.

2. If two-thirds of the state legislatures request that Congress call a national amendment convention, then Congress must call one. The convention may propose amendments to the states for ratification. There has yet to be a successful amendment proposal using this method.

The notion of a national amendment convention is exciting to many people. Many national political and judicial leaders, however, are very uneasy about the prospect of convening a body that conceivably could do what the Constitutional Convention did—create a new form of government.

In two separate instances, the call for a national amendment convention almost became reality. Between 1963 and 1969, thirty-three state legislatures (out of the necessary thirty-four) attempted to call a convention to amend the Constitution to overturn the Supreme Court's "one person, one vote" decisions (see Chapter 11). Since 1975, thirty-two states have asked for a national convention to propose an amendment requiring that the

Independence Hall in Philadelphia.

federal government balance its budget. Generally, the major national convention campaigns have reflected dissatisfaction on the part of conservative and rural groups with the national government's social and economic policies.

METHODS OF RATIFYING AN AMENDMENT There are two methods of ratifying a proposed amendment:

1. Three-fourths of the state legislatures can vote in favor of the proposed amendment. This method is considered the "traditional" ratification method and has been used twenty-six times.

2. The states can call special conventions to ratify the proposed amendment. If three-fourths of the states approve, the amendment is ratified. This method has been used only once—to ratify the Twenty-first Amendment.[26]

You can see the four methods for proposing and ratifying amendments in Figure 2–6 at left. As you can imagine, to meet the requirements for proposal and ratification, any amendment must have wide popular support in all regions of the country.

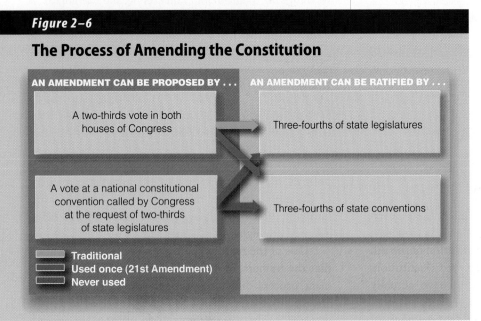

Figure 2–6

The Process of Amending the Constitution

AN AMENDMENT CAN BE PROPOSED BY . . .	AN AMENDMENT CAN BE RATIFIED BY . . .
A two-thirds vote in both houses of Congress	Three-fourths of state legislatures
A vote at a national constitutional convention called by Congress at the request of two-thirds of state legislatures	Three-fourths of state conventions

- Traditional
- Used once (21st Amendment)
- Never used

Americans engaged in intense disputes about the ratification of the Constitution, as you have learned in this chapter. The most important of these disputes was over the relative power of the states and the national government. This dispute is central to the topic of federalism, which we will take up in Chapter 3. Proposed constitutional amendments have also been the source of many controversies throughout U.S. history. These controversies include the following:

- The Equal Rights Amendment of 1972 stated: "Equality of rights under the law shall not be denied or abridged by the United States or by any state on account of sex." The amendment failed to win approval from enough states. Should it be revived—or are equal rights for women unacceptable because women could not then be exempted from a military draft?

- Members of the Tea Party movement have advocated the repeal of the Seventeenth Amendment, which transferred the election of U.S. senators from state legislatures to the people of the respective states. The argument is that giving the choice of senators back to state legislatures would strengthen the relative power of the states. Is this a good argument—or is popular election of senators the superior system?

- Conservatives have campaigned for a constitutional amendment to ban same-sex marriage. Would such a measure be desirable—or repugnant as the first attempt to write a limit on freedoms into the Constitution?

- What about an amendment to ban the destruction of the American flag as an act of protest? Is such a ban important to the dignity of our fallen soldiers—or would it be an unacceptable limit on free speech?

Take Action

As you have read, the founders envisioned that the Constitution, to remain relevant, would need to be changed over time. You can take action over the Constitution by supporting a proposed constitutional amendment. Currently, two organized efforts seek constitutional amendments—the Tea Party movement and a campaign to limit corporate campaign contributions.

Members of the Tea Party movement could be described as obsessed with the Constitution. Some carry copies of the document with them at all times. Perhaps the best summary of Tea Party ideas is expressed in the "Contract *from* America," which you can find at **www.thecontract.org/support**. This document has been endorsed by many local Tea Party organizations. The contract endorses "individual liberty, limited government, and economic freedom." The document also calls for amending the Constitution to require a balanced budget and impose a two-thirds-majority requirement for tax increases. If these ideas appeal to you, the Tea Party Patriots Web site provides a long list of local groups at **www.teapartypatriots.org**.

If you are more concerned about the dangers of big business than big government, several groups support a constitutional amendment to overturn the Supreme Court's 2010 decision *Citizens United v. the Federal Election Commission*. In this ruling, the Court found that corporations (and presumably labor unions) have the same free speech rights as individual persons. The Court therefore overturned decades of legislation governing campaign finance. Many progressives fear that the result will be a tsunami of political corporate cash. Public interest groups opposed to the ruling have organized Free Speech for People, **freespeechforpeople.org**, which offers a wide range of possible ways to get involved in the campaign. Other active groups are Move to Amend at **movetoamend.org** and People for the American Way at **www.pfaw.org/get-involved/take-action**.

SAMUEL PEEBLES/EL DORADO NEWS-TIMES/AP

Amendments that would prohibit the burning of the American flag have been proposed in the past, but none has ever been ratified and become a part of the U.S. Constitution.

POLITICS ON THE
WEB

- A World Wide Web version of the Constitution provides hypertext links to amendments and other changes. Go to **topics.law.cornell.edu/constitution**

- The National Constitution Center in Philadelphia has a Web page at **www.constitutioncenter.org**. The site offers basic facts about the Constitution plus Constitution puzzles.

- James Madison's notes are one of our most important sources for the debates and exchanges that took place during the Constitutional Convention. These notes are now online at **www.thisnation.com/library/madison**

- An online version of the Anti-Federalist Papers is available at the Web site of the West El Paso Information Network (WEPIN). Go to **wepin.com/articles/afp**

- For information on the effect of new computer and communications technologies on the constitutional rights and liberties of Americans, go to the Center for Democracy and Technology at **www.cdt.org**

- The constitutions of almost all of the states are online. You can find them at **www.findlaw. com/11stategov**

- You can find constitutions of other countries at **www.servat.unibe.ch/icl**

CourseMate   Access CourseMate to review and expand on this chapter through quizzes, flashcards, learning objectives, interactive timelines, a crossword puzzle, audio summaries, video, critical-thinking activities, simulations, and more.

{ More Bang for Your Buck }

Federalism

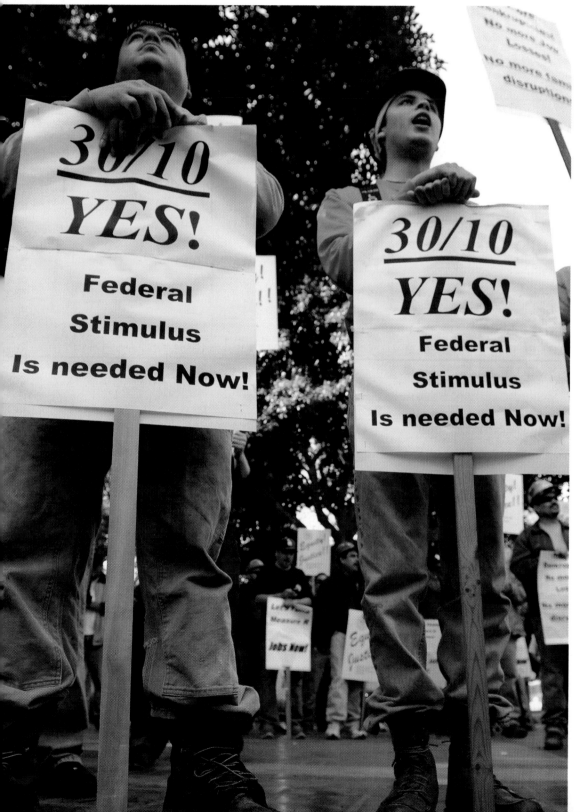

LEARNING OBJECTIVES

LO1 Explain what federalism means, how federalism differs from other systems of government, and why it exists in the United States.

LO2 Indicate how the Constitution divides governing powers in our federal system.

LO3 Summarize the evolution of federal-state relationships in the United States over time.

LO4 Describe developments in federalism in recent years.

LO5 Explain what is meant by the term *fiscal federalism*.

CourseMate

AMERICA AT ODDS

Should the States Lower the Drinking Age?

Our political system is a federal one in which power is shared between the states and the federal government. The Tenth Amendment to the U.S. Constitution reserves all powers not delegated to the national government to the states and to the people. Nonetheless, the federal government has been able to exercise power over matters that traditionally have been under the control of state governments, such as the minimum age for drinking alcoholic beverages. The federal government has been able to do so by its ability to give or withhold federal grants. The provision of grants to the states by the federal government is known as *fiscal federalism,* and these grants give the federal government considerable influence over state policies.

In the 1980s, for example, the national government wanted the states to raise the minimum drinking age to twenty-one years. States that refused to do so were threatened with the loss of federal highway construction funds. The threat worked—it was not long before all of the states had changed their minimum-drinking-age laws. In the 1990s, Congress used the same threat to encourage the states to lower their blood-alcohol limits for drunk driving to 0.08 percent by 2004. Again, states that failed to comply faced reductions in federal highway funds.

It's Time to End This Charade—College Students Still Drink

Underage drinking did not disappear when the minimum-drinking-age requirement was raised to twenty-one years. Indeed, the problem got worse. Millions of young people today are, in effect, criminals, because they are breaking the law by drinking. Moreover, the law encourages young people to binge in secret in order to avoid apprehension and prosecution by the local police. The minimum drinking age of twenty-one years has not reduced drunk driving among teenagers, because it is largely unenforceable. Additionally, it has bred contempt for the law in general among teenagers. That is why a group of 135 U.S. college presidents and chancellors endorsed the Amethyst Initiative, a movement calling for the reconsideration of U.S. drinking-age laws. Prohibition did not work in the 1920s, and prohibiting those under twenty-one from drinking will not work in the twenty-first century. Almost no other country has such a high minimum drinking age. It is time to lower the drinking age everywhere in the United States. Responsible drinking can be taught through role modeling by parents and through educational programs.

Keep the Age-Twenty-One Requirement Because It's Working

Mothers Against Drunk Driving (MADD) leads the opposition to lowering the drinking age. That group contends that the current drinking-age laws have saved more than twenty thousand lives. The National Transportation Safety Board, the American Medical Association, and the Insurance Institute for Highway Safety all agree. After all, young persons' brains are not fully developed, so they are more susceptible to alcohol. When the drinking age limit is twenty-one, it helps to protect young people from being pressured to drink. Teenagers who drink are a danger not only to themselves but also to others—particularly when driving. Young people away at college must deal with enough new responsibilities. They don't need drinking as yet another problem. Fatalities involving eighteen- to twenty-year-old drivers have decreased since the laws establishing the minimum drinking age of twenty-one were enacted. These laws are working as planned, so we should keep them.

WHERE DO YOU STAND?

1. Is it appropriate to compare what happened during the era of Prohibition, when *all* drinking was illegal, to what is happening to teenagers today, when the minimum drinking age is twenty-one? Why or why not?
2. "One can join the military at the age of eighteen and die for this country, so it is absurd not to allow those between the ages of eighteen and twenty-one to drink." Analyze this statement.

EXPLORE THIS ISSUE ONLINE

- Professor David Hanson, of the State University of New York at Potsdam, maintains a Web site that explores alcohol-related issues, including the minimum-drinking-age controversy. You can find it at www2.potsdam.edu/hansondj.
- You can find an academic study of college-age drinking by researchers at the Harvard School of Public Health at www.hsph.harvard.edu/cas/Documents/underminimum/DrinkingBehavior.pdf.
- The Mothers Against Drunk Driving (MADD) site is at www.madd.org. You can find a related organization, Students Against Destructive Decisions (SADD), at www.sadd.org.

Introduction

The controversy over the drinking age is just one example of how different levels of government in our federal system can be at odds with one another. Let's face it—those who work for the national government based in Washington, D.C., would like the states to fully cooperate with the national government in the implementation of national policies. At the same time, those who work in state government don't like to be told what to do by the national government, especially when the implementation of a national policy is costly for the states. Finally, those who work in local governments would like to run their affairs with the least amount of interference from both their state governments and the national government.

Such conflicts arise because our government is based on the principle of **federalism,** which means that government powers are shared by the national government and the states. When the founders of this nation opted for federalism, they created a practical and flexible form of government capable of enduring for centuries. At the same time, however, they planted the seeds for future conflict between the states and the national government over how government powers should be shared. As you will read in this chapter—and throughout this book—many of today's most pressing issues have to do with which level of government should exercise certain powers. Sometimes two levels of government collaborate. For example, California and the federal government jointly manage the Redwood National Park.

The relationship between the national government and the governments at the state and local levels has never been free of conflict. Indeed, even before the Constitution was adopted, the Federalists and Anti-Federalists engaged in a heated debate over the issue of national versus state powers. As you learned in Chapter 2, the Federalists won the day by convincing Americans to adopt the Constitution. The Anti-Federalists' concern for states' rights, however, has surfaced again and again in the course of our history.

LO1 *Federalism and Its Alternatives*

There are various ways of ordering relations between central governments and local units. Federalism is one of these ways. Learning about federalism and how it differs from other forms of government is important to understanding the American political system.

What Is Federalism?

Nowhere in the Constitution does the word *federalism* appear. This is understandable, given that the concept of federalism was an invention of the founders. Since the Federalists and the Anti-Federalists argued more than two hundred years ago about what form of government we should have, hundreds of definitions of federalism have been offered. Basically, though, as mentioned in Chapter 2, in a *federal system*, government powers are divided between a central government and regional, or subdivisional, governments.

Although this definition seems straightforward, its application certainly is not. After all, virtually all nations—even the most repressive totalitarian regimes—have some kind of subnational governmental units. Thus, the existence of national and subnational governmental units by itself does not make a system federal. *For a system to be truly federal, the powers of both the national units and the subnational units must be specified and limited.* Under true federalism, individuals are governed by

> **federalism** A system of shared sovereignty between two levels of government—one national and one subnational—occupying the same geographic region.

Why does lowering the drinking age remain controversial?

unitary system A centralized governmental system in which local or subdivisional governments exercise only those powers given to them by the central government.

confederal system A league of independent sovereign states, joined together by a central government that has only limited powers over them.

two separate governmental authorities (national and state authorities) whose expressly designated powers cannot be altered without changing the fundamental nature of the system—for example, by amending a written constitution. Table 3–1 at right lists some of the countries that the Central Intelligence Agency has classified as having a federal system of government.[1]

Federalism in theory is one thing; federalism in practice is another. As you will read shortly, the Constitution sets forth specific powers that can be exercised by the national government and provides that the national government has the implied power to undertake actions necessary to carry out its expressly designated powers. All other powers are "reserved" to the states. The broad language of the Constitution, though, has left much room for debate over the specific nature and scope of certain powers, such as the national government's implied powers and the powers reserved to the states. Thus, the actual workings of our federal form of government have depended, to a great extent, on the historical application of the broad principles outlined in the Constitution.

To further complicate matters, the term *federal government*, as it is used today, refers to the national, or central, government. When individuals talk of the federal government, they mean the national government based in Washington, D.C. They are *not* referring to the federal *system* of government, which is made up of both the national government and the state governments.

Alternatives to Federalism

Perhaps an easier way to define federalism is to discuss what it is *not*. Most of the nations in the world today have a **unitary system** of government. In such a system, the constitution vests all powers in the national government. If the national government so chooses, it

Table 3–1

Countries That Have a Federal System Today

Country	Population (in Millions)
Argentina	41.3
Australia	21.5
Austria	8.2
Brazil	201.1
Canada	33.8
Ethiopia	88.0
Germany	82.3
India	1,173.1
Malaysia	26.2
Mexico	112.5
Nigeria	152.2
Pakistan	177.3
Switzerland	7.6
United States	310.2
Venezuela	27.2

Source: Central Intelligence Agency, *The World Fact Book;* current edition online at **https://www.cia.gov/library/publications/the-world-factbook**.

can delegate certain activities to subnational units. The reverse is also true: the national government can take away, at will, powers delegated to subnational governmental units. In a unitary system, any subnational government is a "creature of the national government." The governments of Britain, France, Israel, Japan, and the Philippines are examples of unitary systems. In the United States, because the Constitution does not mention local governments (cities and counties), we say that city and county governmental units are "creatures of state government." That means that state governments can—and do—both give powers to and take powers from local governments.

The Articles of Confederation created a confederal system (see Chapter 2). In a **confederal system,** the national government exists and operates only at the direction of the subnational governments. Few true confederal systems are in existence today, although some people contend that the European Union—a group of twenty-seven European nations that has established many common institutions—qualifies as such a system.

Federalism—An Optimal Choice for the United States?

The Articles of Confederation failed because they did not allow for a sufficiently strong central government. The framers of the Constitution, however, were fearful of tyranny and a too-powerful central government. The outcome had to be a compromise—a federal system.

The appeal of federalism was that it retained state powers and local traditions while establishing a strong national government capable of handling common problems, such as national defense. A federal form of government also furthered the goal of creating a division of powers (to be discussed shortly). There are other reasons why the founders opted for a federal system, and a federal structure of government continues to offer many advantages (as well as some disadvantages) for U.S. citizens.

ADVANTAGES OF FEDERALISM One of the reasons a federal form of government is well suited to the United

Figure 3–1

Governmental Units in the United States Today

The most common type of governmental unit in the United States is the special district, which is generally concerned with a specific issue such as solid waste disposal, mass transportation, or fire protection. Often, the jurisdiction of special districts crosses the boundaries of other governmental units, such as cities or counties. Special districts also tend to have fewer restrictions than other local governments as to how much debt they can incur and so are created to finance large building projects.

THE NUMBER OF GOVERNMENTS IN THE UNITED STATES TODAY

Government	Number
Federal government	1
State governments and District of Columbia	51
Local governments	
Counties	3,034
Municipalities (mainly cities or towns)	19,492
Townships (less extensive powers)	16,519
Special districts (water, sewer, and so on)	37,381
School districts	13,051
Subtotal local governments	89,476
Total	**89,528**

PERCENTAGE OF ALL GOVERNMENTS IN THE UNITED STATES TODAY

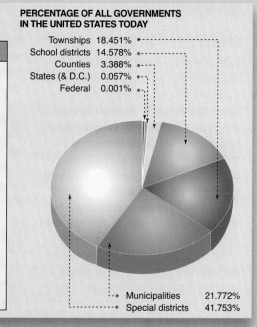

Townships 18.451%
School districts 14.578%
Counties 3.388%
States (& D.C.) 0.057%
Federal 0.001%

Municipalities 21.772%
Special districts 41.753%

Source: U.S. Census Bureau.

States is our country's large size. Even in the days when the United States consisted of only thirteen states, its geographic area was larger than that of England or France. In those days, travel was slow and communication was difficult, so people in outlying areas were isolated. The news of any particular political decision could take several weeks to reach everyone. Therefore, even if the framers of the Constitution had wanted a more centralized system (which most of them did not), such a system would have been unworkable.

Look at Figure 3–1 above. As you can see, to a great extent the practical business of governing this country takes place in state and local governmental units. Federalism, by providing a multitude of arenas for decision making, keeps government closer to the people and helps make democracy possible.

The existence of numerous government subunits in the United States also makes it possible to experiment with innovative policies and programs at the state or local level. Many observers, including Supreme Court justice Louis Brandeis (1856–1941), have emphasized that in a

federal system, state governments can act as "laboratories" for public-policy experimentation. For example, many states have adopted minimum wage laws that establish a higher minimum wage than the one set by national legislation. Several states, including Hawaii and Massachusetts, have experimented with health-care programs that extend coverage to most or all of the states' citizens. Depending on the outcome of a specific experiment, other states may (or may not) implement similar programs. State innovations can also serve as models for federal programs. For instance, California was a pioneer in air-pollution control. Many of that state's regulations were later adapted by other states and eventually by the federal government.

We have always been a nation of different political subcultures. The Pilgrims who founded New England were different from the settlers who established the agricultural society of the South. Both of these groups were different from those who populated the Middle Atlantic states. The groups that founded New England had a religious focus, while those who populated the Middle Atlantic states were more business oriented. Those who settled in the South were more individualistic than the other groups. That is, they were less inclined to act as a collective and more inclined to act independently of each other. A federal system of government allows the political and cultural interests of regional groups to be reflected in the laws governing those groups.

As we noted earlier, nations other than the United States have benefited from the principle of federalism. One of them is Canada, our neighbor to the north. Because federalism permits the expression of varying regional cultures, Canadian federalism naturally differs from the American version, as you will discover in this chapter's *The Rest of the World* feature on the following page.

SOME DRAWBACKS TO FEDERALISM Federalism offers many advantages, but it also has some drawbacks. Consider that although federalism in many ways

Canadian versus American Federalism

Canada has a federal system similar in some ways to that of the United States—but also with some big differences. When the 1867 Constitution Act created modern Canada, the United States had just concluded the Civil War. Canada's founders blamed that war on the weakness of the U.S. central government. Therefore, the Canadian constitution gave far more power to the central government than did the U.S. Constitution.

The Powers of Lower-Level Governments

Our lower levels of government are called states, whereas in Canada they are called provinces. Right there, the powers of the central government are emphasized. The word *state* implies sovereignty. A *province,* however, is never sovereign and is typically set up for the convenience of the central government. The U.S. Constitution limits the powers of the national government to those listed in Article I, Section 8. In the Canadian constitution, it is the powers of the provinces that are limited by a list. The Tenth Amendment to the U.S. Constitution reserves residual powers to the states or to the people. In Canada, residual powers rest with the national government. Under the 1867 Canadian constitution,

the central government could veto any provincial legislation. No such clause appears in the U.S. Constitution.

Changes Over Time

By land area, Canada is the second-largest country in the world. Most people live along the southern edge of the nation, where the climate is the most tolerable. The populated areas of Canada, therefore, are like a ribbon extending from the Atlantic to the Pacific. Physically, the country seems designed for a federal system of government.

Over time, the powers of the U.S. federal government grew at the expense of the states. The opposite happened in Canada. By the end of the nineteenth century, the Canadian government in practice had abandoned the power to veto provincial legislation. The difference between the Canadian and American experiences is well illustrated by the effect of the Great Depression on the federal system. In the United States, the Depression strengthened the federal government. In Canada, it strengthened the provinces.

Two Languages

Another striking difference between Canada and the United States is that

Canada has two national languages. A majority of Canadians speak English, but most of the population of Québec speaks French. The Parti Québécois (PQ), which wants Québec to be a separate country, has gained power in that province twice. Both times, it held referenda on whether Québec should demand "sovereignty-association," a euphemism for independence. In 1995, the PQ almost obtained a majority vote for its position. The party has promised to hold another referendum if it returns to power. The possibility exists, therefore, that Canada could actually break apart.

For Critical Analysis *The Canadian constitution is based on the principles of "peace, order, and good government." Contrast that phrase with the Preamble to the U.S. Constitution. How do the statements differ?*

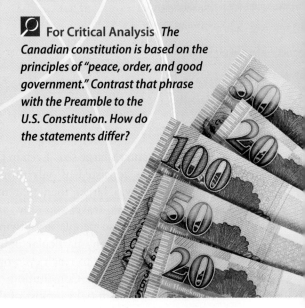

promotes greater self-rule, or democracy, some scholars point out that local self-rule may not always be in society's best interests. These observers argue that the smaller the political unit, the higher the probability that it will be dominated by a single political group, which may or may not be concerned with the welfare of many of the local unit's citizens. For example, entrenched segregationist politicians in southern states denied African Americans their civil rights and voting rights for decades, as we discuss further in Chapter 5.

Powerful state and local interests can block progress and impede national plans. State and local interests often diverge from those of the national government. For example, several of the states have recently been at odds with the national government over how to address the problem of global warming. Finding acceptable solutions to such conflicts has not always been easy. Indeed, as will be discussed shortly, in the 1860s, war—not politics—decided the outcome of a struggle over states' rights.

Federalism has other drawbacks as well. One of them is the lack of uniformity of state laws, which can complicate business transactions that cross state borders. Another problem is the difficulty of coordinating government policies at the national, state, and local levels. Additionally, the simultaneous regulation of business by all levels of government creates red tape that imposes substantial costs on the business community.

Finally, in a federal system, there is always the danger that national power will be expanded at the expense of the states. President Ronald Reagan (1981–1989) once said, "The Founding Fathers saw the federalist system as constructed something like a masonry wall. The States are the bricks, the national government is the mortar. . . . Unfortunately, over the years, many people have increasingly come to believe that Washington is the whole wall."[2]

LO2 The Constitutional Division of Powers

The founders created a federal form of government by dividing sovereign powers into powers that could be exercised by the national government and powers that were to be reserved to the states. Although there is no systematic explanation of this **division of powers** between the national and state governments, the original Constitution, along with its amendments, provides statements on what the national and state governments can (and cannot) do.

The Powers of the National Government

The Constitution delegates certain powers to the national government. It also prohibits the national government from exercising certain powers.

POWERS DELEGATED TO THE NATIONAL GOVERNMENT The national government possesses three types of powers: expressed powers, implied powers, and inherent powers. Article I, Section 8, of the Constitution expressly enumerates twenty-seven powers that Congress may exercise. Two of these **expressed powers,** or *enumerated powers,* are the power to coin money and the power to regulate interstate commerce. Constitutional amendments have provided for other expressed powers. For example, the Sixteenth Amendment, added in 1913, gives Congress the power to impose a federal income tax. Article II, Section 2, of the Constitution expressly delegates certain powers to the president. These powers include making treaties and appointing certain federal officeholders. Laws enacted by Congress can also have the effect of creating additional expressed presidential powers.

The constitutional basis for the **implied powers** of the national government is found in Article I, Section 8, Clause 18, often called the **necessary and proper clause.** This clause states that Congress has the power to make "all Laws which shall be necessary and proper for carrying into Execution the foregoing [expressed] Powers, and all other Powers vested by this Constitution in the Government of the United States, or in any Department or Officer thereof." The necessary and proper clause is often referred to as the *elastic clause,* because it gives elasticity to our constitutional system.

The national government also enjoys certain **inherent powers**—powers that governments must have simply to ensure the nation's integrity and survival as a political unit. For example, any national government must have the inherent ability to make treaties, regulate immigration, acquire territory, wage war, and make peace. While some inherent powers are also enumerated in the Constitution, such as the power to wage war and make treaties, others are not. For example, the Constitution does not speak of regulating immigration or acquiring new territory. Although the national government's inherent powers are few, they are important.

POWERS PROHIBITED TO THE NATIONAL GOVERNMENT The Constitution expressly prohibits the national government from undertaking certain actions, such as imposing taxes on exports, and from passing laws restraining certain liberties, such as the freedom of speech or religion. Most of these prohibited powers are listed in Article I, Section 9, and in the first eight amendments to the Constitution. Additionally, the national government is implicitly prohibited from exercising powers, including

division of powers
A basic principle of federalism established by the U.S. Constitution, by which powers are divided between the federal and state governments.

expressed powers
Constitutional or statutory powers that are expressly provided for by the U.S. Constitution.

implied powers The powers of the federal government that are implied by the expressed powers in the Constitution, particularly in Article I, Section 8.

necessary and proper clause Article I, Section 8, Clause 18, of the Constitution, which gives Congress the power to make all laws "necessary and proper" for the federal government to carry out its responsibilities; also called the *elastic clause.*

inherent powers The powers of the national government that, although not always expressly granted by the Constitution, are necessary to ensure the nation's integrity and survival as a political unit. Inherent powers include the power to make treaties and the power to wage war or make peace.

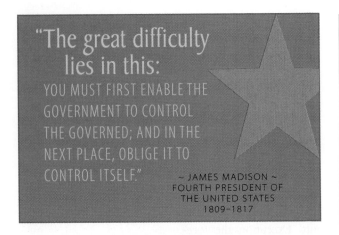

the power to create a national public school system, that are not included among its expressed and implied powers.

The Powers of the States

The Tenth Amendment to the Constitution states that powers that are not delegated to the national government by the Constitution, nor prohibited to the states, "are reserved to the States respectively, or to the people."

POLICE POWERS The Tenth Amendment thus gives numerous powers to the states, including the power to regulate commerce within their borders and the power to maintain a state militia. In principle, each state has the ability to regulate its internal affairs and to enact whatever laws are necessary to protect the health, morals, safety, and welfare of its people. These powers of the states are called **police powers.** The establishment of public schools and the regulation of marriage and divorce have traditionally been considered to be entirely within the purview of state and local governments.

Because the Tenth Amendment does not specify what powers are reserved to the states, these powers have been defined differently at different times in our history. In periods of widespread support for increased regulation by the national government, the Tenth Amendment tends to recede into the background. When the tide turns the other way, the Tenth Amendment is resurrected to justify arguments supporting increased states' rights (see, for example, the discussion of the new federalism later in this chapter). Because the United States Supreme Court is the ultimate arbiter

police powers The powers of a government body that enable it to create laws for the protection of the health, morals, safety, and welfare of the people. In the United States, most police powers are reserved to the states.

of the Constitution, the outcome of disputes over the extent of state powers often rests with the Court.

POWERS PROHIBITED TO THE STATES Article I, Section 10, denies certain powers to state governments, such as the power to tax goods that are transported across state lines. States are also prohibited from entering into treaties with other countries. In addition, the Thirteenth, Fourteenth, Fifteenth, Nineteenth, Twenty-fourth, and Twenty-sixth Amendments prohibit certain state actions. (The complete text of these amendments is included in Appendix B.)

Interstate Relations

The Constitution also contains provisions relating to interstate relations. The states have constant commercial and social interactions among themselves, and these interactions often do not directly involve the national government. The relationships among the states in our federal system of government are sometimes referred to as *horizontal federalism*.

The Constitution outlines a number of rules for interstate relations. For example, the Constitution's full faith and credit clause requires each state to honor every other state's public acts, records, and judicial proceedings. The issue of gay marriage, however, has made this constitutional mandate difficult to follow. If a gay couple legally married in Massachusetts moves to a state that bans same-sex marriage, which state's law takes priority? The federal government attempted to answer that question through the 1996 Defense of Marriage Act (DOMA), which provided that no state

DANIEL BARRY/REDUX

During natural disasters, such as this flooding problem in Fargo, North Dakota, local governments will ask for assistance from other cities, the state, and even the federal government.

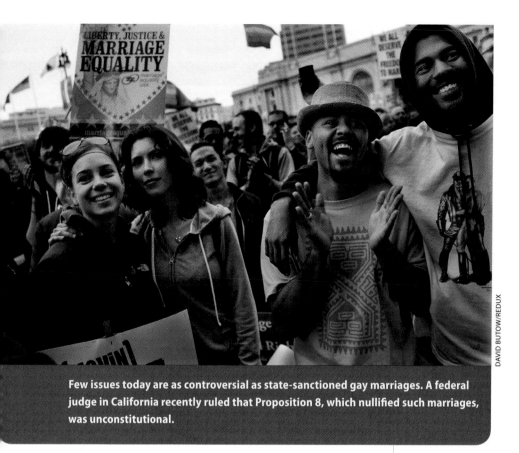

LIBERTY, JUSTICE & MARRIAGE EQUALITY

DAVID BUTOW/REDUX

Few issues today are as controversial as state-sanctioned gay marriages. A federal judge in California recently ruled that Proposition 8, which nullified such marriages, was unconstitutional.

and the negotiation of treaties. An example of a concurrent power is the power to tax. Both the states and the national government have the power to impose income taxes—and a variety of other taxes. States, however, are prohibited from imposing tariffs (taxes on imported goods), and as noted, the federal government may not tax articles exported by any state. Figure 3–2 on the following page, which summarizes the powers granted and denied by the Constitution, lists other concurrent powers.

The Supremacy Clause

The Constitution makes it clear that the federal government holds ultimate power. Article VI, Clause 2, known as the **supremacy clause,** states that the U.S. Constitution and the laws of the federal government "shall be the supreme Law of the Land." In other words, states cannot use their reserved or concurrent powers to counter national policies. Whenever state or local officers, such as judges or sheriffs, take office, they become bound by an oath to support the U.S. Constitution. National government power always takes precedence over any conflicting state action.[3]

is *required* to treat a relationship between persons of the same sex as a marriage, even if the relationship is considered a marriage in another state.

A second part of the law barred the national government from recognizing same-sex marriages in states that legalize them. In July 2010, however, a U.S. district court judge threw out this part of DOMA and ruled that the federal government was required to provide marriage-based benefits to Massachusetts residents who are joined in same-sex marriages. This ruling will certainly be appealed, and ultimately, the United States Supreme Court will have to decide this issue.

Horizontal federalism also includes agreements, known as *interstate compacts,* among two or more states to regulate the use or protection of certain resources, such as water or oil and gas. California and Nevada, for example, have formed an interstate compact to regulate the use and protection of Lake Tahoe, which lies on the border between those states.

Concurrent Powers

Concurrent powers can be exercised by both the state governments and the federal government. Generally, a state's concurrent powers apply only within the geographic area of the state and do not include functions that the Constitution delegates exclusively to the national government, such as the coinage of money

LO3 *The Struggle for Supremacy*

Much of the political and legal history of the United States has involved conflicts between the supremacy of the national government and the desire of the states to preserve their sovereignty. The most extreme example of this conflict was the Civil War in the 1860s. Through the years, because of the Civil War and several important Supreme Court decisions, the national government has increased its power.

concurrent powers Powers held by both the federal and the state governments in a federal system.

supremacy clause Article VI, Clause 2, of the Constitution, which makes the Constitution and federal laws superior to all conflicting state and local laws.

Figure 3–2

The Constitutional Division of Powers

The Constitution grants certain powers to the national government and certain powers to the state governments, while denying them other powers. Some powers, called *concurrent powers,* can be exercised at either the national or the state level, but generally the states can exercise these powers only within their own borders.

POWERS GRANTED BY THE CONSTITUTION

NATIONAL
- ★ To coin money
- ★ To conduct foreign relations
- ★ To regulate interstate commerce
- ★ To declare war
- ★ To raise and support the military
- ★ To establish post offices
- ★ To admit new states
- ★ Powers implied by the necessary and proper clause

CONCURRENT
- ★ To levy and collect taxes
- ★ To borrow money
- ★ To make and enforce laws
- ★ To establish courts
- ★ To provide for the general welfare
- ★ To charter banks and corporations

STATE
- ★ To regulate intrastate commerce
- ★ To conduct elections
- ★ To provide for public health, safety, welfare, and morals
- ★ To establish local governments
- ★ To ratify amendments to the federal Constitution
- ★ To establish a state militia

POWERS DENIED BY THE CONSTITUTION

NATIONAL
- ★ To tax articles exported from any state
- ★ To violate the Bill of Rights
- ★ To change state boundaries without consent of the states in question

CONCURRENT
- ★ To grant titles of nobility
- ★ To permit slavery
- ★ To deny citizens the right to vote

STATE
- ★ To tax imports or exports
- ★ To coin money
- ★ To enter into treaties
- ★ To impair obligations of contracts
- ★ To abridge the privileges or immunities of citizens or deny due process and equal protection of the laws

Early U.S. Supreme Court Decisions

Two Supreme Court cases, both of which were decided in the early 1800s, played a key role in establishing the constitutional foundations for the supremacy of the national government. Both decisions were issued while John Marshall was chief justice of the Supreme Court. In his thirty-four years as chief justice (1801–1835), Marshall did much to establish the prestige and the independence of the Court. In *Marbury v. Madison,*[4] he clearly enunciated the principle of judicial review, which has since become an important part of the checks and balances in the American system of government. Under his leadership, the Supreme Court also established, through the following cases, the superiority of federal authority under the Constitution.

McCULLOCH V. MARYLAND (1819) The issue in *McCulloch v. Maryland,*[5] a case decided in 1819, involved both the necessary and proper clause and the supremacy clause. When the state of Maryland imposed a tax on the Baltimore branch of the Second Bank of the United States, the branch's chief cashier, James McCulloch, declined to pay the tax. The state court ruled that McCulloch had to pay it, and the national government appealed to the United States Supreme Court. The case involved much more than a question of taxes. At issue was whether Congress had the authority under the Constitution's necessary and proper clause to charter and contribute capital to the Second Bank of the United States. A second constitutional issue was also involved: If the bank was constitutional, could a state tax it? In other words, was a state action that conflicted with a national government action invalid under the supremacy clause?

Chief Justice Marshall pointed out that no provision in the Constitution grants the national government the *expressed* power to form a national bank. Nevertheless, if establishing such a bank helps the national government exercise its expressed powers, then the authority to do so could be implied. Marshall also said that the necessary and proper clause included "all means that are appropriate" to carry out "the legitimate ends" of the Constitution.

Having established this doctrine of implied powers, Marshall then answered the other important constitutional question before the Court and established the doctrine of national supremacy. Marshall declared that no state could use its taxing power to tax an arm of the national government. If it could, the Constitution's declaration that the Constitution "shall be the supreme Law

> ## "A LEGISLATIVE ACT
> contrary to the Constitution is not law."
>
> ~ JOHN MARSHALL ~
> CHIEF JUSTICE OF THE UNITED STATES
> SUPREME COURT
> 1801–1835

John Marshall, chief justice of the United States Supreme Court from 1801 to 1835, was instrumental in establishing the supremacy of the national government.

of the Land" would be empty rhetoric without meaning. From that day on, Marshall's decision became the basis for strengthening the national government's power.

GIBBONS V. OGDEN (1824) As Chapter 2 explained, Article I, Section 8, gives Congress the power to regulate commerce "among the several States." But the framers of the Constitution did not define the word *commerce*. At issue in *Gibbons v. Ogden*[6] was how the *commerce clause* should be defined and whether the national government had the exclusive power to regulate commerce involving more than one state. The New York legislature had given Robert Livingston and Robert Fulton the exclusive right to operate steamboats in New York waters, and Livingston and Fulton licensed Aaron Ogden to operate a ferry between New York and New Jersey. Thomas Gibbons, who had a license from the U.S. government to operate boats in interstate waters, decided to compete with Ogden, but he did so without New York's permission. Ogden sued Gibbons in the New York state courts and won. Gibbons appealed.

Chief Justice Marshall defined *commerce* as including all business dealings, including steamboat travel. Marshall also stated that the power to regulate interstate commerce was an *exclusive* national power and had no limitations other than those specifically found in the Constitution. Since this 1824 decision, the national government has used the commerce clause repeatedly to justify its regulation of virtually all areas of economic activity.

The Civil War—The Ultimate Supremacy Battle

The great issue that provoked the Civil War (1861–1865) was the future of slavery. Because people in different sections of the country had radically different beliefs about slavery, the slavery issue took the form of a dispute over states' rights versus national supremacy. The war brought to a bloody climax the ideological debate that had been outlined by the Federalist and Anti-Federalist factions even before the Constitution was ratified.

As just discussed, the Supreme Court headed by John Marshall interpreted the commerce clause in such a way as to increase the power of the national government at the expense of state powers. By the late 1820s, however, a shift back to states' rights had begun, and the question of the regulation of commerce became one of the major issues in federal-state relations. When the national government, in 1828 and 1832, passed laws imposing tariffs (taxes) on goods imported into the United States, southern states objected, believing that such taxes were against their interests.

One southern state, South Carolina, attempted to *nullify* the tariffs, or to make them void. South Carolina claimed that in conflicts between state governments and the national government, the states should have the ultimate authority to determine the welfare of their citizens. President Andrew Jackson was prepared to use force to uphold national law, but Congress reduced the tariffs. The crisis passed.

Additionally, some Southerners believed that democratic decisions could be made only when all the segments of society affected by those decisions were in agreement. Without such agreement, a decision should not be binding on those whose interests it violates. This view was used to justify the **secession**—withdrawal—of the southern states from the Union in 1860 and 1861.

The defense of slavery and the promotion of states' rights were both important elements in the South's decision to secede, and the two concepts were commingled in the minds of Southerners of that era. Which of these two was the more important remains a matter of controversy even today. Modern defenders of states' rights and those who distrust governmental authority often present southern secession as entirely a matter of states' rights. Liberals and those who champion the rights of African Americans see slavery as the sole cause of the crisis. Economic historians can provide helpful insights into the background to secession, as you will learn in this chapter's

> "We here highly resolve that . . .
>
> # THIS NATION . . . SHALL HAVE A NEW BIRTH OF FREEDOM;
>
> and that government of the people, by the people, for the people, shall not perish from the earth."
>
> ~ ABRAHAM LINCOLN ~
> GETTYSBURG ADDRESS
> 1863

Perception versus Reality feature on the facing page.

When the South was defeated in the war, the idea that a state has a right to secede from the Union was defeated also. Although the Civil War occurred because of the South's desire for increased states' rights, the result was just the opposite—an increase in the political power of the national government.

Dual Federalism—From the Civil War to the 1930s

Scholars have devised various models to describe the relationship between the states and the national government at different times in our history. These models are useful in describing the evolution of federalism after the Civil War.

The model of **dual federalism** assumes that the states and the national government are more or less equals, with each level of government having separate and distinct functions and responsibilities. The states exercise sovereign powers over certain matters, and the national government exercises sovereign powers over others.

The Civil War is known in the South as the War between the States, but the official Union designation was the War of the Rebellion. The first shot of the Civil War was fired on April 12, 1861, at Fort Sumter, South Carolina.

LIBRARY OF CONGRESS

secession The act of formally withdrawing from membership in an alliance; the withdrawal of a state from the federal Union.

dual federalism A system of government in which the federal and the state governments maintain diverse but sovereign powers.

PERCEPTION VERSUS REALITY

Did the Civil War Destroy the Economy of the South?

The Civil War imposed great destruction on the South. The Union Army burned Atlanta, Columbia, and Richmond. General Philip Sheridan's cavalry famously destroyed the farms and railroads of Virginia's Shenandoah Valley. In addition to the loss of human life, the South lost livestock, houses, barns, railroads, and bridges. In the cities, Union forces destroyed factories, warehouses, and transportation equipment.

The Perception

The common perception of the South's condition after the Civil War has been heavily influenced by the suffering depicted in *Gone with the Wind* and other popular works. Many Americans have long believed that the destruction of southern wealth by the war made economic recovery impossible. Furthermore, although it was inevitable and proper that the slaves were freed, the North did not compensate the former slave owners for their losses. This immediately destroyed billions of dollars worth of southern capital.

The Reality

The industrial parts of the South actually recovered quite rapidly. For example, by 1867, the railroads between Washington, D.C., and Charleston, South Carolina, were as good as they had been before the war. By 1869, total manufacturing output and investment exceeded their prewar levels.

The South's problem lay in its cotton-based agriculture. You have heard about the huge bubble in housing prices that helped cause the recent Great Recession. There have been many bubbles in the past as well. In the 1850s, the world experienced a cotton bubble. High prices for cotton led to a bubble in the price of slaves. Slave owners believed that even if Abraham Lincoln swore not to interfere with slavery in the states, his presidency still threatened the price of slaves. Secession would serve as a protection. The North could not possibly risk a "war on cotton," and if it did, cotton-dependent Britain would intervene on the

The Mississippi in Time of War, circa 1865, by Currier and Ives.

side of the South. As a southern lady wrote to her daughters, "civil war was *foreign to the original plan.*"[7]

In fact, just before the war, the price of cotton started to fall due to overproduction of cotton textiles. British per-capita consumption of cotton goods did not exceed 1860 levels until after World War I. As a result, after the Civil War, cotton prices fell until almost the end of the century. The Civil War masked the fact that the cotton bubble had burst. Ultra-low cotton prices—with no good economic alternatives for southern farmers—were the true source of the post–Civil War economic distress, not the devastation caused by the Union Army.

Blog On For a vast collection of Civil War materials, see Shotgun's Home of the American Civil War at **www.civilwarhome.com**. For economic history, try **eh.net**, a Web site supported by the Economic History Association. One of the site's most popular services lets you convert modern prices into those of any past year, or vice versa.

For much of our nation's history, this model of federalism prevailed. Certainly, after the Civil War the courts tended to support the states' rights to exercise their police powers and tended to strictly limit the powers of the federal government under the commerce clause. In 1918, for example, the Supreme Court ruled unconstitutional a 1916 federal law excluding from interstate commerce the products created through the use of child labor. The law was held unconstitutional because it attempted to regulate a local problem.[8] The era of dual federalism came to an end in the 1930s, when the United States was in the depths of the greatest economic depression it had ever experienced.

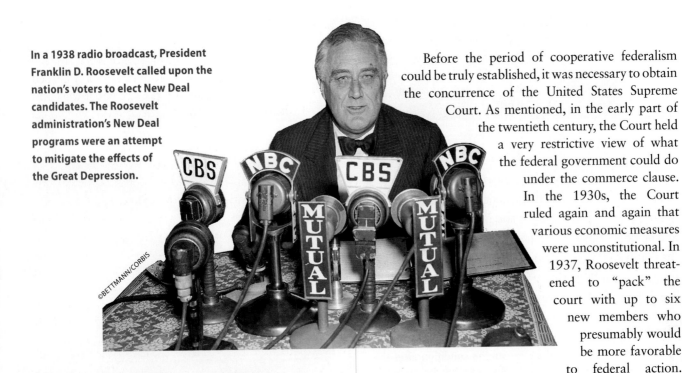

In a 1938 radio broadcast, President Franklin D. Roosevelt called upon the nation's voters to elect New Deal candidates. The Roosevelt administration's New Deal programs were an attempt to mitigate the effects of the Great Depression.

©BETTMANN/CORBIS

Cooperative Federalism and the Growth of the National Government

The model of **cooperative federalism,** as the term implies, involves cooperation by all branches of government. This model views the national and state governments as complementary parts of a single governmental mechanism, the purpose of which is to solve the problems facing the entire United States. For example, federal law enforcement agencies, such as the Federal Bureau of Investigation, lend technical expertise to solve local crimes, and local officials cooperate with federal agencies.

Cooperative federalism grew out of the need to solve the pressing national problems caused by the Great Depression, which began in 1929. To help bring the United States out of the Depression, President Franklin D. Roosevelt (1933–1945) launched his **New Deal,** which involved many government-spending and public-assistance programs. Roosevelt's New Deal legislation not only ushered in an era of cooperative federalism, which has more or less continued until the present day, but also marked the real beginning of an era of national supremacy.

cooperative federalism
The theory that the states and the federal government should cooperate in solving problems.

New Deal The policies ushered in by the Roosevelt administration in 1933 in an attempt to bring the United States out of the Great Depression. The New Deal included many government-spending and public-assistance programs, in addition to thousands of regulations governing economic activity.

picket-fence federalism
A model of federalism in which specific policies and programs are administered by all levels of government—national, state, and local.

Before the period of cooperative federalism could be truly established, it was necessary to obtain the concurrence of the United States Supreme Court. As mentioned, in the early part of the twentieth century, the Court held a very restrictive view of what the federal government could do under the commerce clause. In the 1930s, the Court ruled again and again that various economic measures were unconstitutional. In 1937, Roosevelt threatened to "pack" the court with up to six new members who presumably would be more favorable to federal action. This move was widely considered to be an assault on the Constitution, and Congress refused to support it. Clearly, however, the Court got the message: after 1937, it ceased its attempts to limit the scope of the commerce clause.

COOPERATIVE FEDERALISM AND THE WELFARE STATE The 1960s and 1970s saw an even greater expansion of the national government's role in domestic policy. The Great Society legislation of President Lyndon Johnson's administration (1963–1969) created Medicaid, Medicare, the Job Corps, Operation Head Start, and other programs. The Civil Rights Act of 1964 prohibited discrimination in public accommodations, employment, and other areas on the basis of race, color, national origin, religion, or gender. In the 1970s, national laws protecting consumers, employees, and the environment imposed further regulations on the economy. Today, few activities are beyond the reach of the regulatory arm of the national government.

Nonetheless, the massive social programs undertaken in the 1960s and 1970s also precipitated greater involvement by state and local governments. The national government simply could not implement those programs alone. For example, Head Start, a program that provides preschool services to children of low-income families, is administered by local nonprofit organizations and school systems, although it is funded by federal grants. The model in which every level of government is involved in implementing a policy is sometimes referred to as **picket-fence federalism.** In this model, the policy area is the vertical picket on the fence, while the levels of government are the horizontal support boards. America's welfare system has relied on this

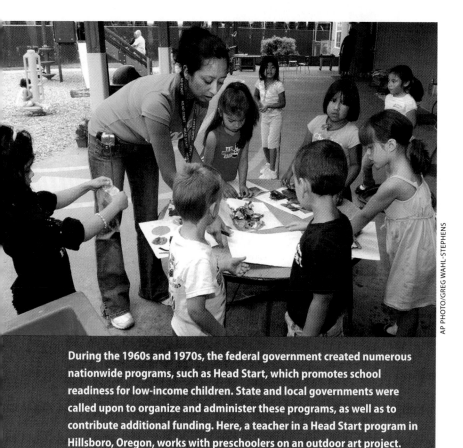

During the 1960s and 1970s, the federal government created numerous nationwide programs, such as Head Start, which promotes school readiness for low-income children. State and local governments were called upon to organize and administer these programs, as well as to contribute additional funding. Here, a teacher in a Head Start program in Hillsboro, Oregon, works with preschoolers on an outdoor art project.

years, though, the Supreme Court has, for the first time since the 1930s, occasionally curbed Congress's regulatory powers under the commerce clause. You will read more about this development shortly.

John Marshall's validation of the supremacy clause of the Constitution has also had significant consequences for federalism. One important effect of the supremacy clause today is that the clause allows for federal **preemption** of certain areas in which the national government and the states have concurrent powers. When Congress chooses to act exclusively in an area in which the states and the national government have concurrent powers, Congress is said to have *preempted* the area. In such cases, the courts have held that a valid federal law or regulation takes precedence over a conflicting state or local law or regulation covering the same general activity.

LO4 *Federalism Today*

By the 1970s, some Americans had begun to question whether the national government had acquired too many powers. Had the national government gotten too big? Had it become, in fact, a threat to the power of the states and the liberties of the people? Should steps be taken to reduce the regulatory power and scope of the national government? Since that time, the model of federalism has evolved in ways that reflect these and other concerns.

The New Federalism— More Power to the States

Starting in the 1970s, several administrations attempted to revitalize the doctrine of dual federalism, which they renamed the "new federalism." The **new federalism** involved a shift from *nation-centered* federalism to *state-centered* federalism. One of the major goals of the new federalism was to return to the states certain powers that had been exercised by the national government since the 1930s. The term

model of federalism, although, as you will read, from time to time there have been attempts to give more power to state and local governments.

UNITED STATES SUPREME COURT DECISIONS AND COOPERATIVE FEDERALISM The two United States Supreme Court decisions discussed earlier, *McCulloch v. Maryland* and *Gibbons v. Ogden,* became the constitutional cornerstone of the regulatory powers that the national government enjoys today. From 1937 on, the Supreme Court consistently upheld Congress's power to regulate domestic policy under the commerce clause. Even activities that occur entirely within a state were rarely considered to be outside the regulatory power of the national government. For example, in 1942 the Supreme Court held that wheat production by an individual farmer intended wholly for consumption on his own farm was subject to federal regulation because the home consumption of wheat reduced the demand for wheat and thus could have an effect on interstate commerce.[9]

In 1980, the Supreme Court acknowledged that the commerce clause had "long been interpreted to extend beyond activities actually in interstate commerce to reach other activities that, while wholly local in nature, nevertheless substantially affect interstate commerce."[10] Today, Congress can regulate almost any kind of economic activity, no matter where it occurs. In recent

preemption A doctrine rooted in the supremacy clause of the Constitution that provides that national laws or regulations governing a certain area take precedence over conflicting state laws or regulations governing that same area.

new federalism A plan to limit the federal government's role in regulating state governments and to give the states increased power to decide how they should spend government revenues.

devolution—the transfer of powers to political subunits—is often used to describe this process. Although a product of conservative thought and initiated by Republicans, the devolutionary goals of the new federalism were also espoused by the Clinton administration (1993–2001). An example of the new federalism is the welfare reform legislation passed by Congress in 1996, which gave the states more authority over welfare programs.

The Supreme Court and the New Federalism

During and since the 1990s, the Supreme Court has played a significant role in furthering the cause of states' rights. In a landmark 1995 decision, *United States v. Lopez*,[11] the Supreme Court held, for the first time in sixty years, that Congress had exceeded its constitutional authority under the commerce clause. The Court concluded that the Gun-Free School Zones Act of 1990, which banned the possession of guns within one thousand feet of any school, was unconstitutional because it attempted to regulate an area that had "nothing to do with commerce." In a significant 1997 decision, the Court struck down portions of the Brady Handgun Violence Prevention Act of 1993, which obligated state and local law enforcement officers to do background checks on prospective handgun buyers until a national instant check system could be implemented. The Court stated that Congress lacked the power to "dragoon" state employees into federal service through an unfunded **federal mandate** of this kind.[12]

Since then, the Court has continued to limit the national government's regulatory powers. In 2000, for example, the Court invalidated a key provision of the federal Violence Against Women Act of 1994, which allowed women to sue in federal court when they were victims of gender-motivated violence, such as rape. The Court upheld a federal appellate court's ruling that the commerce clause did not justify national regulation of noneconomic, criminal conduct.[13]

In the twenty-first century, the United States Supreme Court has been less noticeably guided by an ideology of states' rights, but some of its decisions have had the effect of enhancing the power of the states. For example, in one case, *Massachusetts v. Environmental Protection Agency*,[14] Massachusetts and several other states sued the Environmental Protection Agency (EPA) for failing to regulate greenhouse-gas emissions. The states asserted that the agency was required to do so by the Clean Air Act of 1990. The EPA argued that it lacked the authority under the Clean Air Act to regulate greenhouse-gas emissions alleged to promote global warming. The Court ruled for the states, holding that the EPA did have the authority to regulate such emissions and should take steps to do so.

The Shifting Boundary between Federal and State Authority

Clearly, the boundary between federal and state authority has been shifting. Notably, issues relating to the federal structure of our government, which at one time were not at the forefront of the political arena, have in recent years been the subject of heated debate among Americans and their leaders. The federal government and the states seem to be in a constant tug-of-war over federal regulation, federal programs, and federal demands on the states.

THE POLITICS OF FEDERALISM The Republican Party is often viewed as the champion of states' rights. Certainly, the party has claimed such a role. For example, when the Republicans took control of both chambers of Congress in 1995, they promised devolution—which, as already noted, refers to a shifting of power from the national level to the individual states. Smaller central government and a state-centered federalism have long been regarded as the twin pillars of Republican ideology. In contrast, Democrats usually have sought greater centralization of power in Washington, D.C.

Since the Clinton administration, however, the party tables seem to have turned. As mentioned earlier, it was under Clinton that welfare reform legislation giving more responsibility to the states—a goal that had been endorsed by the Republicans for some time—became a reality. Conversely, the No Child Left Behind Act of 2001, passed at the request of Republican president George W. Bush,

"Don't take your guns to town, son leave your guns at home..."
—Johnny Cash

Taproom Hours
Monday - Saturday
11:00 a.m. til Midnight
Closed

AP PHOTO/JOSH ANDERSON

A nationwide review by The Associated Press found that over the last two years, 24 states, mostly in the South and West, have passed 47 new laws loosening gun restrictions.

devolution The surrender or transfer of powers to local authorities by a central government.

federal mandate A requirement in federal legislation that forces states and municipalities to comply with certain rules. If the federal government does not provide funds to the states to cover the costs of compliance, the mandate is referred to as an *unfunded* mandate.

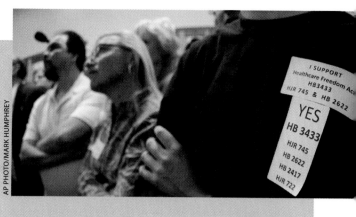

AP PHOTO/MARK HUMPHREY

JOIN THE DEBATE

Is Obamacare Unconstitutional?

In 2010, President Obama signed into law the most significant legislation in decades concerning health care. Some were elated by passage of the legislation, nicknamed "Obamacare." Others were aghast. Some who opposed the new law are raising constitutional issues—twenty state attorney generals have joined together in a suit against the federal government. Others, including those who favor Obamacare, are convinced that no constitutional issues are involved.

The Government Can't Force Us to Buy Anything

The reasoning of those who believe Obamacare is unconstitutional runs as follows: It is true that state governments have the right to require, for example, drivers to buy automobile insurance to travel on the public streets. Nothing in the Constitution, in contrast, gives the federal government the right to impose such requirements. The new laws demand that everyone in the United States purchase health-care insurance or be fined. The Internal Revenue Service will enforce this law. While the commerce clause allows the federal government to regulate interstate commerce, it has never been used to *require* citizens to buy any service or good. Another constitutional argument against the reforms is that a requirement to buy insurance violates the Fifth Amendment's right to due process.

Further constitutional challenges are based on states' rights. Some states have passed legislation barring any of their citizens from being required to purchase medical insurance. A suit by Florida claims that the Medicare expansion provided by the law improperly commandeers state officials. The battle between the states and the federal government is not new. Sometimes the Supreme Court has supported states' rights. Sometimes it hasn't.

There Is No Constitutional Basis for a Challenge

Proponents of health-care reform argue that the constitutional challenges to the new legislation are smoke and mirrors. Congress has spoken—all Americans will eventually have access to medical care. For this to occur, almost all Americans will need to have health insurance of one form or another. Otherwise, those who do have health insurance will pay higher premiums to make up for the missing premiums of those that don't have insurance. The "requirement" to buy insurance simply amounts to a tax on those who do not buy it. It's assumed that some people will pay the tax and go without insurance. The courts have always held that Congress can place tax incentives in the Internal Revenue Code.

As for states' rights, that's an old argument brought up every time some people don't like new legislation. In fact, the supremacy of national law was established in 1819 by *McCulloch v. Maryland,* and the breadth of the commerce clause was settled in 1824 by *Gibbons v. Ogden.* (See pages 56 and 57.) If constitutional arguments against the new legislation make it all the way to the United States Supreme Court, they will be rejected—probably on a nine-to-zero vote.

For Critical Analysis *Who will gain and who will lose because of the new health-care legislation?*

---

gave the federal government a much greater role in education and educational funding than ever before. Many Republicans also supported a constitutional amendment that would ban same-sex marriages nationwide. Liberals, recognizing that it was possible to win support for same-sex marriages only in a limited number of states, took a states' rights position on this issue. Finally, consider that the Bush administration made repeated attempts to block California's medical-marijuana initiative and Oregon's physician-assisted suicide law.

OBAMA AND FEDERALISM The position of the Obama administration has been more ambiguous. Obama has certainly championed measures that

increase the role of government in society, but the new laws have not necessarily shifted power from the states to the federal government. Obama's opponents, however, have frequently invoked states' rights in opposition to such legislation as the health-care reform bills. Officials in a number of states have filed suits claiming that "Obamacare" is unconstitutional. Do these suits have any chance of succeeding? We examine that question in this chapter's *Join the Debate* feature above.

FEDERALISM AND THE "WAR ON TERRORISM" In modern times, terrorism—the use of violence to intimidate or coerce—has become so large-scale and has claimed so many victims that it is hard to consider it an

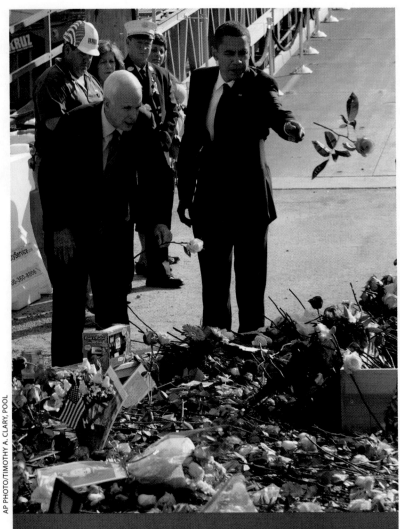

Presidential candidates John McCain and Barack Obama toss flowers into the reflecting pool at Ground Zero in New York City. They were commemorating the seventh anniversary of the September 11 terrorist attacks on the World Trade Center towers.

ordinary crime. Terrorism has many of the characteristics of war, not just of crime—hence the term *war on terrorism*. Unlike war, however, terrorism involves nongovernmental actors. Some authorities suggest thinking of terrorism as a "supercrime."[15]

The U.S. Constitution gives Congress the power and authority to provide for the common defense. Nevertheless, most of the burden of homeland defense falls on state and local governments. These governments are the "first responders" to crises, including terrorist attacks. Additionally, state and local governments are responsible for detecting, preparing for, preventing, and recovering from attacks.

After the terrorist attacks of September 11, 2001, the Bush administration increased demands on state and local governments to participate in homeland security.

As with the implementation of any national policy, the requirements imposed on the states to support homeland security were costly. Firefighting departments needed more equipment and training. Emergency communications equipment had to be purchased. State and local governments were required to secure ports, ensure water safety and airport security, install new bomb-detecting equipment, and take a multitude of other steps. Since 9/11, almost every state law enforcement agency and about a quarter of local agencies (most of them in larger cities) have formed specialized antiterrorism units. Although the federal government has provided funds to the states to cover some of these expenses, much of the cost of homeland security is borne by the states.

The wars in Afghanistan and Iraq also depleted the ranks of state and local police, firefighters, and other emergency personnel. Many individuals working in these areas were also in the National Guard and were called up to active duty.

FEDERALISM AND THE ECONOMIC CRISIS

Unlike the federal government, state governments are required to balance their budgets. This requirement is written into the constitution of every state except Vermont. Such requirements do not, of course, prevent the states from borrowing money, but typically when a state borrows it must follow a strict series of rules laid down in its constitution. Frequently, a vote of the people is required before a state or local government can go into debt by issuing bonds. In contrast, when the federal government runs a budget deficit, the borrowing that results takes place almost automatically—the U.S. Treasury continually issues new Treasury bonds.

A practical result is that when a major recession occurs, the states are faced with severe budget problems. Because state citizens are earning and spending less, state income and sales taxes fall. At the same time, people who have lost their jobs require more state services. The costs of welfare, unemployment compensation, and Medicaid (health care for low-income persons) all rise. During a recession, state governments may be forced either to reduce spending and lay off staff—or to raise taxes. Either choice helps make the recession worse. State spending patterns tend to make economic booms more energetic and busts more painful—in a word, they are *procyclical*.

Unlike the states, the federal government has no difficulty in spending more on welfare, unemployment compensation, and Medicaid during a recession. Even though revenue raised through the federal income tax may fall, the federal government often cuts tax rates in a recession to spur the economy. It makes up the difference by going further into debt, an option not available to the states. The federal government even has the power to reduce its debt by issuing new money, as you learned in the *Our Government Faces a Troubled Economy* feature in Chapter 2 on page 40. In a recession, the actions of the federal government are normally *anticyclical*.

One method of dealing with the procyclical nature of state spending is to increase federal grants to the states during a recession. For more details on how that can work, see this chapter's *Our Government Faces a Troubled Economy* feature on the following page.

LO5 *The Fiscal Side of Federalism*

Since the advent of cooperative federalism in the 1930s, the national government and the states have worked hand in hand to implement programs mandated by the national government. Whenever Congress passes a law that preempts a certain area, the states are, of course, obligated to comply with the requirements of that law. As already noted, a requirement that a state provide a service or undertake some activity to meet standards specified by a federal law is called a *federal mandate*. Many federal mandates concern civil rights or environmental protection. Recent federal mandates require the states to provide persons with disabilities with access to public buildings, sidewalks, and other areas; to establish minimum water-purity and air-purity standards; and to extend Medicaid coverage to all poor children.

To help the states pay for some of the costs associated with implementing national policies, the national government gives back some of the tax dollars it collects to the states—in the form of grants. As you will see, the states have come to depend on grants as an important source of revenue. When taxes are collected

"GIVING MONEY AND POWER TO GOVERNMENT

is like giving whiskey and car keys to teenage boys"

~ P.J. O'ROURKE ~
AMERICAN HUMORIST
1947–PRESENT

by one level of government (typically the national government) and spent by another level (typically state or local governments), we call the process **fiscal federalism.**

Federal Grants

Even before the Constitution was adopted, the national government granted lands to the states to finance education. Using the proceeds from the sale of these lands, the states were able to establish elementary schools and, later, *land-grant colleges*. Cash grants started in 1808, when Congress gave money to the states to pay for the state militias. Federal grants were also made available for other purposes, such as building roads and railroads.

Only in the twentieth century, though, did federal grants become an important source of funds to the states. The major growth began in the 1960s, when the dollar amount of grants quadrupled to help pay for the Great Society programs of the Johnson administration. Grants became available for education, pollution control, conservation, recreation, highway construction and maintenance, and other purposes.

There are two basic types of federal grants: categorical grants and block grants. A **categorical grant** is targeted for a specific purpose as defined by federal law—the federal government defines hundreds of categories of state and local spending. Categorical grants give the national government control over how states use the money by imposing certain conditions. For example, a categorical grant may require that the funds not be used for purposes that discriminate against any group or for construction projects that pay below the local prevailing wage. Depending on the project, the government might require that an environmental impact statement be prepared.

In contrast, a **block grant** is given for a broad area, such as criminal justice or mental-health programs. First issued in 1966, block grants now constitute a growing percentage of all federal aid programs. A block grant gives the states more discretion over how the funds

fiscal federalism The allocation of taxes collected by one level of government (typically the national government) to another level (typically state or local governments).

categorical grant A federal grant targeted for a specific purpose as defined by federal law.

block grant A federal grant given to a state for a broad area, such as criminal justice or mental-health programs.

OUR GOVERNMENT FACES A TROUBLED ECONOMY

Fighting a Recession with Government Spending

In an attempt to prevent the Great Recession from turning into another Great Depression, President Barack Obama called for massive stimulus legislation in 2009. He and his advisers believed that fiscal policy can have profound effects on the nation's economy. Fiscal policy refers to changes in government taxes and spending.

The logic behind fiscal policy is straightforward. When unemployment is rising and the economy is in a recession, fiscal policy should stimulate economic activity by increasing government spending, decreasing tax rates, or both. When unemployment is falling and prices are rising—when there is inflation— the government should curb excessive economic activity by reducing spending, increasing taxes, or both. In other words, the government's budget deficit should rise in a recession and fall in a boom. This view of fiscal policy is based on the theories of the British economist John Maynard Keynes (1883–1946). It's worth noting, by the way, that not all economists agree with Keynes.

Making Grants to the States

It can take a while for the government to realize that a recession has begun. It takes more time for a bill authorizing a tax cut or spending increase to work its way through Congress. It takes still more time for the change in taxation or spending to have an effect. By the time fiscal policy is actually stimulating the economy, the recession may be over. Obama moved quickly, however. He gave the Democrats in Congress

almost total freedom to come up with a bill, as long as they did it fast. Indeed, Congress came up with a massive stimulus bill, initially valued at $787 billion, in record time. How could Congress write a bill so quickly?

State and local governments make grant proposals on a continuing basis. Thousands of such proposals from state and local governments were already in hand. Obama therefore promised the American people that the stimulus bill would concentrate on "shovel-ready" projects—state and local projects that were ready to be started immediately upon the receipt of federal funds.

What the Stimulus Really Funded

America has thousands of bridges that need repair, highways that need resurfacing, and other serious infrastructure problems. Of the $787 billion, however, $264 billion was devoted to tax cuts (mostly for individuals), and the rest to spending. Infrastructure received less than $100 billion. Unemployment compensation, food stamps, and other programs totaled more than $100 billion. Health care received about $150 billion—most of it paid to the states—and education received roughly another $100 billion.

Those economists who supported the stimulus believe that it did have a positive effect on the economy. Clearly, however, it did not solve the unemployment problem. By 2010, the unemployment rate was still almost 10 percent. To the extent that the stimulus had an impact on employment, it reduced layoffs rather than creating new jobs. It especially saved the jobs of health-care workers, teachers, and other state government employees. Spending fueled by tax cuts and unemployment compensation presumably saved some jobs as well, but it was impossible to identify who benefited. As a result, the effects of the stimulus were largely invisible. Most voters concluded that the stimulus had no effect.

You Be the Judge Business tax reductions in the stimulus bill amounted to only $32 billion. Why do you think Obama was reluctant to cut business tax rates further?

will be spent. Nonetheless, the federal government can exercise control over state decision making through these grants by using *cross-cutting requirements*, or requirements that apply to all federal grants. Title VI of the 1964 Civil Rights Act, for example, bars discrimination in the use of all federal funds, regardless of their source.

Using Federal Grants to Control the States

Grants of funds to the states from the national government are one way that the Tenth Amendment to the U.S. Constitution can be bridged. Remember that the

Competitive federalism includes state tax-reduction incentives, through which states offer lower taxes to manufacturing firms that agree to locate in their states. Such an incentive was one reason Toyota opened a plant in Huntsville, Alabama.

the states must comply—but compliance with federal mandates can be costly. The estimated total cost of complying with federal mandates to the states in the 2000s has been calculated as $29 billion annually. Although Congress passed legislation in 1995 to curb the use of unfunded federal mandates, that legislation was more rhetoric than reality.

Competitive Federalism

The debate over federalism is sometimes reduced to a debate over taxes. Which level of government will raise taxes to pay for government programs, and which will cut services to avoid raising taxes?

How states answer that question gives citizens an option: they can move to a state with fewer services and lower taxes, or to a state with more services but higher taxes. Political scientist Thomas R. Dye calls this model of federalism **competitive federalism.** State and local governments compete for businesses and citizens. If the state of Ohio offers tax advantages for locating a factory there, for example, a business may be more likely to build its factory in Ohio, providing more jobs for Ohio residents. If Ohio has very strict environmental regulations, however, that same business may choose not to build there, no matter how beneficial the tax advantages, because complying with the regulations would be costly. Although Ohio citizens lose the opportunity for more jobs, they may enjoy better air and water quality than citizens of the state where the new factory is ultimately built.

Some observers consider such competition an advantage: Americans have several variables to consider when they choose a state in which to live. Others consider it a disadvantage: a state that offers more social services or lower taxes may experience an increase in population as people "vote with their feet" to take advantage of that state's laws. This population

Tenth Amendment reserves all powers not delegated to the national government to the states and to the people. You might well wonder, then, how the federal government has been able to exercise control over matters that traditionally have been under the control of state governments, such as the minimum drinking age. The answer involves the giving or withholding of federal grant dollars.

For example, as noted in the *America at Odds* feature at the beginning of this chapter, the national government forced the states to raise the minimum drinking age to twenty-one by threatening to withhold federal highway funds from states that did not comply. The education reforms embodied in the No Child Left Behind (NCLB) Act also rely on federal funding for their implementation. The states receive block grants for educational purposes and, in return, must meet federally imposed standards for testing and accountability. A common complaint, however, is that the existing NCLB Act is an underfunded federal mandate. Critics argue that the national government does not provide sufficient funds to implement it.

The Cost of Federal Mandates

As mentioned, when the national government passes a law preempting an area in which the states and the national government have concurrent powers, the states must comply with that law in accordance with the supremacy clause of the Constitution. Thus, when such laws require the states to implement certain programs,

> **competitive federalism**
> A model of federalism devised by Thomas R. Dye in which state and local governments compete for businesses and citizens, who in effect "vote with their feet" by moving to jurisdictions that offer a competitive advantage.

increase can overwhelm the state's resources and force it to cut social services or raise taxes.

It appears likely, then, that the debate over how our federal system functions, as well as the battle for control between the states and the federal government, will continue. The Supreme Court, which has played umpire in this battle, will also likely continue to issue rulings that influence the balance of power.

> "Taxes, AFTER ALL, ARE THE DUES THAT WE PAY FOR THE PRIVILEGES OF MEMBERSHIP IN AN organized society."
>
> ~ FRANKLIN D. ROOSEVELT ~
> THIRTY-SECOND PRESIDENT
> OF THE UNITED STATES
> 1933–1945

AMERICA AT ODDS *Federalism*

The topic of federalism raises one of the most enduring disputes in American history—the relative power of the national government versus the governments of the states. As you read in the last two chapters, Americans have been at odds over the strength of the central government since well before the American Revolution. The issue of centralization versus decentralization has taken a number of specific forms:

- Is it right for the national government to use its financial strength to pressure states into taking actions such as raising the drinking age by threatening to withhold subsidies—or are such pressures an abuse of the federal system?

- Should the national government intervene in the issue of legalizing or banning same-sex marriages—or leave such matters strictly to the states?

- Should the commerce clause be interpreted broadly, granting the federal government much power to regulate the economy—or should it be interpreted as narrowly as possible to keep the government from interfering with the rights of business owners?

- Should the federal government have a role in setting national policies for public education—or should that be left entirely to the states?

- Should the federal government establish a national system for funding health care—or should that, too, be left to the states or to the private sector?

Take Action

Many people believe that it's only possible to have a real impact on the problems we face—the economy, poverty, health care, or the environment—at the national level. You can do a lot to address these issues at the state and local level, however. Consider that an individual or a small group can have much more influence on a state government than on the national one, and can make an even bigger impact on a local government.

As the slogan goes, "Think globally, act locally." Your local government controls construction and land-use issues, oversees the police or sheriff's department, and can pass all kinds of local ordinances. Will banning the sale of Styrofoam cups lead to a tidier environment—or is it a ridiculous infringement on personal freedoms? There are hundreds of such issues that you and your friends could take up.

Acting locally does not have to mean political engagement, however. You can also volunteer your services to a cause that concerns you, such as improving the environment or helping the poor or the elderly. Volunteer activities can be very gratifying, and you could make a big difference in the lives that you touch. Try using VolunteerMatch to find volunteer opportunities in your community. Just enter your ZIP code on its Web site (**www.volunteermatch.org**). Other organizations that work to meet critical needs include AmeriCorps (**www.americorps.gov**) and the Corporation for National and Community Service (**www.nationalservice.gov**).

POLITICS ON THE
WEB

- You can access the *Federalist Papers,* as well as state constitutions, information on the role of the courts in resolving issues relating to federalism, and information on international federations, at the following site: **www.constitution.org/cs_feder.htm**

- You can find information on state governments, state laws and pending legislation, and state issues and initiatives at **www.statescape.com**

- Supreme Court opinions, including those discussed in this chapter, can be found at the Court's official Web site. Go to **www.supremecourt.gov**

- A good source of information on state governments and issues concerning federalism is the Web site of the Council of State Governments. Go to **www.csg.org**

- The Brookings Institution, the nation's oldest think tank, is a good source for information on emerging policy challenges, including federal-state issues, and for practical recommendations for dealing with those challenges. To access the institution's home page, go to **www.brookings.edu**

- If you are interested in a libertarian perspective on issues such as federalism, you can visit the Cato Institute's Web site at **www.cato.org**

- The Web site of the National Governors Association offers information on many issues affecting the nation, ranging from health-care reform, to education, to new and innovative state programs. You can access information on these issues, as well as many key issues relating to federalism, at **www.nga.org**

- *Governing* magazine, an excellent source of state and local news, can be found online at **www.governing.com**

CourseMate

Access CourseMate to review and expand on this chapter through quizzes, flashcards, learning objectives, interactive timelines, a crossword puzzle, audio summaries, video, critical-thinking activities, simulations, and more.

Civil Liberties

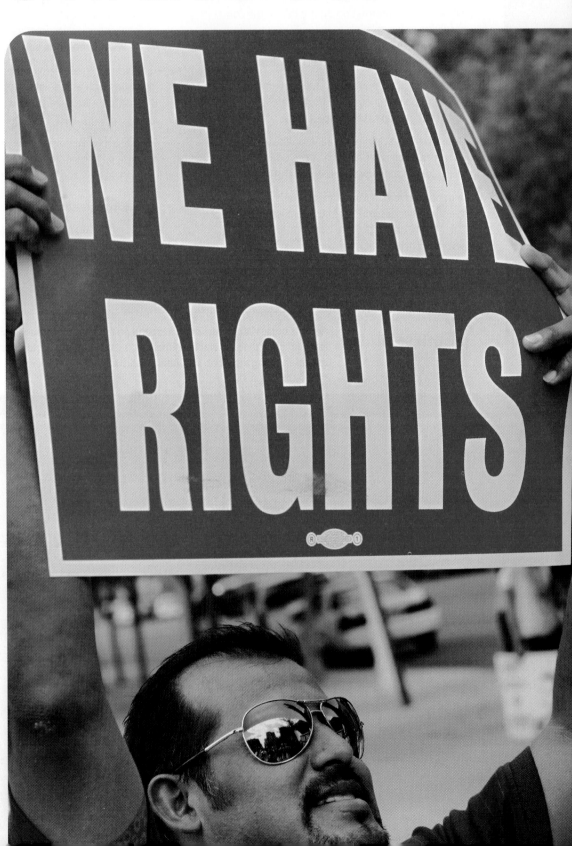

LEARNING OBJECTIVES

LO1 Define the term *civil liberties,* explain how civil liberties differ from civil rights, and state the constitutional basis for our civil liberties.

LO2 List and describe the freedoms guaranteed by the First Amendment and explain how the courts have interpreted and applied these freedoms.

LO3 Discuss why Americans are increasingly concerned about privacy rights.

LO4 Summarize how the Constitution and the Bill of Rights protect the rights of accused persons.

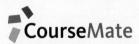
CourseMate

AMERICA AT ODDS

Should Government Entities Enjoy Freedom of Speech?

We all know that the First Amendment to the U.S. Constitution states that Congress shall make no law "abridging the freedom of speech." Indeed, citizens of the United States may enjoy greater freedom of speech than the citizens of any other country. But what about government entities? Do they, too, enjoy freedom of speech? Can government bodies decide without constraint the messages they wish to communicate to the public?

This question becomes important when we consider whether religious displays can be allowed on government property. Until recently, the legal battles over such displays have centered on another part of the First Amendment—the establishment clause, which states: "Congress shall make no law respecting an establishment of religion." On several occasions, the United States Supreme Court has been asked to decide whether Christmas nativity scenes on public property violate the establishment clause. The Court has found that they do, unless equal space is provided for secular displays or the symbols of other religions.

Recently, the Supreme Court grappled with a case in which a small religious group, Summum, wanted to force Pleasant Grove, Utah, to accept a granite monument containing "the Seven Aphorisms of Summum" and place it in a public park. The city had earlier accepted a monument containing the Ten Commandments as one of several dozen displays in the park. Summum claimed that the city had violated the group's free speech rights by refusing to accept its donation. The Court backed the arguments of the city, however, and ruled that "the placement of a permanent monument in a public park is best viewed as a form of government speech and is therefore not subject to scrutiny under the Free Speech Clause." Because it was the city speaking, and not the groups that donated the monuments, none of the organizations could make a free speech claim. In short, government bodies enjoy their own rights to free speech. Is this appropriate?

Obviously, the Government Has a Right to Free Speech

The free speech clause involves government regulation of private speech; it does not regulate government speech. A government entity has the right to "speak for itself" and is entitled to say what it wishes. How could any government body function if it lacked this basic freedom? If citizens had the right to insist that no official paid with public funds could express a view with which that citizen disagreed, debate over issues of public concern would be severely limited. The process of government would be radically transformed. To govern, governments have to say something.

Governments own public land, including parks. Government officials have to decide what expressions of speech should be affixed permanently to public land. If the government did not have the right to decide, every single religious body and special interest group could demand that their monuments be placed on public land. Alongside the Statue of Liberty, New York might be required to erect a "statue of autocracy." In the end, governments would be forced to ban monuments or statues of any description. We cannot take away government bodies' rights to decide in such instances.

It's the Edge of the Wedge

To apply the concept of freedom of speech to governments is asking for trouble. It may be that by accepting a privately financed and donated monument, a government body has exercised a kind of government speech and has implicitly accepted the ideas represented by such monuments. Such thinking raises serious establishment clause issues. If the privately donated monuments are religious in nature, as was true in the Pleasant Grove case, the government is implicitly violating the establishment clause of the First Amendment.

We must make sure that government bodies understand that they cannot even hint at preferring one religion over another. If a government does accept one religious monument, then it had better accept a variety of others. The "government speech doctrine," newly developed by the Supreme Court, must not allow government bodies to escape the establishment clause's ban on discriminating among religious sects or groups. Several Supreme Court justices in the Pleasant Grove case argued that the Court could have ruled for the city without reference to any theory of free speech for governments. The Court's majority should have taken their advice.

WHERE DO YOU STAND?

1. How can voters hold governments accountable for their decisions about which monuments to display and which not to display?
2. Several courts have held that any opinions communicated by specialty license plates are those of the driver, not the state. Why are license plates different from monuments in parks?

EXPLORE THIS ISSUE ONLINE

- The FindLaw Web site lets you browse through recent decisions by the Supreme Court on a wide variety of topics. Civil liberties issues are grouped together with civil rights. To locate cases, use the search box at www.findlaw.com/casecode.
- Adam Liptak, the Supreme Court correspondent of the *New York Times*, writes a regular column called "Sidebar." To see Liptak's perceptive columns, go to www.nytimes.com and type "sidebar" into the search box.

CIVIL LIBERTIES
are legal and constitutional rights that protect citizens from government actions.

Introduction

The debate over government free speech discussed in the chapter-opening *America at Odds* feature is but one of many controversies concerning our civil liberties. **Civil liberties** are legal and constitutional rights that protect citizens from government actions. For example, the First Amendment to the U.S. Constitution prohibits Congress from making any law that abridges the right to free speech. The First Amendment also guarantees freedom of religion, freedom of the press, and freedom to assemble (to gather together for a common purpose, such as to protest against a government policy or action). These and other freedoms and guarantees set forth in the Constitution and the Bill of Rights are essentially *limits* on government action.

Perhaps the best way to understand what civil liberties are and why they are important to Americans is to look at what might happen if we did not have them. If you were a student in China, for example, you would have to exercise some care in what you said and did. That country prohibits a variety of kinds of speech, notably any criticism of the leading role of the Communist Party. If you criticized the government in e-mail messages to your friends or on your Web site, you could end up in court on charges that you had violated the law—and perhaps even go to prison.

Note that some Americans confuse *civil liberties* (discussed in this chapter) with *civil rights* (discussed in the next chapter) and use the terms interchangeably. Nonetheless, scholars make a distinction between the two. They point out that whereas civil liberties are limitations on government action, setting forth what the government *cannot do,* civil rights specify what the government *must* do—to ensure equal protection under the law for all Americans, for example.

LO1 *The Constitutional Basis for Our Civil Liberties*

The founders believed that the constitutions of the individual states contained ample provisions to protect citizens from government actions. Therefore, the founders did not include many references to individual civil liberties in the original version of the Constitution. Many of our liberties were added by the Bill of Rights, ratified in 1791. Nonetheless, the original Constitution did include some safeguards to protect citizens against an overly powerful government.

Safeguards in the Original Constitution

Article I, Section 9, of the Constitution provides that the writ of *habeas corpus* (a Latin phrase that roughly means "produce the body") will be available to all citizens except in times of rebellion or national invasion. A **writ of *habeas corpus*** is an order requiring that an official bring a specified prisoner into court and show the judge why the prisoner is being kept in jail. If the court finds that the imprisonment is unlawful, it orders the prisoner to be released. If our country did not have such a constitutional provision, political leaders could jail their opponents without giving them the opportunity to plead their cases before a judge. Without this opportunity, many opponents might conveniently disappear or be left to rot away in prison.

The Constitution also prohibits Congress and the state legislatures from passing bills of attainder. A **bill of attainder** is a legislative act that directly punishes a specifically named

Corky Ra is the founder of the group Summum, described on the previous page.

AP PHOTO/SUMMUM, HO

civil liberties Individual rights protected by the Constitution against the powers of the government.

writ of *habeas corpus* An order that requires an official to bring a specified prisoner into court and explain to the judge why the person is being held in prison.

bill of attainder A legislative act that inflicts punishment on particular persons or groups without granting them the right to a trial.

individual (or a group or class of individuals) without a trial. For example, no legislature can pass a law that punishes a named Hollywood celebrity for unpatriotic statements.

Finally, the Constitution also prohibits Congress from passing *ex post facto* laws. The Latin term *ex post facto* roughly means "after the fact." An **ex post facto law** punishes individuals for committing an act that was legal when it was committed.

The Bill of Rights

As you read in Chapter 2, one of the contentious issues in the debate over ratification of the Constitution was the lack of protections for citizens from government actions. Although many state constitutions provided such protections, the Anti-Federalists wanted more. The promise of the addition of a bill of rights to the Constitution ensured its ratification.

The Bill of Rights was ratified by the states and became part of the Constitution on December 15, 1791. Look at the text of the Bill of Rights on page 42 in Chapter 2. As you can see, the first eight amendments grant the people specific rights and liberties. The remaining two amendments reserve certain rights and powers to the people and to the states.

Basically, in a democracy, government policy tends to reflect the view of the majority. A key function of the Bill of Rights, therefore, is to protect the rights of those in the minority against the will of the majority. When there is disagreement over how to interpret the Bill of Rights, the courts step in. The United States Supreme Court, as our nation's highest court, has the final say on how the Constitution, including the Bill of Rights, should be interpreted. The civil liberties that you will read about in this chapter have all been shaped over time by Supreme Court decisions. For example, it is the Supreme Court that determines where freedom of speech ends and the right of society to be protected from certain forms of speech begins.

Ultimately, the responsibility for protecting minority rights lies with the American people. Each generation has to learn anew how it can uphold its rights by voting, expressing opinions to elected representatives, and bringing cases to the attention of the courts when constitutional rights are threatened.

The Incorporation Issue

For many years, the courts assumed that the Bill of Rights limited only the actions of the national government, not the actions of state or local governments. In other words, if a state or local law was contrary to a basic freedom, such as the freedom of speech or the right to due process of law, the federal Bill of Rights did not come into play. The founders believed that the states, being closer to the people, would be less likely to violate their own citizens' liberties. Moreover, state constitutions, most of which contain bills of rights, protect citizens against state government actions. The United States Supreme Court upheld this view when it decided, in *Barron v. Baltimore* (1833), that the Bill of Rights did not apply to state laws.[1]

Eventually, however, the Supreme Court began to take a different view. Because the Fourteenth Amendment played a key role in this development, we look next at the provisions of that amendment.

THE RIGHT TO DUE PROCESS   In 1868, three years after the end of the Civil War, the Fourteenth Amendment was added to the Constitution. The **due process clause** of this amendment requires that state governments protect their citizens' rights. (A similar requirement, binding on the federal government, was provided by the Fifth Amendment.) The due process clause reads, in part, as follows:

> No State shall . . . deprive any person of life, liberty, or property, without due process of law.

The right to **due process of law** is simply the right to be treated fairly under the legal system. That system and its officers must follow "rules of fair play" in making decisions, in determining guilt or innocence, and in punishing those who have been found guilty.

Procedural Due Process   *Procedural* due process requires that any governmental decision to take life, liberty, or property be made equitably. For example, the government must use fair procedures in determining whether a person will be subjected to punishment or have some burden imposed on him or her. Fair procedure has been interpreted as requiring that the person have at least an opportunity to object to a proposed action before an impartial, neutral decision maker (which need not be a judge).

ex post facto **law**   A criminal law that punishes individuals for committing an act that was legal when the act was committed.

due process clause   The constitutional guarantee, set out in the Fifth and Fourteenth Amendments, that the government will not illegally or arbitrarily deprive a person of life, liberty, or property.

due process of law   The requirement that the government use fair, reasonable, and standard procedures whenever it takes any legal action against an individual; required by the Fifth and Fourteenth Amendments.

establishment clause
The section of the First Amendment that prohibits Congress from passing laws "respecting an establishment of religion." Issues concerning the establishment clause often center on prayer in public schools, the teaching of fundamentalist theories of creation, and government aid to parochial schools.

free exercise clause The provision of the First Amendment stating that the government cannot pass laws "prohibiting the free exercise" of religion. Free exercise issues often concern religious practices that conflict with established laws.

Table 4–1

Incorporating the Bill of Rights into the 14th Amendment

Year	Issue	Amendment Involved	Court Case
1925	Freedom of speech	I	*Gitlow v. New York*, 268 U.S. 652.
1931	Freedom of the press	I	*Near v. Minnesota*, 283 U.S. 697.
1932	Right to a lawyer in capital punishment cases	VI	*Powell v. Alabama*, 287 U.S. 45.
1937	Freedom of assembly and right to petition	I	*De Jonge v. Oregon*, 299 U.S. 353.
1940	Freedom of religion	I	*Cantwell v. Connecticut*, 310 U.S. 296.
1947	Separation of church and state	I	*Everson v. Board of Education*, 330 U.S. 1.
1948	Right to a public trial	VI	*In re Oliver*, 333 U.S. 257.
1949	No unreasonable searches and seizures	IV	*Wolf v. Colorado*, 338 U.S. 25.
1961	Exclusionary rule	IV	*Mapp v. Ohio*, 367 U.S. 643.
1962	No cruel and unusual punishments	VIII	*Robinson v. California*, 370 U.S. 660.
1963	Right to a lawyer in all criminal felony cases	VI	*Gideon v. Wainwright*, 372 U.S. 335.
1964	No compulsory self-incrimination	V	*Malloy v. Hogan*, 378 U.S. 1.
1965	Right to privacy	Various	*Griswold v. Connecticut*, 381 U.S. 479.
1966	Right to an impartial jury	VI	*Parker v. Gladden*, 385 U.S. 363.
1967	Right to a speedy trial	VI	*Klopfer v. North Carolina*, 386 U.S. 213.
1969	No double jeopardy	V	*Benton v. Maryland*, 395 U.S. 784.
2010	Right to bear arms	II	*McDonald v. Chicago*, 561 U.S. __.

Substantive Due Process

Substantive due process focuses on the content, or substance, of legislation. If a law or other governmental action limits a *fundamental right,* it will be held to violate substantive due process, unless it promotes a *compelling* or *overriding state interest.* All First Amendment rights plus the rights to interstate travel, privacy, and voting are considered fundamental. Compelling state interests could include, for example, the public's safety.

OTHER LIBERTIES INCORPORATED The Fourteenth Amendment also states that no state "shall make or enforce any law which shall abridge the privileges or immunities of citizens of the United States." For some time, the Supreme Court considered the "privileges and immunities" referred to in the amendment to be those conferred by state laws or constitutions, not the federal Bill of Rights.

Starting in 1925, however, the Supreme Court gradually began using the due process clause to say that states could not abridge a civil liberty that the national government could not abridge. In other words, the Court *incorporated* the protections guaranteed by the national Bill of Rights into the liberties protected under the Fourteenth Amendment. As you can see in Table 4–1 above, the Supreme Court was particularly active during the 1960s in broadening its interpretation of the due process clause to ensure that states and localities could not infringe on civil liberties protected by the Bill of Rights. Today, the liberties still not incorporated include the right to refuse to quarter soldiers and the right to a grand jury hearing. The right to bear arms described in the Second Amendment was incorporated only in 2010.

LO2 *Protections under the First Amendment*

As mentioned earlier, the First Amendment sets forth some of our most important civil liberties. Specifically, the First Amendment guarantees the freedoms of religion, speech, the press, and assembly, as well as the right to petition the government. In the pages that follow, we look closely at each of these freedoms and discuss how, over time, Supreme Court decisions have defined their meaning and determined their limits.

Freedom of Religion

The First Amendment prohibits Congress from passing laws "respecting an establishment of religion, or prohibiting the free exercise thereof." The first part of this amendment is known as the **establishment clause.** The second part is called the **free exercise clause.**

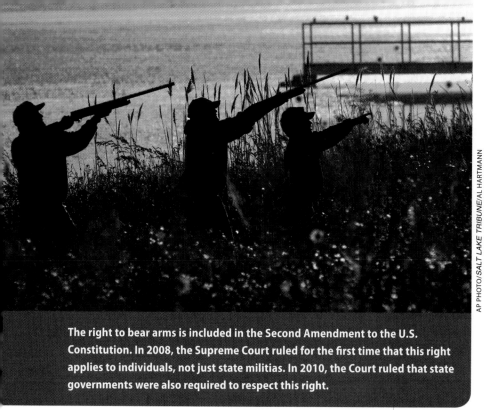

The right to bear arms is included in the Second Amendment to the U.S. Constitution. In 2008, the Supreme Court ruled for the first time that this right applies to individuals, not just state militias. In 2010, the Court ruled that state governments were also required to respect this right.

AP PHOTO/SALT LAKE TRIBUNE/AL HARTMANN

THE ESTABLISHMENT CLAUSE The establishment clause forbids the government to establish an official religion. This makes the United States different from countries that are ruled by religious governments, such as the Islamic government of Iran. It also makes us different from nations that have in the past strongly discouraged the practice of any religion at all, such as the People's Republic of China.

What does this separation of church and state mean in practice? For one thing, religion and government, though constitutionally separated in the United States, have never been enemies or strangers. The establishment clause does not prohibit government from supporting religion in *general*. It remains a part of public life.

Most government officials take an oath of office in the name of God, and our coins and paper currency carry the motto "In God We Trust." Clergy of different religions serve in each branch of the armed forces. Public meetings and even sessions of Congress open with prayers. Indeed, the establishment clause often masks the fact that Americans are, by and large, religious and would like their political leaders to be people of faith.

The "wall of separation" that Thomas Jefferson referred to, however, does exist and has been upheld by the Supreme Court on many occasions. An important ruling by the Supreme Court on the establishment clause came in 1947 in *Everson v. Board of Education*.[2] The case involved a New Jersey law that allowed the state to pay for bus transportation of students who attended parochial schools (schools run by churches or other religious groups). The Court stated as follows: "No tax in any amount, large or small, can be levied to support any religious activities or institutions."

The Court upheld the New Jersey law, however, because it did not aid the church *directly* but provided for the safety and benefit of the students. The ruling both affirmed the importance of separating church and state and set the precedent that not *all* forms of state and federal aid to church-related schools are forbidden under the Constitution.

A full discussion of the various church-state issues that have arisen in American politics would fill volumes. Here we examine three of these issues: prayer in the schools, evolution versus creationism or intelligent design, and government aid to parochial schools.

That freedom of religion was the first freedom mentioned in the Bill of Rights is not surprising. After all, many colonists came to America to escape religious persecution. Nonetheless, these same colonists showed little tolerance for religious freedom within the communities they established. For example, in 1610 the Jamestown colony enacted a law requiring attendance at religious services on Sunday "both in the morning and the afternoon." Repeat offenders were subjected to particularly harsh punishments. For those who twice violated the law, for example, the punishment was a public whipping. For third-time offenders, the punishment was death.

The Maryland Toleration Act of 1649 declared that anyone who cursed God or denied that Jesus Christ was the son of God was to be punished by death. In all, nine of the thirteen colonies had established official religions by the time of the American Revolution.

This context is helpful in understanding why, in 1802, President Thomas Jefferson, a great proponent of religious freedom and tolerance, wanted the establishment clause to be "a wall of separation between church and state." The context also helps to explain why even state leaders who supported state religions might have favored the establishment clause—to keep the national government from interfering in such state matters. After all, the First Amendment says only that *Congress* can make no law respecting an establishment of religion. It says nothing about whether the *states* could make such laws. And, as noted earlier, the protections in the Bill of Rights initially applied only to actions taken by the national government, not the state governments.

Prayer in the Schools On occasion, some public schools have promoted a general sense of religion without proclaiming allegiance to any particular church or sect. Whether the states have a right to allow this was the main question presented in 1962 in *Engel v. Vitale*,[3] also known as the "Regents' Prayer case." The State Board of Regents in New York had composed a nondenominational prayer (a prayer not associated with any particular church) and urged school districts to use it in classrooms at the start of each day. The prayer read as follows:

> Almighty God, we acknowledge our dependence upon Thee, and we beg Thy blessings upon us, our parents, our teachers, and our Country.

Some parents objected to the prayer, contending that it violated the establishment clause. The Supreme Court agreed and ruled that the Regents' Prayer was unconstitutional. Speaking for the majority, Justice Hugo Black wrote that the First Amendment must at least mean "that in this country it is no part of the business of government to compose official prayers for any group of the American people to recite as a part of a religious program carried on by government."

or proposed laws permitting (but not *requiring*, as the Kentucky law did) the display of the Ten Commandments on public property, including public schools. Supporters of such displays contend that they will help reinforce the fundamental religious values that are a part of the American heritage. Opponents claim that the displays blatantly violate the establishment clause.

Another controversial issue is whether "moments of silence" in the schools are constitutional. In 1985, the Supreme Court ruled that an Alabama law authorizing a daily one-minute period of silence for meditation and voluntary prayer was unconstitutional. Because the law specifically endorsed prayer, it appeared to support religion.[5] Since then, the lower courts have generally held that a school may require a moment of silence, but only if it serves a clearly secular purpose (such as to meditate on the day's activities).[6] Yet another issue concerns prayers said before public school sporting events, such as football games. In 2000, the Supreme Court held that student-led pregame prayer using the school's public-address system was unconstitutional.[7]

In sum, the Supreme Court has ruled that the public schools, which are agencies of government, cannot

Prayer in the Schools— The Debate Continues

Since the *Engel v. Vitale* ruling, the Supreme Court has continued to shore up the wall of separation between church and state in a number of decisions. Generally, the Court has had to walk a fine line between the wishes of those who believe that religion should have a more prominent place in our public institutions and those who do not. For example, in a 1980 case, *Stone v. Graham*,[4] the Supreme Court ruled that a Kentucky law requiring that the Ten Commandments be posted in all public schools violated the establishment clause. Many groups around the country opposed this ruling. Today, a number of states have passed

MARILYNN K. YEE/NEW YORK TIMES/REDUX

These students at Trey Whitfield School, in Brooklyn, New York—a private school—are engaged in school-organized prayers. Why is it constitutional to allow prayers in private schools but not in public schools?

sponsor religious activities. It has *not,* however, held that individuals cannot pray, when and as they choose, in schools or in any other place. Nor has it held that the schools are barred from teaching *about* religion, as opposed to engaging in religious practices.

Evolution versus Creationism Certain religious groups have long opposed the teaching of evolution in the schools. These groups contend that evolutionary theory, a theory with overwhelming scientific support, directly counters their religious belief that human beings did not evolve but were created fully formed, as described in the biblical story of the creation. In fact, surveys have repeatedly shown that a majority of Americans believe that humans were directly created by God rather than having evolved from other species. The Supreme Court, however, has held that state laws forbidding the teaching of evolution in the schools are unconstitutional.

For example, in *Epperson v. Arkansas,*[8] a case decided in 1968, the Supreme Court held that an Arkansas law prohibiting the teaching of evolution violated the establishment clause because it imposed religious beliefs on students. In 1987, the Supreme Court also held unconstitutional a Louisiana law requiring that the biblical story of the creation be taught along with evolution. The Court deemed the law unconstitutional in part because it had as its primary purpose the promotion of a particular religious belief.[9]

Nevertheless, some state and local groups continue their efforts against the teaching of evolution. Recently, for example, Alabama approved a disclaimer to be inserted in biology textbooks, stating that evolution is "a controversial theory some scientists present as a scientific explanation for the origin of living things." Laws and policies that discourage the teaching of evolution are also being challenged on constitutional grounds. For example, in Cobb County, Georgia, stickers were inserted into science textbooks stating that "evolution is a theory, not a fact" and that "the theory should be approached with an open mind, studied carefully, and critically considered." When Cobb County's actions were challenged in court as unconstitutional, a federal judge held that the stickers conveyed a "message of endorsement of religion," thus violating the First Amendment.

Evolution versus Intelligent Design Some schools have adopted the concept of "intelligent design" as an alternative to the teaching of evolution. Advocates of intelligent design believe that an intelligent cause, and not an undirected process such as natural selection, lies behind the creation and development of the universe and living things. Proponents of intelligent design claim that it is a scientific theory and thus that its teaching should not violate the establishment clause in any way. Opponents of intelligent design theory claim that it is pseudoscience at best and that, in fact, the so-called theory masks its supporters' belief that God is the "intelligent cause."

Aid to Parochial Schools Americans have long been at odds over whether public tax dollars should be used to fund activities in parochial schools—private schools that have religious affiliations. Over the years, the courts have often had to decide whether specific types of aid do or do not violate the establishment clause. Aid to church-related schools in the form of transportation, equipment, or special educational services for disadvantaged students has been held permissible. Other forms of aid, such as funding teachers' salaries and paying for field trips, have been held unconstitutional.

Since 1971, the Supreme Court has held that, to be constitutional, a state's school aid must meet three requirements: (1) the purpose of the financial aid must be clearly secular (not religious), (2) its primary effect must neither advance nor inhibit religion, and (3) it must avoid an "excessive government entanglement with religion." The Court first used this three-part test in *Lemon v. Kurtzman,*[10] and hence it is often referred to as the **Lemon test.** In the 1971 *Lemon* case, the Court denied public aid to private and parochial

> **Lemon test** A three-part test enunciated by the Supreme Court in the 1971 case of *Lemon v. Kurtzman* to determine whether government aid to parochial schools is constitutional. To be constitutional, the aid must (1) be for a clearly secular purpose; (2) in its primary effect, neither advance nor inhibit religion; and (3) avoid an "excessive government entanglement with religion." The *Lemon* test has also been used in other types of cases involving the establishment clause.

When an Oklahoma school attempted to bar a young Muslim girl from wearing a head scarf to school, the federal government intervened. Why would the U.S. government protect the right to wear religious symbols in public schools? What other civil liberties ensured by the U.S. Constitution might protect the right to wear religious dress in public schools?

school voucher An educational certificate, provided by a government, that allows a student to use public funds to pay for a private or a public school chosen by the student or his or her parents.

schools for the salaries of teachers of secular courses and for textbooks and instructional materials in certain secular subjects. The Court held that the establishment clause is designed to prevent three main evils: "sponsorship, financial support, and active involvement of the sovereign [the government] in religious activity."

In 2000, the Supreme Court applied the *Lemon* test to a federal law that gives public school districts federal funds for special services and instructional equipment. The law requires that the funds be shared with all private schools in the district. A central issue in the case was whether using the funds to supply computers to parochial schools had a clearly secular purpose. Some groups claimed that it did not, because students in parochial schools could use the computers to access religious materials online. Others, including the Clinton administration (1993–2001), argued that giving high-tech assistance to parochial schools did have a secular purpose and was a religiously neutral policy. The Supreme Court sided with the latter argument and held that the law did not violate the establishment clause.[11]

School Voucher Programs   Another contentious issue has to do with the use of **school vouchers**—educational certificates, provided by state governments, that students can use at any school, public or private. In an effort to improve their educational systems, several school districts have been experimenting with voucher systems. Four states now have limited voucher programs under which schoolchildren may attend private elementary or high schools using vouchers paid for by taxpayers' dollars.

In 2002, the United States Supreme Court ruled that a voucher program in Cleveland, Ohio, was constitutional. Under the program, the state provided up to $2,250 to low-income families, who could use the funds to send their children to either public or private schools. The Court concluded that the taxpayer-paid voucher program did not unconstitutionally entangle church and state because the funds went to parents, not to schools. The parents theoretically could use the vouchers to send their children to nonreligious private academies or charter schools, even though 95 percent used the vouchers at religious schools.[12]

Despite the 2002 Supreme Court ruling, several constitutional questions surrounding

school vouchers remain unresolved. For example, some state constitutions are more explicit than the federal Constitution in denying the use of public funds for religious education. Even after the Supreme Court ruling in the Ohio case, a Florida court ruled in 2002 that a voucher program in that state violated Florida's constitution.[13]

The public is very closely divided on this issue. About 30 percent of those responding to a public opinion poll on the subject did not have strong feelings one way or the other; those with opinions were evenly split. Support for vouchers tended to come from Catholics and white evangelicals, which is not surprising—a large number of existing private schools represent either the Catholic or evangelical faiths. Public school teacher unions oppose vouchers strongly, and they are a major constituency for the Democratic Party. With the Democrats in control of the presidency, federal support for vouchers is unlikely in the near future.

THE FREE EXERCISE CLAUSE   As mentioned, the second part of the First Amendment's statement on religion consists of the free exercise clause, which forbids the passage of laws "prohibiting the free exercise of religion." This clause protects a person's right to worship or believe as he or she wishes without government interference. No law or act of government may violate this constitutional right.

Belief and Practice Are Distinct   The free exercise clause does not necessarily mean that individuals can act in any way they want on the basis of their religious beliefs. There is an important distinction between belief and practice. The Supreme Court has ruled consistently

These members of the Texas State Board of Education discuss the teaching of evolution and scientific theory with the state science advisor. What is the controversy?

AP PHOTO/HARRY CABLUCK

that the right to hold any *belief* is absolute. The government has no authority to compel you to accept or reject any particular religious belief. The right to *practice* one's beliefs, however, may have some limits. As the Court itself once asked, "Suppose one believed that human sacrifice were a necessary part of religious worship?"

The Supreme Court first dealt with the issue of belief versus practice in 1878 in *Reynolds v. United States*.[14] Reynolds was a Mormon who had two wives. Polygamy, or the practice of having more than one spouse at a time, was encouraged by the customs and teachings of his religion. Polygamy was also prohibited by federal law. Reynolds was convicted and appealed the case, arguing that the law violated his constitutional right to freely exercise his religious beliefs. The Court did not agree. It said that to allow Reynolds to practice polygamy would make religious doctrines superior to the law.

Student religious organizations at colleges and universities have been the subject of a number of civil liberties controversies over the years. One of the most recent cases focused on a free exercise topic. We discuss it in this chapter's feature *Join the Debate: Should We Let Student Religious Groups Bar Gays from Membership?* on the following page.

THE FREE EXERCISE CLAUSE

protects a person's right to worship or believe as he or she wishes without government interference.

Religious Practices and the Workplace   The free exercise of religion in the workplace was bolstered by Title VII of the Civil Rights Act of 1964, which requires employers to accommodate their employees' religious practices unless such accommodation causes an employer to suffer an "undue hardship." Thus, if an employee claims that his or her religious beliefs prevent him or her from working on a particular day of the week, such as Saturday or Sunday, the employer must attempt to accommodate the employee's needs.

Several cases have come before lower federal courts concerning employer dress codes that contradict the religious customs of employees. For example, in 1999 the Third Circuit Court of Appeals ruled in favor of two Muslim police officers in Newark, New Jersey, who claimed that they were required by their faith to wear beards and would not shave them to comply with the police department's grooming policy. A similar case was brought in 2001 by Washington, D.C., firefighters.[15] Muslims, Rastafarians, and others have refused to change the grooming habits required by their religions and have been successful in court.

Freedom of Expression

No one in this country seems to have a problem protecting the free speech of those with whom they agree. The real challenge is protecting unpopular ideas. The protection needed is, in Justice Oliver Wendell Holmes's words, "not free thought for those who agree with us but freedom for the thought that we hate." The First Amendment is designed to protect the freedom to express *all* ideas, including those that may be unpopular.

The First Amendment has been interpreted to protect more than merely spoken words. It also protects **symbolic speech**—speech involving actions and other nonverbal expressions. Some common examples include picketing in a labor dispute and wearing a black armband in protest of a government policy. Even burning the American flag as a gesture of protest has been held to be protected by the First Amendment.

> **symbolic speech**   The expression of beliefs, opinions, or ideas through forms other than speech or print; speech involving actions and other nonverbal expressions.

This proponent of a school voucher program in Cleveland, Ohio, believes that only the students of rich parents have much school choice. Her implicit argument is that school vouchers will give the same school choice to children who are poor as to those who are rich.

Should We Let Student Religious Groups Bar Gays from Membership?

AP PHOTO/THE JOPLIN GLOBE, T. ROB BROWN

The members of campus student organizations often share common beliefs. Young Republicans do not normally seek to join the Democratic club on campus, and vice versa. You don't expect to find many members of the Association of Muslim Law Students who are not Muslims. Many colleges and universities, however, prohibit certain membership restrictions in student organizations. For example, the Student Conduct Code at Eastern Michigan University (EMU) lists the following violation: "*Discrimination by Student Organizations.* Selecting its membership upon the basis of restrictive clauses involving race, religion, color, national origin, gender, age, sexual orientation or disability unless any given student organization's membership restriction is shown to be specifically allowed by law."

Under such rules, EMU's Democratic club could bar Republicans, because political ideology is an acceptable basis for membership. But what about a Christian group that, as a matter of belief, opposes sex outside of marriage between a man and a woman? Can such student religious groups bar gay men and lesbians from membership? If they do, can the school withdraw official recognition?

This question was at the heart of a recent case involving the University of California's Hastings College of the Law. The Christian Legal Society (CLS) at the school excludes from affiliation anyone who engages in "unrepentant homosexual conduct" or holds religious convictions different from those in the group's Statement of Faith. Hastings, however, requires that all recognized student organizations accept *any* student as a member. (At Hastings, unlike EMU, the campus Republicans could *not* formally exclude Democrats.) Hastings therefore refused to grant recognition to the CLS. The organization sued—and lost at every stage, all the way to the Supreme Court.[16]

Government Bodies Must Oppose Discrimination

Those who support the Court's ruling believe that the ruling is as it should be. The Court's ruling did not force the CLS to accept lesbians or gay men as members. It did not ban the group, which continues to meet on campus despite its lack of official status. But why should a student pay mandatory student-activity fees to fund a group that would reject her as a member? A free society must accept all minorities. Whether discrimination is based on religion, sexual orientation, or race, it should not be subsidized by state universities. Groups should be able to believe—and say—whatever they want, but discrimination is an action, not a belief.

What Happened to Freedom of Association?

Opponents of the Court's decision point out that the Bill of Rights grants us freedom of association. Freedom to associate also means freedom *not* to associate. That's why Hastings's ridiculous open membership rule is wrong. Indeed, there's some evidence that Hastings created the rule specifically to apply to the CLS. In effect, the Court's decision denies freedom of expression when that expression offends prevailing standards of political correctness. If campus organizations cannot choose their members, an African American student group will have to admit members of the Ku Klux Klan. Consider one possibility—everyone opposed to the principles of an organization could join that group and then vote to disband. Is this freedom?

For Critical Analysis *When is it legal for an organization to restrict who may join?*

THE RIGHT TO FREE SPEECH IS NOT ABSOLUTE
Although Americans have the right to free speech, not *all* speech is protected under the First Amendment. Our constitutional rights and liberties are not absolute. Rather, they are what the Supreme Court—the ultimate interpreter of the Constitution—says they are. Although the Court has zealously safeguarded the right to free speech, at times it has imposed limits on speech in the

interests of protecting other rights of Americans. These rights include security against harm to one's person or reputation, the need for public order, and the need to preserve the government.

Generally, throughout our history, the Supreme Court has attempted to balance our rights to free speech against these other needs of society. As Justice Holmes once said, even "the most stringent protection of free speech would not protect a man in falsely shouting fire in a theatre and causing a panic."[17] We look next at some of the ways that the Court has limited the right to free speech.

EARLY RESTRICTIONS ON EXPRESSION At times in our nation's history, various individuals have opposed our form of government. The government, however, has drawn a fine line between legitimate criticism and the expression of ideas that may seriously harm society. Clearly, the government may pass laws against violent acts. But what about **seditious speech,** which urges resistance to lawful authority or advocates overthrowing the government?

As early as 1798, Congress took steps to curb seditious speech when it passed the Alien and Sedition Acts, which made it a crime to utter "any false, scandalous, and malicious" criticism of the government. The acts were considered unconstitutional by many but were never tested in the courts. Several dozen individuals were prosecuted under the acts, and some were actually convicted. In 1801, President Thomas Jefferson pardoned those sentenced under the acts, and Congress soon repealed them.

During World War I, Congress passed the Espionage Act of 1917 and the Sedition Act of 1918. The 1917 act prohibited attempts to interfere with the operation of the military forces, the war effort, or the process of recruitment. The 1918 act made it a crime to "willfully

> ## "FREE SPEECH
> is the whole thing, the whole ball game. Free speech is life itself."
>
> ~ SALMAN RUSHDIE ~
> INDIAN-BORN BRITISH WRITER
> B. 1947

utter, print, write, or publish any disloyal, profane, scurrilous [insulting], or abusive language" about the government. More than two thousand persons were tried and convicted under this act, which was repealed at the end of World War I.

In 1940, Congress passed the Smith Act, which forbade people from advocating the violent overthrow of the U.S. government. In 1951, the Supreme Court first upheld the constitutionality of the Smith Act in *Dennis v. United States,*[18] which involved eleven top leaders of the Communist Party who had been convicted of violating the act. The Court found that their activities went beyond the permissible peaceful advocacy of change. Subsequently, however, the Court modified its position. Since the 1960s, the Court has defined seditious speech to mean only the advocacy of imminent and concrete acts of violence against the government.[19]

LIMITED PROTECTION FOR COMMERCIAL SPEECH Advertising, or **commercial speech,** is also protected by the First Amendment, but not as fully as regular speech. Generally, the Supreme Court has considered a restriction on commercial speech to be valid as long as the restriction "(1) seeks to implement a substantial government interest, (2) directly advances that interest, and (3) goes no further than necessary to accomplish its objective." Problems arise, though, when restrictions on commercial advertising achieve one substantial government interest yet are contrary to the interest in protecting free speech and the right of consumers to be informed. In such cases, the courts have to decide which interest takes priority.

Liquor advertising is a good illustration of this kind of conflict. For example,

Attorney Patrick Coughlin (center) gives a press conference in front of the Supreme Court. He represented activists who sued Nike for false advertising when it defended itself from attacks against its employment policies in Asia. How much free speech do companies enjoy?

KEVIN LAMARQUE/REUTERS /LANDOV

> **seditious speech** Speech that urges resistance to lawful authority or that advocates the overthrowing of a government.
>
> **commercial speech** Advertising statements that describe products. Commercial speech receives less protection under the First Amendment than ordinary speech.

libel A published report of a falsehood that tends to injure a person's reputation or character.

slander The public utterance (speaking) of a statement that holds a person up for contempt, ridicule, or hatred.

obscenity Indecency or offensiveness in speech, expression, behavior, or appearance. Whether specific expressions or acts constitute obscenity normally is determined by community standards.

in one case, Rhode Island argued that its law banning the advertising of liquor prices served the state's goal of discouraging liquor consumption (because the ban discouraged bargain hunting and thus kept liquor prices high). The Supreme Court, however, held that the ban was an unconstitutional restraint on commercial speech. The Court stated that the First Amendment "directs us to be especially skeptical of regulations that seek to keep people in the dark for what the government perceives to be their own good."[20]

UNPROTECTED SPEECH Certain types of speech receive no protection under the First Amendment. These types of speech include defamation (libel and slander) and obscenity.

Libel and Slander No person has the right to libel or slander another. **Libel** is a published report of a falsehood that tends to injure a person's reputation or character. **Slander** is the public utterance (speaking) of a statement that holds a person up for contempt, ridicule, or hatred. To prove libel or slander, however, certain criteria must be met. The statements made must be untrue, must stem from an intent to do harm, and must result in actual harm.

The Supreme Court has ruled that public figures (public officials and others in the public limelight) cannot collect damages for remarks made against them unless they can prove the remarks were made with "reckless" disregard for accuracy. Generally, it is believed that because public figures have greater access to the media than ordinary persons do, they are in a better position to defend themselves against libelous or slanderous statements.

Obscenity Obscene speech is another form of speech that is not protected under the First Amendment. Although the dictionary defines **obscenity** as that which is offensive and indecent, the courts have had difficulty defining the term with any precision. Supreme Court justice Potter Stewart's famous statement, "I know it when I see it," certainly gave little guidance on the issue.

One problem in defining obscenity is that what is obscene to one person is not necessarily obscene to another. What one reader considers indecent, another reader might see as "colorful." Another problem is that society's views on obscenity change over time. Major literary works of such great writers as D. H. Lawrence (1885–1930), Mark Twain (1835–1910), and James Joyce (1882–1941), for example, were once considered obscene in most of the United States.

After many unsuccessful attempts to define obscenity, in 1973 the Supreme Court came up with a three-part test in *Miller v. California*.[21] The Court decided that a book, film, or other piece of material is legally obscene if it meets the following criteria:

1. The average person applying contemporary (present-day) standards finds that the work taken as a whole appeals to the prurient interest—that is, tends to excite unwholesome sexual desire.

2. The work depicts or describes, in a patently (obviously) offensive way, a form of sexual conduct specifically prohibited by an antiobscenity law.

3. The work taken as a whole lacks serious literary, artistic, political, or scientific value.

The very fact that the Supreme Court has had to set up such a complicated test shows how difficult defining obscenity is. The Court went on to state that, in effect, local communities should be allowed to set their own standards for what is obscene. What is obscene to many people in one area of the country might be perfectly acceptable to those in another area.

Obscenity in Cyberspace A hugely controversial issue concerning free speech is the question of obscene and pornographic materials in cyberspace. Such materials can be easily accessed by anyone of any age anywhere in the world at countless Web sites. Many people strongly believe that the government should step in to prevent obscenity on the Internet. Others believe, just as strongly, that speech on the Internet should not be regulated.

The issue came to a head in 1996, when Congress passed the Communications Decency Act (CDA). The law made it a crime to transmit "indecent" or "patently offensive" speech or images to minors (those under the age of eighteen) or to make such speech or images available online to minors. Violators of the act could be fined up to $250,000 or imprisoned for up to two years. In 1997, the Supreme Court held that the law's sections on indecent speech were unconstitutional. According to the Court, those sections of the CDA were too broad in their scope and significantly restrained the constitutionally protected free speech of adults.[22] Congress made a further attempt to regulate Internet speech in 1998 with the Child Online Protection Act. The act imposed criminal penalties on those who distribute material that is "harmful to minors" without using some kind of age-verification system to separate adult and minor Web users. In 2004, the Supreme Court barred enforcement of the act, ruling that the act likely violated constitutionally protected free speech, and sent the case back to the district court for a trial.[23] The district court found the act unconstitutional, and in 2008 a federal appellate court upheld the district court's ruling.

Having failed twice in its attempt to regulate online obscenity, Congress decided to try a different approach. In late 2000, it passed the Children's Internet Protection Act (CIPA). This act requires schools and libraries to use Internet filtering software to protect children from pornography or risk losing federal funds for technology upgrades. The CIPA was also challenged on constitutional grounds, but in 2003 the Supreme Court held that the act did not violate the First Amendment. The Court concluded that because libraries can disable the filters for any patrons who ask, the system was reasonably flexible and did not burden free speech to an unconstitutional extent.[24]

FREE SPEECH FOR STUDENTS? America's schools and college campuses experience an ongoing tension between the guarantee of free speech and the desire to restrain speech that is offensive to others. Typically, cases involving free speech in the schools raise the following question: Where should the line between unacceptable speech and merely offensive speech be drawn? Schools at all levels—elementary schools, high schools, and colleges and universities—have grappled with this issue.

Generally, the courts allow elementary schools wide latitude to define what students may and may not say to other students. At the high school level, the Supreme Court has allowed some restraints to be placed on the freedom of expression. For example, as you will read shortly in the discussion of freedom of the press, the Court does allow school officials to exercise some censorship over high school publications. And, in a controversial 2007 case, the Court upheld a school principal's decision to suspend a high school student who unfurled a banner reading "Bong Hits 4 Jesus" at an event off the school premises. The Court sided with the school officials, who maintained that the banner appeared to advocate illegal

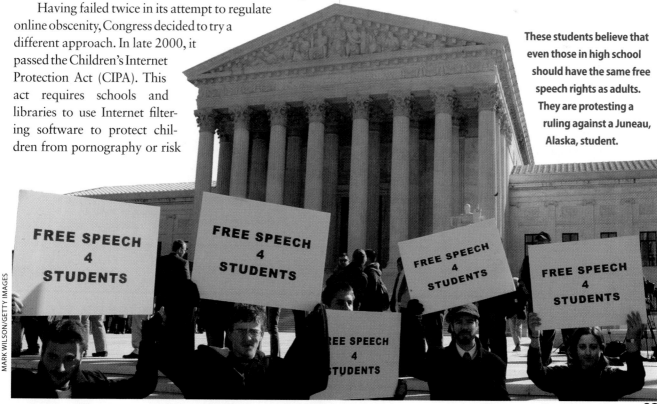

These students believe that even those in high school should have the same free speech rights as adults. They are protesting a ruling against a Juneau, Alaska, student.

drug use in violation of school policy. Many legal commentators and scholars strongly criticized this decision.[25]

A difficult question that many universities face today is whether the right to free speech includes the right to make hateful remarks about others based on their race, gender, or sexual orientation. Some claim that allowing people with extremist views to voice their opinions can lead to violence. In response to this question, several universities have gone so far as to institute speech codes to minimize the disturbances that hate speech might cause. Although these speech codes have often been ruled unconstitutional on the ground that they restrict freedom of speech,[26] such codes continue to exist on many college campuses. For example, the student assembly at Wesleyan University passed a resolution in 2002 stating that the "right to speech comes with implicit responsibilities to respect community standards."[27] Campus rules governing speech and expression, however, can foster the idea that "good" speech should be protected, but "bad" speech should not. Furthermore, who should decide what is considered "hate speech"?

Freedom of the Press

The framers of the Constitution believed that the press should be free to publish a wide range of opinions and information, and generally the free speech rights just discussed also apply to the press. The courts have placed certain restrictions on the freedom of the press, however. Over the years, the Supreme Court has developed various guidelines and doctrines to use in deciding whether freedom of speech and the press can be restrained.

CLEAR AND PRESENT DANGER One guideline the Court has used resulted from a case in 1919, *Schenck v. United States*.[28] Charles T. Schenck was convicted of printing and distributing leaflets urging men to resist the draft during World War I. The government claimed that his actions violated the Espionage Act of 1917, which made it a crime to encourage disloyalty to the government or resistance to the draft. The Supreme Court upheld both the law and the convictions. Justice Holmes, speaking for the Court, stated as follows:

> The question in every case is whether the words used are used in such circumstances and are of such a nature as to create a *clear and present danger* that they will bring about the substantive

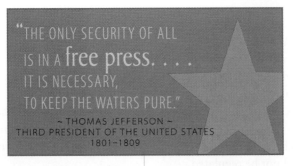

"THE ONLY SECURITY OF ALL IS IN A free press. . . . IT IS NECESSARY, TO KEEP THE WATERS PURE."
~ THOMAS JEFFERSON ~
THIRD PRESIDENT OF THE UNITED STATES
1801–1809

evils that Congress has a right to prevent. It is a question of proximity [closeness] and degree. [Emphasis added.]

Thus, according to the *clear and present danger test,* government should be allowed to restrain speech only when that speech clearly presents an immediate threat to public order. It is often hard to say when speech crosses the line between being merely controversial and being a "clear and present danger," but the principle has been used in many cases since *Schenck.*

The clear and present danger principle seemed too permissive to some Supreme Court justices. Several years after the *Schenck* ruling, in the case of *Gitlow v. New York,*[29] the Court held that speech could be curtailed even if it had only a *tendency* to lead to illegal action. Since the 1920s, however, this guideline, known as the *bad-tendency test,* generally has not been supported by the Supreme Court.

THE PREFERRED-POSITION DOCTRINE Another guideline, called the *preferred-position doctrine,* states that certain freedoms are so essential to a democracy that they hold a preferred position. According to this doctrine, any law that limits these freedoms should be presumed unconstitutional unless the government can show that the law is absolutely necessary. Thus, freedom of speech and the press should rarely, if ever, be diminished, because spoken and printed words are the prime tools of the democratic process.

Brandon Mayfield (left) exits the federal courthouse with his attorney Gerry Spence (right). Mayfield has brought suit against the FBI for wrongful arrest in connection with the Madrid train bombings in 2004.

STEPHEN VOSS/REDUX

PRIOR RESTRAINT Stopping an activity before it actually happens is known as *prior restraint*. With respect to freedom of the press, prior restraint involves *censorship*, which occurs when an official removes objectionable materials from an item before it is published or broadcast. An example of censorship and prior restraint would be a court's ruling that two paragraphs in an upcoming article in the local newspaper had to be removed before the article could be published. The Supreme Court has generally ruled against prior restraint, arguing that the government cannot curb ideas *before* they are expressed.

On some occasions, however, the Court has allowed prior restraint. For example, in a 1988 case, *Hazelwood School District v. Kuhlmeier*,[30] a high school principal deleted two pages from the school newspaper just before it was printed. The pages contained stories on students' experiences with pregnancy and discussed the impact of divorce on students at the school. The Supreme Court, noting that students in school do not have exactly the same rights as adults in other settings, ruled that high school administrators *can* censor school publications. The Court said that school newspapers are part of the school curriculum, not a public forum. Therefore, administrators have the right to censor speech that promotes conduct inconsistent with the "shared values of a civilized social order."

LO3 *The Right to Privacy*

Supreme Court justice Louis Brandeis stated in 1928 that the right to privacy is "the most comprehensive of rights and the right most valued by civilized men."[31] The majority of the justices on the Supreme Court at that time did not agree. In 1965, however, in the landmark case of *Griswold v. Connecticut*,[32] the justices on the Supreme Court held that a right to privacy is implied by other constitutional rights guaranteed in the First, Third, Fourth, Fifth, and Ninth Amendments. For example, consider the words of the Ninth Amendment: "The enumeration in the Constitution, of certain rights, shall not be construed to deny or disparage others retained by the people." In other words, just because the Constitution, including its amendments, does not

> ## "THE RIGHT TO BE LET ALONE
>
> – the most comprehensive of the rights and the right most valued by civilized men."
>
> ~ LOUIS BRANDEIS ~
> ASSOCIATE JUSTICE OF THE UNITED STATES SUPREME COURT
> 1916–1939

specifically mention the right to privacy does not mean that this right is denied to the people.

Since then, the government has also passed laws ensuring the privacy rights of individuals. For example, in 1966 Congress passed the Freedom of Information Act, which, among other things, allows any person to request copies of any information about her or him contained in government files. In 1974, Congress passed the Privacy Act, which restricts government disclosure of data to third parties. In 1994, Congress passed the Driver's Privacy Protection Act, which prevents states from disclosing or selling a driver's personal information without the driver's consent.[33] In late 2000, the federal Department of Health and Human Services issued a regulation ensuring the privacy of a person's medical information. Health-care providers and insurance companies are restricted from sharing confidential information about their patients.

Although Congress and the courts have acknowledged a constitutional right to privacy, the nature and scope of this right are not always clear. For example, Americans continue to debate whether the right to privacy includes the right to have an abortion or the right of terminally ill persons to commit physician-assisted suicide. Since the terrorist attacks of September 11, 2001, another pressing privacy issue has been how to monitor potential terrorists to prevent another attack without violating the privacy rights of all Americans.

The Abortion Controversy

One of the most divisive and emotionally charged issues being debated today is whether the right to privacy means that women can choose to have abortions.

ABORTION AND PRIVACY In 1973, in the landmark case of *Roe v. Wade*,[34] the Supreme Court, using the *Griswold* case as a precedent, held that the "right of privacy . . . is broad enough to encompass a woman's decision whether or not to terminate her pregnancy." The right is not absolute throughout pregnancy, however. The Court also said that any state could impose certain regulations to safeguard the health of the mother after the first three months of pregnancy and, in the final stages of pregnancy, could act to protect potential life.

Since the *Roe v. Wade* decision, the Supreme Court has adopted a more conservative approach and has upheld restrictive state laws requiring counseling, waiting periods, notification of parents, and other actions prior to abortions.[35] Yet the Court has never overturned the *Roe* decision. In fact, in 1997 and again in 2000, the Supreme Court upheld laws requiring "buffer zones" around abortion clinics to protect those entering the clinics from unwanted counseling or harassment by antiabortion groups.[36] In 2000, the Supreme Court invalidated a Nebraska statute banning "partial-birth" abortions, a procedure used during the second trimester of pregnancy.[37]

Abortion continues to be extremely controversial in the United States. Pro-choice supporters demonstrate their desire that abortion remain legal.

Undeterred by the fate of the Nebraska law, President George W. Bush signed the Partial Birth Abortion Ban Act in 2003. In a close (five-to-four) and controversial 2007 decision, the Supreme Court upheld the constitutionality of the 2003 act.[38]

Many were surprised at the Court's decision on partial-birth abortion, given that the federal act banning this practice was quite similar to the Nebraska law that had been struck down by the Court in 2000, just seven years earlier. Since that decision was rendered, however, the Court has become more conservative with the appointment of two new justices by President George W. Bush. Dissenting from the majority opinion in the case, Justice Ruth Bader Ginsburg said that the ruling was an "alarming" departure from three decades of Supreme Court decisions on abortion.

ABORTION AND POLITICS American opinion on the abortion issue is more nuanced than the labels "pro-life" and "pro-choice" would indicate. For example, a 2010 Gallup poll found that 45 percent of the respondents considered themselves pro-choice and 47 percent called themselves pro-life. Yet when respondents were asked whether abortion should be legal or illegal, public opinion was more middle-of-the-road than the attachments to these labels would suggest. About 54 percent thought that abortion should be limited to only certain circumstances, while 19 percent believed it should be

illegal in all circumstances, and 24 percent thought that it should be legal in all circumstances.

Do We Have the "Right to Die"?

Whether it is called euthanasia (mercy killing), assisted suicide, or a dignified way to leave this world, it all comes down to one basic question: Do terminally ill persons have, as part of their civil liberties, a right to die and to be assisted in the process by physicians or others? Phrased another way, are state laws banning physician-assisted suicide in such circumstances unconstitutional?

In 1997, the issue came before the Supreme Court, which characterized the question as follows: Does the liberty protected by the Constitution include a right to commit suicide, which itself includes a right to assistance in doing so? The Court's clear and categorical answer to this question was no. To hold otherwise, said the Court, would be "to reverse centuries of legal doctrine and practice, and strike down the considered policy choice of almost every state."[39] Although the Court upheld the states' rights to ban such a practice, the Court did not hold that state laws *permitting* assisted suicide were unconstitutional. In 1997, Oregon became the first state to implement such a law. In 2008, Washington and Montana became the second and third states, respectively, to allow the practice. Oregon's law was upheld by the Supreme Court in 2006.[40]

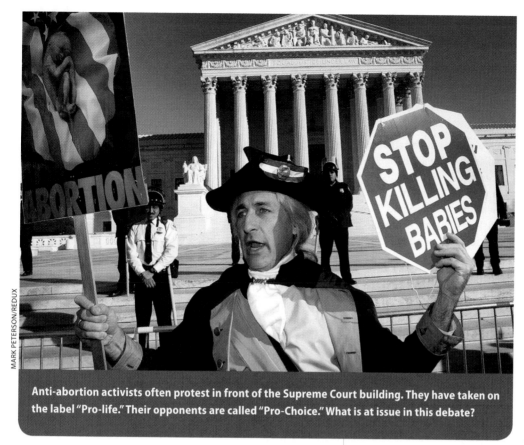

Anti-abortion activists often protest in front of the Supreme Court building. They have taken on the label "Pro-life." Their opponents are called "Pro-Choice." What is at issue in this debate?

The Supreme Court's enunciation of its opinion on this topic has not ended the debate, though, just as the debate over abortion did not stop after the 1973 *Roe v. Wade* decision legalizing abortion. Americans continue to be at odds over this issue.

Personal Privacy and National Security

Since the terrorist attacks of September 11, 2001, a common debate in the news media and on Capitol Hill has been how the United States can address the urgent need to strengthen national security while still protecting civil liberties, particularly the right to privacy. As you will read throughout this book, various programs have been proposed or attempted, and some have already been dismantled after public outcry. For example, the Homeland Security Act passed in late 2002 included language explicitly prohibiting a controversial program called Operation TIPS (Terrorism Information and Prevention System). Operation TIPS was proposed to create a national reporting program for "citizen volunteers" who regularly work in neighborhoods and communities, such as postal carriers and meter readers, to report suspicious activity to the government. The public backlash against the program was quick and resolute—neighbors would not spy on neighbors. Indeed, Americans are protective enough of their privacy to reject the idea of national identification cards, even though such cards are common in other countries. We say more about national ID cards in the feature *The Rest of the World: Fingerprinting 1.2 Billion Citizens of India* on the following page.

THE USA PATRIOT ACT Other laws and programs that infringe on Americans' privacy rights were also created in the wake of 9/11 in the interests of protecting the nation's security. For example, the USA Patriot Act of 2001 gave the government broad latitude to investigate people who are only vaguely associated with terrorists. Under this law, the government can access personal information on American citizens to an extent heretofore never allowed by law. The Federal Bureau of Investigation was also authorized to use "National Security Letters" to demand personal information about individuals from private companies (such as banks and phone companies). In one of the most controversial programs, the National Security Agency (NSA) was authorized to monitor certain domestic phone calls without first obtaining a warrant. When Americans learned of the NSA's actions in 2005, the ensuing public furor

FBI director Robert Mueller often faces questioning in front of congressional hearings on national security. What limits his decisions?

Fingerprinting 1.2 Billion Citizens of India

From time to time, persons who are concerned about our national security propose that the United States create a national identity card. That would mean that all 310 million Americans would be required to have an official federal ID card. Now imagine imposing such a requirement on a nation of more than 1.2 billion people. It sounds like quite a task, but the government of India began work on such a project in 2011.

Lots of Precedent

Quite a few countries, including Belgium, France, Germany, and Spain, already require that their residents have national identity cards. In fact, more than a hundred countries require such cards. Why not India? The big problem, of course, is that few countries have to deal with more than a billion fingerprints to create a biometric identity card for every resident.

All for the Good, According to Some

According to Nandan Nilekani, head of India's Unique Identity Authority, pro-viding a national biometric identity card will change his country. "Every person for the first time will be able to prove who he or she is," he said in a recent interview. "If you are going to have all of this economic growth, people who are marginalized should be given a chance." He was referring to the more than 75 million homeless people who do not even have birth certificates. They cannot obtain government aid or register their children for school. They cannot even obtain phone service or open a bank account.

Are Civil Liberties an Issue?

More than one-sixth of the world's population lives in India. If every single man, woman, and child there is registered in a government database, then more than one-sixth of the world's inhabitants can be found by searching that single database. Civil libertarians argue that there will be no oversight mechanism to defend against the surveillance abuses that will be possible with such a large database. The reality, though, is that India already has a gigantic bureaucracy that oversees its citizens. In some regions, residents must have twenty different ID cards—one to vote, one to obtain food ration tickets, and many others for various purposes.

For Critical Analysis *If more than one hundred countries already require a national identity card for every resident, why doesn't the United States do the same?*

---

forced the Bush administration to agree to henceforth obtain warrants for such monitoring activities.

THE CIVIL LIBERTIES DEBATE Some Americans, including many civil libertarians, are so concerned about the erosion of privacy rights that they wonder why the public outcry has not been even more vehement. They point out that trading off even a few civil liberties, including our privacy rights, for national security is senseless. After all, these liberties are at the heart of what this country stands for. When we abandon any of our civil liberties, we weaken our country rather than defend it. Essentially, say some members of this group, the federal government has achieved what the terrorists were unable to accomplish—the destruction of our freedoms. Other Americans believe that we have little to worry about. Those who have nothing to hide should not be concerned about government surveillance or other privacy intrusions undertaken by the government to make our nation more secure against terrorist attacks. To what extent has the Obama administration revised the policies established under President Bush? We examine that question in this chapter's *Perception versus Reality* feature on page 90.

LO4 *The Rights of the Accused*

The United States has one of the highest murder rates in the industrialized world. It is therefore not surprising that many Americans have extremely strong opinions about the rights of persons accused of criminal offenses. Indeed, some Americans complain that criminal defendants have too many rights.

Why do criminal suspects have rights? The answer is that all persons are entitled to the protections afforded by the Bill of Rights. If criminal suspects were deprived of their basic constitutional liberties, all people would suffer the consequences, because there is nothing to stop the government from accusing anyone of being a criminal. In a criminal case, a state official (such as the district attorney, or D.A.) prosecutes the defendant, and the state has immense resources that it can bring to bear against the accused person. By protecting the rights of accused persons, the Constitution helps to prevent the arbitrary use of power by the government.

The Rights of Criminal Defendants

The basic rights, or constitutional safeguards, provided for criminal defendants are set forth in the Bill of Rights. These safeguards include the following:

■ The Fourth Amendment protection from unreasonable searches and seizures.

■ The Fourth Amendment requirement that no warrant for a search or an arrest be issued without **probable cause**—cause for believing that there is a substantial likelihood that a person has committed or is about to commit a crime.

■ The Fifth Amendment requirement that no one be deprived of "life, liberty, or property, without due process of law." As discussed earlier in this chapter, this requirement is also included in the Fourteenth Amendment, which protects persons against actions by state governments.

■ The Fifth Amendment prohibition against **double jeopardy**—being tried twice for the same criminal offense.

■ The Fifth Amendment provision that no person can be required to be a witness against (incriminate) himself or herself. This is often referred to as the constitutional protection against **self-incrimination.** It is the basis for a criminal suspect's "right to remain silent" in criminal proceedings.

■ The Sixth Amendment guarantees of a speedy trial, a trial by jury, a public trial, and the right to confront witnesses.

■ The Sixth Amendment guarantee of the right to counsel at various stages in some criminal proceedings. The right to counsel was strengthened in 1963 in *Gideon v. Wainwright*.[41] The Supreme Court held that if a person is accused of a felony and cannot afford an attorney, an attorney must be made available to the accused person at the government's expense.

■ The Eighth Amendment prohibitions against excessive bail and fines and against cruel and unusual punishments.

The Exclusionary Rule

Any evidence obtained in violation of the constitutional rights spelled out in the Fourth Amendment normally is not admissible at trial. This rule, which has been applied in the federal courts since at least 1914, is known as the **exclusionary rule.** The rule was extended to state court proceedings in 1961.[42] The reasoning behind the exclusionary rule is that it forces law enforcement personnel to gather evidence properly. If they do not, they will be unable to introduce the evidence at trial to convince the jury that the defendant is guilty.

The *Miranda* Warnings

In the 1950s and 1960s, one of the questions facing the courts was not whether suspects had constitutional rights—that was not in doubt—but how and when those rights could be exercised. For example, could the right to remain silent (under the Fifth Amendment's prohibition against self-incrimination) be exercised during pretrial interrogation proceedings or only during the trial? Were confessions obtained from suspects admissible in court if the suspects had not been advised of their right to remain silent and other constitutional rights? To clarify these issues, in 1966 the Supreme Court issued a landmark decision in *Miranda v. Arizona*.[43] In that case, the Court enunciated the **Miranda warnings** that are now familiar to virtually all Americans:

> Prior to any questioning, the person must be warned that he has a right to remain silent, that any statement he does make may be used against him, and that he has a right to the presence of an attorney, either retained or appointed.

probable cause Cause for believing that there is a substantial likelihood that a person has committed or is about to commit a crime.

double jeopardy The prosecution of a person twice for the same criminal offense; prohibited by the Fifth Amendment in all but a few circumstances.

self-incrimination Providing damaging information or testimony against oneself in court.

exclusionary rule A criminal procedural rule requiring that any illegally obtained evidence not be admissible in court.

***Miranda* warnings** A series of statements informing criminal suspects, on their arrest, of their constitutional rights, such as the right to remain silent and the right to counsel; required by the Supreme Court's 1966 decision in *Miranda v. Arizona*.

During much of the administration of President George W. Bush, civil libertarians denounced the antiterrorism policies of President Bush and his vice president, Dick Cheney. Certainly, after 9/11, the administration's view of civil liberties, especially those relating to privacy, changed substantially. The USA Patriot Act, which Bush signed into law on October 26, 2001, authorized a major expansion in the "snooping" activities of the federal government. In addition, the National Security Agency (NSA) was allowed to engage in domestic wiretapping without obtaining search warrants.

The Perception

During the Bush administration, Bush and Cheney ran a counterterrorism program that violated the civil liberties of Americans, tortured enemy combatants, and committed a variety of other illegal actions. According to Cheney, these practices saved "thousands, perhaps hundreds of thousands" of lives. They were also "legal, essential, justified, successful and the right thing to do." President Barack Obama made the country "less safe," said Cheney, by eliminating them and by attempting to close the prison holding suspected terrorists at the Guantánamo Bay Naval Base.

In contrast, Obama called the Guantánamo prison a "misguided experiment" that actually increased the threats to American national security. "The problem of what to do with Guantánamo detainees was not caused by my decision to close the facility," Obama said. "The problem exists because of the decision to open Guantánamo in the first place."

The Reality

At most, the excessive antiterrorism policies of the Bush administration lasted for three years following 9/11. This nation had been blindsided—our intelligence officials knew almost nothing about the threats against us. The Bush administration frantically attempted to discover and prevent any further threats. It was in this environment that officials such as Cheney could demand—and obtain—policies that seemed to violate traditional American standards.

By 2005, however, members of the Bush administration were trying to rein in the excesses of the earlier post-9/11 period. Secretary of State Condoleezza Rice, National Security Advisor Stephen Hadley, and other officials sought to wean the administration away from the Cheney approach. In 2007, Rice refused to support an executive order reviving the "enhanced" interrogation program. Throughout Bush's second term, officials tried to close Guantánamo and pleaded with foreign governments to take some of its prisoners.

The most famous "enhanced" interrogation technique—waterboarding—was halted long before Obama came to power. Obama castigated the military-commission system used to try captured enemy combatants, but in fact he revived this system with only cosmetic changes. Harvard law professor Jack Goldsmith puts it this way: "The main difference between the Obama and Bush administrations concerns not the substance of terrorism policy, but rather its packaging." In reality, Obama's policies largely represented a continuation of the policies adopted during Bush's second term. Cheney, Bush, and Obama all had an interest in glossing over that fact.

Blog On National security blogs may outnumber the stars you can see on a cloudless night. We can mention only a few. The *National Journal* offers expert posts at **security.nationaljournal.com**. The Heritage Foundation takes a strongly conservative line at **www.heritage.org/Issues/National-Security-and-Defense**. Finally, this blog defends the rights of Guantánamo detainees: **gtmoblog.blogspot.com**.

The Erosion of *Miranda*

As part of a continuing attempt to balance the rights of accused persons against the rights of society, the Supreme Court has made a number of exceptions to the *Miranda* ruling. In 1986, for example, the Court held that a confession need not be excluded even though the police failed to inform a suspect in custody that his attorney had tried to reach him by telephone.[44] In an important 1991 decision, the Court stated that a suspect's conviction will not be automatically overturned if the suspect was coerced into making a confession. If the other evidence admitted at trial was strong enough to justify the conviction without the confession, then the fact that the confession was obtained illegally can be, in effect, ignored.[45] In yet another case, in 1994 the Supreme Court ruled that a suspect must unequivocally and assertively state his right to counsel in order to stop police questioning. Saying "Maybe I should talk to a lawyer" during an interrogation after being taken into custody is not enough. The Court held that police officers are not required to decipher the suspect's intentions in such situations.[46]

Miranda may eventually become obsolete regardless of any decisions made in the courts. A relatively new trend in law enforcement has been for agencies to digitally record interrogations and confessions. Thomas P. Sullivan, a former U.S. attorney in Chicago, and his staff interviewed personnel in more than 230 law enforcement agencies in thirty-eight states that record interviews of suspects who are in custody. Sullivan found that nearly all police officers said the procedure saved time and money, created valuable evidence to use in court, and made it more difficult for defense attorneys to claim that their clients had been illegally coerced.[47] Some scholars have suggested that recording all custodial interrogations would satisfy the Fifth Amendment's prohibition against coercion and in the process render the *Miranda* warnings unnecessary.

ELENA ROORAID/PHOTOEDIT

This police officer is reading the accused his *Miranda* warnings. Since the 1966 *Miranda* decision, the Supreme Court has relaxed its requirements in some situations, such as when a criminal suspect who is not under arrest enters a police station voluntarily.

AMERICA AT ODDS   *Civil Liberties*

Civil liberties is a contentious topic, and Americans are at odds over many of its issues. Almost all Americans claim to believe in individual rights, but how should this freedom be defined? Often, one right appears to interfere with another. Some of the resulting disputes include the following:

• Should the First Amendment's establishment clause be interpreted strictly, so that no one's rights are infringed on by government sponsorship of religion—or should it be interpreted loosely, to recognize that the United States is a very religious country?

• What kinds of religious practices should be allowed under the free exercise clause? In particular, should religious groups that limit or ban participation by gay men and lesbians receive the same government benefits as any other group—or may they be penalized for discrimination?

• Should advertising receive the same free-speech rights as any other kind of speech—or should advertisers be held accountable for making false claims?

• Has the government gone too far in restricting liberties in an attempt to combat terrorism—or are the restrictions trivial compared with the benefits?

• Consider finally the most intense controversy of all. Should women have a privacy right to terminate a pregnancy for any reason—or should abortion be a crime?

Take Action

If you are ever concerned that your civil liberties are being threatened by a government action, you can exercise one of your liberties—the right to petition the government—to object to the action. Often, those who want to take action feel that they are alone in their struggles until they begin discussing their views with others. Brenda Koehler, a writing student attending college in Kutztown, Pennsylvania, relates how one of her friends, whom we will call "Charyn," took action in response to the USA Patriot Act of 2001. Concerned about the extent to which this act infringed on Americans' civil liberties, Charyn began e-mailing her friends and others about the issue. Eventually, a petition against the enforcement of the act in her town was circulated, and the city council agreed to consider the petition. Charyn did not expect anything to come from the review and assumed that the council would dismiss the petition without even reading the three-hundred-page Patriot Act. On the day of the hearing, the council chambers were packed with town citizens who shared Charyn's and her friends' concerns. The council adjourned the meeting for a week so that it could review the act, and when it met the next week, the resolution to oppose enforcing the act was adopted. Although one person's efforts are not always so successful, there will certainly be no successes at all if no one takes action.[48]

POLITICS ON THE WEB

- Almost three dozen First Amendment groups have launched the Free Expression Network, a Web site designed to feature legislation updates, legal briefings, and news on cases of censorship in local communities. Go to **www.freeexpression.org**

- The Web site for the leading civil liberties organization, the American Civil Liberties Union (ACLU), can be found at **www.aclu.org**

- The Liberty Counsel is "a nonprofit religious civil liberties education and legal defense organization established to preserve religious freedom." Its take on civil liberties is definitely right of center. You can access this organization's home page at **www.lc.org**

- For information on the effect of new computer and communications technologies on the constitutional rights and liberties of Americans, go to the Center for Democracy and Technology at **www.cdt.org**

- For information on privacy issues relating to the Internet, go to the Electronic Privacy Information Center's Web site at **www.epic.org/privacy**

- To access United States Supreme Court decisions on civil liberties, go to the Court's official Web site at **www.supremecourt.gov**

- For many people, the YouTube Web site is a favorite destination not only for entertainment but also for information on a host of topics. URLs for locating videos on YouTube take the form of **www.youtube.com/watch?v=** immediately followed by a string of characters that identifies a particular video. Videos on civil liberties topics include **AviKQaEsaDM**, which describes the role of the Jehovah's Witnesses in winning civil liberties cases during the twentieth century. Federal policies on inspecting and seizing laptop computers and MP3 players at the border are described at **rSGDVTk6ra0**.

 CourseMate Access CourseMate to review and expand on this chapter through quizzes, flashcards, learning objectives, interactive timelines, a crossword puzzle, audio summaries, video, critical-thinking activities, simulations, and more.

Civil Rights

LEARNING OBJECTIVES

LO1 Explain the constitutional basis for our civil rights and for laws prohibiting discrimination.

LO2 Discuss the reasons for the civil rights movement and the changes it caused in American politics and government.

LO3 Describe the political and economic achievements of women in this country over time and identify some obstacles to equality that women continue to face.

LO4 Summarize the struggles for equality that other groups in America experience.

LO5 Explain what affirmative action is and why it has been so controversial.

CourseMate

AMERICA AT ODDS

Should the Census Count Be Limited to Citizens?

The 2010 census was the most expensive ever—it cost about $37 per person counted. The U.S. census, which is taken every ten years, is important in part because the number of persons each state sends to the House of Representatives is based on the most recent census count. In addition, the census determines which communities receive a share of the more than $400 billion in federal funds each year for things such as hospitals; schools; job-training centers; and bridges, tunnels, and other public works projects.

Not surprisingly, who should be counted is an often-debated issue. Should census counters ignore unauthorized immigrants? This question is more than academic. In states with many unauthorized immigrants, such as California, counting them increases the state's representation in Congress. Should everyone be counted? Alternatively, should only citizens and legal permanent residents be counted?

Keep It Simple—Unauthorized Immigrants Need Not Apply

The first Census Act in 1790 provided for a counting of "inhabitants." According to a court ruling, the term *inhabitant* meant "a *bona fide* member of a State, subject to all the requisitions of its laws, and entitled to all of the privileges which they confer." Under such a definition, those who are in the country illegally shouldn't be considered inhabitants.

Naturally, leaders in some states that do not have high numbers of unauthorized immigrants and that will lose one or more seats in the House of Representatives after a census have opposed counting such immigrants. By the time you read this, Louisiana, Massachusetts, Michigan, Ohio, and other states may have already lost one or more seats in the House because of counts based on the 2010 census. Every voter is supposed to have an equal voice. If unauthorized immigrants are counted in determining the apportionment of representatives, voters in areas with large numbers of unauthorized immigrants will be overrepresented.

There is a more fundamental issue at stake, though: Who is an American? Presumably, we want to count the people of the United States in our ten-year census. The "people" should not include those who are living here illegally. This logic seems clear to many.

Follow the Constitution—Count Them All

Those who are against counting unauthorized immigrants forget that the basis of the census, Section 2 of the Fourteenth Amendment to the Constitution, states: "Representatives shall be apportioned among the several States according to their respective numbers, counting the whole number of persons in each State." Apportionment is by *persons*, not *citizens*. The Fourteenth Amendment refers to citizens in some clauses, and persons in others. It distinguishes between the two. Unauthorized immigrants are persons, plain and simple. If California therefore picks up extra seats in the House after a census, so be it. There is nothing unconstitutional about this. Bear in mind the rule for counting slaves in the original Constitution. Three-fifths of the slaves in each state were included when apportioning House seats. This means that the founders were deliberately counting people who weren't citizens and, in the founders' opinion, never would be.

Consider also that cities and states of necessity provide services to unauthorized immigrants. If those people are not counted when dividing up federal funds, citizens in areas with many illegal immigrants won't be adequately compensated by the federal government.

WHERE DO YOU STAND?

1. Do you think states that have more unauthorized immigrants should consequently have more representatives in the House? Why or why not?
2. Why did the authors of the Fourteenth Amendment seek to ensure that persons—and not just citizens—would enjoy certain rights?

EXPLORE THIS ISSUE ONLINE

Much of the recent debate over counting unauthorized immigrants is based on a *Wall Street Journal* article written by John Baker, a Louisiana State University law professor, and Elliot Stonecipher, a pollster. The *Journal* deleted many of their legal arguments, but you can find a full version of the piece at the Volokh Conspiracy: **volokh.com/posts/1250274418.shtml.** (Click on a link to pull up the full draft.) You'll also find there a detailed criticism of the Baker/Stonecipher thesis by Eugene Volokh, a law professor at the University of California, Los Angeles.

Introduction

As noted in Chapter 4, people sometimes confuse civil rights with civil liberties. Generally, though, the term **civil rights** refers to the rights of all Americans to equal treatment under the law, as provided for by the Fourteenth Amendment. One of the functions of our government is to ensure—through legislation or other means—that this constitutional mandate is upheld.

Although the democratic ideal is for all people to have equal rights and equal treatment under the law, and although the Constitution guarantees those rights, this ideal has often remained just that—an ideal. It is people who put ideals into practice, and as James Madison (1751–1836) once pointed out (and as we all know), people are not angels. As you will read in this chapter, the struggle of various groups in American society to obtain equal treatment has been a long one, and it still continues. One such group is made up of immigrants—those here both legally and illegally. We discussed an issue that concerns them in this chapter's opening *America at Odds* feature.

In a sense, the history of civil rights in the United States is a history of discrimination against various groups. Discrimination against women, African Americans, and Native Americans dates back to the early years of this nation, when the framers of the Constitution did not grant these groups rights that were granted to others (that is, to white, property-owning males). During our subsequent history, as peoples from around the globe immigrated to this country at various times and for various reasons, each of these immigrant groups faced discrimination in one form or another. More recently, other groups, including persons with disabilities and gay men and lesbians have struggled for equal treatment under the law.

Central to any discussion of civil rights is the interpretation of the equal protection clause of the Fourteenth Amendment to the Constitution. For that reason, we look first at that clause and at how the courts, particularly the United States Supreme Court, have interpreted it and applied it to civil rights issues.

All Americans are entitled to

EQUAL TREATMENT UNDER THE LAW

as provided for by the Fourteenth Amendment.

LO1 *The Equal Protection Clause*

Equal in importance to the due process clause of the Fourteenth Amendment is the **equal protection clause** in Section 1 of that amendment, which reads as follows: "No State shall . . . deny to any person within its jurisdiction the equal protection of the laws." Section 5 of the amendment provides a legal basis for federal civil rights legislation: "The Congress shall have power to enforce, by appropriate legislation, the provisions of this article."

The equal protection clause has been interpreted by the courts, and especially the Supreme Court, to mean that states must treat all persons in an equal manner and may not discriminate *unreasonably* against a particular group or class of individuals. The task of distinguishing between reasonable

civil rights The rights of all Americans to equal treatment under the law, as provided for by the Fourteenth Amendment to the Constitution.

equal protection clause Section 1 of the Fourteenth Amendment, which states that no state shall "deny to any person within its jurisdiction the equal protection of the laws."

These demonstrators are making sure that the residents of New York City remember the goals of Martin Luther King, Jr.—equality for all minorities in America.

REUTERS/CHIP EAST /LANDOV

discrimination and unreasonable discrimination is difficult. Generally, in deciding this question, the Supreme Court balances the constitutional rights of individuals to equal protection against government interests in protecting the safety and welfare of citizens. Over time, the Court has developed various tests, or standards, for determining whether the equal protection clause has been violated.

Strict Scrutiny

If a law or action prevents some group of persons from exercising a **fundamental right** (such as one of our First Amendment rights), the law or action will be subject to the "strict-scrutiny" standard. Under this standard, the law or action must be necessary to promote a *compelling state interest* and must be narrowly tailored to meet that interest. A law based on a **suspect classification,** such as race, is also subject to strict scrutiny by the courts, meaning that the law must be justified by a compelling state interest.

Intermediate Scrutiny

Because the Supreme Court had difficulty deciding how to judge cases in which men and women were treated differently, another test was developed—the "intermediate-scrutiny" standard. Under this standard, laws based on gender classifications are permissible if they are "substantially related to the achievement of an important governmental objective." For example, a law punishing males but not females for statutory rape is valid because of the important governmental interest in preventing teenage pregnancy in those circumstances and because almost all of the harmful and identifiable consequences of teenage pregnancies fall on young females.[1] A law prohibiting the sale of beer to males under twenty-one years of age and to females under eighteen years would not be valid, however.[2]

Generally, since the 1970s, the Supreme Court has scrutinized gender classifications closely and has declared many gender-based laws unconstitutional. In 1979, the Court held that a state law allowing wives to obtain alimony judgments against husbands but preventing husbands from receiving alimony from wives violated the equal protection clause.[3] In 1982, the Court declared that Mississippi's policy of excluding males from the School of Nursing at Mississippi University for Women was unconstitutional.[4] In a controversial 1996 case, *United States v. Virginia,*[5] the Court held that Virginia Military Institute, a state-financed institution, violated the equal protection clause by refusing to accept female applicants. The Court said that the state of Virginia had failed to provide a sufficient justification for its gender-based classification.

The Rational Basis Test (Ordinary Scrutiny)

A third test used to decide whether a discriminatory law violates the equal protection clause is the **rational basis test.** When applying this test to a law that classifies or treats people or groups differently, the justices ask whether the discrimination is rational. In other words, is it a reasonable way to achieve a legitimate government objective? Few laws tested under the rational basis test—or the "ordinary-scrutiny" standard, as it is also called—are found invalid, because few laws are truly unreasonable. A municipal ordinance that prohibits certain vendors from selling their wares in a particular area of the city, for example, will be upheld if the city can meet this rational basis test. The rational basis for the ordinance might be the city's legitimate government interest in reducing traffic congestion in that particular area.

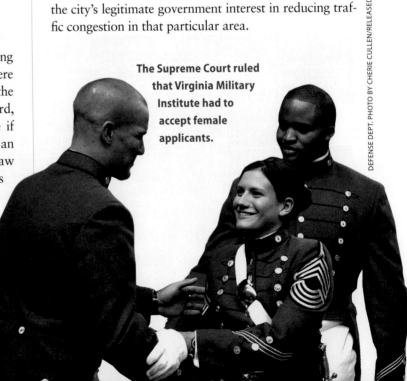

The Supreme Court ruled that Virginia Military Institute had to accept female applicants.

DEFENSE DEPT. PHOTO BY CHERIE CULLEN/RELEASED

LO2 *African Americans*

The equal protection clause was originally intended to protect the newly freed slaves after the Civil War (1861–1865). In the early years after the war, the U.S. government made an effort to protect the rights of blacks living in the former states of the Confederacy. The Thirteenth Amendment (which granted freedom to the slaves), the Fourteenth Amendment (which guaranteed equal protection under the law), and the Fifteenth Amendment (which stated that voting rights could not be abridged on account of race) were part of that effort. By the late 1880s, however, southern legislatures had begun to pass a series of segregation laws—laws that separated the white community from the black community. Such laws were commonly called "Jim Crow" laws (from a song that was popular in minstrel shows that caricatured African Americans). Some of the most common Jim Crow laws called for racial segregation in the use of public facilities, such as schools, railroads, and later, buses. These laws were also applied to housing, restaurants, hotels, and many other facilities.

Separate but Equal

In 1892, a group of Louisiana citizens decided to challenge a state law that required railroads to provide separate railway cars for African Americans. A man named Homer Plessy, who was seven-eighths Caucasian and one-eighth African, boarded a train in New Orleans and sat in the railway car reserved for whites. When Plessy refused to move at the request of the conductor, he was arrested for breaking the law.

Four years later, in 1896, the Supreme Court provided a constitutional basis for segregation laws. In *Plessy v. Ferguson*,[6] the Court held that the law did not violate the equal protection clause if *separate* facilities for blacks were *equal* to those for whites. The lone dissenter, Justice John Marshall Harlan, disagreed: "Our Constitution is colorblind, and neither knows nor tolerates classes among citizens." The majority opinion, however, established the **separate-but-equal doctrine,** which was used to justify segregation in many areas of American life for nearly sixty years. Separate facilities for African Americans, when they were provided at all, were in practice almost never truly equal.

In the late 1930s and the 1940s, the United States Supreme Court gradually moved away from this doctrine. The major breakthrough, however, did not come until 1954, in a case involving an African American girl who lived in Topeka, Kansas.

The *Brown* Decisions and School Integration

In the 1950s, Topeka's schools, like those in many cities, were segregated. Mr. and Mrs. Oliver Brown wanted their daughter, Linda Carol Brown, to attend a white school a few blocks from their home instead of an all-black school that was twenty-one blocks away. With the help of lawyers from the National Association for the Advancement of Colored People (NAACP), Linda's parents sued the board of education to allow their daughter to attend the nearby school.

In *Brown v. Board of Education of Topeka*,[7] the Supreme Court reversed *Plessy v. Ferguson*. The Court unanimously held that segregation by race in public education was unconstitutional. Chief Justice Earl Warren wrote as follows:

> Does segregation of children in public schools solely on the basis of race, even though the physical facilities and other "tangible" factors may be equal, deprive the children of the minority group of equal educational opportunities? We believe that it does. . . . [Segregation generates

> **separate-but-equal doctrine** A Supreme Court doctrine holding that the equal protection clause of the Fourteenth Amendment did not forbid racial segregation as long as the facilities for blacks were equal to those for whites. The doctrine was overturned in the *Brown v. Board of Education of Topeka* decision of 1954.

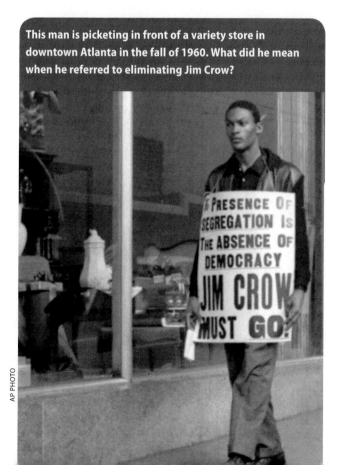

This man is picketing in front of a variety store in downtown Atlanta in the fall of 1960. What did he mean when he referred to eliminating Jim Crow?

AP PHOTO

in children] a feeling of inferiority as to their status in the community that may affect their hearts and minds in a way unlikely ever to be undone. . . . We conclude that in the field of public education the doctrine of "separate but equal" has no place. Separate educational facilities are inherently unequal.

In 1955, in *Brown v. Board of Education*[8] (sometimes called *Brown II*), the Supreme Court ordered desegregation to begin "with all deliberate speed," an ambiguous phrase that could be (and was) interpreted in a variety of ways.

REACTIONS TO SCHOOL INTEGRATION The Supreme Court ruling did not go unchallenged. Bureaucratic loopholes were used to delay desegregation. Another reaction was "white flight." As white parents sent their children to newly established private schools, some formerly white-only public schools became 100 percent black. In Arkansas, Governor Orval Faubus used the state's National Guard to block the integration of Central High School in Little Rock in 1957, which led to increasing violence in the area. A federal court demanded that the troops be withdrawn. Only after President Dwight D. Eisenhower federalized the Arkansas National Guard and sent in troops to help quell the violence did Central High finally become integrated.

By 1970, *de jure* **segregation**—segregation that is established by law—had been abolished by school systems. But that meant only that no public school could legally identify itself as being reserved for all whites or all blacks. It did not mean the end of *de facto* **segregation** (segregation that is not imposed by law but is produced by circumstances, such as the existence of neighborhoods or communities populated primarily by African Americans). Attempts to overcome *de facto* segregation included redrawing school district lines, reassigning pupils, and busing.

de jure **segregation**
Racial segregation that occurs because of laws or decisions by government agencies.

de facto **segregation**
Racial segregation that occurs not as a result of deliberate intentions but because of past social and economic conditions and residential patterns.

busing The transportation of public school students by bus to schools physically outside their neighborhoods to eliminate school segregation based on residential patterns.

BUSING **Busing** is the transporting of students by bus to schools physically outside their neighborhoods in an effort to achieve racially desegregated schools. The Supreme Court first endorsed busing in 1971 in a case involving the school system in Charlotte, North Carolina.[9] Following this decision, the Court upheld busing in several northern cities.[10] Proponents believed that busing improved the educational and career opportunities of minority children and also enhanced the ability of children from different ethnic groups to get along with one another.

Nevertheless, busing was unpopular with many groups from its inception. By the mid-1970s, the courts had begun to retreat from their former support for busing. In 1974, the Supreme Court rejected the idea of busing children across school district lines.[11] In 1986, the Court refused to review a lower court decision that ended a desegregation plan in Norfolk, Virginia.[12] Today, busing orders to end *de facto* segregation are not upheld by the courts. Indeed, *de facto* segregation in America's schools is still widespread.

The Civil Rights Movement

In 1955, one year after the first *Brown* decision, an African American woman named Rosa Parks, a long-time activist in the NAACP, boarded a public bus in Montgomery, Alabama. When it became crowded, she refused to move to the "colored section" at the rear of the bus. She was arrested and fined for violating local segregation laws. Her arrest spurred the local African American community to organize a year-long boycott of the entire Montgomery bus system. The protest was led by a twenty-seven-year-old Baptist minister, the Reverend Dr. Martin Luther King, Jr. During the protest period,

Martin Luther King Jr. acknowledges the crowd at the Lincoln Memorial for his "I Have a Dream" speech during the March on Washington, D.C., on Aug. 28, 1963.

AP PHOTO

he was jailed and his house was bombed. Despite the hostility and what appeared to be overwhelming odds against them, the protesters were triumphant.

In 1956, a federal court prohibited the segregation of buses in Montgomery, and the era of the **civil rights movement**—the movement by minorities and concerned whites to end racial segregation—had begun. The movement was led by a number of groups and individuals, including Martin Luther King and his Southern Christian Leadership Conference (SCLC). Other groups, such as the Congress of Racial Equality (CORE), the NAACP, and the Student Nonviolent Coordinating Committee (SNCC), also sought to secure equal rights for African Americans.

"INJUSTICE

anywhere is a threat to justice everywhere."

~ MARTIN LUTHER KING, JR. ~
U.S. CIVIL RIGHTS LEADER
1929–1968

Civil rights activists were trained in the tools of nonviolence—how to use nonthreatening body language, how to go limp when dragged or assaulted, and how to protect themselves from clubs or police dogs. As the civil rights movement gained momentum, the media images of nonviolent protesters being attacked by police, sprayed with fire hoses, and attacked by dogs shocked and angered Americans across the country. This public backlash led to nationwide demands for reform. The March on Washington for Jobs and Freedom, led by Martin Luther King in 1963, aimed in part to demonstrate the widespread public support for legislation to ban discrimination in all aspects of public life.

NONVIOLENCE AS A TACTIC Civil rights protesters in the 1960s began to apply the tactic of nonviolent **civil disobedience**—the deliberate and public refusal to obey laws considered unjust—in civil rights actions throughout the South. For example, in 1960, in Greensboro, North Carolina, four African American students sat at the "whites only" lunch counter at Woolworth's and ordered food. The waitress refused to serve them, and the store closed early, but more students returned the next day to sit at the counter, with supporters picketing outside. **Sit-ins** spread to other lunch counters across the South. In some instances, students were heckled or even dragged from the store by angry whites. But the protesters never reacted with violence. They simply returned to their seats at the counter, day after day. Within months of the first sit-in, lunch counters began to reverse their policies of segregation.

CIVIL RIGHTS LEGISLATION IN THE 1960s As the civil rights movement demonstrated its strength, Congress began to pass civil rights laws. While the Fourteenth Amendment prevented the *government* from discriminating against individuals or groups, the private sector—businesses, restaurants, and so on—could still freely refuse to employ and serve nonwhites. Therefore, Congress sought to address this issue.

The Civil Rights Act of 1964 was the first and most comprehensive civil rights law. It forbade discrimination on the basis of race, color, religion, gender, and national origin. The major provisions of the act were as follows:

- It outlawed discrimination in public places of accommodation, such as hotels, restaurants, snack bars, movie theaters, and public transportation.

- It provided that federal funds could be withheld from any federal or state government project or facility that practiced any form of discrimination.

These Arkansas African American college students participate in a sit-in at a diner's counter. Why did they feel the need to demonstrate in this fashion? Why don't we see such pictures in the news today?

MPI/GETTY IMAGES

civil rights movement The movement in the 1950s and 1960s, by minorities and concerned whites, to end racial segregation.

civil disobedience The deliberate and public act of refusing to obey laws thought to be unjust.

sit-in A tactic of nonviolent civil disobedience. Demonstrators enter a business, college building, or other public place and remain seated until they are forcibly removed or until their demands are met. The tactic was used successfully in the civil rights movement and in other protest movements in the United States.

- It banned discrimination in employment.

- It outlawed arbitrary discrimination in voter registration.

- It authorized the federal government to sue to desegregate public schools and facilities.

Other significant laws passed by Congress during the 1960s included the Voting Rights Act of 1965, which made it illegal to interfere with anyone's right to vote in any election held in this country (see Chapter 8 for a discussion of the historical restrictions on voting that African Americans faced), and the Civil Rights Act of 1968, which prohibited discrimination in housing.

THE BLACK POWER MOVEMENT Not all African Americans embraced nonviolence. Several outspoken leaders in the mid-1960s were outraged at the slow pace of change in the social and economic status of blacks. Malcolm X, a speaker and organizer for the Nation of Islam (also called the Black Muslims), rejected the goals of integration and racial equality espoused by the civil rights movement. He called instead for black separatism and black pride. Although he later moderated some of his views, his rhetorical style and powerful message influenced many African American young people.

By the late 1960s, with the assassinations of Malcolm X in 1965 and Martin Luther King in 1968, the era of mass acts of civil disobedience in the name of civil rights had come to an end.

Political Participation

As you will read in Chapter 8, in many jurisdictions African Americans were prevented from voting for years after the Civil War, despite the Fifteenth Amendment (1870). These discriminatory practices persisted in the twentieth century. In the early 1960s, only 22 percent of African Americans of voting age in the South were registered to vote, compared with 63 percent of voting-age whites. In Mississippi, the most extreme example, only 6 percent of voting-age African Americans were registered to vote. Such disparities led to the enactment of the Voting Rights Act of 1965, which ended discriminatory voter-registration tests and gave federal voter registrars the power to prevent racial discrimination in voting.

Today, the percentages of voting-age blacks and whites registered to vote are nearly equal. As a result of

this dramatic change, political participation by African Americans has increased, as has the number of African American elected officials.

Today, more than nine thousand African Americans serve in elective office in the United States. At least one congressional seat in each southern state is held by an African American, as are more than 15 percent of the state legislative seats in the South. A number of African Americans have achieved high government office, including Colin Powell, who served as President George W. Bush's first secretary of state, and Condoleezza Rice, his second secretary of state. Of course, in 2008 Barack Obama, a U.S. senator from Illinois, became the first African American president of the United States. Obama's election reflects a significant change in public opinion. Fifty years ago, only 38 percent of Americans said that they would be willing to vote for an African American as president. Today, this number has risen to more than 90 percent. Nonetheless, only two African Americans have been elected to a state governorship, and only a handful of African Americans have been elected to the U.S. Senate since 1900.

Continuing Challenges

Although African Americans no longer face *de jure* segregation, they continue to struggle for income and educational parity with whites. Recent census data show

Black Muslim leader Malcolm X speaks to an audience at a Harlem rally in 1963. His talk, in which he restated the Black Muslim theme of complete separation of whites and African Americans, outdrew a nearby rally sponsored by a civil rights group by ten to one.

LIBRARY OF CONGRESS

that incomes in white households are two-thirds higher than those in black households. The poverty rate for blacks is roughly three times that for whites.

The education gap between blacks and whites also persists despite continuing efforts by educators—and by government, through programs such as the federal No Child Left Behind Act—to reduce it. Recent studies show that on average, African American students in high school can read and do math at only the average level of whites in junior high school. While black adults have narrowed the gap with white adults in earning high school diplomas, the disparity has widened for college degrees.

These problems tend to feed on one another. Schools in poorer neighborhoods generally have fewer educational resources available, resulting in lower achievement levels for their students. Thus, some educational experts suggest that it all comes down to money. In fact, many parents of minority students in struggling school districts are less concerned about integration than they are about funds for their children's schools. A number of these parents have initiated lawsuits against their state governments, demanding that the states give poor districts more resources.

Researchers have known for decades that when students enrolled at a particular school come almost entirely from impoverished families, regardless of race, the performance of the students at that school is seriously depressed. When low-income students attend schools where the majority of the students are middle class, again regardless of race, their performance improves dramatically—without dragging down the performance of the middle-class students. Because of this research and recent U.S. Supreme Court rulings that have struck down some racial integration plans, several school systems have adopted policies that integrate students on the basis of socioeconomic class, not race.[13]

LO3 *Women*

In 1848, Lucretia Mott and Elizabeth Cady Stanton organized the first "woman's rights" convention in Seneca Falls, New York. The three hundred people who attended approved a Declaration of Sentiments: "We hold these truths to be self-evident: that all men *and women* are created equal." In the following years, other women's groups held conventions in various cities in the Midwest and the East. With the outbreak of the Civil War, though, women's rights advocates devoted their energies to the war effort.

President Obama often accepts public speaking engagements. While he has stumped for health-care reform, increased regulation of business and of banks, and other causes, he has rarely talked about race relations. Why not?

The Struggle for Voting Rights

The movement for political rights gained momentum again in 1869, when Susan B. Anthony and Elizabeth Cady Stanton formed the National Woman Suffrage Association. **Suffrage**—the right to vote—became their goal. Members of this association, however, saw suffrage as only one step on the road toward greater social and political rights for women. Lucy Stone and other women, who founded the American Woman Suffrage Association, thought that the right to vote should be the only goal. By 1890, the two organizations had joined forces, and the resulting National American Woman Suffrage Association had indeed only one goal—the enfranchisement of women. When little progress was made, small, radical splinter groups took to the streets. Parades, hunger strikes, arrests, and jailings soon followed.

World War I (1914–1918) marked a turning point in the battle for women's rights. The war offered many opportunities for women. Thousands of women served as volunteers, and about a million women joined the workforce, holding jobs vacated by men who entered military service. After the war, President Woodrow Wilson wrote to Carrie Chapman Catt, one of the leaders of the women's movement: "It is high time that [that] part of our debt should be

suffrage The right to vote; the franchise.

acknowledged." Two years later, in 1920, seventy-two years after the Seneca Falls convention, the Nineteenth Amendment to the Constitution was ratified: "The right of citizens of the United States to vote shall not be denied or abridged by the United States or by any State on account of sex."

> "THE RIGHT OF CITIZENS OF THE UNITED STATES TO VOTE **shall not be denied or abridged . . . on account of sex."**
>
> ~ THE NINETEENTH AMENDMENT TO THE UNITED STATES CONSTITUTION ~
> 1920

The Feminist Movement

After winning the right to vote, women engaged in little independent political activity for many years. In the 1960s, however, a new women's movement arose—the feminist movement. Women who faced discrimination in employment and other circumstances were inspired in part by the civil rights movement and the campaign against the war in Vietnam. The National Organization for Women (NOW), founded in 1966, was the most important new women's organization. But the feminist movement also consisted of thousands of small, independent "women's liberation" and "consciousness-raising" groups established on campuses and in neighborhoods throughout the nation. **Feminism,** the goal of the movement, meant full political, economic, and social equality for women.

During the 1970s, NOW and other organizations sought to win passage of the Equal Rights Amendment (ERA) to the Constitution, which would have written equality into the heart of the nation's laws. The amendment did not win support from enough state legislatures, however, and it failed. Campaigns to change state and national laws affecting women were much more successful. Congress and the various state legislatures enacted a range of measures to provide equal rights for women. The women's movement also enjoyed considerable success in legal action. Courts at all levels accepted the argument that *gender discrimination* violated the Fourteenth Amendment's equal protection clause.

Women in American Politics Today

More than ten thousand members have served in the U.S. House of Representatives. Only 1 percent of them have been women, and women continue to face a "men's club" atmosphere in Congress. In 2002, however, a woman, Nancy Pelosi (D., Calif.), was elected minority leader of the House of Representatives. She was

feminism The belief in full political, economic, and social equality for women.

the first woman to hold this post. Pelosi again made history when, after the Democratic victories in the 2006 elections, she was elected Speaker of the House of Representatives, the first woman ever to lead the House.

FEDERAL OFFICES Women have been underrepresented when receiving presidential appointments to federal offices. Franklin D. Roosevelt (1933–1945) appointed the first woman to a cabinet post—Frances Perkins, who was secretary of labor from 1933 to 1945. Several women have held cabinet posts in more recent administrations, however. All of the last three presidents have appointed women to the most senior cabinet post—secretary of state. Bill Clinton (1993–2001) appointed Madeleine Albright to this position, George W. Bush (2001–2009) picked Condoleezza Rice for the post in his second term, and most recently, Barack Obama chose New York senator Hillary Clinton to be secretary of state.

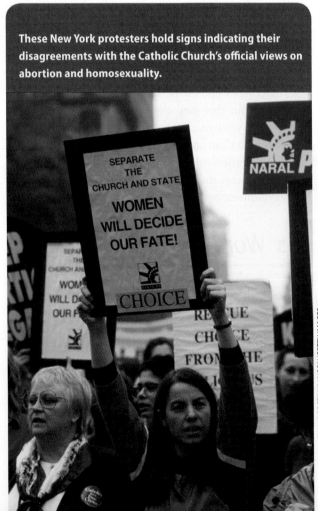

These New York protesters hold signs indicating their disagreements with the Catholic Church's official views on abortion and homosexuality.

EVAN AGOSTINI/LIAISON/GETTY IMAGES

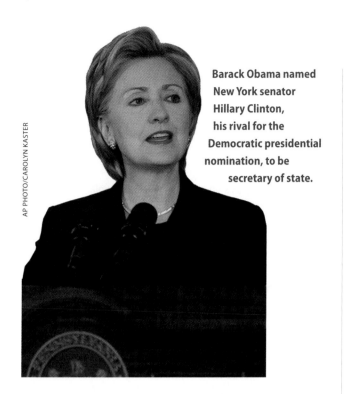

Barack Obama named New York senator Hillary Clinton, his rival for the Democratic presidential nomination, to be secretary of state.

AP PHOTO/CAROLYN KASTER

In addition, Ronald Reagan (1981–1989) appointed the first woman to sit on the Supreme Court, Sandra Day O'Connor. Bill Clinton appointed Ruth Bader Ginsburg to the Supreme Court. Barack Obama selected Sonia Sotomayor for the Court in 2009, and Elena Kagan in 2010.

STATE POLITICS Women have made greater progress at the state level, and the percentage of women in state legislatures has been rising steadily. Women now constitute nearly one-fourth of state legislators. Notably, in 1998, women won races for each of the top five offices

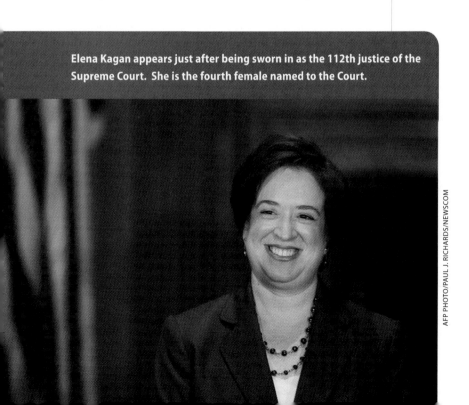

Elena Kagan appears just after being sworn in as the 112th justice of the Supreme Court. She is the fourth female named to the Court.

AFP PHOTO/PAUL J. RICHARDS/NEWSCOM

in Arizona, the first such occurrence in U.S. history. Generally, women have been more successful politically in the western states than elsewhere. In Washington State, more than one-third of the state's legislative seats are now held by women. At the other end of the spectrum are states such as Alabama. In that state, fewer than 10 percent of the lawmakers are women.

Women in the Workplace

An ongoing challenge for American women is to obtain equal pay and equal opportunity in the workplace. In spite of federal legislation and programs to promote equal treatment of women in the workplace, women continue to face various forms of discrimination.

WAGE DISCRIMINATION In 1963, Congress passed the Equal Pay Act. The act requires employers to pay an equal wage for substantially equal work—males cannot be paid more than females who perform essentially the same job. The following year, Congress passed the Civil Rights Act of 1964, Title VII of which prohibits employment discrimination on the basis of race, color, national origin, gender, and religion. Women, however, continue to face wage discrimination.

It is estimated that for every dollar earned by men, women earn about 80 cents. Although the wage gap has narrowed significantly since 1963, when the Equal Pay Act was enacted (at that time, women earned 58 cents for every dollar earned by men), it still remains. This is particularly true for women in management positions and older women. Female managers now earn, on average, only 70 percent of what male managers earn. And women between the ages of forty-five and fifty-four make, on average, only 73 percent of what men in that age group earn. Notably, when a large number of women are in a particular occupation, the wages that are paid in that occupation tend to be relatively low. On the positive side, women are less likely than men to lose their jobs during a recession. We examine that phenomenon in this chapter's feature *Our Government Faces a Troubled Economy: Unemployment among Men* on the following page.

Even though an increasing number of women now hold business and professional jobs once held only by men, relatively few of these women are able to rise to the top of the career ladder in their firms due to the lingering bias against women in the

OUR GOVERNMENT FACES A TROUBLED ECONOMY

Unemployment among Men

One of the most far-reaching and painful aspects of any recession is unemployment. Those who are unemployed lose not only their income but also some of their dignity. Continued unemployment was the number-one issue for most voters throughout the Great Recession.

During this period, many people noticed that more men than women were losing their jobs. From December 2007 to October 2009, net employment fell by 5.8 million for men but only 2.5 million for women. As a result, some called the Great Recession a "mancession." At the height of the unemployment crisis, a full one-fifth of the male population of prime working age was, for one or another reason, not working. The only other time in American history when the share of men not working was this large or larger was during the Great Depression of the 1930s.

The Hardest-Hit Industries Were Dominated by Men

The Great Recession started with the collapse of the housing sector. Construction came to an abrupt halt in most of the United States. Men have always dominated the construction industry—up to 88 percent of the jobs in construction are filled by men. Consequently, many more men than women were put out of work in this sector. Manufacturing was hit harder than any sector other than construction, and more than 71 percent of manufacturing jobs are held by men. In contrast, the industries that suffered least were dominated by women. Employment in education and health services actually edged up through the crisis, and more than 77 percent of the workers in those two fields are women.

These differentials go a long way toward explaining why the Great Recession was a mancession. Some economists have pointed out, however, that men have lost many more jobs than women in every recession since World War II. In that sense, all recessions have been mancessions.

In the Long Run

Although the employment picture for men was especially bleak during the recession, male employment has declined over the last forty years in good times and bad. Before 1970, 92 to 95 percent of the men in the prime employment years—ages 25 to 54—were working. On the eve of the Great Recession, the percentage was about 88. Fewer than half of women aged 25 to 54 were working in 1970. In 2000, female employment peaked at about 75 percent.

Women have pulled ahead of men when it comes to education, and that cannot help men get jobs. Consider how many people aged 25 to 29 have college degrees: In 1964, 17 percent of men in this age group had a degree, compared with 9 percent of women. In 2009, 27 percent of men in this age group had a degree—and 35 percent of women had one. Men in their twenties are actually *less* likely to have a college degree today than in 1975.

The Government Reacts

High unemployment rates are very bad news for politicians. They anger voters and can cost officeholders their jobs. In 2009 and 2010, the Democrats attempted to combat the recession and unemployment through stimulus programs and extending unemployment compensation. Subsidies to the states for education and health care may have preserved some jobs in sectors dominated by women. Saving Chrysler and General Motors helped men (auto employment is 80 percent male). At best, though, such measures blunted the effects of the recession. They did not end it.

You Be the Judge Women continue to receive lower wages than men, on average. What effect might this have on the ability of women to get jobs?

glass ceiling An invisible but real discriminatory barrier that prevents women and minorities from rising to top positions of power or responsibility.

workplace. This bias has been described as the **glass ceiling**—an invisible but real discriminatory barrier that prevents women (or minorities) from rising to top positions of power or responsibility. Today, less than one-sixth of the top executive positions in the largest American corporations are held by women.

SEXUAL HARASSMENT Title VII's prohibition of gender discrimination has also been extended to prohibit sexual harassment. **Sexual harassment** occurs when job opportunities, promotions, salary increases, or even the ability to retain a job depends on whether an employee complies with demands for sexual favors. A special form of sexual harassment, called hostile-environment harassment, occurs when an employee is subjected to sexual conduct or comments in the workplace that interfere with the employee's job performance or that create an intimidating, hostile, or offensive environment.

The Supreme Court has upheld the right of persons to be free from sexual harassment on the job on a number of occasions. In 1998, the Court made it clear that sexual harassment includes harassment by members of the same sex.[14] In the same year, the Court held that employers are liable for the harassment of employees by supervisors unless the employers can show that (1) they exercised reasonable care in preventing such problems (by implementing antiharassment policies and procedures, for example) and (2) the employees failed to take advantage of any corrective opportunities provided by the employers.[15] The Civil Rights Act of 1991 greatly expanded the remedies available for victims of sexual harassment. Under the act, victims can seek damages as well as back pay, job reinstatement, and other compensation.

LO4 *Securing Rights for Other Groups*

In addition to African Americans and women, a number of other groups in U.S. society have faced discriminatory treatment. To discuss all of these groups would require volumes.

Here, we look first at three significant ethnic groups that have had to struggle for equal treatment—Hispanics, Asian Americans, and Native Americans. Then we examine the struggles of several other groups of Americans—persons with disabilities and gay men and lesbians.

Hispanics

Hispanics, or Latinos, constitute the largest ethnic minority in the United States. Whereas African Americans represent about 13 percent of the U.S. population, Hispanics now constitute more than 15 percent. Each year, the Hispanic population grows by nearly 1 million people, one-third of whom are newly arrived legal immigrants. By 2050, Hispanics are expected to constitute about one-fourth of the U.S. population.

Hispanics can be of any race, and to classify them as a single minority group is misleading. Spanish-speaking individuals tend to identify themselves by their country of origin, rather than as Hispanics. As you can see in Figure 5–1 below, the largest Hispanic group consists of Mexican Americans, who constitute about 66 percent of the Hispanic population living in the United States. About 9 percent of Hispanics are Puerto Ricans, and 3.5 percent are Cuban Americans. Most of the remaining Hispanics are from Central and South American countries.

Economically, Hispanic households are often members of this country's working poor. About 20 percent of Hispanic families live below the poverty line, compared with 8 percent of non-Hispanic white families. Hispanic leaders tend to attribute the low income levels to language problems, lack of job training, and continuing immigration. Immigration disguises statistical progress because language problems and lack of job training are usually more notable among new immigrants than among those who have lived in the United States for many years.

> **sexual harassment**
> Unwanted physical contact, verbal conduct, or abuse of a sexual nature that interferes with a recipient's job performance, creates a hostile environment, or carries with it an implicit or explicit threat of adverse employment consequences.

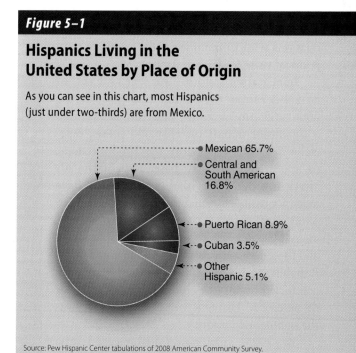

Figure 5–1

Hispanics Living in the United States by Place of Origin

As you can see in this chart, most Hispanics (just under two-thirds) are from Mexico.

- Mexican 65.7%
- Central and South American 16.8%
- Puerto Rican 8.9%
- Cuban 3.5%
- Other Hispanic 5.1%

Source: Pew Hispanic Center tabulations of 2008 American Community Survey.

Minority Group Members and Women

The 2010 election saw a large number of minority and female candidates for the Senate, for the House, for governor, and for seats in state legislatures. The total number of minority candidates for the House and Senate was 123. A record number of African-American Republican congressional candidates sought office and two were successful. The number of Latino members of the House and Senate is now a near-record twenty-seven. Five of them are Republican. The number of Asian-American members of the House and Senate will remain at thirteen, while the number of African-Americans will be forty-one, one less than in the previous Congress.

A total of 154 female candidates sought office in the House and Senate. Campaign spending hit new records, and one of them was set by a woman. Republican Meg Whitman spent $140 million of her own money to defeat Democratic rival Jerry Brown for the governorship of California. (She lost nonetheless.) An estimated seventy-two House seats are now held by women, down one from the previous Congress. The number of female senators remained the same at seventeen. At the state level, for the first time ever, two female minority group members won governorships—in New Mexico and South Carolina—bringing the total number of female governors to seven.

PARTY IDENTIFICATION AND ELECTORAL SIGNIFICANCE In their party identification, Hispanics tend to follow some fairly well-established patterns. Traditionally, Mexican Americans and Puerto Ricans identify with the Democratic Party, which has favored more government assistance and support programs for disadvantaged groups. Cubans, in contrast, tend to identify with the Republican Party. This is largely because of a different history. Cuban émigrés fled from Cuba during and after the Communist revolution led by Fidel Castro. The strong anti-Communist sentiments of the Cubans propelled them toward the more conservative party—the Republicans. Today, relations with Communist Cuba continue to be a key political issue for Cuban Americans.

Immigration reform was the subject of heated debate in the months leading up to the 2006 midterm elections, and this debate had a significant impact on Hispanic voters, especially in California. Before the 2006 elections, to appeal to the party base, Republican ads attacked proposed legislation that would have made it possible for unauthorized immigrants to obtain legal status. According to some observers, many Hispanics perceived the ads as attacking all Hispanics and were motivated to vote against Republicans in the 2006 elections. Exit polls conducted during the elections showed that for 69 percent of Hispanic voters, immigration was the number-one priority.

By 2008, immigration had receded as a national issue—it did not come up at all in the presidential debates. For Hispanics, along with everyone else, economic troubles were the number-one issue. In the fall elections, only 31 percent of Hispanic voters chose Republican John McCain, even though he had been a major proponent of immigration reform. This was down sharply from the almost 40 percent of the Hispanic vote won by George W. Bush in 2004.

POLITICAL PARTICIPATION Generally, Hispanics in the United States have a comparatively low level of political participation. This is understandable, given that one-third of Hispanics are below voting age and another one-fourth are not citizens and thus cannot vote. Although voter turnout among Hispanics is

Sonia Sotomayor was grilled by Republicans during her nomination hearing before the Senate Judiciary Committee. (Here you can see that she didn't always feel under pressure.) Her nomination was easily approved by the Senate, making her the first Hispanic to become a Supreme Court justice.

AP PHOTO/J. SCOTT APPLEWHITE

generally low compared with the population at large, the Hispanic voting rate is rising as more immigrants become citizens and as more Hispanics reach voting age. Indeed, when comparing citizens of equal incomes and educational backgrounds, Hispanic citizens' participation rate is higher than average.

Increasingly, Hispanics hold political office, particularly in those states with large Hispanic populations. Today, more than 5 percent of the state legislators in Arizona, California, Colorado, Florida, New Mexico, and Texas are of Hispanic ancestry. Cuban Americans have been notably successful in gaining local political power, particularly in Dade County, Florida.

President George W. Bush appointed a number of Hispanics to federal offices, including cabinet positions. For example, he named Alberto Gonzales to head the Justice Department and Carlos Gutierrez as secretary of commerce. Barack Obama appointed Senator Ken Salazar (D., Colo.) to head the Interior Department and Representative Hilda Solis (D., Calif.) as secretary of labor. Hispanics are also increasing their presence in Congress, albeit slowly.

Asian Americans

Asian Americans have also suffered, at times severely, from discriminatory treatment. The Chinese Exclusion Act of 1882 prevented persons from China and Japan from coming to the United States to prospect for gold or to work on the railroads or in factories in the West. After 1900, immigration continued to be restricted—only limited numbers of individuals from China and Japan were allowed to enter the United States. Those who were allowed into the country faced racial prejudice from Americans who had little respect for their customs and culture. In 1906, after the San Francisco earthquake, Japanese American students were segregated into special schools so that white children could use their buildings.

The Japanese bombing of Pearl Harbor in 1941, which launched the entry of the United States into World War II (1939–1945), intensified Americans' fear of the Japanese. Actions taken under an executive order issued by President Franklin D. Roosevelt in 1942 subjected many Japanese Americans to curfews, excluded them from certain "military areas," and evacuated most of the West Coast Japanese American population to internment camps (also called "relocation centers").[16]

NEWSCOM

Asian American students routinely score higher on their college-entrance SATs than do other groups. Also, Asian Americans graduate at a higher rate than do other groups. Because they are in a minority, should they nonetheless benefit from affirmative action programs in college admissions and job hiring?

In 1988, Congress provided funds to compensate former camp inhabitants—$1.25 billion for approximately 60,000 people.

Today, Japanese Americans and Chinese Americans lead other ethnic groups in median income and median education. Indeed, Asians who have immigrated to the United States since 1965 (including immigrants from India) represent the most highly skilled immigrant groups in American history. Nearly 40 percent of Asian Americans over the age of twenty-five have college degrees. The image of Asian Americans as a "model minority" has created certain problems for its members, however. Some argue that leading colleges and universities have discriminated against Asian Americans in admissions because so many of them apply. We discuss that issue in this chapter's *Join the Debate* feature on the following page.

More than a million Indochinese war refugees, most from Vietnam, have immigrated to the United States since the 1970s. Many came with relatives and were sponsored by American families or organizations. Thus, they had support systems to help them get started. Some immigrants from other parts of Indochina, however, have experienced difficulties because they come from cultures that have had very little contact with the practices of developed industrial societies.

Native Americans

When we consider population figures since 1492, we see that the Native Americans experienced one catastrophe after another. We cannot know exactly how many people lived in America when Columbus arrived.

Are Admissions at Top Schools Unfair to Asian Americans?

There are 14 million Asian Americans, about 4.5 percent of the U.S. population. They are a diverse group. Outside of the United States, people from China, India, Japan, and Korea have little in common. Only in America are they lumped together—and in this country, people from East and South Asia do have a few things in common. Their average family income is higher than that of whites. They are also well educated. By one estimate, Asian Americans make up as many as 30 percent of the top college candidates as determined by SAT scores, National Merit and AP Scholar awards, and grades. In the Ivy League, however, Asian admissions have consistently run below 20 percent. In other words, many excellent Asian American students are being turned away.

Colleges Admission Isn't Just about Grades and Test Scores

While it may appear to high-scoring Asian Americans who don't get into their college of choice that they have suffered from discrimination, it is not necessarily true. Universities routinely manage admissions to obtain the freshman classes they wish to have. They try to include the right number of football and basketball players, dancers, minorities, and men (the latter are favored in some universities because otherwise campuses might become "too female"). Only if you believe that high test scores should be the sole basis for admission can you argue that university admission preferences constitute discrimination.

The goal of a diverse freshman class is to expose all students to a mix of races, ethnicities, and viewpoints. Vincent Pan, head of Chinese for Affirmative Action, argues that universities "have a public responsibility to prepare future leaders, and we need to prepare a generation of leaders that will look like America." A freshman class that is, say, 40 percent Asian American does not look like America, just as a class that is 80 percent women does not look like America.

Discrimination Is Discrimination—Period

Lately, Ivy League–level universities have established techniques to limit the number of Asian American students admitted to their institutions. These same techniques were used before World War II (and sometimes even after) to limit the number of Jewish students. The basic scheme, then and now, is to award lots of extra points for being "well-rounded" and then to define well-rounded as everything that young Asian Americans aren't (or that the young Jews weren't). A more labor-intensive method of accomplishing the same goal is through a "holistic" review process for all candidates. Schools using this process rely on admissions officers' subjective views of students, which yields an assessment that supposedly evaluates the "whole person."

There is no need to set Asian Americans in competition with other minorities in admissions. More than 20 percent of the spaces at top private universities are currently set aside for legacy students, children of the rich and famous, and athletes. (Legacy students are the children of alumni or alumnae.) If the number of these unjustified preferences were merely cut in half, there would be enough room for qualified Asian youths.

For Critical Analysis *Why do some universities reserve spots for the children of their graduates?*

Current research estimates the population of what is now the continental United States to have been anywhere from 3 million to 8 million, out of a total New World population of 40 million to 100 million. The Europeans brought with them diseases to which these Native Americans had no immunity. As a result, after a series of terrifying epidemics, the population of the continental United States was reduced to perhaps eight hundred thousand people by 1600. Death rates elsewhere in the New World were comparable. When the Pilgrims arrived at Plymouth, the Massachusetts coast was lined with abandoned village sites.[17]

In subsequent centuries, the American Indian population continued to decline, bottoming out at about half a million in 1925. These were centuries in which the European American—and African American—populations experienced explosive growth. By 2000, the Native American population had recovered to about 2 million, or about 3.5 million if we count individuals who are only part Indian.

In 1789, Congress designated the Native American tribes as foreign nations so that the government could sign land and boundary treaties with them. As members of foreign nations, Native Americans had no civil rights under U.S. laws. This situation continued until 1924, when the citizenship rights spelled out in the Fourteenth Amendment to the Constitution were finally extended to American Indians.

EARLY POLICIES TOWARD NATIVE AMERICANS The Northwest Ordinance, passed by the Congress of the Confederation in 1787, stated that "the utmost good faith shall always be observed towards the Indians; their lands and property shall never be taken from them without their consent; and in their property, rights, and liberty, they shall never be invaded or disturbed, unless in just and lawful wars authorized by Congress." Over the next hundred years, these principles were violated more often than they were observed.

In the early 1830s, boundaries were established between lands occupied by Native Americans and those occupied by white settlers. In 1830, Congress instructed the Bureau of Indian Affairs (BIA), which Congress had established in 1824 as part of the War Department, to remove all tribes to lands (reservations) west of the Mississippi River in order to free land east of the Mississippi for white settlement.

In the late 1880s, the U.S. government changed its policy. The goal became the "assimilation" of Native Americans into American society. Each family was given a parcel of land within the reservation to farm. The remaining acreage was sold to whites, thus reducing the number of acres in reservation status from 140 million to about 47 million. Tribes that would not cooperate with this plan lost their reservations altogether. The BIA

also set up Native American boarding schools for children to remove them from their parents' influence. In these schools, American Indian children were taught to speak English, to practice Christianity, and to dress like white Americans.

NATIVE AMERICANS TODAY Native Americans have always found it difficult to obtain political power. In part, this is because the tribes are small and scattered, making organized political movements difficult. Today, American Indians remain fragmented politically because large numbers of their population live off the reservations. Nonetheless, in the 1960s, some Native Americans formed organizations to strike back at the U.S. government and to reclaim their heritage, including their lands.

In the late 1960s, a small group of Indians occupied Alcatraz Island, claiming that the island was part of their ancestral lands. Other militant actions followed. For example, in 1973, supporters of the American Indian Movement took over Wounded Knee, South Dakota, where about 150 Sioux Indians had been killed by the U.S. Army in 1890.[18] The occupation was undertaken to protest the government's policy toward Native Americans and to call attention to the injustices they had suffered.

COMPENSATION FOR INJUSTICES OF THE PAST As more Americans became aware of the sufferings of Native Americans, Congress began to compensate them for past injustices. In 1990, Congress passed the Native American Languages Act, which declared that

> Native American languages are unique and serve an important role in maintaining Indian culture and continuity. Courts, too, have shown a greater willingness to recognize Native American treaty rights. For example, in 1985, the Supreme Court ruled that three tribes of Oneida Indians could claim damages for the use of tribal land that had been unlawfully transferred in 1795.[19]

The Indian Gaming Regulatory Act of 1988 allows Native Americans to have gambling operations on their reservations. Although the profits from casinos have helped to improve the economic and social status of many Native Americans, some Indians feel that this industry has seriously injured their traditional culture. Poverty and unemployment remain widespread on the reservations.

Many Native Americans work at locally owned casinos, such as this one in Biloxi, Mississippi. Has gambling on reservations changed the standard of living of all Native Americans? Why or why not?

JUSTIN SULLIVAN/GETTY IMAGES

Obtaining Rights for Persons with Disabilities

Discrimination based on disability crosses the boundaries of race, ethnicity, gender, and religion. Persons with disabilities, especially those with physical deformities or severe mental impairments, have to face social bias. Although attitudes toward persons with disabilities have changed considerably in the last several decades, such persons continue to suffer from discrimination in all its forms.

Persons with disabilities first became a political force in the 1970s, and in 1973, Congress passed the first legislation protecting this group of persons—the Rehabilitation Act. This act prohibited discrimination against persons with disabilities in programs receiving federal aid. The Individuals with Disabilities Education Act (formerly called the Education for All Handicapped Children Act of 1975) requires public schools to provide children with disabilities with free, appropriate, and individualized education in the least restrictive environment appropriate to their needs. Further legislation in 1978 led to regulations for ramps, elevators, and the like in all federal buildings. The Americans with Disabilities Act (ADA) of 1990, however, is by far the most significant legislation protecting the rights of this group of Americans.

THE AMERICANS WITH DISABILITIES ACT The ADA requires that all public buildings and public services be accessible to persons with disabilities. The act also mandates that employers "reasonably accommodate" the needs of workers or job applicants with disabilities who are otherwise qualified for particular jobs unless to do so would cause the employer to suffer an "undue hardship."

The ADA defines persons with disabilities as persons who have physical or mental impairments that "substantially limit" their everyday activities. Health conditions that have been considered disabilities under federal law include blindness, a history of alcoholism, heart disease, cancer, muscular dystrophy, cerebral palsy, paraplegia, diabetes, and acquired immune deficiency syndrome (AIDS). The ADA, however, does not require employers to hire or retain workers who, because of their disabilities, pose a "direct threat to the health or safety" of their co-workers.

LIMITING THE SCOPE OF THE ADA From 1999 to 2002, the Supreme Court handed down a series of rulings that substantially limited the scope of the ADA. The Court found that any limitation that could be remedied by medication or by corrective devices such as eyeglasses did not qualify as a protected disability. According to the Court, even carpal tunnel syndrome was not a

ROGER L. WOLLENBERG/UPI/LANDOV

In the fall of 2008, Representative Jim Langevin (D., R.I.), in the center of the photo, spoke at a rally after Congress passed important amendments to the Americans with Disabilities Act.

disability.[20] In 2008, however, the ADA Amendments Act overturned most of these limits. Carpal tunnel syndrome and other ailments may again qualify as disabilities. (Eyeglasses were not covered by the new law.)

In 2001, the Supreme Court reviewed a case raising the question of whether suits under the ADA could be brought against state employers. The Court concluded that states are immune from lawsuits brought to enforce rights under this federal law.[21]

Gay Men and Lesbians

Until the late 1960s and early 1970s, gay men and lesbians tended to keep quiet about their sexual preferences because exposure usually meant facing harsh consequences. This attitude began to change after a 1969 incident in New York City, however. When the police raided the Stonewall Inn—a bar popular with gay men and lesbians—on June 27 of that year, the bar's patrons responded by throwing beer cans and bottles at the police. The riot continued for two days. The Stonewall Inn uprising launched the gay power movement. By the end of the year, gay men and lesbians had formed fifty organizations, including the Gay Activist Alliance and the Gay Liberation Front.

A CHANGING LEGAL LANDSCAPE The number of gay and lesbian organizations has grown from fifty in 1969 to several thousand today. These groups have exerted significant political pressure on legislatures, the media, schools, and churches. In the decades following Stonewall, more than half of the forty-nine states that had sodomy laws—laws prohibiting homosexual conduct and certain other forms of sexual activity—repealed them. In seven other states, the courts invalidated such laws. Then, in 2003, the United States Supreme Court issued a ruling that effectively invalidated all remaining sodomy laws in the country.

In *Lawrence v. Texas*,[22] the Court ruled that sodomy laws violated the Fourteenth Amendment's due process clause. According to the Court, "The liberty protected by the Constitution allows homosexual persons the right to choose to enter upon relationships in the confines of their homes and their own private lives and still retain their dignity as free persons."

Today, twenty-five states and more than 180 cities and counties in the United States have laws prohibiting discrimination against homosexuals in at least some contexts. The laws may prohibit discrimination

> "The liberty protected by the Constitution ALLOWS HOMOSEXUAL PERSONS THE RIGHT TO CHOOSE TO ENTER UPON RELATIONSHIPS IN THE CONFINES OF THEIR HOMES AND THEIR OWN PRIVATE LIVES AND STILL RETAIN THEIR dignity as free persons."
>
> ~ UNITED STATES SUPREME COURT ~
> *LAWRENCE V. TEXAS*, 2003

in housing, education, banking, employment, or public accommodations. In a landmark case in 1996, *Romer v. Evans*,[23] the Supreme Court held that a Colorado constitutional amendment that would have invalidated all state and local laws protecting homosexuals from discrimination violated the equal protection clause of the U.S. Constitution. The Court stated that the amendment would have denied to homosexuals in Colorado—but to no other Colorado residents—"the right to seek specific protection from the law."

CHANGING ATTITUDES Laws and court decisions protecting the rights of gay men and lesbians reflect social attitudes that are much changed from the 1960s. Liberal political leaders have been supporting gay rights for at least two decades. In 1984, presidential candidate Walter Mondale openly sought the gay vote, as did Jesse Jackson in his 1988 presidential campaign. As president, Bill Clinton strongly supported gay rights.

Even some conservative politicians have softened their stance on the issue. For example, during his 2000 presidential campaign, George W. Bush met with representatives of gay groups to discuss issues important to them. Although Bush stated that he was opposed to gay marriage, he promised that he would not disqualify anyone from serving in his administration on the basis of sexual orientation.

According to a Gallup poll taken in 2009, public support for gay and lesbian rights has continued to rise. The survey showed that 56 percent of respondents believed that gay or lesbian relations between consenting adults should be legal, up from 43 percent in 1978. Support for employment and domestic partnership rights ran even higher. Among those interviewed, 69 percent believed that openly gay or lesbian individuals should be able to serve in the military, and the same number believed that such persons should be allowed to teach children. Giving domestic partners access to health insurance and other employee benefits was endorsed by 67 percent of Americans, and inheritance rights by 73 percent. Only 40 percent of those interviewed endorsed same-sex marriage, but that was up substantially from 27 percent in 1996.

SAME-SEX MARRIAGE Today, same-sex marriage is legal in five states—Connecticut, Iowa, New Hampshire, Massachusetts, and Vermont—and in the District of

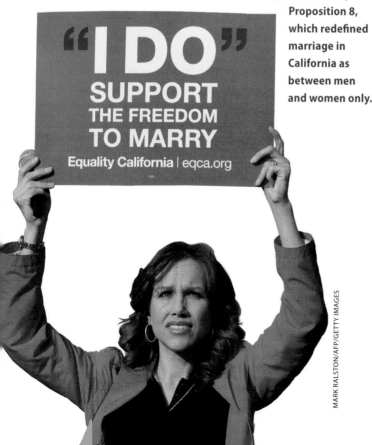

A woman holds up a protest placard during a gay rights rally in Hollywood, California, after the state supreme court upheld Proposition 8, which redefined marriage in California as between men and women only.

"I DO" SUPPORT THE FREEDOM TO MARRY
Equality California | eqca.org

MARK RALSTON/AFP/GETTY IMAGES

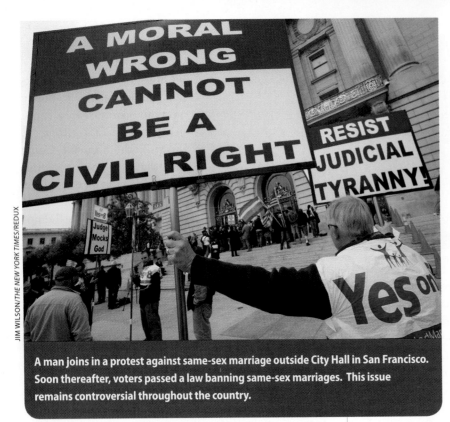

A man joins in a protest against same-sex marriage outside City Hall in San Francisco. Soon thereafter, voters passed a law banning same-sex marriages. This issue remains controversial throughout the country.

more liberal alternatives would not be accepted. During his presidential campaign, Barack Obama pledged to abolish the policy. Later, however, gay and lesbian rights activists accused him of "putting the issue on a back burner."

Generally, attitudes toward gay men and lesbians in the military divide along party lines, with the Democrats approving and the Republicans in opposition. What do soldiers themselves think about serving alongside gay men and lesbians? In a recent survey, three-quarters of the troops polled said that they would have no problem serving with such people. In October 2010, a federal judge ruled that "don't ask, don't tell was unenforceable. The government will appeal.

Columbia. It was temporarily legal in California during part of 2008, between a state supreme court ruling in May that legalized the practice and a constitutional amendment passed by the voters in November that banned it again. California continues to recognize those same-sex couples who married between May and November 2008 as lawfully wedded. New York State and Maryland do not perform same-sex marriages but recognize those performed elsewhere.

A number of states have civil union or domestic partnership laws that grant most of the benefits of marriage to registered same-sex couples. These include California, Nevada, New Jersey, Oregon, and Washington. More limited benefits are provided in Colorado, Hawaii, Maryland, and Wisconsin. Either through a constitutional amendment or through legislation, same-sex marriage is explicitly banned in most states without domestic partnership laws—and even in some of the states just mentioned.

GAYS AND LESBIANS IN THE MILITARY For gay men and lesbians who wish to join the military, one of the battlefields they face is the "Don't ask, don't tell" policy. This policy, which bans openly gay men and lesbians from the military, was implemented in 1993 by President Bill Clinton when it became clear that

affirmative action A policy calling for the establishment of programs that give special consideration, in jobs and college admissions, to members of groups that have been discriminated against in the past.

LO5 Beyond Equal Protection— Affirmative Action

One provision of the Civil Rights Act of 1964 called for prohibiting discrimination in employment. Soon after the act was passed, the federal government began to legislate programs promoting *equal employment opportunity*. Such programs require that employers' hiring and promotion practices guarantee the same opportunities to all individuals. Experience soon showed that minorities often had fewer opportunities to obtain education and relevant work experience than did whites. Because of this, minorities were still excluded from many jobs. Even though discriminatory practices were made illegal, the change in the law did not make up for the results of years of discrimination. Consequently, under President Lyndon B. Johnson (1963–1969), a new policy was developed.

Called **affirmative action,** this policy requires employers to take positive steps to remedy *past* discrimination. Affirmative action programs involve giving special consideration, in jobs and college admissions, to members of groups that have been discriminated against in the past. Until recently, all public and private employers who received federal funds were required to adopt and implement these programs. Thus, the policy of affirmative action has been applied to all agencies of the federal, state, and local governments and to all private employers who sell goods to or perform services for any agency of the federal government. In short, it has covered nearly all of the nation's major employers and many of its smaller ones.

Affirmative Action Tested

The Supreme Court first addressed the issue of affirmative action in 1978 in *Regents of the University of California v. Bakke*.[24] Allan Bakke, a white male, had been denied admission to the University of California's medical school at Davis. The school had set aside sixteen of the one hundred seats in each year's entering class for applicants who wished to be considered as members of designated minority groups. Many of the students admitted through this special program had lower test scores than Bakke. Bakke sued the university, claiming that he was a victim of **reverse discrimination**—discrimination against whites. Bakke argued that the use of a **quota system,** in which a specific number of seats were reserved for minority applicants only, violated the equal protection clause.

The Supreme Court was strongly divided on the issue. Some justices believed that Bakke had been denied equal protection and should be admitted. A majority on the Court concluded that although both the Constitution and the Civil Rights Act of 1964 allow race to be used as a factor in making admissions decisions, race cannot be the *sole* factor. Because the university's quota system was based solely on race, it was unconstitutional. For more

on affirmative action problems elsewhere in the world, see *The Rest of the World* feature on the following page.

Strict Scrutiny Applied

In 1995, the Supreme Court issued a landmark decision in *Adarand Constructors, Inc. v. Peña*.[25] The Court held that any federal, state, or local affirmative action program that uses racial classifications as the basis for making decisions is subject to "strict scrutiny" by the courts. As discussed earlier in this chapter, this means that, to be constitutional, a discriminatory law or action must be narrowly tailored to meet a *compelling* government interest. In effect, the *Adarand* decision narrowed the application of affirmative action programs. An affirmative action program can no longer make use of quotas or preferences and cannot be maintained simply to remedy past discrimination by society in general. It must be narrowly tailored to remedy actual discrimination that has occurred, and once the program has succeeded, it must be changed or dropped.

The Diversity Issue

Following the *Adarand* decision, several lower courts faced cases raising the question of whether affirmative action programs designed to achieve diversity on college campuses were constitutional. For example, in a 1996 case, *Hopwood v. State of Texas*,[26] two white law school applicants sued the University of Texas School of Law in Austin, claiming that they had been denied admission because of the school's affirmative action program. The program allowed admissions officials to take racial and other factors into consideration when determining which students would be admitted.

A federal appellate court held that the program violated the equal protection clause because it discriminated in favor of minority applicants. In its decision, the court directly challenged the *Bakke* decision by stating that the use of race even as a means of achieving diversity on college campuses "undercuts the Fourteenth Amendment." In other words, race could never be a factor, even if it was not the sole factor, in such decisions.

In 2003, the United States Supreme Court reviewed two cases involving issues similar to that in the *Hopwood* case. Both cases involved admissions programs at the University of Michigan. In *Gratz v. Bollinger*,[27] two white

reverse discrimination
Discrimination against those who have no minority status.

quota system A policy under which a specific number of jobs, promotions, or other types of placements, such as university admissions, must be given to members of selected groups.

Any type of affirmative action brings protests from one side or the other. Here, demonstrators oppose a change to current laws that mandate racial integration.

PHOTO BY ALEX WONG/GETTY IMAGES

India Faces an Affirmative Action Nightmare

Affirmative action in the United States has involved a relatively small number of groups, even if some of them have many members—women, for example, make up more than half the population. In India, however, affirmative action is much more complicated due to the caste tradition. Under this millennia-old system, Indians are grouped into thousands of castes and subcastes. Formerly, some groups were considered outside the caste system altogether—these were the "untouchables," or Dalits. In 1950, after India became independent from Britain, the new constitution abolished the practice of untouchability, or discrimination against Dalits, and established a program of rights and quotas for the former untouchables, now officially called the Scheduled Castes. Discrimination remains widespread in rural India, however.

Quotas for Scheduled Castes

Together with the Scheduled Tribes (generally located in the far east of the country), the Scheduled Castes make up about 25 percent of India's population. Quotas were established to bring members of these groups into universities and government jobs in a program that is now about sixty years old. Several

years ago, the government expanded the quota program to include the Other Backward Castes, groups that have suffered impoverishment or discrimination, but not to the degree of the Scheduled Castes and Scheduled Tribes. With the addition of the Other Backward Castes, the favored groups swelled to constitute half of India's population. A nationwide furor resulted.

A Caste of Shepherds Demands to Be Downgraded

In 2007, tens of thousands of members of the Gujjar caste, who traditionally worked as shepherds, blocked the roads in an Indian farming region. The Gujjars were one of the Other Backward Castes, and they were demanding reclassification as one of the Scheduled Castes, or untouchables. Why? The Gujjars realized that if they were classified as Dalits, they would benefit from more generous quotas in schooling and employment, and they would be eligible for more government welfare. This shepherd caste made their demand even though a

lower status might result in increased discrimination, such as not being allowed to use the same water pumps as their neighbors.

For Critical Analysis *An Indian sociologist, Dipankar Gupta, commented, "If you play the caste game, you will end up with caste war." What might he have meant?*

These members of India's Gujjar caste are demonstrating in the Indian state of Rajasthan. They wanted their status to be downgraded from "Other Backward Caste" to "untouchable" so that they could benefit from more generous quotas and receive increased welfare benefits.

AP PHOTO/AMAN SHARMA

applicants who were denied undergraduate admission to the university alleged reverse discrimination. The school's policy gave each applicant a score based on a number of factors, including grade point average, standardized test scores, and personal achievements. The system *automatically* awarded every "underrepresented" minority (African American, Hispanic, and Native American) applicant twenty points—one-fifth of the points needed to guarantee admission. The Court held that this policy violated the equal protection clause.

In contrast, in *Grutter v. Bollinger*,[28] the Court held that the University of Michigan Law School's

admissions policy was constitutional. In that case, the Court concluded that "[u]niversities can, however, consider race or ethnicity more flexibly as a 'plus' factor in the context of individualized consideration of each and every applicant." The significant difference between the two admissions policies, in the Court's view, was that the law school's approach did not apply a mechanical formula giving "diversity bonuses" based on race or ethnicity. In short, the Court concluded that diversity on college campuses was a legitimate goal and that limited affirmative action programs could be used to attain this goal.

The Supreme Court Revisits the Issue

The Michigan cases were decided in 2003. By 2007, when another case involving affirmative action came before the Court, the Court had a new chief justice, John G. Roberts, Jr., and a new associate justice, Samuel Alito, Jr. Both men were appointed by President George W. Bush, and the conservative views of both justices have moved the Court significantly to the right. Justice Alito replaced Sandra Day O'Connor, who had often been the "swing" vote on the Court, sometimes voting with the more liberal justices and sometimes joining the conservative bloc. Hers was the deciding vote in the five-to-four decision upholding the University of Michigan Law School's affirmative action program.

Some claim that the more conservative composition of today's Court strongly influenced the outcome in a case that came before the Court in 2007: *Parents Involved in Community Schools v. Seattle School District No. 1.*[29] The case concerned the policies of two school districts, one in Louisville, Kentucky, and one in Seattle, Washington. Both schools were trying to achieve a more diversified student body by giving preference to minority students if space in the schools was limited and a choice among applicants had to be made. Parents of white children who were turned away from schools in these districts because of these policies sued the school districts, claiming that the policies violated the equal protection clause. Ultimately, the case reached the Supreme Court, and the Court, in a five-to-four vote, held in favor of the parents, ruling that the policies violated the equal protection clause. The Court's decision did not overrule the 2003 case involving the University of Michigan Law School, however, for the Court did not say that race could *not* be used as a factor in university admissions policies. Nonetheless, some claim that the decision represents a significant change on the Court with respect to affirmative action policies.

State Actions

Beginning in the mid-1990s, some states have taken actions to ban affirmative action programs or replace them with alternative policies. For example, in 1996, by a ballot initiative, California amended its state constitution to prohibit any "preferential treatment to any individual or group on the basis of race, sex, color, ethnicity, or national origin in the operation of public employment, public education, or public contracting."

FURTHER ACTIONS Two years later, voters in the state of Washington approved a ballot measure ending all state-sponsored affirmative action. Florida has also ended affirmative action. In 2006, a ballot initiative in Michigan—just three years after the Supreme Court decisions discussed above—banned affirmative action in that state. In the 2008 elections, Nebraska also banned affirmative action, but voters in Colorado rejected such a measure. The 2008 initiatives were spearheaded by Ward

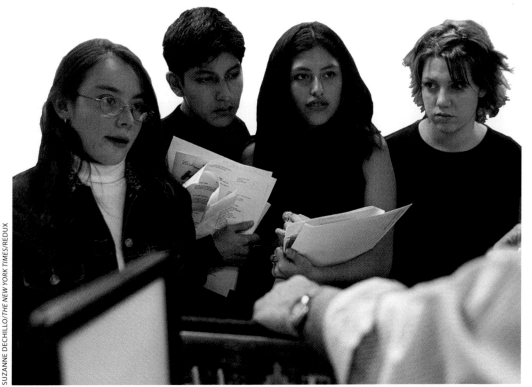

SUZANNE DECHILLO/THE NEW YORK TIMES/REDUX

These high school students are attending a college fair in Queens, New York. Depending on where they are applying, some may benefit from affirmative action admissions policies. There has been a backlash in some states because majority students have argued that affirmative action is equivalent to reverse discrimination.

Connerly, an African American libertarian businessman. In 2010, Arizona also banned affirmative action.

"RACE-BLIND" ADMISSIONS In the meantime, many public universities are trying to find "race-blind" ways to attract more minority students to their campuses. For example, Texas has established a program under which the top students at every high school in the state are guaranteed admission to the University of Texas, Austin. Originally, the guarantee applied to students who were in the top 10 percent of their graduating class. In 2009, the guarantee was limited to students in the top 8 percent of their class.

This policy ensures that the top students at minority-dominated inner-city schools can attend the state's leading public university. It also guarantees admission to the best white students from rural, often poor, communities. Previously, these students could not have hoped to attend the University of Texas. The losers are students from upscale metropolitan neighborhoods or suburbs who have high test scores but are not the top students at their schools. One result is that more students with high test scores enroll in less famous schools, such as Texas Tech University and the University of Texas, Dallas—to the benefit of these schools' reputations.

AMERICA AT ODDS *Civil Rights*

During the first part of the twentieth century, discrimination against African Americans and members of other minority groups was a social norm in the United States. Indeed, much of the nation's white population believed that the ability to discriminate was a constitutionally protected right. Today, the "right to discriminate" has very few defenders. America's laws—and its culture—now hold that discrimination on the basis of race, gender, religion, national origin, and many other characteristics is flatly unacceptable.

Even if civil rights are now broadly supported and protected by law, however, questions remain as to how far these protections should extend. Americans are at odds over a number of civil rights issues, including the following:

- If unauthorized immigrants have certain rights as *persons* under the Fourteenth Amendment to the Constitution, should these rights be construed broadly—or as narrowly as possible?

- Should same-sex marriages by lesbians and gay men be recognized—or prohibited?

- Should we allow lesbians and gay men to serve openly in the nation's armed forces—or should the "Don't ask, don't tell" policy be retained?

- Is affirmative action still a necessary policy—or should it be abandoned?

- When colleges and universities consider admissions, is it legitimate to promote racial, ethnic, gender, or socioeconomic diversity—or are such considerations just new forms of discrimination?

Take Action

Despite the progress that has been made toward attaining equal treatment for all groups of Americans, much remains to be done. Countless activist groups continue to pursue the goal of equality for all Americans. If you wish to contribute your time and effort toward this goal, there are hundreds of ways to go about it. You can easily find activist opportunities just by going to the Web sites of the groups listed in this chapter's *Politics on the Web* section on the following page. There, you will find links to groups that seek to protect and enhance the rights of African Americans, Latinos, women, persons with disabilities, and more.

Other groups you can contact if you would like to get involved include the Leadership Conference on Civil and Human Rights, which encourages people to contact Congress on matters of interest. Its Web site is **www.civilrights.org**. If you are interested in the rights of immigrants, a good place to start is the Justice for Immigrants Web site at **www.justiceforimmigrants.org**, where you can sign up to receive e-mails from the Immigrant Justice Action Network. If there are gatherings or events planned for your neighborhood, such as a demonstration for immigrants' rights, you can participate in them—or volunteer to help organize them. Justice for Immigrants was organized by twenty major Roman Catholic organizations. An additional source of information on Latino issues is the National Council of La Raza at **www.nclr.org**.

Finally, you can search the Web for blogs on a civil rights issue that particularly interests you, read about what others on that site are saying, and "tell the world" your opinion on the issue.

POLITICS ON THE
WEB

- Stanford University's Web site contains primary documents written by Martin Luther King, Jr., as well as secondary documents written about King. The URL for the Martin Luther King, Jr., Research and Education Institute is **mlk-kpp01.stanford.edu**

- If you are interested in learning more about the Equal Employment Opportunity Commission (EEOC), the laws it enforces, and how to file a charge with the EEOC, go to **www.eeoc.gov**

- The home page for the National Association for the Advancement of Colored People (NAACP), which contains extensive information about African American civil rights issues, is **www.naacp.org**

- For information on Hispanics in the United States, the League of United Latin American Citizens is a good source. You can find it at **www.lulac.org**

- The home page of the National Organization for Women (NOW) has links to numerous resources containing information on the rights and status of women both in the United States and around the world. You can find NOW's home page at **www.now.org**

- You can access the Web site of the Feminist Majority Foundation, which focuses on equality for women, at **www.feminist.org**

- For information on the Americans with Disabilities Act, including the text of the act, go to **www.jan. wvu.edu/links/adalinks.htm**

- The Gay and Lesbian Alliance against Defamation has an online news bureau. To find this organization's home page, go to **www.glaad.org**

 CourseMate   Access CourseMate to review and expand on this chapter through quizzes, flashcards, learning objectives, interactive timelines, a crossword puzzle, audio summaries, video, critical-thinking activities, simulations, and more.

{ Explore It Your Way! }

Interactive eBooks • Embedded Study Tools   Take your learning online: **4ltrpress.cengage.com/politicalscience**

6 Interest Groups

LEARNING OBJECTIVES

LO1 Explain what an interest group is, why interest groups form, and how interest groups function in American politics.

LO2 Indicate how interest groups differ from political parties.

LO3 Identify the various types of interest groups.

LO4 Discuss how the activities of interest groups help to shape government policymaking.

LO5 Describe how interest groups are regulated by government.

CourseMate

AMERICA AT
ODDS
Are Secret Ballots Essential in Union Elections?

The National Labor Relations Act of 1935 established the right of employees to form unions and the right of those unions to engage in collective bargaining—negotiation of contracts for the workers the unions represent—along with the right to strike. The decision on whether or not employees should be represented by a union is typically made though a secret-ballot election.

In the early 2000s, with union membership declining, unions began pressuring members of Congress to pass legislation to help unions organize. The result was the proposed Employee Free Choice Act (EFCA), which has commonly been referred to as "card-check" legislation. The card-check system would in most instances replace privately held, federally supervised secret-ballot voting in collective decisions to form unions. Currently, elections are not mandatory, and an employer may voluntarily recognize a union if the union presents evidence that most employees support unionization. This evidence may include cards signed by a majority of employees. But the employer always has a right to ask for an election in spite of this evidence. Under the proposed law, that would no longer be the case. Organizers would simply need to gather signatures from more than 50 percent of the employees in a workplace. Once 50 percent of the workers had signed those cards, the employer would be required to recognize the union and negotiate with it.

Secret Ballots Are a Democracy's Only Choice

Recently, a group of congressional representatives who were concerned about workers' rights in Mexico wrote to officials in that country stating, "We are writing to encourage you to use the secret ballot in all union recognition elections. . . . We feel that the secret ballot is absolutely necessary in order to ensure that workers are not intimidated into voting for a union they might not otherwise choose." Former Democratic presidential candidate George McGovern had this to say about the card-check legislation: "Workers would lose the freedom to express their will in private, the right to make a decision without anyone peering over their shoulder, free from fear of reprisal."

A major reason why unions spent half a billion dollars in the 2008 elections is because they were unified behind one driving goal—passing card-check legislation. In response to the unions' actions, McGovern stated that "part of being a steward of democracy means telling our friends 'no' when they press for a course that in the long run may weaken labor and disrupt a tried and trusted method for conducting honest elections."

Card-Check Union Organizing Will Level the Playing Field

The late senator Ted Kennedy (D., Mass.) claimed that card-check legislation was necessary to "level the playing field" between unions and management. He argued that there are large loopholes in today's labor laws that allow employers to intimidate their employees prior to and during secret elections. Representative George Miller (D., Calif.) contended that management in nonunion companies can "browbeat" workers about unions anytime and anywhere in the workplace. Union backers point out that it may be illegal to fire an employee for supporting a union drive, but it happens again and again. It is very difficult for an employee to prove that he or she was fired for supporting a union rather than for some other reason.

Proponents of the EFCA agree that it will help increase union membership. They argue that this is good not only for union workers but also for other workers. Workers in general, they say, benefit when some of them strengthen their negotiating positions. Whenever a union effectively organizes another workplace, nonunion workers' bargaining positions are strengthened as well.

WHERE DO YOU STAND?

1. How important is it for union elections to be held in secret?
2. Do you believe that an expansion in union membership can benefit all workers? Why or why not?

EXPLORE THIS ISSUE ONLINE

- Employer and conservative groups have organized the Coalition for a Democratic Workplace, a broad umbrella group, to oppose the EFCA card-check legislation. You can find that group's Web site at www.myprivateballot.com.
- The two largest union federations support the EFCA, of course. Find out what the American Federation of Labor–Congress of Industrial Organizations (AFL-CIO) says about it at www.aflcio.org/joinaunion/voiceatwork/efca. Change to Win, the nation's second-largest union alliance, argues for the EFCA at www.changetowin.org/issues/workers-rights/freedom-to-join-together-in-unions.html.

Introduction

The groups supporting and opposing card checks for unionization provide but one example of how Americans form groups to pursue or protect their interests. All of us have interests that we would like to have represented in government: farmers want higher prices for their products, young people want good educational opportunities, and environmentalists want cleaner air and water.

The old saying that there is strength in numbers is certainly true in American politics. Special interests significantly influence American government and politics. Indeed, some Americans think that this influence is so great that it jeopardizes representative democracy. Others maintain that interest groups are a natural consequence of democracy. After all, throughout our nation's history, people have organized into groups to protect special interests. Because of the important role played by interest groups in the American system of government, in this chapter we examine such groups. We look at what they are, why they are formed, and how they influence policymaking.

"Politics is about **PEOPLE,** not politicians."
~ SCOTT SIMMS ~
CANADIAN POLITICIAN
B. 1969

LO1 *Interest Groups and American Government*

An **interest group** is an organized group of people sharing common objectives who actively attempt to influence government policymakers through direct and indirect methods. Whatever their goals—more or fewer social services, higher or lower prices—interest groups pursue these goals on every level and in every branch of government.

On any given day in Washington, D.C., you can see national interest groups in action. If you eat breakfast in the Senate dining room, you might see congressional committee staffers reviewing testimony with representatives from women's groups. Later that morning, you might visit the Supreme Court and watch a civil rights lawyer arguing on behalf of a client in a discrimination suit. Lunch in a popular Washington restaurant might find you listening in on a conversation between an agricultural lobbyist and a congressional representative.

That afternoon you might visit an executive department, such as the Department of Labor, and watch bureaucrats working out rules and regulations with representatives from a business interest group. Then you might stroll past the headquarters of the National Rifle Association (NRA), AARP (formerly the American Association of Retired Persons), or the National Wildlife Federation.

The Constitutional Right to Petition the Government

The right to form interest groups and to lobby the government is protected by the Bill of Rights. The First Amendment guarantees the right of the people "to petition the Government for a redress of grievances." This important right sometimes gets lost among the other, more well-known First Amendment guarantees, such as the freedoms of religion, speech, and the press. Nonetheless, the right to petition the government is as important and fundamental to our democracy as the other First Amendment rights.

The right to petition the government allows citizens and groups of citizens to lobby members of Congress and

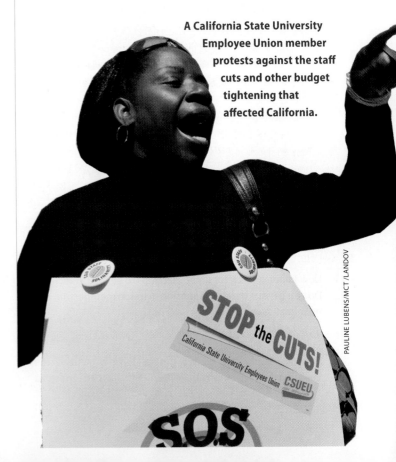

A California State University Employee Union member protests against the staff cuts and other budget tightening that affected California.

PAULINE LUBENS/MCT /LANDOV

interest group An organized group of individuals sharing common objectives who actively attempt to influence policymakers.

other government officials, to sue the government, and to submit petitions to the government. Whenever someone writes to her or his congressional representative for help with a problem, such as not receiving a Social Security payment, that person is petitioning the government.

Why Interest Groups Form

The United States is a vast country of many regions, scores of ethnic groups, and a huge variety of businesses and occupations. The number of potential interests that can be represented is therefore very large. Beyond the sheer size of the country, however, there are a number of specific reasons why the United States has as many interest groups as it does.

It is worth remembering that not all groups are interest groups. A group becomes an interest group when it seeks to affect the policies or practices of the government. Many groups do not meet such a standard. A social group, for example, may be formed to entertain or educate its members, with no broader purpose. Churches, organized to facilitate worship and community, frequently have no political aims. (Indeed, certain political activities, such as campaigning for or against candidates for office, could cost a church its tax-exempt status.)

A group founded with little or no desire to influence the government can become an interest group, however, if its members decide that the government's policies are important to them. Alternatively, lobbying the government may initially be only one of several activities pursued by a group and then grow to become the group's primary purpose. The National Rifle Association (NRA) is an example of this process. From its foundation in 1871 until the 1930s, the group took little part in politics. As late as the 1970s, a large share of the NRA's members joined for reasons that had nothing to do with politics. Many joined solely to participate in firearms training programs or to win marksman certifications. The NRA continues to provide such services today, but it is now so heavily politicized that anyone likely to take out a membership must broadly agree with the NRA's political positions.

MORE GOVERNMENT, MORE INTEREST GROUPS Interest groups may form—and existing groups may become more politically active—when the government expands its scope of activities. More government, in other words, means more interest groups. Prior to the 1970s, for example, the various levels of government were not nearly as active in attempting to regulate the use of firearms as they were thereafter. This change provides one explanation of why the NRA is much more politically active today than it was years ago. Consider another example—AARP, formerly the American Association of

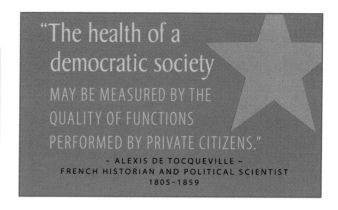

"The health of a democratic society MAY BE MEASURED BY THE QUALITY OF FUNCTIONS PERFORMED BY PRIVATE CITIZENS."
~ ALEXIS DE TOCQUEVILLE ~
FRENCH HISTORIAN AND POLITICAL SCIENTIST
1805–1859

Retired Persons. AARP is a major lobbying force that seeks to preserve or enhance Social Security and Medicare benefits for citizens sixty-five years old and older. Before the creation of Social Security in the 1930s, however, the federal government did not provide income support to the elderly, and there would have been little reason for an organization such as AARP to exist. For more details on the NRA, AARP, and a few other key interest groups, see Figure 6–1 on the following page.

DEFENDING THE GROUP'S INTERESTS Interest groups also may come into existence in response to a perceived threat to a group's interests. In the example of the NRA, the threat was an increase in the frequency of attempts to regulate or even ban firearms. This increase threatened the interests of gun owners. As another example, the National Right to Life Committee formed in response to *Roe v. Wade,* the United States Supreme Court's decision that legalized abortion. Interest groups can also form in reaction to the creation of other interest groups, thus pitting two groups against each other. Political scientist David B. Truman coined the term *disturbance theory* for his description of this kind of defensive formation of interest groups.[1]

THE IMPORTANCE OF LEADERS Political scientist Robert H. Salisbury provided another analysis of the organization of interest groups that he dubbed *entrepreneurial theory.* This line of thought focuses on the importance of the leaders who establish the organization. The desire of such individuals to guarantee a viable organization is important to the group's survival.[2] AARP is an example of a group with an important founder—Dr. Ethel Percy Andrus, a retired high school principal. Andrus organized the group in 1958 to let older Americans purchase health-care insurance collectively. As with the NRA, AARP did not develop into a lobbying powerhouse until years after it was founded.

INCENTIVES TO JOIN A GROUP The French political observer and traveler Alexis de Tocqueville wrote in 1835 that Americans have a tendency to form "associations" and have perfected "the art of pursuing in common the object of

Figure 6-1

Profiles of Selected Interest Groups

Name: AARP
Founded: 1958
Membership: 40 million working or retired persons 50 years of age or older.
Description: AARP strives to better the lives of older people, especially in the areas of health care, worker equity, and minority affairs. AARP sponsors community crime prevention programs, research on the problems of aging, and a mail-order pharmacy.
Budget: $1,140,000,000
Address: 601 E St. N.W., Washington, DC 20049
Phone: (888) 687-2277   **Web site:** www.aarp.org

Name: U.S. Chamber of Commerce
Founded: 1912
Membership: 3 million businesses.
Description: The Chamber is the world's largest business federation, also representing local chambers and industry associations. More than 96 percent of members are small businesses with 100 employees or fewer. The Chamber fights for free enterprise before Congress, the White House, regulatory agencies, and the courts.
Budget: $150,000,000
Address: 1615 H Street N.W., Washington, DC 20062
Phone: (800) 638-6582   **Web site:** www.uschamber.com

Name: National Education Association (NEA)
Founded: 1857
Membership: 3.2 million elementary and secondary school teachers, college and university professors, academic administrators, and others.
Description: The NEA's committees investigate and take action in the areas of benefits, civil rights, educational support, personnel, higher education, human relations, legislation, minority affairs, and women's concerns. Many NEA locals function as labor unions.
Budget: $307,000,000
Address: 1201 16th St. N.W., Washington, DC 20036
Phone: (202) 833-4000   **Web site:** www.nea.org

Name: National Rifle Association (NRA)
Founded: 1871
Membership: Nearly 4 million persons interested in firearms.
Description: The NRA promotes rifle, pistol, and shotgun shooting, as well as hunting, gun collecting, and home firearm safety. It educates police firearm instructors and sponsors teams to participate in international competitions.
Budget: $200,000,000
Address: 11250 Waples Mill Road, Fairfax, VA 22030
Phone: (800) 672-3888   **Web site:** www.nra.org

Name: The Sierra Club (SC)
Founded: 1892
Membership: 1.3 million.
Description: The Sierra Club protects and conserves natural resources; saves endangered areas; and resolves problems associated with wilderness, clean air, energy conservation, and land use. Its committees are concerned with agriculture, economics, environmental education, hazardous materials, the international environment, Native American sites, political education, and water resources.
Budget: $40,000,000
Address: 85 2d St., 2d Floor, San Francisco, CA 94105
Phone: (415) 977-5500   **Web site:** www.sierraclub.org

their common desires." "In no other country of the world," said Tocqueville, "has the principle of association been more successfully used or applied to a greater multitude of objectives than in America."[3] Of course, Tocqueville could not foresee the thousands of associations that now exist in this country. Surveys show that more than 85 percent of Americans belong to at least one group. Table 6–1 on the facing page shows the percentage of Americans who belong to various types of groups today.

Political scientists have identified various reasons why people join interest groups. Often, people have one or more incentives to join such organizations. If a group

Table 6-1

Percentage of Americans Belonging to Various Groups

Health organizations	16%
Social clubs	17
Neighborhood groups	18
Hobby, garden, and computer clubs	19
PTA and school groups	21
Professional and trade associations	27
Health, sport, and country clubs	30
Religious groups	61

Source: AARP.

stands for something that you believe is very important, you can gain considerable satisfaction from taking action. Such satisfaction is referred to as a **purposive incentive.** Some people enjoy the camaraderie and sense of belonging that comes from associating with other people who share their interests and goals. That enjoyment can be called a **solidary incentive.** Finally, some groups offer their members material incentives for joining, such as discounts on products, subscriptions, or group insurance programs. Each of these could be characterized as a **material incentive.** But sometimes none of these incentives is enough to persuade people to join.

Alexis de Tocqueville (1805–1859) was a well-known French political historian. He lived during a time of political upheaval in France and took a keen interest in the new democracy in America. He toured the United States and Canada as a young man and collected his observations in *Democracy in America*, which was published in 1835.

THE GRANGER COLLECTION

THE FREE RIDER PROBLEM   This world in which we live is one of scarce resources that can be used to create *private goods* and *public goods*. Most of the goods and services that you use are private goods. If you consume them, no one else can consume them at the same time. If you eat a sandwich, no one else can have it. With the other class of goods, called public goods, however, your use of a good does not diminish its use by someone else. National defense is a good example. If this country is protected through its national defense system, your protection from enemy invasion does not reduce anybody else's protection.

People cannot be excluded from enjoying a public good, such as national defense, just because they did not pay for it. As a result, public goods are often provided by the government, which can force people to pay for the public good through taxation.

Lobbying, collective bargaining by labor unions, and other forms of representation can also be public goods. If an interest group is successful in lobbying for laws that will improve air quality, for example, everyone who breathes that air will benefit, whether they paid for the lobbying effort or not. The existence of persons who benefit but do not contribute is called the **free rider problem.** Much of what we know about the free rider problem comes from Mancur Olson's classic work of political science, *The Logic of Collective Action.*[4]

In some instances, the free rider problem can be overcome. For example, social pressure may persuade some people to join or donate to a group for fear of being ostracized. For this and other reasons, it is much easier for an interest shared by a relatively small number of people to organize.

The government can also step in to ensure that the burden of lobbying for the public good is shared by all. When the government classifies interest groups as nonprofit organizations, it confers on them tax-exempt status. The groups' operating costs are reduced because they do not have to pay taxes, and the impact of the government's lost revenue is absorbed by all taxpayers.

purposive incentive A reason to join an interest group— satisfaction resulting from working for a cause in which one believes.

solidary incentive A reason to join an interest group— pleasure in associating with like-minded individuals.

material incentive Practical benefits from joining an interest group, such as discounts, subscriptions, or group insurance.

free rider problem The difficulty that exists when individuals can enjoy the outcome of an interest group's efforts without having to contribute, such as by becoming members of the group.

How Interest Groups Function in American Politics

Despite the bad press that interest groups tend to get in the United States, they do serve several purposes in American politics:

- Interest groups help bridge the gap between citizens and government and enable citizens to explain their views on policies to public officials.

- Interest groups help raise public awareness and inspire action on various issues.

- Interest groups often provide public officials with specialized and detailed information that might be difficult to obtain otherwise. This information may be useful in making policy choices.

- Interest groups serve as another check on public officials to make sure that they are carrying out their duties responsibly.

ACCESS TO GOVERNMENT In a sense, the American system of government invites the participation of interest groups by offering many points of access for groups wishing to influence policy. Consider the possibilities at just the federal level. An interest group can lobby members of Congress to act in the interests of the group. If the Senate passes a bill opposed by the group, the group's lobbying efforts can shift to the House of Representatives. If the House passes the bill, the group can try to influence the new law's application by lobbying the executive agency that is responsible for implementing the law. The group might even challenge the law in court, directly (by filing a lawsuit) or indirectly (by filing a brief as an *amicus curiae*,[5] or "friend of the court").

PLURALIST THEORY The **pluralist theory** of American democracy focuses on the participation of groups in a decentralized government structure that offers many points of access to policymakers. According to the pluralist theory, politics is a contest among various interest groups. These groups vie with one another—at all levels of government—to gain benefits for their members. Pluralists maintain that the influence of interest groups on government is not undemocratic because individual interests are indirectly represented in the policymaking process through these groups. Although not every American belongs to an interest group, inevitably some group will represent each individual's interests.

> **pluralist theory** A theory that views politics as a contest among various interest groups—at all levels of government—to gain benefits for their members.

Each interest is satisfied to some extent through the compromises made in settling conflicts among competing interest groups.

Pluralists also contend that because of the extensive number of interest groups vying for political benefits, no one group can dominate the political process. Additionally, because most people have more than one interest, conflicts among groups do not divide the nation into hostile camps. Not all scholars agree that this is how interest groups function, however.

LO2 *How Do Interest Groups Differ from Political Parties?*

Although interest groups and political parties are both groups of people joined together for political purposes, they differ in several important ways. As you will read in Chapter 7, a political party is a group of individuals who organize to win elections, operate the government, and determine policy. Interest groups, in contrast, do not seek to win elections or operate the government, although they do seek to influence policy.

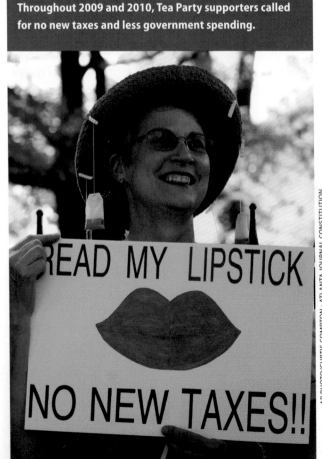

Throughout 2009 and 2010, Tea Party supporters called for no new taxes and less government spending.

READ MY LIPSTICK NO NEW TAXES!!

Interest groups differ from political parties in the following ways:

- Interest groups are often policy *specialists*, whereas political parties are policy *generalists*. Political parties are broad-based organizations that must attract the support of many opposing groups and consider a large number of issues. Interest groups, in contrast, may have only a handful of key policies to push. An environmental group will not be as concerned about the economic status of Hispanics as it is about polluters. A manufacturing group is more involved with pushing for fewer regulations than it is with inner-city poverty.

- Interest groups are usually more tightly organized than political parties. They are often financed through contributions or dues-paying memberships. Organizers of interest groups communicate with members and potential members through conferences, mailings, newsletters, and electronic formats, such as e-mail, Facebook, and Twitter.

- A political party's main sphere of influence is the electoral system. Parties run candidates for political office. Interest groups may try to influence the outcome of elections, but unlike parties, they do not compete for public office. Although a candidate for office may be sympathetic to—or even be a member of—a certain group, he or she does not run for election as a candidate of that group.

LO3 *Different Types of Interest Groups*

American democracy embraces almost every conceivable type of interest group, and the number is increasing rapidly. No one has ever compiled a *Who's Who* of interest groups, but you can get an idea of the number and variety by looking through the annually published *Encyclopedia of Associations*.

Some interest groups have large memberships. AARP, for example, has about 40 million members. Others, such as the Colorado Auctioneers Association, have barely a hundred members. Some, such as the U.S. Chamber of Commerce, are household names and have been in existence for many years, while others crop up overnight. Some are highly structured and are run by full-time professionals, while others are loosely structured and informal.

The most common interest groups are those that promote private interests. These groups seek public policies that benefit the economic interests of their members and work against policies that threaten those interests. Other groups, sometimes called **public-interest groups,** are formed with the broader goal of working for the "public good." The American Civil Liberties Union and Common Cause are examples. Let there be no mistake, though, about the name *public interest*. There is no such thing as a clear public interest in a nation of more than 310 million diverse people. The two so-called public-interest groups just mentioned do not represent all American people but only a relatively small part of the American population. In reality, all lobbying groups, organizations, and other political entities always represent special interests.

> **public-interest group**
> An interest group formed for the purpose of working for the "public good." Examples of public-interest groups are the American Civil Liberties Union and Common Cause.

Business Interest Groups

Business has long been well organized for effective action. Hundreds of business groups are now operating in Washington, D.C., in the fifty state capitals, and at the local level across the country. Table 6–2 below lists some top business interests. Two umbrella organizations that include small and large corporations and businesses are the U.S. Chamber of Commerce and the National Association of Manufacturers (NAM). In addition to representing about 3 million individual businesses, the Chamber has more than three thousand local, state, and regional affiliates. It has become a major voice for millions of small businesses.

Table 6–2
Top Business Campaign Donors, 1989–2010

Firm or Group	Total, 1989–2010
1. AT&T Inc.	$45,279,674
2. National Association of Realtors	36,626,273
3. Goldman Sachs (bank)	32,497,752
4. Citigroup Inc. (bank)	27,448,288
5. National Automobile Dealers Assn.	24,968,258
6. United Parcel Service	24,675,166
7. Altria Group (cigarettes)	24,210,766
8. American Bankers Assn.	23,071,721
9. National Assn. of Home Builders	22,655,655
10. National Beer Wholesalers Assn.	21,822,595

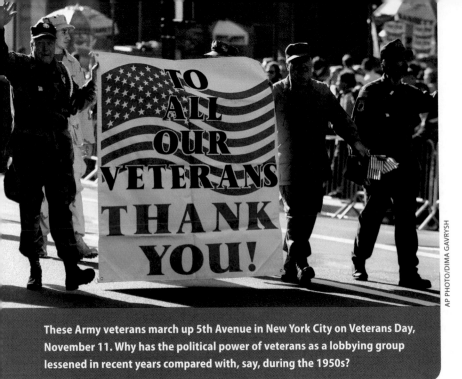

These Army veterans march up 5th Avenue in New York City on Veterans Day, November 11. Why has the political power of veterans as a lobbying group lessened in recent years compared with, say, during the 1950s?

AP PHOTO/DIMA GAVRYSH

TRADE ORGANIZATIONS The hundreds of **trade organizations** are far less visible than the Chamber of Commerce and the NAM, but they are also important in seeking policies that assist their members. Trade organizations usually support policies that benefit specific industries. For example, people in the oil industry work for policies that favor the development of oil as an energy resource. Other business groups work for policies that favor the development of coal, solar power, and nuclear power. Trucking companies work for policies that would lower their taxes. Railroad companies would, of course, not want other forms of transportation to receive special tax breaks, because that would hurt their business.

HOW BUSINESSS INTEREST GROUPS SUPPORT BOTH PARTIES Traditionally, business interest groups have been viewed as staunch supporters of the Republican Party. This is because Republicans are more likely to promote a "hands-off" government policy toward business. Over the last decade, however, donations from corporations to the Democratic National Committee have more than doubled. Why would business groups make contributions to the Democratic National Committee?

One reason is that in some fields, business leaders today are more likely to be Democrats than in the past. Financial industry leaders were once almost entirely Republican, but today many of them support the Democrats. Information technology, a

> **trade organization** An association formed by members of a particular industry, such as the oil industry or the trucking industry, to develop common standards and goals for the industry. Trade organizations, as interest groups, lobby government for legislation or regulations that specifically benefit their groups.

new industry, contains both Republicans and Democrats.

An additional reason why many business interests support both parties is to ensure that they will benefit regardless of who wins the elections. Fred McChesney, a professor of law and business, offers another reason why business interests might want to contribute to both parties. He argues that campaign contributions are often made not to gain political favors but rather to avoid political disfavor. Just as government officials can take away wealth from citizens (in the form of taxes, for example), politicians can extort from private enterprises payments *not* to damage their business.[6]

Business interests have often wielded great power. In recent years, the financial industry has been especially successful in influencing the government. We discuss that issue in this chapter's *Our Government Faces a Troubled Economy* feature on the following page.

Labor Interest Groups

Interest groups representing labor have been some of the most influential groups in our country's history. They date back to at least 1886, when the American Federation of Labor (AFL) was formed. The largest and most powerful labor interest group today is the AFL-CIO (the American Federation of Labor–Congress of Industrial Organizations), a confederation of fifty-six unions representing 11 million members. Unions not affiliated with the AFL-CIO also represent millions of members. The Change to Win federation consists of seven unions and 6 million workers. Dozens of other unions are independent. Examples include the National Education Association, the United Electrical Workers (UE), and the Major League Baseball Players Association. We list some top labor groups in Table 6–3 on page 128.

UNION GOALS Like labor unions everywhere, American unions press for policies to improve working conditions and ensure better pay for their members. Unions may compete for new members. In many states, for example, the National Education Association and the AFL-CIO's American Federation of Teachers compete fiercely for members.

THE DECLINE OF UNIONS Although unions were highly influential in the 1930s, 1940s, and 1950s, their strength and political power have waned in the last

OUR GOVERNMENT FACES A TROUBLED ECONOMY

Lobbying by the Financial Industry

From the beginning, helping out the financial industry was a key part of our government's response to the Great Recession. This help was necessary because finance is the lifeblood of our economy. When the crisis became acute in 2008, financial institutions were the ones immediately threatened. Investment banks were among the hardest hit.

A Little History, First

In 2004, the heads of five major investment banks gathered at the Securities and Exchange Commission (SEC). The bankers convinced the SEC to lift a rule that required them to hold reserves as a cushion against losses on their investments. Those five banks, which included Goldman Sachs, then went on an investment spree the likes of which the world had never seen. They created trillions of dollars of mortgage-backed securities and credit derivatives (a form of insurance for investors). The head of Goldman Sachs at that time was Henry M. Paulson, Jr.

Fast-forward four years. All five banks had either gone bankrupt or been bailed out by the federal government. Who made the bailout decisions? None other than Henry M. Paulson, Jr., secretary of the Treasury under President George W. Bush. A huge share of Paulson's $700 billion bank bailout bill helped his friends and colleagues in the investment banking business. Critics complained that Paulson helped bankers, rather than the banking industry.

Reregulating the Financial Industry

The belief that the financial industry caused the Great Recession became nearly universal. Whether that was true or not, calls for financial industry reforms echoed through Congress. The result was the 2,319-page Restoring American Financial Stability Act of 2010. Throughout the months prior to passage of the act, there was intense lobbying in Congress to shape the new legislation.

The Lobbyists Go to Work

Lobbying on tax issues alone is a business worth more than $3.5 billion a year. The financial reform legislation, the most sweeping package of changes since the New Deal, has been called "a Super Bowl for lobbyists." What do interests get for what they pay to lobbyists? Take one example. The new financial reform law contains a rule to keep banks from putting their own funds into risky ventures. The argument was that this rule would limit practices that led to the financial meltdown in 2008. Many beneficiaries of such deals wanted to modify that rule, and their lobbyists went to work. Most mutual-fund companies won complete exemption from the rule. Another provision lets banks invest up to 3 percent of their own capital. Still another change lets banks make investments in small or start-up businesses that "promote the public welfare."

Consumers versus Finance

The Consumer Federation of America fought hard to make sure the new financial reform law benefited consumers, but that group had only three lawyers working on the entire bill. In contrast, according to the legislative director for the Consumer Federation, "the banking industry can have three people working on just a single paragraph." Lobbyists for the banking and financial industries wrote numerous "white papers" to bolster their arguments. These documents provided an unending flow of alternative-language proposals for the new financial reform bill.

Such lobbying typically weakens a bill as it passes through the legislative process. An odd thing happened with the financial reform bill, however. Even while some provisions became more and more generous to the industry, others actually became tougher. As Congressman Barney Frank (D., Mass.) observed, "The more important an issue is to the public, the less important the lobbyists are." Because the financial industry had become so unpopular, legislators could hope to win votes by appearing to be strict with it.

You Be the Judge Some commentators argue that lobbyists are not the most important reason for the financial industry's influence. Policymakers have simply come to believe that what is good for Wall Street is good for the United States. Many investment bankers go on to become leaders in the executive branch of government. How might such individuals influence policy?

several decades, as you can see in Figure 6–2 on the following page. Today, members of organized labor make up only 12.4 percent of the **labor force**—defined as all of the people over the age of sixteen who are working or actively looking for jobs.

There are several reasons why the power of organized

labor force All of the people over the age of sixteen who are working or actively looking for jobs.

Table 6–3

Top Labor Campaign Donors, 1989–2010

Union or Group	Total, 1989–2010
1. Amer. Fed. of State, County and Municipal Employees	$42,764,261
2. Intl. Brotherhood of Electrical Workers	32,282,895
3. National Education Assn.	30,606,680
4. Laborers Union	29,604,550
5. Teamsters Union	28,510,684
6. Service Employees International Union	28,461,982
7. Carpenters & Joiners Union	28,386,933
8. American Federation of Teachers	27,711,391
9. Communications Workers of America	27,543,796
10. United Auto Workers	26,241,902

labor has declined in the United States. One is the continuing fall in the proportion of the nation's workforce employed in such blue-collar activities as manufacturing and transportation. These sectors have always been among the most heavily unionized. Another important factor in labor's decline, however, is the general political environment. Forming and maintaining unions is more difficult in the United States than in most other industrial nations. Among the world's wealthy democracies, the United States is one of the most politically conservative, at least on economic issues. Economic conservatives are traditionally hostile to labor unions. Further, many business owners in the United States do not accept unions as legitimate institutions and will do anything within their power to ensure that their own businesses remain unorganized.

The impact of the political environment on labor's organizing ability can be easily seen by comparing rates of unionization in various states. These rates are especially low in conservative southern states. Georgia and North Carolina are both major manufacturing states, but in Georgia, unions represent only 4.6 percent of the workforce, and in North Carolina, only 5 percent. Compare these figures with rates in more liberal states, such as California and New York: unions represent 19.5 percent of the workforce in California and 26.6 percent in New York. One factor that depresses unionization rates in many states is the existence of so-called **right-to-work laws.** These laws ban unions from collecting dues or other fees from workers that they represent but who have not actually joined the

right-to-work laws Laws that ban unions from collecting dues or other fees from workers that they represent but who have not actually joined the union.

union. Such laws create a significant free rider problem for unions. Twenty-two states in the South, Great Plains, and Rocky Mountain region have right-to-work laws.

PUBLIC SECTOR UNIONS While labor groups have generally experienced a decline in lobbying power, public employee unions have grown in both numbers and political clout in recent years. Public employees enjoy some of the nation's best health-care and retirement benefits because of the efforts of their labor groups.

Professional Interest Groups

Most professions that require advanced education or specialized training have organizations to protect and promote their interests. These groups are concerned mainly with the standards of their professions, but they also work to influence government policy. Major professional groups include the American Medical Association (AMA), representing physicians; the American Bar Association, representing lawyers; and the American Association for Justice, representing trial lawyers. In addition, there are dozens of less well known and less politically active professional groups, such as the National Association of Social Workers and the American Political Science Association.

Competing interests sometimes divide professional interest groups from one another. For example, consider the issue of tort reform. Advocates of tort reform contend that it is too easy for lawyers to sue physicians, insurance companies, and other businesses, and that generous settlements drive up the cost of health care and other goods. The AMA generally favors tort reform. The American Association for Justice, naturally, opposes it.

Figure 6–2

Union Membership, 1952 to Present

This figure shows the percentage of the workforce who are members of unions from 1952 to the present. As you can see, union membership has declined significantly over the past several decades.

Agricultural Interest Groups

Many groups work for general agricultural interests at all levels of government. Three broad-based agricultural groups represent millions of American farmers, from peanut farmers to dairy producers to tobacco growers. They are the American Farm Bureau Federation (Farm Bureau), the National Grange, and the National Farmers Union. The Farm Bureau, representing more than 5.5 million families (a majority of whom are not actually farm families), is the largest and generally the most effective of the three. Founded in 1919, the Farm Bureau achieved one of its greatest early successes when it helped to obtain government guarantees of "fair" prices during the Great Depression of the 1930s.[7] The Grange, founded in 1867, is the oldest group. It has units in 3,600 communities in thirty-seven states, with a total membership of about 300,000. The National Farmers Union comprises approximately 250,000 farm and ranch families.

Interest groups representing farmers have been spectacularly successful in winning subsidies from the federal government. Farm subsidies cost the taxpayer at least $20 billion per year. Resulting higher prices for food may add another $12 billion to the bill. European farmers, however, have been even more successful in winning subsidies, as we explain in this chapter's feature *The Rest of the World: Europe's Common Agricultural Policy* on the following page.

Producers of various specific farm commodities, such as dairy products, soybeans, grain, fruit, corn, cotton, beef, and sugar beets, have formed their own organizations. These specialized groups, such as the Associated Milk Producers, Inc., also have a strong influence on farm legislation.

Consumer Interest Groups

Groups organized for the protection of consumer rights were very active in the 1960s and 1970s. Some are still active today. The best known and perhaps the most effective are the public-interest groups organized under the leadership of consumer activist Ralph Nader. Another well-known group is Consumers Union, a nonprofit organization started in 1936. In addition to publishing *Consumer Reports,* Consumers Union has been influential in pushing for the removal of phosphates

A number of national interest groups protect the rights of farmers. Through their lobbying efforts and campaign contributions, these groups have wielded significant influence in Congress.

AP PHOTO/MICHAEL CONROY

from detergents, lead from gasoline, and pesticides from food. Consumers Union strongly criticizes government agencies when they appear to act against consumer interests.

Consumer groups have been organized in every city. They deal with such problems as poor housing, discrimination against minorities and women, discrimination in the granting of credit, and business inaction on consumer complaints.

Identity Interest Groups

Americans who share the same race, ethnicity, gender, or other characteristic often have important common interests. African Americans, for example, have a powerful interest in combating the racism and racial discrimination that have marked American history from the beginning. Slaves, of course, were not able to form interest groups. For many years after the abolition of slavery, organizing African American interest groups remained impossibly dangerous. Such groups did not come into existence until the twentieth century. The National Association for the Advancement of Colored People was founded in 1909, and the National Urban League was created in 1910. During the civil rights movement of the 1950s and 1960s, African Americans organized a number of new groups, some of which lasted (the Southern Christian Leadership Conference, founded in 1957) and some of which did not (the Student Nonviolent Coordinating Committee, organized in 1960).

Europe's Common Agricultural Policy

Lobbying efforts by America's farmers have been highly successful—farmers receive tens of billions of dollars of subsidies every year. Consumers in this country pay higher food prices because of such successful lobbying. We are not alone, however. The European Union (EU) doles out agricultural subsidies at an even greater rate than we do.

It's All in the CAP

The EU's agricultural subsidies are part of its Common Agricultural Policy (CAP). The CAP directly pays farmers subsidies for crops and for specific land uses—sometimes for no use at all. The CAP also provides price supports and minimum prices. Specific agricultural goods brought into the EU are taxed, and there are quotas on imports, too. Production quotas limit the supply of certain products such as milk and grain. Not only does the CAP effectively prevent competition from non-European farmers in European markets, but it also injures those farmers by dumping "butter mountains" and "wine lakes" cheaply onto the world market. African and Asian dairy, tomato, and poultry farmers cannot keep up with cheap competition from Europe.

How Successful Are Farm Lobbyists in the EU?

The EU's $130 billion annual budget is paid for by levies on the twenty-seven member nations, which must fund their contributions through taxes. Lobbyists for farming interests have succeeded in capturing 48 percent of this budget. A few brave politicians in Britain and Sweden have called for the abolition of the CAP. The agriculture lobby is strong enough to prevent such a change, however, and farm subsidies in Europe will continue for the foreseeable future.

For Critical Analysis *Farmers make up only about 1 percent of the population in the United States and 5 percent in Europe. Why are they so successful, nonetheless, in winning so many taxpayer dollars?*

The campaigns for dignity and equality of Native Americans, Latinos, women, lesbians and gay men, Americans with disabilities, and many other groups have all resulted in important interest groups. You learned about many of these organizations in Chapter 5. One identity-based group not discussed in that chapter is older Americans. Senior citizens are numerous, are politically active, and have a great deal at stake in debates over certain programs, such as Social Security and Medicare. As a result, groups representing them, such as the AARP, can be a potent political force.

Ideological Interest Groups

Some interest groups are not organized to promote an economic interest or a collective identity but a shared political perspective or ideology. Examples include MoveOn, an Internet-oriented liberal group, and the Club for Growth, a conservative, antitax organization.

The highly decentralized Tea Party movement, which sprang into life in 2009, has been described as an ideological interest group. The activities of the Tea Party movement, however, raise the question of whether it really is an interest group at all. The point is that interest groups, while they are often very concerned about who wins an election and may endorse candidates, do not themselves attempt to gain control of the machinery of government. Most Tea Party leaders claim that the movement is nonpartisan and that it contains not only Republicans but independents, Libertarians, and even some Democrats. Still, some Tea Party groups have attempted to gain control of local Republican Party organizations. It may be only a matter of terminology, but political scientists refer to groups that compete for control of a political party as *factions*, not interest groups. You will learn more about factions in Chapter 7.

Environmental groups have supported pollution controls, wilderness protection, and clean-air legislation. They have opposed strip mining, nuclear power plants, logging activities, chemical waste dumps, and many other potential environmental hazards. In the past, environmental groups have been characterized as single-interest groups, not ideological organizations. Issues such as global warming, however, have led many modern environmental groups to advocate sweeping changes to the entire economy. Groups with such broad agendas could be considered a type of ideological interest group. Environmental interest groups range from traditional organizations such as the National Wildlife Federation, with 4 million members, to more radical groups such as Greenpeace USA, with a membership of 250,000.

Single-Issue Interest Groups

Numerous interest groups focus on a single issue. For example, Mothers Against Drunk Driving (MADD) lobbies for stiffer penalties for drunk driving. Formed in 1980, MADD now boasts more than 3 million members and supporters. The abortion debate has created various single-issue groups, such as the Right to Life organization (which opposes abortion) and NARAL Pro-Choice America (which supports abortion rights). Other examples of single-issue groups are the NRA and the American Israel Public Affairs Committee (a pro-Israel group).

More and more government groups, namely school districts, are using local tax dollars to hire lobbyists. The more the federal government subsidizes state and local activities, the more lobbying by the latter we can expect to occur.

Government Interest Groups

Efforts by state and local governments to lobby the federal government have escalated in recent years. When states experience budget shortfalls, these governments often lobby in Washington, D.C., for additional federal funds. The federal government has sometimes lobbied in individual states, too. During the 2004 elections, for example, the U.S. Attorney General's office lobbied against medical marijuana use in states that were considering ballot measures on the issue.

direct technique Any method used by an interest group to interact with government officials directly to further the group's goals.

lobbying All of the attempts by organizations or by individuals to influence the passage, defeat, or contents of legislation or to influence the administrative decisions of government.

lobbyist An individual who handles a particular interest group's lobbying efforts.

LO4 *How Interest Groups Shape Policy*

Interest groups operate at all levels of government and use a variety of strategies to steer policies in ways beneficial to their interests. Sometimes, they attempt to influence policymakers directly, but at other times they try to exert indirect influence on policymakers by shaping public opinion. The extent and nature of the groups' activities depend on their goals and their resources.

Direct Techniques

Lobbying and providing election support are two important **direct techniques** used by interest groups to influence government policy.

LOBBYING Today, **lobbying** refers to all of the attempts by organizations or by individuals to influence the passage, defeat, or contents of legislation or to influence the administrative decisions of government. (The term *lobbying* arose because, traditionally, individuals and groups interested in influencing government policy would gather in the foyer, or lobby, of the legislature to corner legislators and express their concerns.) A **lobbyist** is an individual who handles a particular interest group's lobbying efforts. Most of the larger interest groups have lobbyists in Washington, D.C. These lobbyists often include former members of Congress or former employees of executive bureaucracies who are experienced in the methods of political influence and who "know people." Many lobbyists also work at state and local levels. In fact, lobbying at the state level has increased in recent years as states have begun to play a more significant role in policymaking. Table 6–4 at right summarizes some of the basic methods by which lobbyists directly influence legislators and government officials.

Lobbying can be directed at the legislative branch of government, at administrative agencies, and even at the courts. For example, pharmaceutical companies may lobby the Food and Drug Administration to speed up the process of approving new prescription drugs. Lobbying can also be directed at changing international policies. For instance, after political changes had opened up Eastern Europe to business in the late 1980s and early 1990s, intense lobbying by Western business groups helped persuade the United States and other industrial powers to reduce controls on the sale of high-technology products, such as personal computers, to Eastern European countries.

PROVIDING ELECTION SUPPORT Interest groups often become directly involved in the election process. Many interest group members join and work with political parties to influence party platforms and the nomination of candidates. Interest groups provide campaign support for legislators who favor their policies and sometimes encourage their own members to try to win posts in party organizations. Most important, interest groups urge their members to vote for candidates who support the views of the group. They can also threaten legislators with the withdrawal of votes. No candidate can expect to have support from all interest groups, but if the candidate is to win, she or he must have support from many of the strongest ones.

Since the 1970s, federal laws governing campaign financing have allowed corporations, labor unions, and special interest groups to raise funds and make campaign contributions through **political action committees (PACs).** Both the number of PACs and the amount of money PACs spend on elections have grown astronomically in recent years. There were about 1,000 PACs in 1976. Today, there are more than 4,500 PACs. In 1973, total spending by PACs amounted to $19 million. In the 2007–2008 presidential election cycle, total spending by PACs exceeded $400 million. We will discuss PACs in more detail in Chapter 9.

Although campaign contributions do not guarantee that officials will vote the way the groups wish, contributions usually do ensure that the groups will have the ear of the public officials they have helped to elect.

political action committee (PAC)

A committee that is established by a corporation, labor union, or special interest group to raise funds and make contributions on the establishing organization's behalf.

Table 6–4

Direct Lobbying Techniques

Technique	Description
Making Personal Contacts with Key Legislators	A lobbyist's personal contacts with key legislators or other government officials—in their offices, in the halls of Congress, or on social occasions such as dinners, boating expeditions, and the like—are one of the most effective direct lobbying techniques. The lobbyist provides the legislators with information on a particular issue in an attempt to convince them to support the interest group's goals.
Providing Expertise and Research Results for Legislators	Lobbyists often have knowledge and expertise that are useful in drafting legislation, and this expertise can be a major strength for an interest group. Because harried members of Congress cannot possibly be experts on everything they vote on and therefore eagerly seek information to help them make up their minds, some lobbying groups conduct research and present their findings to those legislators.
Offering "Expert" Testimony before Congressional Committees	Lobbyists often provide "expert" testimony before congressional committees for or against proposed legislation. A bill to regulate firearms, for example, might concern several interest groups. The NRA would probably oppose the bill, and representatives from that interest group might be asked to testify. Groups that would probably support the bill, such as law enforcement personnel, might also be asked to testify. Each side would offer as much evidence as possible to support its position.
Providing Legal Advice to Legislators	Many lobbyists assist legislators in drafting legislation or prospective regulations. Lobbyists are a source of ideas and sometimes offer legal advice on specific details.
Following Up on Legislation	Because executive agencies responsible for carrying out legislation can often increase or decrease the scope of the new law, lobbyists may also try to influence the bureaucrats who implement the policy. For example, beginning in the early 1960s, regulations outlawing gender discrimination were broadly outlined by Congress. Both women's rights groups favoring the regulations and interest groups opposing the regulations lobbied for years to influence how those regulations were carried out.

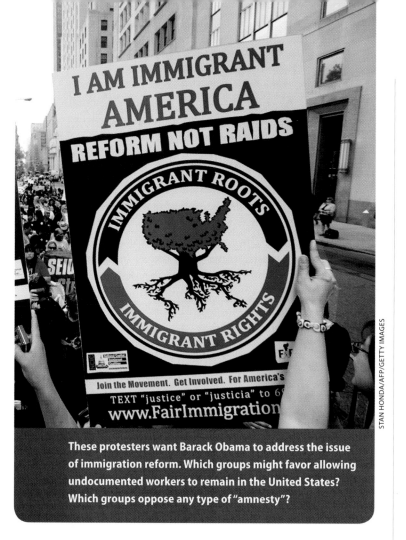

These protesters want Barack Obama to address the issue of immigration reform. Which groups might favor allowing undocumented workers to remain in the United States? Which groups oppose any type of "amnesty"?

Indirect Techniques

Interest groups also try to influence public policy indirectly through third parties or the general public. The effects of such **indirect techniques** may appear to be spontaneous, but indirect techniques are generally as well planned as the direct lobbying techniques just discussed. Indirect techniques can be particularly effective because public officials are often more impressed by contacts from voters than from lobbyists.

SHAPING PUBLIC OPINION   Public opinion weighs significantly in the policymaking process, so interest groups cultivate their public images carefully. If public opinion favors a certain group's interests, then public officials will be more ready to listen and more willing to pass legislation favoring that group. To cultivate public opinion, an interest group's efforts may include online campaigns, television publicity, newspaper and magazine advertisements, mass mailings, and the use of public relations techniques to improve the group's public image.

For example, environmental groups often run television ads to dramatize threats to the environment. Oil companies may respond to criticism about increased gasoline prices with advertising showing their concern

for the public welfare. The goal of all these activities is to influence public opinion.

RATING SYSTEMS   Some interest groups also try to influence legislators through **rating systems.** A group selects legislative issues that it believes are important to its goals and rates legislators according to the percentage of times they vote favorably on that legislation. For example, a score of 90 percent on the Americans for Democratic Action (ADA) rating scale means that the legislator supported that liberal group's position to a high degree. Other groups tag members of Congress who support (or fail to support) their interests to a significant extent with telling labels. For instance, the Communications Workers of America refers to policymakers who take a position consistent with its views as "Heroes" and those who take the opposite position as "Zeroes." Needless to say, such tactics can be an effective form of indirect lobbying, particularly with legislators who do not want to earn a low ADA score or be placed on the "Zeroes" list.

ISSUE ADS AND "527s"   One of the most powerful indirect techniques used by interest groups is the "issue ad"—a television or radio ad taking a position on a particular issue. The Supreme Court has made it clear that the First Amendment's guarantee of free speech protects interest groups' rights to set forth their positions on issues when they are **independent expenditures** that are not coordinated with a candidate's campaign or a political party. Nevertheless, issue advocacy is controversial because the funds spent to air issue ads have had a clear effect on the outcome of elections.

Both parties have benefited from such interest group spending. As you will read in Chapter 9, the Bipartisan Campaign Reform Act of 2002 banned unlimited donations to campaigns and political parties, called *soft money.* In subsequent years, interest groups that had previously given soft money to parties set up new groups called "527s" (after the provision of the tax code that covers them). The 527s engaged

indirect technique   Any method used by interest groups to influence government officials through third parties, such as voters.

rating system   A system by which a particular interest group evaluates (rates) the performance of legislators based on how often the legislators have voted with the group's position on particular issues.

independent expenditure   An expenditure for activities that are independent from (not coordinated with) those of a political candidate or a political party.

in such practices as voter registration, but they also began making large expenditures on issue ads—which were legal so long as the 527s did not coordinate their activities with candidates' campaigns.

In the run-up to the 2008 presidential elections, clever campaign finance lawyers hit upon a new type of group, the 501(c)4 organization, also named after a section of the tax code. Groups such as the Sierra Club and Citizens Against Government Waste have set up special 501(c)4 arms. Lawyers argued that a 501(c)4 group could spend some of its funds on direct campaign contributions as long as most of the group's spending was on issue advocacy. Further, a 501(c)4 group could conceal the identity of its contributors. It was not possible to determine the legality of these claims in time for the 2010 elections. We will discuss this issue in greater depth in Chapter 9.

MOBILIZING CONSTITUENTS   Interest groups sometimes urge members and other constituents to contact government officials—by letter, e-mail, Facebook, or telephone—to show their support for or opposition to a certain policy. Large interest groups can generate hundreds of thousands of letters, e-mail messages, and phone calls. Interest groups often provide form letters or postcards for constituents to fill out and mail. The NRA has successfully used this tactic to fight strict federal gun control legislation by delivering half a million letters to Congress within a few weeks. Policymakers recognize that such communications are initiated by interest groups, however, and are impressed only when the volume of letters or e-mail communications is very large. Campaigns that masquerade as grassroots mobilizations, but are not, have been given the apt label *Astroturf lobbying*.

GOING TO COURT   The legal system offers another avenue for interest groups to influence the political process. In the 1950s and 1960s, civil rights groups paved the way for interest group litigation with major victories in cases concerning equal housing, school desegregation, and employment discrimination. Environmental groups, such as the Sierra Club, have also successfully used litigation to press their concerns. For example, an environmental group might challenge in court an activity that threatens to pollute the environment or that will destroy the natural habitat of an endangered species. The legal challenge forces those engaging in the activity to bear the costs of defending themselves and

> "Never doubt that a small group of thoughtful, committed citizens can
> # CHANGE THE WORLD;
> indeed, it's the only thing that ever has."
> ~ MARGARET MEAD ~
> AMERICAN ANTHROPOLOGIST
> 1901–1978

may delay the project. In fact, much of the success of environmental groups has been linked to their use of lawsuits.

Interest groups can also influence the outcome of litigation without being a party to a lawsuit. Frequently, an interest group files an *amicus curiae* ("friend of the court") brief. The brief states the group's legal argument in support of its desired outcome in a case. For example, in the case *Metro-Goldwyn-Mayer Studios, Inc. v. Grokster, Ltd.*[8]—involving the legality of file-sharing software—hundreds of *amicus* briefs were filed by various groups on behalf of the petitioners. Groups filing *amicus* briefs for the case, which was heard by the Supreme Court in 2005, included the National Basketball Association, the National Football League, the National Association of Broadcasters, the Association of American Publishers, and numerous state governments. Often, interest groups have statistics and research that support their position on a certain issue, and this research can have considerable influence on the judges deciding the case.

DEMONSTRATIONS   Some interest groups stage protests to make a statement in a dramatic way. The Boston Tea Party of 1773, in which American colonists dressed as Native Americans and threw tea into Boston Harbor to protest British taxes, is testimony to how long this tactic has been around. Over the years, many groups have organized protest marches and rallies to support or oppose legalized abortion, gay and lesbian rights, the treatment of Native Americans, restrictions on the use of federally owned lands in the West, and the activities of global organizations, such as the World Trade Organization.

Not all demonstration techniques are peaceful. Some environmental groups, for example, have used such dangerous tactics as spiking trees and setting traps on logging roads that puncture truck tires. Pro-life groups have bombed abortion clinics, and members of the Animal Liberation Front have broken into laboratories and freed animals being used for experimentation. Some evidence exists that violent demonstrations can be counterproductive—that is, that they can hurt the demonstrators' cause by angering the public. Historians continue to debate whether violent demonstrations against the Vietnam War (1964–1975) helped or hurt the antiwar cause.

LO5 *Today's Lobbying Establishment*

Without a doubt, interest groups and their lobbyists have become a permanent feature in the landscape of American government. The major interest groups all have headquarters in Washington, D.C., close to the center of government. Professional lobbyists and staff members of various interest groups move freely between their groups' headquarters and congressional offices and committee rooms. Interest group representatives are routinely consulted when Congress drafts new legislation. As already mentioned, interest group representatives are frequently asked to testify before congressional committees or subcommittees on the effect or potential effect of particular legislation or regulations. In sum, interest groups have become an integral part of the American government system.

As interest groups have become a permanent feature of American government, lobbying has developed into a profession. A professional lobbyist—one who has mastered the techniques of lobbying discussed earlier in this chapter—is a valuable ally to any interest group seeking to influence government. Professional lobbyists can and often do represent a number of different interest groups over the course of their careers.

In recent years, it has become increasingly common for those who leave positions with the federal government to become lobbyists or consultants for the private-interest groups they helped to regulate. In spite of legislation and regulations that have been created in an attempt to reduce this "revolving door" syndrome, it is still functioning quite well.

Why Do Interest Groups Get Bad Press?

Despite their importance to democratic government, interest groups, like political parties, are often criticized by both the public and the press. Our image of interest groups and their special interests is not very favorable. You may have run across political cartoons depicting lobbyists standing in the hallways of Congress with briefcases stuffed with money.

These cartoons are not entirely factual, but they are not entirely fictitious either. President Richard Nixon (1969–1974) was revealed to have responded to the campaign contributions of milk producers by authorizing a windfall increase in milk subsidies. In the early 1990s, it was revealed that a number of senators who

"An honest politician IS ONE WHO, WHEN HE IS BOUGHT, WILL STAY BOUGHT."
~ SIMON CAMERON ~
U.S. FINANCIER AND POLITICIAN
1799–1889

received generous contributions from a particular savings and loan association subsequently supported a "hands-off" policy by savings and loan regulators. The savings and loan association in question later got into financial trouble, costing the taxpayers billions of dollars. (One of the senators criticized for having exercised poor judgment during the savings and loan scandal was John McCain, the 2008 Republican presidential candidate. It may have been this painful experience that inspired McCain to become an ardent advocate of campaign-finance reform.)

Some of the most heated and expensive lobbying in recent years surrounded the health-care reform bills that Congress passed in March 2010. Heavy lobbying may have done its part in causing many Americans to distrust the reforms. Did lobbying damage the health-care legislation? We examine that question in this chapter's *Join the Debate* feature on the following page.

The Regulation of Interest Groups

In an attempt to control lobbying, Congress passed the Federal Regulation of Lobbying Act in 1946. The major provisions of the act are as follows:

- Any person or organization that receives money to influence legislation must register with the clerk of the House and the secretary of the Senate.

"MY GREATEST ASSET IS I'M SO RICH, I CAN'T BE BOUGHT BY ANY INTEREST GROUP."

Did Lobbying Damage the Health-Care Legislation?

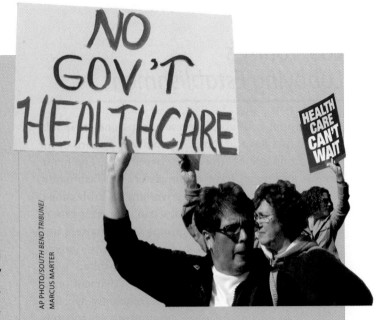

AP PHOTO/SOUTH BEND TRIBUNE/ MARCUS MARTER

Immediately upon taking office in January 2009, President Barack Obama declared that health-care reform "must not wait." One thing that did not wait was perhaps the greatest lobbying spree in American history. Medical interests alone spent almost a billion dollars in lobbying during the following fifteen months. These expenses declined after the passage of the health-care reform legislation, which has been dubbed "Obamacare" by journalists and Republicans. We will, however, see continued lobbying efforts by physicians, the drug industry, and manufacturers of medical products as the government creates thousands of rules and regulations to implement the new policies.

Lobbying Gave Us Imperfect Health-Care Reform

Those who support the reforms contend that every U.S. citizen will soon have the right to obtain health-care insurance at a price she or he can afford, and that this is a blessing. Many supporters, however, believe that lobbying resulted in reforms that were not as good as they could have been. For example, lobbying by the pharmaceutical industry eliminated measures to limit drug prices. Costly brand-name biotech drugs received twelve years of protection against cheaper generic competitors. Pharmaceutical lobbyists also killed a proposal to allow the import of low-cost medicines from abroad.

A major feature of the original plan was a "public option"—a government-sponsored health-care insurance plan that would compete with private insurance companies, presumably holding down their rates. The insurance industry succeeded in eliminating that option. The result of these various lobbying measures was to channel billions of dollars to the pharmaceutical, insurance, and hospital industries. Those sums will come from taxpayers and from everyone who must pay part or all of the cost of their health-care insurance policy.

Intense Lobbying Saved Us from a Worse Fate

Those who funded the lobbying effort argue that lobbying kept the final reform legislation from being even worse than it was. Lobbying efforts reduced restrictions on businesses, especially health-care industry businesses. For example, pharmaceutical companies contend that price controls on their products would be a disaster. Why? Because controls would lower the profits of pharmaceutical companies—which in turn would force these companies to reduce the sums they spend on research and development. The result would be fewer new drugs.

Opponents of the health-care reform legislation see it as a giant mass of new restrictions on the freedoms of businesses and citizens alike. They see the requirement that everyone must purchase health-care insurance—which did survive the legislative process—as the prime example of such restrictions. Any successes that lobbyists had in limiting the scope of the legislation prevented further erosions of our personal and economic freedoms. That is a plus, not a negative.

For Critical Analysis *From the very beginning, much of the lobbying paid for by the health-care industries supported the general concept of reform. Why would these interests have taken this position?*

- Any group or person registering must identify their employer, salary, amount and purpose of expenses, and duration of employment.

- Every registered lobbyist must make quarterly reports on his or her activities.

- Anyone violating this act can be fined up to $10,000 and be imprisoned for up to five years.

The act did not succeed in regulating lobbying to any great degree for several reasons. First, the Supreme Court restricted the application of the law to only those lobbyists who sought to influence federal legislation directly.[9] Any lobbyist seeking to influence legislation indirectly through public opinion did not fall within the scope of the law. Second, only persons or organizations whose principal purpose was to influence legislation were required to register. Many groups avoided registration by claiming that their principal function was something else. Third, the act did not cover those whose lobbying was directed at agencies in the executive branch or lobbyists who testified before congressional committees. Fourth, the public was almost totally unaware of the information in the quarterly reports filed by lobbyists. Not until 1995 did Congress finally address those loopholes by enacting new legislation.

The Lobbying Disclosure Act of 1995

In 1995, Congress passed new lobbying legislation—the Lobbying Disclosure Act—that reformed the 1946 act in the following ways:

- Strict definitions now apply to determine who must register with the clerk of the House and the secretary of the Senate as a lobbyist. A lobbyist is anyone who either spends at least 20 percent of his or her time lobbying members of Congress, their staffs, or executive-branch officials, or is paid more than $5,000 in a six-month period for such work. Any organization that spends more than $20,000 in a six-month period conducting such lobbying activity must also register. These amounts have since been altered to $2,500 and $10,000 per quarter, respectively.

- Lobbyists must report their clients, the issues on which they lobbied, and the agency or chamber of Congress they contacted, although they do not need to disclose the names of those they contacted.

Tax-exempt organizations, such as religious groups, were exempted from these provisions, as were organizations that engage in grassroots lobbying, such as a media campaign that asks people to write or call their congressional representative. Nonetheless, the number of registered lobbyists nearly doubled in the first few years of the new legislation.

Lobbying Scandals and Reform Efforts

In 2005, a number of lobbying scandals in Washington, D.C., came to light. A major figure in the scandals was Jack Abramoff, an influential lobbyist who had ties to many Republicans (and a few Democrats) in Congress and to various officials in the Bush administration.

Abramoff gained access to the power brokers in the capital by giving them campaign contributions, expensive gifts, and exotic trips. Eventually, Abramoff pleaded guilty to charges of fraud, tax evasion, and conspiracy to bribe public officials. Abramoff received a prison sentence in 2006.

Following the midterm elections of 2006, the new Democratic majority in the Senate and House of Representatives undertook a lobbying reform effort. The goal of the reforms was to force lobbyists to disclose their expenditures on House and Senate election campaigns above and beyond straight campaign contributions.

Bundled campaign contributions, in which a lobbyist arranges for contributions from a variety of sources, would have to be reported. Expenditures on the sometimes lavish parties to benefit candidates would have to be reported as well. (Of course, partygoers were expected to pay for their food and drink with a check written out to the candidate.) The new rules covered PACs as well as registered lobbyists, which led one lobbyist to observe sourly that this wasn't lobbying reform but campaign-finance reform.

President Bush signed the resulting Honest Leadership and Open Government Act in September 2007. The new law increased lobbying disclosure and placed further restrictions on the receipt of gifts and travel by members of Congress paid for by lobbyists and the organizations they represent. The act also included provisions requiring the disclosure of lawmakers' requests for earmarks in legislation. (We discuss earmarks in more depth in Chapter 11.)

Lobbyists and the Obama Administration

During his campaign for the presidency, Barack Obama pledged that "lobbyists won't find a job in my White House." Given how many talented individuals with experience in government have served as lobbyists, that pledge turned out to be unenforceable. Senior administration officials soon included dozens of persons who had served as lobbyists within the past five years.

Appointees signed a pledge not to work on issues for which they had lobbied in the previous two years, but given the positions that many of these appointees filled, such a pledge was probably unworkable as well. Interest groups represented by these former lobbyists included the Campaign for Tobacco-Free Kids, the mortgage giant Fannie Mae, the investment bank Goldman Sachs, Mothers Against Drunk Driving, the National Council of La Raza, the defense industry giant Raytheon, and the Service Employees International Union.

Other restrictions imposed by the new administration included a rule that all communications with lobbyists over economic stimulus projects had to be in writing. Many old hands in Washington considered Obama's policies toward lobbyists absurd and predicted that they would not last.

AMERICA AT ODDS *Interest Groups*

Interest groups are one of the most controversial features of our democratic system. The right to lobby may be protected by the First Amendment, but many people consider lobbying by interest groups to be a source of corruption within the political system. Of course, it is simpler for anyone to see the problems with lobbying when it is done for a cause that they oppose. It is easy to support political action for something you believe in, regardless of what others might think of it. Some of the controversies surrounding interest group lobbying include the following:

- Should labor unions be allowed to organize workplaces by obtaining signed cards—or are secret-ballot elections an essential safeguard?

- Are farm subsidies a valid protection for an important industry—or just another giveaway to the politically powerful?

- Does lobbying always harm legislation—or can lobbying improve it?

- Free riders benefit from a particular activity without paying their share of its costs. Is free riding inherently unfair—or is it only a problem when it is so pervasive that it makes the activity in question (for example, lobbying by consumer groups) unaffordable?

- Are there too many lobbyists—or is the real problem that there aren't enough lobbyists for ordinary people?

Take Action

An obvious way to get involved in politics is to join an interest group whose goals you endorse—perhaps one of the organizations on your campus. You can find lists of interest groups operating at the local, state, and national levels by simply going to an online search engine, such as Google, and keying in the words "interest groups." Alternatively, you can go directly to one of the pages that list interest groups. One is **usgovinfo.about.com/blorgs. htm**. Another is **directory.google.com/ Top/Society/Organizations/Advocacy**. Almost all interest groups have Web sites, and you'll want to check them out. A very large number of groups have Facebook pages as well—just type the name of the organization into your Facebook search box.

If you have a particular interest or goal that you would like to promote, consider forming your own group, as some Iowa students did when they formed a group called Students Toward Environmental Protection. In the photo at right, students

from Grinnell College in Iowa are seen staging a protest rally at the state capitol. The students wanted Iowa's lawmakers to issue tougher regulations governing factory farms and to expand the state's bottle deposit requirements.

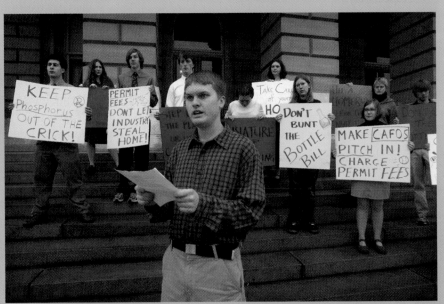

AP PHOTO/CHARLIE NEIBERGALL

POLITICS ON THE
WEB

- To find particular interest groups online, a good point of departure is the Internet Public Library Association, which provides links to hundreds of professional and trade associations. Go to **www.ipl.org/div/aon**

- You can access the National Rifle Association online at **www.nra.org**

- AARP's Web site can be found at **www.aarp.org**

- To learn about the activities of the National Education Association, go to **www.nea.org**

- You can find information on environmental issues and the activities of the National Resources Defense Council at **www.nrdc.org**

Access CourseMate to review and expand on this chapter through quizzes, flashcards, learning objectives, interactive timelines, a crossword puzzle, audio summaries, video, critical-thinking activities, simulations, and more.

GOVT

7

Political Parties

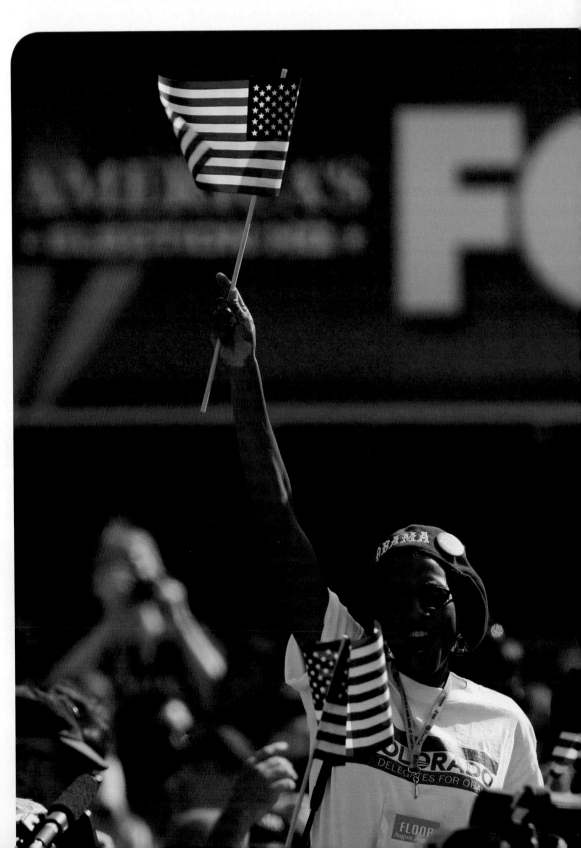

LEARNING OBJECTIVES

LO1 Summarize the origins and development of the two-party system in the United States.

LO2 Describe the current status of the two major parties.

LO3 Explain how political parties function in our democratic system.

LO4 Discuss the structure of American political parties.

LO5 Describe the different types of third parties and how they function in the American political system.

AMERICA AT ODDS

Is the Republican Party Conservative Enough?

The Republican Party lost control of the U.S. House and Senate in 2006, in large part due to the seemingly endless war in Iraq. In 2008, with the economy in crisis, the Republicans lost more seats in Congress and the presidency as well. Not surprisingly, these results touched off a debate within the party. In 2009, a few Republicans argued that their party should moderate its conservatism to attract independent voters. By 2010, however, some Republican activists, many of them part of the Tea Party movement, claimed that incumbent Republican politicians were not conservative enough. Should the Republican Party change its views? And if so, how?

Uncompromising Conservatism Is the Only Way Forward

Uncompromising conservatives believe that the Republicans must steer to the political right. Even though only 29 percent of voters call themselves Republicans, 42 percent say that they are conservatives. In 2009, 39 percent of respondents said that they were becoming more conservative, not less. Support is rising for such conservative positions as the right to bear arms and opposition to abortion. Conservative activists argue that their values are not only popular but also "correct" in a very deep sense. Values such as religious belief, strong families, and individual self-reliance are the foundation of our civilization. Liberalism erodes these values and paves the road to cultural collapse.

Further, as the Tea Party movement has advocated, Republicans must return to their conservative roots on economic issues. Under President George W. Bush, Republicans in Congress abandoned their traditional opposition to government spending. Millions of Americans, including independents, were alarmed at Bush's budget deficits and bank bailouts. They are even more appalled at President Barack Obama's spending programs and his unprecedented federal budget deficits. Americans are starting to rebel against big government and a culture of immorality. If the Republicans don't stand for true conservatism, these Americans won't have anyone to vote for.

Radical Conservatism Spells Disaster in the Long Run

A minority of Republicans argue that the party's improved electoral prospects in 2010 were largely due to Democratic mistakes. The resulting Republican advantage may be only temporary. The face of America is changing. Support for gay rights has risen dramatically. The number of Hispanic voters rises year by year, and after 2050, non-Hispanic whites will be a minority of the U.S. population. Despite these changes, some conservatives seem intent on ensuring that the Republicans are seen as the "nasty party"—the party that hates people. The campaign by leading Republicans against a Muslim cultural center and mosque two blocks from "ground zero" in New York City is an example. In 2000, a majority of Muslims of Middle Eastern background voted Republican because of Islamic cultural conservatism. Today, Muslims are the most Democratic religious group in the nation.

The Republicans must break with the ultraright and stop antagonizing the very people they need to form a majority. Republicans require young voters, but tirades against gays are poison to that constituency. If the vast majority of Latinos come to reject the Republicans because of the party's anti-immigrant rhetoric, eventually the Republicans will fail to carry even Texas. If voters conclude that Republicans see large numbers of their fellow Americans as "the enemy," the party will lose future elections, no matter how well it did in 2010.

WHERE DO YOU STAND?

1. Pastor Rick Warren, author of *The Purpose Driven Life*, accepts that homosexuality is a sin, but he also emphasizes his belief in God's love for all people. Why might some members of the religious right reject Warren's formula?
2. American-style cultural conservatism is not popular in much of Europe. Many of these nations are also facing declines in their populations. Some conservatives would argue that these facts are connected. Is this argument reasonable? Why or why not?

EXPLORE THIS ISSUE ONLINE

- Web sites that advocate a more moderate Republican Party include David Frum's www.newmajority.com. For full-throttle conservatism, try www.rushlimbaugh.com.

Introduction

Political ideology can spark heated debates among Americans, as you read in the chapter-opening *America at Odds* feature. A **political party** can be defined as a group of individuals who organize to win elections, operate the government, and determine policy. Political parties serve as major vehicles for citizen participation in our political system. It is hard to imagine democracy without political parties. Political parties provide a way for the public to choose who will serve in government and which policies will be carried out. Even citizens who do not identify with any political party or who choose not to participate in elections are affected by the activities of parties and their influence on government.

Political parties were an unforeseen development in American political history. The founders defined many other important institutions, such as the presidency and Congress, and described their functions in the Constitution. Political parties, however, are not even mentioned in the Constitution. In fact, the founders decried factions and parties. Thomas Jefferson probably best expressed the founders' antiparty sentiments when he declared, "If I could not go to heaven but with a party, I would not go there at all."[1]

If the founders did not want political parties, though, who was supposed to organize political campaigns and mobilize supporters of political candidates? Clearly, there was a practical need for some kind of organizing group to form a link between citizens and their government. Even our early national leaders, for all their antiparty feelings, realized this. Several of them were active in establishing or organizing the first political parties.

"Both of our political parties . . . agree conscientiously in the same object:
THE PUBLIC GOOD;
but they differ essentially in what they deem the means of promoting that good."

~ THOMAS JEFFERSON ~
IN A LETTER TO
ABIGAIL ADAMS
1804

LO1 A Short History of American Political Parties

political party A group of individuals who organize to win elections, operate the government, and determine policy.

Throughout the course of our history, several parties have formed, and some have disappeared. Even today, although we have only two major political parties, numerous other parties have been organized, as will be discussed later in this chapter.

The First Political Parties

The founders rejected the idea of political parties because they believed, as George Washington said in his Farewell Address, that the "spirit of party . . . agitates the community with ill-founded jealousies and false alarms, kindles the animosity of one part against another, foments occasionally riot and insurrection."[2] At some point in the future, the founders feared, a party leader might even seize power as a dictator. Nonetheless, two major political factions—the Federalists and Anti-Federalists—were formed even before the Constitution was ratified. Remember from Chapter 2 that the Federalists pushed for the ratification of the Constitution because they wanted a stronger national government than the one that had existed under the Articles of Confederation. The Anti-Federalists argued against ratification. They supported states' rights and feared a too-powerful central government.

These two national factions continued, in somewhat altered form, after the Constitution was ratified. Alexander

John Adams (1735–1826) was the Federalists' candidate to succeed George Washington. Adams defeated Thomas Jefferson in 1796, but lost to him in 1800.

Hamilton, the first secretary of the Treasury, became the leader of the Federalist Party, which was also joined by Vice President John Adams. The Federalists supported a strong central government that would encourage the development of commerce and manufacturing. The Federalists generally thought that a republic should be ruled by its wealthiest and best-educated citizens. Opponents of the Federalists and Hamilton's policies referred to themselves as Republicans. Today, they are often referred to as Jeffersonian Republicans, or Democratic Republicans (a name never used at the time), to distinguish this group from the later Republican Party. The Jeffersonian Republicans favored a more limited role for government. They believed that the nation's welfare would be best served if the states had more power than the central government. In their view, Congress should dominate the government, and government policies should serve farming interests rather than promote commerce and manufacturing.

From 1796 to 1860

The nation's first two parties clashed openly in the elections of 1796, in which John Adams, the Federalists' candidate to succeed George Washington as president, defeated Thomas Jefferson. Over the next four years, Jefferson and James Madison worked to extend the influence of the Jeffersonian Republican Party. In the presidential elections of 1800 and 1804, Jefferson won the presidency, and his party also won control of Congress.

TRIUMPH OF THE JEFFERSONIANS The transition of political power from the Federalists to the Republicans

is the first example in American history of what political scientists have called a **realignment.** In a realignment, a substantial number of voters change their political allegiance,

> **realignment** A process in which the popular support for and relative strength of the parties shift and the parties are reestablished with different coalitions of supporters.

which usually also changes the balance of power between the two major parties. In fact, the Federalists never returned to power and thus became the first (but not the last) American party to go out of existence. (See the time line of American political parties in Figure 7–1 on the following page.)

The Jeffersonian Republicans dominated American politics for the next twenty years. Jefferson was succeeded in the White House by two other members of the party— James Madison and James Monroe. In the mid-1820s, however, the Republicans split into two groups. This was the second realignment in American history. Supporters of Andrew Jackson, who was elected president in 1828, called themselves Democrats. The Democrats appealed to small farmers and the growing class of urbanized workers. The other group, the National Republicans (later the Whig Party), was led by John Quincy Adams, Henry Clay, and the great orator Daniel Webster. It had the support of bankers, business owners, and many southern planters.

THE IMPENDING CRISIS As the Whigs and Democrats competed for the White House throughout the 1840s and 1850s, the two-party system as we know it today emerged. Both parties were large, with well-known leaders and supporters across the nation. Both had

Thomas Jefferson (1743–1826) became our third president and served two terms. The Jeffersonian Republicans (not to be confused with the later Republican Party of Abraham Lincoln) dominated American politics for more than two decades.

LIBRARY OF CONGRESS

Andrew Jackson (1767–1845) was part of the newly named party of Democrats. Jackson won the presidential election in 1828, defeating the candidate of the National Republicans.

LIBRARY OF CONGRESS

Figure 7–1

A Time Line of U.S. Political Parties

Many of these parties—including the Constitutional Union Party, Henry Wallace's Progressive Party, and the States' Rights Democrats—were important during only one presidential election.

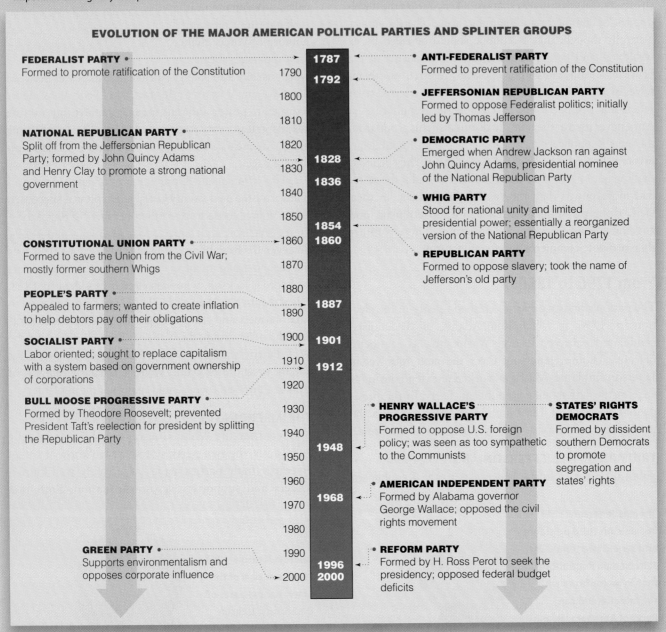

EVOLUTION OF THE MAJOR AMERICAN POLITICAL PARTIES AND SPLINTER GROUPS

FEDERALIST PARTY
Formed to promote ratification of the Constitution

1787

ANTI-FEDERALIST PARTY
Formed to prevent ratification of the Constitution

1792

JEFFERSONIAN REPUBLICAN PARTY
Formed to oppose Federalist politics; initially led by Thomas Jefferson

NATIONAL REPUBLICAN PARTY
Split off from the Jeffersonian Republican Party; formed by John Quincy Adams and Henry Clay to promote a strong national government

1828

DEMOCRATIC PARTY
Emerged when Andrew Jackson ran against John Quincy Adams, presidential nominee of the National Republican Party

1836

WHIG PARTY
Stood for national unity and limited presidential power; essentially a reorganized version of the National Republican Party

CONSTITUTIONAL UNION PARTY
Formed to save the Union from the Civil War; mostly former southern Whigs

1854
1860

REPUBLICAN PARTY
Formed to oppose slavery; took the name of Jefferson's old party

PEOPLE'S PARTY
Appealed to farmers; wanted to create inflation to help debtors pay off their obligations

1887

SOCIALIST PARTY
Labor oriented; sought to replace capitalism with a system based on government ownership of corporations

1901

1912

BULL MOOSE PROGRESSIVE PARTY
Formed by Theodore Roosevelt; prevented President Taft's reelection for president by splitting the Republican Party

HENRY WALLACE'S PROGRESSIVE PARTY
Formed to oppose U.S. foreign policy; was seen as too sympathetic to the Communists

STATES' RIGHTS DEMOCRATS
Formed by dissident southern Democrats to promote segregation and states' rights

1948

AMERICAN INDEPENDENT PARTY
Formed by Alabama governor George Wallace; opposed the civil rights movement

1968

GREEN PARTY
Supports environmentalism and opposes corporate influence

1996
2000

REFORM PARTY
Formed by H. Ross Perot to seek the presidency; opposed federal budget deficits

Time line years: 1790, 1800, 1810, 1820, 1830, 1840, 1850, 1860, 1870, 1880, 1890, 1900, 1910, 1920, 1930, 1940, 1950, 1960, 1970, 1980, 1990, 2000

grassroots organizations of party workers committed to winning as many political offices (at all levels of government) for the party as possible. Both the Whigs and the Democrats tried to avoid the issue of slavery. By the mid-1850s, the Whig coalition had fallen apart, and most northern Whigs were absorbed into the new Republican Party, which opposed the extension of slavery into new territories. Campaigning on this platform, the Republicans succeeded in electing Abraham Lincoln the first president under the banner of the new Republican Party in 1860.

From the Civil War to the Great Depression

When the former Confederate states rejoined the Union after the Civil War, the Republicans and Democrats were roughly even in strength, although the Republicans were

From the election of Abraham Lincoln (shown here) in 1860 until the election of Franklin Delano Roosevelt in 1932, the Republican Party was the more successful party in presidential politics.

LIBRARY OF CONGRESS

The realigning election of 1932 brought Franklin Delano Roosevelt to the presidency and the Democrats back to power at the national level.

LIBRARY OF CONGRESS

more successful in presidential contests. In the 1890s, however, the Republicans gained a decisive advantage. In that decade, the Democrats allied themselves with the Populist movement, which consisted largely of indebted farmers in the West and South. The Populists—the People's Party—advocated inflation as a way of lessening their debts. Urban workers in the Midwest and East strongly opposed this program, which would erode the value of their paychecks. After the election of 1896, the Republicans established themselves in the minds of many Americans as the party that knew how to manage the nation's economy.

As a result of a Republican split, the Democrats under Woodrow Wilson won power from 1912 to 1920. Otherwise, the Republicans remained dominant in national politics until the onset of the Great Depression.

After the Great Depression

The Great Depression of the 1930s destroyed the belief that the Republicans could better manage the economy and contributed to another realignment in the two-party system. In a realignment, the minority (opposition) party may emerge as the majority party, and this is certainly what happened in 1932. (Realignment can also reestablish the majority party in power with a different coalition of supporters or leave the two parties closely balanced.) The election of 1932 brought Franklin D. Roosevelt to the presidency and the Democrats back to power at the national level. The elections of 1860 and 1896 are also considered to represent realignments.

A CIVIL RIGHTS PLANK Roosevelt's programs to fight the Depression were called the *New Deal*. Those who

joined the Democrats during Roosevelt's New Deal included a substantial share of African Americans—Roosevelt's relief programs were open to people of all races. (Until the 1930s, African Americans had been overwhelmingly Republican.) In 1948, for the first time ever, the Democrats adopted a civil rights plank as part of the party platform at their national convention. A number of southern Democrats revolted and ran a separate States' Rights ticket for president.

In 1964, the Democrats, under incumbent president Lyndon Johnson, won a landslide victory, and liberals held a majority in Congress. In the political environment that produced this election result, a coalition of northern Democrats and Republicans crafted the major civil rights legislation that you read about in Chapter 5. The subsequent years were turbulent, with riots and marches in several major cities and student protests against the Vietnam War.

A "ROLLING REALIGNMENT" Conservative Democrats did not like the direction in which their party seemed to be taking them. Under President Richard Nixon, the Republican Party was receptive to these conservative Democrats, and over a period of years, most of them became Republican voters. This was a major alteration in the political landscape, although it was not exclusively associated with a single election. Republican president Ronald Reagan helped cement the new Republican coalition. The Democrats continued to hold majorities in the House and Senate until 1994, but partisan labels were somewhat misleading. During the 1970s and 1980s, a large bloc of Democrats in Congress, mostly from the South, sided with the Republicans on almost all issues. In time, these conservative Democrats were replaced by conservative Republicans.

The result of this "rolling realignment" was that the two major parties were fairly evenly matched. The elections of 2000 were a striking demonstration of how closely the electorate was now divided. Republican George W. Bush won the presidency in that year by carrying Florida with a margin of 538 votes. Democrat Al Gore actually received about half a million more popular votes than Bush. Following the elections, the Senate was made up of 50 Republicans and 50 Democrats. The Republicans controlled the House by a razor-thin margin of seven seats.

LO2 *America's Political Parties Today*

Historically, political parties drew together like-minded individuals. Today, too, individuals with similar characteristics tend to align themselves more often with one or the other major party. Such factors as race, age, income, education, marital status, and geography all influence party identification.

Red States versus Blue States

Geography is one of the many factors that can determine party identification. Examine the national electoral map shown below. In 2008, Republican John McCain did well in the South, on the Great Plains, and in parts of the Mountain West. Democrat Barack Obama did well in the Northeast, in the Midwest, and on the West Coast. Beginning with the presidential elections of 2000, the press has made much of the supposed cultural differences between the "blue" states that vote for the Democratic candidate and the "red" states that vote for the Republican.[3] In reality, though, many states could better be described as "purple"—that is, a mixture of red and blue. These states could give their electoral votes to either party.

For another way to consider the influence of geography, see the map of Ohio on the following page. Most of Ohio is red, and a quick glance might lead you to believe that McCain carried the state. In fact, Obama carried Ohio by a margin of 4.6 percentage points. Ohio looks red because McCain carried almost all of the rural parts of the state. The Obama counties had larger populations. This pattern was seen all over the country: the more urban the county, the more likely it was to vote Democratic.

Shifting Political Fortunes

As noted earlier, by 2000 the two major parties were very closely matched in terms of support. Public opinion polls reported that voters continued to view the parties with roughly equal favor.

TROUBLE FOR THE REPUBLICANS During 2005, however, the partisan deadlock began to break up. The grinding, seemingly endless war in Iraq began to cut into support for the Republicans. By 2006, that party had lost about 5 percentage points in popularity relative to the Democrats, as measured by Gallup. A poll in 2008 found that 51 percent of those surveyed identified with or leaned toward the Democratic Party. Only 37 percent identified with or leaned toward the Republicans. Even before the start of the Great Recession, therefore, the Republicans were in trouble. In 2006, the Democrats regained control of the House and Senate. In 2008, in the shadow of a global financial crisis, the Democrats elected Barack Obama as president.

TROUBLE FOR THE DEMOCRATS Within one year of Obama's inau-

This map shows the 2008 presidential election results by state. Note that Obama won a single electoral vote in Nebraska, which is represented by a symbol.

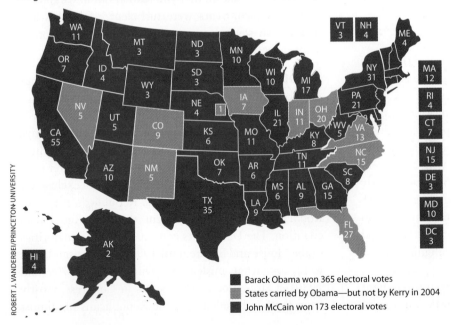

ROBERT J. VANDERBEI/PRINCETON UNIVERSITY

■ Barack Obama won 365 electoral votes
■ States carried by Obama—but not by Kerry in 2004
■ John McCain won 173 electoral votes

This map displays the Ohio counties carried by Barack Obama (blue) and John McCain (red) in the 2008 presidential elections. The cities shown on the map are the ten most populous municipalities in Ohio. Obama did well in urban and suburban counties, but poorly in nonmetropolitan regions. (Note that one nonmetropolitan county that Obama carried contains a major university.)

guration, the Democratic advantage had vanished. The party's favorability ratings dropped about 5 percentage points during 2009. Both parties were now distinctly less popular than they had been five years earlier. Democratic unpopularity was confirmed in January 2010, when Republican Scott Brown won the Massachusetts Senate seat formerly occupied by Democratic legend Ted Kennedy.

Arguments differ as to why the Democrats lost support. Continued high rates of unemployment were very important. Another reason may have been the dramatic increase in the size and scope of government during Obama's first two years. In February 2009, the Democrats adopted a large economic stimulus package.[4] Then came the bailouts of automobile giants Chrysler and General Motors (GM). In March 2010, Congress passed a massive health-care reform package. Millions of voters concluded that the government was growing too big, too fast.

THE TRIUMPH OF PARTISANSHIP A key characteristic of recent politics has been the extreme partisanship of party activists and members of Congress. As noted earlier, in the 1960s party coalitions contained a variety of factions with differing politics. Many Democrats in Congress were conservatives from the South. Likewise, the Republican Party contained a large liberal faction

based in the Northeast. The rolling realignment after the elections of 1968 resulted in parties that were much more homogeneous. Political scientists have calculated that in the 111th Congress (2009–2011), the most conservative Democrat in the House was still to the left of the most moderate Republican.

Ideological uniformity has made it easier for the parties to maintain discipline in Congress. Personal friendships across party lines, once common in Congress, have become rare. The belief has grown that compromise with the other party is a form of betrayal. According to this view, the minority party should not attempt to improve legislation proposed by the majority, but it should oppose majority-party measures in an attempt to make the majority appear ineffective. The Republican Party was able to employ such tactics as early as the 1990s. Democrats soon began to match these capabilities. What impact did extreme partisanship have on the government's attempt to fight the Great Recession? We look at that question in this chapter's *Our Government Faces a Troubled Economy* feature on the following page.

Realignment, Dealignment, and Tipping

Despite the narrowness of the Republican margin after 2000, Republican strategists dreamed of a new realignment that would force the Democrats into the minority. These hopes were not fulfilled. After 2006, many Democrats anticipated a realignment that would benefit the Democrats. These dreams were shattered as well. For a major realignment to take place, a large number of voters must conclude that their party is no longer capable of representing their interests and ideals, and that another party can do better. It is hard to identify large groups of voters who could be swayed to support a different party today.

DEALIGNMENT One political development that may rule out realignment is the growth in the number of independent voters. By 2010, fully 40 percent of the electorate claimed to be independent. True, many of these voters admitted to leaning to the Republicans or the Democrats. Still, anyone claiming to be an independent has a weakened attachment to the parties. Some political scientists argue that with so many independent voters, the concept of realignment becomes irrelevant. Realignment has been replaced by **dealignment.**

TIPPING Realignment is not the only process that can alter the political landscape. What if

dealignment Among voters, a growing detachment from both major political parties.

OUR GOVERNMENT FACES A TROUBLED ECONOMY

No Retreat from Partisan Politics

The Great Recession was America's most serious economic crisis since the Great Depression. You might think that in such a crisis, the major political parties would put partisanship aside to find mutually acceptable solutions. Nothing of the sort happened. When the House took up President Obama's February 2009 stimulus bill, for example, not one Republican voted "yea."

Taxes—and Spending— and More Taxes Still

For many years, the Republicans have beaten the drum for lower taxes. When Republican president George W. Bush took office in 2001, his first major proposal was a series of sweeping tax cuts. Obama's stimulus package did contain some tax cuts. Most of the bill, however, consisted of new spending programs. In contrast, the Republican alternative to the stimulus package consisted entirely of tax cuts. Since that time, Democrats in Congress have enacted a number of tax increases. To pay for universal health care, Congress imposed new taxes on the highest-earning Americans and on the most expensive employer-paid medical plans. In late 2010, Democrats debated whether to let some or all of the Bush tax cuts expire. Republican hostility was severe, given the party's opposition to any tax increase at any time for any reason.

The Mighty, Mighty Deficit

In 2009, Democratic leaders were united in their belief in the necessity of a stimulus program. This belief, based on the theories of John Maynard Keynes, held that the government's budget deficit should rise in a recession and fall in a boom.

Between increased government spending and an abrupt fall in tax revenues resulting from the recession, the nation's budget deficit did indeed rise to levels not seen since World War II (1939–1945). By 2010, the sheer size of the deficit was beginning to cause political problems for the Democrats. Few voters understood or accepted Keynesian arguments in favor of the deficit. Unemployment remained high. As far as most people were concerned, the recession was still on. Keynesians contended that the recession was so powerful that the stimulus could only moderate its effects.

A thumping majority of voters, however, concluded that the stimulus had no effects whatsoever—an idea the Republicans endorsed with enthusiasm. Given these attitudes, it was hard for the Democrats even to extend the duration of unemployment benefits, much less consider another stimulus bill.

Freshwater versus Saltwater Economics

While Keynesianism remains the majority view among experts, a different theory has taken hold at many universities. This alternative has been nicknamed "freshwater economics" because many of its advocates work at schools in the Great Lakes states. Likewise, Keynesianism has been dubbed "saltwater economics" because it is popular at many universities on the East and West Coasts. Many leading Republicans now advocate freshwater theories. Freshwater economists reject the proposition that deficits can be beneficial. They argue that sooner or later, all deficits must be paid off in full by the private sector. Freshwater advocates believe that individuals will react to budget deficits by spending less and saving more in preparation for higher taxes in the future. Indeed, saving in the United States is at record levels.

You Be the Judge If we save more, isn't that good? Could increased savings prolong a recession? If so, how?

the various types of voters maintain their political identifications—but one type of voter becomes substantially more numerous? This can happen due to migration between states or between counties, or even by changes

in education levels and occupations. The result could tip a state from one party to another. Many Democratic strategists believe that such *tipping* will benefit their party greatly in the future.

The Parties and the 2010 Elections

As you learned in Chapter 1, the Democratic Party clearly lost support among American voters. That did not mean, though, that the voters had fallen in love with the Republicans. Rather, a large share of those who went to the polls voted *against* the Democratic Party, and by association, against President Obama. Exit polls showed that many voters did not necessarily seek to put the Republicans back into power but rather sought to punish the Democrats. Both parties were viewed with suspicion by more than half of all eligible voters—in fact, the parties were about tied in negative perceptions.

Whatever their reasons, the voters gave the Republican Party a clear majority in the House and reduced the Democratic advantage in the Senate. With the two chambers in the hands of different parties, it was unlikely that the incoming Congress would be able to accomplish much.

At the state level, more than 680 Republicans won legislative seats. The twenty-nine governorships that were now in Republican hands also strengthened that party at the state level. (One new governor is an independent.) The majorities that Republicans obtained in state legislatures, plus the new Republican governors, yielded one important result. The Republicans were now well-placed to gerrymander election districts in their favor during the upcoming reapportionment based on the 2010 Census.

LO3 *What Do Political Parties Do?*

As noted earlier, the Constitution does not mention political parties. Historically, though, political parties have played a vital role in our democratic system. Their main function has been to link the people's policy preferences to actual government policies. Political parties also perform many other functions.

Selecting Candidates

One of the most important functions of the two political parties is to recruit and nominate candidates for political office. This function simplifies voting choices for the electorate. Political parties take the large number of people who want to run for office and narrow the field. They accomplish this by the use of the **primary,** which is a preliminary election to choose a party's final candidate. This candidate then runs against the opposing party's candidate in the general election.

Voter turnout for primaries is lower than it is for general elections. The voters who do go to the polls are often strong supporters of their party. Indeed, in many states, independents cannot participate in primary elections, even if they lean toward one or the other of the two major parties. As a result, the Republican primary electorate is very conservative, and Democratic primary voters are quite liberal. Candidates often find that they must run to the political right or left during the primaries. Frequently, they then move to the center during the general election campaign. Chapter 9 provides much more detail on primary and general elections.

Informing the Public

Political parties help educate the public about important political issues. In recent years, these issues have included environmental policies, health-care reform, our tax system, education, Social Security, and ways to stimulate the economy. Each party presents its view of these issues through television announcements, newspaper articles or ads, Web site materials, campaign speeches, rallies, debates, and leaflets. These activities help citizens learn about the issues, form opinions, and consider proposed solutions.

Coordinating Policymaking

In our complex government, parties are essential for coordinating policy among the various branches of the government. The political party is usually the major institution through which the executive and legislative branches cooperate with each other. Each president, cabinet head, and member of Congress is normally a member of the Democratic or the Republican Party. The president works through party leaders in Congress to promote the administration's legislative program.

> **primary** A preliminary election held for the purpose of choosing a party's final candidate.

minority party The political party that has fewer members in the legislature than the opposing party.

majority party The political party that has more members in the legislature than the opposing party.

coalition An alliance of individuals or groups with a variety of interests and opinions who join together to support all or part of a political party's platform.

Ideally, the parties work together to fashion compromises—legislation that is acceptable to both parties and that serves the national interest. In recent years, however, there has been little bipartisanship in Congress. (For a more detailed discussion of the role played by political parties in Congress, see Chapter 11.) Parties also act as the glue of our federal structure by connecting the various levels of government—state and national—with a common bond.

Checking the Power of the Governing Party

The party with fewer members in the legislature is the **minority party.** The party with more members is the **majority party.** The party that does not control Congress or a state legislature, or the presidency or a state governorship, also plays a vital function in American politics. The "out party" does what it can to influence the "in party" and its policies, and to check the actions of the party in power. For example, depending on how evenly Congress is divided, the out party, or minority party, may be able to attract to its side some of the members of the majority party to pass or defeat certain legislation. The out party will also work to inform the voters of the shortcomings of the in party's agenda and to plan strategies for winning the next election.

Balancing Competing Interests

Political parties are often described as vast umbrellas under which Americans with diverse interests can gather. Political parties are essentially **coalitions**—individuals and groups with a variety of interests and opinions who join together to support the party's platform, or parts of it.

The Republican Party, for example, includes a number of groups with different views on such issues as health care, immigration, and global warming. The role of party leaders in this situation is to adopt a broad enough view on these issues that the various groups will not be alienated. In this way, different groups can hold their individual views and still come together

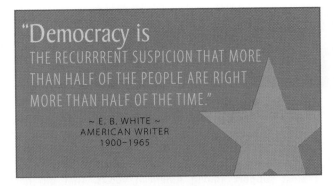

"Democracy is THE RECURRENT SUSPICION THAT MORE THAN HALF OF THE PEOPLE ARE RIGHT MORE THAN HALF OF THE TIME."

~ E. B. WHITE ~
AMERICAN WRITER
1900–1965

under the umbrella of the Republican Party. Leaders of both the Democratic Party and the Republican Party modify contending views and arrange compromises among different groups. In so doing, the parties help to unify, rather than divide, their members.

Running Campaigns

Through their national, state, and local organizations, parties coordinate campaigns. Political parties take care of a large number of small and routine tasks that are essential to the smooth functioning of the electoral process. For example, they work at getting party members registered and at conducting drives for new voters. Sometimes, party volunteers staff the polling places.

LO4 *How American Political Parties Are Structured*

Each of the two major American political parties consists of three components: the party in the electorate, the party organization, and the party in government.

Every political campaign relies on volunteers at the grassroots level, such as these volunteers in Baldwin Park, California. They are tallying votes for their candidate on the evening of election day.

ZUMA PRESS/NEWSCOM

1. The party in the **electorate** is the largest component, consisting of all of those people who describe themselves as Democrats or Republicans. Members of the party in the electorate never need to work on a campaign or attend a party meeting. In most states, they may register as Democrats or Republicans, but registration can be changed at will.

2. Each major party has a nationwide organization with national, state, and local offices. As will be discussed later in this section, the party organizations include several levels of people who maintain the party's strength between elections, make its rules, raise money, organize conventions, help with elections, and recruit candidates.

3. The party in government consists of all of the party's candidates who have won elections and now hold public office. Even though members of Congress, state legislators, presidents, and all other officeholders almost always run for office as either Democrats or Republicans, members of any one party do not always agree with each other on government policy. The party in government helps to organize the government's agenda by coaxing and convincing its own party members to vote for its policies. If the party is to translate its promises into public policies, the job must be done by the party in government.

The Party in the Electorate

Let's look more closely at the largest component of each party—the party in the electorate. What does it mean to belong to a political party? In many European countries, being a party member means that you actually join a political party. You get a membership card to carry in your wallet, you pay dues, and you vote to select your local and national party leaders. In the United States, becoming a member of a political party is far less involved.

In most states, voters may declare a party preference when they register to vote. This declaration allows them to participate in party primaries. Some states do not register party preferences, however. In short, to be a member of a political party, an American citizen has only to think of herself or himself as a Democrat or a Republican (or a member of a third party, such as the Green Party, the Libertarian Party, or the American Independent Party).

"Under democracy one party always devotes its chief energies to trying to prove that the other party is **UNFIT TO RULE**—and both commonly succeed."

~ H. L. MENCKEN ~
AMERICAN JOURNALIST
1880–1956

Members of parties do not have to work for the party or attend party meetings. Nor must they support the party platform.

IDENTIFIERS AND ACTIVISTS Generally, the party in the electorate consists of **party identifiers** (those who identify themselves as being members of a particular party) and **party activists**—party members who choose to work for the party and even become candidates for office. Political parties need year-round support from the latter group to survive. During election campaigns in particular, candidates depend on active party members or volunteers to mail literature, answer phones, conduct door-to-door canvasses, organize speeches and appearances, and, of course, donate money.

Between elections, parties also need active members to plan the upcoming elections, organize fund-raisers, and stay in touch with party leaders in other communities to keep the party strong. The major functions of American political parties are carried out by the party activists.

WHY PEOPLE JOIN POLITICAL PARTIES Generally, in the United States people belong to a political party because they agree with many of its main ideas and support some of its candidates. In a few countries, such as the People's Republic of China, people belong to a political party because they are required to do so to get ahead in life, regardless of whether they agree with the party's ideas and candidates.

People join political parties for a multitude of reasons. One reason is that people wish to express their **solidarity,** or mutual agreement, with the views of friends, loved ones, and other like-minded people. People also join parties because they enjoy the excitement of politics.

In addition, many believe they will benefit materially from joining a party through better employment or personal

electorate All of the citizens eligible to vote in a given election.

party identifier A person who identifies himself or herself as being a supporter of a particular political party.

party activist A party member who helps to organize and oversee party functions and planning during and between campaigns.

solidarity Mutual agreement among the members of a particular group.

During the Denver Democratic National Convention in 2008, presidential candidate Barack Obama, then a senator from Illinois, takes center stage with vice-presidential candidate Joe Biden, then a senator from Delaware.

career advancement. The traditional institution of **patronage**—rewarding the party faithful with government jobs or contracts—lives on, even though it has been limited to prevent abuses.[5] Back in the nineteenth century, when almost all government employees got their jobs through patronage, people spoke of it as the "spoils system," as in "the spoils of war."

Finally, some join political parties because they wish to actively promote a set of ideals and principles that they feel are important to American politics and society. As a rule, people join political parties because of their overall agreement with what a particular party stands for. Thus, when interviewed, people may make the following remarks when asked why they support the Democratic Party: "It seems that the economy is better when the Democrats are in control." "The Democrats are for the working people." People might say about the Republican Party: "The Republicans help small businesses more than the Democrats." "The Republicans deal better with foreign policy and defense issues."

The Party Organization

In theory, each of the major American political parties has a standard, pyramid-shaped organization. This theoretical structure is much like that of a large company, in which the bosses are at the top and the employees are at various lower levels.

Actually, neither major party is a closely knit or

patronage A system of rewarding the party faithful and workers with government jobs or contracts.

highly organized structure. Both parties are fragmented and *decentralized*, which means there is no central power with a direct chain of command. If there were, the national chairperson of the party, along with the national committee, could simply dictate how the organization would be run, just as if it were Microsoft or General Electric. In reality, state party organizations are all very different and are only loosely tied to the party's national structure. Local party organizations are often quite independent from the state organization. There is no single individual or group who directs all party members. Instead, a number of personalities, frequently at odds with one another, form loosely identifiable leadership groups.

STATE ORGANIZATIONS The powers and duties of state party organizations differ from state to state. In general, the state party organization is built around a central committee and a chairperson. The committee works to raise funds, recruit new party members, maintain a strong party organization, and help members running for state offices.

The state chairperson is usually a powerful party member chosen by the committee. In some instances, however, the chairperson is selected by the governor or a senator from that state.

Then Alaska governor Sarah Palin is shown giving her acceptance speech as candidate for vice president at the Republican National Convention in St. Paul, Minnesota, in 2008.

Tim Kaine (left) is currently the chair of the Democratic National Committee and was the governor of Virginia until January 2010. Michael Steele is the chair of the Republican National Committee. What do these men do?

WILLIAM B. PLOWMAN/NBC NEWSWIRE VIA AP IMAGES

LOCAL ORGANIZATIONS Local party organizations differ greatly, but generally there is a party unit for each district in which elective offices are to be filled. These districts include congressional and legislative districts, counties, cities and towns, wards, and precincts.

A **ward** is a political division or district within a city. A **precinct** can be either a political district within a city, such as a block or a neighborhood, or a rural portion of a county. Polling places are located within the precincts. The local, grassroots foundations of politics are formed within voting precincts.

THE NATIONAL PARTY ORGANIZATION On the national level, the party's presidential candidate is considered to be the leader of the party. Well-known members of Congress may also be viewed as national party leaders. In addition to the party leaders, the structure of each party includes four major elements: the national convention, the national committee, the national chairperson, and the congressional campaign committees.

The National Convention Much of the public attention that the party receives comes at the **national convention,** which is held every four years during the summer before the presidential elections. The news media always cover these conventions, and as a result, they have become quite extravagant. Are these extravaganzas worth the cost? We look at that question in this chapter's *Join the Debate* feature on the following page.

The national conventions are attended by delegates chosen by the states in various ways, which we describe in Chapter 9. The delegates' most important job is to choose the party's presidential and vice-presidential candidates, who together make up the **party ticket.** The delegates also write the **party platform,** which sets forth the party's positions on national issues. Essentially, through its platform, the party promises to initiate certain policies if it wins the presidency. Despite the widespread perception that candidates can and do ignore these promises once they are in office, in fact, many of them become law.

The National Committee Each state elects a number of delegates to the **national party committee.** The Republican National Committee and the Democratic National Committee direct the business of their respective parties during the four years between national conventions. The committees' most important duties, however, are to organize the next national convention and to plan how to obtain a party victory in the next presidential elections.

The National Chairperson Each party's national committee elects a **national party chairperson** to serve as administrative head of the national party. The main duty of the national chairperson is to direct the work of the national committee from party headquarters in Washington, D.C. The chairperson is involved in raising

Are National Party Conventions Worth the Cost?

For many decades, national party conventions were important to the nomination of each party's presidential candidate. In modern times, however, each party has already chosen its candidates for president and vice president before the conventions begin. Nonetheless, state delegates continue to attend the four-day extravaganzas that each party holds every four years, and so do the media, political commentators, and quite a few entertainers.

At the 2008 Democratic Party convention in Denver, members of Congress were able to hear singer Kanye West, courtesy of the recording industry. Others were given $5,000 to play poker at a tournament that featured actor Ben Affleck. At the 2008 Republican Party convention, some lucky delegates were invited to the Aqua Nightclub in Minneapolis to hear the band Smash Mouth. Both conventions cost over $100 million. Are national party conventions worth the cost?

It's Not Just Flash and Partying

Those who defend the conventions point out that they inspire and mobilize party members throughout the nation. They provide the voters with an opportunity to see and hear the candidates directly, rather than through the filter of the media or through characterizations provided by supporters and opponents. Candidate speeches draw huge audiences. For example, in 2008, more than 38 million people watched the acceptance speeches of Barack Obama and John McCain.

Don't forget the unifying nature of most national party conventions. At the 2008 Democratic convention in Denver, supporters of Hillary Clinton were not necessarily convinced that they should support Barack Obama. By the end of that convention, many of these voters had decided that they could indeed endorse him. At the 2008 Republican convention in St. Paul, a humorous

and aggressive acceptance speech by vice-presidential candidate Sarah Palin not only electrified the attending delegates but also served as a way to unify the party behind the ticket. In short, conventions are well worth their costs.

No More Wretched Excess

Who needs multimillion-dollar national conventions to ratify the nominations of presidential and vice-presidential candidates who have already been chosen? What party business is there that cannot be done with less time and expense? In 2008, during a period of economic struggle for many Americans, the spending of millions of dollars on superfluous activities in Denver and St. Paul certainly did not send the right signals.

And where did all that money come from? You guessed it—lobbyists, big business, and labor unions. In spite of new congressional ethics rules designed to curb the influence of these groups, they spent more in 2008 than ever before. Those millions are not spent to further the general welfare—they come from companies and associations that depend on government subsidies, tax breaks, or regulatory favors from Washington, D.C.

For Critical Analysis *The parties often pick the states that host their national conventions in the hope of enhancing their performance in those states. Do you think that holding a party's convention in a particular state will win votes from its voters? Why or why not?*

funds, providing for publicity, promoting party unity, encouraging the development of state and local organizations, recruiting new voters, and other activities. In presidential election years, the chairperson's attention is focused on the national convention and the presidential campaign.

The Congressional Campaign Committees Each party has a campaign committee, made up of senators and representatives, in each chamber of Congress. Members are chosen by their colleagues and serve for two-year terms. The committees work to help reelect party members to Congress.

The Party in Government: Developing Issues

When a political party wins the presidency or control of one or more chambers of Congress, it has the opportunity to carry out the party platform it developed at its national convention. The platform represents the official party position on various issues, although as just mentioned, neither all party members nor all candidates running on the party's ticket are likely to share these positions exactly.

HOW PRESIDENTS RESPOND TO PARTY PLATFORMS

Party platforms do not necessarily tell you what candidates are going to do when they take office. For example, although the Democratic Party generally favors social legislation to help low-income individuals, it was a Democratic president, Bill Clinton, who signed a major welfare reform bill in 1996, forcing many welfare recipients off the welfare rolls. The Democrats usually have the support of labor unions, yet President Clinton approved the North American Free Trade Agreement despite bitter opposition from most of the nation's unions. Additionally, the Democrats have traditionally been associated with "big government" and deficit spending, but under President Bill Clinton there was a budget surplus for several years in a row.

Similarly, although the Republican Party has long advocated "small government" and states' rights, federal government spending was taken to new heights during the George W. Bush administration, budget surpluses disappeared, and legislation such as the No Child

"I AM NOT A MEMBER OF ANY ORGANIZED POLITICAL PARTY.
I am a democrat."
~ WILL ROGERS ~
AMERICAN HUMORIST
1879–1935

Left Behind Act effectively transferred power from the states to the federal government.

THE PARTIES RETURN TO THEIR ROOTS   Following the elections of 2008, the Republican Party appeared to regain its traditional appreciation for states' rights. To a considerable extent, this return to tradition was fueled by the dramatic ambitions of President Obama and the Democratic Party. In reality, the new measures adopted by the Democrats in 2009 and 2010 did not tend to strip power away from the states. Rather, the federal government gained power largely at the expense of the private sector.

Many conservatives, however, saw the states as a force that could counter the federal government. This view led to such actions as state lawsuits challenging the Democrat's health-care reform legislation, discussed in the *Join the Debate* feature in Chapter 3.

LO5 *The Dominance of Our Two-Party System*

In the United States, we have a **two-party system.** This means that the two major parties—the Democrats and the Republicans—dominate national politics. Why has the two-party system become so firmly entrenched in the United States? According to some scholars, the first major political division between the Federalists and the Anti-Federalists established a precedent that continued over time and ultimately resulted in the domination of the two-party system.

As noted earlier, about a third of the voters identify themselves as independents (although they may lean toward one party or the other). For these individuals, both of the major parties evidently fail to address issues that are important to them or represent their views. Nonetheless, the two-party system

> **two-party system**   A political system in which two strong and established parties compete for political offices.

Texas delegates at the 2008 Republican Party national convention bow their heads during the invocation on the last day. Do these delegates have any real power to elect their party's presidential candidate when attending this convention?

SARA KRULWICH/THE NEW YORK TIMES/REDUX

Most colleges and universities have mascots that represent their athletic teams. So, too, do the two major political parties. On the left, you see the donkey that became the Democratic Party mascot. On the right, you see the elephant that became the Republican Party mascot.[6]

continues to thrive. A number of factors help to explain this phenomenon.

The Self-Perpetuation of the Two-Party System

One of the major reasons for the perpetuation of the two-party system is simply that there is no alternative. Minor parties, called **third parties,**[7] have found it extremely difficult to compete with the major parties for votes. There are many reasons for this, including election laws and institutional barriers.

ELECTION LAWS FAVORING TWO PARTIES American election laws tend to favor the major parties. In many states, for example, the established major parties need relatively few signatures to place their candidates on the ballot, whereas a third party must get many more signatures. The number of signatures required is often based on the total party vote in the last election, which penalizes a new party competing for the first time.

The rules governing campaign financing also favor the major parties. As you will read in Chapter 9, both major parties receive federal funds for presidential campaigns and for their national conventions. Third parties, in contrast, receive federal funds only if they garner 5 percent of the vote, and they receive the funds only *after* the election.

third party In the United States, any party other than one of the two major parties (Republican and Democratic).

INSTITUTIONAL BARRIERS TO A MULTIPARTY SYSTEM
The structure of many of our institutions prevents third parties from enjoying electoral success. One of the major institutional barriers is the winner-take-all feature of the electoral college system for electing the president (discussed in more detail in Chapter 9). In a winner-take-all system, which applies in all but two of the states (Maine and Nebraska), the winner of a state's popular vote gets all of that state's electoral votes. Thus, third-party candidates have little incentive to run for president, because they are unlikely to get enough popular votes to receive any state's electoral votes.

Another institutional barrier to a multiparty system is the single-member district. Today, all federal and most state legislative districts are single-member districts—that is, voters elect one member from their district to the House of Representatives and to their state legislature.[8] In most European countries, by contrast, districts are drawn as multimember districts and are represented by multiple elected officials from different parties, according to the proportion of the vote their party received.

DUVERGER'S LAW In nations around the world, the association between multimember districts (or proportional representation) and multiple political parties is strong. So is the association between single-member, first-past-the-post districts and two-party systems. These relationships are firm enough that some scholars have called them a "law" of political science—*Duverger's Law,* named after French political scientist Maurice Duverger.

Britain's Coalition Government

Coalition governments are impossible in the United States because we do not have a *parliamentary system*. Britain, Canada, Germany, and many other countries do use parliamentary systems, however.

First, a Few Basics

Britain—the United Kingdom—has a typical parliamentary system. Members of Parliament are elected just as we elect members of Congress. Here the similarity ends. British voters do not choose a chief executive, as we do in the United States when we vote for president. Rather, the chief executive is chosen by the *lower house* of Parliament—the House of Commons, analogous to our House of Representatives. (There is an upper house, the House of Lords, but it has little power.)

Each party selects a leader well before the general elections. The leader then chooses other members of Parliament who, if the party wins, will take cabinet posts, such as minister of defense or minister of justice. If one party wins a majority of the seats in the House of Commons, it can name its leader as the *prime minister*—the chief executive of the nation. The Queen then formally appoints the new government.

In the rare event that no party has a majority in the Commons, two options are possible. The largest party can form a "minority government" with the acquiescence of other parties. Alternatively, two or more parties can agree to form a coalition government. Many countries that use the parliamentary system are normally governed by coalitions, although until 2010 Britain had not had one for decades.

The British Parties

Just as in the United States, British legislators are elected in single-member districts. This system makes it difficult for third parties to organize, but over the last century Britain has always had important third parties. In the nineteenth century, the two major parties were the Conservatives and the Liberals. In the early twentieth century, however, the Liberals lost their position as a major party to the Labour Party. The Liberals never vanished entirely. Under the name Liberal Democrats, they are Britain's main third party today. (Other minor parties contest seats only in particular regions.) The Labour Party is the main left-of-center party in Britain. It was originally organized to defend labor unions, but it soon grew into a broader left-wing movement. On the right is the Conservative Party, often called the Tories.

The New British Coalition Government

In 2010, the unthinkable happened in Britain—the first coalition government in sixty-five years was formed. The prime minister is Conservative David Cameron, the youngest person to hold this post in almost two centuries. The deputy prime minister is Liberal Democrat Nick Clegg. Before the elections that led to the coalition, Britain was governed by Labour.

In short order, the coalition government unveiled a plan to make severe cuts to Britain's huge budget deficit. Although some taxes were raised, most of the deficit reduction will come from spending cuts. Except for the National Health Service, every government department will have to shrink by 20 to 30 percent over the next few years. Will the coalition succeed in reducing the size of Britain's government? The future of this "great gamble" is less than clear.

For Critical Analysis *Why don't sitting members of the U.S. Congress ever join the president's cabinet?*

Still, many nations have single-member constituencies and three or more major political parties. Canada and Britain are examples. To guarantee a two-party system, it is probably necessary also to have directly elected executive officers, such as the president and various state governors in the United States. Third parties may be able to elect a few members to a legislature, but winning a nationwide vote for chief executive is typically hopeless. For a closer look at Britain's multiparty system, see the feature *The Rest of the World: Britain's Coalition Government* above.

Third Parties in American Politics

Despite difficulties, throughout American history, third parties have competed for influence in the nation's two-party system. Indeed, as mentioned earlier, third parties have been represented in most of our national elections.

These parties are as varied as the causes they represent, but all have one thing in common: their members and leaders want to challenge the major parties because they believe that certain needs and values are not being properly addressed.

Some third parties have tried to appeal to the entire nation. Others have focused on particular regions, states, or local areas. Most third parties have been short lived. A few, however, such as the Socialist Party (founded in 1901 and disbanded in 1972), lasted for a long time. The number and variety of third parties make them difficult to classify, but most fall into one of the general categories discussed in the following subsections.

ISSUE-ORIENTED PARTIES An issue-oriented third party is formed to promote a particular cause or timely issue. For example, the Free Soil Party was organized in 1848 to oppose the expansion of slavery into the western territories. The Prohibition Party was formed in 1869 to advocate banning the manufacture and use of alcoholic beverages.

Most issue-oriented parties fade into history as the issue that brought them into existence fades from public attention, is taken up by a major party, or is resolved. Some issue-oriented parties endure, however, when they expand their focus beyond a single area of concern. For example, the Green Party was founded in 1972 to raise awareness of environmental issues, but it is no longer a single-issue party. Ralph Nader, the presidential candidate for the Green Party in 2000, campaigned against alleged corporate greed and the major parties' ostensible indifference to a number of issues, including universal health insurance, child poverty, the excesses of globalism, and the failure of the drug war.

IDEOLOGICAL PARTIES As discussed in Chapter 1, a *political ideology* is a system of political ideas rooted in beliefs about human nature, society, and government. An ideological party supports a particular political doctrine or a set of beliefs. For example, a party such as the (still-existing) Socialist Workers Party may believe that our free enterprise system should be replaced by one in which workers own all of the factories in the economy. The party's members may believe that competition should be replaced by cooperation and social responsibility so as to achieve an equitable distribution of income. In contrast, an ideological party such as the Libertarian Party may oppose virtually all forms of

> "Let us not seek the Republican answer or the Democratic answer, but the
> # RIGHT ANSWER."
> ~ JOHN FITZGERALD KENNEDY ~
> THIRTY-FIFTH PRESIDENT OF THE UNITED STATES
> 1961–1963

government interference with personal liberties and private enterprise.

SPLINTER OR PERSONALITY PARTIES A splinter party develops out of a split within a major party. This split may be part of an attempt to elect a specific person. For example, when Theodore Roosevelt did not receive the Republican Party's nomination for president in 1912, he created the Bull Moose Party (also called the Progressive Party) to promote his candidacy. From the Democrats have come Henry Wallace's Progressive Party and the States' Rights (Dixiecrat) Party, both formed in 1948. In 1968, the American Independent Party was formed to support George Wallace's campaign for president.

Most splinter parties have been formed around a leader with a strong personality, which is why they are sometimes called personality parties. When that person steps aside, the party usually collapses. An example of a personality party is the Reform Party, which was formed in 1996 mainly to provide a campaign vehicle for H. Ross Perot.

The Effects of Third Parties

Although most Americans do not support third parties or vote for their candidates, third parties have influenced American politics in several ways, some of which we examine here.

THIRD PARTIES BRING ISSUES TO THE PUBLIC'S ATTENTION Third parties have brought many political issues to the public's attention. They have exposed

Theodore Roosevelt and his Progressive (Bull Moose) Party changed the outcome of the 1912 election.

Figure 7–2

The Effect of Third Parties on Vote Distribution, 1848–1992

In eight presidential elections, a third party's candidate received more than 10 percent of the popular vote—and in six of those elections, the incumbent party lost. As shown here, only in 1856 and 1924 did the incumbent party manage to hold on to the White House in the face of a significant third-party showing.

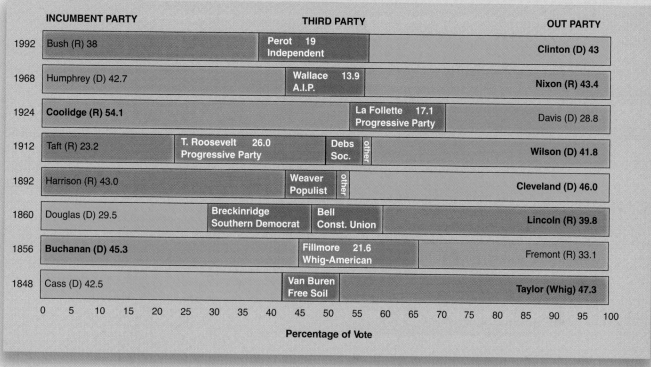

Source: *Congressional Quarterly Weekly Report*, June 13, 1992, p. 1729.

and focused on unpopular or highly debated issues that major parties have preferred to ignore. Third parties are in a position to take bold stands on issues that major parties avoid, because third parties are not trying to be all things to all people. Progressive social reforms such as the minimum wage, women's right to vote, railroad and banking legislation, and old-age pensions were first proposed by third parties. The Free Soilers of the 1850s, for example, were the first true antislavery party, and the Populists and Progressives put many social reforms on the political agenda.

Some people have argued that third parties are often the unsung heroes of American politics, bringing new issues to the forefront of public debate. Some of the ideas proposed by third parties were never accepted, while others were taken up by the major parties as those ideas became increasingly popular.

THIRD PARTIES CAN AFFECT THE VOTE Third parties can also influence election outcomes. Third parties have occasionally taken victory from one major party and given it to another, thus playing the "spoiler" role.

For example, in 1912, when the Progressive Party split off from the Republican Party, the result was

three major contenders for the presidency: Woodrow Wilson, the Democratic candidate; William Howard Taft, the regular Republican candidate; and Theodore Roosevelt, the Progressive candidate. The presence of the Progressive Party "spoiled" the Republicans' chances for victory and gave the election to Wilson, the Democrat. Without Roosevelt's third party, Taft might have won. Similarly, some commentators contended that Ralph Nader "spoiled" the chances of Democratic candidate Al Gore in the 2000 elections, because many of those who voted for Nader would have voted Democratic had Nader not been a candidate.

A significant showing by a minor party also reduces an incumbent party's chances of winning the election, as you can see in Figure 7–2 above. In 1992, for example, third-party candidate H. Ross Perot captured about 19 percent of the vote. Had those votes been distributed between the candidates of the major parties, incumbent George H. W. Bush and candidate Bill Clinton, the outcome of the election might have been different.

THIRD PARTIES PROVIDE A VOICE FOR DISSATISFIED AMERICANS Third parties also provide a voice for voters who are frustrated with and alienated from the

Republican and Democratic parties. Americans who are unhappy with the two major political parties can still participate in American politics through third parties that reflect their opinions on political issues. For example, many new Minnesota voters turned out during the 1998 elections to vote for Jesse Ventura, a Reform Party candidate for governor in that state. Ventura won.

Ultimately, third parties find it difficult to break through in an electoral system that perpetuates their own failure. Because third parties normally do not win elections, Americans tend not to vote for them or to contribute to their campaigns, so they continue not to win elections. As long as Americans hold to the perception that third parties can never win big in an election, the current two-party system is likely to persist.

AMERICA AT ODDS   *Political Parties*

By their very nature, arguments about the parties are some of the most divisive conflicts in politics. We can list only a sampling of the disputes:

- Is the Republican Party driving off voters that it needs by excessive conservatism—or is it failing to uphold basic conservative values? For that matter, are the Democrats too liberal—or not liberal enough?

- Are political parties desirable and inevitable—or should elections be nonpartisan whenever possible?

- Is it better when the two chambers of Congress and the presidency are held by the same party, thus guaranteeing effective government—or is it better when Congress and the presidency are held by

different parties, so that the two parties can check each other?

- Is the increasing importance of political independents a positive development—or is it a sign that citizens are becoming dangerously detached from our political system?

- Is it better to support a third party when you are in greater agreement with its positions than with those of either major party—or should you avoid wasting your vote and always support the major party that is closer to your politics?

- Finally, looking forward, do the Republicans or the Democrats offer the best solutions for our problems?

Take Action

Getting involved in political parties is as simple as going to the polls and casting your vote for the candidate of one of the major parties—or of a third party. If you want to go a step further, you can attend a speech given by a political candidate or even volunteer to assist a political party or a specific candidate's campaign activities.

You can also consider another alternative—becoming a delegate to a party convention. National conventions aren't the only ones that the parties hold. There are state conventions, and most local party units conduct regular conventions as well. Depending on the state, parties may hold conventions by U.S. House district, by county, or by state legislative district. In many states, the lowest-level conventions are open to anyone who shows up.

Voting rights at a convention, however, may be restricted to those who are elected as a precinct delegate in a party primary. In much of the country, precinct delegate slots go unfilled. If this is true in your area, you can become a precinct delegate with a simple write-in campaign. You merely need to write in your own name and persuade a small handful of friends or neighbors to write you in as well. Whether you attend a convention as a voting delegate or as a guest, you'll have a firsthand look at how politics

operates. You'll hear debates on resolutions. You might participate in electing delegates to higher-level conventions—perhaps even the national convention if it is a presidential election year. Few exercises are more educational.

AP PHOTO/CHARLES KRUPA

The government provides election materials in a variety of languages other than English.

POLITICS ON THE
WEB

- For a list of political Web sites available on the Internet, sorted by country and with links to parties, organizations, and governments throughout the world, go to **www.politicalresources.net**

- Ron Gunzburger's Politics1 Web site contains a vast amount of information on American politics. Click on "Political Parties" in the directory box at the top of the home page to see one of the most complete descriptions of major and minor parties to be found anywhere. Gunzburger's site is at **www.politics1.com**

- The Democratic Party is online at **www.democrats.org**

- The Republican National Committee is online at **www.gop.com**

- The Libertarian Party has a Web site at **www.lp.org**

- The Green Party's Web site can be accessed by going to **www.greenparty.org**

CourseMate Access CourseMate to review and expand on this chapter through quizzes, flashcards, learning objectives, interactive timelines, a crossword puzzle, audio summaries, video, critical-thinking activities, simulations, and more.

{ Learning Your Way }

Resources that match your learning style, when and where you need them!
Get them today: **4ltrpress.cengage.com/politicalscience**

Public Opinion and Voting

LEARNING OBJECTIVES

LO1 Explain what public opinion is and how it is measured.

LO2 Describe the political socialization process.

LO3 Summarize the history of polling in the United States, and explain how polls are conducted and how they are used in the political process.

LO4 Indicate some of the factors that affect voter turnout, and discuss what has been done to improve voter turnout and voting procedures.

LO5 Discuss the different factors that affect voter choices.

AMERICA AT ODDS

Should Felons Be Allowed to Vote?

Suppose that you commit a crime that is punishable by a prison term. You serve your time and are released. You are now a felon—someone who has been convicted of a serious crime. When you leave prison, the terms people apply to you are not pretty. You are an "ex-con"—an ex-convict. You may believe that you have "repaid your debt to society" by going to prison, but that does not mean that all of your rights are restored after you have served your sentence. In most states, felons do not have the right to vote. Certainly, many people will agree that those who are actually serving time in prison should not be able to vote. But what about those who have rejoined society?

Because America puts more people behind bars than any other nation, the number of ex-cons is staggering. In Florida alone there are more than 120,000 former convicts. At least 13 percent of the nation's African American male population is disenfranchised. The United States takes a much harder line on this issue than most countries. Many of our allies, in fact, allow most people to vote while they are still in prison. Nations that do that include Canada, France, Germany, and many others. In the United States, Maine and Vermont allow prisoners to vote—and so does Puerto Rico. Among our European allies, only Belgium permanently disenfranchises felons. Should such people have the right to vote?

No One Should Be Denied the Right to Vote

Felony disenfranchisement affects almost 6 million persons in the United States. That means that 6 million Americans cannot express their political beliefs by voting. One negative result of this exclusion is racial discrimination. The percentage of African Americans who are felons is much greater than their share of the total population. The result: compared with whites, a disproportionate number of blacks are excluded from the democratic process because of state laws that prevent felons from voting.

Regardless of race, those who are convicted of felonies are disproportionately poor. By excluding many poor persons and minority group members from the voting rolls, we bias the vote against the poor and the historically disadvantaged. Some question how we can call ourselves a fully democratic country if we disenfranchise so many people. Those who want felons to regain the right to vote contend that our current situation is patently unfair.

When You Break the Rules, You Lose Some Rights

No one questions the right of society to incarcerate those convicted of serious crimes. No one questions the need for punishment when individuals violate our accepted rules of behavior. Therefore, why should anyone question each state's right to prevent convicts and former convicts from exercising all of the rights enjoyed by law-abiding citizens? Felons are not the kind of people we want to choose our leaders and the legislators who make our laws.

Some opponents of felon enfranchisement also contend that proponents are making a mountain out of a molehill. When Florida passed a law allowing former convicts to register to vote, the results were not encouraging. Only about 10,000 out of a potential 120,000 former convicts actually registered. Those in favor of allowing felons to vote are misplacing their efforts. They should instead attempt to reduce incentives for Americans to commit crimes.

WHERE DO YOU STAND?

1. Would you be in favor of allowing individuals currently in prison to be able to register to vote? Why or why not?
2. If the millions of former convicts in America could register to vote, would it make any difference? Why or why not?

EXPLORE THIS ISSUE ONLINE

- The *New York Times* has covered the issue of felon disenfranchisement in considerable depth. You can find some of its stories by entering their titles into a search engine such as Google. Type in "Voting Behind Bars" for a recent article by Linda Greenhouse that raises the question of whether disenfranchisement is unconstitutional. Enter "States Restore Voting Rights for Ex-Convicts" for details about the Florida experience.

Introduction

For a democracy to be effective, members of the public must form opinions and openly express them to their elected officials. Only when the opinions of Americans are communicated effectively to elected representatives can those opinions form the basis of government action. As President Franklin D. Roosevelt once said, "A government can be no better than the public opinion that sustains it."

What exactly is *public opinion*? How do we form our opinions on political issues? How can public opinion be measured accurately? Finally, what factors affect voter participation?

Researchers and scholars have addressed these questions time and again. They are important questions because the backbone of our democracy has always been civic participation—taking part in the political life of the country. Civic participation means many things, but perhaps the most important way that Americans participate in their democracy is through voting—expressing their opinions in the polling places. Who may vote is therefore an important issue, as explained in this chapter's opening *America at Odds* feature.

"A government can be no better than the

PUBLIC OPINION

that sustains it."

~ FRANKLIN DELANO ROOSEVELT ~
THIRTY-SECOND PRESIDENT
OF THE UNITED STATES
1933–1945

significant number of Americans" feel a certain way about an issue, you are probably hearing that a particular opinion is held by a large enough number of people to make government officials turn their heads and listen. For example, public opinion surveys in 2008 revealed that the poor state of the economy was the number-one issue for Americans. Polls also showed that the economy was the main issue in 2010, although it hardly took a poll to discover that fact, given that the unemployment rate was above 9 percent and houses were entering foreclosure in huge numbers.

Politicians were forced to react. In 2008, the outgoing Bush administration obtained a $700 billion bank bailout bill from Congress. After January 2009, the incoming Democrats under President Barack Obama undertook a series of expensive steps in an attempt to combat the Great Recession, beginning with an enormous stimulus package in February. These various measures may have reduced the severity of the recession, but they did not halt it. The voters therefore punished the Republicans in 2008—and turned against the Democrats in 2010.

LO1 *What Is Public Opinion?*

People hold opinions—sometimes very strong ones—about a variety of issues, ranging from the ethics of capital punishment to the latest trends in fashion. In this chapter, however, we are concerned with only a portion of those opinions. For our purposes here, we define **public opinion** as the sum total of a complex collection of opinions held by many people on issues in the public arena, such as taxes, health care, Social Security, clean-air legislation, and unemployment.

When you hear a news report or read a magazine article stating that "a

public opinion The views of the citizenry about politics, public issues, and public policies; a complex collection of opinions held by many people on issues in the public arena.

political socialization The learning process through which most people acquire their political attitudes, opinions, beliefs, and knowledge.

agents of political socialization People and institutions that influence the political views of others.

LO2 *How Do People Form Political Opinions?*

When asked, most Americans are willing to express an opinion on political issues. Not one of us, however, was born with such opinions. Most people acquire their political attitudes, opinions, beliefs, and knowledge through a complex learning process called **political socialization.** This process begins in childhood and continues throughout life.

Most political socialization is informal, and it usually begins during early childhood, when the dominant influence on a child is the family. Although parents normally do not sit down and say to their children, "Let us explain to you the virtues of becoming a Republican," their children nevertheless come to know the parents' feelings, beliefs, and attitudes. The strong early influence of the family later gives way to the multiple influences of school, peers, television, co-workers, and other groups. People and institutions that influence the political views of others are called **agents of political socialization.**

The Importance of Family

As just suggested, most parents or caregivers do not deliberately set out to form their children's political ideas and beliefs. They are usually more concerned with the moral, religious, and ethical values of their offspring. Yet a child first sees the political world through the eyes of his or her family, which is perhaps the most important force in political socialization. Children do not "learn" political attitudes the same way they learn to master in-line skating. Rather, they learn by hearing their parents' everyday conversations and stories about politicians and issues and by observing their parents' actions. They also learn from watching and listening to their siblings, as well as from the kinds of situations in which their parents place them.

The family's influence is strongest when children clearly perceive their parents' attitudes. Parents commonly do communicate their political attitudes to their children. For example, in one study, more high school students could identify their parents' political party affiliation than their parents' other attitudes or beliefs. In many situations, the political party of the parents becomes the political party of the children, particularly if both parents support the same party.

The Schools and Educational Attainment

Education also strongly influences an individual's political attitudes. From their earliest days in school, children learn about the American political system. They say the Pledge of Allegiance and sing patriotic songs. They celebrate national holidays, such as Presidents' Day and Veterans' Day,

This Native American boy poses with his Cub Scout manual. He hopes to obtain a Cub Scout religious emblem that recognizes his faith in the traditional Navajo spiritual way of life. Both his family and the Cub Scouts are socializing influences on him.

AP PHOTO/NAVAJO NATION, GEORGE HARDEEN

and learn about the history and symbols associated with them. In the upper grades, young people acquire more knowledge about government and democratic procedures through civics classes and participation in student government and various clubs. They also learn citizenship skills through school rules and regulations. Generally, those with more education have more knowledge about politics and policy than those with less education. The level of education also influences a person's political values, as will be discussed later in this chapter.

Although the schools have always been important agents of political socialization, many Americans today believe that our schools are not fulfilling this mission. Too many students are graduating from high school—and even college—with too little knowledge of the American system of government.

The Media

The **media**—newspapers, magazines, television, radio, and the Internet—also have an impact on political socialization. The most influential of these media is television, which continues to be a leading source of political and public affairs information for most people.

Some contend that the media's role in shaping public opinion has increased to the point at which the media are as influential as the family, particularly among high school students. For example, in her analysis of the media's role in American politics, media scholar Doris A. Graber points out that high school students, when asked where they obtain the information on which they base their attitudes, mention the mass media far more than they mention their families, friends, and teachers.[1] Graber's conclusion takes on added significance in view of a 2006 Gallup poll showing that only about half of the parents polled

media Newspapers, magazines, television, radio, the Internet, and any other printed or electronic means of communication.

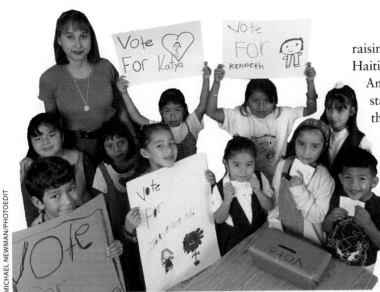

MICHAEL NEWMAN/PHOTOEDIT

Students learn about the political process early on when they participate in class elections.

were concerned about their children's TV-viewing habits, even when their children watched TV "a great deal" or a "fair amount" of time.

Other studies have shown that the media's influence on people's opinions may not be as great as some have thought. Generally, people watch television, read articles, or access online sites with preconceived ideas about the issues. These preconceived ideas act as a kind of perceptual screen that blocks out information that is not consistent with those ideas. For example, if you are already firmly convinced that daily meditation is beneficial for your health, you probably will not change your mind if you watch a TV show that asserts that those who meditate live no longer on average than people who do not. Generally, the media tend to wield the most influence over the views of persons who have not yet formed opinions about certain issues or political candidates. (See Chapter 10 for a more detailed discussion of the media's role in American politics.)

Opinion Leaders

Every state or community has well-known citizens who are able to influence the opinions of their fellow citizens. These people may be public officials, religious leaders, teachers, or celebrities. They are the people to whom others listen and from whom others draw ideas and convictions about various issues of public concern. These opinion leaders play a significant role in the formation of public opinion.

Opinion leaders often include politicians or former politicians. For example, President Barack Obama asked former U.S. presidents George W. Bush (2001–2009) and Bill Clinton (1993–2001) to lead a nationwide fund-

raising drive following the January 2010 earthquake in Haiti, which destroyed much of that country. Certainly, Americans' attitudes are influenced by the public statements of important government leaders such as the president or secretary of state. Sometimes, however, opinion leaders can fall from grace when they express views radically different from what most Americans believe. This was true for President George W. Bush. His insistence on continuing the widely unpopular war in Iraq was a major factor in causing his approval ratings to dip to historically low levels. Another example is former president Jimmy Carter (1977–1981), who lost much popularity after he published a book that harshly criticized Israel's actions toward the Palestinians.[2] (Most Americans of both parties are strongly pro-Israel.)

Americans do not often look to other countries for opinion leaders, but the president of the United States is frequently an opinion leader in other nations. We examine the impact of a new president on citizens of other countries in this chapter's *The Rest of the World* feature on the facing page.

Senator Ted Kennedy (D., Mass.) is shown here shortly before his death in 2009. Kennedy was a major opinion leader for decades while he served in the Senate. He especially tried to form others' opinions on the need for health-care reform. How does a politician become an opinion leader?

AP PHOTO/CHARLES DHARAPAK

THE REST OF THE WORLD

An Improved Image of the United States Abroad?

During George W. Bush's eight years as president, foreign public opinion about the United States in general and Bush in particular fell dramatically. Since the election of Barack Obama, however, the world's view of the United States has, on average, undergone measurable improvement.

U.S. "Favorability" Ratings

While citizens of most countries have looked at the United States more favorably since President Obama took office, attitudes vary from region to region. In Western Europe, "favorability" ratings have soared. According to the Pew Research Center's Global Attitudes Project, the number of Germans with a favorable opinion of the United States jumped from 31 percent in 2008 to 63 percent in 2010. In France, the number climbed from 42 percent to 73 percent. Opinions of America have also become more positive in many nations of Latin America. An exception is Mexico, where favorable opinions of the United States collapsed

after Arizona passed a strict new law in 2010 to control illegal immigration.

It should be understood that in quite a few countries, Bush was never particularly unpopular. These include the nations of Eastern Europe, which for many years were dominated by the Soviet Union. This experience made Eastern Europeans strong supporters of the United States, the longtime rival of the Soviets during the Cold War. By 2008 and 2009, the United States was still popular enough in Eastern Europe that there was little room for improvement. Other nations that did not exhibit strong negativity toward Bush included India, China, South Korea, and Japan.

Bush was actually quite popular in sub-Saharan Africa. Many Americans may not realize that Bush increased foreign aid to Africa dramatically, but Africans know it. Of course, as the son of an African father, Obama has been more popular still.

In contrast, opinions of the United States among Muslims in the Middle East have remained extremely unfavorable. Favorability ratings even fell in Pakistan,

probably due to Obama's use of drones to attack Taliban leaders hiding in the border regions of that country. An exception: favorability ratings have gone up substantially in Indonesia, a predominantly Muslim nation. Obama is something of a "favorite son" in that country—he lived there as a boy and has Indonesian relatives. Russian opinions of the United States have risen somewhat, but remain very low.

For Critical Analysis *Will President Obama's Nobel Peace Prize help improve the United States' image in the rest of the world? Why or why not?*

Major Life Events

Often, the political attitudes of an entire generation of Americans are influenced by a major event. For example, the Great Depression (1929–1939), the most severe economic depression in modern U.S. history, persuaded many Americans who lived through it that the federal government should step in when the economy is in decline. A substantial number of voters came to believe that the New Deal programs and policies of President Franklin Roosevelt showed that the Democratic Party was concerned about the

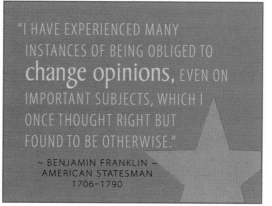

"I HAVE EXPERIENCED MANY INSTANCES OF BEING OBLIGED TO change opinions, EVEN ON IMPORTANT SUBJECTS, WHICH I ONCE THOUGHT RIGHT BUT FOUND TO BE OTHERWISE."

~ BENJAMIN FRANKLIN ~
AMERICAN STATESMAN
1706-1790

fate of ordinary people, and so they became supporters of that party.

The generation that lived through World War II (1939–1945) tends to believe that American intervention in foreign affairs is good. In contrast, the generation that came of age during the Vietnam War (1964–1975) is more skeptical of American interventionism. A national tragedy, such as the terrorist attacks of September 11, 2001, is also likely to influence the political attitudes of a generation, though in what way is difficult to predict. Certainly, the U.S. government's response to 9/11, and particularly the war in Iraq, has elicited

peer group Associates, often close in age to one another; may include friends, classmates, co-workers, club members, or religious group members. Peer group influence is a significant factor in the political socialization process.

public opinion poll A numerical survey of the public's opinion on a particular topic at a particular moment.

sample In the context of opinion polling, a group of people selected to represent the population being studied.

straw poll A nonscientific poll; a poll in which there is no way to ensure that the opinions expressed are representative of the larger population.

biased sample A poll sample that does not accurately represent the population.

deep concern on the part of Americans. Opposition to this war, however, did not lead to the widespread antiwar demonstrations that took place during another unpopular war—in Vietnam—years ago. The recent Great Recession and the financial crisis that struck in September 2008 will surely affect popular attitudes in years to come.

Peer Groups

Once children enter school, the views of friends begin to influence their attitudes and beliefs. From junior high school on, the **peer group**—friends, classmates, co-workers, club members, or religious group members—becomes a significant factor in the political socialization process. Most of this socialization occurs when the peer group is involved in political activities. For example, your political beliefs might be influenced by a peer group with which you are working on a common political cause, such as preventing the clear-cutting of old-growth forests or campaigning for a favorite candidate. Your political beliefs probably would not be as strongly influenced by peers with whom you snowboard regularly or attend concerts.

Economic Status and Occupation

A person's economic status may influence her or his political views. For example, poorer people are more likely to favor government assistance programs. On an issue such as abortion, lower-income people are more likely to be conservative—that is, to be against abortion—than are higher-income groups (of course, there are many exceptions).

Where a person works also affects her or his opinion. Co-workers who spend a great deal of time working together tend to influence one another. For example, labor union members working together for a company may have similar political opinions, at least on issues of government involvement in the economy. Individuals working for a nonprofit agency that

depends on government funds will tend to support government spending in that area. Business managers are more likely to favor tax laws helpful to businesses than are factory workers.

LO3 *Measuring Public Opinion*

If public opinion is to affect public policy, then public officials must be made aware of it. They must know which issues are of current concern to Americans and how strongly people feel about those issues. They must also know when public opinion changes. Public officials commonly learn about public opinion through election results, personal contacts, interest groups, and media reports. The only relatively precise way to measure public opinion, however, is through the use of public opinion polls.

A **public opinion poll** is a numerical survey of the public's opinion on a particular topic at a particular moment. The results of opinion polls are most often cast in terms of percentages: 62 percent feel this way, 31 percent do not, and 7 percent have no opinion. Of course, a poll cannot survey the entire U.S. population. Therefore, public opinion pollsters have devised scientific polling techniques for measuring public opinion through the use of **samples**—groups of people who are typical of the general population.

Early Polling Efforts

Since the 1800s, magazines and newspapers have often spiced up their articles by conducting **straw polls** of readers' opinions. Straw polls try to read the public's collective mind by simply asking a large number of people the same question. The early straw polls were mail surveys. Today, some newspapers and magazines still run "mail-in" polls. Increasingly, though, straw polls make use of telephone technology—encouraging people to call "900" numbers, for example—or the Internet. Visitors to a Web page can instantly register their opinions on an issue with the click of a mouse. The problem with straw polls is that the opinions expressed usually represent an atypical subgroup of the population, or a **biased sample.** A survey of those who read the *Reader's Digest* will most likely produce different results than a survey of those who read *Rolling Stone*.

The most famous of all straw-polling errors was committed by the *Literary Digest* in 1936 when it tried to predict the outcome of that year's presidential elections. The *Digest* had accurately predicted the winning candidates in several earlier presidential elections, but in 1936 the *Digest* forecast that Alfred Landon would easily defeat incumbent Franklin Roosevelt. Instead, Roosevelt won by a landslide. The editors of the *Digest* had sent mail-in cards to citizens whose names appeared in telephone directories, to its own subscribers, and to automobile owners—in all, to a staggering 2,376,000 people. In the mid-Depression year of 1936, however, people who owned a car or a telephone or who subscribed to the *Digest* were not representative of the majority of Americans. The vast majority of Americans could not afford such luxuries. Despite the enormous number of people surveyed, the sample was unrepresentative and consequently inaccurate.

Several newcomers to the public opinion poll industry, however, did predict Roosevelt's landslide victory. Two of these organizations are still at the forefront of the polling industry today: the Gallup Organization, started by George Gallup; and Roper Associates, founded by Elmo Roper and now known as the Roper Center.

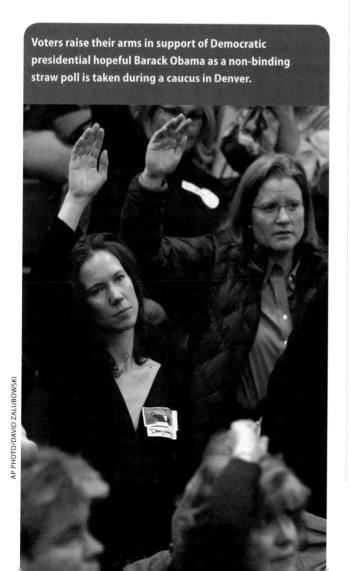

Voters raise their arms in support of Democratic presidential hopeful Barack Obama as a non-binding straw poll is taken during a caucus in Denver.

Polling Today

Today, polling is used extensively by political candidates and policymakers. Politicians and the news media generally place a great deal of faith in the accuracy of poll results. Polls can be remarkably accurate when they are conducted properly. In the last fourteen presidential elections, Gallup polls conducted early in September predicted the eventual winners in eleven of the fourteen races. Even polls taken several months in advance have been able to predict the eventual winner quite well. This success is largely the result of careful sampling techniques.

SAMPLING Today, most Gallup polls sample between 1,500 and 2,000 people. How can interviewing such a small group possibly indicate what millions of voters think? To be successful, a sample must consist of people who are typical of the general population. If the sample is properly selected, the opinions of those in the sample will be representative of the opinions held by the population as a whole. If the sample is not properly chosen, then the results of the poll may not reflect the beliefs of the general population.

The most important principle in sampling is randomness. A **random sample** means that each person within the entire population being polled has an equal chance of being chosen. For example, if a poll is trying to measure how women feel about an issue, the sample should include respondents from all groups within the female population in proportion to their percentage in the entire population. A properly drawn random sample, therefore, would include appropriate numbers of women in terms of age, racial and ethnic characteristics, occupation, geography, household income level, and religious affiliation.

BIAS In addition to trying to secure a random sample, poll takers also want to ensure that there is no bias in their polling questions. How a question is phrased can significantly affect how people answer it. Consider a question about whether high-speed connections to the Internet should be added to the school library's computer center. One way to survey opinions on this issue is simply to ask, "Do you believe that the school district should provide high-speed connections to the Internet?" Another way to ask the same question is, "Are you willing to pay higher property taxes so that the school district can have high-speed connections to the Internet?"

random sample In the context of opinion polling, a sample in which each person within the entire population being polled has an equal chance of being chosen.

Undoubtedly, the poll results will differ depending on how the question is phrased.

Polling questions also sometimes reduce complex issues to questions that simply call for "yes" or "no" answers. For example, a survey question might ask respondents whether they favor giving aid to foreign countries. A respondent's opinion on the issue might vary depending on the recipient country or the purpose and type of the aid. The poll would nonetheless force the respondent to give a "yes" or "no" answer that does not fully reflect his or her opinion.

Respondents to such questions sometimes answer "I don't know" or "I don't have enough information to answer," even when the poll does not offer such options. Interestingly, a study of how polling is conducted on the complex issue of school vouchers (school vouchers were discussed in Chapter 4) found that about 4 percent volunteered the answer "I don't know" when asked if they favored or opposed vouchers. When respondents were offered the option of answering "I haven't heard or read enough to answer," however, the proportion choosing that answer jumped to about 30 percent.[3] One current issue on which members of the public often have complicated opinions is health-care reform, as we explain in this chapter's *Our Government Faces a Troubled Economy* feature on the facing page.

TYPES OF POLLS   In the earliest days of scientific polling, interviewers typically went door-to-door locating respondents. Such in-person surveys were essential in the mid-twentieth century, when a surprisingly large portion of the population did not have a home telephone. Interviews using telephones only would run the danger of replicating the *Literary Digest* disaster mentioned earlier.

In time, however, the number of homes without phones dwindled, and polling organizations determined that they were able to obtain satisfactory samples of voters through telephone interviews alone. In recent years, poll takers have even replaced human interviewers with prerecorded messages that solicit responses. Such methods allow companies to conduct very large numbers of polls at little cost. Questions have arisen as to whether automated polling

"A popular government without popular information, or the means of acquiring it, is but

A PROLOGUE TO A FARCE OR A TRAGEDY,

or perhaps both."

~ JAMES MADISON ~
FOURTH PRESIDENT
OF THE UNITED STATES
1809–1817

is as accurate as polling that uses live interviewers, however. Further complications for telephone poll takers are the increase in the use of cell phones—which not all pollsters bother to call—and the growing number of people who simply refuse to participate in telephone surveys.

Technological advances have opened up a new possibility—the Internet survey. The Harris Poll now specializes in this type of research. As when telephone interviews were introduced, serious questions exist today as to whether the samples obtained by Harris and other Internet polling firms can be representative. Internet usage has become extremely widespread, but it is still not universal.

RELIABILITY OF POLLS   In addition to potential bias, poll takers must also be concerned about the general reliability of their polls. Respondents interviewed may be influenced by the interviewer's personality or tone of voice. They may answer without having any information on the issue, or they may give the answer that they think will please the interviewer. Additionally, any opinion poll contains a **sampling error,** which is the difference between what the sample results show and what the true results would have been had everybody in the relevant population been interviewed. (For a further look at how polling can lead to misleading results, see this chapter's *Perception versus Reality* feature on page 172.)

Opinion polls of voter preferences cannot reflect rapid shifts in public opinion unless they are taken frequently. One example of this problem was the polls taken during the presidential elections of 1980. The candidates in that year were incumbent Democratic president Jimmy Carter and Republican Ronald Reagan. Almost to the end of the campaign, polls showed Carter in the lead. Only the most capable analysts took note of the very large number of undecided voters. In the last week before the elections, these voters broke sharply for Reagan. Few polls were conducted late enough to detect this development.

EXIT POLLS   The reliability of polls was also called into question by the use of exit polls in the 2000 presidential elections. The Voter News Service (VNS)—a consortium of news networks that no longer exists—conducted polls of people exiting polling places on Election Day. These

sampling error In the context of opinion polling, the difference between what the sample results show and what the true results would have been had everybody in the relevant population been interviewed.

Our Government Faces a TROUBLED ECONOMY

The Public's Complicated Attitude toward Health-Care Reform

During the 2008 campaign for the White House, all the presidential candidates agreed that America's health-care system needed reform. After all, we are currently spending about 17 percent of our total national income on health care, and costs have been rising faster than the rate of inflation. A substantial share of the population also lacks health insurance. On taking office, President Barack Obama served notice that one of his major goals was to reform our health-care system, as quickly as possible. He argued that we cannot have a booming economy unless we change the way medical services are insured and paid for in the United States. In March 2009, about three-quarters of the respondents to a Pew Research poll agreed that the health-care system needed either fundamental changes or a complete rebuilding.

Support for Reform Dwindles

With every step toward turning health-care reform into a reality, however, public support for the process fell. Funding the reform was a major problem—it was likely to cost close to a trillion dollars over a ten-year period. The House proposed to fund the reforms with new taxes on the richest taxpayers. The Senate, in contrast, debated a tax on existing employer-provided benefits. Such a tax was widely considered rational by economists, but not by the public. A poll in July 2009 revealed that increasing taxes on upper-income Americans was strongly or somewhat favored by 58 percent of those polled, but 64 percent opposed taxing employer-provided health insurance. (In the end, most of the new taxes were indeed paid by the rich, and only the most elaborate "Cadillac" employer plans suffered a penalty.)

By the end of July 2009, the nation was split in its view of how well President Obama was handling health-care reform, according to most surveys. This was a significant decline in public approval of Obama's efforts. Polling revealed one problem: While only a minority of Americans believed we have a good health-care system, only 14 percent of those currently insured were dissatisfied with their own plan. Similarly, a majority of those polled believed that reform might help someone else, but not them.

Multiple Sources of Opposition

As the health-care legislation moved toward the finish line in 2010, Republicans argued that a majority of Americans opposed the reforms and that passage would be an affront to democracy. In fact, however, popular attitudes were more complicated than the Republicans were suggesting. It is true that in polls taken early in 2010, a majority of those surveyed opposed the legislation—56 percent were opposed in a March 2010 poll, with 39 percent supporting. That same poll, however, also asked respondents whether they opposed the reforms because they were too liberal or not liberal enough. As it turns out, 13 percent thought the reforms did not go far enough, and only 43 percent thought the reforms went too far. In short, the Republican position on the legislation did not have majority support and was barely more popular than the Democratic one.

Since the passage of the two reform bills in March, public opinion has drifted slightly in favor of the legislation. In several August 2010 polls, just over a third of those surveyed supported repeal of the legislation—a position adopted by most Republican candidates. Majorities either favored the reforms or thought they should be given a chance to work. Polls asking whether the reforms are too liberal or not liberal enough continue to yield results similar to the poll described in the previous paragraph.

You Be the Judge Those under the age of 65 are much more supportive of the health-care reform legislation than those aged 65 or older. Why might that be so?

exit polls were used by the news networks to predict the winner of the Florida race—and they were wrong, not just once, but twice. First, they claimed that the Florida vote had gone to Al Gore. Then, a few hours later, they said it had gone to George W. Bush. Finally, they said the Florida race was too close to call.

These miscalls of the election outcome in Florida caused substantial confusion—and frustration—for the

Today, more than ever before, Americans are bombarded with the results of public opinion polls. If you can think of a political candidate, topic, issue, or concept, chances are that one or more public polling organizations can tell you what "Americans really think" about that candidate or topic. Polling organizations increasingly use telephone interviews and the Internet to conduct their polls. Because these polls are much cheaper to conduct than "feet on the street" polling, it is not surprising that more poll results are available every day. If you subscribe to the online services of the Gallup poll, for example, at least once a week Gallup will send you information on approximately a dozen topics on which that organization has sought to discover Americans' opinions.

The Perception

Americans who hear or read about the results of public opinion polls naturally assume that polling organizations undertook those polls in a scientific way and presented accurate results. Those who know a little bit about polling also assume that the small numbers of people polled represented a random sample.

The Reality

Many polls are not based on a random sample, contrary to popular belief. Consider a poll published by the *Military Times* in 2008, which found that 58 percent of respondents opposed military service by openly gay individuals. Further, 10 percent claimed that they would not reenlist if the ban on openly gay service members were lifted. The press gave this survey widespread coverage without questioning its methodology. One pundit claimed, on the basis of the poll, that gays in the military would "destroy" the institution. In fact, the poll was not based on a random sample but on a self-selected pool of *Military Times* readers, who tended to be older and more conservative than the military as a whole. Further, opinions do not necessarily predict behavior. Before Britain and Canada ended their service bans, polls found widespread resistance to openly gay and lesbian soldiers. Upon integration, however, almost no one actually resigned from service.

Think also about how respondents answer interviewers' questions. In one *New York Times*/CBS News poll, voters were asked if they had voted in a specific presidential election. Although 73 percent said yes, the U.S. Census Bureau later determined that only 64 percent of eligible voters actually voted in that election. Analysts concluded that those who had been interviewed wanted to appear to be "good citizens," so not all of them told the truth.

Do not forget about sampling error. For example, say that two candidates for president are neck and neck in the opinion polls, but the sampling error is 4 percent. That means that either candidate could actually be ahead by 54 percent to 46 percent.

Blog On Why, in your opinion, do various publications continue to print unscientific pseudopolls?

candidates, as well as for the voters. They also led to a significant debate over exit polls: Should exit polls be banned, even though they provide valuable information on voter behavior and preferences?

Exit polls again were employed during the 2004 presidential elections. Again the results were troublesome. During the early hours of the elections, exit polls caused the media to conclude that Democratic candidate John Kerry was leading in the race. Preliminary results of exit polls were leaked to the Internet by midafternoon. After the votes were tallied, however, the exit poll results were shown to have inflated Kerry's support by 6.5 percent—the largest margin of error in decades.

In 2008, the television networks were careful about making predictions based on exit polls. It was clear early that Obama was winning, but the networks wanted viewers to keep watching, so they maintained the suspense. Print media exit polls, used to determine the voting preferences of various groups, did better in 2008 than in 2004, when they contained some major errors.

Pollsters had a tough time persuading Americans to participate in surveys leading up to the 2010 elections. Many Americans only use cell phones and therefore are difficult to contact. Nonetheless, the polls were substantially accurate. A survey of polling data from multiple sources predicted that the Democrats would lose fifty-three seats in the House and seven or eight in the Senate. Not a bad prediction—sixty-four Democrats lost in the House and six in the Senate. Polling firms that used real human interviewers had the most accuracy.

MISUSE OF POLLS Today, a frequently heard complaint is that, instead of measuring public opinion, polls can end up creating it. For example, to gain popularity, a candidate might claim that all the polls show that he is ahead in the race. People who want to support the winner may back this candidate despite their true feelings. This is often called the "bandwagon" effect. Presidential approval ratings lend themselves to the bandwagon effect.

The media also sometimes misuse polls. Many journalists take the easy route during campaigns and base their political coverage almost exclusively on poll findings, with no mention of the chance for bias or the margin of error in the poll. A useful checklist for evaluating the quality of opinion polls is presented in Table 8–1 at right. An increasingly common misuse of polls by politicians is the *push poll*, discussed next.

DEFINING A PUSH POLL One tactic in political campaigns is to use **push polls,** which ask "fake" polling questions that are actually designed to "push" voters toward one candidate or another. The use of push polls has become so prevalent today that many states are taking steps to ban them. The problem with trying to ban push polls, or even to report accurately on which candidates are using them, is that defining a push poll can be difficult.

The National Council on Public Polls describes push polls as outright political manipulation—the spreading of rumors and lies by one candidate about another. For example, a push poll might ask, "Do you believe the rumor that Candidate A misused campaign funds to pay for a family vacation to Hawaii?" Push pollsters usually do not give their name or identify the poll's sponsor. The interviews last less than a minute, whereas legitimate pollsters typically interview a respondent for five to thirty minutes. Based on these characteristics, it is sometimes possible to distinguish a push poll from a

---

Table 8–1

Checklist for Evaluating Public Opinion Polls

Because public opinion polls are so widely used by the media and policymakers, and their reliability is so often called into question, several organizations have issued guidelines for evaluating polls. Below is a list of questions that you can ask to evaluate the quality and reliability of a poll. You can find the answers to many, if not all, of these questions in the polling organization's report accompanying the poll results.

1. Who conducted the poll, and who sponsored or paid for it?
2. How many people were interviewed for the survey, and what part of the population did they represent (for example, registered voters, likely voters, persons over age eighteen)?
3. How were these people chosen, and how random was the sample?
4. How were respondents contacted and interviewed (by telephone, by mail-in survey)?
5. Who should have been interviewed but was not (what was the "nonresponse" rate—people who should have been part of the random sample but who refused to be interviewed, do not have telephones, or do not have listed telephone numbers, for example)?
6. What is the margin of error for the poll? (The acceptable margin of error for national polls is usually plus or minus 4 percent.)
7. What questions did the poll ask?
8. In what order were the questions asked?
9. When was the poll conducted?
10. What other polls were conducted on this topic, and do they report similar findings?

---

legitimate poll conducted by a respected research organization. The checklist in Table 8–1 can also help you distinguish between a legitimate poll and a push poll.

Some researchers argue that identifying a push poll is not that straightforward, however. Political analyst Charlie Cook points out that "there are legitimate polls that can ask push questions, which test potential arguments against a rival to ascertain how effective those arguments might be in future advertising. . . . These are not only legitimate tools of survey research, but any political pollster who did not use them would be doing his or her clients a real disservice."[4] Distinguishing between push polls and push questions, then, can be challenging—which is usually the intent of the push pollsters. A candidate does not want to be accused of conducting push polls, because the public considers them a "dirty trick" and may turn against the candidate who uses them. In several recent campaigns, candidates have accused each other of conducting push polls—accusations that could not always be proved or disproved.

> **push poll** A campaign tactic used to feed false or misleading information to potential voters, under the guise of taking an opinion poll, with the intent to "push" voters away from one candidate and toward another.

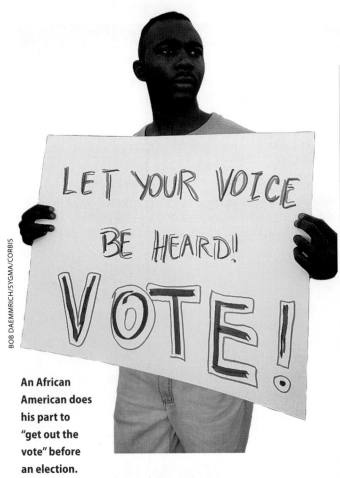

An African American does his part to "get out the vote" before an election.

African Americans faced significant restrictions on voting until the 1950s and 1960s, when new laws and policies helped to end both formal and informal barriers to their voting. Voter turnout among African Americans is increasing, and in 2008 their share of the vote rose from 11 percent to 13 percent.

BOB DAEMMRICH/SYGMA/CORBIS

LO4 *Voting and Voter Turnout*

Voting is arguably the most important way in which citizens participate in the political process. Because we do not live in a direct democracy, Americans use the vote to elect politicians to represent their interests, values, and opinions in government. In many states, public-policy decisions—for example, access to medical marijuana—are decided by voters. Our right to vote also helps keep elected officials accountable to campaign promises because they must face reelection.

Factors Affecting Voter Turnout

literacy test A test given to voters to ensure that they could read and write and thus evaluate political information; a technique used in many southern states to restrict African American participation in elections.

If voting is so important, then why do so many Americans fail to exercise their right to vote? Why is voter turnout—the percentage of those eligible to vote who actually turn out

to vote—relatively low? As you will read shortly, in the past, legal restrictions based on income, gender, race, and other factors kept a number of people from voting. In the last decades of the twentieth century, these restrictions were almost completely eliminated, and yet voter turnout in presidential elections still hovered around 55 percent, as shown in Figure 8–1 on the facing page. In the last two presidential elections, however, turnout has exceeded 60 percent—a welcome, if modest, improvement.

According to a Pew Research Center survey of voter turnout, one of the reasons for low voter turnout is that many nonvoters (close to 40 percent) do not feel that they have a duty to vote. The survey also found that nearly 70 percent of nonvoters said that they did not vote because they lacked information about the candidates.[5] Finally, some people believe that their vote will not make any difference, so they do not bother to become informed about the candidates and issues or go to the polls.

The Legal Right to Vote

In the United States today, citizens who are at least eighteen years of age and who are not felons have the right to vote. This was not always true, however. Recall from Chapter 5 that restrictions on *suffrage,* the legal right to vote, have existed since the founding of our nation. Expanding the right to vote has been an important part of the gradual democratization of the American electoral process. Table 8–2 on page 176 summarizes the major amendments, Supreme Court decisions, and laws that extended the right to vote to various American groups.

HISTORICAL RESTRICTIONS ON VOTING Those who drafted the Constitution left the power to set suffrage qualifications to the individual states. Most states limited suffrage to adult white males who owned property, but these restrictions were challenged early on in the history of the republic. By 1828, laws restricting the right to vote to Christians were abolished in all states, and property ownership and tax-payment requirements gradually began to disappear as well. By 1850, all white males were allowed to vote. Restrictions based on race and gender continued, however.

The Fifteenth Amendment, ratified in 1870, guaranteed suffrage to African American males. Yet, for many decades, African Americans were effectively denied the ability to exercise their voting rights. Using methods ranging from mob violence to economic restrictions, groups of white southerners kept black Americans from voting. Some states required citizens to pass **literacy tests** and to answer complicated questions about government and history before they could register to vote.

Figure 8–1

Voter Turnout since 1968

The figures in this chart show voter turnout as a percentage of the population that is eligible to vote.

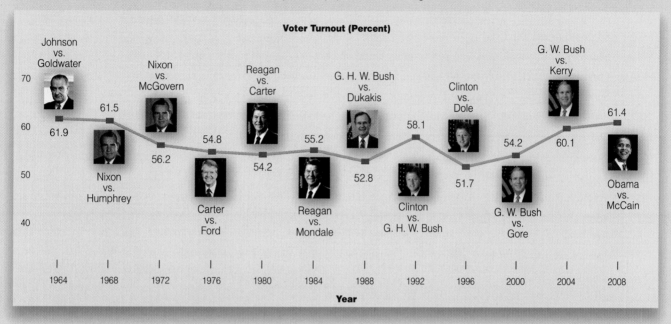

Sources: *Statistical Abstract of the United States,* various issues; the Committee for the Study of the American Electorate; and authors' updates.

Registrars made sure that African Americans would always fail such tests. The **poll tax,** a fee of several dollars, was another device used to prevent African Americans from voting. At the time, this tax was a sizable burden, not only for most blacks but also for poor whites. Another restriction was the **grandfather clause,** which had the effect of restricting voting rights to those whose ancestors had voted before the 1860s. This technique was prohibited by the United States Supreme Court in 1915.[6]

Still another voting barrier was the **white primary**—African Americans were prohibited from voting in the primary elections. The Supreme Court initially upheld this practice on the grounds that the political parties were private entities, not public, and thus could do as they wished. Eventually, in 1944, the Court banned the use of white primaries.[7]

VOTING RIGHTS TODAY Today, these devices for restricting voting rights are explicitly outlawed by constitutional amendments and by the Voting Rights Act of 1965, as discussed in Chapter 5. Furthermore, the Nineteenth Amendment gave women the right to vote in 1920. In 1971, the Twenty-sixth Amendment reduced the minimum voting age to eighteen.

Some restrictions on voting rights still exist. Every state except North Dakota requires voters to register with the appropriate state or local officials before voting. Residency requirements are also usually imposed for voting. Since 1970, however, no state can impose a residency requirement of more than thirty days. Twenty-five states require that length of time, while the other twenty-five states require fewer or no days. Another voting requirement is citizenship. Aliens may not vote in any public election held anywhere in the United States. Most states also do not permit prison inmates, mentally ill people, felons, or election-law violators to vote.

Attempts to Improve Voter Turnout

Attempts to improve voter turnout typically have a partisan dimension. This is because the kinds of people who find it difficult to register to vote tend to be

poll tax A fee of several dollars that had to be paid before a person could vote; a device used in some southern states to prevent African Americans from voting.

grandfather clause A clause in a state law that had the effect of restricting the franchise (voting rights) to those whose ancestors had voted before the 1860s; one of the techniques used in the South to prevent African Americans from exercising their right to vote.

white primary A primary election in which African Americans were prohibited from voting. The practice was banned by the Supreme Court in 1944.

Table 8–2

Extension of the Right to Vote

Year	Action	Impact
1870	Fifteenth Amendment	Discrimination based on race outlawed.
1920	Nineteenth Amendment	Discrimination based on gender outlawed.
1924	Congressional act	All Native Americans given citizenship.
1944	*Smith v. Allwright*	Supreme Court prohibits white primary.
1957	Civil Rights Act of 1957	Justice Department can sue to protect voting rights in various states.
1960	Civil Rights Act of 1960	Courts authorized to appoint referees to assist voter-registration procedures.
1961	Twenty-third Amendment	Residents of District of Columbia given right to vote for president and vice president.
1964	Twenty-fourth Amendment	Poll tax in national elections outlawed.
1965	Voting Rights Act of 1965	Literacy tests prohibited; federal voter registrars authorized in seven southern states.
1970	Voting Rights Act Amendments of 1970	Voting age for federal elections reduced to eighteen years; maximum thirty-day residency required for presidential elections; state literacy tests abolished.
1971	Twenty-sixth Amendment	Minimum voting age reduced to eighteen for all elections.
1975	Voting Rights Act Amendments of 1975	Federal voter registrars authorized in ten more states; bilingual ballots to be used in certain circumstances.
1982	Voting Rights Act Amendments of 1982	Extended provisions of Voting Rights Act amendments of 1970 and 1975; private parties allowed to sue for violations.

disproportionately Democratic in their sympathies. Many, for example, are African Americans, a reliably Democratic voting bloc. As a result, Republicans are generally wary of efforts to make registration easier. For example, most Republicans opposed the passage of the National Voter Registration Act (the "Motor Voter Law") of 1993, which simplified the voter-registration process. The act requires states to provide all eligible citizens with the opportunity to register to vote when they apply for or renew a driver's license. The law also requires that states allow mail-in registration, with forms given at certain public assistance agencies. The law, which took effect on January 1, 1995, has facilitated millions of registrations.

In 1998, Oregon voters approved a ballot initiative requiring that all elections in that state, including presidential elections, be conducted exclusively by mail. In the 2008 presidential elections, 66 percent of Oregonians eligible to vote cast ballots, a figure that is somewhat higher than the national average but not exceptionally so. Some argue that if mail-in voting were allowed nationwide, voter turnout would increase. Others believe that voting by mail has a number of disadvantages, including greater

possibilities for voter fraud. We examine whether voter fraud is a serious issue in the *Join the Debate* feature on the following page.

Civil rights protesters, led by Martin Luther King, Jr., march on the road from Selma to Montgomery, Alabama, in March 1965. During the five-day, fifty-mile march, federal troops were stationed every one hundred yards along the route to protect the marchers from violent attacks by segregationists.

MATT HERON/SMITHSONIAN

DAVID AHNTHOLZ/THE NEW YORK TIMES/REDUX

JOIN THE DEBATE

Voter Fraud—A Real Problem or Much Ado about Nothing?

Cries of voter fraud came from the Democrats in 2000 and again in 2004. The Democrats believed that votes were handled improperly in Florida in 2000 and that this kept Democratic presidential candidate Al Gore from carrying the state and winning the presidency. In 2004, some believed that fraud cost Democratic presidential candidate John Kerry the state of Ohio and the presidency. In 2008, accusations of voter fraud became a major campaign issue when Republican John McCain claimed that a group called Acorn was "on the verge of maybe perpetrating one of the greatest frauds in voter history." Acorn, since dissolved, was a nonprofit group that advocated for the poor. It mounted a voter-registration drive in 2008, and some of its employees handed in registration forms that bore the names of cartoon characters and out-of-state major-league athletes. Strictly speaking, this was not voter fraud, but registration fraud. Voter fraud would occur only if someone using the name Mickey Mouse actually turned up at the polls and tried to vote. Acorn said that it had fired the offending employees and that state laws required it to hand in even obviously bogus registration forms, which it had marked as suspect.

Voter Fraud Is a Myth

Political analyst Harold Meyerson of the *Los Angeles Times* wrote, "Voter fraud is a myth—not an urban or a real myth, as such, but a Republican one." The Justice Department's Ballot Access and Voting Integrity Initiative obtained only eighty-six convictions for voter fraud over a five-year period. Many Americans contend that voter fraud will always exist on a small scale, but it is not a serious problem today. Rather, the Republicans have raised the specter of voter fraud in order to pass laws, such as those requiring photo IDs, that make it harder for disadvantaged persons (mostly Democrats) to vote.

Voter Fraud Is a Real Problem

Other Americans believe that voter fraud is a significant problem. The Election Assistance Commission issued a report indicating that the extent of voter fraud is still open to debate. Lapses in enforcing voting and registration rules continue to occur. Thousands upon thousands of ineligible voters are allowed to vote. Many felons—who are not allowed to vote in most states—end up voting anyway. The only effective method of reducing voter fraud is to require photo IDs at polling places, as is done in states such as Indiana.

For Critical Analysis *Why might people who find it harder to register and vote tend to support the Democratic Party?*

Attempts to Improve Voting Procedures

Because of serious problems in achieving accurate vote counts in recent elections, particularly in the 2000 presidential elections, steps have been taken to attempt to ensure more accuracy in the voting process. In 2002, Congress passed the Help America Vote Act, which, among other things, provided funds to the states to help them purchase new electronic voting equipment. Concerns about the possibility of fraudulent manipulation of electronic voting machines then replaced the worries over inaccurate vote counts caused by the previous equipment.

PROBLEMS IN 2006 In the 2006 elections, about half of the states that were using new electronic voting systems reported problems. Some systems "flipped" votes from the selected candidate to the opposing candidate. In one Florida district, about eighteen thousand votes apparently were unrecorded by electronic equipment, and this may have changed the outcome of a congressional race. Many experts have demanded that electronic

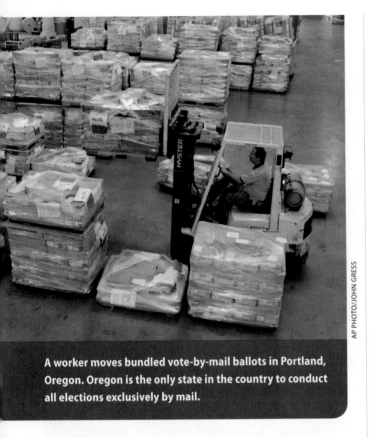

AP PHOTO/JOHN GRESS

A worker moves bundled vote-by-mail ballots in Portland, Oregon. Oregon is the only state in the country to conduct all elections exclusively by mail.

systems create a "paper trail" so that machine errors can be tracked and fixed.

VOTING SYSTEMS IN THE 2008 ELECTIONS   Because of problems with electronic systems, fewer polling places used them in 2008. Indeed, more than half of all votes cast in 2008 used old-fashioned paper ballots. As a result, vote counting was slow. One feature of the elections was the large number of states that allowed early voting at polling places that opened weeks before Election Day. A benefit of early voting was that it allowed election workers time to ensure that all systems were working properly by Election Day.

Who Actually Votes

Just because an individual is eligible to vote does not necessarily mean that the person will actually go to the polls on Election Day and vote. Why do some eligible voters go to the polls while others do not? Although nobody can answer this question with absolute conviction, certain factors, including those discussed next, appear to affect voter turnout.

voting-age population
The number of people residing in the United States who are at least eighteen years old.

EDUCATIONAL ATTAINMENT   Among the factors affecting voter turnout, education appears to be the most important. The more education a person has, the more likely it is that she or he will be a regular voter. People who graduated from high school vote more regularly than those who dropped out, and college graduates vote more often than high school graduates.

INCOME LEVEL AND AGE   Differences in income also lead to differences in voter turnout. Wealthy people tend to be overrepresented among regular voters. Generally, older voters turn out to vote more regularly than younger voters do, although participation tends to decline among the very elderly. Participation likely increases with age because older people tend to be more settled, are already registered, and have had more experience with voting.

MINORITY STATUS   Racial and ethnic minorities traditionally have been underrepresented among the ranks of voters. In several recent elections, however, participation by these groups, particularly African Americans and Hispanics, has increased.

It was expected that with an African American running for president on the Democratic ticket in 2008, voter turnout among African Americans would go through the roof. African American turnout was indeed high, but not as high as some had expected. About 20 percent more African Americans voted in 2008 than in 2004, and their share of the vote rose from 11 percent to 13 percent. African Americans were essential to Obama's victories in North Carolina and Virginia.

In part because the number of Hispanic citizens has grown rapidly, the increase in the Hispanic vote—more than 30 percent—was even larger than the increase in the black vote. Hispanics helped Obama carry Colorado, Indiana, Nevada, and New Mexico.

IMMIGRATION AND VOTER TURNOUT   The United States has experienced high rates of immigration in recent decades, and that has had an effect on voter turnout figures. In the past, voter turnout was often expressed as a percentage of the **voting-age population,** the number of people residing in the United States who are at least eighteen years old. Due to legal and illegal immigration, however, there are many people of voting age who are not eligible to vote because they are not citizens. Millions more cannot vote because they are felons. Additionally, the voting-age population excludes Americans abroad, who are eligible to cast absentee ballots.

Today, political scientists calculate the **vote-eligible population,** the number of people who are actually entitled to vote in American elections. They have found that there may be 20 million fewer eligible voters than the voting-age population suggests. Therefore, voter turnout is actually greater than the percentages sometimes cited. Some experts have argued that the relatively low levels of voter turnout often reported for the years between 1972 and 2000 were largely due to immigration.[8] Beginning in 2004, voter turnout has improved by any calculation method.

LO5 *Why People Vote as They Do*

What prompts some citizens to vote Republican and others to vote Democratic? What persuades voters to choose certain kinds of candidates? Obviously, more is involved than measuring one's own position against the candidates' positions and then voting accordingly. Voters choose candidates for many reasons. Researchers have collected more information on voting than on any other form of political participation in the United States. These data shed some light on why people decide to vote for particular candidates.

Party Identification

Many voters have a standing allegiance to a political party, or a party identification, although the proportion of the population that does so has fallen in recent decades. For established voters, party identification is one of the most important and lasting predictors of how a person will vote. Party identification is an emotional attachment to a party that is influenced by family, age, peer groups, and other factors that play a role in the political socialization process discussed earlier.

A large number of voters call themselves independents. Despite this label, many independents actually support one or the other of the two major parties quite regularly. Figure 8–2 on the following page shows how those who identified themselves as Democrats,

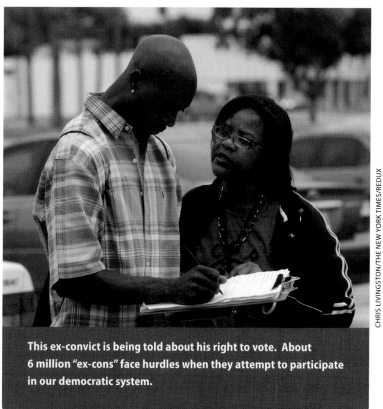

This ex-convict is being told about his right to vote. About 6 million "ex-cons" face hurdles when they attempt to participate in our democratic system.

Republicans, and independents voted in the 2008 presidential elections.

Perception of the Candidates

Voters often base their decisions on the perceived character of the candidates rather than on their qualifications or policy positions. Such perceptions were important in the 2008 presidential elections. At first, some observers saw Democrat Barack Obama as aloof or even arrogant. During the economic crisis, however, Obama's calm temperament was viewed as "presidential." Six out of ten voters reported that they had no idea what Obama would do to get the country out of its financial mess, but they were sure he could do it. Republican John McCain sought to portray himself as a fighter for America. Sometimes he simply came across as angry, however. As Republican strategist Karl Rove put it, "When was the last time Americans elected an angry president?" Falling behind in the polls, McCain repeatedly changed direction in an attempt to alter the nature of the race. These moves, however,

> **vote-eligible population**
> The number of people who are actually eligible to vote in an American election.

played into the impression that he was erratic and unpredictable. His choice of Sarah Palin as a running mate also seemed impulsive.

Policy Choices

When people vote for candidates who share their positions on particular issues, they are engaging in policy voting. If a candidate for senator in your state opposes gun control laws, for example, and you decide to vote for her for that reason, you have engaged in policy voting.

Historically, economic issues have had the strongest influence on voters' choices. When the economy is doing well, it is very difficult for a challenger, particularly at the presidential level, to defeat the incumbent. In contrast, when the country is experiencing inflation, rising unemployment, or high interest rates, the incumbent will likely be at a disadvantage. The main issue in the 2008 presidential elections and the 2010 midterm elections was the financial crisis facing all Americans.

Some of the most heated debates in American political campaigns have involved social issues, such as abortion, gay and lesbian rights, the death penalty, and religion in the schools. Often, presidential candidates prefer to avoid emphasizing their stand on these types of issues, because voters who have strong opinions about such issues are likely to be offended if a candidate does not share their views.

Socioeconomic Factors

Some factors that influence how people vote can be described as socioeconomic. These factors include educational attainment, income level, age, gender, religion, and geographic location. Some of these factors have to do with the circumstances into which individuals are born. Others have to do with personal choices. Figure 8–3 on the facing page shows how various groups voted in the 2008 presidential elections.

EDUCATIONAL ATTAINMENT As a general rule, people with more education are more likely to vote Republican, although in recent years, voters with post-graduate degrees have tended to vote Democratic. Typically, those with less education are also more inclined to vote for the Democratic nominee. Educational attainment, of course, can be linked to income level. Recent studies show that among students from families with income in the bottom fifth of the population, only 12 percent earn a bachelor's degree by the age of twenty-four. In the top fifth, the figure is 73 percent.

OCCUPATION AND INCOME LEVEL Businesspersons tend to vote Republican and have done so for many years. Recently, professionals (such as attorneys, professors, and physicians) have been more likely to vote Democratic than in earlier years. Manual laborers, factory workers, and especially union members are more likely to vote Democratic. In the past, the higher the income, the more likely it was that a person would vote Republican. Conversely, a much larger percentage of low-income individuals voted Democratic. But this pattern is also breaking down, and there are no hard-and-fast rules. Some very poor individuals are

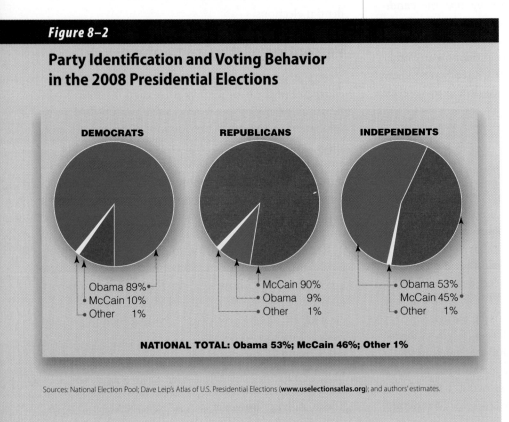

Figure 8–2

Party Identification and Voting Behavior in the 2008 Presidential Elections

DEMOCRATS

Obama 89%
McCain 10%
Other 1%

REPUBLICANS

McCain 90%
Obama 9%
Other 1%

INDEPENDENTS

Obama 53%
McCain 45%
Other 1%

NATIONAL TOTAL: Obama 53%; McCain 46%; Other 1%

Sources: National Election Pool; Dave Leip's Atlas of U.S. Presidential Elections (**www.uselectionsatlas.org**); and authors' estimates.

Figure 8–3

Voting by Groups in the 2008 Presidential Elections

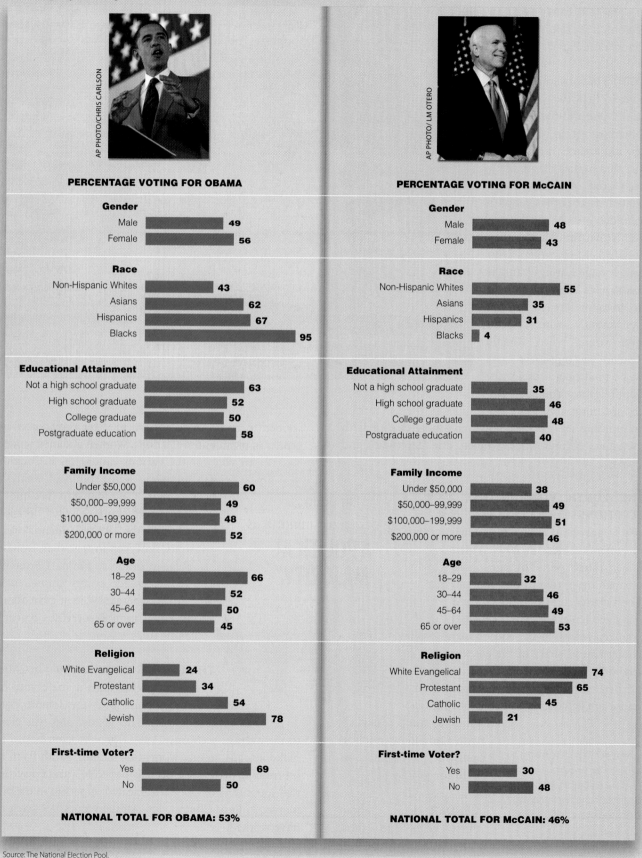

AP PHOTO/CHRIS CARLSON

AP PHOTO/ LM OTERO

PERCENTAGE VOTING FOR OBAMA

PERCENTAGE VOTING FOR McCAIN

Gender
	Obama
Male	49
Female	56

Gender
	McCain
Male	48
Female	43

Race
	Obama
Non-Hispanic Whites	43
Asians	62
Hispanics	67
Blacks	95

Race
	McCain
Non-Hispanic Whites	55
Asians	35
Hispanics	31
Blacks	4

Educational Attainment
	Obama
Not a high school graduate	63
High school graduate	52
College graduate	50
Postgraduate education	58

Educational Attainment
	McCain
Not a high school graduate	35
High school graduate	46
College graduate	48
Postgraduate education	40

Family Income
	Obama
Under $50,000	60
$50,000–99,999	49
$100,000–199,999	48
$200,000 or more	52

Family Income
	McCain
Under $50,000	38
$50,000–99,999	49
$100,000–199,999	51
$200,000 or more	46

Age
	Obama
18–29	66
30–44	52
45–64	50
65 or over	45

Age
	McCain
18–29	32
30–44	46
45–64	49
65 or over	53

Religion
	Obama
White Evangelical	24
Protestant	34
Catholic	54
Jewish	78

Religion
	McCain
White Evangelical	74
Protestant	65
Catholic	45
Jewish	21

First-time Voter?
	Obama
Yes	69
No	50

First-time Voter?
	McCain
Yes	30
No	48

NATIONAL TOTAL FOR OBAMA: 53%

NATIONAL TOTAL FOR McCAIN: 46%

Source: The National Election Pool.

devoted Republicans, just as some extremely wealthy persons are supporters of the Democratic Party.

AGE   The conventional wisdom is that the young are liberal and the old are conservative, yet in years past age differences in support for the parties have often been quite small. One age-related effect is that people's attitudes are shaped by the events that unfolded as they grew up. Many voters who came of age during Franklin Roosevelt's New Deal held on to a preference for the Democrats. Voters who were young when Ronald Reagan was president have had a tendency to prefer the Republicans. Younger voters are noticeably more liberal on one set of issues, however—those dealing with the rights of minorities, women, and gay males and lesbians.

THE YOUTH VOTE IN THE 2008 ELECTIONS   In contrast with past years, age had a striking impact on voters' choices in 2008. Voters under thirty years of age chose Obama by a two-to-one margin. The Obama campaign hoped for a massive increase in the turnout of younger voters. In the end, though, young voters' share of the electorate rose only modestly, from 17 percent to 18 percent. What made the youth vote important was not turnout, but Obama's enormous margin, a result with ominous implications for the Republicans in future years.

GENDER   Until about thirty years ago, there

Barack Obama supporters hold signs during a "Women's Rally for the Change We Need" in Coral Gables, Florida. Was there a gender gap in 2008 voting?

EMMANUEL DUNAND/AFP/GETTY IMAGES

"In politics, an organized minority is **A POLITICAL MAJORITY."**

~ REV. JESSE JACKSON ~
CIVIL RIGHTS ACTIVIST
1941–PRESENT

gender gap   The difference between the percentage of votes cast for a particular candidate by women and the percentage of votes cast for the same candidate by men.

seemed to be no fixed pattern of voter preferences by gender in presidential elections. Women and men tended to vote for the various candidates in roughly equal numbers. Some political analysts believe that a **gender gap** became a major determinant of voter decision making in the 1980 presidential elections, however. In that year, Ronald Reagan outdrew Jimmy Carter by 16 percentage points among male voters, whereas women gave about an equal number of votes to each candidate.

THE GENDER GAP IN 2008   In 2008, Barack Obama carried the male vote by one percentage point and the female vote by a 13 percent margin. This gender gap was close to the average seen since 1980. John McCain hoped to make inroads among women by naming Sarah Palin as his running mate. He especially hoped to attract disgruntled supporters of Obama's defeated opponent in the primaries, Hillary Clinton. This strategy does not seem to have worked.

RELIGION AND ETHNIC BACKGROUND A century ago, at least in the northern states, white Catholic voters were likely to be Democrats and white Protestant voters were likely to be Republicans. There are a few places around the country where this pattern continues to hold, but for the most part, white Catholics are now almost as likely as their Protestant neighbors to support the Republicans.

In recent years, a different religious variable has become important in determining voting behavior. Regardless of their denomination, white Christian voters who attend church regularly have favored the Republicans by substantial margins. White voters who attend church rarely or who find religion less important in their lives are more likely to vote Democratic. Jewish voters are strongly Democratic, regardless of whether they attend services.

Most African Americans are Protestants, but African Americans are one of the most solidly Democratic constituencies in the United States. This is a complete reversal of the circumstances that existed a century ago. As noted in Chapter 7, for many years after the Civil War, those African Americans who could vote were overwhelmingly Republican. Not until President Franklin Roosevelt's New Deal did black voters begin to turn to the Democrats. Hispanic voters have

> "Whenever a fellow tells me he is bipartisan, I KNOW HE IS GOING TO VOTE AGAINST ME."
>
> ~ HARRY TRUMAN ~
> THIRTY-THIRD PRESIDENT
> OF THE UNITED STATES
> 1945–1953

supported the Democrats by margins of about two to one, with some exceptions: Cuban Americans are strongly Republican. Asian Americans tend to favor the Democrats, although Vietnamese Americans are strongly Republican.

GEOGRAPHIC REGION In today's presidential contests, states in the South, the Great Plains, and parts of the Rocky Mountains are strongly Republican. The Northeast, the West Coast, and Illinois are firmly Democratic. Many of the swing states that decide elections are located in the Midwest, although several Rocky Mountain states swing between the parties as well. This pattern is an almost complete reversal of the one that existed a century ago. In those years, most white southerners were Democrats, and people spoke of the **Solid South**—solidly Democratic, that is. The Solid South lasted for a century after the Civil War and in large part was the result of southern resentment of the Republicans for their role in the "War between the States" and their support of African Americans in the postwar era. At the end of the nineteenth century, the Republicans were strong in the Northeast and much of the Midwest, while the Democrats were able to find support outside of the South in the Great Plains and the Far West.

The ideologies of the two parties have likewise undergone something of a reversal. One hundred years ago, the

A member of the League of Women Voters participates in a demonstration to protest the lack of voting rights for the citizens of Washington, D.C., on the 90th Anniversary of the 19th Amendment, guaranteeing women the right to vote.

KEVIN DIETSCH/UPI/LANDOV

Solid South A term used to describe the tendency of the southern states to vote Democratic after the Civil War.

The Vote by Demographic Groups

The 2010 national exit poll was organized ABC, CBS, CNN, Fox, NBC, and the Associated Press, and it contacted more than 17,000 voters in twenty-six states. Some of the results were expected. The gender gap continues to exist—women were six percentage points more likely to vote Democratic than were men. African Americans cast 90 percent of their votes for Democrats. The Hispanic vote was 64 percent Democratic, and Asian Americans voted Democratic by 56 percent. Non-Hispanic whites, however, cast 60 percent of their votes for Republicans. A piece of good news for the Democrats was that the youngest voters, those aged 18 to 29, preferred the Democrats by 57 to 40 percent. Unfortunately for the Democrats, the percentage of youth among the voters who turned out was half what it was in 2008. Voters above the age of 65, in contrast, preferred Republicans by 59 percent to 38 percent. Backing for Republicans among the elderly was 48 percent in 2008—which means the Democrats lost the support of 11 percent of this group in two years. Clearly, the health-care bill, unpopular among seniors, took its toll. The elderly also made up 24 percent of the voters, the highest figure in years. A final point: high family income was a better predictor of Republican support in 2010 than it had been in 2008.

Democrats were seen as *less* likely than the Republicans to support government intervention in the economy. The Democrats were also the party that opposed civil rights. Today, the Democrats are often regarded as the party that supports "big government" and affirmative action programs.

Ideology

Ideology is another indicator of voting behavior. A significant percentage of Americans today identify themselves as moderates. Recent polls indicate that 44 percent of Americans consider themselves to be moderates, 22 percent consider themselves liberals, and 34 percent identify themselves as conservatives.

For many Americans, where they fall in the political spectrum is a strong indicator of how they will vote: liberals vote for Democrats, and conservatives vote for Republicans. The large numbers of Americans who fall in the political center do not adhere strictly to an ideology. In most elections, the candidates compete aggressively for these voters because they know their "base"—on the left or right—is secure.

vital center The center of the political spectrum; those who hold moderate political views. The center is vital because without it, it may be difficult, if not impossible, to reach the compromises that are necessary to a political system's continuity.

THE VITAL CENTER In 1949, historian Arthur Schlesinger, Jr., described the position between the political extremes as the **vital center.** The center is vital because without it, necessary compromises may be difficult, if not impossible, to achieve. One problem with activating the vital center is that voter apathy and low voter turnout are found most commonly among those in the center. The most motivated voters are the "ideologically zealous."[9]

IDEOLOGY IN THE 2008 ELECTIONS According to 2008 exit polls, 89 percent of voters who identified themselves as liberals voted for Barack Obama, who also received the votes of 20 percent of self-identified conservatives. Obama carried self-described moderates by 60 percent to 49 percent, a result that was crucial to his victory.

These figures raise some interesting questions. John McCain tried very hard to portray Obama as "too liberal," and to a certain extent he succeeded. Among all voters, 42 percent thought that Obama was too liberal, compared with 50 percent who thought that his positions were about right. Only 4 percent of those questioned thought that he was too conservative. In another poll, most respondents believed that McCain's ideological positions were closer to their own than Obama's. Still, a majority of these voters supported Obama.

It is clear from these results that there are limits to the power of ideology to determine election outcomes.

Many moderate and even some conservative voters supported Obama because they thought he was better suited to be president—regardless of ideology. In this sense, Obama won the support of the vital center.

AMERICA AT ODDS   *Public Opinion and Voting*

Public opinion polls reveal that Americans are in broad agreement on many issues, such as the basic political structure of our nation. Nevertheless, polls also report that Americans are at odds with one another on many other issues. After all, the questions posed by poll takers are typically divisive ones. Issues surrounding who votes and why can also be contentious. Some examples include the following:

- Is the disenfranchisement of felons a form of racial discrimination—or a rational part of the punishment process?

- Given that historical events shape popular attitudes toward the parties, when all is said and done, will the impact of the Great Recession benefit the Republican Party—or will the effects of the recession prove trivial?

- Should legislators follow public opinion as faithfully as they can—or, as the Democrats did on health-care reform, should lawmakers do what they think is best for the country regardless of the polls?

- We discussed *push polls* on page 173. Should push polls be banned—or would that violate First Amendment guarantees of free speech?

- Should voters be most concerned with the policy positions of the presidential candidates—or are the presidential candidates' personalities and personal characteristics of equal or greater concern?

Take Action

"Citizens at the polls are the most powerful agents of change." Thus say political analysts Thomas Mann and Norman Ornstein.[10] But if citizens are not informed about the political issues of the day or the candidates' qualifications, there is little sense in going to the polls. Indeed, as mentioned in this chapter, one of the reasons for the relatively low voter turnout in this country is a sense on the part of some citizens that they lack information. As also noted, peer groups are important in the political socialization process. But just as you might be influenced by your peers, you can also influence them.

If you would like to take action to increase interest in our political life, one thing you might do is host a political salon. This would be a gathering, either in your home or at some other place, that would focus on learning about political issues and opinions. You could invite friends, other students, co-workers, or other persons who might be interested to attend the salon, which could be held weekly, monthly, or at some other interval. At the first meeting, you could set the "rules" for the salon. What topics do you want to discuss? How much time do you want to devote to each topic? What reading or research, if any, should be undertaken before the meetings? Depending on the views and energies of those who attend the salon, you might also devise an activist agenda to increase voter turnout. For example, you could plan a get-out-the-vote drive for the next election.

©HARLEY SCHWADRON

POLITICS ON THE
WEB

- Recent polls conducted and analyzed by the Roper Center for Public Opinion Research can be found at **www.ropercenter.uconn.edu**

- At the Gallup Organization's Web site, you can find the results of recent polls, as well as an archive of past polls and information on how polls are conducted. Go to **www.gallup.com**

- You can find poll data and material on major issues at the following site: **www.publicagenda.org**

- In addition to its enormous collection of recent articles on politics, the Real Clear Politics Web site has one of the most comprehensive collections of election polls available. For the polls, go to **www.realclearpolitics.com/polls**

- Nate Silver gained fame in 2008 for his analysis of polls taken by major firms. His election predictions were outstandingly accurate. Silver and his colleagues at the FiveThirtyEight blog now work under the aegis of the *New York Times*—go to **fivethirtyeight.blogs.nytimes.com**

- You'll find a poll-lover's dream at Mark Blumenthal's Pollster blog site, where readers debate about all the recent polls. Go to **www.pollster.com/blogs**

- Pollster.com's main page is also a trove of information about polls. See it at **www.pollster.com**

- Another site that collects polls and analyzes them is run by Scott Elliott, who is known as the "blogging Caesar." See it at **www.electionprojection.com**

Access CourseMate to review and expand on this chapter through quizzes, flashcards, learning objectives, interactive timelines, a crossword puzzle, audio summaries, video, critical-thinking activities, simulations, and more.

Campaigns and Elections

LEARNING OBJECTIVES

LO1 Explain how elections are held and how the electoral college functions in presidential elections.

LO2 Discuss how candidates are nominated.

LO3 Indicate what is involved in launching a political campaign today, and describe the structure and functions of a campaign organization.

LO4 Describe how the Internet has transformed political campaigns.

LO5 Summarize the laws that regulate campaign financing and the role of money in modern political campaigns.

LO6 Describe what took place during recent presidential elections and what these events tell us about the American electoral system.

CourseMate

AMERICA AT ODDS

Should We Elect the President by Popular Vote?

When Americans go to the polls every four years to cast their ballots for president, many are unaware that they are not, in fact, voting directly for the candidates. Rather, they are voting for electors—individuals chosen in each state by political parties to cast the state's electoral votes for the candidate who wins that state's popular vote. The system by which electors cast their votes for president is known as the *electoral college.*

Each state is assigned electoral votes based on its number of members in the U.S. Senate and House of Representatives. Each state has the same number of senators in the Senate (two), and the number of representatives a state has in the House is determined by the size of its population. As a result, there are currently 538 electoral votes.[1]

To win in the electoral college, a presidential candidate must win 270 of these 538 electoral votes. Most states have a "winner-take-all" system in which the candidate who receives a plurality of the popular votes (more than any other candidate) in a state receives all of that state's electoral votes, even if the margin of victory is very slight. A candidate who wins the popular vote nationally may yet lose in the electoral college—and vice versa. Many Americans believe that we should let the popular vote, not the electoral college, decide who becomes president.[2] Others are not so sure.

Let the People Elect Our President

In 2000, Democratic candidate Al Gore won the popular vote yet narrowly lost to Republican George W. Bush in the electoral college. Many Americans questioned the legitimacy of Bush's election. In 2004, a 120,000-vote swing in Ohio to Democrat John Kerry would have made him the president, even though Republican George W. Bush had a 2.5 percent lead in the popular vote nationally. If the 2008 presidential elections had been closer than it was, Democrat Barack Obama could easily have been elected with fewer popular votes than Republican John McCain—or McCain could have been elected with fewer votes than Obama.

Opponents decry the electoral college as an outdated invention of the late 1700s. To be sure, among the reasons for the system's original design was to ensure that the interests of smaller states were not totally overshadowed by their more populous neighbors. Yet the electoral college gives the smaller states a disproportionate amount of clout. Consider, for example, that one electoral vote in California now corresponds to roughly 675,000 people, while an electoral vote in more sparsely settled Wyoming represents only about 180,000 individuals. Clearly, the votes of Americans are not weighted equally, and this voting inequality is contrary to the "one person, one vote" principle of our democracy.

The Electoral College Protects the Small States and Ensures Stability

Supporters of the electoral college argue that if the system were abolished, small states would suffer. Because each state has as many electors as its total number of members in Congress, even the smallest states get two votes based on their representation in the Senate. Therefore, the electoral college helps to protect the small states from being overwhelmed by the large states.

The electoral college also helps to maintain a relatively stable and coherent party system. If the president were elected by popular vote, we might have multiple parties vying for the nation's highest office—as occurs in such nations as France, Germany, and Italy. The current system helps to discourage single-issue or regional candidates—candidates who are not focused on the interests of the nation as a whole. To prevail in the electoral college, a candidate must build a national coalition, campaign in Santa Fe as well as New York City, and propose policies that unite, rather than divide, the nation.

Finally, the electoral college vote has diverged from the popular vote in only three elections during our nation's history—in 1876, 1888, and 2000. These exceptions do not justify abolishing the system.

WHERE DO YOU STAND?

1. Do you believe that a candidate elected by the popular vote would be more representative of the entire nation than a candidate elected by the electoral college? Why or why not?
2. Suppose that instead of using the "winner-take-all" system, all states awarded their electoral votes according to the proportion of the popular vote each candidate received. How would this affect the final outcome in the electoral college?

EXPLORE THIS ISSUE ONLINE

- For critical views of the electoral college, go to the Web site of the Center for Voting and Democracy at www.fairvote.org/fair-elections and click on "National Popular Vote for President."
- For an article making a case for the electoral college, go to the Web site of Accuracy in Media (a conservative media watchdog group) at www.aim.org/briefing/making-a-case-for-the-electoral-college.

Introduction

During elections, candidates vie to become representatives of the people in both national and state offices. The population of the United States is now more than 310 million. Clearly, all citizens who are eligible to vote cannot gather in one place to make laws and run the government. We have to choose representatives to govern the nation and to act on behalf of our interests. We accomplish this through popular elections.

Campaigning for election has become an arduous task for every politician. As you will see in this chapter, American campaigns are long and expensive undertakings. The rules that govern our elections can be complicated, as you read in the chapter-opening *America at Odds* feature. Yet America's campaigns are an important part of our political process because it is through campaigns that citizens learn about the candidates and decide how they will cast their votes.

LO1 *How We Elect Candidates*

The ultimate goal of a political campaign and the associated fund-raising efforts is, of course, winning the election. The most familiar kind of election is the **general election,** which is a regularly scheduled election held in even-numbered years on the Tuesday after the first Monday in November. During general elections, the voters decide who will be the U.S. president, vice president, and senators and representatives in Congress. The president and vice president are elected every four years, senators every six years, and representatives every two years. General elections are also held to choose state and local government officials, often at the same time as those for national offices. A **special election** is held at the state or local level when the voters must decide an issue before the next general election or when vacancies occur by reason of death or resignation.

Most American citizens still case their ballots in paper form. Why hasn't this technology changed?

Types of Ballots

Since 1888, all states in the United States have used the **Australian ballot**—a secret ballot that is prepared, distributed, and counted by government officials at public expense. As its name implies, this ballot was first developed in Australia in 1856. An Australian innovation that we do not use in this country is compulsory voting, which we describe in this chapter's *The Rest of the World* feature on the following page.

Two variations of the Australian ballot are used today. Most states use the **party-column ballot** (also called the Indiana ballot), which lists all of a party's candidates together in a single column under the party label. In some states, the party-column ballot allows voters to vote for all of a party's candidates for local, state, and national offices by making a single "X" or pulling a single lever. The major parties favor this ballot form because it encourages straight-ticket voting.

Other states use the **office-block ballot** (also called the Massachusetts ballot), which lists together all of the candidates for each office. Parties tend to dislike the office-block ballot because it places more emphasis on the office than on the party and thus encourages split-ticket voting.

general election A regularly scheduled election to choose the U.S. president, vice president, and senators and representatives in Congress. General elections are held in even-numbered years on the Tuesday after the first Monday in November.

special election An election that is held at the state or local level when the voters must decide an issue before the next general election or when vacancies occur by reason of death or resignation.

Australian ballot A secret ballot that is prepared, distributed, and counted by government officials at public expense; used by all states in the United States since 1888.

party-column ballot A ballot (also called the Indiana ballot) that lists all of a party's candidates under the party label. Voters can vote for all of a party's candidates for local, state, and national offices by making a single "X" or pulling a single lever.

office-block ballot A ballot (also called the Massachusetts ballot) that lists together all of the candidates for each office.

DAVID PAUL MORRIS/GETTY IMAGES

Compulsory Voting Elsewhere Improves Voter Turnout

No matter what the election is, no matter what the issues are, and no matter who is running, voter turnout in the United States is low compared with that in many other countries. Obviously, the United States would have higher voter participation if we had a compulsory voting law. Australia is a good example of how such a system works.

Compulsory Voting in Australia

In Australia, citizens over the age of eighteen must register to vote, and they must show up at the polls on Election Day. Otherwise, they are subject to fines. This law has been in effect since 1924. Australia does make voting easier than it is in America, however. Elections are always held on Saturday, not Tuesday. Voters can vote from anywhere in the country. Citizens who live in remote areas can vote before Election Day or send in their ballots by mail.

The Effects of Australia's Law

Before 1924, in a typical year Australia saw a turnout of registered voters that was about on par with the United States—an average of 47 percent. Currently, voter turnout is roughly 95 percent. Candidates or organizations in Australia do not have to engage in "get out the vote" activities. In other words, candidates and their supporters can focus on issues rather than on encouraging voters to go to the polls. In the United States, much effort goes into getting citizens to register and then getting them to go to the polls to vote.

One odd result of compulsory voting is popularly known as the "donkey vote." Citizens who do not care about the elections may simply vote for the first name on a list of candidates. Before 1984, when lists were typically in alphabetical order, candidates could obtain a detectable advantage if their last name began with the letter A. Since that year, however, names have been listed in random order.

Compulsory Voting in Other Countries

Australia is not alone in enforcing compulsory voting. The following nations also do so:

Argentina	Liechtenstein
Brazil	Nauru
Chile	Peru
Congo (Kinshasa)	Singapore
Ecuador	Turkey
Fiji	Uruguay

Twenty other countries have compulsory voting laws but do not attempt to enforce them.

AGENCIA ESTADO VIA AP IMAGES

Like Australia, Brazil has compulsory voting laws. Here voters line up outside an election office in Sao Paulo, Brazil, on the last day of registration to vote in 2010.

For Critical Analysis *Some critics of compulsory voting claim that it is undemocratic. Why do you think they would make this argument?*

Conducting Elections and Counting the Votes

Recall from Chapter 8 that local units of government, such as cities, are divided into smaller voting districts, or precincts. Within each precinct, voters cast their ballots at a designated polling place.

An election board supervises the polling place and the voting process in each precinct. The board sets hours for the polls to be open according to the laws of the state and sees that ballots or voting machines are available. In most states, the board provides the list of registered voters and makes certain that only qualified voters cast ballots in each precinct. When the polls close, staff members count the votes and report the results, usually to the county clerk or the board of elections. Representatives from each party, called **poll watchers,** are allowed at each polling place to make sure the election is run fairly and to avoid fraud.

poll watcher A representative from one of the political parties who is allowed to monitor a polling place to make sure that the election is run fairly and to avoid fraud.

Figure 9–1

State Electoral Votes in 2004 and 2008

This map of the United States is distorted to show the relative weights of the states in terms of their electoral votes in 2004 and 2008, following changes required by the 2000 census. A candidate must win 270 electoral votes, cast by the electors, to become president through the electoral college system.

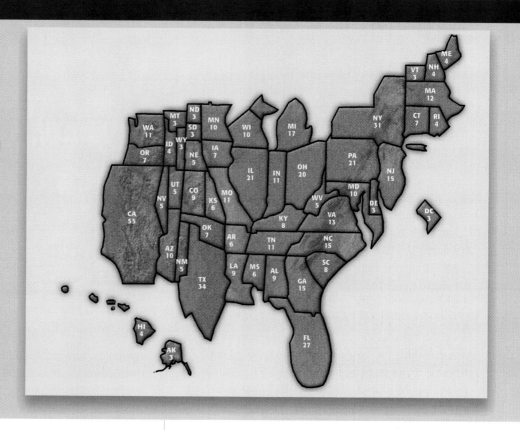

Presidential Elections and the Electoral College

When citizens vote for president and vice president, they are not voting directly for the candidates. Instead, they are voting for **electors** who will cast their ballots in the **electoral college.** The electors are selected during each presidential election year by the states' political parties, subject to the laws of the state. Each state has as many electoral votes as it has U.S. senators and representatives (see Figure 9–1 above). In addition, there are three electors from the District of Columbia, even though it is not a state. Should D.C. also have the right to a representative with a full vote in the House of Representatives? We look at that question in this chapter's *Join the Debate* feature on the following page.

The electoral college system is primarily a **winner-take-all system,** in which the candidate who receives the largest popular vote in a state is credited with all that state's electoral votes. The only exceptions are Maine and Nebraska.[3]

In December, after the general election, electors (either Republicans or Democrats, depending on which candidate has won the state's popular vote) meet in their state capitals to cast their votes for president and vice president. When the Constitution was drafted, the framers intended that the electors would use their own discretion in deciding who would make the best president. Today, however, the electors usually vote for the candidates to whom they are pledged. The electoral college ballots are then sent to the U.S. Senate, which counts and certifies them before a joint session of Congress held early in January. The candidates who receive a majority of the electoral votes are officially declared president and vice president. To be elected, a candidate must receive more than half of the 538 electoral votes available. Thus, a candidate needs 270 votes to win. If no presidential candidate gets an electoral college majority (which has happened twice—in 1800 and 1824), the House of Representatives votes on the candidates, with each state delegation casting only a single vote. If no candidate for vice president gets a majority of

elector A member of the electoral college.

electoral college The group of electors who are selected by the voters in each state to elect officially the president and vice president. The number of electors in each state is equal to the number of that state's representatives in both chambers of Congress.

winner-take-all system A system in which the candidate who receives the most votes wins. In contrast, proportional systems allocate votes to multiple winners.

Should D.C. Residents Have a Representative?

I f you are a resident of Washington, D.C., you can vote for president. You also can vote for a delegate who sits in the House of Representatives. That delegate, though, cannot vote on issues that come before the full House. The District of Columbia has no voting representation in Congress.

It's Only Fair

In 2009, Congress debated the D.C. Voting Rights Act. That act would make the District's current delegate a voting member of the House. Such a change seems quite fair, especially to those who live in the District. After all, everybody else who lives in the fifty states is represented by a voting member of the House (and two senators to boot). Whether or not granting full voting privileges to the delegate from the District is fair, one thing is certain. Any representative from D.C. will probably be a Democrat. Why? Because the District has an African American majority, and African Americans for many years have been among the Democrats' most loyal supporters.

Please Respect the Constitution

Others argue that the framers of the Constitution deliberately established the federal capital as a nonstate over which Congress would have exclusive legislative authority. This geographic and political entity has become Washington, D.C., which has been the nation's capital since 1800.

The Constitution requires that House members be elected by the people of the states. The District is not a state, and therefore its residents cannot have a voting member of the House. In other words, the D.C. Voting Rights Act is unconstitutional, and the legislation could never withstand even the first judicial test of its legitimacy.

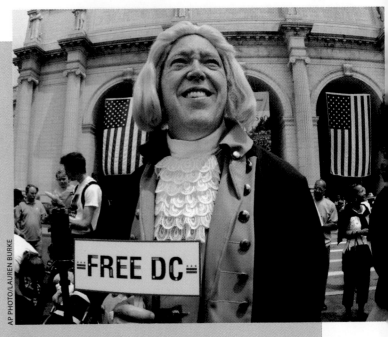

AP PHOTO/LAUREN BURKE

Why the Real Solution Won't Work

There's an obvious solution to the D.C. representation issue: admit the District as a state. Such a proposal would be perfectly constitutional. It is, in fact, the solution that D.C. residents prefer. If the District became a state, it would join Wyoming as one of the most overrepresented states in the Senate. A second possible solution would be to give the District back to Maryland.[4] The city of Washington would then have enough people to dominate its own House district, and Washington residents could vote for Maryland's U.S. senators.

If the District were a state or part of a state, the national government would still have full authority over all federal facilities, just as it controls such facilities in the states today. What Congress would give up, however, is the right to interfere in the District's business when federal questions are not involved. Clearly, Congress finds that right too precious to lose.

🔍 **For Critical Analysis** *In what ways might Congress want to interfere with the government of the District?*

electoral votes, the vice president is chosen by the Senate, with each senator casting one vote.

Even when a presidential candidate wins by a large margin in the electoral college and in the popular vote—a *landslide election*—it does not follow that the candidate has won the support of the majority of those eligible to vote. We explore this paradox in this chapter's *Perception versus Reality* feature on page 194.

LO2 How We Nominate Candidates

T he first step on the long road to winning an election is the nomination process. Nominations narrow the field of possible candidates and limit each political party's choice to one person. For many local government posts, which are often nonpartisan, self-nomination is the most common way to become a candidate. Such a procedure is frequently used in lightly populated areas. A self-proclaimed candidate usually files a petition to be listed on the ballot. Each state has laws that specify how many signatures a candidate must obtain to show that he or she has some public support. An alternative is to be a write-in candidate—voters write the candidate's name on the ballot on Election Day.

Candidates for major offices are rarely nominated in these ways, however. As you read in Chapter 7, most candidates for high office are nominated by a political party and receive considerable support from party activists throughout their campaigns.

Party Control over Nominations

The methods used by political parties to nominate candidates have changed during the course of American history. Broadly speaking, the process has grown more open over the years, with the involvement of ever-greater numbers of local leaders and ordinary citizens. Today, any voter can participate in choosing party candidates. This was not true as recently as 1968, however, and was certainly not possible during the first years of the republic.

George Washington was essentially unopposed in the first U.S. presidential elections in 1789—no other candidate was seriously considered in any state. By the end of Washington's eight years in office, however, political divisions among the nation's leaders had solidified into political parties, the Federalists and the Jeffersonian (or Democratic) Republicans (see Chapter 7). These early parties were organized by gatherings of important persons, who often met in secret. The meetings came to be called **caucuses.**[5] Beginning in 1800, members of Congress who belonged to the two parties held caucuses to nominate candidates for president and vice president. The Republican caucus chose Thomas Jefferson in 1800, as expected, and the Federalist caucus nominated the incumbent president, John Adams. By 1816, the Federalist Party had ceased to exist, and the Jeffersonian Republican congressional caucus was in complete control of selecting the president of the United States.

The congressional caucus system collapsed in 1824.[6] It was widely seen as undemocratic—opponents derided it as "King Caucus." A much-diminished caucus nominated

> "A politician should have three hats: ONE FOR THROWING INTO THE RING, ONE FOR TALKING THROUGH, AND ONE FOR PULLING RABBITS OUT OF IF ELECTED."
>
> ~ CARL SANDBURG ~
> AMERICAN POET AND HISTORIAN
> 1878–1967

a presidential candidate who then came in third in the electoral vote. The other three major candidates were essentially self-nominated.[7] The four candidates split the electoral vote so completely that the House of Representatives had to decide the contest. It picked John Quincy Adams, even though Andrew Jackson had won more popular and electoral votes.

The Party Nominating Convention

In the run-up to the 1828 elections, two new parties grew up around the major candidates. Adams's supporters called themselves the National Republicans (later known as the Whigs). Jackson's supporters organized as the Democratic Party, which won the election. In 1832, both parties settled on a new method of choosing candidates for president and vice president—the national nominating convention. A number of state parties had already adopted the convention system for choosing state-level candidates. New Jersey held conventions as early as 1800.

A **nominating convention** is an official meeting of a political party to choose its candidates. Those who attend the convention are called **delegates,** and they are chosen to represent the people of a particular geographic area. Conventions can take place at multiple levels. A county convention might choose delegates to attend a state convention. The state convention in turn might select delegates to the national convention. By 1840, the convention system was the most common method of nominating political party candidates at the state and national levels.

While the convention system drew in a much broader range of leaders than had the caucus, it was not a particularly democratic institution. Convention delegates were rarely chosen by a vote of the party's local members. Typically, they were appointed by local party officials, who were usually, with good reason, called bosses. These local leaders often gained

caucus A meeting held to choose political candidates or delegates.

nominating convention An official meeting of a political party to choose its candidates. Nominating conventions at the state and local levels also select delegates to represent the citizens of their geographic areas at a higher-level party convention.

delegate A person selected to represent the people of one geographic area at a party convention.

PERCEPTION VERSUS
REALITY

Presidents and the "Popular Vote"

Some presidential contests are very close, such as the 2000 race between Al Gore and George W. Bush. Others are less so, such as the one between Lyndon B. Johnson and Barry Goldwater in 1964. When a presidential candidate wins the race by a wide margin, as Johnson did, we may hear the result referred to as a *landslide election* or a *landslide victory* for the winning candidate.

The Perception

The traditional perception has been that, in general, our presidents are elected by a majority of eligible American voters. A president who has been swept into office by a so-called landslide victory may claim to have received a "mandate from the people" to govern the nation. A president may assert that a certain policy or program she or he endorsed in campaign speeches is backed by popular support simply because she or he was elected to office by a majority of the voters.

The Reality

In reality, the "popular vote" is not all that popular, in the sense of representing the wishes of a majority of American citizens who are eligible to vote. In fact, the president of the United States has never received the votes of a majority of all eligible adults. Lyndon Johnson, in 1964, came the closest of

Lyndon B. Johnson came the closest of any candidate ever to winning a majority of the votes of all citizens eligible to cast a ballot.

any president in history, and even he won the votes of less than 40 percent of those who were eligible to cast a ballot.

The hotly contested presidential elections of 2000 and 2004 were divisive, leaving the millions of Americans who had voted for the losing candidates unhappy with the results. Indeed, in winning the election of 2000, Bush received the votes of a mere 26.0 percent of those with the right to vote. Nonetheless, Bush assumed that his reelection in 2004 was a signal from the American people to push his controversial domestic ideas, such as Social Security reform, as well as an endorsement of his foreign policy and the war on terrorism. Barack Obama likewise claimed a personal mandate based on his strong performance in 2008, and he parlayed it into a sweeping program of domestic initiatives. Yet Obama had won the support of only 32.9 percent of eligible voters.

It is useful to keep these figures in mind whenever a president claims to have received a mandate from the people. The truth is, no president has ever been elected with sufficient popular backing to make this a serious claim.

Blog On Dave Leip's Atlas of U.S. Presidential Elections provides detailed figures on presidential election results. Find the Atlas at **www.uselectionatlas.org.**

---

their positions in ways that were far from democratic. Not until 1972 did ordinary voters in all states gain the right to select delegates to the national presidential nominating conventions.

Primary Elections and the Loss of Party Control

The corruption that so often accompanied the convention system led re-

primary election An election in which voters choose the candidates of their party, who will then run in the general election.

formers to call for a new way to choose candidates— the **primary election,** in which voters go to the polls to decide among candidates who seek the nomination of their party. Candidates who win a primary election then go on to compete against the candidates from other parties in the general election. The first primary election may have been held in 1842 by Democrats in Crawford County, Pennsylvania. The technique was not widely used, however, until the end of the nineteenth century and the beginning of the twentieth. These were years in which reform was a popular cause.

California Republican candidate for governor Meg Whitman, left, and Republican U.S. Senate candidate Carly Fiorina at a rally in Anaheim, Calif. Both candidates were formerly heads of major corporations before turning to politics.

> **direct primary** An election held within each of the two major parties— Democratic and Republican—to choose the party's candidates for the general election. Voters choose the candidate directly, rather than through delegates.

DIRECT AND INDIRECT PRIMARIES The rules for conducting primary elections are highly variable, and a number of different types of primaries exist. One major distinction is between a direct primary and an indirect primary. In a **direct primary,** voters cast their ballots directly for candidates. In an *indirect primary,* voters choose delegates, who in turn choose the candidates. The delegates may be pledged to a particular candidate but sometimes run as *unpledged delegates.* The major parties use indirect primaries to elect delegates to the national nominating conventions that choose candidates for president and vice president. The elections that nominate candidates for Congress and for state or local offices are almost always direct primaries.

THE ROLE OF THE STATES Primary elections are normally conducted by state governments. States set the dates and conduct the elections. They provide polling places, election officials, and registration lists, and they then count the votes. By sponsoring the primaries, state governments have obtained considerable influence over the rules by which the primaries are conducted. The power of the states is limited, however, by the parties' First Amendment right to freedom of association, a right that has been repeatedly confirmed by the United States Supreme Court.[8] On occasion, parties that object to the rules imposed by state governments have opted out of the state-sponsored primary system altogether.[9] Note that third parties typically do not participate in state-sponsored primaries, but hold nominating conventions instead. The major parties rarely opt out of state elections, however, because the financial—and political—costs of going it alone are high. (When primary elections are used to choose candidates for local *nonpartisan* positions, state control is uncontested.)

PRIMARY VOTERS Voter turnout for primaries is lower than it is in general elections. The voters who do go to the polls are often strong supporters of their party. Indeed, as you will learn shortly, independents cannot participate in primary elections in some states, even if they lean toward one or the other of the two major parties. As a result, the Republican primary electorate is very conservative, and Democratic primary voters are quite liberal. Candidates often find that they must run to the political right or left during the primaries. Frequently, they then move to the center during the general election campaign.

New York Democratic candidate for governor, state Attorney General Andrew Cuomo, receives the endorsement of NARAL Pro-Choice New York in the governor's race, at New York's City Hall.

INSURGENT CANDIDATES Primary elections were designed to take nominations out of the hands of the party bosses, and indeed, the most important result of the primary system has been to dramatically reduce the power of elected and party officials over the nominating process. Ever since primary elections were established, the insurgent candidate who runs against the party "establishment" has been a common phenomenon. Running against the "powers that be" is often a very effective campaign strategy, and many insurgents have won victories at the local, state, and national levels.

Insurgent campaigns often replace incumbent leaders who are out of touch with the party rank and file, sometimes because the incumbents are too liberal or too conservative. Occasionally, an insurgent's platform is strikingly different from that of the party as a whole. Yet even when an insurgent's politics are abhorrent to the rest of the party—for example, an insurgent might make an outright appeal to racism—the party has no way of denying the insurgent the right to the party label in the general election.

OPEN AND CLOSED PRIMARIES Primaries can be classified as closed or open. In a **closed primary,** only party members can vote to choose that party's candidates, and they may vote only in the primary of their own party. Thus, only registered Democrats can vote in the Democratic primary to select candidates of the Democratic Party. Only registered Republicans can vote for the Republican candidates. A person usually establishes party membership when she or he registers to vote. Some states have a *semiclosed* primary, which allows voters to register with a party or change their party affiliations on Election Day. Regular party workers favor the closed primary because it promotes party loyalty. Independent voters usually oppose it because it forces them to select a party if they wish to participate in the nominating process.

In an **open primary,** voters can vote for a party's candidates regardless of whether they belong to the party. In most open primaries, all voters receive both a Republican ballot and a Democratic ballot. Voters then choose either the Democratic or the Republican ballot in the privacy of the voting booth. In a *semiopen* primary, voters request the ballot for the party of their choice.

The fifty states have developed dozens of variations on the open and closed primary plans. In some states, primaries are closed only to persons registered to another party, and independents can vote in either primary. In several states, an independent who votes in a party primary is automatically enrolled in that party. In other states, the voter remains an independent. The two major parties often have different rules. For example, in two states, the Democrats allow independents to vote in the primaries, but the Republicans do not.

BLANKET AND "TOP TWO" PRIMARIES Until 2000, California and a few other states employed a *blanket primary,* in which voters could choose the candidates of more than one party. A voter might participate in choosing the Republican candidate for governor, for example, and at the same time vote to pick the Democratic candidate for the U.S. Senate. In that year, however, the Supreme Court ruled that the blanket primary violated the parties' right to freedom of association.[10] Similar primary systems in Washington State and Alaska were struck down in later cases.

Louisiana has for many years had a unique system in which all candidates participate in the same primary, regardless of party. The two candidates receiving the most votes then proceed on to the general election. In 2008, Louisiana abandoned this system for the U.S. House and Senate, but kept it for state and local offices.

Even as Louisiana was backing away from this system, however, other states began picking it up. Washington State adopted the Louisiana system in 2004, and in 2008 the Supreme Court ruled that it was constitutional.[11] In June 2010, California voters adopted a system known as the *"top two" primary* that was patterned on the one in Washington State. Political parties continue to have the right to designate preferred candidates, using conventions or other means, but such endorsements do not appear on the ballot. An insurgent Republican and a "regular" Republican, for example, would both be labeled simply "Republican." The California system will go into effect in 2011, and given California's size and importance, its top two primary will be closely watched.

Nominating Presidential Candidates

In some respects, being nominated for president is more difficult than being elected. The nominating process narrows a very large number of hopefuls down to a single candidate from each party. Choosing a presidential candidate is unlike nominating candidates for any other office. One reason for this is that the nomination process combines several different methods.

---

closed primary A primary in which only party members can vote to choose that party's candidates.

open primary A primary in which voters can vote for a party's candidates regardless of whether they belong to the party.

PRESIDENTIAL PRIMARIES   Most of the states hold presidential primaries, beginning early in the election year. For a candidate, a good showing in the early primaries results in plenty of media attention as television networks and newspaper reporters play up the results. Subsequent state primaries tend to serve as contests to eliminate unlikely candidates.

The presidential primaries do not necessarily follow the same rules the states use for nominating candidates for the U.S. Congress or for state and local offices. Often, the presidential primaries are not held on the same date as the other primaries. States frequently hold the presidential primaries early in hopes of exercising greater influence on the outcome.

CAUCUSES   The caucus system is an alternative to primary elections. Strictly speaking, the caucus system is a convention system. The caucuses are party conventions held at the local level that elect delegates to conventions at the county or congressional district level. These midlevel conventions then choose the delegates to the state convention, which finally elects the delegates to the national party convention. Unlike the caucuses of two centuries ago, modern caucuses are open to all party members. It is not hard to join a party. At the famous Iowa caucuses, you become a party member simply by attending a local caucus.

Senator John McCain and then-Senator Barack Obama during the presidential campaign.

AP PHOTO/ALEX BRANDON

While some states, such as Iowa and Minnesota, rely on the caucus/convention system to nominate candidates for state and local positions, the system is more frequently used only to choose delegates to the Democratic and Republican national conventions. Most states with presidential caucuses use primaries to nominate state and local candidates. Twelve states choose national convention delegates through caucuses. Four states use caucuses to allocate some of the national convention delegates and use primaries to allocate the others.

PRIMARIES—THE RUSH TO BE FIRST   Traditionally, states have held their presidential primaries at various times over the first six months of a presidential election year. In an effort to make their primaries prominent in the media and influential in the political process, however, many states have moved the date of their primary to earlier in the year—a practice known as *front-loading*. In 1988, a group of southern states created a "Super Tuesday" by holding their primaries on the same day in early March. Then, other states moved their primaries to an earlier date, too.

The practice of front-loading primaries has gained momentum over the last decade. The states with later primary dates found that most nominations were decided early in the season, leaving their voters "out of the action." As more states moved up their primary dates, the early primaries became even more important, and other states, to compete, also moved up their primaries.

This rush to be first was particularly notable in the year or so preceding the 2008 presidential primaries. By 2007, about half the states had moved their primaries to earlier dates. Many of these states opted for February 5—or "Super-Super Tuesday," as some called it—as the date for their primaries.

THE IMPACT OF FRONT-LOADING   Many Americans worried that with a shortened primary season, long-shot candidates would no longer be able to propel themselves into serious contention by doing well in small, early-voting states, such as New Hampshire and Iowa. Traditionally, a candidate who had a successful showing in the New Hampshire primary had time to obtain enough financial backing to continue in the race. The fear was that an accelerated schedule of presidential primaries would favor the richest candidates.

In practice, front-loading did not have this effect in 2008. On the Republican side, the early primaries might have benefited a front-runner—if there had been a Republican front-runner in January 2008. As it happened, the candidate with the most funds, former Massachusetts governor Mitt Romney, did not win the most votes. After February 5, Arizona senator John McCain had a clear lead. The Republican primaries were mostly conducted on a winner-take-all basis, a rule that allowed McCain to wrap up the nomination on March 4.

The Democrats, however, allocated delegates on a proportional basis, so that each candidate received delegates based on his or her share of the vote. That rule made an early decision impossible, and Barack Obama did not obtain a majority of the Democratic delegates until June 3. As a result, many of the most important Democratic primaries took place late in the season. States that had moved their primaries to February 5 discovered that they were lost in the crowd of early contests. Front-loading, in other words, had become counterproductive.

NATIONAL PARTY CONVENTIONS Born in the 1830s, the American national political convention is unique in Western democracies. Elsewhere, candidates for prime minister or chancellor are chosen within the confines of party councils. That is actually closer to the way the framers of the Constitution wanted it done.

At one time, the conventions were indeed often giant free-for-alls. It wasn't always clear who the winning presidential and vice-presidential candidates would be until the delegates voted. As more states opted to hold presidential primaries, however, the drama of national conventions diminished. Today, the conventions have been described as massive pep rallies. Nonetheless, each convention's task remains a serious one. In late summer, two thousand to three thousand delegates gather at each convention to represent the wishes of the voters and political leaders of their home states. They adopt the official party platform and declare their support for the party's presidential and vice-presidential candidates.

On the first day of the convention, delegates hear the reports of the **Credentials Committee,** which inspects each prospective delegate's claim to be seated as a legitimate representative of her or his state. When the eligibility of delegates is in question, the committee decides who will be

Credentials Committee
A committee of each national political party that evaluates the claims of national party convention delegates to be the legitimate representatives of their states.

> **"THERE IS NO EXCITEMENT**
> anywhere in the world . . . to match the excitement of an American presidential campaign."
> ~ THEODORE H. WHITE ~
> AMERICAN JOURNALIST AND HISTORIAN
> 1915–1986

seated. In the evening, there is usually a keynote speaker to whip up enthusiasm among the delegates. The second day includes committee reports and debates on the party platform. The third day is devoted to nominations and voting. Balloting begins with an alphabetical roll call in which states and territories announce their votes. By midnight, the convention's real work is over, and the presidential candidate has been selected. The vice-presidential nomination and the acceptance speeches occupy the fourth day. We provided more details on the national party conventions in Chapter 7 on pages 153 and 154.

LO3 *The Modern Political Campaign*

Once nominated, candidates focus on their campaigns. The term *campaign* originated in the military context. Generals mounted campaigns, using their scarce resources (soldiers and materials) to achieve military objectives. Using the term in a political context is apt. In a political campaign, candidates also use scarce resources (time and funds) in an attempt to defeat their adversaries in the battle for votes.

Responsibilities of the Campaign Staff

To run a successful campaign, the candidate's campaign staff must be able to raise funds for the effort, get media coverage, produce and pay for political ads, schedule the candidate's time effectively with constituent groups and potential supporters, convey the candidate's position on the issues, conduct research on the opposing candidate, and persuade the voters to go to the polls. When party identification was firmer and TV campaigning was still in its infancy, a strong party organization on the local, state, or national level could furnish most of the services and expertise that the candidate needed. Less effort was spent on advertising each candidate's position and character, because the party label communicated that information to many of the voters.

Today, party labels are no longer as important as they once were. In part, this is because fewer people identify with the major parties, as evidenced by the rising number of independent voters. Instead of relying so

Kentucky U.S. Senator Mitch McConnell (right) puts an arm around fellow Republican and senatorial candidate Rand Paul as they wave to the crowd at the Fancy Farm Picnic in Graves County, Ky.

extensively on political parties, candidates now turn to professionals to manage their campaigns.

The Professional Campaign Organization

With the rise of candidate-centered campaigns in the past two decades, the role of the political party in managing campaigns has declined. Professional **political consultants** now manage nearly all aspects of a presidential candidate's campaign. President Barack Obama, for example, relied heavily on his longtime political adviser David Axelrod in crafting his 2008 election victory. Most candidates for governor, the House, and the Senate also rely on consultants. Political consultants generally specialize in a particular area of the campaign, such as researching the opposition, conducting polls, developing the candidate's advertising, or organizing "get out the vote" efforts. Nonetheless, most candidates have a campaign manager who coordinates and plans the **campaign strategy.** Figure 9–2 on the following page shows a typical presidential campaign organization. The political party also continues to play an important role in recruiting volunteers and getting out the vote.

A major development in contemporary American politics is the focus on reaching voters through effective use of the media, particularly television. At least half of the budget for a major political campaign is consumed by television advertising. Media consultants are therefore pivotal members of the campaign staff. The nature of political advertising is discussed in more detail in Chapter 10.

LO4 The Internet Campaign

Over the years, political leaders have benefited from understanding and using new communications technologies. In the 1930s, command of a new medium—radio—gave President Franklin D. Roosevelt an advantage. In 1960, Democratic presidential candidate John F. Kennedy gained an edge on Republican Richard Nixon because Kennedy had a better understanding of the visual requirements of television. Today, the ability to make effective use of e-mail and the Web is essential to a candidate. In the 2008 presidential elections, Barack Obama gained a margin over his rivals in part because of his use of the new technologies. His team relied on the Internet for several tasks, which included fund-raising, targeting potential supporters, and creating local political organizations.

Fund-Raising on the Internet

Internet fund-raising grew out of an earlier technique: the direct-mail campaign. In direct mailings, campaigns send solicitations to large numbers of likely prospects, typically seeking contributions. Developing good lists of prospects is central to an effective direct-mail operation. Postage, printing, and the rental of address lists push the marginal cost of each additional letter well above a dollar. Response rates are low—a 1 percent response rate is a tremendous success. In many direct-mail campaigns, most of the funds raised are used up by the costs of the campaign itself. From the 1970s on, conservative organizations became especially adept at managing direct-mail campaigns. This expertise gave conservative causes and candidates a notable advantage over liberals.

To understand the old system is to recognize the superiority of the new one. The marginal cost of each additional e-mail message is essentially zero. Lists of prospects need not be prepared as carefully, because e-mail sent to unlikely prospects does not waste resources. E-mail fund-raising did face one

political consultant
A professional political adviser who, for a fee, works on an area of a candidate's campaign. Political consultants include campaign managers, pollsters, media advisers, and "get out the vote" organizers.

campaign strategy The comprehensive plan developed by a candidate and his or her advisers for winning an election. The strategy includes the candidate's position on issues, slogan, advertising plan, press events, personal appearances, and other aspects of the campaign.

Figure 9–2

A Typical Presidential Campaign Organization

Most aspects of a candidate's campaign are managed by professional political consultants, as this figure illustrates.

CANDIDATE

Campaign Manager
Develops overall campaign strategy, manages finances, oversees staff

Campaign Staff
Undertakes the various tasks associated with campaigning

MEDIA CONSULTANTS	FUND-RAISERS	SPEECHWRITERS	PRESS SECRETARY	POLICY EXPERTS
Help to shape candidate's image, manage campaign advertising	Raise money to subsidize campaign	Prepare speeches for candidate's public appearances	Maintains press contacts, is responsible for disseminating campaign news	Provide input on foreign and domestic policy issues

LAWYERS AND ACCOUNTANTS	PRIVATE POLLSTER	RESEARCHERS	TRAVEL PLANNER	WEB CONSULTANT
Monitor legal and financial aspects of campaign	Gathers up-to-the-minute data on public opinion	Investigate opponents' records and personal history	Arranges for candidate's transportation and accommodations	Oversees the candidate's Internet presence

State Chairpersons
Monitor state and local campaigns

Local Committees
Direct efforts of local volunteers

Volunteers
Publicize candidates at local level through personal visits, phone calls, direct mailings, and online activities

---

problem when it was new—many people were not yet online. Today, that issue is no longer so important.

The new technology brought with it a change in the groups that benefited the most. Conservatives were no longer the most effective fund-raisers. Instead, liberal and libertarian organizations enjoyed some of the greatest successes.

Obama Online

Barack Obama took Internet fund-raising to a new level during his 2008 presidential bid. One of the defining characteristics of his fund-raising was its decentralization. The Obama campaign attempted to recruit as many supporters as possible to act as fund-raisers who would solicit contributions from their friends and neighbors. As a result, Obama was spared much of the personal fund-raising effort that consumes the time of most national politicians.

In the first half of 2007, Obama's campaign raised $58 million, $16.4 million of which was made up of donations of less than $200. The total sum was a record, and the small-donation portion was unusually large. In August 2008, the Obama campaign set another record, raising $66 million—the most ever raised in one month by a presidential campaign. By then, 2.5 million people had donated to Obama's campaign. Most of them had been contacted through the Internet.

Targeting Supporters

In 2004, President George W. Bush's chief political adviser, Karl Rove, pioneered a new campaign technique known as *microtargeting*. The process involves collecting as much information as possible about voters in a gigantic database and then filtering out various groups for special attention. Through microtargeting, for example, the Bush campaign could identify Republican prospects living in heavily Democratic neighborhoods—potential supporters whom the campaign might have neglected because the neighborhood as a whole seemed so unpromising.

EXAMPLES OF MICROTARGETING Microtargeting could also reveal groups that might be receptive to specific appeals. For example, the Republican campaign identified a group of education-conscious Hispanic mothers in New Mexico, and it plied them with mailings and phone calls that touted Bush's No Child Left Behind legislation. Although Rove's operation frequently contacted such voters in traditional ways, much of the data necessary for microtargeting was collected through the Internet. In 2004, the Democrats had nothing to match Rove's efforts. By 2008, however, microtargeting was employed by all major candidates.

BEHAVIORAL TARGETING In 2008, both the Democratic and Republican general election campaigns supplemented microtargeting with a new and somewhat controversial targeting method—behavioral targeting. This technique is entirely Web-based. It uses information about people's online behavior, such as the pages they visit and the searches they make, to tailor the advertisements that they see. What is controversial about the practice is that it involves placing a cookie in the cookie folder of a person's computer, without that person's knowledge, to collect information on the person's online behavior. Later, the person may see online advertisements based on what the cookie "knows" about the person's preferences. Behavioral targeting raises privacy concerns, and both Congress and the Federal Trade Commission have held hearings on the practice.

Support for Local Organizing

Perhaps the most effective use of the Internet has been as an organizing tool. One of the earliest Internet techniques was to use the site Meetup.com to organize real-

> ## "IN CONSTANT PURSUIT OF MONEY
> to finance campaigns, the political system is simply unable to function. Its deliberative powers are paralyzed."
>
> ~ JOHN RAWLS ~
> AMERICAN EDUCATOR
> 1921–2000

world meetings. In this way, campaigns were able to gather supporters without relying on the existing party and activist infrastructure.

OBAMA'S CAMPAIGN As with fund-raising, Barack Obama took Web-based organizing to a new level. In part, his campaign used existing sites such as Facebook and MySpace. By June 2008, Obama had 953,000 Facebook backers to John McCain's 142,000. He also had 394,000 supporters on MySpace, seven times McCain's total. On YouTube, Obama's videos were viewed 50 million times, compared with 4 million for McCain's. Obama's own Web site was especially important to the campaign. My.BarackObama.com eventually racked up more than a million members.

LOCAL SUPPORT GROUPS By gathering information on large numbers of potential supporters, the Obama campaign was able to create local support groups in towns and counties across the country. For example, the Obama campaign assembled a group of forty volunteers in Avery County, North Carolina, a locality in the Blue Ridge Mountains traditionally carried by Republican presidential candidates at rates of more than three to one. The volunteers were often surprised to discover that neighbors they had known for years were fellow Democrats. Several had thought they were the only Democrats in town. The group coordinated its activities by e-mail, in part because of rugged terrain and poor local cell phone reception.

Obama's national Internet fund-raising success meant that he could field hundreds of paid organizers in North Carolina, some of whom supported local groups of volunteers such as this one. In the end, McCain easily carried Avery County, but Obama carried the state.[12]

LO5 *What It Costs to Win*

The modern political campaign is an expensive undertaking. Candidates must spend huge sums for professional campaign managers and consultants, television and radio ads, the printing of campaign literature, travel, office rent, equipment, and other necessities.

To get an idea of the cost of waging a campaign for Congress today, consider that in the 2010 mid-term election cycle, the average House incumbent raised about $1.7 million. The average House challenger raised close to $700,000. In the Senate, a typical incumbent took in more than $13 million. The average challenger spent almost $5 million. Of course, some contests were much more expensive than the average. Barbara Boxer, the incumbent running for reelection to the Senate from California raised over $26 million, while her challenger, Carly Fiorina, spent over $16 million.

Presidential campaigns are even more costly. In 2004, presidential campaign expenditures amounted to nearly $830 million. In the 2007–2008 election cycle, these costs reached about $2.4 billion, making the 2008 presidential campaigns the most expensive in history.

The high cost of campaigns gives rise to the fear that campaign contributors and special interest groups will try to buy favored treatment from those who are elected to office. In an attempt to prevent these abuses, the government regulates campaign financing.

All campaigns involve supporters and volunteers who make up the grass roots backing for every politician who seriously wishes to win. These volunteers are waiting for the ballot count results during a primary election in St. Paul, Minnesota.

AP PHOTO/JIM MONE

The Federal Election Campaign Act

Congress passed the Federal Election Campaign Act (FECA) of 1971[13] in an effort to curb abuses in the ways political campaigns were financed. The 1971 act placed no limit on overall spending but restricted the amount that could be spent on mass media advertising, including television. It limited the amount that candidates and their families could contribute to their own campaigns and required disclosure of all contributions and expenditures of more than $100. In principle, the 1971 act limited the role of labor unions and corporations in political campaigns. Also in 1971, Congress passed a law that provided for a $1 checkoff on federal income tax returns for general campaign funds to be used by major-party presidential candidates. This law was first applied in the 1976 campaign. (Since then, the amount of the checkoff has been raised to $3.)

AMENDMENTS IN 1974 Amendments to the act passed in 1974 did the following:

- *Created the Federal Election Commission (FEC) to administer and enforce the act's provisions.*

- *Provided public financing for presidential primaries and general elections.* Presidential candidates who

raise some money on their own can get funds from the U.S. Treasury to help pay for primary campaigns. For the general election campaign, presidential candidates receive federal funding for almost all of their expenses if they are willing to accept campaign-spending limits.

- *Limited presidential campaign spending.* Candidates accepting federal support must limit spending to amounts set by law.

- *Required disclosure.* Candidates must file periodic reports with the FEC that list the contributors to the campaign and indicate how the funds were spent.

- *Limited contributions.* Limits were placed on how much individuals and groups could contribute to candidates.

A recent development in presidential campaign finance has been the tendency of candidates to reject public funding on the grounds that they can raise larger sums outside the system. By 2008, a majority of the leading Democratic and Republican presidential candidates were refusing public funding for the primaries. That year, Barack Obama became the first major-party candidate in decades to refuse federal funding for the general election as well.

BUCKLEY v. VALEO In a 1976 case, *Buckley v. Valeo*,[14] the United States Supreme Court declared unconstitutional the provision in the 1971 act that limited the amount each individual could spend on his or her own campaign. The Court held that a "candidate, no less than any other person, has a First Amendment right to engage in the discussion of public issues and vigorously and tirelessly to advocate his own election."

THE RISE OF PACS The FECA allows corporations, labor unions, and special interest groups to set up national *political action committees (PACs)* to raise money for candidates. For a PAC to be legitimate, the money must be raised from at least fifty volunteer donors and must be given to at least five candidates in the national elections. PACs can contribute up to $5,000 per candidate in each election, but there is no limit on the total amount of PAC contributions during an election cycle. As discussed in Chapter 6, the number of PACs has grown significantly since the 1970s, as have their campaign contributions. In the 2004 election cycle, about 36 percent of campaign funds spent on House races came from PACs.[15] Since 2004, however, other methods of raising campaign funds have reduced the relative importance of PACs.

Skirting the Campaign-Financing Rules

Individuals and corporations have found **loopholes**— legitimate ways of evading legal requirements—in the federal laws limiting campaign contributions.

SOFT MONEY The biggest loophole in the FECA and its amendments was that they did not prohibit individuals or corporations from contributing to political *parties*.

Senator Ron Wyden, (D., Ore.) and Senator Charles Schumer, right, (D., N.Y.) take part in a campaign finance news conference in front of the Supreme Court in Washington, D.C.

AP PHOTO/HARRY HAMBURG

Contributors could make donations to the parties to cover the costs of registering voters, printing flyers, advertising, developing campaigns to "get out the vote," and holding fund-raising events. Contributions to political parties were called **soft money.** Even though soft money clearly was used to support the candidates, it was difficult to track exactly how this was happening.

loophole A legitimate way of evading a certain legal requirement.

soft money Campaign contributions not regulated by federal law, such as some contributions that are made to political parties instead of to particular candidates.

independent expenditure An expenditure for activities that are independent from (not coordinated with) those of a political candidate or a political party.

By 2000, the parties raised nearly $463 million through soft money contributions. Soft dollars became the main source of campaign money in the presidential race until after the 2002 elections, when they were banned, as you will read shortly.

INDEPENDENT EXPENDITURES Another major loophole in campaign-financing laws was that they did not prohibit corporations, labor unions, and special interest groups from making **independent expenditures** in an election campaign. Independent expenditures, as the term implies, are expenditures for activities that are independent from (not coordinated with) those of the candidate or a political party. In other words, interest groups can wage their own "issue" campaigns so long as they do not go so far as to say "Vote for Candidate X."

The problem is, where do you draw the line between advocating a position on a particular issue and contributing to the campaign of a candidate who endorses that position? In addressing this thorny issue, the United States Supreme Court has developed two determinative tests. Under the first test, a group's speech is a campaign "expenditure" only if it explicitly calls for the election of a particular candidate. Using this test, the courts repeatedly have held that interest groups have the right to advocate their positions. For example, the Christian Coalition has the right to publish voter guides informing voters of candidates' positions. The second test applies when a group or organization has made expenditures explicitly for the purpose of endorsing a candidate. Such expenditures are permissible unless they were made in "coordination" with a campaign. According to the Supreme Court, an issue-oriented group has a First Amendment right to advocate the election of its preferred candidates as long as it acts independently.

In 1996, the Supreme Court held that these guidelines apply to expenditures by political parties as well. Parties may spend money on behalf of candidates if they do so independently—that is, if they do not let the candidates know how, when, or for what the money was spent.[16] As critics of this decision have pointed out, parties generally work closely with candidates, so establishing the "independence" of such expenditures is difficult.

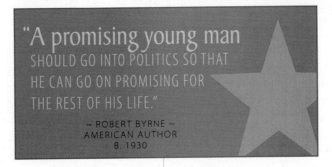

"A promising young man SHOULD GO INTO POLITICS SO THAT HE CAN GO ON PROMISING FOR THE REST OF HIS LIFE."

~ ROBERT BYRNE ~
AMERICAN AUTHOR
B. 1930

The Bipartisan Campaign Reform Act of 2002

Demand for further campaign-finance reform had been growing for several years, and in 2002, Congress passed, and the president signed, the Bipartisan Campaign Reform Act. The measure is also known as the McCain-Feingold Act after its chief sponsors, senators John McCain (R., Ariz.) and Russell Feingold (D., Wisc.).

The new law banned soft money. It also regulated campaign ads paid for by interest groups and prohibited any such issue advocacy commercials within thirty days of a primary election or sixty days of a general election.

The 2002 act set the amount that an individual can contribute to a federal candidate at $2,000 and the amount that an individual can give to all federal candidates at $95,000 over a two-year election cycle. (Under the law, some individual contribution limits are indexed for inflation and thus may change slightly with every election cycle.) Individuals can still contribute to state and local parties, so long as the contributions do not exceed $10,000 per year per individual. The new law went into effect the day after the 2002 general elections.

CONSTITUTIONAL CHALLENGES TO THE 2002 LAW

Several groups immediately filed lawsuits challenging the constitutionality of the new law. Supporters of the restrictions on campaign ads by special interest groups argued that the large amounts of funds spent on these ads create an appearance of corruption in the political process. In contrast, an attorney for the National Rifle Association (NRA) argued that because the NRA represents "millions of Americans speaking in unison . . . [it] is not a *corruption* of the democratic political process; it *is* the democratic political process."[17] In December 2003, the Supreme Court upheld nearly

all of the clauses of the act in *McConnell v. Federal Election Commission*.[18]

In 2007, however, in *Federal Election Commission v. Wisconsin Right to Life, Inc.*, the Supreme Court invalidated a major part of the 2002 law and overruled a portion of its own 2003 decision upholding the act. In the four years since the earlier ruling, Chief Justice John Roberts, Jr., and Associate Justice Samuel Alito, Jr., had been appointed, and both were conservatives. In a five-to-four decision, the Court held that issue ads could not be prohibited in the time period preceding elections (thirty days before primary elections and sixty days before general elections) *unless* they were "susceptible of no reasonable interpretation other than as an appeal to vote for or against a specific candidate."[19] The Court concluded that restricting *all* television ads paid for by corporate or union treasuries in the weeks before an election amounted to censorship of political speech.

INDEPENDENT COMMITTEES AFTER 2002

As you read in Chapter 6, "issue advocacy" groups soon attempted to exploit loopholes in the 2002 act. A major technique was to establish independent 527 committees, named after the provision of the tax code that covers them. Spending by 527s rose rapidly after 2002, and in the 2004 election cycle, the committees spent about $612 million to "advocate positions."

By 2008, the relative importance of 527 committees began to decline. The reason was the creation of a new kind of body, the 501(c)4 organization. According to some lawyers, a 501(c)4 could make limited contributions directly to campaigns and—perhaps more importantly—could conceal the identity of its donors. So far, the Federal Election Commission (FEC) has refused to rule on the legality of this technique.

CITIZENS UNITED v. FEDERAL ELECTION COMMISSION

In January 2010, the Supreme Court took a major step toward freeing up corporate funding of political advertisements. In the *Wisconsin Right to Life* case described earlier, the Court ruled out bans on issue ads placed by corporations and other organizations in the run-up to an election. In the new case, *Citizens United v. FEC*,[20] the Court extended this protection to ads that attack or praise specific candidates, including ads that advise people for whom they should vote in an election. As long as corporations, labor unions, or nonprofit groups do not contribute directly to a candidate's campaign, there is now no limit on their ability to fund advertising. In issuing this decision, the Court not only invalidated key portions of the 2002 act, but also overturned laws dating back to Theodore Roosevelt's presidency (1901–1909).

Republican leaders applauded the ruling as a victory for free speech, but most Democratic leaders were appalled. Their fear was that the ruling would result in a tidal wave of new corporate spending on elections. Presumably, unions and nonprofits are already giving as much as they can, but the ability of corporations to provide new funds for political causes—should they so desire—is vast. Another problem: The Court ruled that it is acceptable to require organizations to disclose the sources of their political spending. Groups such as the 501(c)4 committees mentioned earlier, however, have the right, under current law, to hide the identity of their contributors. Major spenders, in other words, can fund independent ads and conceal such funding from the public.

Campaign Contributions and Policy Decisions

Considering the passion on both sides of the debate about campaign-finance reform, one might wonder how much campaign contributions actually influence policy decisions. Table 9–1 above lists leading industries and other groups contributing to either party in the 2010 midterm election cycle. These contributors must want something in return for their dollars, but what, exactly, do their contributions buy? Do these donations influence government policymaking?

Despite popular suspicions, we cannot assume that a member of Congress who received financial contributions from certain groups while campaigning for Congress will vote differently on policy issues than she or he would otherwise vote. After all, many groups make contributions not so much to influence a candidate's views as to ensure that a candidate whose views the group supports will win the elections.

Many groups routinely donate to candidates from both parties so that, regardless of who wins, the groups

Table 9–1

Top Industries and Other Groups Contributing Funds in the 2010 Midterm Election Cycle

Industry/Group	Total	To Democrats	To Republicans
1 Retired individuals	$108,971,141	43%	56%
2 Lawyers & law firms	102,839,147	76	22
3 Securities & investment firms	65,799,887	53	46
4 Candidate committees	57,393,283	66	33
5 Real estate	55,449,021	52	46
6 Health professionals	55,002,518	48	50
7 Leadership PACs	32,579,556	50	49
8 Insurance	31,278,892	48	52
9 Business services	24,895,601	61	38
10 Lobbyists	23,545,783	65	34
11 Democratic/liberal	22,670,421	100	0
12 TV, movies & music	21,735,793	72	27
13 Pharm. & health products	19,643,925	54	46
14 Oil & gas	19,588,091	25	73
15 Misc. manufacturing & distrib.	17,757,910	43	57
16 Computers & the Internet	17,219,782	64	36
17 Electric utilities	16,230,025	56	42
18 General contractors	15,601,092	36	62
19 Education	15,431,168	75	23
20 Commercial banks	15,413,738	41	59

The numbers are based on contributions from PACs and individuals giving $200 or more.
Source: Center for Responsive Politics, OpenSecrets.org.

will have access to the officeholder. Note that many of the groups listed in Table 9–1 contributed to both parties. Not surprisingly, campaign contributors find it much easier than other constituents to get in to see politicians or to get them to return phone calls. Because politicians are more likely to be influenced by those with whom they have personal contacts, access is important for those who want to influence policymaking.

LO6 The Closeness of Recent Presidential Elections

The 2000 presidential elections were the first since 1888 in which the electoral college system gave Americans a president who had not won the popular vote. Was the outcome an anomaly? The 2004 elections again were close, but in 2008, the pattern changed.

The Campaigns

Two records were broken during the latest election cycle. The first was the amount of spending in a mid-term election. Estimates are not final, but it appears that campaign and independent committees together will have spent almost $4 billion by the time the last dollar is counted. The other record was the share of television campaign ads that were negative.

Some candidates personally spent unprecedented sums in their search for election. As mentioned earlier, Meg Whitman, the former CEO of eBay, spent $140 million of her own funds to become governor of California—an all-time record. Note, though, that none of the five candidates who spent $6 million or more of their own funds, including Whitman, won.

Researchers estimated that about two-thirds of all campaign ads were negative. Back in 2008, Republicans used more ads personally attacking their opponents than the Democrats did. In 2010, the tables were turned, with the Democrats making the larger number of personal attacks. Finally, ads by independent campaign groups set an all-time record. Because they were not, in principle, linked to a particular candidate, they could publicize as much "dirt" as they wanted to—and they did.

The 2000 Presidential Elections

In 2000, then vice president Al Gore won the popular vote by 540,000 votes. Nonetheless, on election night, the outcome in Florida, which would have given Gore the winning votes in the electoral college, was deemed "too close to call." Controversy erupted over the types of ballots used, and some counties in Florida began recounting ballots by hand. This issue ultimately came before the United States Supreme Court: Did manual recounts of some ballots but not others violate the Constitution's equal protection clause? On December 12, five weeks after the election, the Supreme Court ruled against the manual recounts.[21] The final vote tally in Florida gave Bush a 537-vote lead, all of Florida's twenty-five electoral votes, and the presidency.

The 2004 Presidential Elections

The 2004 presidential elections produced another close race, with President Bush edging out Democratic challenger John Kerry by a mere thirty-five electors. In contrast to the situation in 2000, Bush won the popular vote in 2004, defeating Kerry by a 2.5 percentage point margin. Many commentators argued that the elections were decided by the closely contested vote in Ohio.

From early in the 2004 election cycle, Ohio had been viewed as a *battleground state*—a state where voters were not clearly leaning toward either major candidate leading up to the elections. Political analysts and news media outlets placed a great deal of emphasis on the battleground states, arguing that these states could potentially decide the outcome.

At the end of each election, the winning presidential candidate appears with his family for a victory celebration. Here Barack Obama continued the tradition at Grant Park in Chicago on November 4, 2008.

AP PHOTO/PABLO MARTINEZ MONSIVAIS

The 2008 Presidential Elections

At times during the campaign, the 2008 presidential contest appeared to be close. The financial panic that struck on September 15, however, tipped the elections decisively. Barack Obama's victory in 2008 reversed the trend of extremely close elections established in 2000 and 2004. Obama won 365 electoral votes, and his popular-vote margin over John McCain was about 7.2 percentage points, nearly a 10-point swing to the Democrats from the elections of 2004. With approximately 52.9 percent of the total popular vote, Obama was the first Democrat to win an absolute majority (more than 50 percent) of the popular vote since Jimmy Carter did so in 1976. Indeed, Obama won a larger share of the popular vote than any Democrat since Lyndon Johnson's 61 percent victory in 1964.

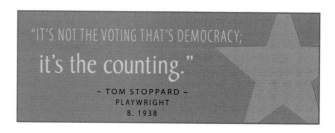

"IT'S NOT THE VOTING THAT'S DEMOCRACY;

it's the counting."

~ TOM STOPPARD ~
PLAYWRIGHT
B. 1938

AMERICA AT ODDS   *Campaigns and Elections*

Some observers believe that if the founders could see how presidential campaigns are conducted today, they would be shocked at how candidates "pander to the masses." Whether they would be shocked at the costliness of modern campaigns is not as clear. After all, the founders themselves were an elitist, wealthy group, as are many of today's successful candidates for high political office. In any event, Americans today are certainly stunned by how much it takes to win an election. Some of the specific controversies concerning campaigns that divide Americans are the following:

- Is the Electoral College a dangerous anachronism—or a force for stability within our political system?

- Should all voters be free to participate in any party primary—or does such a step make it too difficult for the parties to present a coherent group of candidates and policies?

- Should states retain their treasured right to set the dates of their presidential primaries—or should the national parties assume responsibility for establishing a rational primary schedule?

- Are campaign contributions a constitutionally protected form of free speech—or are they too often a thinly veiled method of bribing public officials?

- Should all politically active groups be required to furnish the identities of their major contributors—or should we allow contributors to remain anonymous because they might suffer reprisals due to their contributions?

Take Action

The most obvious way you can take action in political campaigns or elections is to join the campaign of a candidate you support. Any campaign has an insatiable desire for volunteers. Consider that by volunteering, you are in effect making a substantial political contribution that does not have to be reported to anyone. Volunteers can assemble mailings, answer the telephone, or make calls to encourage voters to support their candidate. Even if you have little free time or are not comfortable talking to strangers, most campaigns will be able to find a way in which you can participate.

An alternative is to work for a public-interest group. Many groups

AP PHOTO/ED ANDRIESKI

have worked toward reforming the way campaign funds are raised and spent in politics today. One nonprofit, nonpartisan, grassroots organization that lobbies for campaign-finance reform is Common Cause. In the photo to the left, a participant in Colorado Common Cause's effort to reform campaign financing displays a mock-up of a TV remote control with a large mute button at a news conference. The group was asking voters to "mute" attack ads directed against a Colorado initiative to amend the state constitution to limit campaign financing and set contribution limits.

POLITICS ON THE
WEB

- Dave Leip's Atlas of U.S. Presidential Elections hosts a major discussion site where hundreds of guests discuss election results. You can find detailed figures to back up your arguments elsewhere on Leip's site, along with an electoral college calculator that lets you figure out how many electoral votes a candidate will receive if he or she carries a particular share of the states. Find the Atlas at **www.uselectionatlas.org**

- You can find out exactly what the laws are that govern campaign financing by accessing the Federal Election Commission's Web site. The commission has provided an online "Citizens' Guide" that spells out what is and is not legal. You can also download actual data on campaign donations from the site. Go to **www.fec.gov**

- To look at data from the Federal Election Commission presented in a more user-friendly way, you can access the following nonpartisan, independent site that allows you to type in an elected official's name and receive large amounts of information on contributions to that official. Go to **moneyline.cq.com/pml/home.do**

- Another excellent source for information on campaign financing, including who's contributing what amounts to which candidates, is the Center for Responsive Politics. You can access its Web site at **www.opensecrets.org**

- Common Cause offers additional information about campaign financing on its Web site at **www.commoncause.org**

- Project Vote Smart offers information on campaign financing, as well as voting, on its Web site at **www.votesmart.org**

 CourseMate Access CourseMate to review and expand on this chapter through quizzes, flashcards, learning objectives, interactive timelines, a crossword puzzle, audio summaries, video, critical-thinking activities, simulations, and more.

Politics and the Media

LEARNING OBJECTIVES

LO1 Explain the role of the media in a democracy.

LO2 Summarize how television influences the conduct of political campaigns.

LO3 Explain why talk radio has been described as the Wild West of the media.

LO4 Describe types of media bias and explain how such bias affects the political process.

LO5 Indicate the extent to which the Internet is reshaping news and political campaigns.

AMERICA AT ODDS
Can We Do without Newspapers?

The *New York Times*. The *Washington Post*. The *Wall Street Journal*. The *Christian Science Monitor*. These and hundreds of other major and minor newspapers have generated and disseminated the nation's news for more than one hundred years. Already in 1783, at the end of the Revolutionary War, America had forty-three newspapers. Not until 1910, though, did all of the essential features that we recognize in today's newspapers become commonplace.

Gradually, radio and television supplanted newspapers as this country's primary information source. Relatively recently, some great newspapers have filed for bankruptcy protection. The following newspapers no longer exist: the *Tucson Citizen*, the *Rocky Mountain News,* the *Baltimore Examiner,* the *Cincinnati Post,* and the *Albuquerque Tribune*. Additional newspapers have reduced their printing schedules or have gone completely online.

The online revolution has certainly changed the newspaper business—and perhaps will eventually eliminate it. The godfather of the U.S. investing community, Warren Buffett, has said that the newspaper business faces "just unending losses." His recommendation to investors—stay away. With newspapers in so much trouble, the question arises: Does it matter if newspapers disappear?

Who Cares about Newspapers When Free Content Is Everywhere?

Those who do not mourn the loss of newspapers—particularly the younger generation—point out the obvious. Americans have more access to more news than ever before. Online news is available and updated day and night. An enormous number of citizen bloggers will help you find out what is happening anywhere in the world anytime you want. So who needs newspapers?

Even if your hometown newspaper shuts down, "hyperlocal" Web sites are increasingly available to deliver local news. Many of these sites are organized by companies such as EveryBlock, Outside.In, Placeblogger, and Patch.

Newspapers have always had a "slant," anyway, and in the past most Americans had to put up with whatever point of view their local newspaper provided. That is no longer the case. You can find the news—presented in whatever way you like—on thousands of Internet news sites and millions of blogs (short for "Web logs"). Variety is the spice of life, and we certainly have more variety in news gathering and presentation than ever before.

Newspapers are dead. Long live the news.

Without Newspapers, the News Is Just Background Noise

The reality of this world is that people have to be paid to do a good job no matter what that job is. Journalists have families to feed. Rarely are they independently wealthy amateurs. Where does all that free content on the Web come from? Most of it can ultimately be traced back to journalists working for the print media. This is true of hyperlocal sites as well. Even today, newspapers employ the overwhelming majority of all journalists. How many bloggers bother to attend city council meetings and report what happens? Precious few do.

A British reporter sums up the entire argument: "The real value that newspapers provide, whether in print or online, is organization, editing, and reputation." The issue is not the survival of the newspaper industry, but the survival of an informed citizenry. If citizens believe that all information, no matter where it comes from—blogs, tweets, Web sites that promote conspiracy theories—is of the same value, then these citizens are in trouble.

We need to change the way newspapers work. We need to figure out ways in which online versions of publications can earn enough revenue to be self-supporting. If we do this, we can ensure that newspapers remain the mainstay of American news gathering and distribution.

WHERE DO YOU STAND?

1. Most young people rarely, if ever, read a newspaper. Does that mean they are not getting any news? Why or why not?
2. How much do you think the reputation of a news source really matters?

EXPLORE THIS ISSUE ONLINE

- Newspapers have been harder hit in Michigan than in any other state. Ann Arbor, home of the University of Michigan, with a metro population of almost 350,000, may be the largest urban area in the country to lose its only daily newspaper. Papers in Flint, Saginaw, and Bay City, Michigan, now publish only three times a week. The Detroit papers have drastically cut back their distribution as well. Statewide coverage is now provided by the online service www.mlive.com. For details of how the *Ann Arbor News* came to close its doors, see www.mlive.com/annarbornews.

Introduction

The debate over the survival of newspapers, described in the chapter-opening *America at Odds* feature, is just one aspect of an important topic: the role of the media in American politics. Strictly defined, the term *media* means communication channels. It is the plural form of *medium*, as in medium of communication. In this strict sense, any method used by people to communicate—including the telephone—is a communication medium. In this chapter, though, we look at the **mass media**—channels through which people can communicate to large audiences. These channels include the **print media** (newspapers and magazines) and the **electronic media** (radio, television, and the Internet).

The media are a dominant presence in our lives largely because they provide entertainment. Americans today enjoy more leisure than at any time in history, and we fill it up with books, movies, Web surfing, and television—a huge amount of television. But the

> "The press may not be successful much of the time in telling people what to think, but it is stunningly successful in telling its readers
>
> **WHAT TO THINK ABOUT."**
>
> ~ BERNARD C. COHEN ~
> AMERICAN POLITICAL SCIENTIST
> B. 1926

mass media Communication channels, such as newspapers and radio and television broadcasts, through which people can communicate to large audiences.

print media Communication channels that consist of printed materials, such as newspapers and magazines.

electronic media Communication channels that involve electronic transmissions, such as radio, television, and the Internet.

media play a vital role in our political lives as well, particularly during campaigns and elections. Politicians and political candidates have learned—often the hard way—that positive media exposure and news coverage are essential to winning votes.

As you read in Chapter 4, one of the most important civil liberties protected in the Bill of Rights is freedom of the press. Like free speech, a free press is considered a vital tool of the democratic process. If people are to cast informed votes, they must have access to a forum in which they can discuss public affairs fully and assess the conduct and competency of their officials. The

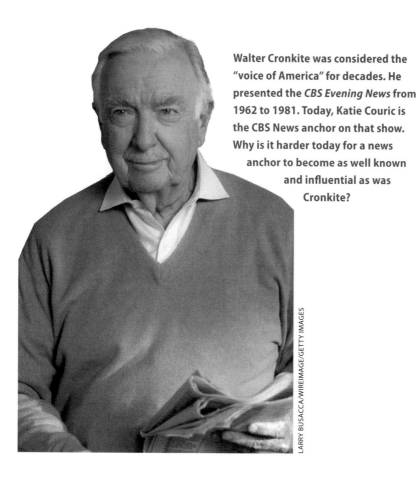

Walter Cronkite was considered the "voice of America" for decades. He presented the *CBS Evening News* from 1962 to 1981. Today, Katie Couric is the CBS News anchor on that show. Why is it harder today for a news anchor to become as well known and influential as was Cronkite?

LARRY BUSACCA/WIREIMAGE/GETTY IMAGES

JIM WATSON/AFP/GETTY IMAGES

Social Networking Becomes a Political Force in Indonesia

You might be surprised to learn that the Southeast Asian nation of Indonesia has the world's third-largest number of Facebook users. (The United States is first and Britain is second). There are now more than 21 million Facebook users in that country—close to 10 percent of the population. Most Indonesians are too poor to own computers and instead rely on inexpensive cell phones or Internet cafés for online access.

Indonesians are not just using social networking to interact with their friends. Facebook, Twitter, and local social networking systems have become a political power in Indonesia. For example, the government recently erected a statue of Barack Obama as a ten-year-old in a local park in the capital, Jakarta. (Obama lived in that city from the time he was six until he was ten.) Almost sixty thousand online protestors demanded that the statue be taken down, arguing that the park should be limited to honoring Indonesians. City officials soon took down the statue. Protests on Facebook also helped stop an attempt to cripple Indonesia's main anti-corruption agency.

Of course, social networking systems such as Facebook are a political force in

the United States as well. When Obama sought to build support for his presidential campaign, he got a considerable boost when he began using Facebook. So too did recently elected Senator Scott Brown (R., Mass.) during his campaign.

The Government Is Afraid

Many Indonesians welcome Facebook and Twitter as ways of democratizing the country's often corrupt political system. In contrast, Indonesian politicians worry that social networking will become an unpredictable and perhaps undesirable political force. Indonesia's minister of communication and information technology, Tifatul Sembiring, states that online content should be regulated to preserve "our values, also our culture and also our norms." Online movements have proved unsettling to bureaucrats and politicians because they are an effective way to challenge governmental authority.

The Indonesian government has recently passed laws that can be used against participants in social networking protest movements. More such laws are possible in the future. Under one new law, a person convicted of online defamation

can receive a maximum sentence of six years in prison.

China as an Example to Avoid

Internet use is subject to strict control in many countries. For example, Chinese users must contend with what has been called the "Great Firewall of China," which severely limits access to foreign Web sites. Some Indonesians fear that the authorities in their country might emulate China. "I think we are between China and the United States," says Sembiring. "Yes, we are free. But with freedom comes responsibility."

For Critical Analysis *Why might online protests against government corruption be more effective than traditional methods of protest?*

media provide this forum. In contrast, government censorship of the press is common in many nations around the globe. One example is China, where the Web is heavily censored even though China now has more Internet users than any other country on earth. One reason dictatorships fear a free press is that people can use it to organize against the authorities. For an example of how citizens in Indonesia have used new forms of media for such purposes, see this chapter's *The Rest of the World* feature above.

LO1 *The Role of the Media in a Democracy*

What the media say and do has an impact on what Americans think about political issues. But just as clearly, the media also *reflect* what Americans think about politics. Some scholars argue that the media is the fourth "check" in our political system—checking and balancing the power of the president, the Congress, and the courts. The power of the media today is enormous, but how the media use their power is an issue about which Americans are often at odds.

The Media and the First Amendment

As just noted, freedom of the press is essential if the media are to play their role in supporting the democratic process. The concept of freedom of the press has been applied to print media since the adoption of the Bill of Rights. Such freedoms were not, however, immediately extended to other types of media as they came into existence. Film was one of the first types of new media to be considered under the First Amendment, and in 1915 the United States Supreme Court ruled that "as a matter of common sense," freedom of the press did not apply to the movies.[1] Radio received no protection upon its development, and neither did television.

The Court did not extend First Amendment protections to the cinema until 1952.[2] Although the Court has stated that the First Amendment is relevant to broadcast media such as radio and television, to this day it has not granted these media complete protection. For example, the Court has never ruled that the *fairness doctrine,* enforced by the Federal Communications Commission (FCC) from 1949 to 1987, is unconstitutional. Talk radio was essentially impossible until the doctrine was repealed. (You will learn more about the fairness doctrine and talk radio later in this chapter.)

In contrast, the Court extended First Amendment protections to the Internet in 1997, in its first opportunity to rule on the issue.[3] Cable TV received substantial protections in 2000.[4] In recent years, the courts have also shown some willingness to expand the freedoms of broadcast media.

The Agenda-Setting Function of the Media

One of the criticisms often levied against the media is that they play too large a role in determining the issues, events, and personalities that are in the public eye. When people take in the day's top news stories, they usually assume automatically that these stories concern the most important issues facing the nation. In actuality, the media decide the relative importance of issues by publicizing some issues and ignoring others, and by giving some stories high priority and others low priority. By helping to determine what people will talk and think about, the media set the *political agenda*—the issues that politicians will address. In other words, to borrow from Bernard Cohen's classic statement on the media and public opinion, the press (media) may *not* be successful in telling people what to think, but it is "stunningly successful in telling its readers what to think about."[5]

For example, television played a significant role in shaping public opinion about the Vietnam War (1964–1975), which has been called the first "television war." Part of the public opposition to the war in the late 1960s came about as a result of the daily portrayal of the war's horrors on TV news programs. Film footage and narrative accounts of the destruction, death, and suffering in Vietnam brought the war into living rooms across the United States. (To examine whether the press is doing its job, see the *Join the Debate* feature on the following page.)

Events in Iraq were also the subject of constant news coverage. Some believe that the media played a crucial role in influencing public opinion at the outset of the war. Indeed, the media have been sharply criticized by media watchdog groups for failing to do more fact checking prior to the invasion of Iraq. Instead of investigating the Bush administration's assertions that Iraq had weapons of mass destruction and links to al Qaeda, the media just passed this information on to the public. If the media had done their job, claim these critics, there would have been much less public support for going to war with Iraq.

The degree to which the media influence public opinion is not always all that clear, however. As you read in Chapter 8, some studies show that people filter the information they receive from the media through their own preconceived ideas

CNN news anchor Anderson Cooper.

BRYAN BEDDER/GETTY IMAGES FOR IMG

Is the Press Living Up to Its Role as a "Watchdog"?

Thomas Jefferson said in 1787 that he'd rather have newspapers without a government than a government without newspapers. Not surprisingly, the First Amendment to the Constitution upholds the important role of a free press. The news media have been placed in a specially protected position in our complicated country to serve as a watchdog against abuses of government. Some Americans believe that the press has lost its ability to act in this way. Others, however, believe that the government scandals unearthed by the media in years past show that the media are doing their job.

The Press Is Not Doing Its Job

Americans who believe that the media are not acting as proper watchdogs contend that journalists are frequently intimidated by the politicians and public officials that they cover. To write stories that catch the reader's eye, journalists must have access to government officials and political candidates. If the journalists are excessively critical, they may lose this access. Journalists are also addicted to "balanced" coverage that "gives both sides" of an issue. The problem is, sometimes there aren't two sides to a story. If a politician makes a statement that is obviously untrue, reporters do the public no favors by neglecting to point that out. Yet it is very rare for the media to challenge a politician on even the most preposterous falsehoods.

During the run-up to the Iraq War, most journalists were reluctant to dispute the Bush administration's arguments in favor of military action. A number of reporters afterwards admitted that they were afraid of being characterized as "unpatriotic" if they questioned the administration's actions. Later, both before the 2008 elections and after President Barack Obama took office, conservatives argued that mainstream journalists were so personally enamored of Obama that they were giving him a "free ride." For their part, liberals complained that the press had largely failed to challenge a series of obviously false statements that Republican leaders made about Democratic health-care proposals.

The Truth Will Come Out Eventually

Those who take the other side of this debate believe that we still have the freest press in the world. Currently, few regulations control what members of the media can say, report, or film. Even if the traditional media do not do a good job, the truth will come out in the blogosphere. Indeed, bloggers have done a better job of investigating some news stories than have the mainstream media. In some instances, the mainstream press has been forced to publish information on stories that first became big in the blogosphere.

When reporting is erroneous, it is quickly exposed—first by bloggers and then by the established media—and the perpetrators are often punished. Some former media superstars, such as Dan Rather, have been relieved of their duties when critics determined that their news reports were unfounded. Also, let's not forget the role of media watchdog groups. They are numerous and represent both conservative and liberal viewpoints. All in all, it's hard to imagine that with current communications possibilities, our government is not being watched enough.

For Critical Analysis *We discussed the crisis of the newspaper business in the chapter-opening* America at Odds *feature. What impact might these problems have on the ability of the press to serve as a watchdog?*

about issues. Scholars who try to analyze the relationship between American politics and the media inevitably confront the chicken-and-egg conundrum: Do the media cause the public to hold certain views, or do the media merely reflect views that are formed independently of the media's influence?

The Medium Does Affect the Message

Of all the media, television has the greatest impact. Television reaches into almost every home in the United States. Virtually all homes have televisions. Even outside their homes, Americans can watch television—in airports, shopping malls, golf clubhouses, and medical offices. People can view television shows on their computers, and they can download TV programs to their iPods, iPhones, or Windows Phone 7 and view the programs whenever and wherever they want.

For some time, it was predicted that as more people used the Internet, fewer people would turn to television for news or entertainment. This prediction turned out to be off the mark. Today, Americans watch more television than ever, and it is the primary news source

Figure 10–1

Media Usage by Consumers, 1988 to Present

Hours shown for Internet usage include only those for "pure-play Internet services"—that is, they do not include time spent at the Web sites of TV networks or print media, including e-books. They also do not include hours for Internet services provided by cable TV companies. All of these hours are included in the totals for the traditional media. If they were included with Internet services, the number of Internet hours in 2010 would approximately double. Internet services would then be in the same range as broadcast TV.

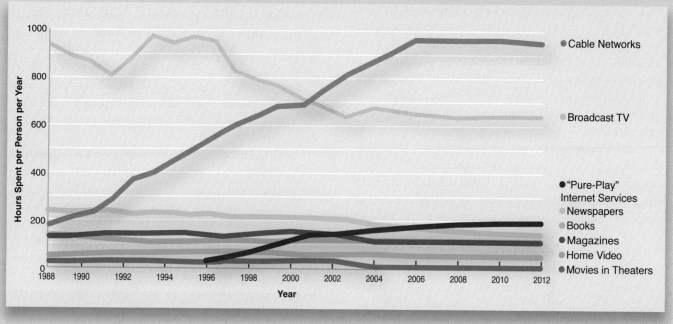

Sources: U.S. Census Bureau, *Statistical Abstract of the United States, 2008* (Washington, D.C.: U.S. Government Printing Office, 2010), and authors' updates.

for more than 65 percent of the citizenry. Figure 10–1 above shows the prominence of television when compared with other media.

As you will read shortly, politicians take maximum advantage of the power and influence of television. But does the television medium alter the presentation of political information in any way? Compare the coverage given to an important political issue by the print media—including the online sites of major newspapers and magazines—with the coverage provided by broadcast and cable TV networks. You will note some striking differences. For one thing, the print media (particularly leading newspapers such as the *Washington Post,* the *New York Times,* and the *Wall Street Journal*) treat an important issue in much more detail. In addition to news stories based on reporters' research, you will find editorials taking positions on the issue and arguments supporting those positions. Television news, in contrast, is often criticized as being too brief and too superficial.

TIME CONSTRAINTS The medium of television necessarily imposes constraints on how political issues are presented. Time is limited. News stories must be reported quickly, in only a few minutes or occasionally in only a **sound bite,** a televised comment lasting for just a few seconds that captures a thought or a perspective and has an immediate impact on the viewers.

A VISUAL MEDIUM Television reporting also relies extensively on visual elements, rather than words, to capture the viewers' attention. Inevitably, the photos or videos selected to depict a particular political event have exaggerated importance. The visual aspect of television contributes to its power, but it also creates a potential bias. Those watching the news presentation do not know what portions of a video being shown have been deleted, what other photos may have been taken, or whether other records of the event exist. This kind of "selection bias" will be discussed in more detail later in this chapter.

TELEVISION IS BIG BUSINESS Today's TV networks compete aggressively with one another to air "breaking news" and to produce interesting news

sound bite A televised comment, lasting for only a few seconds, that captures a thought or a perspective and has an immediate impact on the viewers.

political advertising

Advertising undertaken by or on behalf of a political candidate to familiarize voters with the candidate and his or her views on campaign issues; also advertising for or against policy issues.

programs. Competition in the television industry understandably has had an effect on how the news is presented. To make profits, or even stay in business, TV stations need viewers. And to attract viewers, the news industry has turned to "infotainment"—programs that inform and entertain at the same time. Slick sets, attractive reporters, and animated graphics that dance across the television screen are now commonplace on most news programs, particularly on the cable news channels.

TV networks also compete with one another for advertising income. Although the media in the United States are among the freest in the world, their programming nonetheless remains vulnerable to the influence of their advertising sponsors.

Concentrated ownership of media is another concern. Many mainstream media outlets are owned by giant corporations, such as Time Warner, Rupert Murdoch's News Corporation, and even General Electric. Concentrated ownership may be a more serious problem at the local level than at the national level. If only one or two companies own a city's newspaper and its TV stations, these outlets may not present a diversity of opinion. Further, the owners are unlikely to air information that could be damaging either to their advertisers or to themselves, or even to publicize views that they disagree with politically. For example, TV networks have refused to run antiwar commercials created by religious groups. Still, some media observers are not particularly concerned about concentrated ownership of traditional outlets, because the Internet has generated a massive diversification of media.

LO2 *The Candidates and Television*

Given the TV-saturated environment in which we live, it should come as no surprise that candidates spend a great deal of time—and money—obtaining a TV presence through political ads, debates, and general news coverage. Candidates and their campaign managers realize that the time and money are well spent because television has an important impact on the way people see the candidates, understand the issues, and cast their votes.

Political Advertising

Today, televised **political advertising** consumes at least half of the total budget for a major political campaign. In the 2004 election cycle, $1.4 billion was spent for political advertising on broadcast TV. As you can see in Figure 10–2 below, this was almost five times the amount spent in the 1992 election cycle. For the 2006 elections, the figure climbed to $1.7 billion. According to the research firm PQ Media, spending on all forms of political advertising reached $4.5 billion in the 2007–2008 election cycle, including $2.3 billion for broadcast TV in 2008 alone. Even without an expensive presidential race, spending in 2010 substantially surpassed the 2008 figure.

Political advertising first appeared on television during the 1952 presidential campaign. At that time, there were only about 15 million television sets. Today, there are almost as many TV sets as people. Initially, political TV commercials were more or less like any other type of advertising. Instead of focusing on the positive qualities of a product, thirty-second or sixty-second ads focused

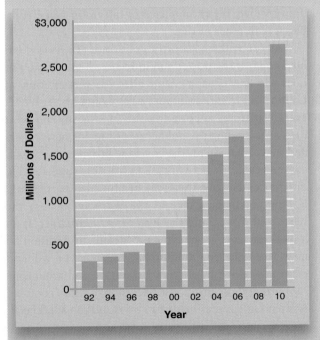

Figure 10–2

Political Ad Spending on Broadcast Television, 1992–2010

As you can see in this figure, spending for political advertising has increased steadily during recent elections.

Sources: Television Bureau of Advertising, as presented in Lorraine Woellert and Tom Lowry, "A Political Nightmare: Not Enough Airtime," *Business Week*, November 23, 2000, p. 111; and authors' updates.

on the positive qualities of a political candidate. Within the decade, however, **negative political advertising** began to appear on TV.

ATTACK ADS Despite the barrage of criticism levied against the candidates' use of negative political ads during recent election cycles, such ads are not new. Indeed, **personal attack ads**—advertising that attacks the character of an opposing candidate—have a long tradition. In 1800, an article in the *Federalist Gazette of the United States* described Thomas Jefferson as having a "weakness of nerves, want of fortitude, and total imbecility of character." After the terrorist attacks of September 11, 2001, candidates found that ads involving fear of terrorism resonated with voters. As a result, candidates routinely accused their opponents of lacking the fortitude to wage war on terrorism.

In 2008, the Republicans understood that after eight years of President Bush, voters wanted something new. For John McCain to win, voters had to see Democrat Barack Obama as an unacceptable alternative. The McCain campaign therefore aired a series of personal attack ads that portrayed Obama as a dangerous radical with unsavory associates. The ads may have enhanced voter turnout among Republicans at the cost of alienating some independent voters. On the Democratic side, the Obama campaign generally employed issue ads, which were also largely negative.

ISSUE ADS Candidates use negative **issue ads** to focus on flaws in the opponents' positions on issues. Candidates level criticisms at each other's stated positions on various issues, such as health care and the bank-bailout legislation. Candidates also try to undermine their opponents' credibility by pointing to discrepancies

Our Country Deserves Better PAC

OPPOSE ObamaCare

www.OurCountryPAC.org

Paid for and authorized by Our Country Deserves Better PAC, which is responsible for the content of this ad. Not authorized by any candidate or candidate's committee.

Negative advertising has become a staple in American political campaigns, whether for political races or for issues to be decided by Congress and the president. As much as voters claim that negative ads are offensive, these ads are effective. Why?

between what the opponents say in their campaign speeches and their political records, such as voting records, which are available to the public and thus can easily be verified. As noted in Chapters 6 and 9, issue ads are also used by interest groups to gather support for candidates who endorse the groups' causes.

Issue ads can be even more devastating than personal attacks—as Barry Goldwater learned in 1964 when his opponent in the presidential race, President Lyndon Johnson, aired the "daisy girl" ad. This ad, a new departure in negative advertising, showed a little girl standing quietly in a field of daisies. She held a daisy and pulled off the petals, counting to herself. Suddenly, a deep voice was heard counting: "10, 9, 8, 7, 6, . . ." When the countdown hit zero, the unmistakable mushroom cloud of an atomic explosion filled the screen. Then President Johnson's voice was heard saying, "These are the stakes: to make a world in which all of God's children can live, or to go into the dark. We must either

negative political advertising Political advertising undertaken for the purpose of discrediting an opposing candidate in the eyes of the voters. Attack ads are one form of negative political advertising.

personal attack ad A negative political advertisement that attacks the character of an opposing candidate.

issue ad A political advertisement that focuses on a particular issue. Issue ads can be used to support or attack a candidate.

"The thing to do now, Senator, is to hit back with some negative advertising of our own."

love each other or we must die." A message on the screen then read: "Vote for President Johnson on November 3." The implication, of course, was that Goldwater would lead the country into a nuclear war.[6]

NEGATIVE ADVERTISING—IS IT GOOD OR BAD FOR OUR DEMOCRACY? The debate over the effect of negative advertising on our political system is ongoing. Some observers argue that negative ads can backfire. Extreme ads may create sympathy for the candidate being attacked rather than support for the attacker, particularly when the charges against the candidate being attacked are not credible. Many people fear that attack ads and "dirty tricks" used by both parties during a campaign may alienate citizens from the political process itself and thus lower voter turnout in elections.

Yet candidates and their campaign managers typically assert that they use negative advertising simply because it works. Negative TV ads are more likely than positive ads to grab the viewers' attention and make an impression. Also, according to media expert Shanto Iyengar, "the more negative the ad, the more likely it is to get free media coverage. So there's a big incentive to go to extremes."[7] Others believe that negative advertising is a force for the good because it sharpens public debate, thereby enriching the democratic process. This is the position taken by Vanderbilt University political science professor John Geer. He contends that negative ads are likely to focus on substantive political issues instead of candidates' personal characteristics. Thus, negative ads do a better job of informing the voters about important campaign issues than positive ads do.[8]

Television Debates

Televised debates have been a feature of presidential campaigns since 1960, when presidential candidates Republican Richard M. Nixon and Democrat John F. Kennedy squared off in four great TV debates. Television debates provide an opportunity for voters to find out how candidates differ on issues. They also allow candidates to capitalize on the power of television to improve their images or point out the failings of their opponents.

It is widely believed that Kennedy won the first of the 1960 debates in large part because of Nixon's haggard appearance and poor makeup—many people who heard the debate on the radio thought that Nixon had done well. No presidential debates were held during the general election campaigns of 1964, 1968, or 1972, but the debates have been a part of every election since 1976. The 1992 debates, which starred Republican George H. W. Bush and Democrat Bill Clinton, also included a third-party candidate, H. Ross Perot. Since 1996, however, the Commission on Presidential Debates, which now organizes the events, has limited the participants to candidates of the two major parties.[9] The commission also organizes debates between the vice-presidential candidates.

Many contend that the presidential debates help shape the outcome of the elections. Others doubt that the debates—or the postdebate "spin" applied by campaign operatives and political commentators—have changed many votes. Evidence on this question is mixed.

Gallup polling figures suggest that in 1960 the debates helped Kennedy to victory. In 1980, Republican Ronald Reagan did well in a final debate with Democratic incumbent Jimmy Carter. Reagan impressed many voters with his sunny temperament, which helped dispel fears that he was a right-wing radical. In Gallup's

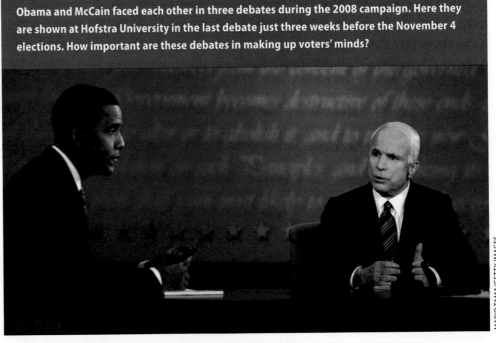

Obama and McCain faced each other in three debates during the 2008 campaign. Here they are shown at Hofstra University in the last debate just three weeks before the November 4 elections. How important are these debates in making up voters' minds?

MARIO TAMA/GETTY IMAGES

PETER KRAMER/GETTY IMAGES

Jon Stewart hosts *The Daily Show* on the Comedy Central channel. A significant number of young people obtain their political ideas from this show.

opinion, however, Reagan would have won the election even without the debate.

The 2008 Presidential Debates

The first debate between Republican John McCain and Democrat Barack Obama was supposed to focus on foreign policy. It took place, however, in one of the worst weeks of the 2008 financial crisis. Inevitably, much time was spent on economics.

The second debate was steered by questions from undecided voters in a town hall format, which was usually McCain's strong suit. Because the financial meltdown in the economy had gotten worse, many questions related to economics. The debate had a tougher tone than the first one.

In the third and final debate, Obama appeared to be "playing it safe," given that he was so far ahead in the polls. McCain accused Obama of advocating too much redistribution of wealth—in his opinion, a socialist idea. In the end, surveys showed that Obama's performance in all three debates was better received than McCain's.

News Coverage

Whereas political ads are expensive, coverage by the news media is free. Accordingly, the candidates try to take advantage of the media's interest in campaigns to increase the quantity and quality of news coverage. This is not always easy. Often, the media devote the lion's share of their coverage to polls and other indicators of which candidate is ahead in the race.

In recent years, candidates' campaign managers and political consultants have shown increasing sophistication in creating newsworthy events for journalists and TV camera crews to cover. This effort is commonly referred to as **managed news coverage.** For example, typically one of the jobs of the campaign manager is to create newsworthy events that demonstrate the candidate's strong points so that the media can capture this image of the candidate.[10]

Besides considering how camera angles and lighting affect a candidate's appearance, the political consultant plans political events to accommodate the press. The campaign staff attempts to make what the candidate is doing appear interesting. The staff also knows that journalists and political reporters compete for stories and that these individuals can be manipulated. Hence, they often are granted favors, such as exclusive personal interviews with the candidate. Each candidate's press advisers, often called **spin doctors,** also try to convince reporters to give the story or event a **spin,** or interpretation, that is favorable to the candidate.[11]

"Popular" Television

Although not normally regarded as a forum for political debate, television programs such as dramas, sitcoms, and late-night comedy shows often use political themes. For example, the popular courtroom drama *Law & Order* regularly broaches controversial topics such as the death penalty, the USA Patriot Act, and the rights of the accused. For years, the sitcom *Will and Grace* consistently brought to light issues regarding gay and lesbian rights. The dramatic *West Wing* series gave viewers a glimpse into national politics as it told the story of a fictional presidential administration. Late-night shows and programs such as *The Daily Show with Jon Stewart* provide a forum for politicians to demonstrate their lighter sides.

managed news coverage News coverage that is manipulated (managed) by a campaign manager or political consultant to gain media exposure for a political candidate.

spin doctor A political candidate's press adviser, who tries to convince reporters to give a story or event concerning the candidate a particular "spin" (interpretation, or slant).

spin A reporter's slant on, or interpretation of, a particular event or action.

Rush Limbaugh is considered the dean of conservative talk-show hosts. Limbaugh's ratings are consistently the highest in the business.

TV host Glenn Beck addresses the Conservative Political Action Conference (CPAC) in Washington D.C.

LO3 *Talk Radio—The Wild West of the Media*

Ever since Franklin D. Roosevelt held his first "fireside chats" on radio, politicians have realized the power of that medium. From the beginning, radio has been a favorite outlet for the political right. During the 1930s, for example, the nation's most successful radio commentator was Father Charles Edward Coughlin, a Roman Catholic priest based at the National Shrine of the Little Flower church in Royal Oak, Michigan. Coughlin's audience numbered more than 40 million listeners—this in a nation that had only 123 million inhabitants in 1930. Coughlin started out as a Roosevelt supporter, but he soon moved to the far right, advocating anti-Semitism and expressing sympathy for Adolf Hitler. Coughlin's fascist connections eventually destroyed his popularity.

Modern talk radio took off in the United States during the 1990s. In 1988, there were 200 talk-show radio stations. Today, there are more than 1,200. The growth of talk radio was made possible by the Federal Communications Commission's repeal of the fairness doctrine in 1987. Introduced in 1949, the fairness doctrine required the holders of broadcast licenses to present controversial issues of public importance in a manner that was (in the commission's view) honest, equitable, and balanced. That doctrine would have made it difficult for radio stations to broadcast conservative talk shows exclusively, as many now do. Nine of the top ten talk-radio shows, as measured by Arbitron

ratings, are politically conservative. No liberal commentator ranks higher than twentieth place in the ratings. (Several of the shows ranked higher than twentieth, are not political, but deal with subjects such as personal finance and paranormal activities.)

Audiences and Hosts

The Pew Research Center for the People and the Press reports that 17 percent of the public regularly listens to talk radio. This audience is predominantly male, middle-aged, and conservative. Among those who regularly listen to talk radio, 41 percent consider themselves Republicans and 28 percent, Democrats.

Talk radio is sometimes characterized as the Wild West of the media. Talk-show hosts do not attempt to hide their political biases. If anything, they exaggerate them for effect. No journalistic conventions are observed. Leading shows, such as those of Rush Limbaugh, Glenn Beck, Sean Hannity, Andrew Wilkow, and Michael Savage, espouse a brand of conservatism that is robust, even radical. Opponents are regularly characterized as Nazis, Communists, or both at the same time. Limbaugh, for example, consistently refers to feminists as "feminazis." Talk-show hosts appear to care far more about the entertainment value of their statements than whether they are, strictly speaking, true. Hosts often publicize fringe beliefs such as the contention that President Barack Obama was not really born in the United States. The government of Britain actually banned Michael Savage from entry into that country based on his remarks about Muslims.

> "FOR A POLITICIAN TO COMPLAIN ABOUT THE PRESS IS LIKE **a ship's captain complaining about the sea.**"
>
> ~ ENOCH POWELL ~
> BRITISH POLITICIAN
> 1912–1998

The Wild West Migrates to Television

Commentators at Fox News have always been predominantly conservative, just as liberals are the rule at the smaller MSNBC network. Still, until recently it was widely seen as inappropriate for television personalities to employ the radical style characteristic of such talk-show hosts as Rush Limbaugh. That understanding began to crumble after October 2008, when Fox News hired conservative commentator Glenn Beck.

Beck's audience is smaller than those of his Fox colleagues Bill O'Reilly and Sean Hannity. In short order, however, Beck transformed himself into one of the nation's most politically polarizing figures. Beck's emotional style—he frequently breaks into tears—his over-the-top statements, and his apocalyptic views were a new development on television. As one example, Beck stated that President Obama had "a deep-seated hatred for white people" and was a racist.

Beck gained further attention by using his on-air pulpit as a political organizing tool. Throughout 2009, Beck promoted the Tea Party movement, and in August 2010 he sponsored the Restoring Honor rally at the Lincoln Memorial in Washington, D.C., which was attended by close to 200,000 people. The apparent aim of the rally was to bring together the Tea Party and Christian conservative movements.

The Impact of Talk Radio

The overwhelming dominance of strong conservative voices on talk radio is justified by supporters as a good way to counter what they perceive as the liberal bias in the mainstream print and TV media (we discuss the question of bias in the media in the following section). Supporters say that such shows are simply a response to consumer demand. Those who think that talk radio is good for the country argue that talk shows, taken together, provide a great populist forum. Others are uneasy because they fear that talk shows empower fringe groups, perhaps magnifying their rage.

Certainly, prominent hosts have had great fun organizing potentially disruptive activities. For example, during the 2008 presidential primaries, Limbaugh called for conservatives to reregister as Democrats and vote for Obama. The theory was that Obama would be easier

for a Republican to beat than Hillary Clinton. In 2009, Beck (who is on radio as well as television) promoted attempts to shout down Democratic members of Congress at town hall meetings set up to discuss health-care reform.

Those who claim that talk-show hosts go too far ultimately have to deal with the constitutional issue of free speech. While the courts have always given broad support to freedom of expression, broadcast media have been something of an exception, as was explained in Chapter 4. The United States Supreme Court, for example, upheld the fairness doctrine in a 1969 ruling.[12] Presumably, the doctrine could be reinstated. In 2009, after the Democratic victories in the 2008 elections, a few liberals advocated doing just that. President Obama and the Democratic leadership in Congress, however, quickly put an end to this notion. Americans have come to accept talk radio as part of the political environment, and any attempt to curtail it would be extremely unpopular.

> "A nation that is afraid to let its people judge truth and falsehood in an **OPEN MARKET** is a nation that is afraid of its people."
>
> ~ JOHN FITZGERALD KENNEDY ~
> THIRTY-FIFTH PRESIDENT
> OF THE UNITED STATES
> 1961–1963

LO4 The Question of Media Bias

The question of media bias is important in any democracy. After all, for our political system to work, citizens must be well informed. And they can be well informed only if the news media, the source of much of their information, do not slant the news. Today, however, relatively few Americans believe that the news media are unbiased in their reporting. Accompanying this perception is a notable decline in the public's confidence in the news media in recent years.

In a 2010 Gallup poll measuring the public's confidence in various institutions, only 25 percent of the respondents stated that they had "a great deal" or "quite a lot" of confidence in newspapers, and 22 percent had such a degree of confidence in television news. Because of these low percentages, some analysts believe that the media are facing a crisis of confidence.

Partisan Bias

For years, conservatives have argued that there is a liberal bias in the media, and liberals have complained that the media reflect a conservative bias. The majority of Americans think that the media reflect a bias in one direction or another. According to a recent poll, 50 percent of the respondents believed that the news media leaned left, whereas only 22 percent thought that the news media had a conservative bias.

Surveys and analyses of the attitudes and voting habits of reporters have suggested that journalists do indeed hold liberal views. In 2007, MSNBC was able to identify 125 journalists who made political contributions to Democrats or liberal causes, according to Federal Election Commission records. Only 16 gave to Republicans. Two gave to both parties. Still, members of the press are likely to view themselves as moderates. In a 2005 study, the Pew Research Center for the People and the Press found that 64 percent of reporters in both national and local media applied the term "moderate" to themselves. Among journalists working for national outlets, 22 percent described themselves as liberal and only 5 percent as conservative.

In contrast, 14 percent of local reporters called themselves liberals, and 18 percent adopted the conservative label. There is substantial evidence that top journalists working for the nation's most famous newspapers and networks do tend to be liberal. Many journalists themselves perceive the *New York Times* as liberal (although an even larger number view Fox News as conservative).

Nonetheless, a number of media scholars, including Kathleen Hall Jamieson, suggest that even if many reporters hold liberal views, these views are not reflected in their reporting. Based on an extensive study of media coverage of presidential campaigns, Jamieson, director of the Annenberg Public Policy Center of the University of Pennsylvania, concludes that there is no systematic liberal or Democratic bias in news coverage.[13] Media analysts Debra Reddin van Tuyll and Hubert P. van Tuyll have similarly concluded that left-leaning reporters do not automatically equate to left-leaning news coverage. They point out that reporters are only the starting point for news stories. Before any story goes to print or is aired on television, it has to go through a progression of editors and perhaps even the publisher. Because employees at the top of the corporate ladder in news organizations are more right leaning than left leaning, the end result of the editorial and oversight process is more balanced coverage.[14]

The Bias against Losers

Kathleen Hall Jamieson believes that media bias does play a significant role in shaping presidential campaigns and elections, but she argues that it is not a partisan bias. Rather, it is a bias against losers. A candidate who falls behind in the race is immediately labeled a "loser," making it even more difficult for the candidate to regain favor in the voters' eyes.[15]

Jamieson argues that the media use the winner-loser paradigm to describe events throughout the campaigns. Even a presidential debate is regarded as a "sporting match" that results in a winner and a loser. In the days leading up to the 2008 debates, reporters focused on what each candidate had to do to "win" the debate. When the debate was over, reporters immediately speculated about who had "won" as they waited for post-debate polls to answer that question. According to Jamieson, this approach "squanders the opportunity to reinforce learning." The debates are an important source of political information for the voters, and this fact is eclipsed by the media's win-lose focus.

"Selection Bias"

As mentioned earlier, television is big business, and maximizing profits from advertising is a major consideration in what television stations choose to air. After all, a station or network that incurs losses will eventually go bankrupt. The expansion of the media universe to include cable channels and the Internet has also increased the competition among news sources. As a result, news directors *select* programming they believe will attract the largest audiences and garner the highest advertising revenues.

Competition for viewers and readers has become even more challenging in the wake of a declining news audience. A recent survey and analysis of reporters' attitudes conducted by the Pew Research Center's Project for Excellence in Journalism found that all media sectors except two are losing popularity. The two exceptions are the ethnic press, such as Latino newspapers and TV programs, and online sources—and even the online sector has stopped growing.[16]

SELECTION BIAS AND THE BOTTOM LINE   The Pew study also indicated that news organizations' struggles to stay afloat are having a notable effect on news coverage. The survey showed that a larger number of reporters than ever before (about 66 percent) agreed that "increased bottom-line pressure is seriously hurting the quality of news coverage." About one-third of the journalists—again, more than in previous surveys—stated that they have felt pressure from either advertisers or corporate owners concerning what to write or broadcast. In other words, these journalists

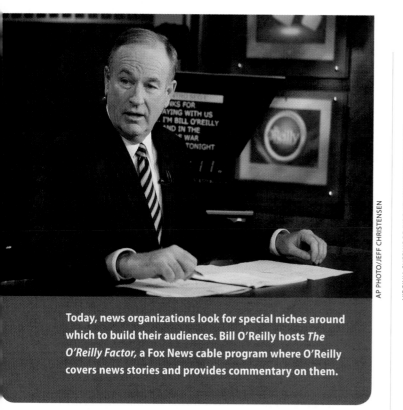

Today, news organizations look for special niches around which to build their audiences. Bill O'Reilly hosts *The O'Reilly Factor,* a Fox News cable program where O'Reilly covers news stories and provides commentary on them.

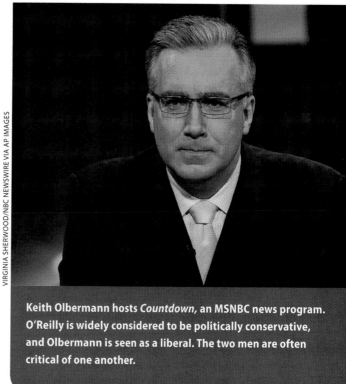

Keith Olbermann hosts *Countdown,* an MSNBC news program. O'Reilly is widely considered to be politically conservative, and Olbermann is seen as a liberal. The two men are often critical of one another.

believe that economic pressure—the need for revenues—is making significant inroads on independent editorial decision making. Generally, the study found that news reporters are not too confident about the future of journalism.

A CHANGING NEWS CULTURE   A number of studies, including the Pew study just cited, indicate that today's news culture is in the midst of change. News organizations are redefining their purpose and increasingly looking for special niches in which to build their audiences. According to the Pew study, for some markets, the niche is *hyperlocalism*—that is, narrowing the focus of news to the local area. For others, it is personal commentary, revolving around highly politicized TV figures such as Bill O'Reilly and Keith Olbermann. In a sense, news organizations have begun to base their appeal less on *how* they cover the news and more on *what* they cover. Traditional journalism—fact-based reporting instead of opinion and punditry—is becoming a smaller part of this mix.

Another development is the move toward highly specific subject matter that appeals strongly to a limited number of viewers. Magazines have always done this—consider the many magazine titles on topics such as model railroading or home decorating. With the large number of cable channels, *narrowcasting* has become important on television as well. Networks now

appeal to members of particular ethnic groups (BET—Black Entertainment Television), hobbyists (Cooking Channel), or history buffs (Military Channel).

LO5 *Political News and Campaigns on the Web*

Cyberspace is getting bigger every day. More than one-quarter of the world's inhabitants currently use the Internet, a total of about 2 billion people. According to Technorati, bloggers around the world update their blogs with new posts in eighty-one languages at a rate of almost a million posts every day. Among U.S. Internet users, 77 percent read blogs, and one blog tracker, BlogPulse, has identified more than 146 million blogs. In addition, popular networking sites have enormous numbers of personalized pages—Twitter has 190 million members, and Facebook has more than 500 million.

Not surprisingly, the Internet is now a major source of information for many people. Gone are the days when you and your friends tromped to the library to research a paper. Why should you? You can go online and in a matter of seconds look up practically any subject. Of course, all major newspapers are online, as are

The Fox News site brings the network's conservative take on the news to the Internet.

transcripts of major television news programs. About two-thirds of Internet users consider the Internet to be an important source of news. Certainly, news abounds on the Web, and having an Internet strategy has become an integral part of political campaigning.

News Organizations Online

Almost every major news organization, both print and broadcast, delivers news via the Web. Indeed, an online presence is required to compete effectively with other traditional news companies for revenues. Studies of the media, including the study by the Pew Research Center's Project for Excellence in Journalism mentioned earlier, note that the online share of newspaper company revenues has increased over the years. Today, 12 percent of U.S. newspaper revenues come from online sources.

Web sites for newspapers, such as those of the *Washington Post* and the *New York Times,* have a notable advantage over their printed counterparts. They can add breaking news to their sites, informing readers of events that occurred just minutes ago. Another advantage is that they can link the reader to more extensive reports on particular topics. According to the Pew study, though, many papers shy away from in-text linking, perhaps fearing that if readers leave the news organization's site, they might not return.

citizen journalism The collection, analysis, and dissemination of information online by independent journalists, scholars, politicians, and the general citizenry.

"The citizen CAN BRING OUR POLITICAL AND GOVERNMENTAL INSTITUTIONS BACK TO LIFE, MAKE THEM RESPONSIVE AND ACCOUNTABLE, AND KEEP THEM HONEST. No one else can."

~ JOHN GARDNER ~
AMERICAN NOVELIST
1933–1982

Although some newspaper sites simply copy articles from their printed versions, the Web sites for major newspapers, including those for the *Washington Post* and the *New York Times,* offer a different array of coverage and options than their printed counterparts. Indeed, the Pew study noted that the online versions of competing newspapers tend to be much more similar than their printed versions are.

A major problem facing these news organizations is that readers or viewers of online newspapers and news programs are typically the same people who read the printed news editions and view news programs on TV. Web-only readers of a particular newspaper make up a relatively small percentage of those going online for their news. Therefore, investing heavily in online news delivery may not be a solution for news companies seeking to increase readership and revenues.

In fact, the additional revenues that newspapers have gained from their online editions do not come close to making up for the massive losses in advertising revenue suffered by their print editions. In many instances, publications have not sold enough advertising in their online editions even to make up for the additional expense of publishing on the Web.

Blogs and the Emergence of Citizen Journalism

As mentioned earlier, the news culture is changing, and at the heart of this change—and of most innovation in news delivery today—is the blogosphere. There has been a virtual explosion of blogs in recent years. To make their Web sites more competitive and appealing, and to counter the influence of blogs run by private citizens and those not in the news business, the mainstream news organizations have themselves been adding blogs to their Web sites.

Blogs are offered by independent journalists, various scholars, political activists, and the citizenry at large. Anyone who wants to can create a blog and post news or information, including videos, to share with others. Many blogs are political in nature, both reporting political developments and discussing politics. Taken as a whole, the collection, analysis, and dissemination of information online by the citizenry is referred to as **citizen journalism.** Other terms that have been used to

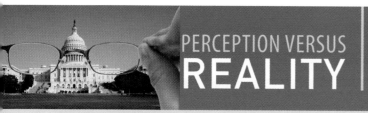

Back in 2006, Jack Dorsey created Twitter, a free social networking and microblogging service. As just about everyone now knows, Twitter posts—or tweets—are text-based messages that cannot exceed 140 characters. Today, Twitter users can send and receive messages through Twitter.com as well as through other media and applications.

The Perception

What can be more useless than twittering about what you are doing? What can be more superfluous than accessing Paris Hilton's Twitter site to find out that she thinks Jimmy Kimmel is funny, or discovering that Denise Richards just had her breakfast coffee? Twitter appears to be for those who don't value their time very highly—it's even more of a time waster than text messaging and blogging. Just because 90 million tweets are posted every day doesn't mean that it has much value to the world. Some believe that tweeting has simply replaced reading *People* magazine and talking on the phone about, well, nothing.

The Reality

Today, Twitter is an important news and political vehicle. Often, breaking news stories are first reported on Twitter and then picked up by major media sources. In addition, many media outlets use Twitter to measure public sentiment on various issues. And Twitter was used by both candidates in the 2008 U.S. presidential campaign, particularly by Barack Obama.

Look at some of the important messages Twitter made possible. When graduate journalism student James Buck was arrested in Egypt for photographing an antigovernment protest, he used Twitter to get out the message. He was able to send updates about his condition while being detained. He was released the next day. During the 2008 terrorist attacks in Mumbai, India, eyewitnesses twittered every five seconds, letting the rest of the world know what was happening. After the 2009 presidential elections in Iran were deemed fraudulent by many citizens, the Iranian government shut off most Internet outlets. But it wasn't able to shut off Twitter. Indeed, Twitter was almost the only communication medium for protesters in Iran. Much of what the rest of the world saw came through TwitPics.

Blog On You can sign up for Twitter at **twitter.com**. Want to know the demographics of who's on Twitter? The site Quantcast has the answer—go to **www.quantcast.com/twitter.com**. You can follow in-depth reporting on Twitter at **www.telegraph.co.uk/technology/twitter**.

---

describe the news blogosphere include *people journalism* and *participatory journalism*. When blogs focus on news and developments in a specific community, the term *community journalism* is often applied.

The increase in news blogs and do-it-yourself journalism on the Web clearly poses a threat to mainstream news sources. Compared with the operational costs faced by a major news organization, the cost of creating and maintaining blogs is trivial. How can major news sources adhere to their traditional standards and still compete with this new world of news generated by citizens?

Podcasting the News

Another nontraditional form of news distribution is **podcasting**—the distribution of audio or video files to personal computers or mobile devices, such as iPhones.[17] Though still a relatively small portion of the overall news-delivery system, podcasts are becoming increasingly popular. Almost anyone can create a podcast and make it available for downloading onto computers or mobile devices, and like blogging, podcasting is inexpensive. As you will read next, political candidates are using both blogging and podcasting as part of their Internet campaign strategy.

Still another relatively new Internet technology is Twitter, a method for sending short messages to large numbers of people. How useful is Twitter? We discuss that question in this chapter's *Perception versus Reality* feature above.

Cyberspace and Political Campaigns

Today's political parties and candidates realize the benefits of using the Internet to conduct online campaigns and

podcasting The distribution of audio or video files to a personal computer or a mobile device, such as an iPod.

MoveOn.ORG
DEMOCRACY IN ACTION ®

CAMPAIGNS | DONATE | SIGN UP | ABOUT

MOVEON.ORG POLITICAL ACTION

Something terrible is happening!

Will anyone stand up for the "real" health care victims:
the super-rich health insurance executives!?!
Thankfully, Will Ferrell and friends are - check it out:

Watch the video »

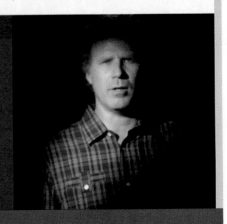

WWW.MOVEON.ORG

MoveOn is a progressive advocacy group. Like other such groups, it uses the Web.

raise funds. Voters also are increasingly using the Web to access information about parties and candidates, promote political goals, and obtain political news. Generally, the use of the Internet is an inexpensive way for candidates to contact, recruit, and mobilize supporters, as well as disseminate information about their positions on issues. In effect, the Internet can replace brochures, letters, and position papers. Individual voters or political party supporters can use the Internet to avoid having to go to special meetings or to a campaign site to do volunteer work or obtain information on a candidate's positions.

That the Internet is now a viable medium for communicating political information and interacting with voters was made clear in the campaigns preceding the 2004, 2006, and 2008 elections. According to a Pew Research Center survey following the 2008 presidential elections, 55 percent of Americans said that they went online for election news—up from 4 percent who did so in the 1996 campaign. Among Internet users, 18 percent posted political comments in a blog or on a social networking site. Fully 45 percent of users watched online videos related to the campaigns. One in three forwarded political content to someone else.

ONLINE FUND-RAISING The Internet can be an effective—and inexpensive—way to raise campaign funds. Fund-raising on the Internet by presidential candidates became widespread after the Federal Election Commission decided, in June 1999, that the federal government could distribute matching funds for credit-card donations received by candidates via the Internet.

In the 2008 presidential contest, however, the candidates took online fund-raising to an entirely new level, especially in the Democratic primaries. The fund-raising effort of Hillary Clinton would have been considered

outstanding in any previous presidential election cycle. Yet it was eclipsed by the organization put together by Barack Obama.

Obama's online operation was the heart of his fund-raising success. One of its defining characteristics was its decentralization. The Obama campaign attempted to recruit as many supporters as possible to act as fundraisers who solicited contributions from their friends and neighbors. As a result, Obama personally was spared much of the fund-raising effort that consumes the time of most national politicians. In the first half of 2007, Obama's campaign raised $58 million, $16.4 million of which was made up of donations of less than $200. The total sum was a record, and the small-donation portion was unusually large. In September 2008, the Obama campaign set another fund-raising record with $150 million, the most ever raised in one month by a presidential campaign. By then, 2.9 million people had donated to Obama's campaign.

THE RISE OF THE INTERNET CAMPAIGN An increasingly important part of political campaigning today is the Internet campaign. Candidates typically hire Web managers to manage their Internet campaigns. The job of the Web manager, or Web strategist, is to create a well-designed, informative, and user-friendly campaign Web site to attract viewers, hold their attention, manage their e-mails, and track their credit-card contributions. The Web manager also hires bloggers to promote the candidate's views, arranges for podcasting of campaign information and updates to supporters, and hires staff to monitor the Web for news about the candidates and to track the online publications of *netroots groups*— online activists who support the candidate but are not controlled by the candidate's organization.

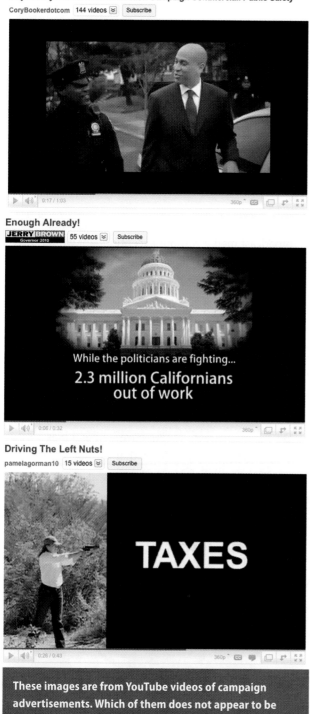

Mayor Cory Booker 2010 Reelection Campaign Commercial: Public Safety

CoryBookerdotcom 144 videos Subscribe

0:17 / 1:03   360p

Enough Already!

JERRY BROWN Governor 2010   55 videos   Subscribe

While the politicians are fighting...

2.3 million Californians out of work

0:06 / 0:32   360p

Driving The Left Nuts!

pamelagorman10 15 videos Subscribe

TAXES

0:26 / 0:43   360p

WWW.YOUTUBE.COM

These images are from YouTube videos of campaign advertisements. Which of them does not appear to be an example of negative advertising?

CONTROLLING THE NETROOTS One of the challenges facing candidates today is trying to deliver a consistent campaign message to voters. Netroots groups may publish online promotional ads or other materials that do not represent a candidate's position. Similarly, online groups may attack the candidate's opponent in ways that the candidate does not approve. Yet no candidate wants to alienate these groups, because they can

raise significant sums of money and garner votes for the candidate. For example, the group MoveOn.org raised $28 million for Democrats prior to the 2006 elections. Yet MoveOn.org is more left leaning on issues than the most competitive Democratic presidential candidates in 2008 wanted to appear—because those candidates hoped to gain the votes of more moderate voters.

CANDIDATES' 24/7 EXPOSURE Just as citizen journalism, discussed earlier, has altered the news culture, so have citizen videos changed the traditional campaign. For example, a candidate can never know when a comment that she or he makes may be caught on camera by someone with a cell phone or digital camera and published on the Internet for all to see. At times, such exposure can be devastating, as George Allen, the former Republican senator from Virginia, learned in the 2006 midterm elections. He was captured on video making a racial slur about one of his opponent's campaign workers. The video was posted on YouTube, and within a short time the major news organizations picked up the story. Many news commentators claimed that this video exposé gave Allen's Democratic opponent, Jim Webb, enough votes to win the race.

A candidate's opponents may post on YouTube or some other Web site a compilation of video clips showing the candidate's inconsistent comments over time on a specific topic, such as abortion or the health-care reform legislation. The effect can be very damaging by making the candidate's "flip-flopping" on the issue apparent.

This 24/7 exposure also makes it difficult for the candidates to control their campaigns. The potential for citizen videos to destroy a candidate's chances is always there, creating a new type of uncertainty in political campaigning.

OBAMA'S DIFFICULTIES Barack Obama certainly learned about the dangers of 24/7 exposure during his campaign for president. In one incident, while speaking at a gathering of supporters that he believed to be private, Obama described many small towns in Pennsylvania: "Each successive administration has said that somehow these communities are going to regenerate and they have not. And it's not surprising, then, they get bitter, they cling to guns or religion or antipathy to people who aren't like them." When these remarks became public, they were widely criticized as condescending.

A more serious problem surfaced when ABC News downloaded an online collection of sermons preached by the Reverend Jeremiah Wright of Chicago, who had been Obama's personal pastor for twenty years. Some of Wright's comments were highly inflammatory, notably this one: "The government . . . wants us to sing God Bless America. No, no, no, not God Bless America. God damn America . . . for killing innocent people." When these quotes were publicized, support for Obama fell. In a well-regarded speech, Obama repudiated Wright's remarks, but not Wright himself. After further indiscretions by the minister, however, Obama broke with Wright completely and left the Chicago church.

AMERICA AT ODDS *Politics and the Media*

Americans love to hate the media, possibly because we spend so much time watching and reading them. Without a doubt, the media are undergoing a revolution today. With the loss of classified ads to the Internet, newspapers are in serious financial jeopardy. Online news sources, meanwhile, have yet to hit upon a reliable method of generating adequate income. In this changing environment, Americans are at odds over a number of media topics:

- Do the difficulties faced by newspapers threaten the existence of competent journalism—or is this not an important problem?

- Is the media's agenda-setting function a vital contribution to the democratic process—or an improper attempt to manipulate viewers?

- Should First Amendment protections be extended to broadcast media without exception—or would such a move threaten the morals of the country and make it impossible for viewers to avoid sexual content?

- Are negative advertisements an inevitable and unremarkable aspect of political campaigns—or should the voters punish politicians who employ them?

- Does talk radio add to the vigor of our political discourse—or is it a corrupting influence that divides the nation?

- Do the mainstream media have a liberal bias—or do they merely publicize facts that do not square with conservative beliefs?

Take Action

Today, the media are wide open for citizen involvement. You, too, can report or comment on the news. Millions of people, especially students, are already halfway to becoming bloggers through their Facebook pages. You might consider turning political discussions on Facebook into an actual blog. Such a project is more easily undertaken if several friends share the responsibility for creating the content. That way, one person does not have to carry the entire load. You can set up links to articles or videos of interest at other sites, but an attractive blog isn't just links but also a place to view unique content.

A variety of other online projects are possible. You can create videos of events that you believe are newsworthy and post them online. You can podcast video or audio coverage of an event from a Web site that you have created. You, by yourself or with others, can set up a "radio station" to spread your views using the Internet. For example, in the photo shown here, two citizens who supported a proposed Tennessee state tax reform set up their own radio station in Nashville to mock local radio personalities who were opposed to the reform. Lining the street nearby are other supporters of the tax reform.

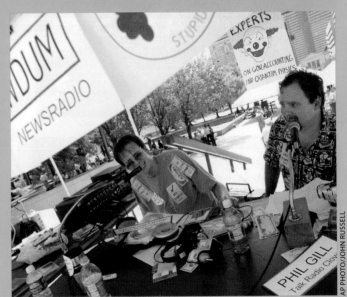

AP PHOTO/JOHN RUSSELL

Local talk-radio and news programs abound. They are often irreverent and operated by young people.

- Newspapers.com features links to more than ten thousand newspapers nationwide. You can also search by categories, such as business, college newspapers, and industry. Go to **www.newspapers.com**

- A blog search engine with links to blogs in a variety of categories can be accessed at **www.blogsearchengine.com**

- A number of watchdog groups monitor the media in an attempt to expose bias, partisanship, or factual errors. Accuracy in Media is a conservative group. Find it at **www.aim.org**

- Fairness and Accuracy in Reporting is a liberal watchdog group. Its Web site is at **www.fair.org**

- With the growth of YouTube, it is now possible to see historically important political videos of all kinds.

These include attack ads, videos of candidates making embarrassing statements, presidential debates, and famous speeches. The easiest way to find a video is to enter a string of descriptive terms into a search engine such as Google. For example, to find the "daisy girl" ad mentioned on pages 217 and 218, enter the following words: **daisy girl video youtube**

- To see an advertisement that Republican presidential candidate George H. W. Bush deployed to great effect against Democratic candidate Michael Dukakis in 1988, enter the following in a search engine: **willie horton ad youtube**

- Quotation marks force a search engine to look for an entire phrase. To see Barack Obama's speech responding to the Jeremiah Wright crisis described on pages 227 and 228, enter **Obama "a more perfect union" full**

Access CourseMate to review and expand on this chapter through quizzes, flashcards, learning objectives, interactive timelines, a crossword puzzle, audio summaries, video, critical-thinking activities, simulations, and more.

{ Studying on the run? }

Audio downloads you can take anywhere, only at
4ltrpress.cengage.com/politicalscience

GOVT

11 Congress

LEARNING OBJECTIVES

LO1 Explain how seats in the House of Representatives are apportioned among the states.

LO2 Describe the power of incumbency.

LO3 Identify the key leadership positions in Congress, describe the committee system, and indicate some important differences between the House of Representatives and the Senate.

LO4 Summarize the specific steps in the lawmaking process.

LO5 Identify Congress's oversight functions and explain how Congress fulfills them.

LO6 Indicate what is involved in the congressional budgeting process.

CourseMate

230

AMERICA AT ODDS

Should It Take Sixty Senators to Pass Important Legislation?

If there is a magic number in politics, it is sixty. Why? Because sixty is the number of Senate votes required to force an end to a filibuster. A filibuster takes place when senators use the chamber's tradition of unlimited debate to block legislation. In years past, filibustering senators would speak for hours—even reading names from the telephone book—to prevent a vote on a proposed bill. In recent decades, however, Senate rules have permitted filibusters in which actual continuous floor speeches are not required. Senators merely announce that they are filibustering. The threat of a filibuster has created an *ad hoc* rule that important legislation needs the support of sixty senators. (There are exceptions. Budget bills are handled using a special "reconciliation" rule that does not permit filibusters.)

If one party can elect sixty or more U.S. senators, assuming they all follow the party line, they can force through any legislation they want by invoking "cloture," which ends filibusters. The Democrats, in fact, enjoyed a supermajority in the Senate for seven months, from July 7, 2009, until February 4, 2010. It began when Al Franken (D., Minn.) joined the Senate after a long-contested race was finally decided in his favor. Shortly after a January 2010 special election, Scott Brown (R., Mass.) was sworn in to a seat formerly held by a Democrat, and that party's supermajority ended.

The question remains, though, whether the magic number of sixty is an appropriate requirement for passing important legislation in the Senate. Should the number be reduced to fifty-five or even to fifty-one—a simple majority of all sitting senators?

Don't Let the Majority Trample on the Minority

The long history of the filibuster in the United States Senate and the consequent need for a supermajority to pass legislation has served us well. Filibusters, or even the threat of filibusters, provide the minority with an effective means of preventing the majority from ramrodding legislation down the throats of American voters.

Rule by a simple majority can be scary. Support for a measure can shift between 49 percent and 51 percent very quickly. Should such small changes be the basis for passing major legislation? A simple majority does not signify an adequate degree of consensus. When it comes to major issues, something more weighty than simple majority rule should prevail.

Many states require supermajorities for passing any legislation that would raise taxes. In California, for example, a tax increase must win two-thirds approval in both chambers of the state legislature. It takes two-thirds of both chambers of Congress to override a veto by the president. That's another supermajority. Changing the Constitution requires a very substantial supermajority—three-quarters of the state legislatures. If these supermajority rules were good enough for the founders, then the principle still is good enough for the Senate.

Don't Let Obstructionists Determine Legislation

Just because supermajorities were required in jury deliberations in classical Rome and for the election of a pope in the Catholic Church does not mean they are necessary in the Senate. Supermajorities make it harder to achieve needed changes. Supermajorities allow a minority to block the preference of the majority. Even James Madison, who worried about the tyranny of the majority over the minority, recognized the opposite possibility. He said that "the fundamental principle of free government" might be reversed by supermajorities. "It would be no longer majority that would rule: the power would be transferred to the minority."

Furthermore, the sixty-vote requirement in the Senate has led to a significant increase in "pork"—that is, special spending provisions inserted into legislation. Senators working on bills find that they must fill them with pork to attract the votes of their colleagues. Without the pork, the bills won't pass. The Senate should reduce the votes required for cloture of a filibuster to fifty-five or even fifty-one. Let's get on with government by the majority, not the supermajority.

EXPLORE THIS ISSUE ONLINE

William Greider denounces the tradition of the filibuster in the pages of *The Nation,* a strongly liberal publication. See his article at www.thenation.com/article/stop-senator-no. Nick Dranias, a conservative, defends the supermajority concept at www.goldwaterinstitute.org/article/3244.

WHERE DO YOU STAND?

1. Why might it be appropriate to require supermajority voting for important legislation?
2. Under what circumstances do supermajority voting rules prevent democracy from being fully realized?

Introduction

Congress is the lawmaking branch of government. When someone says, "There ought to be a law," at the federal level it is Congress that will make that law. The framers had a strong suspicion of a powerful executive authority. Consequently, they made Congress—not the executive branch (the presidency)—the central institution of American government. Yet, as noted in Chapter 2, the founders created a system of checks and balances to ensure that no branch of the federal government, including Congress, could exercise too much power.

Many Americans view Congress as a largely faceless, anonymous legislative body that is quite distant and removed from their everyday lives. Yet the people you elect to Congress represent and advocate for your interests at the very highest level of power. Furthermore, the laws created by the men and women in the U.S. Congress affect the daily lives of every American in one way or another. Getting to know your congressional representatives and how they are voting in Congress on issues that concern you is an important step toward becoming an informed voter. Even the details of how Congress makes law—such as the Senate rules described in the chapter-opening *America at Odds* feature—should be of interest to the savvy voter.

LO1 *The Structure and Makeup of Congress*

The framers agreed that the Congress should be the "first branch of the government," as James Madison said, but they did not immediately agree on its organization. Ultimately, they decided on a *bicameral legislature*—a Congress consisting of two chambers. This was part of the Great Compromise, which you read about in Chapter 2.

---

apportionment The distribution of House seats among the states on the basis of their respective populations.

The framers favored a bicameral legislature so that the two chambers, the House and the Senate, might serve as checks on each other's power and activity. The House was to represent the people as a whole, or the majority. The Senate was to represent the states and would protect the interests of small states by giving them the same number of senators (two per state) as the larger states.

Apportionment of House Seats

The Constitution provides for the **apportionment** (distribution) of House seats among the states on the basis of their respective populations. States with larger populations, such as California, have many more representatives than states with smaller populations, such as Wyoming. California, for example, currently has fifty-three representatives in the House—Wyoming has only one.

Every ten years, House seats are reapportioned based on the outcome of the decennial (ten-year) census conducted by the U.S. Census Bureau. Figure 11–1 on the facing page indicates the states that gained and lost seats based on population changes reported by the 2000 census. This redistribution of seats took effect with the 108th Congress, which was elected in 2002.

Each state is guaranteed at least one House seat, no matter what its population. Today, seven states have only one representative.[1] The District of Columbia, American Samoa, Guam, and the U.S. Virgin Islands all send nonvoting delegates to the House. Puerto Rico, a self-governing possession of the United States, is represented by a nonvoting resident commissioner.

A Senate committee begins work on the health-care reform bill. Most of the work of Congress occurs in committees like this one. Some bills end up being over a thousand pages long. Why do you think they end up being so lengthy?

STEPHEN CROWLEY/THE NEW YORK TIMES/REDUX

Congressional Districts

Whereas senators are elected to represent all of the people in a state, representatives are elected by the voters of a particular area known as a **congressional district.** The Constitution makes no provisions for congressional districts, and in the early 1800s each state was given the right to decide whether to have districts at all. Most states set up single-member districts, in which voters in each district elected one of the state's representatives. In states that chose not to have districts, representatives were chosen at large, from the state as a whole. In 1842, however, Congress passed an act that required all states to send representatives to Congress from single-member districts, as you read in Chapter 7.

For many years, the number of House members increased as the population expanded. In 1929, however, a federal law fixed House membership at 435 members. Thus, today the 435 members of the House are chosen by the voters in 435 separate congressional districts across the country. If a state's population allows it to have only one representative, the entire state is one congressional district. In contrast, states with large populations have many districts. California, for example, because its population entitles it to send fifty-three representatives to the House, has fifty-three congressional districts.

By default, the lines of the congressional districts are drawn by the state legislatures. Alternatively, the task may be handed off to a designated body such as an independent commission. States must meet certain requirements in drawing district boundaries. To ensure equal representation in the House, districts must contain, as nearly as possible, equal numbers of people. Additionally, each district must have contiguous boundaries and must be "geographically compact," although this last requirement is not enforced very strictly.

THE REQUIREMENT OF EQUAL REPRESENTATION

If congressional districts are not made up of equal populations, the value of people's votes is not the same. In

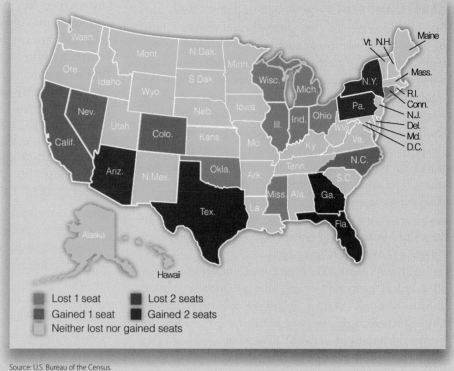

Figure 11–1

Reapportionment of House Seats following the 2000 Census

Lost 1 seat
Gained 1 seat
Neither lost nor gained seats
Lost 2 seats
Gained 2 seats

Source: U.S. Bureau of the Census.

the past, state legislators often used this fact to their advantage. For example, traditionally, many state legislatures were controlled by rural areas. By drawing districts that were not equal in population, rural leaders attempted to curb the number of representatives from growing urban centers. At one point in the 1960s, in many states the largest district had twice the population of the smallest district. In effect, this meant that a person's vote in the largest district had only half the value of a person's vote in the smallest district.

For some time, the United States Supreme Court refused to address this problem. In 1962, however, in *Baker v. Carr,*[2] the Court ruled that the Tennessee state legislature's **malapportionment** was an issue that could be heard in the federal courts because it affected the constitutional requirement of equal protection under the law. Two years later, in *Wesberry v. Sanders,*[3] the Supreme Court held that congressional districts must have equal populations. This

congressional district
The geographic area that is served by one member in the House of Representatives.

malapportionment
A condition in which the voting power of citizens in one district is greater than the voting power of citizens in another district.

principle has come to be known as the **"one person, one vote" rule.** In other words, one person's vote has to count as much as another's vote.

GERRYMANDERING Although in the 1960s the Supreme Court ruled that congressional districts must be equal in population, it continued to be silent on the issue of gerrymandered districts. **Gerrymandering** occurs when a district's boundaries are drawn to maximize the influence of a certain group or political party. Where a party's voters are scarce, the boundaries can be drawn to include as many of the party's voters as possible. Where the party is strong, the lines are drawn so that the opponent's supporters are spread across two or more districts, thus diluting the opponent's strength. (The term *gerrymandering* was originally used to describe the district lines drawn to favor the party of Governor Elbridge Gerry of Massachusetts prior to the 1812 elections—see Figure 11–2 on the facing page.)

Although there have been constitutional challenges to political gerrymandering,[4] the practice continues. It was certainly evident following the 2000 census. Sophisticated computer programs can now analyze the partisan leanings of individual neighborhoods and city blocks. District lines are drawn to "pack" the opposing party's voters into the smallest number of districts or "crack" the opposing party's voters into several different districts. Packing and cracking make congressional races less competitive. In 2003, for example, Texas adopted a controversial redistricting plan that was spearheaded by then House majority leader Tom DeLay (R., Tex.). DeLay and Texas Republicans used pack and crack tactics to redraw districts that had formerly leaned toward Democratic candidates. The

plan effectively cost four Democratic representatives their seats in the 2004 elections.[5]

Racial Gerrymandering Although political gerrymandering has a long history, gerrymandering to empower minority groups is a relatively new phenomenon. In the early 1990s, the U.S. Department of Justice instructed state legislatures to draw district lines to maximize the voting power of minority groups. As a result, several **minority-majority districts** were created. Many of these districts took on bizarre shapes. For example, North Carolina's newly drawn Twelfth Congressional District was 165 miles long—a narrow strip that, for the most part, followed Interstate 85. Georgia's new Eleventh District stretched from Atlanta to the Atlantic, splitting eight counties and five municipalities. The practice of racial gerrymandering has generated heated argument on both sides of the issue.

Some groups contend that minority-majority districts are necessary to ensure equal representation of minority groups, as mandated by the Voting Rights Act of 1965. They further contend that these districts have been instrumental in increasing the number of African Americans holding political office. Minority-majority districts in the South contain, on average, 45 percent non-black voters, whereas before 1990, redistricting plans in the South often created only white-majority districts.[6]

Limiting Racial Gerrymandering Opponents of racial gerrymandering argue that such race-based districting is unconstitutional because it violates the equal protection clause. In a series of cases in the 1990s, the Supreme Court agreed and held that when race is the dominant factor in the drawing of congressional district lines, the districts are unconstitutional and must be redrawn.[7]

In 2001, however, the Supreme Court issued a ruling that seemed—at least to some observers—to be out of step with its earlier rulings. North Carolina's Twelfth District, which had been redrawn in 1997, was again challenged in court as unconstitutional, and a lower court agreed. When the case reached the Supreme Court, however, the justices concluded that there was insufficient evidence that race had been the dominant factor in redrawing the district's boundaries.[8]

Elbridge Gerry, governor of Massachusetts, 1810–1812.

LIBRARY OF CONGRESS

"one person, one vote" rule A rule, or principle, requiring that congressional districts have equal populations so that one person's vote counts as much as another's vote.

gerrymandering The drawing of a legislative district's boundaries in such a way as to maximize the influence of a certain group or political party.

minority-majority district A district in which minority groups make up a majority of the population.

Figure 11–2

The First "Gerrymander"

Prior to the 1812 elections, the Massachusetts legislature divided up Essex County in a way that favored Governor Elbridge Gerry's party. The result was a district that looked something like a salamander. A newspaper editor of the time referred to it as a "gerrymander," and the name stuck.

Source: *Congressional Quarterly's Guide to Congress*, 3d ed. (Washington, D.C.: Congressional Quarterly Press, 1982), p. 695.

"When a man assumes a public trust, he should consider himself a **PUBLIC PROPERTY.**"

~ THOMAS JEFFERSON ~
THIRD PRESIDENT OF
THE UNITED STATES
1801–1809

The Representation Function of Congress

Of the three branches of government, Congress has the closest ties to the American people. Members of Congress represent the interests and wishes of the constituents in their home states. At the same time, they must also consider larger national issues such as the economy and the environment. Often, legislators find that the interests of their constituents are at odds with the demands of national policy.

For example, limits on emissions of carbon dioxide might help reduce global warming, to the benefit of all Americans and the people of the world generally. Yet members of Congress who come from states where most electricity comes from coal-burning power plants might fear that new laws would hurt the local economy and cause companies to lay off workers. All members of Congress face difficult votes that set representational interests against lawmaking realities. There are several views on how legislators should decide such issues.

THE TRUSTEE VIEW OF REPRESENTATION Some believe that representatives should act as **trustees** of the broad interests of the entire society rather than serving only the narrow interests of their constituents. Under the trustee view, a legislator should act according to her or his conscience and perception of national needs. For example, a senator from North Carolina might support laws regulating the tobacco industry even though the state's economy could be negatively affected.

THE INSTRUCTED-DELEGATE VIEW OF REPRESENTATION In contrast, others believe that members of Congress should behave as **instructed delegates.** The instructed-delegate view requires representatives to mirror the views of their constituents, regardless of their opinions. Under this view, a senator from Nebraska would strive to obtain subsidies for corn growers, and a representative from the Detroit area would seek to protect the automobile industry.

THE PARTISAN VIEW OF REPRESENTATION Because the political parties often take different positions on legislative issues, there are times when members of Congress are very attentive to the wishes of the party leadership. Especially on matters that are controversial, the Democratic members of Congress will be more likely to vote in favor of policies endorsed by a Democratic president, while Republicans will be more likely to oppose them.

THE POLITICO STYLE Typically, members of Congress combine these three approaches in what

> **trustee** A representative who tries to serve the broad interests of the entire society and not just the narrow interests of his or her constituents.
>
> **instructed delegate** A representative who deliberately mirrors the views of the majority of his or her constituents.

These female members of the House of Representatives wave to the delegates at the Democratic National Convention in Denver in 2008. While women have made serious inroads into the halls of political power, they are still underrepresented relative to their 51 percent share of our population.

is often called the "politico" style. Legislators may take a trustee approach on some issues, adhere to the instructed-delegate view on other matters, and follow the party line on still others.

LO2 *Congressional Elections*

The U.S. Constitution requires that representatives to Congress be elected every second year by popular vote. Senators are elected every six years, also by popular vote (since the ratification of the Seventeenth Amendment). Under Article I, Section 4, of the Constitution, state legislatures control the "Times, Places and Manner of holding Elections for Senators and Representatives." Congress, however, "may at any time by Law make or alter such Regulations." As you read in Chapter 9, control over the process of nominating congressional candidates has largely shifted from party conventions to direct primaries in which the party's supporters select the candidates who will carry that party's endorsement into the general election.

Who Can Be a Member of Congress?

The Constitution sets forth only a few qualifications that those running for Congress must meet. To be a member of the House, a person must have been a citizen of the United States for at least seven years prior to his or her election, must be a legal resident of the state from which he or she is to be elected, and must be at least twenty-five years of age. To be elected to the Senate, a person must have been a citizen for at least nine years, must be a legal resident of the state from which she or he is to be elected, and must be at least thirty years of age. The Supreme Court has ruled that neither the Congress nor the states can add to these three qualifications.[9]

Once elected to Congress, a senator or representative receives an annual salary from the government, $174,000 for rank-and-file members as of 2010. He or she also enjoys certain perks and privileges. Additionally, if a member of Congress wants to run for reelection in the next congressional elections, that person's chances are greatly enhanced by the power that incumbency brings to a reelection campaign.

The Power of Incumbency

The power of incumbency has long been noted in American politics. Typically, incumbents win so often and by such large margins that some observers have claimed that our electoral system involves something similar to a hereditary entitlement. As you can see in Table 11–1 on the facing page, most incumbents in Congress are reelected if they run.

Incumbent politicians enjoy several advantages over their opponents. A key advantage is their fund-

Table 11-1

The Power of Incumbency

House	Presidential-Year Elections							Midterm Elections							
	1984	1988	1992	1996	2000	2004	2008	1982	1986	1990	1994	1998	2002	2006	2010
Number of incumbent candidates	411	409	368	384	403	404	404	393	394	406	387	402	393	405	397
Reelected	392	402	325	361	394	397	381	354	385	390	349	395	383	382	338
Percentage of total	95.4	98.3	88.3	94.0	97.8	98.3	94.3	90.1	97.7	96.0	90.2	98.3	97.5	94.3	85.1
Defeated	19	7	43	23	9	7	23	39	9	16	38	7	10	23	59
Senate															
Number of incumbent candidates	29	27	28	21	29	26	30	30	28	32	26	29	28	29	24
Reelected	26	23	23	19	23	25	26	28	21	31	24	26	24	23	20
Percentage of total	89.6	85.2	82.1	90.5	79.3	96.2	86.7	93.3	75.0	96.9	92.3	89.7	85.7	79.3	83.3
Defeated	3	4	5	2	6	1	4	2	7	1	2	3	4	6	4

Sources: Norman Ornstein, Thomas E. Mann, and Michael J. Malbin, *Vital Statistics on Congress, 2001–2002* (Washington, D.C.: The AEI Press, 2002); and authors' updates.

raising ability. Most incumbent members of Congress have a much larger network of contacts, donors, and lobbyists than their opponents. Incumbents raise, on average, twice as much in campaign funds as their challengers. Other advantages that incumbents can put to work to aid their reelection include:

- *Congressional franking privileges*—members of Congress can mail newsletters and other correspondence to their constituents at the taxpayers' expense.

- *Professional staffs*—members have large administrative staffs both in Washington, D.C., and in their home districts.

- *Lawmaking power*—members can back legislation that will benefit their states or districts, and then campaign on that legislative record in the next election.

- *Access to the media*—because they are elected officials, members have many opportunities to stage events for the press and thereby obtain free publicity.

- *Name recognition*—incumbent members are usually far better known to the voters than challengers are.

Critics argue that the advantage enjoyed by incumbents reduces the competition necessary for a healthy democracy. It also suppresses voter turnout. Voters are less likely to turn out when an incumbent candidate is virtually guaranteed reelection. The solution often proposed to eliminate the power of incumbency is term limits, a topic we discuss shortly.

Congressional Terms and Term Limits

As noted earlier, members of the House of Representatives serve two-year terms, and senators serve six-year terms. This means that every two years, we hold congressional elections: the entire House of Representatives and a third of the Senate are up for election. In January of every odd-numbered year, a "new" Congress convenes (of course, two-thirds of the senators are not new, and most House incumbents are reelected, so they are not new to Congress either). Each Congress has been numbered consecutively, dating back to 1789. The Congress that convened in 2011 is the 112th.

Each congressional term is divided into two regular sessions, or meetings—one for each year. Until about 1940, Congress remained in session for only four or five months, but the complicated rush of legislation and increased demand for services from the public in recent years have forced Congress to remain in session through most of each year.[10] Both chambers, however, schedule short recesses, or breaks, for holidays and vacations. The president may call a *special session* during a recess, but because Congress now meets on nearly a year-round basis, such sessions are rare.

As you will read in Chapter 12, the president can serve for no more than two terms in office, due to the Twenty-second Amendment. There is no limit on the number of terms a senator or representative can serve, however. For example, Strom Thurmond (R., S.C.) served eight terms in the U.S. Senate, from 1955 until he retired, at the age of one hundred, in 2003.

When the Republicans took control of the House after the 2010 elections, former minority leader John Boehner (R., Ohio), left, was the leading candidate for Speaker of the House. Eric Cantor (R., Va.) was the leading contender for House majority leader. It was widely expected that former Speaker Nancy Pelosi (D., Calif.), right, would serve as the House minority leader.

As mentioned, some observers favor term limits for Congress. Persuading incumbent politicians to vote for term limits, however, is difficult. At the national level, the Supreme Court has ruled that state-level attempts to impose term limits on members of the U.S. House or Senate are unconstitutional.[11] Efforts to pass a constitutional amendment that would impose term limits on members of Congress have had little success.

LO3 *Congressional Leadership, the Committee System, and Bicameralism*

The Constitution provides for the presiding officers of both the House and the Senate, and each chamber has added other leadership positions as it has seen fit. Leadership and organization in both chambers are based on membership in the two major political parties. The majority party in each chamber chooses the major officers of that chamber, controls debate on the floor, selects all committee chairpersons, and has a majority on all committees.

House Leadership

The Constitution states that members of the House are to choose their Speaker and other officers but says nothing more about these positions. Today, important "other officers" include the majority and minority leaders and whips.

SPEAKER OF THE HOUSE Chief among the leaders in the House of Representatives is the **Speaker of the House.** This office is filled by a vote taken at the beginning of each congressional term. The Speaker has traditionally been a longtime member of the majority party who has risen in rank and influence through years of service in the House. The candidate for Speaker is selected by the majority-party caucus. The House as a whole then approves the selection.

As the presiding officer of the House and the leader of the majority party, the Speaker has a great deal of power. In the nineteenth century, the Speaker had even more power and was known as the "king of the congressional mountain." Speakers known by such names as "Uncle Joe Cannon" and "Czar Reed" ruled the House with almost unchallengeable power. A revolt in 1910 reduced the Speaker's powers and gave some of those powers to various committees. Today, the Speaker still has many important powers, including the following:

- The Speaker has substantial control over what bills get assigned to which committees.

Control of Congress after the Elections

Following the 2010 elections, President Obama was in a much weaker position to pursue the rest of his legislative agenda. The Republican margin in the House exceeded fifty. In the Senate, the fifty-three Democrats (this includes two Independents who caucus with the Democrats) would have difficulty attaining the sixty votes needed to end a filibuster and force through any additional legislation.

In the House, Democratic Speaker Nancy Pelosi of California had to step aside for Republican John Boehner of Ohio. Pelosi was expected to run for the post of House minority leader. All committee chairs in the House also changed, with Republicans replacing Democrats. The Senate leadership was not expected to change, however. The Democrats retained their control, and Senate majority leader Harry Reid won a close race for re-election against a Tea Party enthusiast.

Numerous observers predicted that Congress would experience legislative gridlock. Many Democratic moderates—those most willing to compromise with Republicans—lost. On the Republican side, the new Tea Party members were philosophically opposed to any compromise with the Democrats. The result was a more liberal set of Democrats and a more conservative set of Republicans, not a good formula for bipartisan consensus. In those states that now have Republican governors and Republican-dominated state legislatures, however, there should be very little gridlock.

- The Speaker may preside over the sessions of the House, recognizing or ignoring members who wish to speak.

- The Speaker votes in the event of a tie, interprets and applies House rules, rules on points of order (questions about procedures asked by members), puts questions to a vote, and interprets the outcome of most of the votes taken.

- The Speaker plays a major role in making important committee assignments, which all members desire.

- The Speaker schedules bills for action.

The Speaker may choose whether to vote on any measure. If the Speaker chooses to vote, he or she appoints a temporary presiding officer (called a Speaker *pro tempore*), who then occupies the Speaker's chair. Under the House rules, the only time the Speaker *must* vote is to break a tie. Otherwise, a tie automatically defeats a bill. The Speaker does not often vote, but by choosing to vote in some cases, the Speaker can actually cause a tie and defeat a proposal.

MAJORITY LEADER The **majority leader** of the House is elected by the caucus of majority party members to act as spokesperson for the party and to keep the party together. The majority leader's job is to help plan the party's legislative program, organize other party members to support legislation favored by the party, and make sure the chairpersons on the many committees finish work on bills that are important to the party. The House majority leader makes speeches on important bills, stating the majority party's position.

MINORITY LEADER The House **minority leader** is the leader of the minority party. Although not as powerful as the majority leader, the minority leader has similar responsibilities. The primary duty of the minority leader is to maintain solidarity within the party. The minority leader persuades influential members of the party to follow its position and organizes fellow party members in criticism of the majority party's policies and programs.

WHIPS The leadership of each party includes assistants to the majority and minority leaders known as **whips.** Whips originated in the British House of Commons, where they were named after the "whipper in," the rider who keeps the hounds together in a fox hunt. The term is applied to assistant party leaders because of the pressure

majority leader The party leader elected by the majority party in the House or in the Senate.

minority leader The party leader elected by the minority party in the House or in the Senate.

whip A member of Congress who assists the majority or minority leader in the House or in the Senate in managing the party's legislative preferences.

AP/CAROLYN KASTER

MCCONNELL.SENATE.GOV/OFFICIAL_PHOTOS.CFM

In 2006, Democratic senator Harry Reid of Nevada, left, became the Senate majority leader, and Republican senator Mitch McConnell of Kentucky became Senate minority leader. Both are expected to retain their offices when the new Senate votes on its leaders in late 2010.

by the whole Senate and is ordinarily the member of the majority party with the longest continuous term of service in the Senate. In the absence of both the president pro tem and the vice president, a temporary presiding officer is selected from the ranks of the Senate, usually a junior member of the majority party.

PARTY LEADERS The real power in the Senate is held by the majority leader, the minority leader, and their whips. The majority leader is the most powerful individual and chief spokesperson of the majority party. The majority leader directs the legislative program and party strategy. The minority leader commands the minority party's opposition to the policies of the majority party and directs the legislative strategy of the minority party.

that they place on party members to uphold the party's positions. Whips try to determine how each member is going to vote on certain issues and then advise the party leaders on the strength of party support. Whips also try to see that members are present when important votes are to be taken and that they vote with the party leadership. For example, if the Republican Party strongly supports a tax-cut bill, the Republican Party whip might meet with other Republican Party members in the House to try to persuade them to vote with the party.

Senate Leadership

The Constitution makes the vice president of the United States the president of the Senate. As presiding officer, the vice president may call on members to speak and put questions to a vote. The vice president is not an elected member of the Senate, however, and may not take part in Senate debates. The vice president may cast a vote in the Senate only in the event of a tie.

PRESIDENT PRO TEMPORE Because vice presidents are rarely available (or desire) to preside over the Senate, senators elect another presiding officer, the president pro tempore ("pro tem"), who serves in the absence of the vice president. The president pro tem is elected

standing committee
A permanent committee in Congress that deals with legislation concerning a particular area, such as agriculture or foreign relations.

Congressional Committees

Thousands of bills are introduced during every session of Congress, and no single member can possibly be adequately informed on all the issues that arise. The committee system is a way to provide for specialization, or a division of the legislative labor. Members of a committee concentrate on just one area or topic—such as agriculture or transportation—and develop sufficient expertise to draft appropriate legislation when needed. The flow of legislation through both the House and the Senate is determined largely by the speed with which the members of these committees act on bills and resolutions. The permanent and most powerful committees of Congress are called **standing committees;** their names are listed in Table 11–2 on the facing page.

Before any bill can be considered by the entire House or Senate, it must be approved by a majority vote in the standing committee to which it was assigned. As mentioned, standing committees are controlled by the majority party in each chamber. Committee membership is generally divided between the parties according to the number of members in each chamber. In both the House and the Senate, committee *seniority*—the length of continuous service on a particular committee—typically plays a role in determining the committee chairpersons.

Table 11–2

Standing Committees in the 112th Congress, 2011–2013

House Committees	Senate Committees
Agriculture	Agriculture, Nutrition, and Forestry
Appropriations	Appropriations
Armed Services	Armed Services
Budget	Banking, Housing, and Urban Affairs
Education and Labor	Budget
Energy and Commerce	Commerce, Science, and Transportation
Financial Services	Energy and Natural Resources
Foreign Affairs	Environment and Public Works
Homeland Security	Finance
House Administration	Foreign Relations
Judiciary	Health, Education, Labor, and Pensions
Natural Resources	Homeland Security and Governmental Affairs
Oversight and Government Reform	Judiciary
Rules	Rules and Administration
Science and Technology	Small Business and Entrepreneurship
Small Business	Veterans' Affairs
Standards of Official Conduct	
Transportation and Infrastructure	
Veterans' Affairs	
Ways and Means	

Most House and Senate committees also have **subcommittees** with limited areas of jurisdiction. Today, there are more than two hundred subcommittees. There are also other types of committees in Congress. Special, or select, committees, which may be either permanent or temporary, are formed to study specific problems or issues. Joint committees are created by the concurrent action of both chambers of Congress and consist of members from each chamber. Joint committees have dealt with the economy, taxation, and the Library of Congress. There are also conference committees, which include members from both the House and the Senate. They are formed for the purpose of achieving agreement between the House and the Senate on the exact wording of legislative acts when the two chambers pass legislative proposals in different forms. No bill can be sent to the White House to be signed into law unless it first passes both chambers in identical form.

Most of the actual work of legislating is performed by the committees and subcommittees (the "little legislatures"[12]) within Congress. In creating or amending laws, committee members work closely with relevant interest groups and administrative agency personnel. (For more details on the interaction among these groups, see the discussion of "issue networks" and "iron triangles" in Chapter 13.)

The Differences between the House and the Senate

To understand what goes on in the chambers of Congress, we need to look at the effects of bicameralism. Each chamber of Congress has developed certain distinct features. The major differences between the House and the Senate are listed in Table 11–3 on the following page.

SIZE MATTERS Obviously, with 435 voting members, the House cannot operate the same way as the Senate, which has only 100 members. With its larger size, the House needs both more rules and more formality—otherwise, no work would ever get done. The most obvious formal rules have to do with debate on the floor.

The Senate normally permits extended debate on all issues that arise before it. In contrast, the House uses an elaborate system: the House **Rules Committee** normally proposes time limits on debate for any bill, which are accepted or modified by the House. Despite its greater size, as a consequence of its stricter time limits on debate, the House is often able to act on legislation more quickly than the Senate.

IN THE SENATE, DEBATE CAN JUST KEEP GOING AND GOING At one time, both the House and the Senate allowed unlimited debate, but the House ended this practice in 1811. The use of unlimited debate in the Senate to obstruct legislation is called **filibustering**

subcommittee A division of a larger committee that deals with a particular part of the committee's policy area. Most standing committees have several subcommittees.

Rules Committee A standing committee in the House of Representatives that provides special rules governing how particular bills will be considered and debated by the House. The Rules Committee normally proposes time limits on debate for any bill.

filibustering The Senate tradition of unlimited debate undertaken for the purpose of preventing action on a bill.

cloture A method of ending debate in the Senate and bringing the matter under consideration to a vote by the entire chamber.

(see the chapter-opening feature). The longest filibuster was waged by Senator Strom Thurmond of South Carolina, who held forth on the Senate floor for twenty-four hours and eighteen minutes in an attempt to thwart the passage of the 1957 Civil Rights Act.

Today, under Senate Rule 22, debate may be ended by invoking **cloture**—a method of closing debate and bringing the matter under consideration to a vote in the Senate. Sixteen senators must sign a petition requesting cloture, and then, after two days have elapsed, three-fifths of the entire membership must vote for cloture. Once cloture is invoked, each senator may speak on a bill for no more than one hour before a vote is taken. Additionally, a final vote must take place within one hundred hours after cloture has been invoked.

THE SENATE WINS THE PRESTIGE RACE, HANDS DOWN Because of the large number of representatives, few can garner the prestige that a senator enjoys. Senators have relatively little difficulty in gaining access to the media. Members of the House, who run for reelection every two years, have to survive many reelection campaigns before they can obtain recognition for their activities. Usually, a representative has to become an important committee leader before she or he can enjoy the consistent attention of the national news media.

LO4 *The Legislative Process*

Look at Figure 11–3 on the facing page, which shows the basic process through which a bill becomes law at the national level. Not all of the complexities of the process are shown, to be sure. For example, the figure does not indicate the extensive lobbying and media politics that are often involved in the legislative process. There is also no mention of the informal negotiations and "horse trading" that occur to get a bill passed. Few types of legislation are more contentious than those that set tax rates, as you can see in this chapter's *Our Government Faces a Troubled Economy* feature on page 244.

Table 11–3

Major Differences between the House and the Senate

House*	Senate*
Members chosen from local districts	Members chosen from entire state
Two-year term	Six-year term
Always elected by voters	Originally (until 1913) elected by state legislatures
May impeach (accuse, indict) federal officials	May convict federal officials of impeachable offenses
Larger (435 voting members)	Smaller (100 members)
More formal rules	Fewer rules and restrictions
Debate limited	Debate extended
Floor action controlled	Unanimous consent rules
Less prestige and less individual notice	More prestige and media attention
Originates bills for raising revenues	Power of "advice and consent" on presidential appointments and treaties
Local or narrow leadership	National leadership

*Some of these differences, such as term of office, are provided for in the Constitution, while others, such as debate rules, are not.

The basic steps in the process are as follows:

1. *Introduction of legislation.* Most bills are proposed by the executive branch, although individual members of Congress or their staffs can come up with ideas for new legislation—so, too, can private citizens or lobbying groups. Only a member of Congress can formally introduce legislation, however. In reality, many bills are proposed, developed, and often written by the White House or an executive agency. Then

Senators Richard Burr of North Carolina, left, and John Thune of South Dakota talk as they leave a Senate Republican lunch in the Mansfield Room of the Capitol.

BILL CLARK/ROLL CALL/GETTY IMAGES

Figure 11-3

How a Bill Becomes a Law

This illustration shows the most typical way in which proposed legislation is enacted into law. The process is illustrated with two hypothetical bills, House bill No. 100 (HR 100) and Senate bill No. 200 (S 200). Bills must be passed by both chambers in identical form before they can be sent to the president. The path of HR 100 is traced by an orange line, and that of S 200 by a purple line. In practice, most bills begin as similar proposals in both chambers.

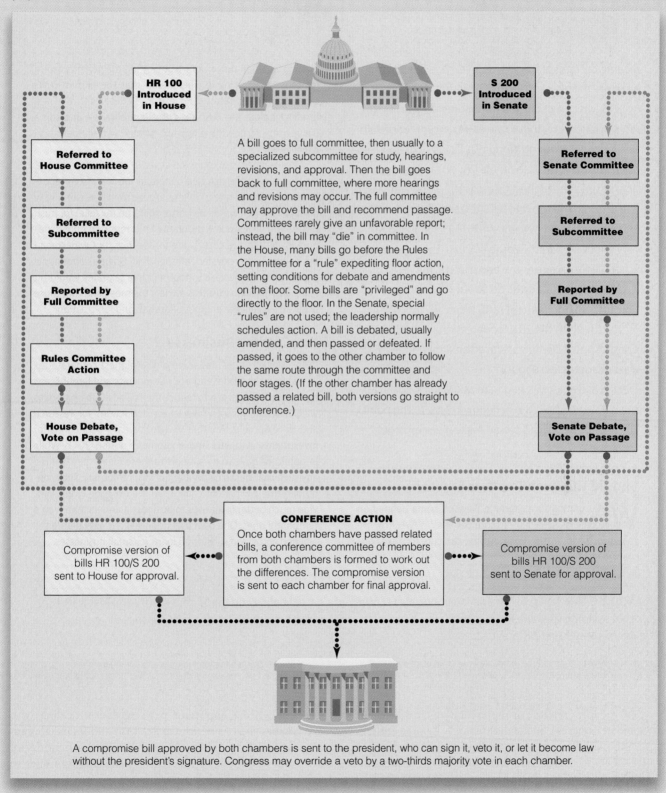

HR 100 Introduced in House

Referred to House Committee

Referred to Subcommittee

Reported by Full Committee

Rules Committee Action

House Debate, Vote on Passage

S 200 Introduced in Senate

Referred to Senate Committee

Referred to Subcommittee

Reported by Full Committee

Senate Debate, Vote on Passage

A bill goes to full committee, then usually to a specialized subcommittee for study, hearings, revisions, and approval. Then the bill goes back to full committee, where more hearings and revisions may occur. The full committee may approve the bill and recommend passage. Committees rarely give an unfavorable report; instead, the bill may "die" in committee. In the House, many bills go before the Rules Committee for a "rule" expediting floor action, setting conditions for debate and amendments on the floor. Some bills are "privileged" and go directly to the floor. In the Senate, special "rules" are not used; the leadership normally schedules action. A bill is debated, usually amended, and then passed or defeated. If passed, it goes to the other chamber to follow the same route through the committee and floor stages. (If the other chamber has already passed a related bill, both versions go straight to conference.)

Compromise version of bills HR 100/S 200 sent to House for approval.

CONFERENCE ACTION
Once both chambers have passed related bills, a conference committee of members from both chambers is formed to work out the differences. The compromise version is sent to each chamber for final approval.

Compromise version of bills HR 100/S 200 sent to Senate for approval.

A compromise bill approved by both chambers is sent to the president, who can sign it, veto it, or let it become law without the president's signature. Congress may override a veto by a two-thirds majority vote in each chamber.

OUR GOVERNMENT FACES A TROUBLED ECONOMY

Should We Cut Taxes— and If So, How?

Income tax rates at the federal level have been as low as zero—that was before the Sixteenth Amendment in 1913, which established the income tax. Income tax rates reached a marginal rate of 94 percent for certain rich individuals during World War II (1941–1945). (The *marginal rate* is the rate on the last dollar reported on a return.) The highest rate was still 91 percent as late as 1963. The top rate fell substantially thereafter, and it has been 35 percent since 2003, following tax cuts under President George W. Bush. Those cuts were scheduled to expire at the end of 2010, however.

What would Congress do about the expiring tax cuts? Unemployment rates were still very high in the run-up to the 2010 congressional elections. Congressional Democrats faced an angry public and a set of aggressive Republican candidates in the elections. Democrats began to ask, What kinds of tax policies would help the economy? More to the point, What kinds of policies would make it easier to get reelected?

Should the Bush Tax Cuts Expire?

While running for president, Barack Obama defined an income of $250,000 or more per year as "wealthy." He called for keeping the Bush income tax cuts for taxpayers making less than that amount, but letting the benefits expire for those making more. This meant that the highest marginal income tax rate would rise to 39.6 percent, the rate in effect before the Bush tax cuts. Republicans—and some Democrats—argued that any tax increase was dangerous in a recession.

Obama stuck to his guns, however. In speech after speech, he argued that the rich had benefited too long from reductions in their tax rates. Obama argued that the sums now going to the rich would be better spent on tax relief for businesses and on spending programs. Polls reported public support for letting the cuts expire for the rich, but widespread opposition to any new federal spending. Obama's opponents argued that an increase in top marginal tax rates would hit small and medium business owners the most, and that those businesses were the engines of growth and job creation.

Tax Cuts for Businesses?

The United States has some of the highest corporate tax rates in the world, and both Democrats and Republicans have talked about ways to reduce them. One of Obama's ideas was to let businesses take larger deductions for research and development. Another was to increase deductions for investments in plants and equipment during 2011. While Republicans gave some support to these ideas, they wanted any such changes to be permanent, not temporary. They contended that permanent changes in the tax code would provide much better incentives to business planners than would temporary ones. One plan that Congress did pass before the elections provided subsidized loans for small businesses.

You Be the Judge The administration also considered a partial holiday on the Social Security and Medicare taxes paid by employees and employers. Obama rejected this idea as too radical. Why might such a plan receive support from both conservatives and liberals?

a "friendly" senator or representative introduces the bill in Congress. Such bills are rarely ignored entirely, although they are often amended or defeated.

To a degree not seen for some decades, the Obama administration has let Congress take the lead on writing important new legislation dealing with issues such as health-care reform and financial regulation. Even under Obama, however, a majority of the legislation considered by Congress continues to come from the executive branch.

2. **Referral to committees.** As soon as a bill is introduced and assigned a number, it is sent to the appropriate standing committee. In the House, the Speaker assigns the bill to the appropriate committee. In the Senate, the presiding officer assigns the bill to the proper committee. For example, a farm bill in the House would be sent to the Agriculture Committee and a gun control bill would be sent to the Judiciary Committee. A committee chairperson will typically send the bill on to a subcommittee. For example, a Senate bill concerning additional involvement in NATO (the North Atlantic Treaty Organization) in Europe would be sent to the Senate Foreign Relations Subcommittee on European Affairs. Alternatively, the chairperson may decide to put the bill aside and ignore it. Most bills that are pigeonholed in this manner receive no further action.

If a bill is not pigeonholed, committee staff members go to work researching the bill. The committee may hold public hearings during which people who support or oppose the bill can express their views. Committees also have the power to order witnesses to testify at public hearings. Witnesses may be executive agency officials, experts on the subject, or representatives of interest groups concerned about the bill.

The subcommittee must meet to approve the bill as it is, add new amendments, or draft a new bill. This meeting is known as the **markup session.** If members cannot agree on changes, a vote is taken. When a subcommittee completes its work, the bill goes to the full standing committee, which then meets for its own markup session. The committee may hold its own hearings, amend the subcommittee's version, or simply approve the subcommittee's recommendations.

3. **Reports on a bill.** Finally, the committee will report the bill back to the full chamber. It can report the bill favorably, report the bill with amendments, or report a newly written bill. It can also report a bill unfavorably, but usually such a bill will have been pigeonholed earlier instead. Along with the bill, the committee will send to the House or Senate a written report that explains the committee's actions, describes the bill, lists the major changes made by the committee, and gives opinions on the bill.

4. **The Rules Committee and scheduling.** Scheduling is an extremely important part of getting a bill enacted

Senator Max Baucus (D., Mont.) on the left discusses pending legislation with Senator Bill Nelson (D., Fla.) during a Finance committee hearing on health-care reform in the fall of 2009. At the same moment, other committees in the House and the Senate were creating their own versions of that legislation.

into law. A bill must be put on a calendar. Typically, in the House the Rules Committee plays a major role in the scheduling process. This committee, along with the House leaders, regulates the flow of the bills through the House. The Rules Committee will also specify the amount of time to be spent on debate and whether amendments can be made by a floor vote.

In the Senate, a few leading members control the flow of bills. The Senate brings a bill to the floor by "unanimous consent," a motion by which all members present on the floor set aside the formal Senate rules and consider a bill. In contrast to the procedure in the House, individual senators have the power to disrupt work on legislation.

5. **Floor debate.** Because of its large size, the House imposes severe limits on floor debate. The Speaker recognizes those who may speak and can force any member who does not "stick to the subject" to give up the floor. Normally, the chairperson of the standing committee reporting the bill will take charge of the session during which it is debated. You can often watch such debates on C-SPAN.

Only on rare occasions does a floor debate change

markup session A meeting held by a congressional committee or subcommittee to approve, amend, or redraft a bill.

anybody's mind. The written record of the floor debate completes the legislative history of the proposed bill in the event that the courts have to interpret it later on. Floor debates also give the full House or Senate the opportunity to consider amendments to the original version of the bill.

6. *Vote.* In both the House and the Senate, the members present generally vote for or against the bill. There are several methods of voting, including voice votes, standing votes, and recorded votes (also called roll-call votes). Since 1973, the House has had electronic voting. The Senate does not have such a system, however.

7. *Conference committee.* To become a law, a bill must be passed in identical form by both chambers. When the two chambers pass differing versions of the same bill, the measure is turned over to a special committee called a **conference committee**—a temporary committee with members from the two chambers, as mentioned earlier.

Most members of the committee are drawn from the standing committees that handled the bill in both chambers. In theory, the conference committee can consider only those points in a bill on which the two chambers disagree. No proposals are supposed to be added. In reality, however, the conference committee sometimes makes important changes in the bill or adds new provisions.

Once the conference committee members agree on the final compromise bill, a **conference report** is submitted to each chamber.

conference committee
A temporary committee that is formed when the two chambers of Congress pass differing versions of the same bill. The conference committee, which consists of members from both the House and the Senate, works out a compromise form of the bill.

conference report A report submitted by a congressional conference committee after it has drafted a single version of a bill.

pocket veto A special type of veto power used by the chief executive after the legislature has adjourned. Bills that are not signed die after a specified period of time.

The bill must be accepted or rejected by both chambers as it was written by the committee, with no further amendments made. If the bill is approved by both chambers, it is ready for action by the president.

8. *Presidential action.* All bills passed by Congress have to be submitted to the president for approval. The president has ten days to decide whether to sign the bill or veto it. If the president does nothing, the bill goes into effect unless Congress has adjourned before the ten-day period expires. In that case, the bill dies in what is called a **pocket veto.**

9. *Overriding a veto.* If the president decides to veto a bill, Congress can still get the bill enacted into law. With a two-thirds majority vote in both chambers, Congress can override the president's veto.

LO5 *Investigation and Oversight*

Steps 8 and 9 of the legislative process described above illustrate the integral role that the executive and the legislative branches play in making laws. The relationship between Congress and the president is at the core of our system of government, although, to be sure, the judicial branch plays a vital role as well (see Chapter 14).

One of the most important functions of Congress is its oversight (supervision) of the executive branch and its many federal departments and agencies. The executive bureaucracy, which includes the president's cabinet departments, wields tremendous power, as you will read in Chapters 12 and 13. Congress can rein in that power by choosing not to provide the money necessary for the bureaucracy to function (the budgeting process will be discussed later in this chapter).

The Investigative Function

Congress also has the authority to investigate the actions of the executive branch, the need for certain legislation, and even the actions of its own members. The Congressional Research Service and the Congressional Budget Office, for example, provide members of Congress with vital information about policies and economic projections. The numerous congressional committees and subcommittees regularly hold hearings to investigate the actions of the executive branch. Congressional committees receive opinions, reports, and assessments on a broad range of issues. A widely held belief is that

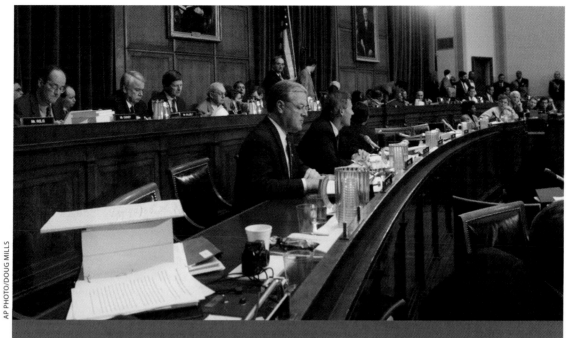
In 1998, for only the third time in history, the House Judiciary Committee debated impeachment articles to oust a president. Republicans and Democrats bitterly clashed over articles accusing President Clinton of perjury, obstruction of justice, and abuse of power.

between 2001 and 2007, when Republicans controlled both the two chambers of Congress and the presidency, Congress neglected its oversight function out of deference to President Bush. Some believe that Congress also neglected its oversight function from 2009 to 2011, when the Democrats controlled both chambers of Congress and the presidency. Can oversight also become excessive? We look at this issue in this chapter's *Perception versus Reality* feature on the following page.

Impeachment Power

Congress has the power to impeach and remove from office the president, vice president, and other "civil officers," such as federal judges. To *impeach* means to accuse a public official of, or charge him or her with, improper conduct in office. The House of Representatives is vested with this power and has exercised it twice against a president—the House voted to impeach Andrew Johnson in 1868 and Bill Clinton in 1998. After a vote to impeach in the full House, the president is then tried in the

"LAWS ARE LIKE SAUSAGES.

It is better if the public does not see how they are made."

~ JOHN GODFREY SAXE ~
AMERICAN POET 1869;
MISATTRIBUTED TO OTTO VON BISMARCK,
CHANCELLOR OF GERMANY
1871–1890

Senate. If convicted by a two-thirds vote, the president is removed from office. Both Johnson and Clinton were acquitted by the Senate. A vote to impeach President Richard Nixon was pending before the full House of Representatives in 1974 when Nixon chose to resign. Nixon is the only president ever to resign from office.

Congress, as mentioned, can also take action to remove other officials. For example, the House of Representatives voted to impeach Judge Alcee Hastings in 1988, and the Senate removed him from the bench (he was later elected to the House in 1992). Only one United States Supreme Court justice has ever been impeached. The House impeached Samuel Chase in 1804, although he was later acquitted by the Senate.

Senate Confirmation

Article II, Section 2, of the Constitution states that the president may appoint ambassadors, justices of the Supreme Court, and other officers of the United

Our political system relies on checks and balances. One of the checks on the executive branch is congressional oversight. This refers to the supervision and monitoring of federal programs, agencies, and activities, as well as of policy implementation by the executive branch. Congress has dozens of committees through which it carries out its oversight function. These committees and subcommittees routinely hold hearings on various issues that involve the executive branch. While nothing in the U.S. Constitution explicitly gives Congress oversight authority, Congress has taken on this duty as one of its implied powers.

The Perception

While few Americans doubt the value of congressional oversight of the executive branch, many believe that Congress engages in too little of it. Certainly, until 2007, Congress seemed to have "rubber-stamped" the Bush administration's agenda. Americans got the impression that the executive branch was out of control from 2001 until the Democrats took control of Congress in 2007. From 2009, when a Democratic president was matched up with a Democratic Congress, many people believed that Congress went back to sleep.

The Reality

The biggest oversight problem faced by Congress since 2009 has been evaluating the impact of the enormous spending measures advanced by the new administration. Certainly, the Democratic majority had a political interest in putting the best face possible on the Obama administration's proposals.

One way in which Congress has "kept itself honest" is by establishing oversight bodies separate from—but responsible to—Congress. These include the Congressional Budget Office (CBO), which evaluates the impact of proposed legislation on the federal budget and the budget deficit. The CBO was much in the news in 2009 due to its "scoring" of the various health-care reform proposals considered by the House and Senate. Members of Congress found themselves tailoring the measures to earn a better score from the CBO.

It is also true that some parts of the executive branch have had so much oversight that they cannot run efficiently. Consider the Department of Homeland Security, which was created by combining more than twenty separate agencies. Each of those agencies had roughly four committees and subcommittees overseeing them. When those agencies were consolidated into one executive department, there was no parallel consolidation of the congressional oversight system. Consequently, about eighty committees and subcommittees now oversee Homeland Security. (Compare this with the Department of Defense, which deals with only four committees on a regular basis.) In a typical year, officials in the Department of Homeland Security must testify in over two hundred congressional hearings. They must also provide more than 2,500 briefings to legislators and their staffs. Much of this time could be used to devise more efficient agency policies.

Blog On Virginia L. Thomas, a conservative, calls for strong oversight of the Internal Revenue Service at **www.heritage.org/press/commentary/ed042899.cfm**. For a left-leaning argument in favor of oversight, see Chuck Collins at **www.thenation.com/blogs/congress2/154082**.

States "with the Advice and Consent of the Senate." The Constitution leaves the precise nature of how the Senate will give this "advice and consent" up to the lawmakers. In practice, the Senate confirms the president's nominees for the Supreme Court, other federal judgeships, and members of the president's cabinet. Nominees appear first before the appropriate Senate committee—the Judiciary Committee for federal judges or the Foreign Relations Committee for the secretary of state, for example. If the individual committee approves the nominee, the full Senate will vote on the nomination.

As you will read further in Chapters 12 and 14, Senate confirmation hearings have been very politicized at times. Judicial appointments often receive the most intense scrutiny by the Senate, because the judges

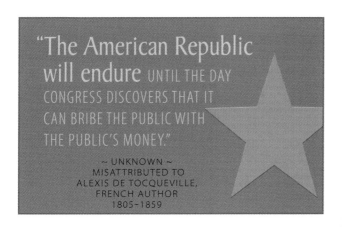

serve on the bench for life. The president has a somewhat freer hand with cabinet appointments, because the heads of executive departments are expected to be loyal to the president. Nonetheless, Senate confirmation remains an important check on the president's power. We will discuss the relationship between Congress and the president in more detail in Chapter 12.

LO6 *The Budgeting Process*

The Constitution makes it very clear that Congress has the power of the purse. Only Congress can impose taxes, and only Congress can authorize expenditures. To be sure, the president submits a budget, but all final decisions are up to Congress.

The congressional budget is, of course, one of the most important determinants of what policies will or will not be implemented. For example, the president might order executive agencies under presidential control to undertake specific programs, but these orders are meaningless if there is no money to pay for their execution. It is Congress that has the power of the "purse strings," and this power is significant. Congress can nullify a president's ambitious program by simply refusing to allocate the necessary money to executive agencies to implement it.

Authorization and Appropriation

The budgeting process is a two-part procedure. **Authorization** is the first part. It involves the creation of the legal basis for government programs. In this phase, Congress passes authorization bills outlining the rules governing the expenditure of funds. Limits may be placed on how much money can be spent and for what period of time.

Appropriation is the second part of the budgeting process. In this phase, Congress determines how many dollars will actually be spent in a given year on a particular set of government activities. Appropriations must never exceed the authorized amounts, but they can be less.

Many **entitlement programs** operate under open-ended authorizations that, in effect, place no limits on how much can be spent. The government is obligated to provide benefits, such as Social Security benefits, veterans' benefits, and the like, to persons who qualify under entitlement laws. The remaining federal programs fall under discretionary spending and can be altered at will by Congress. National defense is the most important item in the discretionary-spending part of the budget. Discretionary spending also includes earmarks, or pork, as described in this chapter's feature *Join the Debate: Should "Earmarks" Be Banned?* on the following page.

authorization A part of the congressional budgeting process that involves the creation of the legal basis for government programs.

appropriation A part of the congressional budgeting process that involves determining how many dollars will be spent in a given year on a particular set of government activities.

entitlement program A government program (such as Social Security) that allows, or entitles, a certain class of people (such as elderly persons) to receive benefits. Entitlement programs operate under open-ended budget authorizations that, in effect, place no limits on how much can be spent.

U.S. Treasury secretary Timothy Geithner testifies during a hearing before the Senate Banking Committee. Geithner testified on international economic and exchange rate policies.

ALEX WONG/GETTY IMAGES

Should "Earmarks" Be Banned?

In recent years, Congress has voted to fund a "bridge to nowhere" in Alaska, a program to combat wild hogs in Missouri, and payment of storage fees for Georgia peanut farmers, among many other special projects. Every year, virtually every bill coming out of Congress includes "earmarked funds" for special projects that are important to individual legislators. This special interest spending is impolitely called *pork-barrel* spending. The term *pork* comes from the idea that members of Congress "bring home the bacon" to their home states, usually in the form of additional federal spending that benefits local businesses and workers. In 2009, earmarks cost taxpayers $16.5 billion. The total for 2010 was estimated to be $11 billion. Should earmarks be banned altogether?

We Must End the Pork

Yes, argue most Americans, it is time to end this unsightly "feeding frenzy" in Congress. Earmarks took off in Congress in the 1990s and rose astronomically thereafter. The bridge to nowhere in Alaska mentioned earlier would have cost more than $200 million. This would have been an obscene use of taxpayers' dollars. (The bridge project was eventually killed.) If pork were banned, legislators would no longer be able to "bribe" other legislators with such requests. In other words, so-called *logrolling* would be much more difficult without earmarks.

Not So Fast

Those in favor of keeping earmarks point out that every member of Congress has constituents who benefit from earmarked funds. Banning earmarks would reduce the value of members of Congress to their constituents and thereby weaken the ties between elected officials and their constituents. Also, without congressional earmarks, Congress would have to accept the decisions of the executive branch as to how each agency or program should allocate its funds among projects. Why should the president and the bureaucracy be the only ones allowed to identify worthy projects?

A less dramatic alternative is to provide for greater disclosure. In the past, the general public often never learned which member of Congress demanded any particular piece of pork. In 2007, Congress changed the rules to require the disclosure of lawmakers' earmark requests. It turns out, however, that many members are quite proud of their pork and want their constituents to know all about it.

For Critical Analysis *Given that pork-barrel spending actually amounts to only a small percentage of the federal government's budget, why are these earmarks so controversial?*

AP PHOTO/HALL ANDERSON/KETCHIKAN DAILY NEWS

The Actual Budgeting Process

fiscal year A twelve-month period that is established for bookkeeping or accounting purposes. The government's fiscal year runs from October 1 through September 30.

Look at Figure 11–4 on the facing page, which outlines the lengthy budgeting process. The process runs from January, when the president submits a proposed federal budget for the next **fiscal year,** to the start of that fiscal year on October 1. In actuality, about eighteen months prior to October 1, the executive agencies submit their requests to the Office of Management and Budget (OMB), and the OMB outlines a proposed budget. If the president approves it, the budget is officially submitted to Congress.

Figure 11–4

The Budgeting Process

The legislative budgeting process begins eight to nine months before the start of the fiscal year. The **first budget resolution** is supposed to be passed in May. It sets overall revenue goals and spending targets and, by definition, the size of the federal budget deficit or surplus. The **second budget resolution,** which sets "binding" limits on taxes and spending, is supposed to be passed in September, before the beginning of the fiscal year on October 1. Whenever Congress is unable to pass a complete budget by October 1, it passes **continuing resolutions,** which enable the executive agencies to keep on doing whatever they were doing the previous year with the same amount of funding. Even continuing resolutions have not always been passed on time.

The budget process involves making predictions about the state of the U.S. economy for years to come. This process is necessarily very imprecise. Since 1996, both Congress and the president

have attempted to make ten-year projections for income (from taxes) and spending, but no one can really know what the financial picture of the United States will look like in ten years. The workforce could grow or shrink, which would drastically alter government revenue from taxes. Any

"WE THE PEOPLE are the rightful masters of both Congress and the courts."

~ ABRAHAM LINCOLN ~
SIXTEENTH PRESIDENT
OF THE UNITED STATES
1861–1865

first budget resolution A budget resolution, which is supposed to be passed in May, that sets overall revenue goals and spending targets for the next fiscal year, which begins on October 1.

second budget resolution A budget resolution, which is supposed to be passed in September, that sets "binding" limits on taxes and spending for the next fiscal year.

continuing resolution A temporary resolution passed by Congress when an appropriations bill has not been passed by the beginning of the new fiscal year.

number of emergencies could arise that would require increased government spending—from going to war against terrorists to inoculating federal employees against smallpox.

In any event, when you read about what the administration predicts the budget deficit (or surplus) will be in five or ten years, take such predictions with a grain of salt. There has never been such a long-term prediction that has come close to being accurate. Moreover, most times, the longest-term predictions made by administrations will depend on decisions made when *another* administration is in office later on.

AMERICA AT ODDS | *Congress*

The founders thought that Congress would be the branch of government that was closest to the people. Yet Congress is one of the least popular institutions in America. It seems that anything that Congress does annoys a substantial share of the electorate. Needless to say, Americans are at odds over Congress on a variety of issues:

- Is the Senate's filibuster rule a legitimate safeguard of minority rights—or a disastrous handicap on Congress's ability to address the nation's problems?

- Is political gerrymandering just a normal part of the political game—or does it deprive voters of their rights?

- Does racial gerrymandering allow the voices of minority groups to be heard—or is it an unconstitutional violation of the equal protection clause?

- When voting on legislation, should members of Congress faithfully represent the views of their constituents—or should they stay true to their own beliefs about what is good for the nation?

- Should legislative earmarks, or "pork," be banned as a waste of taxpayers' resources—or is it appropriate for members of Congress to support specific projects in their own districts?

Take Action

During each session of Congress, your senators and your representative in the House debate the pros and cons of proposed laws, some of which may affect your daily life or the lives of those you care about. If you want to let your voice be heard, you can do so simply by phoning or e-mailing your senators or your representative. You can learn the names and contact information for the senators and the representative from your area by going to the Web sites of the Senate and the House, which are given in this chapter's *Politics on the Web* feature. Your chances of influencing your members of Congress will be greater if you can convince others, including your friends and family members, to do likewise. Citizens often feel that such efforts are useless. Yet members of Congress *do* listen to their constituents and often *do* act in response to their constituents' wishes. Indeed, next to voting, contacting those who represent you in Congress is probably the most effective way to influence government decision making.

KAYTE M. DEIOMA/PHOTOEDIT

Contacting U.S. representatives and senators is much easier today using the Internet. Next to voting, the most effective ways to influence decision making in Washington, D.C., are phoning, writing to, or e-mailing members of Congress.

POLITICS ON THE
WEB

- There is an abundance of online information about Congress and congressional activities. The THOMAS site (named for Thomas Jefferson), maintained by the Library of Congress, provides a record of all bills introduced into Congress, information about each member of Congress and how he or she voted on specific bills, and other data. Go to **thomas.loc.gov**

- The U.S. Government Printing Office (GPO) Access on the Web offers information on the Congress in session, bills pending and passed, and a history of the bills at **www.gpoaccess.gov**

- To learn more about how a bill becomes a law, go to **www.vote-smart.org**

    Click on "Political Resources" and scroll down to "Vote Smart Classroom." Select "An Introduction to

the U.S. Government," and then choose "How a Bill Becomes Law."

- You can find e-mail addresses and home pages for members of the House of Representatives at **www.house.gov**

- For e-mail addresses and home pages for members of the Senate, go to **www.senate.gov**

- To have your local congressional representative's votes e-mailed to you every week, to post letters online and read what others are saying about elected officials, or to create and post a "soapbox action alert" to get others on your side of an issue, explore your options at **www.congress.org**

CourseMate

Access CourseMate to review and expand on this chapter through quizzes, flashcards, learning objectives, interactive timelines, a crossword puzzle, audio summaries, video, critical-thinking activities, simulations, and more.

GOVT
12
The Presidency

LEARNING OBJECTIVES

LO1 List the constitutional requirements for becoming president.

LO2 Explain the roles that a president adopts while in office.

LO3 Indicate the scope of presidential powers.

LO4 Describe advantages enjoyed by Congress and by the president in their institutional relationship.

LO5 Discuss the organization of the executive branch and the role of cabinet members in presidential administrations.

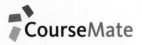

AMERICA AT
ODDS

Just How Effective Is President Obama?

During the 2008 presidential campaign, Barack Obama clearly stood to the political left of his Republican opponent, John McCain. Nonetheless, one of Obama's messages was that of uniting this country and avoiding the divisive partisanship that had marked the years of George W. Bush's presidency. Some observers thought that Obama truly did envision a new bipartisan spirit in Washington.

When in office, however, Obama rolled out sweeping domestic policy initiatives, including a giant stimulus bill, an automobile industry bailout, and a huge reform of the health-care system. These programs convinced conservatives that Obama was the most left-wing president in memory, and Obama was able to win almost no Republican votes for his legislation. The administration made compromises—but principally with the most conservative Democrats, not with Republicans. Given these compromises, plus unified Republican opposition, how effective was Obama in carrying out his agenda?

Obama Has Compromised His Progressive Agenda

Liberals soon came to believe that Obama was making too many compromises. For one example, as a candidate Obama promised to close the prison at Guantánamo Bay Naval Base. Two years later, the prison was still in business. Obama also upheld the Bush policy of detaining some prisoners indefinitely without trial.

Health-care reform was the biggest issue of Obama's first two years in office, and progressives grew alarmed at the compromises that the president was willing to make on this issue. Liberals believed that the so-called public option—a government-run health insurance company that would compete with private insurance companies—was key to the reforms. Obama endorsed the public option, but it was not included in the final legislation. True, Republicans opposed the health-care reforms, but the measures that passed actually bore a strong resemblance to plans that many Republicans had supported in earlier years. How progressive was that? Dramatic reform to the nation's energy industry was another key part of Obama's agenda. It died in the Senate. Immigration reform is yet another issue that went nowhere.

Obama's stand on gay rights also disturbed liberals. During his campaign, Obama called for the repeal of the "don't ask, don't tell" policy that prevented lesbians and gay men from serving openly in the armed forces. Unlike closing the Guantánamo prison, this measure enjoyed strong public support. The courts wound up addressing "don't ask, don't tell" before the administration took any actions to repeal it.

Obama's Changes Are Fundamental—and Dangerous

Conservatives paid little attention to liberal criticism of Obama's compromises. They firmly believed that he was indeed the most liberal president we have ever had. Ominously, he was also one of the most successful. Congress passed 96.7 percent of all legislation requested by the president, an all-time record (see page 268). Conservatives argued that Obama wanted to fundamentally change the American social compact. Mainstream conservatives believed that Obama envisioned the kind of social democratic institutions we see in Western Europe. Radical conservatives went so far as to accuse Obama of seeking some kind of dictatorship.

Consider legislative specifics. In the past, stimulus measures had consisted entirely of tax cuts, but the greater share of Obama's stimulus bill was made up of spending programs. This was a sure-fire way of running up the size of the federal government. Obama was willing to make the government (that is, the taxpayers) the owner of banks, insurance companies, and automobile companies. If government ownership of private companies isn't left-wing, then what is?

Conservatives argued that Obama's version of health-care reform was no more than a road to the complete federal takeover of medical care. Yet Obama was able to win the reforms even after the Democrats lost their sixtieth vote in the Senate. That should put to rest any arguments that Obama was somehow ineffective.

WHERE DO YOU STAND?

1. Has Obama made so many compromises with his original progressive agenda that he could be called a moderate?
2. How effective can Obama be during the second half of his term, given the results of the 2010 elections?

EXPLORE THIS ISSUE ONLINE

- Dozens of progressive bloggers are prepared to take Obama to task for compromises on health care and other issues. We can name only a few—**www.talkingpointsmemo.com**, **www.dailykos.com**, and **www.democracyforamerica.com**.
- A vast number of conservative sites vehemently oppose Obama's programs. Examples include **www.americanthinker.com**, **www.clubforgrowth.org**, and **www.cwfa.org** (Concerned Women for America).

Introduction

President Lyndon B. Johnson (1963–1969) stated in his autobiography[1] that "of all the 1,886 nights I was President, there were not many when I got to sleep before 1 or 2 A.M., and there were few mornings when I didn't wake up by 6 or 6:30." President Harry Truman (1945–1953) once observed that no one can really understand what it is like to be president: there is no end to "the chain of responsibility that binds him," and he is "never allowed to forget that he is president." These responsibilities are, for the most part, unremitting. Unlike Congress, the president never adjourns.

Given the demands of the presidency, why would anyone seek the office? There are some very special perks associated with the presidency. The president enjoys, among other things, the use of the White House. The White House has 132 rooms located on 18.3 acres of land in the heart of the nation's capital. At the White House, the president in residence has a staff of more than eighty persons, including chefs, gardeners, maids, butlers, and a personal tailor. Amenities also include a tennis court, a swimming pool, bowling lanes, and a private movie theater. Additionally, the president has at his or her disposal a fleet of automobiles, helicopters, and jets (including *Air Force One*, which costs about $70,000 an hour to run). For relaxation, the presidential family can go to Camp David, a resort hideaway in the Catoctin Mountains of Maryland. Other perks include free dental and medical care.

These amenities are only a minor motivation for wanting to be president of the United States, of course. A greater motivation is that the presidency is at the apex of the political ladder. It is the most powerful and influential political office that any one individual can hold. Presidents can help to shape not only domestic policy but also global developments. Since the demise of the Soviet Union and its satellite Communist countries in the early 1990s, the president of the United States has been the leader of the most powerful nation on earth. The president heads the greatest military force anywhere. Presidents have more power to reach their political objectives than any other players in the American political system. (We discussed President Barack Obama's political agenda in this chapter's opening *America at Odds* feature.) It is not surprising, therefore, that many Americans aspire to attain this office.

> "No man will ever bring out of the Presidency the reputation which carries him into it. To myself personally, it brings nothing but increasing **DRUDGERY AND DAILY LOSS OF FRIENDS."**
>
> ~ THOMAS JEFFERSON ~
> THIRD PRESIDENT OF
> THE UNITED STATES
> 1801–1809

Ronald Reagan was an actor before he became a politician. Here he is shown with actresses Lucille Barkley on the left and Wanda Hendrix. They were promoting a movie in Hollywood in 1950. How did Reagan's acting career help him in politics?

AP PHOTO

LO1 Who Can Become President?

The notion that anybody can become president of this country has always been a part of the American mythology. Certainly, the requirements for becoming president set forth in Article II, Section 1, of the Constitution are not difficult to meet:

No Person except a natural born Citizen, or a Citizen of the United States, at the time of the Adoption of this Constitution, shall be eligible to the Office of President; neither shall any Person be eligible to that Office who shall not

JOIN THE DEBATE

A Foreign-Born President?

As you just read, Article II of the Constitution states that "[n]o Person except a natural born Citizen . . . shall be eligible to the Office of President." This restriction has long been controversial, for it has kept many otherwise qualified Americans from running for president. These persons include California governor Arnold Schwarzenegger, who was born in Austria, and Michigan governor Jennifer M. Granholm, who was born in Canada, both of whom have been U.S. citizens for decades. In all, some 13 million Americans born outside the United States are excluded by this provision. The requirement of native birth has come up most recently because of claims by conspiracy theorists that President Obama was not born in the United States. These individuals claim that Obama's Hawaiian birth certificate was forged, and they are undeterred by the fact that Obama's birth was also announced in Honolulu newspapers.

An Obsolete Provision

America is a nation of immigrants, so it strikes some as odd that a foreign-born person would be barred from aspiring to the presidency. Naturalized U.S. citizens are allowed to vote, to serve on juries, and to serve in the military. They are also allowed to serve as secretary of state and represent the nation in foreign affairs. Why can't they run for president? Critics of the Constitution's citizenship requirement think that the requirement should be abolished by a constitutional amendment. They point out that the clause was initially included in the Constitution to prevent European princes from attempting to force the young republic back under monarchical rule in the late 1700s. Clearly, the clause is now obsolete and should no longer apply.

A Requirement Still Valid Today

Other Americans believe that the constitutional ban should remain. They argue that national security could be compromised by a foreign-born president. With the immense power that the president wields, especially in the realm of foreign policy, loyalty is of the utmost concern. The current war on terrorism only heightens the need to ensure that the president does not have divided loyalties.

In addition, the Constitution is quite difficult to amend, requiring support from two-thirds of both chambers of Congress and ratification by three-fourths of the fifty states. The need for an amendment that would allow Schwarzenegger and other immigrants to run for president is hardly as pressing as the need for past anti-discrimination amendments such as those abolishing slavery and giving women the right to vote, opponents argue.

For Critical Analysis *Some have suggested that a foreign-born president probably would be more nationalistic than a president born in this country. Why might that be so?*

CERTIFICATION OF LIVE BIRTH

STATE OF HAWAII HONOLULU — DEPARTMENT OF HEALTH HAWAII U.S.A.

CHILD'S NAME BARACK HUSSEIN OBAMA II

DATE OF BIRTH August 4, 1961

CHICAGO TRIBUNE/MCT/LANDOV

ANY ALTERATIONS INVALIDATE THIS CERTIFICATE

---

have attained to the Age of thirty-five Years, and been fourteen Years a Resident within the United States. (See this chapter's *Join the Debate* feature above.)

It is true that modern presidents have included a haberdasher (Harry Truman), a peanut farmer (Jimmy Carter), and an actor (Ronald Reagan), although all of these men also had significant political experience before assuming the presidency. If you look at Appendix E, though, you will see that the most common previous occupation of U.S. presidents has been the legal profession. Out of forty-four presidents, twenty-seven have been lawyers. Many presidents have also been wealthy. Additionally, although the Constitution states that anyone who is thirty-five years of age or older can become president, the average age at inauguration has been fifty-five. The youngest person elected president was John F. Kennedy (1961–1963), who assumed the presidency at the age of forty-three (the youngest person to hold the office was Theodore Roosevelt, who was forty-two when he became president after the assassination of William McKinley). The oldest was Ronald Reagan (1981–1989), who was sixty-nine years old when he became president.

For most of American history, all presidential candidates, even those of minor parties, were white, male, and of the Protestant religious tradition. In recent years, however, the pool of talent has expanded. In 1928, Democrat Al Smith became the first Catholic to run for president on a major-party ticket, and in 1960 Democrat John F. Kennedy became the first Catholic president. Among recent unsuccessful Democratic presidential candidates, Michael Dukakis was Greek Orthodox and John Kerry was Catholic. In 2008, the doors swung wide in the presidential primaries as the Democrats chose between a white woman, Hillary Clinton, and an African American man, Barack Obama. By that time, about 90 percent of Americans told pollsters that they would be willing to support an African American for president, and the same number would support a woman.

LO2 *The President's Many Roles*

The president has the authority to exercise a variety of powers. Some of these are explicitly outlined in the Constitution, and some are simply required by the office—such as the power to persuade. In the course of exercising these powers, the president performs a variety of roles. For example, as commander in chief of the armed services, the president can exercise significant military powers. Which roles a president executes successfully usually depends on what is happening domestically and internationally, as well as on the president's personality. Some presidents,

chief executive The head of the executive branch of government; in the United States, the president.

including Bill Clinton (1993–2001) during his first term, have shown much more interest in domestic policy than in foreign policy. Others, such as George H. W. Bush (1989–1993), were more interested in foreign affairs than in domestic ones.

Table 12–1 on the facing page summarizes the major roles of the president. An important role is, of course, that of chief executive. Other roles include those of commander in chief, head of state, chief diplomat, chief legislator, and political party leader.

Chief Executive

According to Article II of the Constitution,

> The executive Power shall be vested in a President of the United States of America. . . . [H]e may require the Opinion, in writing, of the principal Officer in each of the executive Departments, upon any Subject relating to the Duties of their respective Offices . . . and he shall nominate, and by and with the Advice and Consent of the Senate, shall appoint . . . Officers of the United States . . . . [H]e shall take Care that the Laws be faithfully executed.

This constitutional provision makes the president of the United States the nation's **chief executive,** or the head of the executive branch of the federal government. When the framers created the office of the president, they created a uniquely American institution. Nowhere else in the world at that time was there a democratically elected chief executive. The executive branch is also unique among the branches of government because it is headed by a single individual—the president.

President Woodrow Wilson throwing out the first pitch on the opening day of the major league baseball season in 1916. This action is part of the president's role as head of state.

NATIONAL PHOTO COMPANY COLLECTION/LIBRARY OF CONGRESS

Table 12–1

Roles of the President

Role	Description	Examples
Chief executive	Enforces laws and federal court decisions, along with treaties signed by the United States	• Can appoint, with Senate approval, and remove high-ranking officers of the federal government • Can grant reprieves, pardons, and amnesty • Can handle national emergencies during peacetime, such as riots or natural disasters
Commander in chief	Leads the nation's armed forces	• Can commit troops for up to ninety days in response to a military threat (War Powers Resolution) • Can make secret agreements with other countries • Can set up military governments in conquered lands • Can end fighting by calling a cease-fire (armistice)
Head of state	Performs ceremonial activities as a personal symbol of the nation	• Decorates war heroes • Dedicates parks and post offices • Throws out first pitch of baseball season • Lights national Christmas tree
Chief diplomat	Directs U.S. foreign policy and is the nation's most important representative in dealing with foreign countries	• Can negotiate and sign treaties with other nations, with Senate approval • Can make pacts (executive agreements) with other heads of state, without Senate approval • Can accept the legal existence of another country's government (power of recognition) • Receives foreign heads of state
Chief legislator	Informs Congress about the condition of the country and recommends legislative measures	• Proposes legislative program to Congress in traditional State of the Union address • Suggests budget to Congress and submits annual economic report • Can veto a bill passed by Congress • Can call special sessions of Congress
Political party leader	Heads political party	• Chooses a vice president • Makes several thousand top government appointments, often to party faithful (patronage) • Tries to execute the party's platform • May attend party fund-raisers • May help reelect party members running for office as mayors, governors, or members of Congress

Commander in Chief

The Constitution states that the president "shall be Commander in Chief of the Army and Navy of the United States, and of the Militia of the several States, when called into the actual Service of the United States." As **commander in chief** of the nation's armed forces, the president exercises tremendous power.

Under the Constitution, war powers are divided between Congress and the president. Congress was given the power to declare war and the power to raise and maintain the country's armed forces. The president, as commander in chief, was given the power to deploy the armed forces. The president's role as commander in chief has evolved over the last century. We will examine this shared power of the president and Congress in more detail later in this chapter.

Head of State

Traditionally, a country's monarch has performed the function of **head of state**—the country's representative to the rest of the world. The United States, of course, has no king or queen to act as

commander in chief The supreme commander of a nation's military force.

head of state The person who serves as the ceremonial head of a country's government and represents that country to the rest of the world.

The Unusual Role of the French President

Earlier in this text, you read about the parliamentary system used by many countries. In that system, the chief executive is chosen by the legislature, not the people. A few countries, however, have a hybrid system that is part parliamentary and part presidential. The best-known example of such a system is France.

The Presidential-Parliamentary System

France has a president, currently Nicolas Sarkozy, and a prime minister. Both represent the "center-right" party in France, the Union for a Popular Movement. In France, the president names the prime minister and the members of the cabinet. The prime minister and the cabinet, though, are responsible to the legislature, not the president. The National Assembly, which is the lower house of Parliament, can force the entire cabinet to resign by passing a motion of no confidence. In other words, "the government"—the prime minister and the other cabinet members—cannot survive politically unless a majority in the National Assembly supports them, regardless of the president's preferences.

The Unique French Practice of Cohabitation

For much of the history of the modern French Republic, the legislature's ability to throw out the government was not important, because the president's party had a majority in the National Assembly. French legislators were willing to let the president—the head of their party—choose the government. In 1981, the French elected a Socialist president for the first time, and they also gave the Socialists a majority in the National Assembly. In the 1986 elections, however, France voted for a center-right Assembly majority. The Socialist president, François Mitterrand, still had two years left in his term of office. The French have a quaint term for the resulting situation: "cohabitation." During cohabitation, the prime minister and the rest of the cabinet are from one party and the president is from another.

Who Does What?

Nowhere in the French constitution is there an explicit statement of the division of powers between the president and the prime minister. The division of duties that exists today has evolved over time. Typically, the president is responsible for foreign policy and the prime minister for domestic policy. This distinction is most carefully observed during periods of cohabitation. When one party is in full control of the government, however, the president tends to take over completely. President Sarkozy meddles in every type of policy. This may be one reason why Sarkozy has become increasingly unpopular since 2007, when he was elected.

For Critical Analysis *Does our president fill too many roles? Would our government work better if a prime minister served under the president?*

President Nicolas Sarkozy is shown with his wife, Carla Bruni, who continues to have a singing career.

AP PHOTO/CHARLES DHARAPAK

head of state. Thus, the president of the United States fulfills this role. The president engages in many symbolic or ceremonial activities, such as throwing out the first pitch to open the baseball season and turning on the lights of the national Christmas tree. The president also decorates war heroes, dedicates parks and post offices, receives visiting heads of state at the White House, and goes on official state visits to other countries. Some argue that presidents should not perform such ceremonial duties because they take time that the president should be spending on "real work." (See this chapter's *The Rest of the World* feature above for more information on how one other country handles this issue.)

Chief Diplomat

A **diplomat** is a person who represents one country in dealing with representatives of another country. In the United States, the president is the nation's **chief diplomat.** The Constitution did not explicitly reserve this role to the president, but since the beginning of this nation, presidents have assumed the role based on their explicit constitutional powers to recognize foreign governments and, with the advice and consent of the Senate, to appoint ambassadors and make treaties. As chief diplomat, the president directs the foreign policy of the United States and is our nation's most important representative.

Chief Legislator

Nowhere in the Constitution do the words *chief legislator* appear. The Constitution, however, does require that the president "from time to time give to the Congress Information of the State of the Union, and recommend to their Consideration such Measures as he shall judge necessary and expedient." The president has, in fact, become a major player in shaping the congressional agenda—the set of measures that actually get discussed and acted on. This was not always the case. In the nineteenth century, some presidents preferred to let Congress lead the way

The current and last three presidents are shown in the Oval Office of the White House. What can a president do after she or he leaves office?

in proposing and implementing policy. Since the administration of Theodore Roosevelt (1901–1909), however, presidents have taken an activist approach. Presidents are now expected to develop a legislative program and propose a budget to Congress every year.

In the past, this shared power has often put Congress and the president at odds. President Bill Clinton's administration, for example, drew up a health-care reform package in 1993 and presented it to Congress almost on a take-it-or-leave-it basis. Congress left it. To avoid such confrontations, President Obama has frequently let Congress determine much of the content of important new legislation, such as the health-care reform bills. In the example of health-care reform, such deference had several negative consequences. These included an unusually large number of earmarks, a protracted and unpopular legislative process, and opportunities for conservatives to mobilize against the reforms. Still, in the end, Obama succeeded where Clinton had failed.

Political Party Leader

The president of the United States is also the *de facto* leader of his or her political party. The Constitution, of course, does not mention this role because, in the eyes of the founders, parties should have no place in the American political system.

As party leader, the president exercises substantial powers. For example, the president chooses the chairperson of the party's national committee. The president can also exert political power within the party by using presidential appointment and removal powers. Naturally, presidents are beholden to the party members who put them in office, and usually presidents indulge in the practice of **patronage**—appointing individuals to government or public jobs to reward those who helped them win the presidential contest. The president may also reward party members with fund-raising assistance (campaign financing was discussed in Chapter 9). The

---

diplomat A person who represents one country in dealing with representatives of another country.

chief diplomat The role of the president of the United States in recognizing and interacting with foreign governments.

patronage The practice of giving government jobs to individuals belonging to the winning political party.

president is, in a sense, "fund-raiser in chief" for his or her party, and recent presidents, including Bill Clinton, George W. Bush, and Barack Obama, have proven themselves to be prodigious fund-raisers. Understandably, the use of patronage within the party system gives the president extraordinary powers.

LO3 *Presidential Powers*

The president exercises numerous powers. Some of these powers are set forth in the Constitution. Others, known as *inherent powers,* are those that are necessary to carry out the president's constitutional duties. We look next at these powers, as well as at the expansion of presidential powers over time.

The President's Constitutional Powers

As you have read, the constitutional source for the president's authority is found in Article II of the Constitution, which states, "The executive Power shall be vested in a President of the United States of America." The Constitution then sets forth the president's relatively limited constitutional responsibilities. Just how much power should be entrusted to the president was debated at length by the framers of the Constitution. On the one hand, they did not want a king. On the other hand, they believed that a strong executive was necessary if the republic was to survive. The result of their debates was an executive who was granted enough powers in the Constitution to balance those of Congress.

Article II grants the president broad but vaguely described powers. From the very beginning, there were different views as to what exactly the "executive Power" clause enabled the president to do. Nonetheless, Sections 2 and 3 of Article II list the following specific presidential powers. These powers parallel the roles of the president discussed in the previous section:

- To serve as commander in chief of the armed forces and the state militias.

- To appoint, with the Senate's consent, the heads of the executive departments, ambassadors, justices of the Supreme Court, and other top officials.

- To grant reprieves and pardons, except in cases of impeachment.

- To make treaties, with the advice and consent of the Senate.

treaty A formal agreement between the governments of two or more countries.

President John F. Kennedy (right) and Prime Minister Harold Macmillan of the United Kingdom stop just outside the White House office in 1961 to discuss problems in Southeast Asia. What role is the president playing here?

AP PHOTO

- To deliver the annual State of the Union address to Congress and to send other messages to Congress from time to time.

- To call either house or both houses of Congress into special sessions.

- To receive ambassadors and other representatives from foreign countries.

- To commission all officers of the United States.

- To ensure that the laws passed by Congress "be faithfully executed."

In addition, Article I, Section 7, gives the president the power to veto legislation. We discuss some of these powers in more detail below. As you will see, many of these powers are balanced by the powers of Congress. We address the complex relationship between the president and Congress later in this chapter.

PROPOSAL AND RATIFICATION OF TREATIES A **treaty** is a formal agreement between two or more countries. The president has the sole power to negotiate

President Jimmy Carter (center) met with Egyptian president Anwar Sadat (left) and Israeli prime minister Menachem Begin (right) at the White House for the signing of the Camp David Accords on September 18, 1978. Since then, Egypt and Israel have remained at peace with each other.

> **veto** A Latin word meaning "I forbid"; the refusal by an official, such as the president of the United States or a state governor, to sign a bill into law.

and sign treaties with other countries. The Senate, however, must approve a treaty by a two-thirds vote of the members present before it becomes effective. If the treaty is approved by the Senate and signed by the president, it becomes law.

Presidents have not always succeeded in winning the Senate's approval for treaties. Woodrow Wilson (1913–1921) lost his effort to persuade the Senate to approve the Treaty of Versailles,[2] the peace treaty that ended World War I in 1918. Among other things, the treaty would have made the United States a member of the League of Nations. In contrast, Jimmy Carter (1977–1981) convinced the Senate to approve a treaty returning the Panama Canal to Panama by the year 2000 over such objections as those of Senator S. I. Hayakawa, Republican from California, who said, "We stole it fair and square." The treaty was approved by a margin of a single vote.

THE POWER TO GRANT REPRIEVES AND PARDONS
The president's power to grant a pardon serves as a check on judicial power. A *pardon* is a release from punishment or the legal consequences of a crime. It restores a person to the full rights and privileges of citizenship. In 1925, the United States Supreme Court upheld an expansive interpretation of the president's pardon power in a case involving an individual convicted for contempt of court. The Court held that the power covers all offenses "either before trial, during trial, or after trial, by individuals, or by classes, conditionally or absolutely, and this without modification or regulation by Congress."[3] The president can grant a pardon for any federal offense, except in cases of impeachment.

One of the most controversial pardons was that granted by President Gerald Ford (1974–1977) to former president Richard Nixon (1969–1974) after the Watergate affair (to be discussed later in the chapter), before any formal charges were brought in court. Sometimes pardons are granted to a class of individuals, as a general amnesty. For example, President Jimmy Carter granted amnesty to tens of thousands of people who had resisted the draft during the Vietnam War by failing to register for the draft or by moving abroad. Just before he left office in 2001, President Bill Clinton pardoned 140 individuals. Some of these pardons were controversial.

A more recent controversy followed President George W. Bush's decision, in 2007, to commute the prison sentence received by Lewis ("Scooter") Libby, Vice President Dick Cheney's chief of staff. Libby was convicted of crimes in connection with a leak to the press that exposed the identity of a Central Intelligence Agency agent. Bush administration critics alleged that the exposure of the agent's identity was an attempt to punish the agent's husband for criticisms of the war in Iraq.

THE PRESIDENT'S VETO POWER As noted in Chapter 11, the president can **veto** a bill passed by Congress. Congress can override the veto with a two-thirds vote by the members present in each chamber. The result of a veto override is that the bill becomes law against the wishes of the president. If the president does not send a bill back to Congress after ten congressional working days, the bill becomes law without the president's signature. If the president refuses to sign the bill and Congress adjourns within ten working days after the bill has been submitted to the president, however, the bill is killed for that session of Congress. As mentioned in Chapter 11, this is called a *pocket veto*.

Presidents used the veto power sparingly until the administration of Andrew Johnson (1865–1869). Johnson vetoed twenty-one bills. Franklin D. Roosevelt (1933–1945) vetoed more bills by far than any of his

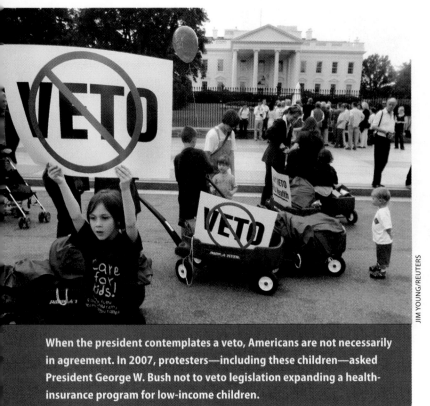

When the president contemplates a veto, Americans are not necessarily in agreement. In 2007, protesters—including these children—asked President George W. Bush not to veto legislation expanding a health-insurance program for low-income children.

JIM YOUNG/REUTERS

predecessors or successors in the presidency. During his administration, there were 372 regular vetoes, 9 of which were overridden by Congress, and 263 pocket vetoes.

The Veto in Recent Administrations President George W. Bush, in contrast, used his veto power very sparingly. Indeed, during the first six years of his presidency, Bush vetoed only one bill—a proposal to expand the scope of stem-cell research. Bush vetoed so few bills, in large part, because the Republican-led Congress during those years strongly supported his agenda. After the Democrats took control of Congress in 2007, however, Bush vetoed eleven bills. Congress overrode four of them.

With a Congress led by his own party, President Obama faced circumstances similar to those enjoyed by George W. Bush during most of his presidency. In his first two years of office, Obama exercised the veto power very rarely.

The Line-Item Veto Many presidents have complained that they cannot control "pork-barrel" legislation—federal expenditures tacked onto bills to "bring home the bacon" to a particular congressional member's district. For example, expenditures on a specific sports stadium might be added to a bill involving crime. The reason is simple: the president would have to veto the entire bill to eliminate the pork—and that might not be feasible politically. Presidents have often argued in favor of a *line-item veto* that would enable them to veto just one (or several) items in a bill. In 1996, Congress passed and President Clinton signed a line-item veto bill. The Supreme Court concluded in 1998 that it was unconstitutional, however.[4]

The President's Inherent Powers

In addition to the powers explicitly granted by the Constitution, the president also has *inherent powers*—powers that are necessary to carry out the specific responsibilities of the president as set forth in the Constitution. The presidency is, of course, an institution of government, but it is also an institution that consists, at any one moment in time, of one individual. That means that the lines between the presidential office and the person who holds that office often become blurred. Certain presidential powers that today are considered part of the rights of the office were simply assumed by strong presidents to be inherent powers of the presidency, and their successors then continued to exercise these powers.

President Woodrow Wilson clearly indicated this interplay between presidential personality and presidential powers in the following statement:

President Bill Clinton used line-item veto powers to eliminate nearly forty projects worth $287 million from a military construction bill in 1997. The line-item veto legislation, passed in 1996, was ruled unconstitutional by the United States Supreme Court in 1998.

AP PHOTO/GREG GIBSON

As chief diplomat, George Washington made foreign policy decisions without consulting Congress. This action laid the ground work for an active presidential role in foreign policy.

By the time Abraham Lincoln gave his Inauguration Day speech, seven southern states had already seceded from the Union. Some scholars believe that Lincoln's skillful and vigorous handling of the Civil War increased the power and prestige of the presidency.

In its attempts to counter the effects of the Great Depression, Franklin D. Roosevelt's administration not only extended the role of the national government in regulating the nation's economic life but also further increased the power of the president.

The President is at liberty, both in law and conscience, to be as big a man as he can. His capacity will set the limit; and if Congress be overborne by him, it will be no fault of the makers of the Constitution—it will be from no lack of constitutional powers on his part, but only because the President has the nation behind him, and Congress has not.[5]

In other words, because the Constitution is vague as to the actual carrying out of presidential powers, presidents are left to define the limits of their authority—subject, of course, to obstacles raised by the other branches of government.

The Expansion of Presidential Powers

The Constitution defines presidential powers in very general language, and even the founders were uncertain just how the president would perform the various functions. George Washington (1789–1797) set many of the precedents that have defined presidential power. For example, he removed officials from office, interpreting the constitutional power to appoint officials as implying power to remove them as well.[6] He established the practice of meeting regularly with the heads of the three departments that then existed and of turning to them for political advice. He set a precedent for the president to act as chief legislator by submitting proposed legislation to Congress. Abraham Lincoln (1861–1865), confronting the problems of the Civil War during the 1860s, took several important actions while Congress was not

in session. He suspended certain constitutional liberties, spent funds that Congress had not appropriated, blockaded southern ports, and banned "treasonable correspondence" from the U.S. mail. Lincoln carried out all of these actions in the name of his power as commander in chief and his constitutional responsibility to "take Care that the Laws be faithfully executed."[7]

Other presidents, including Thomas Jefferson, Andrew Jackson, Woodrow Wilson, Franklin D. Roosevelt, and George W. Bush, also greatly expanded the powers of the president. The power of the president continues to evolve, depending on the person holding the office, the relative power of Congress, and events at home and abroad.

THE PRESIDENT'S EXPANDED LEGISLATIVE POWERS

Congress has come to expect the president to develop a legislative program. From time to time, the president submits special messages on certain subjects. These messages call on Congress to enact laws that the president thinks are necessary. The president also works closely with members of Congress to persuade them to support particular programs. The president writes, telephones, and meets with various congressional leaders to discuss pending bills. The president also sends aides to lobby on Capitol Hill. One study of the legislative process found that "no other single actor in the political system has quite the capability of the president to set agendas in given policy areas." As one lobbyist told a researcher, "Obviously, when a president sends up a bill [to Congress], it takes first place in the queue. All other bills take second place." As noted earlier, however, compared with some recent presidents, Barack Obama has shown a surprising willingness to let Congress determine the details of important legislation.

The Power to Persuade   The president's political skills and ability to persuade others play a large role in determining the administration's success. According to Richard Neustadt in his classic work *Presidential Power*, "Presidential power is the power to persuade."[8] For all of the resources at the president's disposal, the president still must rely on the cooperation of others if the administration's goals are to be accomplished. After three years in office, President Harry Truman made this remark about the powers of the president:

> The president may have a great many powers given to him in the Constitution and may have certain powers under certain laws which are given to him by the Congress of the United States; but the principal power that the president has is to bring people in and try to persuade them to do what they ought to do without persuasion. That's what the powers of the president amount to.[9]

Persuasive powers are particularly important when divided government exists. If a president from one political party faces a Congress dominated by the other party, the president must overcome more opposition than usual to get legislation passed.

Going Public   The president may also use a strategy known as "going public"[10]—that is, using press conferences, public appearances, and televised events to arouse public opinion in favor of certain legislative programs. The public may then pressure legislators to support the administration's programs. A president who has the support of the public can wield significant persuasive power over Congress. Presidents who are voted into office through "landslide" elections have increased bargaining power because of their widespread popularity. Those with less popular support have less bargaining leverage.

The ability of the president to go public effectively is dependent on popular attitudes toward the president. Such attitudes may be quite rational. For example, voters may rate a president based on the state of the economy. Experts have observed that the president's ability to control the level of economic activity is subject to severe limits. From the public's point of view, however, evaluating its leaders based on results makes good sense. Other views of the president may be highly irrational. We provide an example in this chapter's feature *Perception versus Reality: The Mythical Barack Obama* on the facing page.

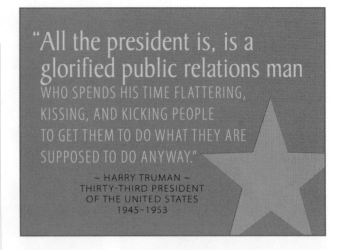

"All the president is, is a glorified public relations man WHO SPENDS HIS TIME FLATTERING, KISSING, AND KICKING PEOPLE TO GET THEM TO DO WHAT THEY ARE SUPPOSED TO DO ANYWAY."

~ HARRY TRUMAN ~
THIRTY-THIRD PRESIDENT
OF THE UNITED STATES
1945–1953

The Power to Influence the Economy   Some of the greatest expansions of presidential power occurred during Franklin D. Roosevelt's administration. Roosevelt claimed the presidential power to regulate the economy during the Great Depression in the 1930s. Since that time, Americans have expected the president to be actively involved in economic matters and social programs. That expectation becomes especially potent during a major economic downturn, such as the Great Recession that began in December 2007.

Congress annually receives from the president a suggested budget and the *Economic Report of the President*. The budget message suggests what amounts of money the government will need for its programs. The *Economic Report of the President* presents the state of the nation's economy and recommends ways to improve it.

The Legislative Success of Various Presidents
Look at Figure 12–1 on page 268. It shows the success records of presidents in getting their legislation passed. Success is defined as how often the president won his way on roll-call votes on which he took a clear position. As you can see, typically a president's success record was very high when he first took office and then gradually declined. This is sometimes attributed to the president's "honeymoon period," when Congress may be most likely to work with the president to achieve the president's legislative agenda. The media often put a great deal of emphasis on how successful a president is during the "first hundred days" in office. Ironically, this is also the period when the president is least experienced in the ways of the White House, particularly if the president was a Washington outsider, such as a state governor, before becoming president.

In 2009, President Obama had the most successful legislative year of any president in half a century. Obama's four years in the Senate may have helped him learn the ways of Washington. Large Democratic majorities in both chambers of Congress were surely

When Barack Obama was running for president, his enemies—and there were plenty of them—attempted to "prove" that he could not legally run for president. They contended that Obama was not a native-born citizen, despite ample proof of his birth in Hawaii. Entire Web sites were devoted to creating a perception of Obama as someone who was unfit to become president. One myth propagated by bloggers and radio talk-show hosts was that Obama was a Muslim.

The Perception

In a recent public opinion poll, the number of respondents who said that Obama is a Muslim was 18 percent, up from 12 percent in 2008. Only 34 percent believed that he was a Christian, down from 51 percent. The belief that Obama is a Muslim has increased most sharply among conservative Republicans—up 16 points, to 34 percent. When asked how they learned about Obama's religion, 60 percent cited the media.

One argument employed by bloggers is based on Obama's Kenyan father, who was Muslim by birth (although apparently irreligious later in life). The bloggers argue that in the Muslim world, the father's religion determines the religion of the child. Therefore, Obama is a Muslim, even if he went to a Christian church for most of his adult life.

The Reality

Contrary to the claims of American bloggers, no authority in the Islamic world has ever said that Obama's ancestry

makes him a Muslim or a Muslim apostate. Obama lived in Indonesia—a Muslim country—for four years as a young boy, but that proves nothing. As president, he reads a daily Christian devotional message, converses with pastors on the phone, and regularly attends Christian services in a military chapel at Camp David. His mother, who raised him, was an atheist, not a Muslim. Obama was baptized as a Christian in his twenties.

The argument that Obama is not a Christian is odd given that one of his most serious problems during his presidential campaign was his relationship with the Reverend Jeremiah Wright, his longtime pastor. Wright served at Trinity United Church of Christ (UCC) in Chicago. (The UCC, one of America's oldest denominations, is the direct descendent of the church founded by the Puritans.) A key to this contradiction is that a large number of Americans also believe that Wright is a Muslim. Some apparently identify Wright with the Black Muslims because they are both African American, politically radical, and from Chicago.

Of one thing we can probably be certain: as the economy improves, the misperception of Obama's attachment to Islam will decline.

🔊 **Blog On** One of the best sources for debunking rumors and urban legends is snopes.com. For analysis of the Obama-is-a-Muslim legend, see **www.snopes.com/politics/obama/muslim.asp**. To see how talk-show host Rush Limbaugh perpetrates the myth, enter "Rush Limbaugh Obama Muslim" into a search engine such as Google.

---

even more important in explaining Obama's ability to obtain the legislation that he sought.

THE INCREASING USE OF EXECUTIVE ORDERS As the nation's chief executive, the president is considered to have the inherent power to issue **executive orders,** which are presidential orders to carry out policies described in laws that have been passed by Congress. These orders have the force of law. Presidents have issued executive orders for a variety of purposes, including to establish procedures for appointing noncareer administrators, restructure the White House bureaucracy, ration consumer goods and administer wage and price controls under emergency conditions, classify government information as secret, implement affirmative action policies, and regulate the

export of certain items. Presidents issue executive orders frequently, sometimes as many as one hundred a year.

AN UNPRECEDENTED USE OF SIGNING STATEMENTS
A **signing statement** is a written statement issued by a president at the time he or she signs a bill into law. James Monroe (1817–1825) was the first president to issue such a statement. For many years, signing statements were rare—prior to the presidency of Ronald

> **executive order** A presidential order to carry out a policy or policies described in a law passed by Congress.
>
> **signing statement** A written statement, appended to a bill at the time the president signs it into law, indicating how the president interprets that legislation.

Figure 12–1

Presidential Success Records

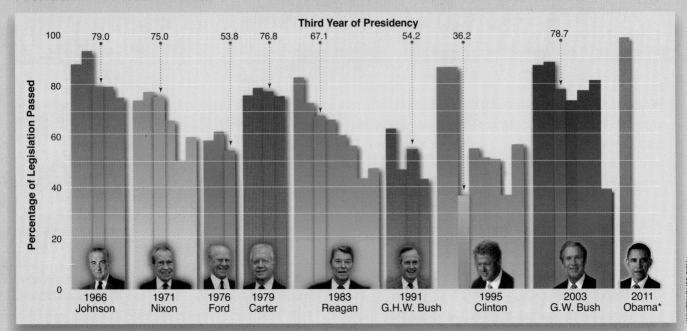

Third Year of Presidency

Percentage of Legislation Passed

79.0 — 75.0 — 53.8 — 76.8 — 67.1 — 54.2 — 36.2 — 78.7

| 1966 Johnson | 1971 Nixon | 1976 Ford | 1979 Carter | 1983 Reagan | 1991 G.H.W. Bush | 1995 Clinton | 2003 G.W. Bush | 2011 Obama* |

WHITEHOUSE.GOV

*Obama's first-year success rate (2009) was 96 percent, the highest on record.

Source: *Congressional Quarterly Almanac.*

Reagan, only seventy-five were issued. Most were "rhetorical" in character. They might praise the legislation or the Congress that passed it, or criticize the opposition. On occasion, however, the statements noted constitutional problems with one or more clauses of a bill or provided details as to how the executive branch would interpret legislative language.

Reagan issued a grand total of 249 signing statements. For the first time, each statement was published in the *U.S. Code Congressional and Administrative News,* along with the text of the bill in question. A substantial share of the statements addressed constitutional issues. Reagan staff member Samuel Alito, Jr.—who now sits on the United States Supreme Court—issued a memo in favor of using signing statements to "increase the power of the Executive to shape the law." Reagan's successors George H. W. Bush and Bill Clinton made similar use of the statements.

President George W. Bush took the use of signing statements to an entirely new level. Bush's 161 statements challenged more than 1,100 clauses of federal law—more legal provisions than were challenged by all previous presidents put together. Many legal scholars and members of Congress considered Bush's use of signing statements to be a constitutional crisis. They believed that Bush was attempting by stealth to re-institute the line-item veto that the Supreme Court had ruled unconstitutional in 1998. The powers that the

statements claimed for the president were also alarming. One statement rejected Congress's authority to ban torture. Another affirmed that the president could have anyone's mail opened without a warrant.

As a presidential candidate, Barack Obama criticized Bush's use of signing statements and promised to limit his use of them. As president, he reduced the number of statements substantially during his first

President George W. Bush is shown here approving a signing statement attached to a piece of legislation. During his two terms as president, Bush made unprecedented use of signing statements to assert presidential authority.

AP PHOTO/THE WHITE HOUSE/CHRIS GREENBERG

two years in office, writing only ten of them through October 2010.

EVOLVING PRESIDENTIAL POWER IN FOREIGN AFFAIRS

The precise extent of the president's power in foreign affairs is constantly evolving. The president is commander in chief and chief diplomat, but only Congress has the power to formally declare war, and the Senate must ratify any treaty that the president has negotiated with other nations. George Washington laid the groundwork for our long history of the president's active role in foreign policy. For example, when war broke out between Britain and France in 1793, Washington chose to disregard a treaty of alliance with France and to pursue a course of strict neutrality. Since that time, on many occasions presidents have taken military actions and made foreign policy without consulting Congress.

Executive Agreements In foreign affairs, presidential power is enhanced by the ability to make **executive agreements,** which are pacts between the president and other heads of state. Executive agreements do not require Senate approval (even though Congress may refuse to appropriate the necessary money to carry out the agreements), but they have the same legal status as treaties.

Presidents form executive agreements for a wide range of purposes. Some involve routine matters, such as promises of trade or assistance to other countries. Others concern matters of great importance. In 1940, for example, President Franklin D. Roosevelt formed an important executive agreement with British prime minister Winston Churchill. The agreement provided that the United States would lend American destroyers to Britain to help protect that nation and its shipping during World War II. In return, the British allowed the United States to use military and naval bases on British territories in the Western Hemisphere.

To prevent presidential abuse of the power to make executive agreements, Congress passed a law in 1972 that requires the president to inform Congress within sixty days of making any executive agreement. The law did not limit the president's power to make executive agreements, however, and they continue to be used far more than treaties in making foreign policy.

Military Actions As you have read, the U.S. Constitution gives Congress the power to declare war. Consider however, that although Congress has declared war in only five different conflicts during our nation's history,[11] the United States has engaged in more than two hundred activities involving the armed services. Before the United States entered World War II in 1941, Franklin D. Roosevelt ordered the Navy to "shoot on sight" any German submarine that appeared in the Western Hemisphere security zone. Without a congressional declaration of war, President Truman sent U.S. armed forces to Korea in 1950, thus involving American troops in the conflict between North and South Korea.

> "If one morning I walked on top of the water across the Potomac River, the headline that afternoon would read: **'PRESIDENT CAN'T SWIM.'"**
>
> ~ LYNDON B. JOHNSON ~
> THIRTY-SIXTH PRESIDENT
> OF THE UNITED STATES
> 1963–1969

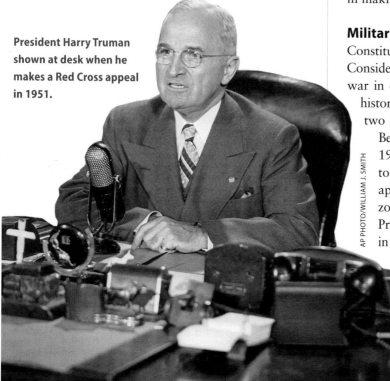

President Harry Truman shown at desk when he makes a Red Cross appeal in 1951.

AP PHOTO/WILLIAM J. SMITH

executive agreement A binding international agreement, or pact, that is made between the president and another head of state and that does not require Senate approval.

The United States also entered the Vietnam War (1964–1975) without a congressional declaration. President Nixon did not consult Congress when he made the decision to invade Cambodia in 1970. Neither did President Reagan when he sent troops to Lebanon and Grenada in 1983 and ordered American fighter planes to attack Libya in 1986 in retaliation for terrorist attacks on American soldiers. No congressional vote was taken before President George H. W. Bush sent troops into Panama in 1989. Bush did, however, obtain congressional approval to use American troops to force Iraq to withdraw from Kuwait in 1991. Without Congress, President Clinton made the decision to send troops to Haiti in 1994 and to Bosnia in 1995, as well as to bomb Iraq in 1998. In 1999, he also decided on his own authority to send U.S. forces under the command of NATO (North Atlantic Treaty Organization) to bomb Yugoslavia.

In 1991, the United States, along with other nations, used military force to expel Iraqi troops that had invaded Kuwait. Here, President George H. W. Bush (left) meets with General Colin Powell to discuss whether the coalition forces should occupy Baghdad, the capital of Iraq.

The War Powers Resolution As commander in chief, the president can respond quickly to a military threat without waiting for congressional action. This power to commit troops and to involve the nation in a war upset many members of Congress as the undeclared war in Vietnam dragged on for years into the 1970s. Criticism of the president's role in the Vietnam conflict led to the passage of the War Powers Resolution of 1973, which limits the president's warmaking powers. The law, which was passed over President Nixon's veto, requires the president to notify Congress within forty-eight hours of deploying troops. It also prevents the president from sending troops abroad for more than sixty days (or ninety days, if more time is needed for a successful withdrawal). If Congress does not authorize a longer period, the troops must be removed.

The War on Terrorism President George W. Bush did not obtain a declaration of war from Congress for the war against terrorism that began on September 11, 2001. Instead, Congress passed a joint resolution authorizing the president to use "all necessary and appropriate force against those nations, organizations, or persons he determines planned, authorized, committed, or aided the terrorist attacks that occurred on September 11, 2001."

This resolution was the basis for America's subsequent involvement in Afghanistan. Also, in October 2002, Congress passed a joint resolution authorizing the use of U.S. armed forces against Iraq. As a consequence of these resolutions, the president was able to invoke certain emergency wartime measures. For example, through executive order the president created military tribunals for trying terrorist suspects. The president also held American citizens as "enemy combatants," denying them access to their attorneys.

Nuclear Weapons Since 1945, the president, as commander in chief, has been responsible for the most difficult of all military decisions—if and when to use nuclear weapons. In 1945, Harry Truman made the awesome decision to drop atomic bombs on the Japanese cities of Hiroshima and Nagasaki. "The final decision," he said, "on where and when to use the atomic bomb was up to me. Let there be no mistake about it." Today, the president travels at all times with the "football"—the briefcase containing the codes used to launch a nuclear attack.

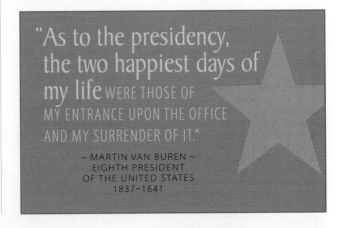

"As to the presidency, the two happiest days of my life WERE THOSE OF MY ENTRANCE UPON THE OFFICE AND MY SURRENDER OF IT."

~ MARTIN VAN BUREN ~
EIGHTH PRESIDENT
OF THE UNITED STATES
1837–1841

LO4 *Congressional and Presidential Relations*

Despite the seemingly immense powers at the president's disposal, the president is limited in what he or she can accomplish, or even attempt. In our system of checks and balances, the president must share some powers with the legislative and judicial branches of government. The president's power is checked not only by these institutions but also by the media, public opinion, and the voters. The founders hoped that this system of shared power would lessen the chance of tyranny.

Some scholars believe the relationship between Congress and the president is the most important one in the American system of government. Congress traditionally has had the upper hand in some areas, primarily in passing legislation. In some other areas, though, particularly in foreign affairs, the president can exert tremendous power that Congress is virtually unable to check.

Advantage: Congress

Congress has the advantage over the president in the areas of legislative authorization, the regulation of foreign and interstate commerce, and some budgetary matters. Of course, as you have already read, the president today proposes a legislative agenda and a budget to Congress every year. Nonetheless, only Congress has the power to pass the legislation and appropriate the money. The most the president can do constitutionally is veto an entire bill if it contains something that he or she does not like. (As noted, however, recent presidents have frequently used signing statements in an attempt to avoid portions of bills that they did not approve.)

Presidential popularity is a source of power for the president in dealings with Congress. Presidents spend a great deal of time courting public opinion, eyeing the "presidential approval ratings," and meeting with the press. Much of this activity is for the purpose of gaining leverage with Congress. The president can put all of his or her persuasive powers to work in achieving a legislative agenda, but Congress still retains the ultimate lawmaking authority.

DIVIDED GOVERNMENT When government is divided—with at least one house of Congress controlled by a different party than the White House—the president can have difficulty even getting a legislative agenda to the floor for a vote. President Bill Clinton

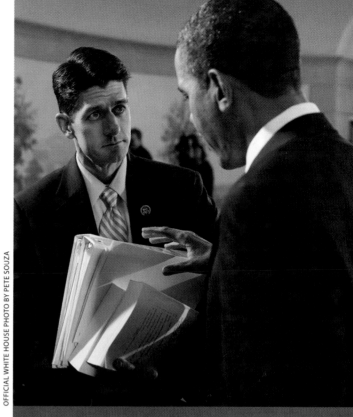

OFFICIAL WHITE HOUSE PHOTO BY PETE SOUZA

President Obama talks with Representative Paul Ryan (R., Wisc.) during a nationally televised bipartisan meeting on health-care reform in February 2010.

found this to be so after the congressional elections of 1994 brought the Republicans to power in Congress. Clinton's success rate in implementing his legislative agenda dropped to 36.2 percent in 1995, after a high of 86.4 the previous year (see Figure 12–1 on page 268).

President George W. Bush faced a similar problem in 2007, when the Democrats gained a majority in Congress. During his first six years as president, Bush had worked with an extremely cooperative Republican-led Congress.[12] After the Democrats became the majority, however, divided government existed again.

DIFFERENT CONSTITUENCIES Congress and the president have different constituencies, and this fact influences their relationship. Members of Congress represent a state or a local district, and this gives them a regional focus. As we discussed in Chapter 11, members of Congress like to have legislative successes of their own to bring home to their constituents—military bases that remain operative, public-works projects that create local jobs, or trade rules that benefit a big local employer. Ideally, the president's focus should be on the nation as a whole: national defense, homeland security, the national economy. At times, this can put the president at odds even

executive privilege An inherent executive power claimed by presidents to withhold information from, or to refuse to appear before, Congress or the courts. The president can also accord the privilege to other executive officials.

Watergate scandal A scandal involving an illegal break-in at the Democratic National Committee offices in 1972 by members of President Nixon's reelection campaign staff. Before Congress could vote to impeach Nixon for his participation in covering up the break-in, Nixon resigned from the presidency.

with members of his or her own party in Congress.

Furthermore, members of Congress and the president face different election cycles (every two years in the House, every six years in the Senate, and every four years for the president), and the president is limited to two terms in office. Consequently, the president and Congress sometimes feel a different sense of urgency about implementing legislation. For example, the president often senses the need to demonstrate legislative success during the first year in office, when the excitement over the elections is still fresh in the minds of politicians and the public.

Advantage: The President

The president has the advantage over Congress in dealing with a national crisis, in setting foreign policy, and in influencing public opinion. In times of crisis, the presidency is arguably the most crucial institution in government because, when necessary, the president can act quickly, speak with one voice, and represent the nation to the world. George W. Bush's presidency was unquestionably changed by the terrorist attacks of September 11, 2001.

Some scholars have argued that recent presidents have abused the powers of the presidency by taking advantage of crises. Others have argued that there is an unwritten "doctrine of necessity" under which presidential powers can and should be expanded during a crisis. When this has happened in the past, however, Congress has always retaken some control when the crisis was over, in a natural process of institutional give-and-take.

A problem faced during the Bush administration was that the "war on terrorism" had no obvious end or conclusion. It was not clear when the crisis would be over and the nation could return to normal government relations and procedures. In fact, several of Bush's most troubling initiatives, such as support for brutal interrogation methods, were ended during his second term. Many supporters of Barack Obama believed that upon election, he would restore civil liberties lost during Bush's war on terrorism. As it turned out, the Obama administration kept most of Bush's policies in place. (You learned about this issue in greater detail in the Chapter 4 *Perception versus Reality* feature on page 90.)

Executive Privilege

As you read in Chapter 11, Congress has the authority to investigate and oversee the activities of other branches of government. Nonetheless, both Congress and the public have accepted that a certain degree of secrecy by the executive branch is necessary to protect national security. Some presidents have claimed an inherent executive power to withhold information from, or to refuse to appear before, Congress or the courts. This is called **executive privilege,** and it has been invoked by presidents from the time of George Washington to the present.

One of the problems with executive privilege is that it has been used for more purposes than simply to safeguard the national security. President Nixon invoked executive privilege in an attempt to avoid handing over taped White House conversations to Congress during the **Watergate scandal.** President Clinton invoked the privilege in an attempt to keep details of his sexual relationship with Monica Lewinsky a secret.

After the Democrats took control of Congress in 2007 and began to investigate various actions undertaken by the Bush administration, they were frequently blocked in their attempts to obtain information by the claim of executive privilege. For example, during Congress's investigation of the Justice Department's firing of several U.S. attorneys for allegedly political reasons, the Bush administration raised the claim of executive privilege to prevent several people from testifying or submitting requested documents to Congress.

While campaigning, Barack Obama promised that his administration would be much more open than that of President Bush. Many of Obama's own supporters, however, do not believe that he has done enough to carry out that promise.

LO5 *The Organization of the Executive Branch*

In the early days of this nation, presidents answered their own mail, as George Washington did. Only in 1857 did Congress authorize a private secretary for the president, to be paid by the federal government. Even Woodrow Wilson typed most of his correspondence, although by that time several secretaries were assigned to the president. When Franklin D. Roosevelt became president in 1933, the entire staff consisted of thirty-seven employees. Only during Roosevelt's New Deal and World War II did the presidential staff become a sizable organization.

The President's Cabinet

The Constitution does not specifically mention presidential assistants and advisers. The Constitution states only that the president "may require the Opinion, in writing, of the principal Officer in each of the executive Departments." Since the time of our first president, however, presidents have had an advisory group, or **cabinet,** to turn to for counsel. Originally, the cabinet consisted of only four officials—the secretaries of state, treasury, and war and the attorney general.

Today, the cabinet includes fourteen department secretaries, the attorney general, and a number of other officials. (See Table 12–2 at right for the names of the major executive departments represented in the cabinet.) Additional cabinet members vary from one presidency to the next. Typically, the vice president is a member.

President Barack Obama speaks at the swearing-in of Commerce Secretary Gary Locke and Health and Human Services Secretary Kathleen Sebelius in the East Room of the White House.

CHIP SOMODEVILLA/GETTY IMAGES

Table 12–2

The Major Executive Departments

The heads of all of these departments are members of the president's cabinet.

Department	Year of First Establishment
Department of State	1789
Department of the Treasury	1789
Department of Defense*	1789
Department of Justice (headed by the Attorney General)[†]	1789
Department of the Interior	1849
Department of Agriculture	1889
Department of Commerce[‡]	1903
Department of Labor[‡]	1903
Department of Health and Human Services[§]	1953
Department of Housing and Urban Development	1965
Department of Transportation	1967
Department of Energy	1977
Department of Education	1979
Department of Veterans Affairs	1989
Department of Homeland Security	2002

*Established in 1947 by merging the Department of War, created in 1789, and the Department of the Navy, created in 1798.
[†]Formerly the Office of the Attorney General; renamed and reorganized in 1870.
[‡]Formed in 1913 by splitting the Department of Commerce and Labor, which was created in 1903.
[§]Formerly the Department of Health, Education, and Welfare; renamed when the Department of Education was spun off in 1979.

President Clinton added ten officials to the cabinet, and George W. Bush added five. Barack Obama added the following members in addition to the vice president:

- The administrator of the Environmental Protection Agency.

- The chair of the Council of Economic Advisers.

- The director of the Office of Management and Budget.

- The United States ambassador to the United Nations.

- The United States trade representative.

- The White House chief of staff.

USE OF THE CABINET

Because the Constitution does not require the president to consult with the cabinet, the use of this body is purely discretionary. Some presidents have relied on the

cabinet An advisory group selected by the president to assist with decision making. Traditionally, the cabinet has consisted of the heads of the executive departments and other officers whom the president may choose to appoint.

counsel of their cabinets. Other presidents solicited the opinions of their cabinets and then did what they wanted to do anyway. After a cabinet meeting in which a vote was seven nays against his one aye, President Lincoln supposedly said, "Seven nays and one aye, the ayes have it."[13] Still other presidents have sought counsel from so-called **kitchen cabinets.** A kitchen cabinet is a very informal group of persons to whom the president turns for advice. The term *kitchen cabinet* originated during the presidency of Andrew Jackson, who relied on the counsel of close friends who allegedly met with him in the kitchen of the White House.

In general, few presidents have relied heavily on the advice of the formal cabinet. The department heads are at times more responsive to the wishes of their own staffs or to their own political ambitions than they are to the president. They may be more concerned with obtaining resources for their departments than with helping presidents achieve their goals.

OBAMA'S CABINET President Obama's response to the need to seek advice has been to centralize the advisory function within the White House Office (discussed below) by appointing a large number of in-house "czars." Each of these White House czars has responsibility for a certain policy area. Critics of the Obama administration believe that the czar system tends to undercut the authority of cabinet members. Congress also loses leverage, because cabinet members must be confirmed by the Senate, whereas czars are responsible only to the president.

The Executive Office of the President

In 1939, President Franklin D. Roosevelt set up the **Executive Office of the President (EOP)** to cope with the increased responsibilities brought

Table 12–3

The Executive Office of the President as of 2010

Department
Council of Economic Advisers
Council on Environmental Quality
Executive Residence
National Security Council and Homeland Security Council
Office of Administration
Office of Management and Budget
Office of National Drug Control Policy
Office of Science and Technology Policy
Office of the U.S. Trade Representative
Office of the Vice President
The White House
White House Office

Source: www.whitehouse.gov.

on by the Great Depression. Since then, the EOP has grown significantly to accommodate the expansive role played by the national government, including the executive branch, in the nation's economic and social life.

The EOP is made up of the top advisers and assistants who help the president carry out major duties. Over the years, the EOP has changed according to the needs and leadership style of each president. It has become an increasingly influential and important part of the executive branch. Table 12–3 above lists various offices within the EOP as of 2010. Note that the organization of the EOP is subject to change. Presidents have frequently added new bodies to its membership and subtracted others. President Obama made a number of changes to the EOP's table of organization during his first two years in office.

THE WHITE HOUSE OFFICE Of all of the executive staff agencies, the **White House Office** has the most direct contact with the president. The White House Office is headed by the **chief of staff,** who advises the president on important matters and directs the operations of the presidential staff. A number of other top officials, assistants, and special assistants to the president also aid him or her in such areas as national security, the economy, and political affairs. The **press secretary** (under Obama, Robert Gibbs) meets with reporters and makes public statements for the president. The counsel to the president serves as the White House lawyer and handles the president's legal matters.

The White House staff also includes speechwriters, researchers, the president's physician, and a

kitchen cabinet The name given to a president's unofficial advisers. The term was coined during Andrew Jackson's presidency.

Executive Office of the President (EOP) A group of staff agencies that assist the president in carrying out major duties. Franklin D. Roosevelt established the EOP in 1939 to cope with the increased responsibilities brought on by the Great Depression.

White House Office The personal office of the president. White House Office personnel handle the president's political needs and manage the media.

chief of staff The person who directs the operations of the White House Office and advises the president on important matters.

press secretary A member of the White House staff who holds news conferences for reporters and makes public statements for the president.

correspondence secretary. Altogether, the White House Office has more than four hundred employees.

The White House staff has several duties. First, the staff investigates and analyzes problems that require the president's attention. Staff members who are specialists in certain areas, such as diplomatic relations or foreign trade, gather information for the president and suggest solutions. White House staff members also screen the questions, issues, and problems that people present to the president, so matters that can be handled by other officials do not reach the president's desk. Additionally, the staff provides public relations support. For example, the press staff handles the president's relations with the White House press corps and schedules news conferences. Finally, the White House staff ensures that the president's initiatives are effectively transmitted to the relevant government personnel. Several staff members are usually assigned to work directly with members of Congress for this purpose.

The White House Office also includes the staff of the president's spouse. First Ladies have at times taken important roles within the White House. For example, Franklin D. Roosevelt's wife, Eleanor, advocated the rights of women, labor, and African Americans. As First Lady, Hillary Clinton developed an unsuccessful plan for a national health-care system. In 2008, she was a leading contender for the Democratic presidential nomination. Had she won the presidency, Bill Clinton would have become the nation's First Gentleman.

THE OFFICE OF MANAGEMENT AND BUDGET The **Office of Management and Budget (OMB)** was originally the Bureau of the Budget. Under recent presidents, the OMB has become an important and influential unit of the Executive Office of the President. The main function of the OMB is to assist the president in preparing the proposed annual budget, which the president must submit to Congress in January of each year (see Chapter 11 for details). The federal budget lists the revenues and expenditures expected for the coming year. It indicates which programs the federal government will pay for and how much they will cost. Thus, the budget is an annual statement of the public policies of the United States translated into dollars and cents. Making changes in the budget is a key way for presidents to influence the direction and policies of the federal government.

The president appoints the director of the OMB with the consent of the Senate. The director oversees the OMB's work and argues the administration's positions before Congress. The director also lobbies members of Congress to support the president's budget or to accept key features of it. Once the budget is approved by Congress, the OMB has the responsibility of putting it into practice. The OMB oversees the execution of the budget, checking the federal agencies to ensure that they use funds efficiently.

Beyond its budget duties, the OMB also reviews new bills prepared by the executive branch. It checks all legislative matters to be certain that they agree with the president's own positions.

> **Office of Management and Budget (OMB)** An agency in the Executive Office of the President that assists the president in preparing and supervising the administration of the federal budget.
>
> **National Security Council (NSC)** A council that advises the president on domestic and foreign matters concerning the safety and defense of the nation; established in 1947.

THE NATIONAL SECURITY COUNCIL The **National Security Council (NSC)** was established in 1947 to manage the defense and foreign policy of the United States. Its members are the president, the vice president, and the secretaries of state and defense; it also has several informal advisers. The NSC is the president's link to his or her key foreign and military advisers. The president's special assistant for national security affairs heads the NSC staff.

The Vice Presidency and Presidential Succession

As a rule, presidential nominees choose running mates who balance the ticket or whose appointment rewards or appeases party factions. For example, to balance the ticket geographically, a presidential candidate from the South may solicit a running mate from the West. George W. Bush, who had little experience in national government, picked Dick Cheney, a well-known Republican with extensive political experience in Washington, D.C.

In 2008, unsuccessful Republican candidate John McCain chose as his running mate Alaska governor Sarah Palin. He hoped, in part, to capture a larger share of the female vote. Palin also shored up McCain's support among cultural conservatives. President Barack Obama picked Senator Joe Biden, who had thirty-five years of experience in Congress. Obama wished to counter detractors who claimed that he was too inexperienced.

THE ROLE OF VICE PRESIDENTS For much of our history, the vice president has had almost no responsibilities. Still, the vice president is in a position to become the nation's chief executive should the president die, be impeached, or resign the presidential office. Nine vice presidents have become president because of the death or resignation of the president.

In recent years, the responsibilities of the vice president have grown immensely. The vice president has become one of the most—if not *the* most—important of the president's advisers. The first modern vice president to act as a major adviser was Walter Mondale, who served under Jimmy Carter. Later, Bill Clinton relied heavily on Vice President Al Gore, who shared many of Clinton's values and beliefs.

Without question, however, the most powerful vice president in American history was Dick Cheney, who served under George W. Bush. A consummate bureaucratic strategist, Cheney was able to place his supporters in important positions throughout the government, giving him access to information and influence. This unprecedented delegation of power, of course, would not have been possible without the president's agreement, and Bush clearly approved of it. Vice President Joe Biden is one of President Barack Obama's most important advisers, but not at the level of Cheney.

PRESIDENTIAL SUCCESSION One of the questions left unanswered by the Constitution was what the vice president should do if the president becomes incapable of carrying out necessary duties while in office. The

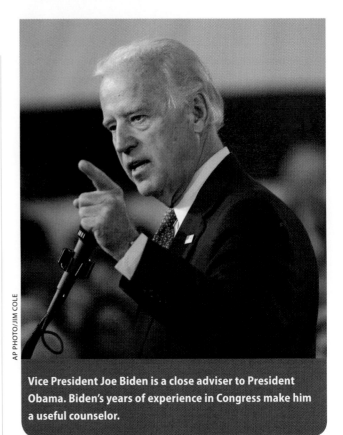

AP PHOTO/JIM COLE

Vice President Joe Biden is a close adviser to President Obama. Biden's years of experience in Congress make him a useful counselor.

Twenty-fifth Amendment to the Constitution, ratified in 1967, filled this gap. The amendment states that when the president believes that he or she is incapable of performing the duties of the office, he or she must inform Congress in writing of this fact. Then the vice president serves as acting president until the president can resume his or her normal duties.

When the president is unable to communicate, a majority of the cabinet, including the vice president, can declare that fact to Congress. Then the vice president serves as acting president until the president resumes normal duties. If a dispute arises over the return of the president's ability to discharge the normal functions of the presidential office, a two-thirds vote of both chambers of Congress is required if the vice president is to remain acting president. Otherwise, the president resumes these duties.

The Twenty-fifth Amendment also addresses the question of how the president should fill a vacant vice presidency. Section 2 of the amendment states, "Whenever there is a vacancy in the office of the Vice President, the President shall nominate a Vice President who shall take office upon confirmation by a majority vote of both Houses of Congress."

In 1973, Gerald Ford became the first appointed vice president of the United States after Spiro Agnew was forced to resign. One year later, President Richard Nixon resigned, and Ford advanced to the office of president. President Ford named Nelson Rockefeller

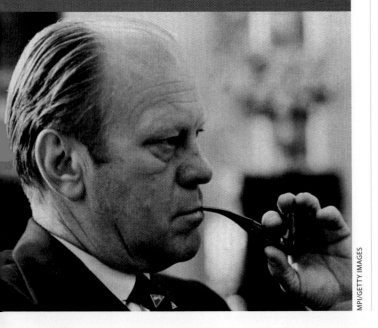

Gerald Ford, the 38th president of the United States. He succeeded Richard Nixon after the Watergate scandal, and one of his first public acts was to pardon the former president for his alleged crimes.

MPI/GETTY IMAGES

as his vice president. For the first time in U.S. history, neither the president nor the vice president had been elected to his position.

What if both the president and the vice president die, resign, or are disabled? According to the Succession Act of 1947, the Speaker of the House of Representatives will then act as president on his or her resignation as Speaker and as representative. If the Speaker is unavailable, next in line is the president pro tem of the Senate, followed by the permanent members of the president's cabinet in the order of the creation of their departments (see Table 12–2 on page 273).

AMERICA AT ODDS   *The Presidency*

The president is the most conspicuous figure in our political system. Everyone has opinions about what the president should do—and in a presidential election year, who the president should be. To an extent not seen in regard to other offices, the public also has a serious interest in the president's personality and character. The president, after all, represents all of us. Americans are at odds over a variety of questions relating to the presidency. These include the following:

- Should the president try, whenever possible, to compromise with other political players such as the Congress—or should the president generally stand on principle?

- Should the president seek to expand his or her authority so as to deal more effectively with the nation's problems—or should the president try to adhere to a strict constitutional understanding of the powers of the office?

- Is it appropriate for the president to rely primarily on staff members within the White House Office when determining policy—or should the president offer the cabinet a substantial policymaking role?

- Should voters evaluate presidential candidates primarily on the positions they take on the issues—or are the president's character and decision-making style more important considerations?

- Should the president be the "moral leader" of the country and base policies on religious values—or should the president avoid any intermingling of religion and policy?

Take Action

President James Madison (1809–1817) once said, "The citizens of the United States are responsible for the greatest trust ever confided to a political society." Notice that Madison laid the responsibility for this trust on the "citizens," not the "government." Even though it may seem that one person can do little to affect government policymaking and procedures, this assumption has been proved wrong time and again. If you would like to influence the way things are done in Washington, D.C., you can do so by helping to elect a president and members of Congress whose views you endorse and who you think would do a good job of running the country. Clearly, you will want to vote in the next elections. Before then, though, you could join others who share your political beliefs and work on behalf of one of the candidates. You could support a candidate in your home state or join others in "adopting" a candidate from another state who is facing a close race for a congressional seat. You can access that candidate's Web site and offer your services, such as calling voters of the candidate's party and urging them to go to the polls and vote for the candidate. You can also help raise funds for the candidate's campaign and, if you can afford it, even donate some money yourself.

President Obama shares a laugh with other world leaders after they posed for the family photo at the G8 Summit in Muskoka, Canada, in June 2010.

OFFICIAL WHITE HOUSE PHOTO BY PETE SOUZA

POLITICS ON THE
WEB

- The White House home page offers links to many sources of information on the presidency. You can access this site at **www.whitehouse.gov**

- If you are interested in reading the inaugural addresses of American presidents from George Washington to Barack Obama, go to **www.bartleby.com/124**. In addition to the full text of the inaugural addresses, this site provides biographical information on the presidents.

- If you would like to research documents and academic resources concerning the presidency, a good Internet site to consult is provided by the University of Virginia's Miller Center of Public Affairs at **millercenter.org/academic/americanpresident**

- To access the various presidential libraries, visit the National Archives site at **www.archives.gov/presidential-libraries**

 CourseMate

Access CourseMate to review and expand on this chapter through quizzes, flashcards, learning objectives, interactive timelines, a crossword puzzle, audio summaries, video, critical-thinking activities, simulations, and more.

GOVT

The Bureaucracy

13

LEARNING OBJECTIVES

LO1 Describe the size and functions of the U.S. bureaucracy.

LO2 Discuss the structure and basic components of the federal bureaucracy.

LO3 Indicate when the federal civil service was established and explain how bureaucrats get their jobs.

LO4 Explain how regulatory agencies make rules and how issue networks affect policymaking in government.

LO5 Identify some of the ways in which the government has attempted to curb waste and improve efficiency in the bureaucracy.

CourseMate

How Much Regulation Do We Need?

Many people believe that the financial crisis of 2008 and 2009 was caused by inadequate regulation of financial enterprises. As a result, these businesses took on far too much risk. It's not surprising, therefore, that in July 2010, Congress imposed a large number of new regulations on the financial industry. Compliance will be costly. The health-care reform legislation adopted earlier in 2010 also involves a substantial body of new regulations.

In the distant past, there was very little government regulation of health care or other industries. One hundred years ago, drugs were not tested before they were put on the market. Hospitals had no uniform standards. Physicians were licensed, but that's about it. Today, the cost of complying with federal rules regulating health care has been estimated at about $350 billion per year.

The Small Business Administration has calculated that the annual cost of all federal regulations is about $1.75 trillion, or 14 percent of the national income. The average cost of regulation for large businesses is $7,755 per employee each year. For small businesses, which do not benefit from economies of scale, the cost is $10,585.

Unbridled Capitalism Is Dead

The law of the capitalist jungle is what got us into the biggest financial crisis since the Great Depression. The events leading up to the credit meltdown in 2008 and the massive federal bailout of banks and insurance companies were caused by unregulated financial entities. Investment banking firms created ever-riskier financial assets, which they sold to unsuspecting individuals and even to local governments as solid, gold-plated investments. In the mortgage industry, unscrupulous salespeople who earned big commissions tricked unsuspecting families into buying homes that were too expensive for their modest means. When house payments went up, those families lost their homes and sometimes their life savings.

We have lived through a time when a president—George W. Bush—scornfully ignored a Supreme Court decision on the regulation of greenhouse gas emissions. Even with something as important as the prescription drugs that we take, the government is not giving us enough protection. Recently, despite its staff members' misgivings, the Food and Drug Administration (FDA) allowed a drug named Avandia to hit the market. That drug turned out to have potential cardiac side effects, and no safety statement on the drug's label warned of them. Regulation is here to stay. Indeed, we need more regulation to protect our lives and our pocketbooks.

Too Much of Anything Is Bad

While no one argues that regulation should be eliminated, many today believe that it is too costly relative to the actual benefits received. Consider the health-care industry regulatory costs mentioned above. By one estimate, the dollar value of the benefits from those regulations is only $170 billion per year. That means that with a total cost of $350 billion, the regulations generate a net cost to society of about $180 billion, or about $1,500 per U.S. household.

Consider another example. We all want safer products, but the Consumer Product Safety Commission now requires that warning labels appear on even common products. A standard ladder has six hundred words of warning pasted on it, including a warning not to place it in front of a swinging door. What are we, idiots? Every toy has a warning that says, "Small parts may cause a choking risk." Parents don't know this? Studies indicate that virtually no one reads warning labels anymore because they are either obvious or too long. What happened to personal responsibility in America? With excessive regulation, the average American no longer appears to be responsible for any of her or his purchases, activities, or actions. Regulation has its place, but it shouldn't control the entire life of a nation.

WHERE DO YOU STAND?

1. How much do you think you benefit from regulation in our economy? Give some examples.
2. Are there any circumstances under which warning labels on consumer products could help you? Give some examples.

EXPLORE THIS ISSUE ONLINE

1. For arguments that the FDA is not strict enough in approving medicines, go to the Public Citizen's Health Research Group site at **www.citizen.org/hrg**.
2. The Competitive Enterprise Institute believes the FDA is too slow to approve drugs. See its articles at **cei.org/issues/economic-regulation**.

Introduction

Did you eat breakfast this morning? If you did, **bureaucrats**—individuals who work in the offices of government—had a lot to do with that breakfast. If you had bacon, the meat was inspected by federal agents. If you drank milk, the price was affected by rules and regulations of the Department of Agriculture. If you looked at a cereal box, you saw fine print about fat and vitamins, which was the result of regulations made by several other federal agencies, including the Food and Drug Administration. If you ate leftover pizza for breakfast, state or local bureaucrats made sure that the kitchen of the pizza eatery was sanitary and safe. Other bureaucrats ensured that the employees who put together (and perhaps delivered) the pizza were protected against discrimination in the workplace.

Today, the word *bureaucracy* often evokes a negative reaction. For some, it conjures up visions of depersonalized automatons performing chores without any sensitivity toward the needs of those they serve. For others, it is synonymous with government "red tape." A **bureaucracy,** however, is simply a large, complex administrative organization that is structured hierarchically in a pyramid-like fashion.[1] Government bureaucrats carry out the policies of elected government officials. Members of the bureaucracy—government employees—deliver our mail, clean our streets, teach in our public schools, run our national parks, and attempt to ensure the safety of our food and the prescription drugs that we take. Life as we know it would be quite different without the bureaucrats who keep our governments—federal, state, and local—in operation. Still, Americans disagree over how much regulation is necessary, as discussed in the chapter-opening *America at Odds* feature.

GOVERNMENT BUREAUCRACY:
"A marvelous labor-saving device which enables ten men to do the work of one."

~ JOHN MAYNARD KEYNES ~
BRITISH ECONOMIST
1883–1946

LO1 The Nature and Size of the Bureaucracy

The concept of a bureaucracy is not confined to the federal government. Any large organization has to have a bureaucracy. In each bureaucracy, everybody (except the head of the bureaucracy) reports to at least one other person. In the federal government, the head of the bureaucracy is the president of the United States, and the bureaucracy is part of the executive branch.[2]

A bureaucratic form of organization allows each person to concentrate on her or his area of knowledge and expertise. In your college or university, for example, you do not expect the basketball coach to solve the problems of the finance department. The reason the federal government bureaucracy exists is that Congress, over time, has delegated certain tasks to specialists. For example, in 1914, Congress

The man in the center is a food inspector who is responsible for the quality and safety of what we eat.

MIKE MERGEN/BLOOMBERG NEWS/GETTY IMAGES

bureaucrat An individual who works in a bureaucracy. As generally used, the term refers to a government employee.

bureaucracy A large, complex, hierarchically structured administrative organization that carries out specific functions.

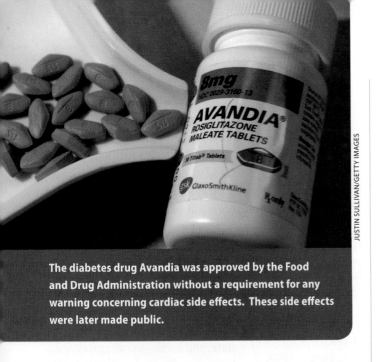

The diabetes drug Avandia was approved by the Food and Drug Administration without a requirement for any warning concerning cardiac side effects. These side effects were later made public.

passed the Federal Trade Commission Act, which established the Federal Trade Commission to regulate deceptive and unfair trade practices. Those appointed to the commission were specialists in this area. Similarly, Congress passed the Consumer Product Safety Act in 1972, which established the Consumer Product Safety Commission to investigate the safety of consumer products. The commission is one of many federal administrative agencies.

Another key aspect of any bureaucracy is that the power to act resides in the *position* rather than in the *person*. In your college or university, the person who is president now has more or less the same authority as any previous president. Additionally, bureaucracies usually entail standard operating procedures—directives on what procedures should be followed in specific circumstances. Bureaucracies normally also have a merit system, meaning that people are hired and promoted on the basis of demonstrated skills and achievements.

The Growth of Bureaucracy

The federal government that existed in 1789 was small. It had three departments, each with only a few employees: (1) the Department of State (nine employees), (2) the Department of War (two employees), and (3) the Department of the Treasury (thirty-nine employees). By 1798, nine years later, the federal bureaucracy was still quite small. The secretary of state had seven clerks. His total expenditures on stationery and printing amounted to $500, or about $8,830 in 2011 dollars. The Department of War spent, on average, a grand total of $1.4 million each year, or about $25.8 million in 2011 dollars.

Times have changed. Figure 13–1 below shows the number of government employees at the local, state, and national levels from 1982 to 2010. Most growth has been at the state and local levels. All in all, the three levels of government employ about 16 percent of the civilian labor force. Today, more Americans are employed by government (at all three levels) than by the entire manufacturing sector of the U.S. economy.

During election campaigns, politicians throughout the nation claim they will "cut big government and red tape" and "get rid of overlapping and wasteful bureaucracies." For the last several decades, virtually every president has campaigned on a platform calling for a reduction in the size of the federal bureaucracy. Yet, at the same time, candidates promise to establish programs that require new employees.

The Costs of Maintaining the Government

The costs of maintaining the government are high and growing. In 1929, government at all levels accounted for about 11 percent of the nation's gross domestic product (GDP). Today, that figure exceeds 40 percent. Average citizens pay a significant portion of their income to federal, state, and local governments. They do this by paying income taxes, sales

Figure 13–1

Government Employment at the Local, State, and National Levels

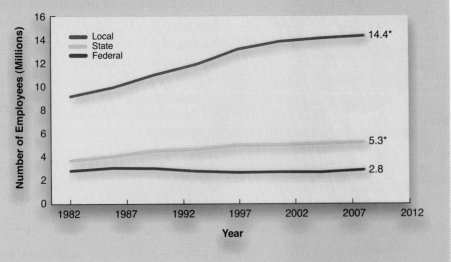

*Estimated
Source: U.S. Census Bureau.

OUR GOVERNMENT FACES A TROUBLED ECONOMY

Spending More on Health Care—and Less

The heath-care reform bills that President Barack Obama signed into law in March 2010 become effective over a period of several years. The most important parts do not take effect until January 1, 2014. From that day on, subsidies will help citizens purchase health-care insurance if they are not covered by an employer's plan. Individuals and families with incomes up to four times the federal poverty level will be eligible for at least some subsidies. (Currently, the income cutoff would be $88,200 for a family of four, but the exact value will surely change.)

About 32 million Americans who do not have health-care insurance will gain coverage. How will the government pay for that? One method is straightforward—the reforms raise the taxes of the wealthiest taxpayers. Part of the necessary funds, however, come from reducing the growth rate of health-care spending by the federal government. Between the new taxes and the reduced spending, the reforms are expected to shrink the size of the federal budget deficit slightly, thus fulfilling one of President Obama's promises. But what will be cut?

Cost Cutting Is Already Part of the System

In fact, some attempts to restrain spending are built into the existing system. Now, as in the past, most federal health-care spending goes for two programs: Medicare, which provides health-care insurance to those aged sixty-five or older, and Medicaid, which funds health care for the poor. In 2010, a federal agency called the Centers for Medicare and Medicaid Services (CMS) proposed a rate reduction for more than 1 million physicians and non-physician practitioners. This 6.1 percent rate reduction for 2011 applies to everyone paid under the Medical Physician Fee Schedule (MPFS). The MPFS determines Medicare and Medicaid payment rates for seven thousand types of services in physicians' offices and hospitals. Of course, some physicians were not happy about this decision.

Cutting Back on Medicare Advantage

Some of the biggest cuts will come from a program called Medicare Advantage. This program lets seniors use Medicare funds to buy private insurance plans. More than 20 percent of American seniors have already enrolled in Medicare Advantage. The program is somewhat more expensive than standard Medicare, which is a government-administered health-insurance program. Polls also show that Medicare Advantage enrollees are more satisfied with their care than those who are enrolled in the regular Medicare program. In the future, those who wish to continue with Medicare Advantage can expect to pay higher premiums and receive fewer benefits.

Polls show that well over 70 percent of individuals aged sixty-five or over approve of Medicare. A majority consider it to be well run. The question is, will Medicare enrollees continue to report high levels of satisfaction as the government attempts to control the program's costs?

You Be the Judge Why might persons aged sixty-five and over be more likely than younger Americans to oppose the recent health-care reforms?

taxes, property taxes, and many other types of taxes and fees. To fully understand the amount of money spent by federal, state, and local governments each year, consider that the same sum of money could be used to purchase all of the farmland in the United States plus all of the assets of the one hundred largest American corporations.

The government is costly, to be sure, but it also provides numerous services for Americans. Cutting back on the size of government inevitably means a reduction in those services. The trade-off between government spending and popular services was central to the debate over health-care reform. Even as the Obama administration advocated substantial new health-care spending, it also tried to limit costs. We discuss that issue in this chapter's *Our Government Faces a Troubled Economy* feature above.

LO2 How the Federal Bureaucracy Is Organized

A complete organization chart of the federal government would cover an entire wall. A simplified version is provided in Figure 13–2 below. The executive branch consists of a number of bureaucracies that provide services to Congress, to the federal courts, and to the president directly.

The executive branch of the federal government includes four major types of structures:

■ Executive departments.

■ Independent executive agencies.

■ Independent regulatory agencies.

■ Government corporations.

Each type of structure has its own relationship to the president and its own internal workings.

Figure 13–2

The Organization of the Federal Government

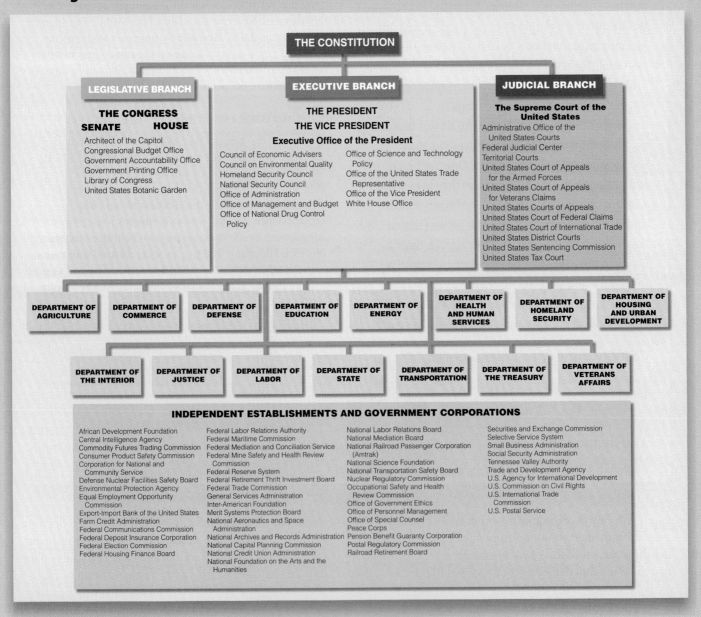

Sources: *United States Government Manual*, 2008–09 (Washington, D.C.: U.S. Government Printing Office, 2008); and **whitehouse.gov**.

The Executive Departments

You were introduced to the various executive departments in Chapter 12, when you read about how the president works with the cabinet and other close advisers. The fifteen executive departments, which are directly accountable to the president, are the major service organizations of the federal government. They are responsible for performing government functions, such as training troops (Department of Defense), printing money (Department of the Treasury), and enforcing federal laws setting minimum safety and health standards for workers (Department of Labor).

Table 13–1 on the following two pages provides an overview of each of the departments within the executive branch. The table lists a few of the many activities undertaken by each department. Because the president appoints the department heads, they are expected to help carry out the president's policy objectives. Often, they attempt to maximize the president's political fortunes as well. Is this a problem when the cabinet member in question is the U.S. attorney general? We discuss that issue in this chapter's *Join the Debate* feature on page 288.

Each executive department was created by Congress as the perceived need for it arose, and each department manages a specific policy area. In 2002, for example, Congress created the Department of Homeland Security to deal with the threat of terrorism. The head of each department is known as the secretary, except for the Department of Justice, which is headed by the attorney general. Each department head is appointed by the president and confirmed by the Senate.

A Typical Departmental Structure

Each cabinet department consists of the department's top administrators (the secretary of the department, deputy secretary, undersecretaries, and the like), plus a number of agencies. For example, the National Park Service is an agency within the Department of the Interior. The Drug Enforcement Administration is an agency within the Department of Justice.

Although there are organizational differences among the departments, each department generally follows a typical bureaucratic structure. The Department of Agriculture provides a model for how an executive department is organized (see Figure 13–3 on page 289).

One aspect of the secretary of agriculture's job is to carry out the president's agricultural policies. Another aspect, however, is to promote and protect the department. The secretary spends time ensuring that Congress allocates enough money for the department to work effectively. The secretary also makes sure that constituents, or the people the department serves—farmers and major agricultural corporations—are happy. In general, the secretary tries to maintain or improve the status of the department with respect to all of the other departments and units of the federal bureaucracy.

The secretary of agriculture is assisted by a deputy secretary and several assistant secretaries and undersecretaries, all of whom are nominated by the president and put into office with Senate approval. The secretary and assistant secretaries have staffs that help with all sorts of jobs, such as hiring new people and generating positive public relations for the Department of Agriculture.

Independent Executive Agencies

Independent executive agencies are federal bureaucratic organizations that have a single function. They are independent in the sense that they are not located within a cabinet department. Rather, independent executive agency heads report directly to the president. A new federal independent executive agency can be created only through cooperation between the president and Congress.

Prior to the twentieth century, the federal government did almost all of its work through the executive departments. In the twentieth century, in contrast, presidents began to ask for certain executive agencies to be kept separate, or independent, from existing departments. Today, there are more than two hundred independent executive agencies.

Sometimes, agencies are kept independent because of the sensitive nature of their functions. At other times, Congress creates independent agencies to protect them from **partisan politics**—politics in support of a particular party. The U.S. Commission on Civil Rights, which was created in 1957, is a case in point. Congress wanted to protect the work of the commission from the influences not only of Congress's own political interests but also of the president. The Central Intelligence Agency (CIA), which was formed in 1947, is another good example. Both Congress and the president know that the intelligence activities of the CIA could be abused if it were not independent. Finally, the General

---

independent executive agency A federal agency that is not located within a cabinet department.

partisan politics Political actions or decisions that benefit a particular party.

Table 13–1

Executive Departments

DEPARTMENT (Year of Original Establishment)		PRINCIPAL DUTIES	SELECTED SUBAGENCIES
State (1789)		Negotiates treaties; develops our foreign policy; protects citizens abroad.	Passport Services Office; Bureau of Diplomatic Security; Foreign Service; Bureau of Human Rights and Humanitarian Affairs; Bureau of Consular Affairs.
Treasury (1789)		Pays all federal bills; borrows money; collects federal taxes; mints coins and prints paper currency; supervises national banks.	Internal Revenue Service; U.S. Mint.
Defense (1789)*		Manages the armed forces (Army, Navy, Air Force, Marines); operates military bases.	National Security Agency; Joint Chiefs of Staff; Departments of the Air Force, Navy, Army; Defense Intelligence Agency; the service academies.
Justice (1789)†		Furnishes legal advice to the president; enforces federal criminal laws; supervises the federal corrections system (prisons).	Federal Bureau of Investigation; Drug Enforcement Administration; Bureau of Prisons; U.S. Marshals Service.
Interior (1849)		Supervises federally owned lands and parks; operates federal hydroelectric power facilities; supervises Native American affairs.	U.S. Fish and Wildlife Service; National Park Service; Bureau of Indian Affairs; Bureau of Land Management.
Agriculture (1889)		Provides assistance to farmers and ranchers; conducts research to improve agricultural efficiency and to prevent plant disease; works to protect forests from fires and disease.	Soil Conservation Service; Agricultural Research Service; Food Safety and Inspection Service; Federal Crop Insurance Corporation; Forest Service.
Commerce (1903)‡		Grants patents and trademarks; conducts national census; monitors the weather; protects the interests of businesses.	Bureau of the Census; Bureau of Economic Analysis; Minority Business Development Agency; Patent and Trademark Office; National Oceanic and Atmospheric Administration.

Table 13–1

Executive Departments—(Continued)

DEPARTMENT (Year of Original Establishment)	PRINCIPAL DUTIES	SELECTED SUBAGENCIES
Labor (1903)‡	Administers federal labor laws; promotes the interests of workers.	Occupational Safety and Health Administration; Bureau of Labor Statistics; Employment Standards Administration; Employment and Training Administration.
Health and Human Services (1953)§	Promotes public health; enforces pure food and drug laws; sponsors health-related research.	Food and Drug Administration; Centers for Disease Control and Prevention; National Institutes of Health; Administration for Children and Families; Centers for Medicare and Medicaid Services.
Housing and Urban Development (1965)	Is concerned with the nation's housing needs; develops and rehabilitates urban communities; oversees resale of mortgages.	Government National Mortgage Association; Office of Multifamily Housing Development; Office of Single Family Program Development; Office of Fair Housing and Equal Opportunity.
Transportation (1967)	Finances improvements in mass transit; develops and administers programs for highways, railroads, and aviation.	Federal Aviation Administration; Federal Highway Administration; National Highway Traffic Safety Administration; Federal Transit Administration.
Energy (1977)	Promotes the conservation of energy and resources; analyzes energy data; conducts research and development.	Office of Civilian Radioactive Waste Management; National Nuclear Security Administration; Energy Information Administration.
Education (1979)	Coordinates federal programs and policies for education; administers aid to education; promotes educational research.	Office of Special Education and Rehabilitation Services; Office of Elementary and Secondary Education; Office of Postsecondary Education; Office of Vocational and Adult Education.
Veterans Affairs (1989)	Promotes the welfare of veterans of the U.S. armed forces.	Veterans Health Administration; Veterans Benefits Administration; National Cemetery Administration.
Homeland Security (2002)	Works to prevent terrorist attacks within the United States, control America's borders, and minimize the damage from potential attacks and natural disasters.	U.S. Customs and Border Protection; U.S. Citizenship and Immigration Services; U.S. Coast Guard; Secret Service; Federal Emergency Management Agency.

*Established in 1947 by merging the Department of War, created in 1789, and the Department of the Navy, created in 1798.
†Formerly the Office of the Attorney General; renamed and reorganized in 1870.
‡Formed in 1913 by splitting the Department of Commerce and Labor, which was created in 1903.
§Formerly the Department of Health, Education, and Welfare; renamed when the Department of Education was spun off in 1979.

Should the Attorney General Be Independent of the President?

The attorney general is a member of the president's cabinet. As such, he or she is nominated by the president and must be approved by the Senate before taking office. Traditionally, the attorney general has been a close political ally of the president. Ronald Reagan and Jimmy Carter both named reliable cronies to head up the Justice Department. Richard Nixon's attorney general John Mitchell was even sentenced to prison for corrupt politicization of his office. George W. Bush's attorney general Alberto Gonzales deferred completely to the White House. One result was a politically motivated "midnight massacre" during which eight U.S. attorneys were fired supposedly for purely partisan reasons.

Is it right for the attorney general to be so close to the president? What if it becomes necessary to investigate members of the president's own administration? Shouldn't the nation's chief law enforcement officer be independent and nonpartisan? One way to accomplish this would be to remove the attorney general position from the president's cabinet and appoint that official for a fixed term of years that transcends the term of any one president. That is exactly what we have done with the position of Federal Bureau of Investigation (FBI) director, so why not do it with the position of attorney general?

Yes, Let's Make the Attorney General Independent

We do not need another attorney general like Alberto Gonzales or John Mitchell. Any president needs a personal attorney, but that official should be a member of the White House staff, not the head of the Justice Department. Presidents appoint FBI directors for a fixed term of ten years, which ensures that directors do not serve under a single president. If the FBI director wants to be reappointed, the director must consider that the president making the reappointment could belong to either political party. In the same way, if the attorney general were removed from the cabinet and appointed to a fixed term, the attorney general would have less political allegiance to any one president.

The attorney general should not be the handmaiden of presidential policy. The attorney general should be able to give the White House frank, independent advice whenever the administration is considering actions that might overreach the bounds of what is permitted by law. We should stop allowing our president to appoint cronies to such an important position.

We Don't Want a Nonpolitical Attorney General

Those who accept the current situation argue that we don't want a nonpolitical attorney general. We elect a president based on his or her policy proposals. We expect the agenda of the Justice Department to reflect the policies that got the president elected. If the president is an advocate of civil liberties, those who elected the president expect the attorney general to reflect this position. If a president has made a strong commitment to reduce illegal immigration, voters expect the attorney general to follow through on this pledge.

The comparison with an independent FBI director is not valid. The FBI director is in charge of the closest thing we have to a national police force. We obviously do not want that position to be politicized. The attorney general is a different type of creature. The president should be able to name an attorney general whose views reflect the president's.

For Critical Analysis *If a president does not like what the attorney general is doing, does the president have any recourse?*

Services Administration (GSA) was created as an independent executive agency in 1949 to provide services and office space for most federal agencies. To serve all parts of the government, it has to be an independent agency.

Among the more than two hundred independent executive agencies, a few stand out in importance either because of the mission they were established to accomplish or because of their large size. We list selected independent executive agencies in Table 13–2 on page 290.

independent regulatory agency A federal organization that is responsible for creating and implementing rules that regulate private activity and protect the public interest in a particular sector of the economy.

Independent Regulatory Agencies

Independent regulatory agencies are responsible for a specific type of public policy. Their function is to create and implement rules that regulate private activity and protect the public interest in a particular sector of the economy. They are sometimes called the "alphabet soup"

Figure 13-3

The Organization of the Department of Agriculture

SECRETARY
DEPUTY SECRETARY

| Chief Information Officer | Chief Financial Officer | Inspector General | Executive Operations | Director of Communications | General Counsel |

Undersecretary for Natural Resources and Environment
- Forest Service
- Natural Resources Conservation Service

Undersecretary for Farm and Foreign Agricultural Services
- Farm Service Agency
- Foreign Agricultural Service
- Risk Management Agency

Undersecretary for Rural Development
- Rural Utilities Service
- Rural Housing Service
- Rural Business Cooperative Service

Undersecretary for Food, Nutrition, and Consumer Services
- Food and Nutrition Service
- Center for Nutrition Policy and Promotion

Undersecretary for Food Safety
- Food Safety and Inspection Service

Undersecretary for Research, Education, and Economics
- Agricultural Research Service
- Cooperative State Research, Education, and Extension Service
- Economic Research Service
- National Agricultural Statistics Service

Undersecretary for Marketing and Regulatory Programs
- Agricultural Marketing Service
- Animal and Plant Health Inspection Service
- Grain Inspection, Packers, and Stockyards Administration

Assistant Secretary for Congressional Relations

Assistant Secretary for Administration

Assistant Secretary for Civil Rights

Source: *United States Government Manual, 2009–2010* (Washington, D.C.: U.S. Government Printing Office, 2010).

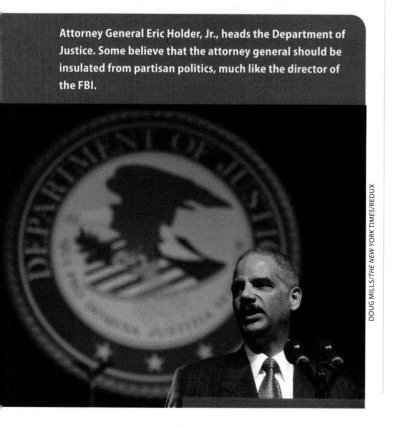

Attorney General Eric Holder, Jr., heads the Department of Justice. Some believe that the attorney general should be insulated from partisan politics, much like the director of the FBI.

DOUG MILLS/*THE NEW YORK TIMES*/REDUX

of government because most such agencies are known in Washington by their initials.

One of the earliest independent regulatory agencies was the Interstate Commerce Commission (ICC), established in 1887. (This agency was abolished in 1995.) After the ICC was formed, other agencies were created to regulate aviation (the Civil Aeronautics Board, or CAB, which was abolished in 1985), communication (the Federal Communications Commission, or FCC), the stock market (the Securities and Exchange Commission, or SEC), and many other areas of business. Table 13–3 on page 291 lists some major independent regulatory agencies.

Government Corporations

Another form of federal bureaucratic organization is the **government corporation,** a business that is owned by the

government corporation
An agency of the government that is run as a business enterprise. Such agencies engage primarily in commercial activities, produce revenues, and require greater flexibility than most government agencies receive.

Table 13–2

Selected Independent Executive Agencies

Name	Date Formed	Principal Duties
Central Intelligence Agency (CIA)	1947	Gathers and analyzes political and military information about foreign countries so that the United States can improve its own political and military status; conducts covert operations outside the United States.
General Services Administration (GSA)	1949	Purchases and manages property of the federal government; acts as the business arm of the federal government, overseeing federal government spending projects; discovers overcharges in government programs.
National Science Foundation (NSF)	1950	Promotes scientific research; provides grants to all levels of schools for instructional programs in the sciences.
Small Business Administration (SBA)	1953	Promotes the interests of small businesses; provides low-cost loans and management information to small businesses.
National Aeronautics and Space Administration (NASA)	1958	Responsible for the U.S. space program, including building, testing, and operating space vehicles.
Environmental Protection Agency (EPA)	1970	Undertakes programs aimed at reducing air and water pollution; works with state and local agencies to fight environmental hazards.
Social Security Administration (SSA)*	1995	Manages the government's Social Security programs, including Retirement and Survivors Insurance, Disability Insurance, and Supplemental Security Income.

*Separated from the Department of Health and Human Services in 1979 that year; originally established in 1946.

government. Government corporations are not exactly like corporations in which you buy stock, become a shareholder, and share in the profits by collecting dividends. The U.S. Postal Service is a government corporation, but it does not sell shares. If a government corporation loses money in the course of doing business, taxpayers, not shareholders, foot the bill.

Government corporations are like private corporations in that they provide a service that could be handled by the private sector. They are also like private corporations in that they charge for their services, though sometimes they charge less than private-sector corporations charge for similar services. Table 13–4 on the facing page lists selected government corporations.

A number of intermediate forms of organization exist that fall between a government corporation and a private one. In some circumstances, the government can take control of a private corporation. When a company goes bankrupt, for example, it is subject to the supervision of a federal judge until it exits from bankruptcy or is liquidated. The government can purchase stock in a private corporation—the government used this technique to funnel funds into major banks during the financial crisis that began in September 2008. The government can also set up a corporation and sell stock to the public.

The Federal Home Loan Mortgage Corporation (Freddie Mac) and the Federal National Mortgage Association (Fannie Mae) are examples of stockholder-

Homeland Security Secretary Janet Napolitano.

SHAWN THEW/EPA /LANDOV

Table 13-3

Selected Independent Regulatory Agencies

Name	Date Formed	Principal Duties
Federal Reserve System (Fed)	1913	Determines policy with respect to interest rates, credit availability, and the money supply.
Federal Trade Commission (FTC)	1914	Works to prevent businesses from engaging in unfair trade practices and to stop the formation of monopolies in the business sector; protects consumers' rights.
Securities and Exchange Commission (SEC)	1934	Regulates the nation's stock exchanges, where shares of stocks are bought and sold; requires full disclosure of the financial profiles of companies that wish to sell stocks and bonds to the public.
Federal Communications Commission (FCC)	1934	Regulates interstate and international communications by radio, television, wire, satellite, and cable.
National Labor Relations Board (NLRB)	1935	Protects employees' rights to join unions and to bargain collectively with employers; attempts to prevent unfair labor practices by both employers and unions.
Equal Employment Opportunity Commission (EEOC)	1964	Works to eliminate discrimination that is based on religion, gender, race, color, national origin, age, or disability; examines claims of discrimination.
Nuclear Regulatory Commission (NRC)	1974	Ensures that electricity-generating nuclear reactors in the United States are built and operated safely; regularly inspects operations of such reactors.

owned government-sponsored enterprises. Fannie Mae (founded in 1938) and Freddie Mac (created in 1970) buy, resell, and guarantee home mortgages. In September 2008, the government placed the two businesses into a conservatorship—effectively a bankruptcy overseen by the Federal Housing Finance Agency instead of a federal judge. The government also took an 80 percent share of the stock of each firm. Fannie Mae and Freddie Mac had become examples of almost every possible way that the government can intervene in a private company.

Table 13-4

Selected Government Corporations

Name	Date Formed	Principal Duties
Tennessee Valley Authority (TVA)	1933	Operates a Tennessee River control system and generates power for a seven-state region and for U.S. aeronautics and space programs; promotes the economic development of the Tennessee Valley region; controls floods and promotes the navigability of the Tennessee River.
Federal Deposit Insurance Corporation (FDIC)	1933	Insures individuals' bank deposits up to $250,000* and oversees the business activities of banks.
Export/Import Bank of the United States (Ex/Im Bank)	1933	Promotes American-made goods abroad; grants loans to foreign purchasers of American products.
National Railroad Passenger Corporation (AMTRAK)	1970	Provides a national and intercity rail passenger service network; controls more than 23,000 miles of track with about 505 stations.
U.S. Postal Service (formed from the old U.S. Post Office department—the Post Office itself is older than the Constitution)	1971	Delivers mail throughout the United States and its territories. Is the largest government corporation.

*This limit, previously $100,000, was raised in October 2008 in response to the financial crisis of that year.

LO3 How Bureaucrats Get Their Jobs

As already noted, federal bureaucrats holding top-level positions are appointed by the president and confirmed by the Senate. These bureaucrats include department and agency heads, their deputy and assistant secretaries, and so on. The list of positions that are filled by appointments is published after each presidential election in a document called *Policy and Supporting Positions*. The volume is more commonly known as the "Plum Book," because the eight thousand jobs it summarizes are known as "political plums." Normally, these jobs go to those who supported the winning presidential candidate.

The rank-and-file bureaucrats—the rest of the federal bureaucracy—are part of the **civil service** (nonmilitary employees of the government). They obtain their jobs through the Office of Personnel Management (OPM), an agency established by the Civil Service Reform Act of 1978. The OPM recruits, interviews, and tests potential government workers and determines who should be hired. The OPM makes recommendations to individual agencies as to which persons meet relevant standards (typically, the top three applicants for a position), and the agencies then generally decide which of the recommended individuals it will hire. The 1978 act also created the Merit Systems Protection Board (MSPB) to oversee promotions, employees' rights, and other employment matters. The MSPB evaluates charges of wrongdoing, hears employee appeals from agency decisions, and can order corrective action against agencies and employees.

The idea that the civil service should be based on a merit system dates back more than a century. The Civil Service Reform Act of 1883 established the principle of government employment on the basis of merit through open, competitive examinations. Initially, only about 10 percent of federal employees were covered by the merit system. Today, more than 90 percent of the federal civil service is recruited on the basis of

civil service Nonmilitary government employees.

legislative rule An administrative agency rule that carries the same weight as a statute enacted by a legislature.

enabling legislation A law enacted by a legislature to establish an administrative agency. Enabling legislation normally specifies the name, purpose, composition, and powers of the agency being created.

merit. Are public employees paid as well as workers in the private sector? For a discussion of this question, see this chapter's *Perception versus Reality* feature on the facing page.

LO4 Regulatory Agencies: Are They the Fourth Branch of Government?

In Chapter 2, we considered the system of checks and balances among the three branches of the U.S. government—executive, legislative, and judicial. Recent history, however, shows that it may be time to regard the regulatory agencies as a fourth branch of the government. Although the U.S. Constitution does not mention regulatory agencies, these agencies can and do make **legislative rules** that are as legally binding as laws passed by Congress. With such powers, this administrative branch has an influence on the nation's businesses that rivals that of the president, Congress, and the courts. Indeed, most Americans do not realize how much of our "law" is created by regulatory agencies.

Regulatory agencies have been on the American political scene since the nineteenth century, but their golden age came during the regulatory explosion of the 1960s and 1970s. Congress itself could not have overseen the actual implementation of all of the laws that it was enacting at that time to control pollution and deal with other social problems. It therefore chose (and still chooses) to delegate to administrative agencies the tasks involved in implementing its laws. By delegating some of its authority to an administrative agency, Congress may indirectly monitor a particular area in which it has passed legislation without becoming bogged down in the details relating to the enforcement of that legislation—details that are often best left to specialists. In recent years, the government has been hiring increasing numbers of specialists to oversee its regulatory work.

Agency Creation

To create a federal administrative agency, Congress passes **enabling legislation,** which specifies the name, purpose, composition, and

LAWRENCE MIGDALE/STONE/GETTY

Most parents do not jump for joy at the thought of their children going to work for the government. Government work in general in the United States has never been considered the road to riches. Indeed, the common picture of government employment is quite negative.

The Perception

It is often assumed that only individuals working in the private sector can hope to receive large paychecks. Even a member of Congress makes far less than most operations officers in midlevel corporations. Top-level staff members in the executive branch of the federal government also make much less than senior executives in the private sector. (This disparity is not really due to low pay for federal executives—it exists because the salaries of private-sector executives have skyrocketed in recent years.) Although even rank-and-file workers in the public sector receive paid-for medical insurance and a generous retirement program, the perception is that these benefits do not make up for the lower pay they earn.

The Reality

The Employee Benefit Research Institute has discovered that overall compensation costs for state and local governments are almost 50 percent higher than for private-sector employers. A recent study showed that a typical hour's work costs state and local governments $26 in wages and salaries, plus more than $13 in benefits. For that same hour of work, on average, a private-sector employer pays only about $19 in wages and salaries, plus $8 in benefits.

Move now to the federal government. The U.S. Bureau of Economic Analysis estimates that federal civilian government workers earn an average of $123,049 a year in total compensation (salaries plus benefits), which is twice the $61,051 in compensation for the average private-sector worker. This is one reason why Washington, D.C.—which is loaded with federal employees—is the fourth richest among this nation's 360 metropolitan areas. The gap between federal and private wages appears to have grown in recent years. Public-sector workers also enjoy pay bonuses amounting to 30 percent more than the bonuses received in the private sector. In addition, federal civil service rules bestow lifetime job security in the sense that it is extremely difficult to fire a federal employee.

One reason why government workers are paid so well is that, on average, they don't do exactly the same kind of work as employees in the private sector. When federal and private salaries are compared on an occupation-by-occupation basis, some of the income disparity goes away. Of course, if many federal employees have jobs that are also well paid in the private sector, that is another reality that contradicts the negative myths concerning government employment.

Blog On Arguments that government employees are overpaid are a constant theme of conservative blogs. Warren Meyer's Coyote Blog pays more attention to the topic than most. Visit it at **www.coyoteblog.com/coyote_blog/government**. The magazine *Government Executive* is a good place to find out how government employees, especially ones in the defense and technological fields, feel about their work. See it at **www.govexec.com**.

---

powers of the agency being created. The Federal Trade Commission (FTC), for example, was created in 1914 by the Federal Trade Commission Act, as mentioned earlier. The act prohibits unfair and deceptive trade practices. The act also describes the procedures that the agency must follow to charge persons or organizations with violations of the act, and it provides for judicial review of agency orders.

Other portions of the act grant the agency powers to "make rules and regulations for the purpose of carrying out the Act," to conduct investigations of business practices, to obtain reports on business practices from interstate corporations, to investigate possible violations of federal antitrust statutes, to publish findings of its investigations, and to recommend new legislation. The act also empowers the FTC to hold trial-like hearings and to **adjudicate** (formally resolve) certain kinds of disputes that involve FTC regulations or federal antitrust laws. When adjudication takes place, within the FTC or any other regulatory agency, an administrative law judge (ALJ) conducts the hearing and, after weighing

> **adjudicate** To render a judicial decision. In regard to administrative law, it is the process in which an administrative law judge hears and decides issues that arise when an agency charges a person or firm with violating a law or regulation enforced by the agency.

the evidence presented, issues an *order*. Unless it is overturned on appeal, the ALJ's order becomes final.

Enabling legislation makes the regulatory agency a potent organization. For example, the Securities and Exchange Commission (SEC) imposes rules regarding the disclosures a company must make to those who purchase its stock. Under its enforcement authority, the SEC also investigates and prosecutes alleged violations of these regulations. Finally, the SEC sits as judge and jury in deciding whether its rules have been violated and, if so, what punishment should be imposed on the offender (although the judgment may be appealed to a federal court).

Rulemaking

A major function of a regulatory agency is **rulemaking**—the formulation of new regulations. The power that an agency has to make rules is conferred on it by Congress in the agency's enabling legislation. For example, the Occupational Safety and Health Administration (OSHA) was authorized by the Occupational Safety and Health Act of 1970 to develop and issue rules governing safety in the workplace. Under this authority, OSHA has issued various safety standards. For example, OSHA deemed it in the public interest to issue a rule regulating the health-care industry to prevent the spread of certain diseases, including acquired immune deficiency syndrome (AIDS). The rule specified various standards—on how contaminated instruments should be handled, for instance—with which employers in that industry must comply. Agencies cannot just make a rule whenever they wish, however. Rather, they must follow certain procedural requirements, particularly those set forth in the Administrative Procedure Act of 1946.

Agencies must also make sure that their rules are based on substantial evidence and are not "arbitrary and capricious." Therefore, before proposing a new rule, an agency may engage in extensive investigation (through research, on-site inspections of the affected industry, surveys, and the like) to obtain data on the problem to be addressed by the rule. Based on this information, the agency may undertake a cost-benefit analysis of a new rule to determine whether its benefits outweigh its costs. For example, when issuing new rules governing electrical equipment, OSHA predicted that they would cost business $21.7 billion annually but would save 60 lives and eliminate 1,600 worker injuries a year. The agency also estimated that its safety equipment regulations for manufacturing workers would cost $52.4 billion, save 4 lives, and prevent 712,000 lost workdays because of injuries each year.

Don't get the idea that rulemaking is isolated from politics. As you will read shortly, bureaucrats work closely with members of Congress, as well as interest groups, when making rules.

Policymaking

Bureaucrats in federal agencies are expected to exhibit **neutral competency,** which means that they are supposed to apply their technical skills to their jobs without regard to political issues. In principle, they should not be swayed by the thought of personal or political gain. In reality, each independent agency and each executive department is interested in its own survival and expansion. Each is constantly battling the others for a larger share of the budget. All agencies and departments wish to retain or expand their functions and staffs. To do this, they must gain the goodwill of both the White House and Congress.

Although administrative agencies of the federal government are prohibited from directly lobbying Congress, departments and agencies have developed techniques to help them gain congressional support. Each organization maintains a congressional information office, which specializes in helping members of Congress by supplying any requested information and solving casework problems. For example, if a member of the House of Representatives receives a complaint from a constituent that his Social Security checks are not arriving on time, that member of Congress may go to the Social Security Administration and ask that something be done. Typically, requests from members of Congress receive immediate attention.

IRON TRIANGLES Analysts have determined that one way to understand the bureaucracy's role in policymaking is to examine the **iron triangle,** which is a three-way alliance among legislators (members of Congress), bureaucrats, and interest groups. (Iron triangles are also referred to as *subgovernments* or *policy communities*.) Presumably, the laws that are passed and the policies that are established benefit the interests of all three sides of the iron triangle. Iron triangles are well established in almost every part of the bureaucracy.

rulemaking The process undertaken by an administrative agency when formally proposing, evaluating, and adopting a new regulation.

neutral competency The application of technical skills to jobs without regard to political issues.

iron triangle A three-way alliance among legislators, bureaucrats, and interest groups to make or preserve policies that benefit their respective interests.

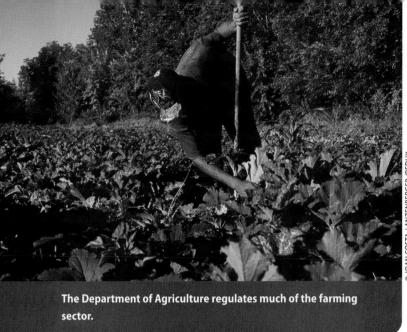

The Department of Agriculture regulates much of the farming sector.

© JOAN COSTA / ANZENBERGER /REDUX

AGRICULTURE AS AN EXAMPLE As an example, consider agricultural policy. Be aware first that the bureaucracy within the Department of Agriculture consists of more than 100,000 individuals working directly for the federal government and thousands of other individuals who work indirectly for the department as contractors, subcontractors, or consultants. Now think about the various interest groups and client groups that are concerned with what the bureaus and agencies in the Agriculture Department can do for them. Some of these groups are the American Farm Bureau Federation, the National Cattlemen's Beef Association, the National Milk Producers Federation, the National Corn Growers Association, and the various regional citrus growers associations. Finally, take a look at Congress, and you will see that two major committees are concerned with agriculture: the House Committee on Agriculture and the Senate Committee on Agriculture, Nutrition, and Forestry. Each committee has several specialized subcommittees.

The bureaucrats, interest groups, and legislators who make up this iron triangle cooperate to create mutually beneficial regulations and legislation. Because of the connections between agricultural interest groups and policymakers within the government, the agricultural industry has benefited greatly over the years from significant farm subsidies.

CONGRESS'S ROLE The Department of Agriculture is headed by the secretary of agriculture, who is nominated by the president (and confirmed by the Senate). But that secretary cannot even buy a desk lamp if Congress does not approve the appropriations for the department's budget. Within Congress, the responsibility for considering the Department of Agriculture's request for funding belongs first to the House and Senate appropriations committees and then to the agriculture subcommittees under them. The members of those subcommittees, most of whom represent agricultural states, have been around a long time and have their own ideas about what is appropriate for the Agriculture Department's budget. They carefully scrutinize the ideas of the president and the secretary of agriculture.

THE INFLUENCE OF INTEREST GROUPS The various interest groups—including producers of farm chemicals and farm machinery, agricultural cooperatives, grain dealers, and exporters—have vested interests in what the Department of Agriculture does and in what Congress lets the department do. Those interests are well represented by the lobbyists who crowd the halls of Congress. Many lobbyists have been working for agricultural interest groups for decades. They know the congressional committee members and Agriculture Department staff extremely well and routinely meet with them.

Issue Networks

The iron triangle relationship does not apply to all policy domains. When making policy decisions on environmental and welfare issues, for example, many members of Congress and agency officials rely heavily on "experts." Legislators and agency heads tend to depend on their staff members for specialized knowledge of rules, regulations, and legislation. These experts have frequently served variously as interest group lobbyists and as public-sector staff members during their careers, creating a revolving-door effect. They often have strong opinions and interests regarding the direction of policy and are thus able to exert a great deal of influence on legislators and bureaucratic agencies.

The relationships among these experts, which are less structured than iron triangles, are often referred to as **issue networks.** Like iron triangles, issue networks are made up of people with similar policy concerns. Issue networks are less interdependent and unified than iron triangles, however, and often include more players, such as media outlets.[3] (See Figure 13–4 on the following page.) A key characteristic of issue networks is that there can be more than one network in a given policy

issue networks Groups of individuals or organizations—which consist of legislators and legislative staff members, interest group leaders, bureaucrats, the media, scholars, and other experts—that support particular policy positions on a given issue.

Figure 13-4

Issue Network: The Environment

Executive Departments and Agencies
- Environmental Protection Agency
- Agriculture Department
- Energy Department
- Department of the Interior
- National Oceanic and Atmospheric Admin.
- Bureau of Land Management
- Army Corps of Engineers

Key Congressional Committees
- **Senate**
  Appropriations; Energy and Natural Resources; Environment and Public Works; Finance; Commerce, Science, and Transportation
- **House of Representatives**
  Agriculture; Appropriations; Natural Resources; Transportation and Infrastructure

Selected Interest Groups
- **Environmental Groups**
  Environmental Defense; Friends of the Earth; National Audubon Society; Clean Water Action; National Wildlife Federation; The Ocean Conservancy; American Forests
- **Industry Groups**
  Citizens for a Sound Economy; Edison Electric Institute; U.S. Chamber of Commerce; National Food Processors Association; International Wood Products Association; National Mining Association; American Resort Development Association

be almost unimaginable in the United States. We discuss that problem in this chapter's *The Rest of the World* feature on the facing page.

Helping Out the Whistleblowers

The term **whistleblower,** as applied to the federal bureaucracy, has a special meaning: it is someone who blows the whistle, or reports, on gross governmental inefficiency, illegal activities, or other wrongdoing. Federal employees are often reluctant to blow the whistle on their superiors, however, for fear of reprisals.

area. To take the example of the environment, one issue network tends to advocate greater environmental regulation, while another network opposes such regulations as undue burdens on businesses and landowners.

LO5 Curbing Waste and Improving Efficiency

There is no doubt that our bureaucracy is costly. There is also little doubt that at times it can be wasteful and inefficient. The government has made several attempts to reduce waste, inefficiency, and wrongdoing. For example, federal and state governments have passed laws requiring more openness in government. Other laws encourage employees to report any waste and wrongdoing that they observe.

Despite the difficulties involved in reforming the bureaucracy, our nation at least enjoys a civil service that is relatively impartial and free from corruption. This is not true of many nations. For example, Mexico, our immediate neighbor to the south, has had difficulties that would

whistleblower In the context of government employment, someone who "blows the whistle" (reports to authorities) on gross governmental inefficiency, illegal action, or other wrongdoing.

LAWS PROTECTING WHISTLEBLOWERS To encourage federal employees to report government wrongdoing, Congress has passed laws to protect whistleblowers. The 1978 Civil Service Reform Act included some protection by prohibiting reprisals against whistleblowers by their superiors. The act set up the Merit Systems Protection Board as part of this protection. The Whistle-Blower Protection Act of 1989 authorized the Office of Special Counsel (OSC), an independent agency, to investigate complaints of reprisals against whistleblowers. Many federal agencies also have toll-free hotlines that employees can use to anonymously report bureaucratic waste and inappropriate behavior.

WHISTLEBLOWERS CONTINUE TO FACE PROBLEMS In spite of these laws, there is little evidence that whistleblowers are adequately protected against retaliation. According to a study conducted by the Government Accountability Office, 41 percent of the whistleblowers who turned to the OSC for protection during a recent three-year period reported that they were no longer employed by the agencies on which they blew the whistle. Indeed, given how difficult it is to fire a federal employee under normal circumstances, it is amazing how quickly most whistleblowers are "shown the door."

Many federal employees who have blown the whistle say that they would not do so again because it

Mexico's Security Problem—The Drug Wars

The United States has 225 law enforcement officers for every 100,000 people. Mexico, in contrast, has 370 officers per 100,000 residents. You might think, then, that citizens of our neighbor to the south would enjoy even more personal security than we do in the United States. The reality is quite different. Crime rates in Mexico on average greatly exceed those in the United States.

Why? For one thing, the United States has far more effective, professional, and trustworthy police forces than Mexico. In addition, Mexico is fighting drug cartels that are also fighting each other. Drug cartel enforcers in Mexico have at their disposal the highest-grade, most sophisticated weapons available—almost all purchased in the United States and smuggled across the border. In September 2010, U.S. secretary of state Hillary Clinton characterized Mexico's drug violence as similar to an insurrection.

Estimates of drug cartel earnings range from $14 billion to $50 billion. With this wealth, the cartels have corrupted many of Mexico's customs agents, army commanders, and local police forces. For example, police in the city of Nuevo Laredo have reportedly participated in kidnapping members of the Gulf cartel and handing them over to the Zetas organization. The Zetas then hold them for ransom or torture them for information about drug deals. Mexico's Federal Investigative Agency (AFI) has 7,000 agents in total. Recently, almost 1,500 of these agents were under investigation, and 457 were facing criminal charges. Some agents were believed to work as enforcers for the Sinaloa cartel.[4]

The Mérida Initiative— U.S. Aid for What?

During the last few years, American taxpayers have provided the Mexican government with aid to combat drug trafficking under a program called the Mérida Initiative. Of the $1.4 billion in assistance, however, only about a third is targeted toward repairing Mexico's crumbling law enforcement and judicial systems. Much of the rest goes to equipment. The results have not been encouraging. Let's face it: buying attack helicopters with the funds (as the Mexican government has done) is not going to solve the drug-wars problem.

A House Cleaning

There are signs that some institutional reform may be taking place in Mexico. In the summer of 2009, the Mexican federal government fired all 700 customs agents, a group notorious for corruption and dereliction of duty, and replaced them with 1,400 new personnel. The new agents had to take drug tests and undergo scrutiny to make sure that they did not have criminal records. Seventy percent of the new agents have a college education, compared with only 10 percent of the old group. Customs agents are responsible for curbing the smuggling of arms into the country.

For Critical Analysis *Will it ever be possible to eradicate police corruption in Mexico when bribes can sometimes be ten to twenty times an average officer's annual salary? Why are the bribes so high?*

© DAVID FRANKLIN/ISTOCKPHOTO

---

was so difficult to get help, and even when they did, the experience was a stressful ordeal. Creating more effective protection for whistleblowers remains an ongoing goal of the government. The basic problem, though, is that most organizations, including federal government agencies, do not like to have their wrongdoings and failings exposed, especially by insiders.

Improving Efficiency and Getting Results

The Government Performance and Results Act, which went into effect in 1997, has forced the federal government to change the way it does business. Since 1997, virtually every agency (except the intelligence agencies) has had to describe its goals and methods for evaluating how well those goals are met. A goal of an agency could be as broad as lowering the number of highway traffic deaths or as narrow as reducing the number of times an agency's phone rings before it is answered.

As one example, consider the National Oceanic and Atmospheric Adminstration (NOAA). It improved the effectiveness of its short-term forecasting services, particularly in issuing warnings of tornadoes. The warning time has increased from seven to nine minutes. This may seem insignificant, but it provides additional critical time for those in the path of a tornado.

President Obama's contribution to the attempt to improve government effectiveness has been to create a chief performance officer. This individual reports directly to the president and works with other economic officials in an attempt to increase efficiency and eliminate waste in government.

Another Approach— Pay-for-Performance Plans

For some time, the private sector has used pay-for-performance plans as a means to increase employee productivity and efficiency. About one-third of the major firms in this country use some kind of alternative pay system, such as team-based pay, skill-based pay, profit-sharing plans, or individual bonuses. In contrast, workers for the federal government traditionally have received fixed salaries; promotions and salary increases are given on the basis of seniority, not output.

The federal government has been experimenting with pay-for-performance systems. For example, the U.S. Postal Service has implemented an Economic Value Added program, which ties bonuses to performance. As part of a five-year test of a new pay system, three thousand scientists working in Air Force laboratories received salaries based on actual results. Also, the Department of Veterans Affairs launched a skill-based pay project at its New York regional office.

Many hope that by offering such incentives, the government will be able to compete more effectively with the private sector for skilled and talented employees. Additionally, according to some, pay-for-performance plans will go a long way toward countering the entitlement mentality that has traditionally characterized employment within the bureaucracy.

Privatization

Another idea for reforming government bureaucracies is **privatization,** which means turning over certain types of

> **privatization** The transfer of the task of providing services traditionally provided by government to the private sector.

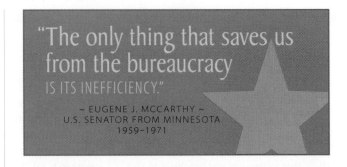

"The only thing that saves us from the bureaucracy IS ITS INEFFICIENCY."

~ EUGENE J. MCCARTHY ~
U.S. SENATOR FROM MINNESOTA
1959–1971

government work to the private sector. Privatization can take place by contracting out (outsourcing) work to the private sector or by "managed competition," in which the task of providing public services is opened up to competition. In managed competition, both the relevant government agency and private firms can compete for the work. Vouchers are another way in which certain services traditionally provided by government, such as education, can be provided on the open market. The government pays for the vouchers, but the services are provided by the private sector.

State and local governments have been experimenting with privatization for some time. Virtually all of the states have privatized at least a few of their services, and some states, including California, Colorado, and Florida, have privatized more than one hundred activities formerly undertaken by government. In Scottsdale, Arizona, the city contracts for fire protection. In

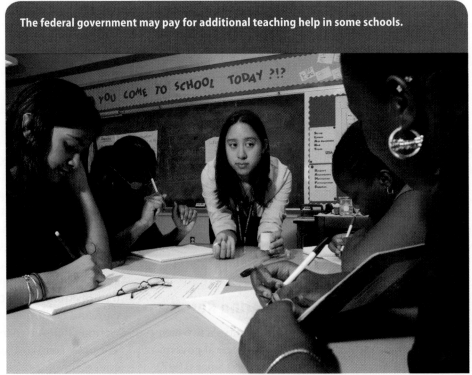

The federal government may pay for additional teaching help in some schools.

Baltimore, Maryland, nine of the city's schools are out-sourced to private entities. In other cities, services ranging from janitorial work to management of recreational facilities are handled by the private sector.

Government in the Sunshine

The past four decades saw a trend toward more openness in government. The theory was that because Americans pay for the government, they own it—and they have a right to know what the government is doing with the taxpayers' dollars.

In response to pressure for more government openness and disclosure, Congress passed the Freedom of Information Act in 1966. This act requires federal agencies to disclose any information in agency files, with some exceptions, to any persons requesting it. Since the 1970s, "sunshine laws," which require government meetings to be open to the public, have been enacted at all levels of American government. During the Clinton administration (1993–2001), Americans gained even greater access to government information as federal and state agencies went online.

The trend toward greater openness in government came to an abrupt halt on September 11, 2001. In the wake of the terrorist attacks on the World Trade Center and the Pentagon, the government began tightening its grip on information. In the months following the attacks, hundreds of thousands of documents were removed from government Web sites.

No longer can the public access plans of nuclear power plants, descriptions of airline security violations, or maps of pipeline routes. Agencies were instructed to be more cautious about releasing information in their files and were given new guidelines on what should be considered public information. State and local agencies followed the federal government's lead. Some states barred access to such information as emergency preparedness evacuation plans. Others established commissions or panels whose activities are exempt from state sunshine laws. All in all, the Bush administration made it much more difficult to obtain information about the government than under previous administrations. During the 2008 presidential campaign, Barack Obama championed the restoration of open government. In practice, however, the Obama administration has shown little interest in pursuing this goal.

> "BUREAUCRACY DEFENDS THE STATUS QUO
> long past the time when the quo has lost its status."
>
> ~ LAURENCE J. PETER ~
> AMERICAN EDUCATOR
> 1919–1990

An Expanding Bureaucracy

The Great Recession reached its crisis point on September 15, 2008, while George W. Bush was still president. As a result, the federal government took on substantial new responsibilities even before Barack Obama was sworn in as president. In early October 2008, Congress passed a $700 billion bank bailout bill. The key activity established by this legislation was the Troubled Asset Relief Program, or TARP. New federal staff members were required to administer this program. Oversight personnel were hired to inform Congress whether TARP funds were being loaned out or distributed wisely.

EXPANDED GOVERNMENT UNDER PRESIDENT OBAMA A series of legislative enactments in 2009 and 2010 swelled the rolls of the federal bureaucracy. The stimulus bill of February 2009 was followed by the federal takeover of two automobile manufacturers, Chrysler and General Motors. In March 2010, Congress passed health-care reform. The two reform bills were officially named the Patient Protection and Affordable Care Act and the Health Care and Education Reconciliation Act. Friends of reform shortened this mouthful to the Affordable Care Act. Conservative opponents—and irreverent journalists—dubbed it "Obamacare." Major new regulations covering the financial industry followed in July.

These and other expansions of federal authority had an impact on the bureaucracy. By the middle of 2010, almost every executive department of the federal government had more employees than in 2009. The increased staffing occurred even in departments that were not central to the new legislation. For example, the Department of Agriculture now had 111,987 employees, up from 108,018 in 2009. Across the executive branch, the number of new staff members totaled about 86,000, not counting those hired on a temporary basis to conduct the 2010 census. Layoffs by state and local governments, however, tended to counterbalance the expansion of the federal government as the recession continued to slash state tax receipts.

A NEW SPIRIT IN CONGRESS The 2010 elections dramatically changed the composition of Congress. The new legislators were conspicuously hostile to "big government" and unlikely to support major new programs. As one example, in 2009 the Democrats advocated massive changes to the nation's energy system to reduce the amount of carbon dioxide (CO_2) emitted by American industry. CO_2 emissions are believed to be a major cause of global warming. The bill in question died in the Senate, however, and there seemed to be no chance that any important legislation on this topic could pass the new Congress. The federal government remained on course to hire new bureaucrats to administer programs already created, but additional expansion of the government was no longer on the table.

AMERICA AT ODDS *The Bureaucracy*

Although the story is often told about red tape and wasteful spending generated by our bureaucracy, all in all, the U.S. bureaucracy compares favorably with bureaucracies in other countries. Citizens typically overestimate the amount of "government waste" by very large margins. Still, the U.S. government faces the same problems with its bureaucracy—sluggishness, inefficiency, and even incompetence—that large businesses and organizations throughout the country also face. The major difference is the size and scope of the U.S. bureaucracy—and the effect that its actions can have on the daily lives of all Americans. Americans are at odds over a number of issues relating to the bureaucracy, including the following:

- Can new financial regulations eliminate the danger of a catastrophe such as the one we experienced in September 2008—or will clever financiers find ways around any new regulations?

- Do the recent health-care reforms provide vital protection to the citizenry—or are they an example of excessive government meddling in the private sector?

- Are government employees overpaid—or is their pay appropriate given their responsibilities?

- Is the contracting-out of governmental services a way to improve efficiency—or does it mostly serve to hide the true cost and scope of government?

- Should our leaders focus on openness and transparency in government—or are such measures dangerous during the war on terrorism?

Take Action

Although this chapter's focus is on the federal bureaucracy, realize that all levels of government require bureaucracies to implement their goals. In virtually every community, however, there are needs that government agencies cannot meet. Often, agencies simply lack the funds to hire more personnel or to provide assistance to those in need. To help address these needs, many Americans do volunteer work. If you want to take action in this way, check with your local government offices and find out which agencies or offices have volunteer programs. Volunteer opportunities on the local level can range from helping the homeless and mentoring children in a local school to joining a local environmental clean-up effort. Decide where your interests lie, and consider volunteering your time in a local bureaucracy.

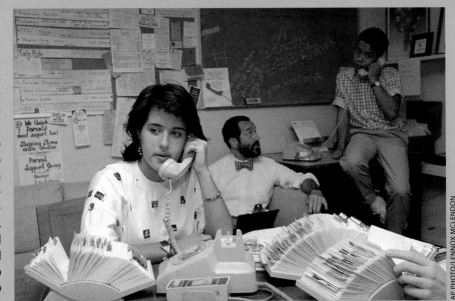

AP PHOTO/LENNOX MCLENDON

Volunteers answer hotlines that teenagers can call when they need help. Many volunteers at such hotline services have found this type of work especially rewarding.

POLITICS ON THE
WEB

- For information on the government, including the Web sites for federal agencies, go to the federal government's "gateway" Web site at **www.usa.gov**

- The Web site of the Office of Management and Budget offers information on increasing the government's efficiency—and, of course, on the federal budget. You can access the OMB at **www.whitehouse.gov/omb**

- To learn more about the mission of the General Services Administration (GSA) and its role in managing the federal bureaucracy, go to **www.gsa.gov**

- If you want to see an example of what federal agencies are putting on the Web, you can go to the Department of Commerce's Web site at **www.commerce.gov**

- The *Federal Register* is the official publication for executive-branch documents. This publication, which includes the orders, notices, and rules of all federal administrative agencies, is online at **www.gpoaccess.gov/fr**

- The *United States Government Manual* contains information on the functions, organization, and administrators of every federal department. You can access the most recent edition of the manual online at **www.gpoaccess.gov/gmanual**

 CourseMate

Access CourseMate to review and expand on this chapter through quizzes, flashcards, learning objectives, interactive timelines, a crossword puzzle, audio summaries, video, critical-thinking activities, simulations, and more.

{ Test coming up? Now what? }

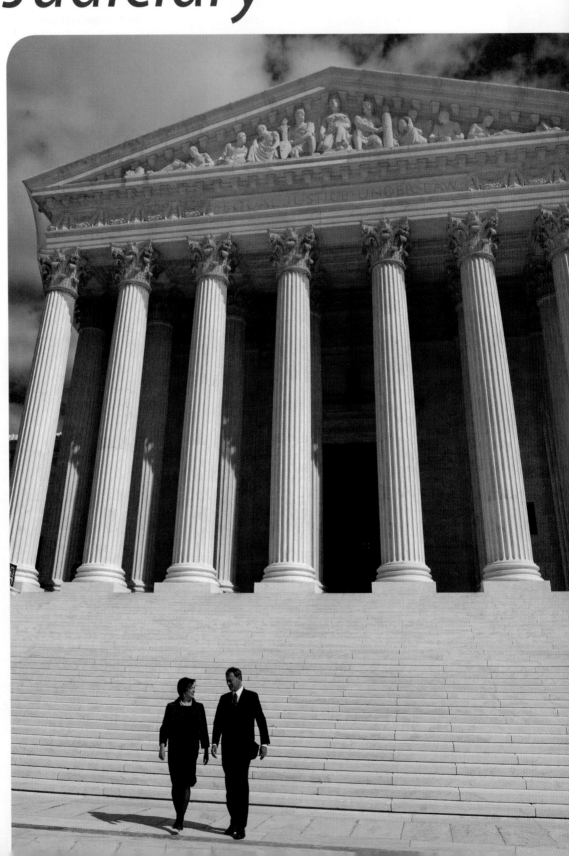

LEARNING OBJECTIVES

LO1 Summarize the origins of the American legal system and the basic sources of American law.

LO2 Delineate the structure of the federal court system.

LO3 Indicate how federal judges are appointed.

LO4 Explain how the federal courts make policy.

LO5 Describe the role of ideology and judicial philosophies in judicial decision making.

LO6 Identify some of the criticisms of the federal courts and some of the checks on the power of the courts.

CourseMate

AMERICA AT ODDS

Are There Prisoners We Must Detain without Trial?

After the September 11, 2001, attacks in the United States, the George W. Bush administration interred hundreds of suspected terrorists at the Guantánamo Bay Naval Base in Cuba. Most of them were foreign fighters captured during the war in Afghanistan, a war initiated just after 9/11. A few suspected terrorists from elsewhere ended up at Guantánamo as well. All prisoners were labeled *unlawful enemy combatants* and therefore were afforded neither the legal protections guaranteed to prisoners of war (POWs) under the Geneva Conventions nor the protections required under the conventions for dealing with civilians who commit crimes. Indeed, the Bush administration established the prison at Guantánamo in the belief that the facility would lie outside the reach of American law. President Barack Obama promised to close the Guantánamo prison, but he has failed to do so. Obama furthermore stated that it may be necessary to hold some of the detainees more or less forever without bringing them to trial. There are those who object to this policy, but many who agree with it.

We Release Terrorists at the Civilized World's Peril

Look back over U.S. history. Federal judges never heard cases brought by Confederate prisoners of war held during the Civil War. During World War II, no civilian courts reviewed the cases of the thousands of German prisoners housed in the United States. At the end of that war, the Supreme Court agreed that enemy aliens held by the United States in Europe and Asia had no right to appear in front of an American judge.

Today, if the president deems that certain terrorist prisoners are too dangerous to be tried and perhaps freed, that is the president's prerogative. After all, under our Constitution, the president has wartime decision-making powers. We also have evidence that at least thirty detainees released from the Guantánamo prison rejoined terrorist organizations and have been responsible for the deaths of innocent people overseas.

Who will be responsible for the deaths caused by terrorists if they cannot be convicted and we then let them go? Terrorists do not deserve the civil liberties we offer to fellow Americans. If we cannot be sure that a trial will result in a conviction, we must not let these people stand trial at all.

WHERE DO YOU STAND?

1. Could Congress fashion a law providing a procedure to determine when an alleged terrorist should never be let out of prison? Could such a law withstand Supreme Court review?[1] Why or why not?
2. Why is it easier to falsely arrest a purported terrorist than a regular military soldier?

EXPLORE THIS ISSUE ONLINE

- The editorial page of the *Wall Street Journal* favors indefinite detention. One of the strongest voices on that page has been John Yoo, who served in President Bush's Justice

Indefinite Detention Is Unconstitutional and Damages Our Image Abroad

It is wrong to hold persons deemed "dangerous" by the government indefinitely. How can we know that the government is correct in its allegations against these people? We have learned that some of the Afghans held at Guantánamo and elsewhere were arrested due to false accusations resulting from long-standing feuds between rival families. U.S. officials were reluctant to release these innocents because it meant admitting that the officials had made a mistake.

The way our government has handled prisoners of war (POWs) in the past is irrelevant. Traditional POWs were picked up during battle, on the field, in uniform. The potential for picking up a POW by mistake was minimal. In contrast, the danger of error when picking up an alleged unlawful enemy combatant is enormous. Most of the Guantánamo detainees were arrested nowhere near a battlefield. How can we know whether such detainees are truly dangerous if there is no trial? Furthermore, as the blog site Digby's Hullabaloo puts it: "There are literally tens of thousands of potential terrorists all over the world who could theoretically harm America. We cannot protect ourselves from that possibility by keeping the handful we have in custody locked up forever."

Department when the detention policies were crafted. You'll find some of Yoo's articles if you perform a Google search on "john yoo wall street journal."

- Two of the many bloggers who oppose indefinite detentions are Digby and Glenn Greenwald. You can find their work at digbysblog.blogspot.com and www.salon.com/opinion/greenwald. Digby writes on many topics, and you may need to search his site using "terrorism."

Introduction

As you read in this chapter's opening *America at Odds* feature, the question of whether certain alleged terrorists should be imprisoned indefinitely without trial has elicited a great deal of controversy. Also controversial is the policymaking function of the United States Supreme Court. After all, when the Court renders an opinion on how the Constitution is to be interpreted, it is, necessarily, making policy on a national level. To understand the nature of this controversy, you first need to understand how the **judiciary** (the courts) functions in this country. We begin by looking at the origins and sources of American law. We then examine the federal court system, at the apex of which is the United States Supreme Court, and consider various issues relating to the courts.

LO1 The Origins and Sources of American Law

The American colonists brought with them the legal system that had developed in England over hundreds of years. Thus, to understand how the American legal system operates, we need to go back in time to the early English courts and the traditions they established.

The Common Law Tradition

After the Normans conquered England in 1066, William the Conqueror and his successors began the process of unifying the country under their rule. One of the methods they used was the establishment of the "king's courts," or *curiae regis*. Before the Norman Conquest, disputes had been settled according to the local legal customs and traditions in various regions of the country. The law developed in the king's

courts, however, applied to the country as a whole. What evolved in these courts was the beginning of the **common law**—a body of general rules that was applied throughout the entire English realm. Trial by jury is a famous part of the common law tradition. Juries are less common outside the English-speaking world, but some countries with different legal traditions have begun to introduce them, as you will learn in this chapter's *The Rest of the World* feature on the facing page.

THE RULE OF PRECEDENT The early English courts developed the common law rules from the principles underlying judges' decisions in actual legal controversies. Judges attempted to be consistent, and whenever possible, they based their decisions on the principles applied in earlier cases. They sought to decide similar cases in a similar way and considered new kinds of cases with care, because they knew that their decisions would make new law. Each interpretation became part of the law on the subject and served as a legal **precedent**—that is, a decision that furnished an example or authority for deciding subsequent cases involving identical or similar legal principles or facts.

U.S. attorneys are appointed by the president with the advice and consent of the Senate. They serve under the direction of the attorney general.

AP PHOTO/DENNIS COOK

---

judiciary The courts; one of the three branches of government in the United States.

common law The body of law developed from judicial decisions in English and U.S. courts, not attributable to a legislature.

precedent A court decision that furnishes an example or authority for deciding subsequent cases involving identical or similar facts and legal issues.

Jury Trials Introduced in Asian Courts

The U.S. Constitution provides for jury trials in Article III and in the Bill of Rights, so most of us take jury trials for granted. Yet juries do not exist in most parts of the world, including many democracies. The right to a jury trial for a criminal defendant seems so obvious that it's hard for us to imagine how greatly the United States differs from many other countries on this issue.

South Korea and Japan Take the Plunge

Until 2008, South Korea had never had a jury trial in a criminal case. The first one was held in the small city of Taegu. It concerned a twenty-seven-year-old man who was charged with the petty criminal offenses of assault and trespass. A dozen South Korean citizens aided the presiding judge. The jury found the defendant guilty.

Until that moment in South Korean judicial history, no one in that country could have imagined that citizens without legal training and with no accountability could decide the fate of a criminal defendant. The South Korean jury system is similar to that in the United States, but with some modifications. The more complex the case, the more jurors there are. Also, jury verdicts are based on majority vote rather than on unanimous decisions, as required in almost all American criminal cases. Finally, at least for the next few years, the vote of the jurors is not binding on the judge.

In 2009, Japan reinstated trials by jury after a sixty-five-year absence. The first individual to be tried under the new system was a seventy-two-year-old man who had confessed to stabbing a neighbor. A panel of ordinary citizens stood in judgment of the accused, alongside professional judges. Despite Japan's tradition of deferring to authority, the citizen judges participated actively, cross-examining the accused and the victim's son. The audience at the trial exceeded two thousand people.

Why the Sudden Desire to Have Jury Trials?

In Japan, those who are prosecuted are almost inevitably convicted—the conviction rate is over 99 percent. Confessions, made in police custody without a lawyer present, are very common. A spate of executions of persons later found to be innocent led to demands for a new system.

Legal scholars analyzing the trend toward jury trials in Asia point out several additional reasons why they are now becoming more common. One is that many of these countries have opened themselves up to a growing influence from the United States.

Another explanation is that some formerly authoritarian countries that are now democracies believe that juries might be a way to foster stronger democratic values. Juries seem to serve as a check on governmental power. They build trust in legal institutions.

For Critical Analysis *In many jurisdictions in the United States, the defendant can waive his or her right to a jury trial. Why might a defendant waive this important right?*

This Japanese judicial officer is attempting to explain the use of juries at a seminar organized by that country's Justice Ministry.

AP PHOTO/KATSUMI KASAHARA

The practice of deciding new cases with reference to former decisions, or precedents, eventually became a cornerstone of the English and American judicial systems. The practice forms a doctrine called **stare decisis** ("to stand on decided cases"). Under this doctrine, judges are obligated to follow the precedents established in their jurisdictions. For example, if the Supreme Court of Georgia holds that a state law requiring candidates for state office to pass drug tests is unconstitutional, that decision will control the outcome of future cases on that issue brought before the state

stare decisis A common law doctrine under which judges normally are obligated to follow the precedents established by prior court decisions. Pronounced *ster*-ay dih-*si*-sis.

courts in Georgia. Similarly, a decision on a given issue by the United States Supreme Court (the nation's highest court) is binding on all inferior (lower) courts. For example, if the Georgia case on drug testing is appealed to the United States Supreme Court and the Court agrees that the Georgia law is unconstitutional, the high court's ruling will be binding on *all* courts in the United States. In other words, similar drug-testing laws in other states will be invalid and unenforceable.

DEPARTURES FROM PRECEDENT   Sometimes a court will depart from the rule of precedent if it decides that a precedent is simply incorrect or that technological or social changes have rendered the precedent inapplicable. Cases that overturn precedent often receive a great deal of publicity. For example, in 1954, in *Brown v. Board of Education of Topeka,*[2] the United States Supreme Court expressly overturned precedent when it concluded that separate educational facilities for African Americans, which had been upheld as constitutional in many earlier cases under the "separate-but-equal" doctrine[3] (see Chapter 5), were inherently unequal and violated the equal protection clause. The Supreme Court's departure from precedent in *Brown* received a tremendous amount of publicity as people began to realize the political and social ramifications of this change in the law.

More recently, the Supreme Court departed from precedent when it held in a 2003 case, *Lawrence v. Texas,*[4] that a Texas sodomy law (see Chapter 5) violated the U.S. Constitution. In that case, the Court concluded that consensual sexual conduct, including homosexual conduct, was part of the liberty protected by the due process clause of the Fourteenth Amendment. This decision overturned the Court's established precedent on such laws—specifically, its ruling in *Bowers v. Hardwick,*[5] a 1986 case in which the Court upheld a Georgia sodomy statute.

"IT IS BETTER, so the Fourth Amendment teaches, **THAT THE GUILTY SOMETIMES GO FREE** than that citizens be subject to easy arrest."

~ WILLIAM O. DOUGLAS ~
ASSOCIATE JUSTICE OF THE
UNITED STATES SUPREME COURT
1939–1975

priority of these sources when particular laws come into conflict.

CONSTITUTIONAL LAW   The U.S. government and each of the fifty states have separate written constitutions that set forth the general organization, powers, and limits of their respective governments. **Constitutional law** consists of the rights and duties set forth in these constitutions.

The U.S. Constitution is the supreme law of the land. As such, it is the basis of all law in the United States. Any law that violates the Constitution is invalid and unenforceable. Because of the paramount importance of the U.S. Constitution in the American legal system, the complete text of the Constitution is found in Appendix B.

The Tenth Amendment to the U.S. Constitution reserves to the states and to the people all powers not granted to the federal government. Each state in the union has its own constitution. Unless they conflict with the U.S. Constitution or a federal law, state constitutions are supreme within the borders of their respective states.

STATUTORY LAW   Statutes enacted by legislative bodies at any level of government make up another source of law, which is generally referred to as **statutory law.** Federal statutes—laws enacted by the U.S. Congress—apply to all of the states. State statutes—laws enacted by state legislatures—apply only within the state that enacted the law. Any state statute that conflicts with the U.S. Constitution, with federal laws enacted by Congress, or with the state's constitution will be deemed invalid, if challenged in court, and will not be enforced. Statutory law also includes the ordinances (such as local zoning or housing-construction laws) passed by cities and counties, none of which can violate the U.S.

primary source of law A source of law that establishes the law. Primary sources of law include constitutions, statutes, administrative agency rules and regulations, and decisions rendered by the courts.

constitutional law Law based on the U.S. Constitution and the constitutions of the various states.

statutory law The body of law enacted by legislatures (as opposed to constitutional law, administrative law, or case law).

Sources of American Law

In any governmental system, the primary function of the courts is to interpret and apply the law. In the United States, the courts interpret and apply several sources of law when deciding cases. We look here only at the **primary sources of law**—that is, sources that *establish* the law—and the relative

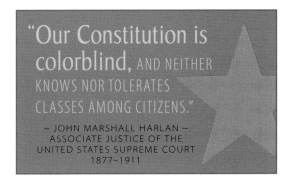

Constitution, the relevant state constitution, or any existing federal or state laws.

ADMINISTRATIVE LAW   Another important source of American law consists of **administrative law**—the rules, orders, and decisions of administrative agencies. As you read in Chapter 13, at the federal level, Congress creates executive agencies, such as the Food and Drug Administration and the Environmental Protection Agency, to perform specific functions. Typically, when Congress establishes an agency, it authorizes the agency to create rules that have the force of law and to enforce those rules by bringing legal actions against violators. Rules issued by various government agencies now affect virtually every aspect of our economy. For example, almost all of a business's operations, including the firm's capital structure and financing, its hiring and firing procedures, its relations with employees and unions, and the way it manufactures and markets its products, are subject to government regulation.

Government agencies exist at the state and local levels as well. States commonly create agencies that parallel federal agencies. Just as federal statutes take precedence over conflicting state statutes, federal agency regulations take precedence over conflicting state regulations.

CASE LAW   As is evident from the earlier discussion of the common law tradition, another basic source of American law consists of the rules of law announced in court decisions, or **case law.** These rules of law include interpretations of constitutional provisions, of statutes enacted by legislatures, and of regulations issued by administrative agencies. Thus, even though a legislature passes a law to govern a certain area, how that law is interpreted and applied depends on the courts. The importance of case law, or judge-made law, is one of the distinguishing characteristics of the common law tradition.

Civil Law and Criminal Law

All of the sources of law just discussed can be classified in other ways as well. One of the most significant classification systems divides all law into two categories:

civil law and criminal law. **Civil law** spells out the duties that individuals in society owe to other persons or to their governments, excluding the duty not to commit crimes. Typically, in a civil case, a private party sues another private party (although the government can also sue a party for a civil law violation). The object of a civil lawsuit is to make the defendant—the person being sued—comply with a legal duty (such as a contractual promise) or pay money damages for failing to comply with that duty.

Criminal law, in contrast, has to do with wrongs committed against the public as a whole. Criminal acts are prohibited by local, state, or federal government statutes. Thus, criminal defendants are prosecuted by public officials, such as a district attorney (D.A.), on behalf of the government, not by their victims or other private parties. In a criminal case, the government seeks to impose a penalty (a fine and/or imprisonment) on a person who has violated a criminal law. For example, when someone robs a convenience store, that person has committed a crime and, if caught and proved guilty, will normally spend time in prison.

Basic Judicial Requirements

A court cannot decide just any issue at any time. Before a court can hear and decide a case, specific requirements must be met. To a certain extent, these requirements act as restraints on the judiciary because they limit the types of cases that courts can hear and decide. Courts also have procedural requirements that frame the judicial process.

JURISDICTION   In Latin, *juris* means "law," and *diction* means "to speak." Therefore, **jurisdiction** literally refers to the power "to speak the law." Jurisdiction applies either to the geographic area in which a court has the right and power to decide

administrative law   The body of law created by administrative agencies (in the form of rules, regulations, orders, and decisions) in order to carry out their duties and responsibilities.

case law   The rules of law announced in court decisions. Case law includes the aggregate of reported cases that interpret judicial precedents, statutes, regulations, and constitutional provisions.

civil law   The branch of law that spells out the duties that individuals in society owe to other persons or to their governments, excluding the duty not to commit crimes.

criminal law   The branch of law that defines and governs actions that constitute crimes. Generally, criminal law has to do with wrongful actions committed against society for which society demands redress.

jurisdiction   The authority of a court to hear and decide a particular case.

cases, or to the right and power of a court to decide matters concerning certain persons, types of property, or subjects. Before any court can hear a case, it must have jurisdiction over the person against whom the suit is brought, the property involved in the suit, and the subject matter.

A state trial court, for example, usually has jurisdictional authority over the residents of a particular area of the state, such as a county or district. (A **trial court** is, as the term implies, a court in which a trial is held and testimony taken.) A state's highest court (often called the state supreme court)[6] has jurisdictional authority over all residents within the state. In some cases, if an individual has committed an offense such as injuring someone in an automobile accident or selling defective goods within the state, the court can exercise jurisdiction even if the individual is a resident of another state. State courts can also exercise jurisdiction over people who do business within the state. A New York company that distributes its products in California, for example, can be sued by a California resident in a California state court.

Because the federal government is a government of limited powers, the jurisdiction of the federal courts is limited. Article III, Section 2, of the Constitution states that the federal courts can exercise jurisdiction over all cases "arising under this Constitution, the Laws of the United States, and Treaties made, or which shall be made, under their Authority." Whenever a case involves a claim based, at least in part, on the U.S. Constitution, a treaty, or a federal law, a federal question arises. Any lawsuit involving a **federal question** can originate in a federal court.

Federal courts can also exercise jurisdiction over cases involving **diversity of citizenship.** Such cases may arise when the parties in a lawsuit live in different states or when one of the parties is a foreign government or a foreign citizen. Before a federal court can take jurisdiction in a diversity case, the amount in controversy must be more than $75,000.

STANDING TO SUE To bring a lawsuit before a court, a person must have **standing to sue,** or a sufficient "stake" in the matter to justify bringing a suit. Thus, the party bringing the suit must have suffered a harm or been threatened with a harm by the action at issue, and the issue must be justiciable. A **justiciable controversy** is one that is real and substantial, as opposed to hypothetical or academic.

The requirement of standing clearly limits the issues that can be decided by the courts. Furthermore, both state and federal governments can specify by law when an individual or group has standing to sue. Variations in state laws have led to some interesting consequences. In New York State, for example, to have standing to sue a lawyer for making a mistake on a legal document, you must be the person who hired the lawyer. As a result, if an attorney makes a mistake when drafting a will, the beneficiaries have no standing to sue. In 2009, a New

trial court A court in which trials are held and testimony taken.

federal question A question that pertains to the U.S. Constitution, acts of Congress, or treaties. A federal question provides a basis for federal court jurisdiction.

diversity of citizenship A basis for federal court jurisdiction over a lawsuit that arises when (1) the parties in the lawsuit live in different states or when one of the parties is a foreign government or a foreign citizen, and (2) the amount in controversy is more than $75,000.

standing to sue The requirement that an individual must have a sufficient stake in a controversy before he or she can bring a lawsuit. The party bringing the suit must demonstrate that he or she has either been harmed or been threatened with a harm.

justiciable controversy A controversy that is not hypothetical or academic but real and substantial; a requirement that must be satisfied before a court will hear a case. *Justiciable* is pronounced jus-*tish*-a-bul.

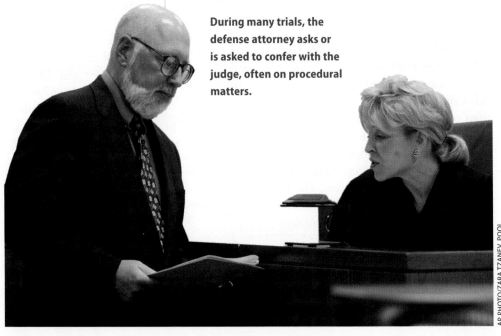

During many trials, the defense attorney asks or is asked to confer with the judge, often on procedural matters.

AP PHOTO/ZARA TZANEV, POOL

Figure 14–1

The Organization of the Federal Court System

Note: Some specialized courts, such as the Tax Court, are not included in this figure.

apply in criminal and civil cases. Generally, criminal procedural rules attempt to ensure that defendants are not deprived of their constitutional rights.

Parties involved in civil or criminal cases must comply with court procedural rules or risk being held in contempt of court. A party who is held in contempt of court can be fined, taken into custody, or both. A court must take care to ensure that the parties—and the court itself—comply with procedural requirements. Procedural errors often serve as grounds for a mistrial or for appealing the court's decision to a higher tribunal.

LO2 *The Federal Court System*

The federal court system is a three-tiered model consisting of U.S. district courts (trial courts), U.S. courts of appeals, and the United States Supreme Court. Figure 14–1 above shows the organization of the federal court system.

Bear in mind that the federal courts constitute only one of the fifty-two court systems in the United States. Each of the fifty states has its own court system, as does the District of Columbia. No two state court systems are exactly the same, but usually each state has different levels, or tiers, of courts, just as the federal system does. Generally, state courts deal with questions of state law, and the decisions of a state's highest court on matters of state law are normally final. If a federal question is involved, however, a decision of a state supreme court may be appealed to the United States Supreme Court. We will discuss the federal court system in the pages that follow.

U.S. District Courts

On the lowest tier of the federal court system are the U.S. district courts, or federal trial courts—the courts in which cases involving federal laws begin. The cases in these courts are decided by a judge or a jury (if it is a jury trial). There is at least one federal district court in every state, and there is one in the District of Columbia. The number of judicial districts varies over time, primarily owing to population changes and corresponding caseloads. Currently, there are ninety-four judicial districts. Figure 14–2 on the following page shows their

York lawyer did in fact make a mistake that cost the beneficiaries of a will millions of dollars, and a state judge affirmed the lawyer's immunity. The court ruled that the only person with standing was the deceased, who was obviously not going to sue anyone.

In complete contrast, the California legislature has placed no restrictions whatsoever on who has standing to file a suit seeking the appointment of a guardian for children. As a result, in 2009, Paul Petersen, a former child actor and head of a child advocacy group called A Minor Consideration, was able to proceed with a lawsuit calling for a guardian to protect the children of Nadya Suleman even though Petersen had no connection at all with the Suleman family. Suleman, also known as the "Octomom," gave birth to octuplets at a time when she was already the mother of six children. Suleman was single, unemployed, and receiving public assistance, and her fitness as a parent was widely questioned in the media.

COURT PROCEDURES Both the federal and the state courts have established procedural rules that apply in all cases. These procedures are designed to protect the rights and interests of the parties, ensure that the litigation proceeds in a fair and orderly manner, and identify the issues that must be decided by the court—thus saving court time and costs. Different procedural rules

Figure 14–2

U.S. Courts of Appeals and U.S. District Courts

Source: Administrative Office of the United States Courts.

geographic boundaries. The federal system also includes other trial courts, such as the Court of International Trade and others shown in Figure 14–1 on the previous page. These courts have limited, or specialized, subject-matter jurisdiction—that is, they can exercise authority only over certain kinds of cases.

appellate court A court having appellate jurisdiction. An appellate court normally does not hear evidence or testimony but reviews the transcript of the trial court's proceedings, other records relating to the case, and attorneys' arguments as to why the trial court's decision should or should not stand.

U.S. Courts of Appeals

On the middle tier of the federal court system are the U.S. courts of appeals. Courts of appeals, or **appellate courts,** do not hear evidence or testimony. Rather, an appellate

court reviews the transcript of the trial court's proceedings, other records relating to the case, and attorneys' arguments as to why the trial court's decision should or should not stand. In contrast to a trial court, where normally a single judge presides, an appellate court consists of a panel of three or more judges. The task of the appellate court is to determine whether the trial court erred in applying the law to the facts and issues involved in a particular case.

There are thirteen federal courts of appeals in the United States. The courts of appeals for twelve of the circuits, including the Court of Appeals for the D.C. Circuit, hear appeals from the U.S. district courts located within their respective judicial circuits (see Figure 14–2 above). Decisions made by federal administrative agencies can in some cases be appealed directly to the U.S. courts of appeals. The Court of Appeals for the Federal Circuit has national jurisdiction over certain types of cases, such as those concerning patent law and some claims against the national government.

The decisions of the federal appellate courts may be appealed to the United States Supreme Court. If a decision is not appealed, or if the high court declines to review the case, the appellate court's decision is final.

The United States Supreme Court

The highest level of the three-tiered model of the federal court system is the United States Supreme Court. According to Article III of the U.S. Constitution, there is only one national Supreme Court. Congress is empowered to create additional ("inferior") courts as it deems necessary. The inferior courts that Congress has created include the second tier in our model—the U.S. courts of appeals—as well as the district courts and any other courts of limited, or specialized, jurisdiction.

The United States Supreme Court consists of nine justices—a chief justice and eight associate justices—although that number is not mandated by the Constitution. The Supreme Court has original, or trial, jurisdiction only in rare instances (set forth in Article III, Section 2). In other words, only rarely does a case originate at the Supreme Court level. Most of the Court's work is as an appellate court. The Supreme Court has appellate authority over cases decided by the U.S. courts of appeals, as well as over some cases decided in the state courts when federal questions are at issue.

THE WRIT OF *CERTIORARI* To bring a case before the Supreme Court, a party may request that the Court issue a **writ of *certiorari*,** often called "cert.," which is an order that the Supreme Court issues to a lower court requesting the latter to send it the record of the case in question. Parties can petition the Supreme Court to issue a writ of *certiorari*, but whether the Court will do so is entirely within its discretion. The Court will not issue a writ unless at least four of the nine justices approve. In no instance is the Court required to issue a writ of *certiorari*.[7]

Figure 14–3

The Number of Supreme Court Opinions

The number of Supreme Court opinions peaked at 151 in the Court's 1982 term and declined more or less steadily through 1995 and then leveled off. During the 2009 term (ending in June 2010), the Court issued 92 opinions.

Most petitions for writs of *certiorari* are denied. A denial is not a decision on the merits of a case, nor does it indicate that the Court agrees with a lower court's opinion. Furthermore, the denial of a writ has no value as a precedent. A denial simply means that the decision of the lower court remains the law within that court's jurisdiction.

WHICH CASES REACH THE SUPREME COURT? There is no absolute right to appeal to the United States Supreme Court. Although thousands of cases are filed with the Supreme Court each year, on average the Court hears fewer than one hundred. As Figure 14–3 above shows, the number of cases heard by the Court each year has declined significantly since the 1980s. In large part, this has occurred because the Court has raised its standards for accepting cases in recent years.

Typically, the Court grants petitions for cases that raise important policy issues that need to be addressed. In its 2009–2010 term, for example, the Court heard cases involving such pressing issues as the following:

- Whether long-standing campaign finance laws violate the First Amendment free speech rights of corporations and labor unions. (The Court determined that they did.)[8]

- Whether state and local governments are bound to recognize the right to bear arms as an individual right,

> **writ of *certiorari*** An order from a higher court asking a lower court for the record of a case. *Certiorari* is pronounced sur-shee-uh-*rah*-ree.

and not as a right that is limited to state militias. (The Court ruled that state and local governments are so bound.)[9]

- Whether juveniles who commit crimes in which no one is killed may be sentenced to life in prison without the possibility of parole. (The Court found that they may not.)[10]

If the lower courts have rendered conflicting opinions on an important issue, the Supreme Court may review one or more cases involving that issue to define the law on the matter. For example, in 2002 the Court agreed to review two cases raising the issue of whether affirmative action programs (see Chapter 5) violate the equal protection clause of the Constitution. Different federal appellate courts had reached conflicting opinions on this issue.

SUPREME COURT OPINIONS Like other appellate courts, the United States Supreme Court normally does not hear any evidence. The Court's decision in a particular case is based on the written record of the case and the written arguments (legal briefs) that the attorneys submit. The attorneys also present **oral arguments**—spoken arguments presented in person rather than on paper—to the Court, after which the justices discuss the case in **conference.** The conference is strictly private—only the justices are allowed in the room.

When the Court has reached a decision, the chief justice, if in the majority, assigns the task of writing the Court's **opinion** to one of the justices. When the chief justice is not in the majority, the most senior justice voting with the majority assigns the writing of the Court's opinion. The opinion outlines the reasons for the Court's decision, the rules of law that apply, and the judgment.

Often, one or more justices who agree with the Court's decision do so for reasons different from those outlined in the majority opinion. These justices may write

---

oral argument A spoken argument presented to a judge in person by an attorney on behalf of her or his client.

conference In regard to the Supreme Court, a private meeting of the justices in which they present their arguments concerning a case under consideration.

opinion A written statement by a court expressing the reasons for its decision in a case.

concurring opinion A statement written by a judge or justice who agrees (concurs) with the court's decision, but for reasons different from those in the majority opinion.

dissenting opinion A statement written by a judge or justice who disagrees with the majority opinion.

> ## "AS NIGHTFALL DOESN'T COME AT ONCE, NEITHER DOES OPPRESSION.
>
> In both instances, . . . we must be aware of change in the air, however slight, lest we become unwitting victims of the darkness."
>
> ~ WILLIAM O. DOUGLAS ~
> ASSOCIATE JUSTICE OF THE
> UNITED STATES SUPREME COURT
> 1939–1975

concurring opinions, setting forth their own legal reasoning on the issue. Frequently, one or more justices disagree with the Court's conclusion. These justices may write **dissenting opinions,** outlining the reasons they feel the majority erred in arriving at its decision.

Although a dissenting opinion does not affect the outcome of the case before the Court, it may be important later. In a subsequent case concerning the same issue, a jurist or attorney may use the legal reasoning in the dissenting opinion as the basis for an argument to reverse the previous decision and establish a new precedent.

LO3 *Federal Judicial Appointments*

Unlike state court judges, who are often elected, all federal judges are appointed. Article II, Section 2, of the Constitution authorizes the president to appoint the justices of the Supreme Court with the advice and consent of the Senate. Laws enacted by Congress provide that the same procedure is to be used for appointing judges to the lower federal courts as well.

Federal judges receive lifetime appointments (because under Article III of the Constitution they "hold their Offices during good Behaviour"). Federal judges may be removed from office through the impeachment process, but such proceedings are extremely rare and are usually undertaken only if a judge engages in blatantly illegal conduct, such as bribery. In the history of this nation, only thirteen federal judges have been

Table 14-1

Backgrounds of United States Supreme Court Justices through 2011

	Number of Justices (112 = Total)
Occupational Position before Appointment	
Private legal practice	25
State judgeship	21
Federal judgeship	31
U.S. attorney general	7
Deputy or assistant U.S. attorney general	2
U.S. solicitor general	3
U.S. senator	6
U.S. representative	2
State governor	3
Federal executive post	9
Other	3
Religious Affiliation	
Protestant	83
Roman Catholic	14
Jewish	7
Unitarian	7
No religious affiliation	1
Age on Appointment	
Under 40	5
41–50	33
51–60	60
61–70	14
Political Party Affiliation	
Federalist (to 1835)	13
Jeffersonian Republican (to 1828)	7
Whig (to 1861)	1
Democrat	46
Republican	44
Independent	1
Education	
College graduate	96
Not a college graduate	16
Gender	
Male	108
Female	4
Race	
White (non-Hispanic)	109
African American	2
Hispanic	1

Sources: *Congressional Quarterly's Guide to the U.S. Supreme Court* (Washington, D.C.: Congressional Quarterly Press, 1997); and authors' updates.

impeached, and only seven of them were removed from office. Normally, federal judges serve until they resign, retire, or die.

Although the Constitution sets no specific qualifications for those who serve on the Supreme Court, those who have done so share one characteristic: all have been attorneys. The backgrounds of the Supreme Court justices have been far from typical of the characteristics of the American public as a whole. Table 14–1 at left summarizes the backgrounds of all of the 112 United States Supreme Court justices through 2011.

The Nomination Process

The president receives suggestions and recommendations as to potential nominees for Supreme Court positions from various sources, including the Justice Department, senators, other judges, the candidates themselves, state political leaders, bar associations, and other interest groups. After selecting a nominee, the president submits her or his name to the Senate for approval. The Senate Judiciary Committee then holds hearings and makes its recommendation to the Senate, where it takes a majority vote to confirm the nomination.

SENATORIAL COURTESY When judges are nominated to the district courts (and, to a lesser extent, the U.S. courts of appeals), a senator of the president's political party from the state where there is a vacancy traditionally has been allowed to veto the president's choice. This practice is known as **senatorial courtesy.** At times, senatorial courtesy even permits senators from the opposing party to veto presidential choices. Because of senatorial courtesy, home-state senators of the president's party may be able to influence the choice of the nominee.

PARTISANSHIP It should come as no surprise that partisanship plays a significant role in the president's selection of nominees to the federal bench, particularly to the Supreme Court, the crown jewel of the federal judiciary. Traditionally, presidents have attempted to strengthen their legacies by appointing federal judges with political and philosophical views similar to their own. In the history of the Supreme Court, fewer than 13 percent of the justices nominated by a president have been from an opposing political party.

senatorial courtesy A practice that allows a senator of the president's party to veto the president's nominee to a federal court judgeship within the senator's state.

That said, presidents have often discovered that the justices they appointed took very different positions than expected. President Dwight D. Eisenhower (1953–1961), for example, had no idea when he appointed Chief Justice Earl Warren that Warren would seek to overturn the system of racial segregation. The Court accomplished this goal through rulings such as *Brown v. Board of Education* (see Chapter 5).[11]

COURTS OF APPEALS Appointments to the U.S. courts of appeals can also have a lasting impact. Recall that these courts occupy the level just below the Supreme Court in the federal court system. Also recall that the decisions rendered by these courts—about 60,000 per year—are final unless overturned by the Supreme Court. Given that the Supreme Court renders opinions in fewer than one hundred cases a year, the decisions of the federal appellate courts have a wide-reaching effect on American society. For example, a decision interpreting the federal Constitution by the U.S. Court of Appeals for the Ninth Circuit, if not overruled by the Supreme Court, establishes a precedent that will be followed in the states of Alaska, Arizona, California, Hawaii, Idaho, Montana, Nevada, Oregon, and Washington.

Confirmation or Rejection by the Senate

The president's nominations are not always confirmed. In fact, almost 20 percent of presidential nominations for the Supreme Court have been either rejected or not acted on by the Senate. The process of nominating and confirming federal judges, especially Supreme Court justices, often involves political debate and controversy. Many bitter battles over Supreme Court appointments have ensued when the Senate and the president have disagreed on political issues.

From 1893 until 1968, the Senate rejected only three Court nominees. From 1968 through 1986, however, two presidential nominees to the highest court were rejected, and two more nominations, both by President Ronald Reagan, failed in 1987. The most significant of these nominees was Robert Bork, who faced hostile questioning about his views on the Constitution during the confirmation hearings. The Bork hearings are often considered to be a turning point after which confirmation hearings became much more contentious.

One of President George H. W. Bush's nominees to the Supreme Court—Clarence Thomas—was also the subject of considerable controversy. The nation watched on television as Anita Hill, a former aide, leveled charges of sexual harassment at Thomas, who nevertheless was confirmed.

AP PHOTO/RON EDMONDS

Sonia Sotomayor became only the third woman to serve on the Supreme Court and the first Latina (as she prefers to call herself).

GEORGE W. BUSH'S APPOINTMENTS During George W. Bush's second term, Chief Justice William Rehnquist died, and Sandra Day O'Connor, the Court's first woman, retired. These events allowed Bush to nominate John G. Roberts, Jr., to replace Rehnquist and Samuel A. Alito, Jr., to replace O'Connor. Both nominations were confirmed by the Senate with relatively little difficulty. The appointment of Alito in particular changed the character of the Court, because he was distinctly more conservative than O'Connor.

OBAMA'S NOMINEES In May 2009, as a result of a judicial retirement, President Barack Obama named Sonia Sotomayor to the Court. Sotomayor had served for more than a decade as a judge of the U.S. Court of Appeals for the Second Circuit and was the first Hispanic woman ever nominated to the Supreme Court. Due to the large Democratic majority in the Senate, Sotomayor was confirmed without difficulty. Conservatives, however, turned up several statements she had made that they used to challenge the nomination. For example, Sotomayor had said that a "wise Latina woman" might, because of her background, be able to make better decisions in discrimination cases than a white man. On the basis of that remark, talk-show host Rush Limbaugh called Sotomayor a racist.

A second retirement gave Obama an additional chance to pick a nominee in May 2010. He chose Elena Kagan, his solicitor general. At her confirmation hearings, several Republicans seized on an incident that occurred when Kagan was dean of Harvard Law School. In line with Harvard policy, Kagan placed restrictions on military recruiters. The restrictions were in response to the military's "don't ask, don't tell" policy that prevents lesbians and gay men from serving openly. Still, Kagan was confirmed. It was a sign of the increased political polarization in the Senate that neither Sotomayor nor Kagan received more than a handful of votes from Republican senators.

LO4 *The Courts as Policymakers*

I n the United States, judges and justices play a major role in government. Unlike judges in some other countries, U.S. judges have the power to decide on the constitutionality of laws or actions undertaken by the other branches of government.

Clearly, the function of the courts is to interpret and apply the law, not to make law—that is the function of the legislative branch of government. Yet judges can and do "make law"; indeed, they cannot avoid making law in some cases because the law does not always provide clear answers to questions that come before the courts. The text of the U.S. Constitution, for example, is set forth in broad terms. When a court interprets a constitutional provision and applies that interpretation to a specific

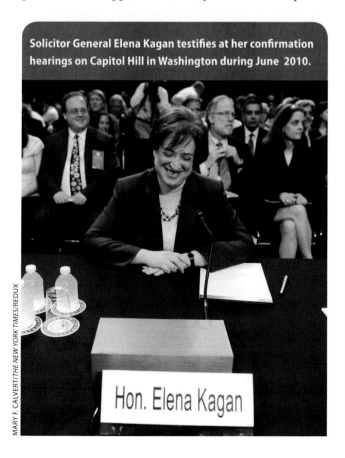

Solicitor General Elena Kagan testifies at her confirmation hearings on Capitol Hill in Washington during June 2010.

Hon. Elena Kagan

set of circumstances, the court is essentially "making the law" on that issue. Examples of how the courts, and especially the United States Supreme Court, make law abound. Consider privacy rights, which we discussed in Chapter 4. Nothing in the Constitution or its amendments specifically states that we have a right to privacy. Yet the Supreme Court, through various decisions, has established such a right by deciding that it is implied by several constitutional amendments. The Court has also held that this right to privacy includes a number of specific rights, such as the right to have an abortion.

Statutory provisions and other legal rules also tend to be expressed in general terms, and the courts must decide how those general provisions and rules apply to specific cases. The Americans with Disabilities Act of 1990 is an example. The act requires employers to reasonably accommodate the needs of employees with disabilities. But the act does not say exactly what employers must do to "reasonably accommodate" such persons. Thus, the courts must decide, on a case-by-case basis, what this phrase means. Additionally, in some cases there is no relevant law or precedent to follow. In recent years, for example, courts have been struggling with new kinds of legal issues stemming from new communications technologies, including the Internet. Until legislative bodies enact laws governing these issues, it is up to the courts to fashion the law that will apply—and thus make policy.

The Impact of Court Decisions

As already mentioned, how the courts interpret particular laws can have a widespread impact on society. For example, in 1996, in *Hopwood v. Texas*,[12] the U.S. Court of Appeals for the Fifth Circuit held that an affirmative action program implemented by the University of Texas School of Law in Austin was unconstitutional. The court's decision in *Hopwood* set a precedent for all federal courts within the Fifth Circuit's jurisdiction (which covers Louisiana, Mississippi, and Texas).

Decisions rendered by the United States Supreme Court, of course, have an even broader impact, because all courts in the nation are obligated to follow precedents set by the high court. For example, in 2003 the Supreme Court issued two rulings on affirmative action programs at the University of Michigan. Unlike the appeals court in the *Hopwood* case, the Supreme Court held that diversity on college campuses is a legitimate goal and that affirmative action programs that take race into consideration as part of an examination of each applicant's background do not necessarily violate the equal protection clause of the Constitution.[13] This decision rendered any contrary ruling, including the ruling by the court in the *Hopwood* case, invalid. In 2007, however, the Court retreated somewhat from its position in the University of Michigan cases when it declared that Seattle schools could not use race as a determining factor when assigning students to schools.[14]

Thus, when the Supreme Court interprets laws, it establishes national policy. If the Court deems that a law passed by Congress or a state legislature violates the Constitution, for example, that law will be void and unenforceable in any court within the United States.

The Power of Judicial Review

Recall from Chapter 2 that the U.S. Constitution divides government powers among the executive, legislative, and judicial branches. This division of powers is part of our system of checks and balances. Essentially, the founders gave each branch of government the constitutional authority to check the other two branches. The federal judiciary can exercise a check on the actions of either of the other branches through its power of **judicial review.**

The Constitution does not actually mention judicial review. Rather, the Supreme Court claimed the power for itself in *Marbury v. Madison.*[15] In that case, which was decided by the Court in 1803, Chief Justice John Marshall held that a provision of a 1789 law affecting the Supreme Court's jurisdiction violated the Constitution and was thus void. Marshall declared, "It is emphatically the province and duty of the judicial department [the courts] to say what the law is. . . . If two laws conflict with each other, the courts must decide on the operation of each. . . . So if a law be in opposition to the constitution . . . the court must determine which of these conflicting rules governs the case. This is the very essence of judicial duty."

Most constitutional scholars believe that the framers intended that the federal courts should have the power of judicial review. In *Federalist Paper* No. 78, Alexander Hamilton clearly espoused the doctrine. Hamilton stressed the importance of the "complete independence" of federal judges and their special duty to "invalidate all acts contrary to the manifest

judicial review The power of the courts to decide on the constitutionality of legislative enactments and of actions taken by the executive branch.

PHOTO BY MIKE SIMONS/GETTY IMAGES

The U.S. Supreme Court has often faced cases that deal with affirmative action questions. This University of Cincinnati student supports the continuation of affirmative action programs. What are the arguments in her favor? What are the arguments against?

tenor of the Constitution." Without judicial review by impartial courts, there would be nothing to ensure that the other branches of government stayed within constitutional limits when exercising their powers, and "all the reservations of particular rights or privileges would amount to nothing." Chief Justice Marshall shared Hamilton's views and adopted Hamilton's reasoning in *Marbury v. Madison.*

Judicial Activism versus Judicial Restraint

As already noted, making policy is not the primary function of the federal courts. Yet it is unavoidable that courts do, in fact, influence or even establish policy when they interpret and apply the law. Further, the

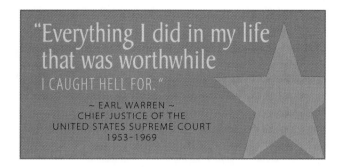

"Everything I did in my life that was worthwhile I CAUGHT HELL FOR."

~ EARL WARREN ~
CHIEF JUSTICE OF THE
UNITED STATES SUPREME COURT
1953-1969

power of judicial review gives the courts, and particularly the Supreme Court, an important policymaking tool. When the Supreme Court upholds or invalidates a state or federal statute, the consequences for the nation can be profound.

One issue that is often debated is how the federal courts should wield their policymaking power, particularly the power of judicial review. Often, this debate is couched in terms of judicial activism versus judicial restraint.

ACTIVIST VERSUS RESTRAINTIST JUSTICES Although the terms *judicial activism* and *judicial restraint* do not have precise meanings, generally an activist judge or justice believes that the courts should actively use their powers to check the legislative and executive branches to ensure that they do not exceed their authority. A restraintist judge or justice, in contrast, generally assumes that the courts should defer to the decisions of the legislative and executive branches, because members of Congress and the president are elected by the people, whereas federal court judges are not. In other words, the courts should not thwart the implementation of legislative acts unless those acts are clearly unconstitutional.

POLITICAL IDEOLOGY AND JUDICIAL ACTIVISM/ RESTRAINT One of the Supreme Court's most activist eras occurred during the period from 1953 to 1969 under the leadership of Chief Justice Earl Warren. The Warren Court propelled the civil rights movement forward by holding, among other things, that laws permitting racial segregation violated the equal protection clause (see Chapter 5).

Because of the activism of the Warren Court, the term *judicial activism* has often been linked with liberalism. Indeed, many liberals are in favor of an activist federal judiciary because they believe that the judiciary can "right" the "wrongs" that result from unfair laws or from "antiquated" legislation at the state and local levels. Neither judicial activism nor judicial restraint is

necessarily linked to a particular political ideology, however. In fact, many observers claim that today's Supreme Court is activist on behalf of a conservative agenda.

Still, in handling certain issues, the courts—especially at the state level—have continued to engage in activism that can be characterized as liberal. One such issue is the question of equal rights for lesbians and gay men. Today, the general public supports a variety of rights for such individuals, but the question of same-sex marriage remains extremely controversial. Are the courts an appropriate venue for deciding whether same-sex marriages should be recognized? We address that issue in the *Join the Debate* feature on the following page.

LO5 *Ideology and the Courts*

The policymaking role of the courts gives rise to an important question: To what extent do ideology and personal policy preferences affect judicial decision making? Numerous scholars have attempted to answer this question, especially with respect to Supreme Court justices.

Ideology and Supreme Court Decisions

Few doubt that ideology affects judicial decision making, although, of course, other factors play a role as well. Different courts (such as a trial court and an appellate court) can look at the same case and draw different conclusions as to what law is applicable and how it should be applied. Certainly, there are numerous examples of ideology affecting Supreme Court decisions. As new justices replace old ones and new ideological alignments are formed, the Court's decisions are affected. Yet many scholars argue that there is no real evidence that personal preferences influence Supreme Court decisions to an *unacceptable* extent.

Keep in mind that judicial decision making, particularly at the Supreme Court level, can be very complex. When deciding cases, the Supreme Court often must consider any number of sources of law, including constitutions, statutes, and administrative agency regulations—as well as cases interpreting relevant portions of those sources. At times, the Court may also take demographic data, public opinion, foreign laws, and other factors into account. How much weight is given to each of these sources or factors will vary from justice to justice. After all, reasoning of any kind, including judicial

JOIN THE DEBATE

Should Judges Be the Ones to Decide Whether Same-Sex Couples Can Marry?

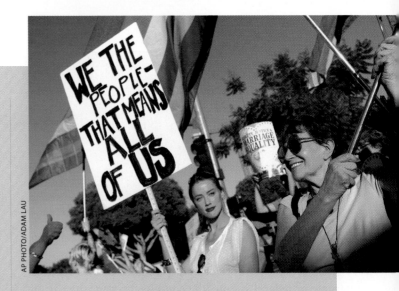

AP PHOTO/ADAM LAU

Until recently, the idea of marriages by same-sex couples never even entered the consciousness of most people. During the last few decades, however, gay marriage has become a sensitive and newsworthy topic. A few states have passed laws that authorize same-sex marriages. In a few more states, such marriages have been mandated by the state supreme court. A majority of the states, however, have passed laws or adopted constitutional amendments banning the practice.

The California experience is particularly noteworthy. In May 2008, the California Supreme Court ruled that the state constitution required the recognition of same-sex marriages. To overturn this ruling, opponents of gay marriage placed an amendment to the state constitution on the ballot. This was Proposition 8, which passed in November 2008. Same-sex marriage was again illegal in California. Supporters of same-sex marriage then sued to reverse Proposition 8 in a federal district court. In August 2010, Judge Vaughn R. Walker ruled that Proposition 8 violated the U.S. Constitution. The United States Supreme Court may ultimately resolve this conflict. Yet many people have asked, Why should judges be the ones to decide this issue, as opposed to legislators or the people?

Let the People or Their Representatives Decide

Why shouldn't the people of a state or their elected representatives decide whether to legitimize same-sex marriages? The federal government should have no say. Whether same-sex marriages should exist is a political question, not a constitutional one. We have a federal system of government, which means that the states have certain powers that the national government cannot touch. One such power is to create the rules for legal marriages. Whether you are in favor of or against same-sex marriages is irrelevant. The decision on whether to approve such marriages, once made by the people in a referendum or by the legislature in a state capital, must stand

as law. There is no reason for judges to intervene and decide whether the people or the legislatures were right or wrong. In the example of California's Proposition 8, the people spoke—against same-sex marriages. As a free people, that was their right.

If Judges Cannot Determine Constitutionality, Who Can?

The interpretation of the Constitution is always a matter for the courts. Individual citizens can have their own opinions, but it is up to the judiciary to carefully assess the constitutionality of any law. Supporters of same-sex marriage argue that the question of whether the Fourteenth Amendment to the U.S. Constitution prohibits states from banning such marriages is a real one.

No level of government may enforce a law that violates the Fourteenth Amendment's equal protection clause unless the law is "rationally related" to a "legitimate" government interest. Satisfying popular prejudices is not a legitimate interest. After careful investigation, Judge Walker found no legitimate interest that justified the banning of same-sex marriages. There will be those who dispute this finding, and they will have a chance to make their arguments through the federal appeals system. However this case turns out, judges ultimately must decide the constitutionality of bans on same-sex marriages. There is no other way.

For Critical Analysis *Why is it unlikely that the U.S. Congress would pass a law making all same-sex marriages legal?*

reasoning, does not take place in a vacuum. It is only natural that a justice's life experiences, personal biases, and intellectual abilities and predispositions will touch on the reasoning process. Nevertheless, when reviewing

a case, a Supreme Court justice does not start out with a conclusion (such as "I don't like this particular law that Congress passed") and then look for legal sources to support that conclusion.

Chief Justice John Roberts, Jr.

Justice Samuel Alito, Jr.

Ideology and the Roberts Court

In contrast to the liberal Supreme Court under Earl Warren, today's Court is generally conservative. The Court began its rightward shift after President Ronald Reagan (1981–1989) appointed conservative William Rehnquist as chief justice in 1986, and the Court moved further to the right as other conservative appointments to the bench were made by Reagan and George H. W. Bush (1989–1993).

Many Supreme Court scholars believe that the appointments of John Roberts (as chief justice) and Samuel Alito (as associate justice) caused the Court to drift even further to the right.[16] Certainly, the five conservative justices on the bench during the Roberts Court's first five terms voted together and cast the deciding votes in numerous cases. The remaining justices held liberal to moderate views and often formed an opposing bloc.

A notable change in the Court occurred when Alito replaced retiring justice Sandra Day O'Connor. O'Connor had often been the "swing" vote on the Court, sometimes voting with the liberal bloc and at other times siding with the conservatives. On the Roberts Court, the swing voter is Justice Anthony Kennedy, who is generally more conservative in his views than O'Connor was. Although Justice Kennedy dislikes being described as a swing voter, he often decides the outcome of a case. In the 2009–2010 term, for example, Kennedy was in the majority in nearly 75 percent of the closely decided cases.

Today's Court is strongly divided ideologically. In the Court term ending in June 2007, one-third of the decisions rendered by the Court were reached by five-

to-four votes—the highest share of such votes in more than a decade. In the 2009–2010 term, however, only seventeen out of ninety-two cases were decided by five-to-four votes.[17]

Approaches to Legal Interpretation

It would be a mistake to look at the judicial philosophy of today's Supreme Court solely in terms of the political ideologies of liberalism and conservatism. In fact, some Supreme Court scholars have suggested that other factors are as important as, or even more important than, the justices' political philosophies in determining why they decide as they do. These factors include the justices' attitudes toward legal interpretation and their perceptions of the Supreme Court's role in the federal judiciary.

STRICT VERSUS BROAD CONSTRUCTION Legal scholars have often used the terms *strict* and *broad* construction to describe how judges and justices interpret the law. Generally, strict constructionists look to the letter of the law as written when trying to decipher its meaning, whereas broad constructionists look more to the purpose and context of the law. Broad constructionists believe that the law is an evolving set of standards and is not fixed in concrete. Generally, broad constructionists are more willing to "read between the lines" of a law to serve what they perceive to be the law's intent and purpose.

Strict construction of the law is often linked with conservative views, and broad construction with liberal views. The conservative justices on today's Supreme Court are often labeled strict constructionists because they give great weight to the text of the law. Of course,

Although often considered a conservative when he served on the Rehnquist Court, Justice Anthony Kennedy has typically held the "swing" vote on the closely divided Roberts Court.

Justice Stephen Breyer.

Justice Antonin Scalia.

Justice Clarence Thomas.

Justice Ruth Bader Ginsburg.

as with judicial activism and judicial restraint, it is possible for these links to be reversed. There have been cases in which the Court appeared to be taking a conservative broad-constructionist or a liberal narrow-constructionist approach.

ORIGINAL INTENT VERSUS MODERNISM   The terms *strict construction* and *broad construction* describe different approaches to interpreting the law generally. These approaches may be used when determining the meaning of any law, whether it be a statutory provision, a specific regulation, or a constitutional clause. When discussing *constitutional* interpretation, however, the terms *original intent* and *modernism* are also used to describe the differences in Supreme Court justices' reasoning.

Original Intent   Some of the justices believe that to determine the meaning of a particular constitutional phrase, the Court should look to the intentions of the founders. What did the framers of the Constitution themselves intend when they included the phrase in the document? In other words, what was the "original intent" of the phrase? To discern the intent of the founders, the justices should look to sources that shed light on the founders' views. These sources include contemporary writings by the founders, newspaper articles, the *Federalist Papers*, and notes taken during the Constitutional

Convention. Justice Antonin Scalia, one of the Court's most conservative justices, gives some insight into this approach to constitutional interpretation in his book *A Matter of Interpretation.*[18] In response to those who maintain that the Constitution is a "living Constitution" and should be interpreted in light of society's needs and practices today, Scalia contends that constitutional principles are fixed, not evolving: "The Constitution that I interpret and apply is not living, but dead."

Modernism   Other justices, sometimes referred to as "modernists," believe that the Constitution is indeed a living document that evolves to meet changing times and new social needs. Otherwise, how could the Constitution be relevant to today's society? How could the opinions of a small group of white men who drafted the document more than two hundred years ago possibly apply to today's large and diverse population? Moreover, the founders themselves often disagreed on what the Constitution should mean. Additionally, if original intent is the goal, what about the intentions of those who ratified the Constitution? Shouldn't they be taken into consideration also? The modernist approach to constitutional interpretation thus looks at the Constitution in the context of today's society and considers how today's life affects the words in the document. Modernists also defend their approach by stating that the founders intentionally left many constitutional provisions vague so

"THE CONSTITUTION ITSELF SHOULD BE OUR GUIDE, not our own concept of what is fair, decent, and right."

~ HUGO L. BLACK ~
ASSOCIATE JUSTICE OF THE
UNITED STATES SUPREME COURT
1937–1971

Our Constitution gives legislative powers to the Congress exclusively. All executive powers are granted to the president. And all judicial powers are given to the judiciary. The United States Supreme Court is the final arbiter and interpreter of what is and is not constitutional. Because of its power of judicial review, it has the ability to "make law," or so it seems.

The Perception

Using the power of judicial review, the Supreme Court creates new laws. In 1954, the Court determined that racial segregation is illegal, a position that is universally accepted today but was hugely controversial back in the 1950s. The Court has also legalized sexual acts between same-sex adults and, of course, abortion. These decisions, especially the legalization of abortion, remain very controversial today. Such decisions have had a major impact on the nature of American society. Because citizens elect members of Congress and the president only—and not members of the Supreme Court—it is undemocratic to allow these nine justices to determine laws for our nation.

The Reality

The Supreme Court cannot actually write new laws. It can only eliminate old ones. When the Court threw out laws that criminalized adult sexual activity by gay men and lesbians, it was abolishing laws, not creating them. The Court does not have the power to legislate—to create new laws. Consider what would happen if the Court decided that some basic level of health care is a constitutional right—a highly unlikely event. Could the Court establish mechanisms by which such a right

could be enforced? It could not. It takes members of Congress months of hard work to craft bills that affect our health-care system. Such legislation fills thousands of pages and can only be developed with the assistance of large numbers of experts and lobbyists. The federal courts could not undertake such projects even if they wanted to.

Supreme Court justice Sonia Sotomayor once said: "The courts of appeals are where policy is made." Indeed, most cases never make it to the Supreme Court, and this fact limits the ability of Supreme Court justices to make policy decisions. More to the point, however, in referring to policy, Sotomayor was speaking of judicial policy, not policy in general. The courts must decide how they will handle the cases that are brought before them. To do so establishes judicial policy. It does not constitute lawmaking.

In any event, we have no alternative to judicial review when it comes to determining what is or is not constitutional. Without the Supreme Court, Congress and the president could make all sorts of laws that violate our Constitution and infringe on our rights, and there would be nothing to stop them. As Chief Justice John Roberts said during his confirmation hearings, "Judges are like umpires. Umpires don't make the rules; they apply them."

Blog On Plenty of bloggers follow the activities of the Supreme Court, but for sophisticated commentary, try **www.scotusblog.com**, produced by the law firm of Akin, Gump, Strauss, Hauer, and Feld. Another choice is **ussc.blogspot.com**, by Paul M. Rashkind, a Florida lawyer.

that future generations could interpret the document in a manner that would meet the needs of a growing nation.

LO6 Assessing the Role of the Federal Courts

The federal courts have often come under attack, particularly in the last decade or so, for many reasons. This should come as no surprise in view of the

policymaking power of the courts. After all, a Supreme Court decision can establish national policy on such issues as abortion, racial segregation, and gay rights. Critics, especially on the political right, frequently accuse the judiciary of "legislating from the bench." We discuss these criticisms in this chapter's *Perception versus Reality* feature above.

Criticisms of the Federal Courts

Certainly, policymaking by unelected judges and justices in the federal courts has serious implications in a democracy. Some Americans, including many conservatives, contend that making policy from the bench has upset the balance of powers envisioned by the framers of the Constitution. They cite Thomas Jefferson, who once said, "To consider the judges as the ultimate arbiters of all constitutional questions [is] a very dangerous doctrine indeed, and one which would place us under the despotism of an oligarchy."[19] This group believes that we should rein in the power of the federal courts, and particularly judicial activism.

Indeed, from the the mid-1990s until 2007, when the Republicans controlled Congress, a number of bills to restrain the power of the federal judiciary were introduced in Congress. Among other things, it was proposed that Congress, not the Supreme Court, should have the ultimate say in determining the meaning of the Constitution; that judges who ignore the will of Congress or follow foreign precedents should be impeached; that federal courts should not be allowed to decide certain types of cases, such as those involving abortion or the place of religion in public life; and that Congress should be empowered to use its control over the judiciary to punish judges who overstep their authority.

The Case for the Courts

On the other side of the debate over the courts are those who argue in favor of leaving the courts alone. Several federal court judges have sharply criticized congressional efforts to interfere with their authority. They claim that such efforts violate the Constitution's separation of powers. James M. Jeffords, a former independent senator from Vermont, likened the federal court system to a referee: "The first lesson we teach children when they enter competitive sports is to respect the referee, even if we think he [or she] might have made the wrong call. If our children can understand this, why can't our political leaders?"[20]

Others argue that there are already sufficient checks on the courts, some of which we look at next.

JUDICIAL TRADITIONS AND DOCTRINES One check on the courts is judicial restraint. Supreme Court justices traditionally have exercised a great deal of self-restraint. Justices sometimes admit to making decisions that fly in the face of their personal values and policy preferences, simply because they feel obligated to do so in view of existing law. Self-restraint

is also mandated by various established judicial traditions and doctrines, including the doctrine of *stare decisis,* which theoretically obligates the Supreme Court to follow its own precedents. Furthermore, the Supreme Court will not hear a meritless appeal just so it can rule on the issue. Finally, more often than not, the justices narrow their rulings to focus on just one aspect of an issue, even though there may be nothing to stop them from broadening their focus and thus widening the impact of their decisions.

OTHER CHECKS The judiciary is subject to other checks as well. Courts may make rulings, but they cannot force federal and state legislatures to appropriate the funds necessary to carry out those rulings. For example, if a state supreme court decides that prison conditions must be improved, the state legislature has to find the funds to carry out the ruling, or the improvements will not take place.

Additionally, legislatures can revise old laws or pass new ones in an attempt to negate a court's ruling. This may happen when a court interprets a statute in a way that Congress did not intend. Congress may also propose amendments to the Constitution to reverse Supreme Court rulings, and Congress has the authority to limit or otherwise alter the jurisdiction of the lower federal courts. Finally, although it is most unlikely, Congress could even change the number of justices on the Supreme Court, in an attempt to change the ideological balance on the Court. (President Franklin D. Roosevelt proposed such a plan in 1937, without success.)

THE PUBLIC'S REGARD FOR THE SUPREME COURT As mentioned, some have proposed that Congress, not the Supreme Court, be the final arbiter of the Constitution. In debates on this topic, one factor is often overlooked: the American public's high regard for the Supreme Court and the federal courts generally. The Court continues to be respected as a fair arbiter of conflicting interests and the protector of constitutional rights and liberties. Even when the Court issued its decision to halt the manual recount of votes in Florida following the 2000 elections, which effectively handed the presidency to George W. Bush, Americans respected the Court's decision-making authority—although many disagreed with the Court's decision. Polls continue to show that Americans have much more trust and confidence in the Supreme Court than they do in Congress.

A Supreme Court decision can affect the lives of millions of Americans. For example, in 1973, the Supreme Court, in *Roe v. Wade,* held that the constitutional right to privacy included the right to have an abortion. The influence wielded by the Court today is a far cry from the Court's relative obscurity at the founding of this nation. Initially, the Supreme Court was not even included in the plans for government buildings in the national capital. It did not have its own building until 1935. Over time, however, the Court has established a reputation with the public for dispensing justice in a fair and reasonable manner. Still, Americans are at odds over a number of judicial issues:

- Are there terrorist suspects who must be detained indefinitely without trial to protect our safety—or is such an act a violation of our Constitution that does us more damage in the world than a detainee could possibly accomplish if freed?

- Should the United States Supreme Court accept more cases to provide a greater number of definitive rulings—or should it take on relatively few cases so that it can treat each one thoroughly?

- Should senators accept a Supreme Court nomination by a president of the opposing party whenever the nominee appears to have sound judicial temperament—or should senators vote only for those nominees who share their political philosophies?

- Should judges defer to the decisions of legislatures and administrative agencies whenever possible—or should they strictly police the constitutionality of legislative and executive decisions?

- Is it crucial that the Constitution be interpreted in terms of the beliefs of the founders—or should justices take full account of modern circumstances that the founders could not have envisioned?

Take Action

The founders deliberately attempted to insulate the federal judiciary from popular opinion, so it might seem difficult to take action in regard to it. There are points at which the public can exercise leverage, however. One possibility is to lobby senators over judicial appointments. Especially if one or more of your senators is of a different political party than the president, that senator is probably of two minds over a presidential nomination to the Supreme Court or any of the lesser courts. Such senators will pay special attention to letters and e-mail from constituents who oppose or support a nomination. If you have voted for the senator or the senator's party in the past, it is helpful to point that out.

Greater opportunities to take action exist at the state level, especially in the majority of states in which judges are either elected or must face the voters after appointment. An important characteristic of state judicial elections is that most voters typically know nothing about the candidates. You can have a significant impact if you gather information and distribute it. Together with a group of your friends, you could research the candidates and pass on what you have learned, perhaps through an opinion piece in the campus newspaper. You may even be able to get academic credit for such an effort. It is

very useful if you can determine who is providing a candidate with campaign funds. A judicial candidate who receives large contributions from businesses such as insurance companies that fear lawsuits may handle cases one way. A candidate who receives most of his or her funds from trial lawyers (who do the suing) may handle cases differently.

Parents confer with a judge during jury deliberations at the trial of their daughter's murderer. He was found guilty and sentenced to death. (He had also killed several other young people.)

AP PHOTO/LARRY KOLVOORD, POOL

POLITICS ON THE
WEB

- An excellent Web site for information on the justices of the United States Supreme Court is **www.oyez. org**. This site offers biographies of the justices, links to opinions they have written, and, for justices who have served after 1920, video and audio materials. Oral arguments before the Supreme Court are also posted on this site.

- Another helpful Web site is **www.law.cornell.edu/ supct**. This collection of United States Supreme Court cases includes recent Court decisions, as well as selected historic decisions rendered by the Court.

- The Supreme Court makes its opinions available online at its official Web site. Go to **www.supremecourt.gov**

- FindLaw offers a free searchable database of Supreme Court decisions since 1907 at **www.findlaw.com**

- Increasingly, decisions of the state courts are available online. You can search through the texts of state cases that are on the Internet, as well as federal cases, state and federal laws, and the laws of other countries, by accessing WashLaw at **www.washlaw.edu**

- To learn more about the federal court system, go to **www.uscourts.gov**. This is the home page for the federal courts. Among other things, you can follow the path a case takes as it moves through the federal court system.

Access CourseMate to review and expand on this chapter through quizzes, flashcards, learning objectives, interactive timelines, a crossword puzzle, audio summaries, video, critical-thinking activities, simulations, and more.

Domestic Policy

LEARNING OBJECTIVES

LO1 Explain what domestic policy is and summarize the steps in the policymaking process.

LO2 Discuss the issue of health-care funding and recent legislation on universal health insurance.

LO3 Summarize the issues of energy independence, global warming, and alternative energy sources.

LO4 Describe the two major areas of economic policymaking.

CourseMate

AMERICA AT
ODDS

Do We Send Too Many People to Prison?

Currently, there are about 2.4 million U.S. residents in prison or jail. That's roughly one in every one hundred adults. We are setting records—we have twelve times the share of our population in prison as Japan, nine times more than in Germany, and five times more than in Britain. Federal prisons currently hold in excess of 60 percent of their rated capacity. Yet in 1970, the proportion of Americans behind bars—the *incarceration rate*—was only one-fourth of what it is today. Not surprisingly, the number of drug offenders in prison is responsible for much of this increase. Such lockups have multiplied thirteenfold since 1980.

Holding that many prisoners is not cheap. It costs about $50,000 a year to house a convicted criminal in a state prison. As defense attorney Jim Felman of Tampa, Florida, said, America is conducting "an experiment in imprisoning first-time non-violent offenders for periods of time previously reserved only for those who had killed someone." We can expect that more U.S. residents will go to prison in the future. The federal government currently has 4,400 crimes on the books, and that number rises every year. So, do we send too many Americans to prison?

Keep Criminals Behind Bars—It Works

Supporters of aggressive incarceration policies argue that still more criminals should be behind bars. Putting more people in prison reduces crime rates. After all, incentives matter. If potential criminals know that they will be thrown in jail more readily and stay there longer, they will have less incentive to engage in illegal activities. Also, the crime rate is strongly determined by the number of criminals at large. When we remove a criminal from the streets and put that person in prison, the prisoner can no longer commit crimes that harm the public. This effect of removal is called *incapacitation*. The evidence shows that during the 1960s, when incarceration rates fell, the crime rate more than doubled. As incarceration rates rose sharply in the 1990s, the crime rate went steadily down. As a comparison, the risk of criminal punishment in England has been falling. As a consequence, crime rates have risen in England while they have fallen in the United States.

Tough sentencing is effective. We should not turn career criminals loose on the streets.

Too Many Laws and Too Many Prisoners

Those who argue against our high rates of incarceration point out that many individuals are convicted of nonviolent crimes. The government should not be spending $50,000 a year or more to keep such people in prison. Too many acts have been criminalized, particularly at the federal level. Many crimes are so vaguely defined that most Americans would not know if they were breaking the law or not. Granted, hard-core criminals should be behind bars. But what about the casual pot smoker? Or someone convicted under a federal statute designed to protect the environment? Lying to a federal official is a felony. Who can say how many people could be imprisoned based on such an act?

Many states have so-called habitual-offender laws. In California, for example, almost 4,000 individuals are serving life sentences because they were convicted of a third offense—one that was neither violent nor serious. Furthermore, the cost to society of putting drug users behind bars is much greater than the benefits. Wouldn't that money be better spent on rehabilitation?

WHERE DO YOU STAND?

1. Could other factors underlie the apparent relationship between high incarceration rates and low crime rates? What might they be?
2. Why do you think federal, state, and local governments arrest so many drug-law violators?

EXPLORE THIS ISSUE ONLINE

- You can find several articles arguing that we imprison too many people in the *Economist,* a British magazine. One such article is at www.economist.com/node/16640389.
- The Criminal Justice Legal Foundation is among the few groups that advocate increased rates of incarceration. See its arguments at www.cjlf.org/publctns/ConfiningCriminals.pdf.

Introduction

Whether we send too many people to prison is just one of the issues that confront our nation's policymakers today. How are questions of national importance, such as this one, decided? Who are the major participants in the decision-making process?

To learn the answers to these questions, we need to delve into the politics of policymaking. Policy, or public policy, can be defined as a plan or course of action taken by the government to respond to a political issue or to enhance the social or political well-being of society. Public policy is the end result of the policymaking process, which will be described shortly. **Domestic policy,** in contrast to foreign policy, consists of public policy concerning issues *within* a national unit.

In this chapter, after discussing how policy is made through the policymaking process, we look at several aspects of domestic policy, including health-care policy, energy policy, and economic policy. We focus on these policy areas because they have been the Obama administration's top priorities. An additional priority for the administration is immigration reform. It is an open question, however, as to when this subject can be addressed. We consider immigration reform in this chapter's *Join the Debate* feature on the following page.

Overcrowding in state and federal prisons, such as this one in California, has placed the issue on the policymaking agenda. One response has been early release of nonviolent offenders.

AP PHOTO/CALIFORNIA DEPARTMENT OF CORRECTIONS

Bear in mind that although the focus here is on policy and policymaking at the national level, state and local governments also engage in policymaking and establish policies to achieve goals relating to activities within their boundaries. This is certainly true in relation to the criminal justice issues discussed in this chapter's opening *America at Odds* feature.

domestic policy Public policy concerning issues within a national unit, such as national policy concerning health care or the economy.

policymaking process The procedures involved in getting an issue on the political agenda; formulating, adopting, and implementing a policy with regard to the issue; and then evaluating the results of the policy.

LO1 *The Policymaking Process*

A new law does not appear out of nowhere. First, the problem addressed by the new law has to become part of the political agenda—that is, the problem must be defined as a political issue to be resolved by government action. Furthermore, once the issue gets on the political agenda, proposed solutions to the problem have to be formulated and then adopted. Issue identification and agenda setting, policy formulation, and policy adoption are all parts of the **policymaking process.** The process does not end there, however. Once the law is passed, it has to be implemented and then evaluated.

Each phase of the policymaking process involves interactions among various individuals and groups. The president and members of Congress are obviously important participants in the process. Remember from Chapter 6 that interest groups also play a key role. Groups that may be affected adversely by a new policy will try to convince Congress not to adopt the policy. Groups that will benefit from the policy will exert whatever influence they can on Congress to do the opposite. Congressional committees and subcommittees may investigate the problem to be addressed by the policy and, in so doing, solicit input from members of various groups or industries.

The participants in policymaking and the nature of the debates involved depend on the particular policy being proposed, formed, or implemented. Whatever the policy, however, debate over its pros and cons occurs during each stage of the policymaking process. Additionally, making policy decisions

Should Unauthorized Immigrants Be Given a Path to Citizenship?

The United States is a land of immigrants. Apart from Native Americans, all of us are either current immigrants or the descendants of immigrants. Yet immigration remains one of the most divisive issues facing Americans and their elected representatives today.

Congress has reacted in various ways to the issue of illegal immigration. At one time, it established an amnesty program to allow unauthorized immigrants who had been working in the United States for five years to obtain legal residency. More recently, it voted in favor of a large, secure fence on the U.S.-Mexican border to keep illegal immigrants out. President Barack Obama's immigration proposals require undocumented immigrants who do not otherwise violate the law to pay a fine, learn English, and go to the back of the line for the opportunity to become citizens. Obama also favors crackdowns on employers who hire illegal immigrants and steps to make legal immigration easier.

Today, there are up to 12 million illegal immigrants living and working in this country. Should they be given a path to citizenship?

How Can Any American Be against Immigration?

Some find the "close the door after me" mentality to be very un-American. Just remember, standards of living in the United States have been improving for decades not in spite of immigration but because of it. It's true that an unauthorized immigrant is not playing by the rules.

But that is because the rules are so difficult to follow. We should make it easier for current unauthorized immigrants to become legal. The vast majority of illegal immigrants are working and adding to this nation's well-being. The net taxpayer cost per immigrant is negative. They are normally not eligible to receive welfare benefits. They come here to work, not to receive government handouts.

A Path to Citizenship Sends the Wrong Signals

Illegal immigrants have broken the law. If we give them a path to citizenship or even to legal status, we are sending the wrong signals to the rest of the world. As a result, we will end up with even more illegal immigrants, all of them hoping to find a path to citizenship one day.

Most unauthorized immigrants have few job skills. Immigrants without high school diplomas now head about a third of immigrant households. Certainly, this country can use more high-skilled immigrants—those with scientific degrees and PhDs. Low-skilled immigrants, in contrast, simply take jobs away from Americans. To send the right signals to the rest of the world, we should also crack down on employers who hire illegal immigrants. These employers are making a real contribution to the problem. Then there is the issue of security. We have to protect our borders if we are to prevent terrorists from entering the United States.

For Critical Analysis *How might we rationalize the inconsistency between our being a country of immigrants and wanting to keep out new ones?*

---

inevitably involves *trade-offs,* in which policymakers must sacrifice one goal to achieve another because of budget constraints.

Issue Identification and Agenda Setting

If no one recognizes a problem, then no matter how important the problem may be, politically it does not yet really exist. Thus, *issue identification* is part of the first stage of the policymaking process. Some

agenda setting Getting an issue on the political agenda to be addressed by Congress; part of the first stage of the policymaking process.

group—whether it be the media, the public, politicians, or even foreign commentators—must identify a problem that can be solved politically. The second part of this stage of the policymaking process involves getting the issue on the political agenda to be addressed by Congress. This is called **agenda setting,** or agenda building.

A problem in society can be identified as an issue and included on the political agenda in a number of different ways. An event or series of events may lead to a call for action. For example, the failure of a major bank may lead to the conclusion that the financial industry is in trouble and that the government should take action to rectify the problem. Dramatic increases

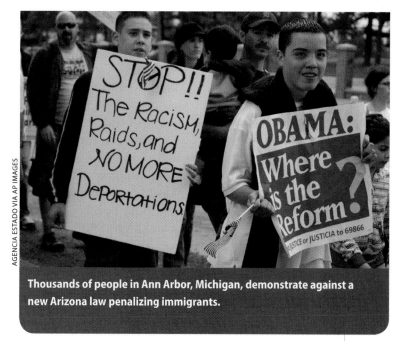

Thousands of people in Ann Arbor, Michigan, demonstrate against a new Arizona law penalizing immigrants.

in health-care costs may cause the media or other groups to consider health care a priority that should be on the national political agenda. Sometimes, the social or economic effects of a national calamity, such as the Great Depression of the 1930s or the terrorist attacks of September 11, 2001, create a pressing need for government action.

Policy Formulation and Adoption

The second stage in the policymaking process involves the formulation and adoption of specific plans for achieving a particular goal, such as health-care reform. The president, members of Congress, administrative agencies, and interest group leaders typically are the key participants in developing proposed legislation. Remember from Chapter 13 that iron triangles and issue networks work together in forming mutually beneficial policies. To a certain extent, the courts also establish policies when they interpret statutes passed by legislative bodies or make decisions concerning disputes not yet addressed by any law, such as disputes involving new technology.

Note that some issues may get on the political agenda but never proceed beyond that stage of the policymaking process. Usually, this happens when it is impossible to achieve a consensus over what policy should be adopted.

Policy Implementation

Because of our federal system, the implementation of national policies necessarily requires the cooperation of the federal government and the various state and local governments. A case in point is the 1996 Welfare Reform Act. The act required the states to develop plans for implementing the new welfare policy within their borders. The federal government, though, retained some authority over the welfare system by providing that state welfare plans had to be certified, or approved, by the federal government. In addition, successful implementation usually requires the support of groups outside the government. For example, the work requirements of the Welfare Reform Act meant that the business sector would also play a key role in the policy's implementation.

Policy implementation also involves agencies in the executive branch (see Chapter 13). Once Congress establishes a policy by enacting legislation, the executive branch, through its agencies, enforces the new policy. Furthermore, the courts are involved in policy implementation, because the legislation and administrative regulations enunciating the new policy must be interpreted and applied to specific situations by the courts.

Policy Evaluation

The final stage of policymaking involves evaluating the success of a policy during and following its implementation. Once a policy has been implemented, groups both inside and outside the government evaluate the policy. Congress may hold hearings to obtain feedback from different groups on how a statute or regulation has affected them. Scholars and scientists may conduct studies to determine whether a particular law, such as an environmental law designed to reduce air pollution, has actually achieved the desired result—less air pollution. Sometimes, feedback obtained in these or other ways indicates that a policy has failed, and a new policymaking process may be undertaken to modify the policy or create a more effective one.

Policymaking versus Special Interests

The policymaking steps just discussed seem straightforward, but they are not. Every bill that passes through Congress is a compromise. Every bill that passes through Congress is also an opportunity for individual members of Congress to help constituents, particularly those who were kind enough to contribute financially to the members' reelection campaigns.

Consider the Emergency Economic Stabilization Act of 2008, a $700 billion financial rescue plan that the U.S. Treasury Department urgently demanded on

September 19, 2008. After the House defeated the initial "clean" version of the bailout bill, the Senate drafted a second version. This second version included a landmark health-care provision requiring that insurance companies provide coverage for mental health treatment equivalent to that provided for the treatment of physical illnesses. The bill also contained almost $14 billion in tax-break extensions for businesses. Special provisions benefited rural schools, film and television producers, makers of toy wooden arrows, victims of the 1989 *Exxon Valdez* oil spill in Alaska, rum distillers in the Virgin Islands and Puerto Rico, auto racetracks, and wool researchers. The second bill passed the House on October 3. Clearly, policymaking, particularly on the economic front, remains a complicated process.

LO2 *Health-Care Policy*

In March 2010, Congress passed major health-care reform legislation. The two bills containing the reforms, which President Barack Obama immediately signed, were among the most consequential government initiatives in many years. Health-care reform is one of the most important topics that the government can address. Even before the new legislation was adopted, the federal government was paying the health-care costs of more than 100 million Americans. When President Obama took office, the government was picking up the tab for about 50 percent of the nation's health-care costs. Private insurance was responsible for about a third of all health-care payments, and the rest was met either by patients themselves or by charity. Paying for health-care expenses, in other words, was already a major federal responsibility, and questions about how the government should carry out that function in the future were unavoidable.

Our system for funding health care suffers from two major problems. One is that health care is expensive. About 17.6 percent of national spending in the United States goes to health care, compared with 10 percent in Canada, 9 percent in Sweden, and 8 percent in Japan. Also, almost 42 million Americans—close to 16 percent of the population—have no health-care insurance. Lack of coverage means that people may neglect preventive care, put off seeing a physician until it is too late, or be forced into bankruptcy due to large medical bills. One study has estimated that 20,000 people each year die prematurely because they lack health insurance.[1] (Others dispute these findings.) All other economically advanced nations provide health insurance to everyone, typically through a government program similar to Social Security or Medicare in the United States.

Before discussing the recently passed health-care reforms, let's first look at the programs that are already in place. The most important of these is **Medicare,** which provides health-care insurance to Americans aged sixty-five or over, and **Medicaid,** which funds health-care coverage for the poor.

Medicaid and Medicare

The federal government pays for health care in a variety of ways. Like many major employers, it buys health-care insurance for its employees. In addition, members of the armed forces, veterans, and Native Americans receive medical services provided directly by the government. Most federal spending on health care, however, is accounted for by Medicare and Medicaid. Both are costly, and each, in its own way, poses a serious financial problem to the government.

MEDICAID A joint federal-state program, Medicaid provides health-care subsidies to low-income persons. The federal government provides about 60 percent of the Medicaid budget, and the states provide the rest. More than 60 million people are in the program, which currently costs all levels of government well over $300 billion per year. The cost of Medicaid has doubled in the last decade, and this has put a considerable strain on the budgets of many states. About 17 percent of the average state general fund budget now goes to Medicaid. Recent cost-containment measures have slowed the

Medicare A federal government program that pays for health-care insurance for Americans aged sixty-five years or over.

Medicaid A joint federal-state program that pays for health-care services for low-income persons.

growth of Medicaid spending, however. Another program, the **State Children's Health Insurance Program (SCHIP)**, covers children in families with incomes that are modest but too high to qualify for Medicaid.

The Great Recession put a considerable strain on the states' ability to pick up their share of Medicaid payments. The Obama administration's February 2009 stimulus package, therefore, included $87 billion to reduce temporarily the Medicaid burden on the states. Congressional Democrats also substantially increased the size of SCHIP within weeks of Obama's inauguration.

MEDICARE Medicare is the federal government's health-care program for persons over the age of sixty-five. Medicare is now the government's second-largest domestic spending program, after Social Security. In 1970, Medicare accounted for only 0.7 percent of total annual U.S. national income (gross domestic product, or GDP). It currently accounts for about 3.2 percent of the GDP, and costs are expected to soar as millions of "baby boomers" retire over the next two decades. By 2030, the sixty-five-and-older population is expected to double. Further, technological developments in health care and the advancement of medical science are driving medical costs up every year. There are simply more things that medical science can do to keep people alive—and Americans naturally want to take advantage of these services.

This senior citizen lives in a nursing home in North Smithfield, Rhode Island. Most of her living and medical expenses are paid for by the government through Medicaid. Rhode Island is one of many states that are facing record Medicaid expenses.

The Democrats Propose Universal Coverage

As noted earlier, the United States is the only economically advanced nation that does not provide universal health-insurance coverage to its citizens. Universal insurance is not a new idea. German chancellor Otto von Bismarck implemented the first such plan in Germany in 1883. (A staunch conservative, Bismarck sought to use social legislation to "steal the thunder" of the German socialists, who were quite popular.) Democratic president Bill Clinton (1993–2001) and then First Lady Hillary Clinton made a serious push for a universal plan during President Clinton's first term, but the project failed to pass Congress.

Many universal health insurance plans—for example, the systems in Canada and France—involve government monopolies. In these nations, the government is responsible for providing basic health-care insurance to everyone through **national health insurance.** The plan that the United States has adopted, however, provides a larger role for the private sector.

The legislative process began in 2009 with hearings in multiple committees in the House and Senate. Still, all the proposals had common features. All assumed that employer-provided health insurance would continue to be a major part of the system. Large employers

State Children's Health Insurance Program (SCHIP) A joint federal-state program that provides health-care insurance for low-income children.

national health insurance A program, found in many of the world's economically advanced nations, under which the central government provides basic health-care insurance coverage to everyone in the country. Some wealthy nations, such as the Netherlands and Switzerland, provide universal coverage through private insurance companies instead.

who did not offer a plan would be required to pay a penalty. Medicaid would be available to individuals with incomes up to about 1.5 times the federal poverty level. (In 2010, the poverty level for a family of four was $22,050.) A new health-insurance marketplace, the Health Insurance Exchange, would allow individuals and small employers to shop for plans. Insurance companies would not be allowed to deny anyone coverage. Most individuals would be required to obtain coverage or pay an income-tax penalty. This requirement is known as the **individual mandate,** or the *personal mandate*. Those with low-to-middle incomes would receive help in paying their premiums. Subsidies would be phased out for those earning more than four times the federal poverty level.

House legislation called for a government-sponsored insurance plan known as the **public option.** This plan would compete against private plans in the Health Insurance Exchange. The public option, however, was rejected by the Senate. The House passed a plan in November 2009. In December, the Senate version passed with votes from all sixty Democrats and no Republicans.

The Health-Care Debate

Republicans were quite hostile toward the public option. A caucus of conservative Democrats in the House, known as the **Blue Dog Coalition,** also opposed it, as did a half-dozen Democrats in the Senate. Advocates of the public option contended that it would provide needed competition to private plans.

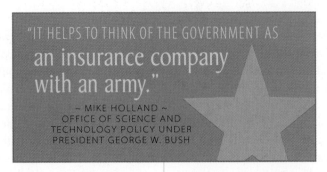

"IT HELPS TO THINK OF THE GOVERNMENT AS **an insurance company with an army.**"

~ MIKE HOLLAND ~
OFFICE OF SCIENCE AND
TECHNOLOGY POLICY UNDER
PRESIDENT GEORGE W. BUSH

Opponents argued that it could lead to the destruction of private-sector health insurance. Polls, however, reported considerable support for the public option.

The individual mandate was also controversial, because it would require all Americans to have health insurance whether they wanted it or not. The mandate would impose a burden on young, healthy persons who chose not to buy insurance. Supporters of reform, however, pointed out that without an individual mandate, reform would not work. Without a mandate, people might wait until they became sick before they purchased insurance. Any system that let healthy people avoid buying insurance would face financial collapse.

SUPPORT AND OPPOSITION The Obama administration won considerable support for reform from interest groups that had opposed universal health-care systems in the past. For the first time, the American Medical Association was on board. Pharmaceutical companies gave general support. The greater part of the opposition came not from interest groups but from conservatives.

Over the course of 2009, conservative hostility to the legislation grew in strength and fervor. Opponents

individual mandate In the context of health-care reform, a requirement that all persons obtain health-care insurance from one source or another. Those failing to do so would pay a penalty.

public option In the context of health-care reform, a government-sponsored health-care insurance program that would compete with private insurance companies.

Blue Dog Coalition A caucus that unites most of the moderate-to-conservative Democrats in the House of Representatives.

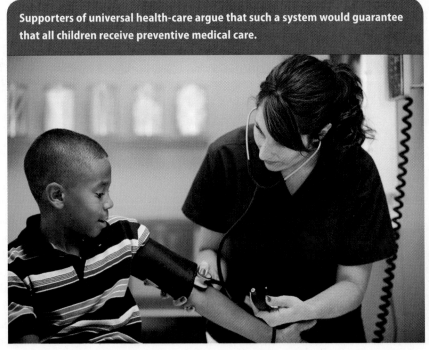

Supporters of universal health-care argue that such a system would guarantee that all children receive preventive medical care.

© SEAN LOCKE/ISTOCKPHOTO

were not only hostile to health-care reform; most were upset over what they saw as the growing power of government in general. They believed that health-care reform was only one of several steps toward a vast federal leviathan that would crush individual freedoms.

In time, a second reason emerged for opposing reform—Democratic plans to curb increases in Medicare spending. Many older persons receiving Medicare were afraid that their benefits would be cut. (See Chapter 13's *Our Government Faces a Troubled Economy* feature on page 283.) By 2010, health-care reform had lost much of its earlier support among the public.

The growing unpopularity of reform was confirmed in January 2010, when Republican Scott Brown won a special election to fill a U.S. Senate seat in Massachusetts. Brown's victory cost the Democrats in the Senate their sixty-vote supermajority.

HOW THE LEGISLATION PASSED Brown's victory came at a time when two different health-care reform bills had passed the House and Senate. Normally, a conference committee of House and Senate leaders would agree to a compromise that would then have to be passed by both chambers. With only fifty-nine votes in the Senate, however, the Democrats would be unable to pass such a bill. Republicans celebrated in the belief that they had successfully killed the health-care legislation. They celebrated too soon, however. If the House passed the Senate version of reform without any changes, no conference committee would be necessary. The bill could go immediately to the president for his signature. House Speaker Nancy Pelosi and President Obama were able to find enough votes in the House to pass the Senate's Patient Protection and Affordable Care Act.

RECONCILIATION The House then passed a second bill, the Health Care and Education Reconciliation Act. **Reconciliation** acts are a special kind of legislation that cannot be filibustered in the Senate. To qualify, an act must deal only in financial matters. This measure amended the Senate's bill in a number of ways. It split the difference between the House and Senate funding mechanisms. Both high-income taxpayers and high-end "Cadillac" health plans would be taxed. The **Congressional Budget Office (CBO),** an agency set up by Congress to evaluate the impact of proposed measures on the federal budget, scored the result as costing $940 billion over ten years and reducing the deficit by $138 billion. The Senate quickly adopted the reconciliation act with fifty-six votes in favor. On Obama's signature, health-care reform was law.

THE CONSERVATIVE REACTION Conservatives argued that the Democrats had ignored the will of the people, who were against the reform legislation. In a typical poll in March 2010, 56 percent of respondents opposed the legislation. That figure was slightly misleading, however. Only 43 percent opposed the reforms because they were "too liberal." Another 13 percent opposed them because they were "not liberal enough."

One last-ditch method of opposing the reforms was to challenge their constitutionality. Attorney generals in twenty states challenged the measure on the basis that the individual mandate violated the Constitution. (See Chapter 3's *Join the Debate* feature on page 63.)

A second method of attack would be to repeal the legislation, and the Republicans made repeal part of their platform for the 2010 elections. Republicans have plenty of time to win repeal, because full universal coverage does not go into effect until 2014. Repeal, however, would require specific legislation passed by Congress and signed by the president. To prevent a veto, a Republican president would be necessary. The Republicans also would have to control the House. Finally, they would need sixty votes in the Senate to override a Democratic filibuster.[2]

LO3 *Energy Policy*

As a priority for the Obama administration, energy policy was second only to health-care policy. Energy policy is important because of two problems: (1) our reliance on imported oil and (2) the possibility of global warming.

The Problem of Imported Oil

Our nation imports about three-fifths of its petroleum supply. Oil imports are a potential problem largely because many of the nations that export oil are not particularly friendly to the United States. Some, such as Iran, are outright adversaries. Other oil exporters that could pose difficulties include Iraq, Libya, Nigeria, Russia, and Venezuela. Even Saudi Arabia, nominally a U.S. friend, is something of a question mark. Most of the terrorists

reconciliation A special kind of legislation not subject to filibuster in the Senate. A reconciliation act must deal only with financial matters.

Congressional Budget Office (CBO) An agency established by Congress to evaluate the impact of proposed legislation on the federal budget.

Corporate Average Fuel Economy (CAFE) standards A set of federal standards under which each manufacturer must meet a miles-per-gallon benchmark averaged across all cars or trucks that it sells.

global warming An increase in the average temperature of the Earth's surface over the last half century and its projected continuation.

greenhouse gas A gas that, when released into the atmosphere, traps the sun's heat and slows its release into outer space. Carbon dioxide (CO_2) is a major example.

who attacked the United States on 9/11 were Saudis, and many Saudis have anti-Western attitudes. A change of regime in Saudi Arabia could spell big trouble. Some exporters, including Iraq, Nigeria, and Venezuela, have recently experienced drops in oil production due to internal disturbances. Fortunately for the United States, half of our oil imports come from Canada and Mexico, stable and friendly neighbors to the north and south. Venezuela, however, is also a major American supplier. In addition, many of our European and Asian allies are dependent on imports from questionable regimes.

THE PRICE OF OIL Until fairly recently, the price of oil was low, and the U.S. government was under little pressure to address our dependence on imports. In 1998, the price per barrel fell below $12. In July 2008, however, on the eve of the collapse of the Lehman Brothers investment bank, the price of oil spiked to more than $125 a barrel, forcing U.S. gasoline prices above $4 per gallon. Thereafter, oil prices fell dramatically when demand collapsed due to the global economic panic. Experts believe, however, that oil prices will rise again as economic activity resumes.

U.S. ENERGY POLICIES The federal government responded to an earlier spurt in oil prices, in the 1970s, by imposing fuel-mileage standards on cars and trucks sold in this country. Under the **Corporate Average Fuel Economy (CAFE) standards,** each manufacturer had to meet a miles-per-gallon benchmark, which was averaged across all cars and trucks that it sold. Under the rules, trucks were allowed to consume more fuel. One unintended result was that when oil prices dropped in the 1980s, Americans began turning away from automobiles and toward pickups and SUVs, which were considered trucks under the standards.

> **"NATURE PROVIDES A FREE LUNCH**
> but only if we control
> our appetites."
> ~ WILLIAM DOYLE RUCKELSHAUS ~
> FIRST HEAD OF THE ENVIRONMENTAL
> PROTECTION AGENCY
> 1970–1973

Many economists have long argued that the best way to encourage fuel economy would be to impose a new federal tax on gasoline and diesel fuel, perhaps fifty cents per gallon. The resulting revenues could be used to lower other taxes. European nations have much higher taxes on fuel than the United States does, and as a result, Europeans tend to favor smaller, more fuel-efficient vehicles. Very few American politicians have been willing to endorse such a concept, however. They rightly judged that it would be political poison.

The steep rise in oil prices in 2007 and 2008, plus the election of a Democratic Congress and president, meant that measures to restrain U.S. fuel consumption were on the agenda again. In 2009, President Obama issued higher fuel-efficiency standards for cars and trucks. By 2016, the standards will be thirty-nine miles per gallon for cars and thirty miles per gallon for light trucks. The standards began to take effect in 2010. Because of this government mandate, along with expected high fuel prices, vehicles that are more fuel efficient will almost certainly be part of America's future. Many of the new vehicles will run at least partially on electric power.

Global Warming

Observations collected by agencies such as the National Aeronautics and Space Administration (NASA) suggest that during the last century, average global temperatures increased by about 0.74 degrees Celsius (1.33 degrees Fahrenheit). Figure 15–1 on the facing page illustrates this phenomenon. Most climatologists believe that this **global warming** is the result of human activities, especially the release of **greenhouse gases** into the atmosphere. A United Nations body, the Intergovernmental Panel on Climate Change (IPCC), estimated that during the twenty-first century, global temperatures could rise an additional 1.1 to 6.4 degrees Celsius (2.0 to 11.5 degrees Fahrenheit). Warming may continue in subsequent centuries.

The predicted outcomes of global warming vary depending on the climate models on which they are based. If the oceans grow warmer, seawater will expand and polar ice will melt. These two developments will cause sea levels to rise, possibly drowning some coastal areas. Rainfall patterns are expected to change, turning some areas into desert but allowing agriculture to expand elsewhere. Other likely effects include increases in extreme weather and the extinction of some plants and animals.

THE GLOBAL WARMING DEBATE Some scientists actively working on climate issues dispute the consensus view of global warming. Those who dispute the consensus argue that any observed warming is due largely to natural causes and may not continue into the future. Although skepticism is rare among relevant scientists, it is extremely common in the broader community of Americans.

A Gallup poll in 2009 revealed that only 49 percent of those with an opinion believed that global warming is the result of human activities. Furthermore, attitudes toward global warming have become highly politicized. Some commentators on the political right contend that global warming is a giant liberal hoax designed to clear the way for increased government control of the economy and society. At the same time, many on the political left believe that the right-wing refusal to accept the existence of global warming threatens the very future of the human race. Members of Congress are influenced by these attitudes even if they do not necessarily share them, and as a result, congressional Republicans and Democrats have almost no common ground on questions of how global warming might be reduced or its effects mitigated.

RENEWABLE ENERGY Not all methods of supplying the economy with energy depend on burning carbon and thus releasing greenhouse gases into the environment. For example, hydroelectric energy, generated by water flowing through dams, is a widely used technology that employs no coal, natural gas, oil, or other fossil fuels. Energy from such technologies is referred to as **renewable energy,** because it does not rely on extracted resources, such as oil and coal, that can run out. Obviously, the use of renewable energy has many

Figure 15–1

Global Warming

Temperature change in degrees Celsius (°C) from 1951–1980 to 2000–2010.

Source: NASA/GISS (Goddard Institute for Space Studies).

benefits. For one thing, it can be an effective method of reducing potential global warming. The problem is that most existing renewable technologies, such as solar power cells, are expensive. Hydropower is an exception, but the number of feasible locations for new dams in the United States is small, and dams create their own environmental problems.

Wind Energy One renewable technology that is almost as economical as conventional power sources is wind energy, and both the Bush and Obama administrations have subsidized wind power. Windmills are now under construction in many locations. Of course, even if the price is right, wind power suffers from one obvious problem: the wind does not always blow, so wind cannot provide more than a modest share of the nation's electrical needs. Still, Obama's February 2009 stimulus package set aside billions of dollars that could be used for high-tension lines to transport electricity from rural wind farms to major cities.

Nuclear Energy An additional energy source that does not contribute to global warming is nuclear power. This

> **renewable energy**
> Energy from technologies that do not rely on extracted resources, such as oil and coal, that can run out.

technology is not actually renewable, because high-quality deposits of uranium ore could be depleted someday. Still, nuclear power does not release greenhouse gases. Due to concern over possible dangers and the difficulty of storing spent nuclear fuel, no new nuclear power plants have been built in the United States in more than thirty years. Construction of new plants, however, has the support of most Republicans and some Democrats, including President Obama. As a result, we may see new nuclear power plants in the near future.

CAP-AND-TRADE The chief Democratic proposal to respond to possible global warming was known as **cap-and-trade.** The Obama administration hoped to see movement on cap-and-trade legislation as soon as work on health-care legislation was complete. The House of Representatives approved such legislation in June 2009.

Under the bill, the government would establish a cap for CO_2 emissions. Major emitters would need permits, which they could buy and sell—or trade—on the open market. Over time, the cap would decline, resulting in a reduction in emissions. Cap-and-trade died in the Senate, however, and there appears to be no possibility that it could be resurrected during the 2011–2013 Congress.

OFFSHORE DRILLING One possible method of decreasing our reliance on foreign oil is additional exploration and drilling in waters off the American coastline. For twenty years, however, the federal government prohibited offshore drilling in much of the ocean. The concern was that oil spills could have severely damaging consequences for the environment. Indeed, the only coastal areas open to drilling were off the southern coast of Alaska, in the western two-thirds of the Gulf of Mexico, and in a small patch off the coast of Southern California.

In 2008, President George W. Bush opened a small additional area off the coast of Virginia. During the 2008 elections, Republicans demanded that vast areas be made available for drilling. Barack Obama also endorsed additional drilling, but in fewer areas. In March 2010, Obama proposed opening up the Atlantic seaboard from Delaware to northern Florida, portions of the eastern Gulf of Mexico, and waters off the northern coast of Alaska.

THE BP OIL SPILL IN THE GULF OF MEXICO On April 20, 2010, three weeks after Obama's announcement, an offshore drilling platform in the Gulf of Mexico exploded and sank. Eleven workers died, and a torrent of oil and gas began flowing into the Gulf. Before long, tar balls began floating ashore on the Louisiana coast. The drilling platform was leased to BP, formerly known as British Petroleum. BP made multiple attempts to block the undersea leak, all of which failed. A major problem was that the leak was 5,000 feet below the surface. BP also funded a massive cleanup effort by local workers and the federal government.

In May, Obama placed a six-month moratorium on deepwater drilling projects. A federal district court judge ruled the moratorium illegal—so the Department of Interior issued a new one. In June, Obama secured BP's promise to establish a $20 billion fund to pay damage claims. In mid-July, BP was finally able to stop the leak.

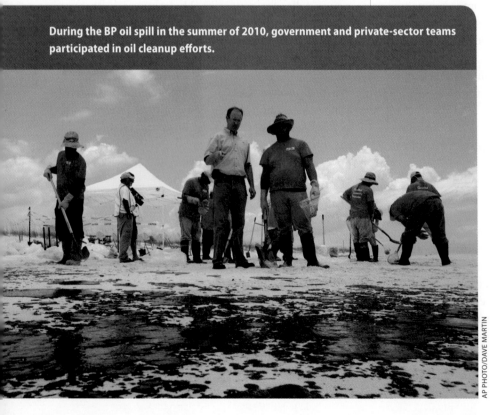

During the BP oil spill in the summer of 2010, government and private-sector teams participated in oil cleanup efforts.

AP PHOTO/DAVE MARTIN

The well was permanently plugged via relief wells in September. By that time, 4.9 million barrels of oil had spilled into the sea—the largest oil spill in American history. In October, the government lifted the moratorium one month before it was due to expire.

During the period before the leak was plugged, the federal government was widely derided for its inability to deal with the problem. This criticism was somewhat unfair, because oil leaks and fires had always been the responsibility of the petroleum industry, and thus the federal government had no particular competence in addressing such disasters. It soon became obvious, however, that the federal agency in charge of overseeing drilling safety was fatally corrupt. It was dissolved and replaced with a new one. By the time of the 2010 elections, the oil spill had receded as a national political issue, although it remained powerful in Louisiana and other Gulf states. The negative impact on the offshore oil drilling industry was more long-lasting.

LO4 *Economic Policy*

Economic policy consists of all actions taken by the government to address the ups and downs in the nation's level of business activity. National economic policy is solely the responsibility of the national government.

Federal Reserve chair Ben Bernanke (left) sits with U.S. Treasury secretary Tim Geithner at a meeting of twenty leading nations (the so-called G-20) in 2009. In the past, the Fed and the U.S. Treasury rarely worked together because the Fed is supposed to be an independent agency.

PHOTO BY GEOFF CADDICK/WPA POOL/GETTY IMAGES

One of the tools used in this process is **monetary policy**, which involves changing the amount of money in circulation so as to affect interest rates, credit markets, the rate of inflation, the rate of economic growth, and the rate of unemployment. You read about monetary policy in the *Our Government Faces a Troubled Economy* feature in Chapter 2 (see page 40). There, we explained that monetary policy is under the control of the Federal Reserve System, an independent regulatory agency.

The national government also controls **fiscal policy**, which involves changes in government expenditures and taxes to alter national economic variables. These variables include the rate of unemployment, the total number of those in the labor market, labor force participation rates, and the rate of economic growth.

In this section, we look briefly at the politics of monetary and fiscal policy, as well as the federal tax system and the issue of deficit spending.

Monetary Policy

The Federal Reserve System (the Fed) was established by Congress as the nation's central banking system in 1913. The Fed is governed by a board of seven governors, including the very powerful chairperson. The president appoints the members of the board of governors, and the Senate must approve the nominations. Members of the board serve for fourteen-year terms. Although the Fed's board of governors acts independently, the Fed has, on occasion, yielded to presidential pressure, and the Fed's chairperson must follow a congressional resolution requiring him or her to report monetary targets over each six-month period. Nevertheless, until recently, the Fed has remained one of the truly independent sources of economic power in the government.

The Fed and its **Federal Open Market Committee (FOMC)** make decisions about monetary policy several times each year. In theory, monetary policy is relatively

economic policy All actions taken by the national government to smooth out the ups and downs in the nation's level of business activity.

monetary policy Actions taken by the Federal Reserve Board to change the amount of money in circulation so as to affect interest rates, credit markets, the rate of inflation, the rate of economic growth, and the rate of unemployment.

fiscal policy The use of changes in government expenditures and taxes to alter national economic variables.

Federal Open Market Committee (FOMC) The most important body within the Federal Reserve System. The FOMC decides how monetary policy should be carried out by the Federal Reserve.

easy-money policy A monetary policy that involves stimulating the economy by expanding the rate of growth of the money supply. An easy-money policy supposedly will lead to lower interest rates and induce consumers to spend more and producers to invest more.

Keynesian economics An economic theory proposed by British economist John Maynard Keynes that is typically associated with the use of fiscal policy to alter national economic variables.

straightforward. In periods of recession and high unemployment, we should pursue an **easy-money policy** to stimulate the economy by expanding the rate of growth of the money supply. An easy-money policy supposedly will lead to lower interest rates and induce consumers to spend more and producers to invest more. In periods of rising inflation, the Fed does the reverse: it reduces the rate of growth in the amount of money in circulation. This policy should cause interest rates to rise, thus inducing consumers to spend less and businesses to invest less. In theory, this sounds quite simple. The reality, however, is not simple at all. To give one example, if times are hard enough, people and businesses may not want to borrow even if interest rates go down to zero, and an easy-money policy will have little effect.

An additional difficulty is the length of time it takes for a change in monetary policy to become effective. There is usually a lag of about fourteen months between the time the economy slows down (or speeds up) and the time the economy begins to feel the effects of a policy change. Therefore, by the time a change in policy becomes effective, a different policy may be needed.

Fiscal Policy

The principle underlying fiscal policy, like the one that underlies monetary policy, is relatively simple: when unemployment is rising and the economy is going into a recession, fiscal policy should stimulate economic activity by increasing government spending, decreasing taxes, or both. When unemployment is decreasing and prices are rising (that is, when we have inflation), fiscal policy should curb economic activity by reducing government spending, increasing taxes, or both. In Chapter 3's *Our Government Faces a Troubled Economy* feature (see page 66), we explained that this view of fiscal policy is an outgrowth of the economic theories of the British economist John Maynard Keynes (1883–1946). Keynes's theories were the result of his study of the Great Depression of the 1930s.

Keynesian economics suggests that the forces of supply and demand operate too slowly in recessions, and therefore the government should undertake actions to stimulate the economy during such periods. Keynesian economists maintain that the Great Depression resulted from a serious imbalance in the economy. The public was saving more than usual, and businesses were investing less than usual. According to Keynesian theory, at the beginning of the Depression, the government should have filled the gap that was created when businesses began limiting their investments. The government could have done so by increasing government spending or cutting taxes.

One of the problems with fiscal policy is that, just as with monetary policy, typically a lag exists between the government's decision to institute fiscal policy and the actual implementation of that policy. It is up to Congress, through its many committees, to enact the legislation necessary to implement fiscal policy.

The Federal Tax System

The government raises money to pay its expenses in two ways: through taxes levied on business and personal income and through borrowing. In 1960, individuals paid 52 percent of total federal tax revenues. By 2009, this proportion was more than 80 percent (adding income taxes and Social Security payments together). The American income tax system is progressive—meaning that as you earn more income, you pay a higher tax rate on the additional income earned. The 2010 tax rates are shown in Table 15–1 on the facing page. The tax rates for 2011 will not be known until Congress decides whether to extend some or all of the tax cuts enacted under President George W. Bush in 2003. The cuts were set to expire at the end of 2010. (See Chapter 11's *Our Government Faces a Troubled Economy* feature on page 244.) About 40 percent of American families earn so little that they

British economist John Maynard Keynes developed theories of how to pull the world out of the Great Depression in the 1930s. His work was cited frequently during the Great Recession that started in December 2007.

WALTER STONEMAN/SAMUEL BOURNE/GETTY IMAGES

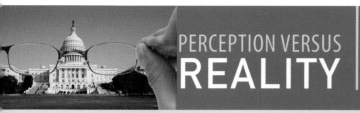
As the saying goes, only two things are certain—death and taxes. In recent years, though, different presidents have instituted a number of tax-rate cuts. The last one occurred in 2003 under the administration of George W. Bush.

The Perception

You often hear or read that the Bush tax-rate cuts favored the rich. After all, it's the rich who received the lion's share of the benefits from these tax-rate cuts.

The Reality

First, we must distinguish between tax rates and taxes paid. It is true that the Bush tax cuts lowered the top marginal tax rate from 39.6 percent to 35 percent and that the long-term capital gains tax rate dropped from 20 percent to 15 percent. Also, the rate applied to dividends fell. Therefore, the tax rates on the highest-income individuals did indeed fall after the tax cuts of 2003 were enacted.

At the same time, though, the percentage of taxes paid by the rich went up, not down. Indeed, the share of individual income tax liabilities paid by the top 1 percent of income earners rose steadily from about 1981 to 2000, dropped off a bit from 2000 to 2003, and has risen ever since. According to the nonpartisan Congressional Budget Office, the top 40 percent of income earners in the United States pay 99.1 percent of all income taxes. The top 10 percent pay more than 70 percent of all income taxes. At the bottom end of the scale, about 40 percent of this nation's households pay no income taxes at all (though they do pay Social Security contributions). Finally, it is true that the rich have been getting richer in the United States. Nevertheless, their share of income has gone up more slowly than their share of individual tax liabilities.

These data give us some indication of what may happen if Congress fails to extend the Bush tax cuts on the upper tax brackets. If these cuts expire, capital gains taxes will rise from 15 percent to 20 percent. The income tax rate for those making more than $250,000 per year will go up from 35 percent to 39.6 percent. What we may see is an ironic reversal in the percentage of taxes (not the tax rate) paid by the rich—it could actually decrease when higher tax rates become reality.

Blog On Scott Adams, creator of the *Dilbert* comic strip, makes hilarious and fresh observations about all sorts of things on his blog. Taxing the rich is just one of his topics—see **dilbertblog.typepad.com/ the_dilbert_blog/2007/07/how-to-tax-the-.html**. The blog of Harvard economics professor Greg Mankiw has an interesting discussion at **gregmankiw.blogspot. com/2006/04/are-rich-paying-enough.html**.

Table 15–1			
Tax Rates for Single Persons and Married Couples (2010)			
Single Persons		**Married Filing Jointly**	
Tax Bracket ($)	**Marginal Tax Rate (%)**	**Tax Bracket ($)**	**Marginal Tax Rate (%)**
0–8,350	10	0–16,700	10
8,350–33,950	15	16,700–67,900	15
33,950–82,250	25	67,900–137,050	25
82,250–171,550	28	137,050–208,850	28
171,550–372,950	33	208,850–372,950	33
372,950 and higher	35	352,950 and higher	35

Source: Internal Revenue Service.

have no income tax liability at all. (For a discussion of the amount of taxes paid by the rich versus other groups in American society, see this chapter's *Perception versus Reality* feature above.)

THE ACTION-REACTION SYNDROME The Internal Revenue Code consists of thousands of pages, thousands of sections, and thousands of subsections. In other words, our tax system is not simple. Part of the reason for this is that tax policy has always been plagued by the **action-reaction syndrome**, a term describing the following phenomenon: *for every government action, there will be a reaction*

action-reaction syndrome For every government action, there will be a reaction by the public. The government then takes a further action to counter the public's reaction—and the cycle begins again.

by the public. Eventually, the government will react with another action, and the public will follow with further reaction. The ongoing action-reaction cycle is clearly operative in policymaking on taxes.

TAX LOOPHOLES   Generally, the action-reaction syndrome means that the higher the tax rate—the action on the part of the government—the greater the public's reaction to that tax rate. Individuals and corporations facing high tax rates will react by making concerted attempts to get Congress to add various loopholes to the tax law that will allow them to reduce their taxable incomes.

Years ago, when Congress imposed very high tax rates on high incomes, it also provided for more loopholes. These loopholes enabled many wealthy individuals to decrease their tax bills significantly. For example, special tax provisions allowed investors in oil and gas wells to reduce their taxable income. Additional loopholes permitted individuals to shift income from one year to the next—which meant that they could postpone the payment of their taxes for one year. Still more loopholes let U.S. citizens form corporations outside the United States in order to avoid some taxes completely.

WILL WE EVER HAVE A TRULY SIMPLE TAX SYSTEM?
The Tax Reform Act of 1986 was intended to lower taxes and simplify the tax code—and it did just that for most taxpayers. A few years later, however, large federal deficits forced Congress to choose between cutting spending and raising taxes, and Congress opted to do the latter. Tax increases occurred under the administrations of both George H. W. Bush (1989–1993) and Bill Clinton. In fact, the tax rate for the highest income bracket rose from 28 percent in 1986 to 39.6 percent in 1993. Thus, the effective highest marginal tax rate increased significantly.

In response to this sharp increase in taxes, those who were affected lobbied Congress to legislate special exceptions and loopholes so that the full impact of the rate increase would not be felt by the wealthiest Americans. As a result, the tax code is more complicated than it was before the 1986 Tax Reform Act.

Some people see the complications of our tax code as a limitation on our economic freedom. For a look at the issue of economic freedom around the world, see this chapter's *The Rest of the World* feature on the facing page.

While in principle everyone is for a simpler tax code, in practice Congress rarely is able to pass tax-reform legislation. Why?

> **public debt**   The total amount of money that the national government owes as a result of borrowing; also called the *national debt.*

The reason is that those who now benefit from our complicated tax code will not give up their tax breaks without a fight. These groups include homeowners who deduct interest on their mortgages (and therefore the home-building industry as well), charities that receive tax-deductible contributions, and businesses that get tax breaks for research and development. Two other groups also benefit greatly from the current complicated tax code: tax accountants and tax lawyers.

The Public Debt

When the government spends more than it receives, it has to finance this shortfall. Typically, it borrows. The U.S. Treasury sells IOUs on behalf of the U.S. government. They are called U.S. Treasury bills, notes, or bonds, depending on how long the funds are borrowed. All are commonly called *treasuries.* The sale of these obligations to corporations, private individuals, pension plans, foreign governments, foreign companies, and foreign individuals is big business. After all, except for a few years in the late 1990s and early 2000s, federal government expenditures have always exceeded federal government revenues.

Every time there is a federal government deficit, there is an increase in the total accumulated **public debt** (also called the *national debt*), which is defined as the total value of all outstanding federal government borrowing. If the existing public debt is $5 trillion and the

Every year, millions of Americans go see their tax preparers to help them figure out the complicated forms that must be submitted to the Internal Revenue Service. The Tax Code consists of about 70,000 pages of less-than-easy-to-understand rules about taxes.

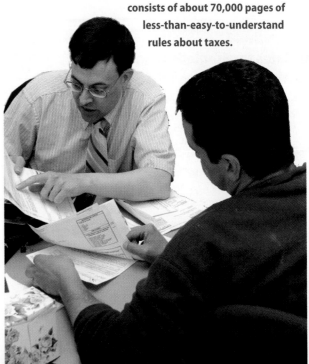

The Relationship between Economic Freedom and Prosperity

For decades, political scientists and economists, as well as sociologists, have examined the key differences between developing countries and developed countries. For decades, the consensus has been that developed countries must transfer more wealth to less developed countries if these poorer nations are to experience economic growth. International institutions such as the World Bank have argued for investments in infrastructure such as roads, sewers, and the like. Some specialists in development argue that impoverished people in developing countries will remain in permanent misery unless the richer countries transfer more wealth to them.

Freedom Enters the Picture

A small but growing band of development specialists see a different path out of misery for the world's poorest countries. They look at the degree of economic freedom and find some powerful correlations. As it turns out, freedom and prosperity are positively related. The freedom we are referring to here is economic freedom, not necessarily political freedom. (Note that in countries where citizens have obtained economic freedom, political freedom often follows after a number of years.)

The 2010 Index of Economic Freedom ranks countries from Hong Kong (number one) to North Korea (last on the list) in terms of how much economic freedom the citizens really have. It turns out that the freest 20 percent of the world's economies have average per-person incomes that are five times greater than those of the least free 20 percent.

Why Economic Freedom Matters

Development specialists who stress the positive relationship between economic freedom and prosperity offer several reasons why such freedom is so important. They believe that the degree of efficiency with which any society uses its scarce resources to produce goods and services is a key element in the speed of economic growth for all citizens. If there is little economic freedom in a society, entrepreneurs face huge barriers to innovation and to starting new businesses.

The result is very little economic growth. This analysis holds true for such economically stagnant countries as Belarus, Myanmar (Burma), Cuba, Iran, North Korea, and Zimbabwe. Despite their oil wealth, Russia and Venezuela appear to be headed in this direction as well.

For Critical Analysis *Why do you think multinational agencies such as the World Bank are in favor of massive foreign aid programs for developing countries?*

Children eat mangoes in a suburb of Harare, Zimbabwe.

---

government runs a deficit of $100 billion, then at the end of the year the public debt is $5.1 trillion. Table 15–2 at right shows what has happened to the *net* public debt over time. (The net public debt doesn't count sums that the government owes to itself.)

THE BURDEN OF THE PUBLIC DEBT We often hear about the burden of the public debt. Some even maintain that the government will eventually go bankrupt. As long as the government can collect taxes to pay interest on its public debt, however, that will never happen. What happens instead is that when treasuries come due, they are simply "rolled over," or refinanced. That is, if a $1 million Treasury bond comes due today and is cashed in, the U.S. Treasury pays it off with the money it gets from selling another $1 million bond.

Table 15–2

The Public Debt

Year	Net Public Debt (Billions of Current Dollars)	Year	Net Public Debt (Billions of Current Dollars)
1945	235.2	2003	3,924.1
1950	219.0	2004	4,307.3
1960	236.8	2005	4,601.2
1970	283.2	2006	4,843.1
1980	811.9	2007	5,049.3
1990	2,411.6	2008	5,808.7
1995	3,604.4	2009	7,551.9
2000	3,405.3	2010	9,022.8*
2001	3,339.3	2011	10,120.1*
2002	3,553.2		

*Estimate.
Sources: 1945–1995, U.S. Office of Management and Budget; 2000–2011, U.S. Treasury.

OUR GOVERNMENT FACES A
TROUBLED ECONOMY

Red Ink Forever?

A response of the federal government to the Great Recession has been to increase spending. Not since the buildup to World War II has the government increased its spending as fast as it did in late 2008 and in 2009. At the same time, the economy was shrinking, so tax revenues were shrinking, too. Between increased spending and lower revenues, the federal budget deficit shot up. The estimated deficit for 2010 was $1.3 trillion. That was almost 9 percent of the entire economy. For 2011, the estimated deficit was about the same. Take all levels of government together: For every five dollars of spending, three were backed up by tax receipts. The other two were borrowed.

Deficit Spending to Fight the Great Recession

As you read in this chapter, many economists accept the theories of John Maynard Keynes. They advocate government spending and tax cuts to fight a recession, paid for by running up the deficit. When Obama took office, his advisers recommended this solution. Obama's February 2009 stimulus bill was the result. Despite the stimulus, the unemployment rate reached 10 percent in 2009—the highest in decades. Keynesian economists argued that the stimulus had been too small. Not surprisingly, most voters concluded that it was not helping at all.

Short-Term versus Long-Term Deficits

Even if you believe that a Keynesian stimulus doesn't work—and there are economists as well as voters who

think that—the deficits are meant to be temporary. Once the recession is over, the government should cut back or even abolish the deficits. No Keynesian economist advises running huge budget deficits until the end of time. But that is what we see in President Obama's budget forecast. Even when the recession is over, the deficit is predicted to remain at $0.7 trillion to $0.8 trillion more or less forever. In a few years, that will run the national debt up past 100 percent of GDP. Peter Orszag, Obama's budget director in 2009 and 2010, admitted that such deficits were "unsustainable." But the Democrats have not shown the courage necessary to address this issue.

A Republican Alternative?

Do the Republicans offer an alternative? They definitely made the deficit a major campaign issue in 2010. Republican policy positions, however, tend to contradict the goal of fixing the long-term deficit. For example, as part of the recent health-care reform legislation, Democrats proposed reducing the rate at which future Medicare spending would rise. Republicans saw the cost curbs as a reason to oppose the program. The Republican platform for the 2010 elections put Medicare, military spending, and Social Security off limits, and it opposed any new taxes. Yet with that much spending "ring-fenced" and with no new revenues, it would have been necessary to shut down the rest of the federal government to balance the budget in 2011 or 2012.

Given the positions of both parties, many citizens wonder: What will happen in the future? How will we pay for these huge deficits? And will the federal government crowd out the rest of the economy?

You Be the Judge What kind of spending cuts, if any, would you be willing to accept to bring down the long-term deficit? What kind of tax increases, if any?

The interest on treasuries is paid by federal taxes. Even though much of the interest is being paid to American citizens, the more the federal government borrows to meet these payments, the greater the percentage of its budget that is committed to making interest payments. This reduces the government's ability to

supply funds for anything else, including transportation, education, housing programs, and the military.

PUBLIC DEBT EXPLOSION IN 2008 AND 2009 Due to the financial meltdown that began in 2008, Congress passed historic legislation that involved hundreds of billions of dollars in additional spending. Ultimately, the net public debt will rise by trillions of dollars. Just how much trouble is this explosion in public debt likely to cause? We consider that issue in this chapter's *Our Government Faces a Troubled Economy* feature on the facing page.

PERCENTAGE OF THE DEBT HELD BY FOREIGNERS

An additional problem with a growing federal debt involves how much non-Americans own. Today, more than 55 percent of the U.S. net public debt is owned by foreign individuals, foreign businesses, and foreign central banks. Some worry that these foreigners might not want to keep all of this U.S. debt. If that were ever to

happen, their efforts to sell U.S. government treasuries might lead to a collapse in the markets for government obligations in this country. The result would be much higher interest rates.

There does not appear to be much evidence, however, that such a disaster will happen anytime soon. During the recent economic crises, frightened investors bought more treasuries in the belief that they were the safest possible investment. As a result, the government has been able to borrow at very low interest rates. For example, the September 2010 rate for four-week bills, the shortest-term obligations, dipped below 0.1 percent. (The rate for five-year notes was 1.25 percent and the rate for thirty-year bonds was 3.875 percent.)

AMERICA AT ODDS   *Domestic Policy*

The Preamble to the U.S. Constitution states that one of the goals of the new government was to "promote the general Welfare." Domestic policy is certainly the main way in which our government seeks to promote the general welfare. But how should this be done? Americans are at odds over many domestic issues. A few of them are listed here:

- Do we send too many people to prison—or do our current incarceration policies protect the public?

- Should unauthorized immigrants be given the opportunity to regularize their position—or would such a measure merely increase the number of illegal immigrants in the future?

- Should universal health-care insurance be a right of all citizens—or does such a program sap individual initiative and lead to an over-mighty government?

- Is global warming a serious problem that must be addressed now—or are the risks overblown and the proposed solutions a danger to our economy?

- Is new offshore drilling essential to our energy independence—or is it an unacceptable threat to the environment?

- Is budgetary stimulus a necessary tool to fight recessions—or does it simply worsen the long-term budget deficit?

Take Action

In 2007, John Kerry and Teresa Heinz Kerry published a book titled *This Moment on Earth: Today's New Environmentalists and Their Vision for the Future.*[3] The book details, in an eminently readable fashion, how numerous individuals and groups have successfully taken action over the years to help protect the health of the environment. If you want to take action to help protect the environment, read through the Kerrys' book. You, like many others, may find the stories of other people's successful actions inspiring. For a list of simple changes you can make in your day-to-day life to preserve energy—from buying energy-efficient appliances to turning off electric lights and electrical appliances when they're not in use—see Appendix B in their book, which is titled "What You Can Do." The appendix also includes a list of environmental groups, with contact information for each group.

Linda Ziedrich, author of *The Joy of Pickling*, is shown in her garden in Scio, Oregon.

POLITICS ON THE
WEB

- The size of the national debt is a hot topic. You can find out more about the size of the national debt and other subjects at **www.treasurydirect.gov**

- The U.S. Census Bureau provides "USA Statistics in Brief" at **www.census.gov/compendia/statab/brief. html**. If you can't find the data you're looking for here, start with the Census Bureau's home page at **www.census.gov**

- If you are interested in reading the *Economic Report of the President,* go to **www.gpoaccess.gov/eop**

- For a conservative view of domestic policy issues, including economic policy, see the Heritage Foundation site at **www.heritage org**

- Economist Paul Krugman is one of the most readable and entertaining advocates of Keynesian economics and other liberal domestic policies. His blog is at **krugman.blogs.nytimes.com**

CourseMate

Access CourseMate to review and expand on this chapter through quizzes, flashcards, learning objectives, interactive timelines, a crossword puzzle, audio summaries, video, critical-thinking activities, simulations, and more.

Foreign Policy

中美战略与经济对话
U.S.-CHINA STRATEGIC AND ECONOMIC DIALOGUE

LEARNING OBJECTIVES

LO1 Discuss how foreign policy is made and identify the key players in this process.

LO2 Summarize the history of American foreign policy through the years.

LO3 Identify the foreign policy challenges presented by terrorism and the consequences of the "Bush doctrine" with respect to Iraq.

LO4 Describe the principal issues dividing the Israelis and the Palestinians and the solutions proposed by the international community.

LO5 Outline some of the actions taken by the United States to curb the threat of nuclear weapons.

LO6 Discuss China's emerging role as a world leader.

CourseMate

AMERICA AT ODDS

Do Russia's Ambitions Mean Trouble?

In August 2008, the Russian army invaded the small neighboring country of Georgia. The invasion was Russia's first use of troops outside of its own borders since the dissolution of the Soviet Union in 1991. Many people around the world drew the obvious conclusion: the "Russian bear" was back—and it posed a threat to world peace.

During the years of the Cold War, which lasted from the late 1940s until the end of the 1980s, the Russian-dominated Soviet Union clearly was a threat to peace. The Soviets had occupied Eastern Europe. By the 1960s, even the Chinese were worried that the Soviets might attack them. In 1985, the Soviets had more personnel in uniform than any other nation. Its nuclear weapons were at least equal to those of the United States. In 1985, the Soviet Union also had a population of 278 million, compared with 238 million in the United States.

The impact of the Soviet breakup on Russian power was almost beyond belief. With the loss of the fourteen other Soviet republics, Russia stood alone. Its population in 1995 was 150 million. Its economy was in a state of collapse. Its army had only 40 percent as many soldiers as the Soviet army had had, and its inventory of main battle tanks had fallen from 51,000 to 19,500.[1] Russia was unable to prevent its former "satellite states" in Eastern Europe from joining NATO, the American-led alliance originally established to defend the West against the Soviets.

Russia today is nowhere near as formidable as the Soviet Union was—but how much of a threat is it, really? Americans who take an interest in foreign affairs are at odds over this issue.

A Stronger Russia Is Bad News

Those who believe that Russia poses a substantial threat to world peace point to its attack on Georgia, threats made against Ukraine, and the cyberwar it recently launched against the tiny nation of Estonia. Furthermore, Russia is regaining the economic power needed to support a large military. Its economy experienced a substantial recovery during the presidency of Vladimir Putin (2000–2008). Naturally, Putin was popular, and his popularity was not damaged by the way he undermined Russia's democratic institutions.

Russia is the world's largest exporter of natural gas and the second-largest oil exporter. It is Europe's biggest supplier of oil and natural gas, currently providing 33 percent of Europe's oil imports and 38 percent of its natural gas. Ominously, Russia has repeatedly used its energy exports for political purposes. It has temporarily cut off gas supplies to Belarus, the Czech Republic, Georgia, Lithuania, and Ukraine.

Russia's Future as a Great Power Looks Grim

Those who are less worried about the return of the Russian bear point out several factors that may undermine its future as a world power. In many countries, oil wealth has led to gross corruption and inefficiency, and this has happened in Russia. The greatest threat to Russia's future, however, is its collapsing population. Russia's population is now down to 140 million, and the United Nations estimates that it will fall to a mere 109 million by 2050. Many developed nations expect to lose people in forthcoming years. No nation, however, is experiencing losses that come close to what is predicted for Russia. If Russia is no longer one of the world's most populous countries, it will not be able to maintain its position as a great power. Russia not only has a low birth rate, but a very high death rate. The life expectancy of a Russian male is only about fifty-eight years. Experts attribute this in part to extremely high rates of alcoholism among men.

WHERE DO YOU STAND?

1. What factors might cause Russia to take a belligerent stand toward neighboring countries?
2. In 2009, President Barack Obama and Secretary of State Hillary Clinton stated that they would "push the reset button" in relations with Russia, in an attempt to move beyond the negative feelings that had developed during the Bush administration. Later, Obama canceled a missile system scheduled to be built in Czechoslovakia and Poland. While the system was designed to protect Europe from Iranian missiles, the Russians were convinced it was directed at them. Are these steps likely to prove beneficial? Why or why not?

EXPLORE THIS ISSUE ONLINE

- You can find a vast amount of information on Russia, much of it written from a relatively sympathetic point of view, at www.russiaprofile.org.
- John Bolton is one of America's best-known foreign policy "hawks." For his criticism of Obama's missile decision, see www.aei.org/article/101060.

Introduction

What we call **foreign policy** is a systematic and general plan that guides a country's attitudes and actions toward the rest of the world. Foreign policy includes all of the economic, military, commercial, and diplomatic positions and actions that a nation takes in its relationships with other countries. Although foreign policy may seem quite removed from the concerns of everyday life, it can and does have a significant impact on the day-to-day lives of Americans.

American foreign policy has been shaped by two principles that are often seen as contradicting each other. One is **moral idealism,** the belief that the most important goal in foreign policy is to do what is right. Moral idealists think that it is possible for nations to relate to each other as part of a rule-based community. Moral idealism appeals to the American belief that our nation is special and should provide an example to the rest of the world.

A contrasting view is **political realism,** the belief that nations are inevitably selfish. Foreign countries, therefore, are by definition dangerous. Foreign policy must be based on protecting our national security, regardless of moral arguments. Although there have been times when one or the other of these two principles has dominated, U.S. foreign policy has usually been a mixture of both.

LO1 Who Makes U.S. Foreign Policy?

The framers of the Constitution envisioned that the president and Congress would cooperate in developing American foreign policy. The Constitution did not spell out exactly how this was to be done, though. As commander in chief, the president has assumed much of the decision-making power in the area of foreign policy. Nonetheless, members of Congress, a number of officials, and a vast national security bureaucracy help to shape the president's decisions and to limit the president's powers.

The President's Role

Article II, Section 2, of the Constitution names the president commander in chief of the armed forces. As commander in chief, the president oversees the military and guides defense policies. Presidents have interpreted

JOHN MOORE/GETTY IMAGES

Village elders speak with a U.S. Marine in the Korengal Valley of Kunar Province in eastern Afghanistan. The United States has had active troops in this country for almost a decade as part of its attempt to prevent the Taliban from regaining control.

this role broadly and have sent American troops, ships, and weapons to trouble spots at home and around the world. The Constitution also authorizes the president to make treaties, which must be approved by two-thirds of the Senate. In addition, the president is empowered to form executive agreements—pacts between the president and the heads of other nations. Executive agreements do not require Senate approval. Furthermore, the president's foreign policy responsibilities take on special significance because the president has ultimate control over the use of nuclear weapons.

As head of state, the president also influences foreign policymaking. As the symbolic head of our government, the president represents the United States to the rest of the world. When a serious foreign policy issue or international question arises, the nation expects the president to make a formal statement on the matter.

The Cabinet

Many members of the president's cabinet concern themselves with international problems and recommend policies to deal with them. As U.S. power in the world has grown and as economic

foreign policy A systematic and general plan that guides a country's attitudes and actions toward the rest of the world. Foreign policy includes all of the economic, military, commercial, and diplomatic positions and actions that a nation takes in its relationships with other countries.

moral idealism In foreign policy, the belief that the most important goal is to do what is right. Moral idealists think that it is possible for nations to cooperate as part of a rule-based community.

political realism In foreign policy, the belief that nations are inevitably selfish, and that we should seek to protect our national security regardless of moral arguments.

factors have become increasingly important, the departments of Commerce, Agriculture, Treasury, and Energy have become more involved in foreign policy decisions. The secretary of state and the secretary of defense, however, are the only cabinet members who concern themselves with foreign policy matters on a full-time basis.

THE DEPARTMENT OF STATE

The Department of State is, in principle, the government agency most directly involved in foreign policy. The department is responsible for diplomatic relations with nearly two hundred independent nations around the globe, as well as with the United Nations and other multilateral organizations, such as the Organization of American States. Most U.S. relations with other countries are maintained through embassies, consulates, and other U.S. offices around the world.

As the head of the State Department, the secretary of state has traditionally played a key role in foreign policymaking, and many presidents have relied heavily on the advice of their secretaries of state. Since the end of World War II, though, the preeminence of the State Department in foreign policy has declined dramatically.

THE DEPARTMENT OF DEFENSE

The Department of Defense is the principal executive department that establishes and carries out defense policy and protects our national security. The secretary of defense advises the president on all aspects of U.S. military and defense policy, supervises all of the military activities of the U.S. government, and works to see that the decisions of the president as commander in chief are carried out. The secretary advises and informs the president on the nation's military forces, weapons, and bases and works closely with the U.S. military, especially the Joint Chiefs of Staff, in gathering and studying defense information.

The Joint Chiefs of Staff include the chief of staff of the Army, the chief of staff of the Air Force, the chief of naval operations, and the commandant of the Marine Corps. The chairperson of the Joint Chiefs of Staff is appointed by the president for a four-year term. The joint chiefs regularly serve as the key military advisers to the president, the secretary of defense, and the National Security Council (described next). They are responsible for handing down the president's orders to the nation's military units, preparing strategic plans,

> ### "TO BE PREPARED FOR WAR
>
> is one of the most effectual means of preserving peace."
>
> ~ GEORGE WASHINGTON ~
> COMMANDER OF THE CONTINENTAL ARMY
> AND FIRST PRESIDENT OF THE
> UNITED STATES
> 1789–1797

and recommending military actions. They also propose military budgets, new weapons systems, and military regulations.

Other Agencies

Several other government agencies are also involved in the foreign relations of the United States. Two key agencies in the area of foreign policy are the National Security Council and the Central Intelligence Agency.

THE NATIONAL SECURITY COUNCIL

The National Security Council (NSC) was established by the National Security Act of 1947. The formal members of the NSC include the president, the vice president, the secretary of state, and the secretary of defense, but meetings are often attended by the chairperson of the Joint Chiefs of Staff, the director of the Central Intelligence Agency, and representatives from other departments. The national security adviser, who is a member of the president's White House staff, is the director of the NSC. The adviser informs the president, coordinates advice and information on foreign policy, and serves as a liaison with other officials.

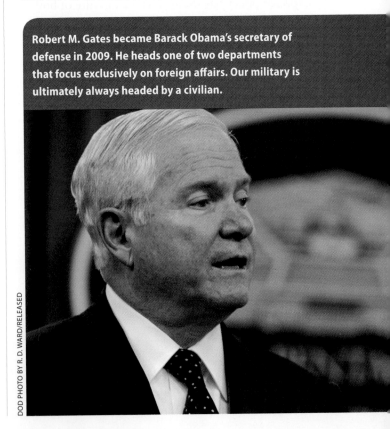

Robert M. Gates became Barack Obama's secretary of defense in 2009. He heads one of two departments that focus exclusively on foreign affairs. Our military is ultimately always headed by a civilian.

DOD PHOTO BY R. D. WARD/RELEASED

The NSC and its members can be as important and powerful as the president wants them to be. Some presidents have made frequent use of the NSC, whereas others have convened it infrequently. Similarly, the importance of the role played by the national security adviser in shaping foreign policy can vary significantly, depending on the administration and the adviser's identity.

THE CENTRAL INTELLIGENCE AGENCY The Central Intelligence Agency (CIA) was created after World War II to coordinate American intelligence activities abroad. The CIA provides the president and his or her advisers with up-to-date information about the political, military, and economic activities of foreign governments. The CIA gathers much of its intelligence from overt sources, such as foreign radio broadcasts and newspapers, people who travel abroad, the Internet, and satellite photographs. Other information is gathered from covert activities, such as the CIA's own secret investigations into the economic or political affairs of other nations. In addition to its intelligence-gathering functions, the CIA engages in covert operations. It may secretly supply weapons to a force rebelling against an unfriendly government or seize suspected terrorists in a clandestine operation and hold them for questioning.

The CIA has tended to operate autonomously, and the nature of its work, methods, and operating funds is kept secret. Intelligence reform passed by Congress in 2004, however, makes the CIA accountable to a national intelligence director. The CIA is required to cooperate more with other U.S. intelligence agencies and has lost a degree of the autonomy it once enjoyed.

Congress's Powers

Although the executive branch takes the lead in foreign policy matters, Congress also has some power over foreign policy. Remember that Congress alone has the power to declare war. It also has the power to appropriate funds to build new weapons systems, equip the U.S. armed forces, and provide for foreign aid. The Senate has the power to approve or reject the implementation of treaties and the appointment of ambassadors.

In 1973, Congress passed the War Powers Resolution, which limits the president's use of troops in military action without congressional approval. Presidents since then, however, have not interpreted the resolution to mean that Congress must be consulted before military action is taken. On several occasions, presidents have ordered military action and then informed Congress after the fact.

A few congressional committees are directly concerned with foreign affairs. The most important are the Armed Services Committee and the Committee on Foreign Affairs in the House, and the Armed Services Committee and the Foreign Relations Committee in the Senate. Other congressional committees deal with matters, such as oil, agriculture, and imports, that indirectly influence foreign policy.

LO2 A Short History of American Foreign Policy

Although many U.S. foreign policy initiatives have been rooted in moral idealism, a primary consideration in U.S. foreign policy has also been national security—the protection of the independence and political integrity of the nation. Over the years, the United States has attempted to preserve its national security in many ways. These ways have changed over time and are not always internally consistent. This is because foreign policymaking, like domestic policymaking, reflects the influence of various political groups in the United States. These groups—including the voting public, interest groups, Congress, and the president and relevant agencies of the executive branch—are often at odds over what the U.S. position should be on particular foreign policy issues.

Isolationism

The nation's founders and the early presidents believed that avoiding political involvement with other nations—**isolationism**—was the best way to protect American interests. The colonies were certainly not yet strong enough to directly influence European developments. As president of the new nation, George Washington did little in terms of foreign policy. Indeed, in his Farewell Address in 1797, he urged Americans to "steer clear of permanent alliances with any portion of the foreign world." During the 1700s and 1800s, the United States generally attempted to avoid conflicts and political engagements elsewhere.

In 1823, President James Monroe proclaimed what became known as the **Monroe Doctrine.** In his message to Congress in December 1823, Monroe stated

isolationism A political policy of noninvolvement in world affairs.

Monroe Doctrine A U.S. policy, announced in 1823 by President James Monroe, that the United States would not tolerate foreign intervention in the Western Hemisphere, and in return, the United States would stay out of European affairs.

President James Monroe (1817–1825) said that the United States would not accept foreign intervention in the Western Hemisphere.

position as a world power. For example, in the early 1900s, President Theodore Roosevelt proposed that the United States could invade Latin American countries when it was necessary to guarantee political or economic stability.

The World Wars

When World War I broke out in 1914, President Woodrow Wilson initially proclaimed a policy of **neutrality**—the United States would not take sides in the conflict. The United States did not enter the war until 1917, after U.S. ships in international waters were attacked by German submarines that were blockading Britain. Wilson called the war a way to "make the world safe for democracy." In his eyes, Germany was not merely dangerous but evil. Wilson, in short, was our most famous presidential advocate of moral idealism. After World War I ended in 1918, the United States returned to a policy of isolationism. We refused to join the League of Nations, an international body intended to resolve peacefully any future conflicts between nations.

The U.S. policy of isolationism lasted only until the Japanese attacked Pearl Harbor in 1941. The United States joined the Allies—Australia, Britain, Canada, China, France, and the Soviet Union—that fought the Axis nations of Germany, Italy, and Japan. One of the most significant foreign policy actions during World War II was the dropping of atomic bombs on the Japanese cities of Hiroshima and Nagasaki in August 1945.

The Cold War

After World War II ended in 1945, the wartime alliance between the United States and the Soviet Union began to deteriorate quickly. The Soviet Union opposed America's political and economic systems. Many Americans considered Soviet attempts to spread Communist systems to other countries a major threat to democracy. After the war ended, countries in Eastern Europe—Bulgaria, Czechoslovakia, East Germany, Hungary, Poland, and Romania—fell under Soviet domination, forming what became known as the **Soviet bloc.**

THE IRON CURTAIN Britain's wartime minister, Winston Churchill, established the tone for a new relationship between the Soviet Union and the Western allies in a famous speech in 1946:

> An iron curtain has descended across the Continent. Behind that line all are subject in one form or another, not only to Soviet influence but to a very high . . . measure of control from Moscow.

that the United States would not tolerate foreign intervention in the Western Hemisphere. In return, promised Monroe, the United States would stay out of European affairs. The Monroe Doctrine buttressed the policy of isolationism toward Europe.

The Beginning of Interventionism

Isolationism gradually gave way to **interventionism** (direct involvement in foreign affairs). The first true step toward interventionism occurred with the Spanish-American War of 1898. The United States fought this war to free Cuba from Spanish rule. Spain lost and subsequently ceded control of several of its possessions, including Guam, Puerto Rico, and the Philippines, to the United States. The United States acquired a **colonial empire** and was acknowledged as a world power.

The growth of the United States as an industrial economy also confirmed the nation's

interventionism Direct involvement by one country in another country's affairs.

colonial empire A group of dependent nations that are under the rule of a single imperial power.

neutrality A position of not being aligned with either side in a dispute or conflict, such as a war.

Soviet bloc The group of Eastern European nations that fell under the control of the Soviet Union following World War II.

Left Photo: The United States entered World War II after the surprise Japanese attack on Pearl Harbor, Hawaii, on December 7, 1941. Right Photo: World War II came to an end shortly after the United States dropped atomic bombs on Hiroshima and Nagasaki, Japan, in 1945.

The reference to an **iron curtain** described the political boundaries between the democratic countries in Western Europe and the Soviet-controlled Communist countries in Eastern Europe.

THE MARSHALL PLAN AND THE POLICY OF CONTAINMENT In 1947, when it appeared that local Communists, backed by the Soviets, would take over Greece and Turkey, President Harry Truman took action. He convinced Congress to appropriate $400 million ($3.9 billion in 2011 dollars) in aid for those countries to prevent the spread of communism. The president also proclaimed what became known as the *Truman Doctrine*. It would be "the policy of the United States to support free peoples who are resisting attempted subjugation by armed minorities or by outside pressures."[2]

The Truman administration also instituted a policy of economic assistance to war-torn Europe, called the **Marshall Plan** after George Marshall, who was then the U.S. secretary of state. During the next five years, Congress appropriated $17 billion (about $160 billion in 2011 dollars) for aid to sixteen European countries. By 1952, the nations of Western Europe, with U.S. help, had recovered and were again prospering.

These actions marked the beginning of a policy of **containment**—a policy designed to contain the spread of communism by offering threatened nations U.S. military and economic aid.[3] To make the policy of containment effective, the United States initiated a program of collective security involving the formation of mutual defense alliances with other nations. In 1949, through the North Atlantic Treaty, the United States, Canada, and ten European nations formed a military alliance—the North Atlantic Treaty Organization (NATO)—and declared that an attack on any member of the alliance would be considered an attack against all members.

Thus, by 1949, almost all illusions of friendship between the Soviet Union and the Western allies had disappeared. The United States became the leader of a bloc of democratic nations in Western Europe, the Pacific, and elsewhere. The tensions between the Soviet Union and the United States became known as the **Cold War**—a war of words, warnings, and ideologies that lasted from the late 1940s through the early 1990s. The term *iron curtain*, from Churchill's speech in 1946, became even more appropriate

iron curtain A phrase coined by Winston Churchill to describe the political boundaries between the democratic countries in Western Europe and the Soviet-controlled Communist countries in Eastern Europe.

Marshall Plan A plan providing for U.S. economic assistance to European nations following World War II to help those nations recover from the war; the plan was named after George C. Marshall, secretary of state from 1947 to 1949.

containment A U.S. policy designed to contain the spread of communism by offering military and economic aid to threatened nations.

Cold War The war of words, warnings, and ideologies between the Soviet Union and the United States that lasted from the late 1940s through the early 1990s.

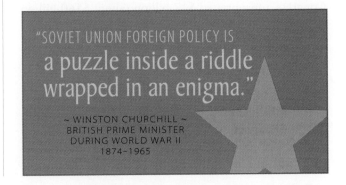

deterrence A policy of building up military strength for the purpose of discouraging (deterring) military attacks by other nations; the policy of "building weapons for peace" that supported the arms race between the United States and the Soviet Union during the Cold War.

mutually assured destruction (MAD) A phrase referring to the assumption, on which the policy of deterrence was based, that if the forces of two nations are equally capable of destroying each other, neither nation will take a chance on war.

Cuban missile crisis A nuclear standoff that occurred in 1962 when the United States learned that the Soviet Union had placed nuclear warheads in Cuba, ninety miles off the U.S. coast. The crisis was defused diplomatically, but it is generally considered the closest the two Cold War superpowers came to a nuclear confrontation.

détente French word meaning a "relaxation of tensions." Détente characterized the relationship between the United States and the Soviet Union in the 1970s, as the two Cold War rivals attempted to pursue cooperative dealings and arms control.

Prime Minister Winston Churchill led the United Kingdom during World War II.

LIBRARY OF CONGRESS

in 1961, when Soviet-dominated East Germany constructed the Berlin Wall, which separated East Berlin from West Berlin.

Although the Cold War was mainly a war of words and belief systems, the wars in Korea (1950–1953) and Vietnam (1964–1975) grew out of the efforts to contain communism.

THE ARMS RACE AND DETERRENCE The tensions induced by the Cold War led both the Soviet Union and the United States to try to surpass each other militarily. They began competing for more and better weapons, particularly nuclear weapons, with greater destructive power. This phenomenon, known as the *arms race,* was supported by a policy of **deterrence**—of rendering ourselves and our allies so strong militarily that our very strength would deter (stop or discourage) any attack on us. Out of deterrence came the theory of **mutually assured destruction (MAD),** which held that if the forces of both nations were equally capable of destroying each other, neither nation would take a chance on war.

THE CUBAN MISSILE CRISIS In 1962, the United States and the Soviet Union came close to a nuclear confrontation in what became known as the **Cuban missile crisis.** The United States learned that the Soviet Union

had placed nuclear weapons on the island of Cuba, ninety miles from the coast of Florida. The crisis was defused diplomatically: a U.S. naval blockade of Cuba convinced the Soviet Union to agree to remove the missiles. The United States also agreed to remove some of its missiles near the Soviet border in Turkey. Both sides recognized that a nuclear war between the two superpowers was unthinkable.

DÉTENTE AND ARMS CONTROL In 1969, the United States and the Soviet Union began negotiations on a treaty to limit the number of anti-ballistic missiles (ABMs) and offensive missiles that each country could develop and deploy. In 1972, both sides signed the Strategic Arms Limitation Treaty (SALT I). This event marked the beginning of a period of **détente,** a French word that means a "relaxation of tensions."

In 1983, President Ronald Reagan (1981–1989) nearly reignited the arms race by proposing a missile defense system known as the strategic defense initiative (SDI, or "Star Wars"). Nonetheless, Reagan and Soviet leader Mikhail Gorbachev pursued arms control agreements, as did Reagan's successor, President George H. W. Bush (1989–1993).

THE DISSOLUTION OF THE SOVIET UNION In the late 1980s, the political situation inside the Soviet Union began to change rapidly. Mikhail Gorbachev had initiated an effort to democratize the Soviet political system and decentralize the economy. The reforms quickly spread to other countries in the Soviet bloc. In 1989, the Berlin Wall, constructed nearly thirty years earlier, was torn down, and East Germany and West Germany were reunited.

In August 1991, a number of disgruntled Communist Party leaders who wanted to reverse the reforms briefly seized control of the Soviet central government. Russian

> "SOVIET UNION FOREIGN POLICY IS
> **a puzzle inside a riddle wrapped in an enigma."**
>
> ~ WINSTON CHURCHILL ~
> BRITISH PRIME MINISTER
> DURING WORLD WAR II
> 1874–1965

citizens rose up in revolt and defied those leaders. The democratically elected president of the Russian republic (the largest republic in the Soviet Union), Boris Yeltsin, confronted troops in Moscow that were under the control of the conspirators. The attempted coup collapsed after three days. The Communist Party in the Soviet Union lost virtually all of its power.

The fifteen republics constituting the Soviet Union—including the Russian republic—declared their independence, and by the end of the year, the Union of Soviet Socialist Republics (USSR) no longer existed.

Post–Cold War Foreign Policy

The demise of the Soviet Union altered the framework and goals of U.S. foreign policy. During the Cold War, the moral underpinnings of American foreign policy were clear to all—the United States was the defender of the "free world" against the Soviet aggressor. When the Cold War ended, U.S. foreign policymakers were forced, for the first time in decades, to rethink the nation's foreign policy goals and adapt them to a world arena in which, at least for a time, the United States was the only superpower. Some have argued that the European Union, an economic and political organization of twenty-seven European states, could in time rival the United States. Others are skeptical, as you'll see in the *Perception versus Reality* feature on the following page.

U.S. foreign policymakers have struggled since the end of the Cold War to determine the degree of intervention that is appropriate and prudent for the U.S. military. Should we intervene in a humanitarian crisis, such as a famine? Should the U.S. military participate in peacekeeping missions, such as those instituted after civil or ethnic strife in other countries? Americans have faced these questions in Bosnia, Kosovo, Rwanda, Somalia, and Sudan. Yet no overriding framework emerged in U.S. foreign policy until September 11, 2001. Since that date, our goal has been to capture and punish the terrorists who planned and perpetrated the events of that day and to prevent future terrorist attacks against Americans—even if that means "regime change," which was one of the goals of the second Gulf War against Iraq in 2003.

LO3 *The War on Terrorism*

One of the most difficult challenges faced by governments around the world is how to control terrorism. Terrorism is defined as the use of staged violence, often against civilians, to achieve political goals. International terrorism has occurred in virtually every region of the world. The most devastating terrorist attack in U.S. history occurred on September 11, 2001, when radical Islamist terrorists used hijacked airliners as missiles to bring down the World Trade Center towers in New York City and to destroy part of the Pentagon building in Washington, D.C. A fourth airplane crashed in a Pennsylvania field after passengers fought back against the hijackers. In all, almost three thousand innocent civilians were killed as a result of these terrorist acts.

Terrorist attacks have occurred with increasing frequency during the past three decades. Other examples of terrorist acts include the Palestinian attacks on Israeli Olympic athletes in Munich in 1972; the Libyan suitcase bombing of an American airliner over Lockerbie, Scotland, in 1988; the bombing of two U.S. embassies in Africa in 1998; the bombing of the navy ship USS *Cole* in a Yemeni port in 2000; and coordinated bomb attacks on London's transportation system in 2005.

Somalia has been the battleground for fighting between rival Islamist factions. The United States has supported a United Nations–backed government, but that regime remains almost powerless. The Islamic Party combatants shown here rest after a fully armed conflict exercise.

AP PHOTO/FARAH ABDI WARSAMEH

PERCEPTION VERSUS REALITY | *A United Europe?*

Decades ago, European leaders had a dream of forging a common European union of nations so that world war would never occur again. To that end, they created the Common Market and later the European Union (EU), which now consists of twenty-seven nations, a third of which are former Communist countries.

The Perception

If you read the newspapers and listen to the TV talk shows in America, you get the impression that the EU represents a bloc of more than 500 million people that acts as a counterweight to America's 310 million citizens. The EU is portrayed as an economic and foreign policy powerhouse today.

The Reality

While the twenty-seven members of the EU have given up some of their sovereignty, particularly over manufacturing standards, food safety, and the like, they are still twenty-seven sovereign nations. This is most evident in the efforts of EU members to protect their own citizens' economic livelihood.

The latest so-called minitreaty among the EU nations, conceived in 2007, is a case in point. France succeeded in removing from the treaty's preamble a statement to the effect that the EU was all about free competition in all countries. Instead, the French substituted the concept that each country must protect its "national champions" and preserve the jobs of its citizens.

In the United States, in contrast, no matter what the individual states would like to do, they cannot raise protectionist walls to prevent job losses due to competition from other states. The U.S. Constitution forbids that.

Europe's disunity, relative to the United States and other full-fledged nations, was clearly revealed by the Great Recession. Of the twenty-seven members of the EU, sixteen use a common currency, the euro. (That eleven countries do not use the euro immediately shows the limits to European unity.)

When the recession struck, it became obvious that in Greece, Ireland, Portugal, and Spain, businesses and individuals had borrowed far too many euros and would now have trouble paying them back. The problem was especially bad in Greece, where the government, as well as the private sector, had borrowed irresponsibly. In 2010, investors became afraid of making additional loans to the Greek government, and the possibility arose that Greece might default on its debts.

"Eurozone" countries with stronger economies, such as France and Germany, were extremely reluctant to help out the Greeks. Germans clearly did not see the Greeks as fellow Europeans, but rather as foreigners. Greece's problems, however, threatened to spread to other troubled economies. In the end, the EU was forced to come up with a huge bailout package to defend Greece and other troubled nations. Compare the situation in the United States, where no state-government crisis could possibly threaten the dollar.

◖ Blog On *The Economist,* published in London, is one of the most highly regarded news magazines in the world. You can find its blogs on Europe at **www.economist.com/blogs**. Politics in Europe generally is tilted further left than in the United States. Find out what left-of-center Europeans are thinking at **www.social-europe.eu**.

Varieties of Terrorism

Terrorists are willing to destroy others' lives and property, and often sacrifice their own lives, for a variety of reasons. Terrorist acts generally fall into one of the three broad categories discussed next.

LOCAL OR REGIONAL TERRORISM Some terrorist acts have been committed by extremists who are motivated by the desire to obtain freedom from a nation or government that they regard as an oppressor. Terrorists have sometimes acted to disrupt peace talks. In Israel, for example, numerous suicide bombings by Palestinians against Israeli civilians have helped to stall efforts to forge a lasting peace between Israel and the Palestinians. The Irish Republican Army, which sought to unite British-governed Northern Ireland with the independent Republic of Ireland, conducted bombings and other terrorist acts in Northern Ireland and England over a period of many years. The attacks came to an end in 1997 as part of a peace process that lasted from 1995 until 2005. Basque separatists in Spain have engaged in terrorism for decades. The separatists were initially—and incorrectly—blamed for bombing a commuter train in Madrid, Spain, on March 11, 2004. That

A hijacked airliner approaches New York's World Trade Center moments before striking the second tower, as seen from downtown Brooklyn on September 11, 2001. The 110-story towers collapsed in a shower of rubble and dust after two hijacked airliners slammed into them. Nearly three thousand people were killed on that day.

the terrorists were and for whom they were working. Then it must decide what type of retribution is warranted.

FOREIGN TERRORIST NETWORKS

A relatively new phenomenon in the late 1990s and early 2000s was the emergence of nonstate terrorist networks, such as al Qaeda. Al Qaeda is the nongovernmental terrorist organization that planned and carried out the terrorist attacks of September 11, 2001. Its leader is the Saudi dissident Osama bin Laden. Throughout the 1990s, al Qaeda conducted training camps in the mountains of Afghanistan, which was ruled by an ultraconservative Islamic faction known as the Taliban. After their training, al Qaeda operatives dispersed into small units across the globe, connected by e-mail and the Internet.

Before September 11, the U.S. government had monitored the activities and movements of al Qaeda operatives and had connected the terrorist attacks on two U.S. embassies in Africa and the bombing of the USS *Cole* to al Qaeda. In 1998, President Bill Clinton (1993–2001) ordered the bombing of terrorist camps in Afghanistan in retaliation for the embassy bombings, but with little effect. Al Qaeda cells continued to operate largely unimpeded until the terrorist attacks of September 11.

terrorist attack, actually perpetrated by Islamic radicals, killed 191 people and injured hundreds of others.

The United States has also been the victim of homegrown terrorists. The bombing of the Oklahoma City federal building in 1995 was the act of vengeful extremists in the United States who claimed to fear an oppressive federal government. Although Timothy McVeigh and Terry Nichols, who were convicted of the crime, were not directly connected to a particular political group, they expressed views characteristic of the extreme right-wing militia movement in the United States.

STATE-SPONSORED TERRORISM Some terrorist attacks have been planned and sponsored by governments. For example, the bombing of Pan Am Flight 103, which exploded over Lockerbie, Scotland, in 1988, killing all 259 people on board and 11 on the ground, was later proved to be the work of an intelligence officer working for Libya. The United Nations imposed economic sanctions against Libya in an effort to force Libyan dictator Muammar Qaddafi to extradite those who were suspected of being responsible for the bombing. More than a decade after the bombing, Libya agreed to hand the men over for trial.

The case of Pan Am Flight 103 illustrates the difficulty in punishing the perpetrators of state-sponsored terrorism. The victim country must first prove who

In 2004, terrorists detonated explosives in two packed commuter trains in Madrid, Spain. One hundred and ninety-one people were killed, and hundreds of others were injured.

Glossary

coalition An alliance of nations formed to undertake a foreign policy action, particularly a military action. A coalition is often a temporary alliance that dissolves after the action is concluded.

weapons of mass destruction Chemical, biological, or nuclear weapons that can inflict massive casualties.

preemptive war A war launched by a nation to prevent an imminent attack by another nation.

preventive war A war launched by a nation to prevent the possibility that another nation might attack at some point in the future; not supported by international law.

neoconservatism A philosophy of foreign policy based on moral idealism. Neoconservatives support the use of economic and military power to bring democracy and human rights to other countries.

> # "FIGHTING TERRORISM IS LIKE BEING A GOALKEEPER.
> You can make a hundred brilliant saves but the only shot that people remember is the one that gets past you."
>
> ~ PAUL WILKINSON ~
> BRITISH TERRORISM EXPERT
> B. 1937

The U.S. Response to 9/11—The War in Afghanistan

Immediately after the 9/11 terrorist attacks, Congress passed a joint resolution authorizing President George W. Bush to use "all necessary and appropriate force" against nations, organizations, or individuals that the president determined had "planned, authorized, committed, or aided the terrorist attacks." In late 2001, supported by a **coalition** of allies, the U.S. military attacked al Qaeda camps in Afghanistan and the ruling Taliban regime that harbored those terrorists. Once the Taliban had been ousted, the United States helped to establish a government in Afghanistan that did not support terrorism. Instead of continuing the hunt for al Qaeda members in Afghanistan, however, the Bush administration increasingly looked to Iraq as a threat to U.S. security.

The Focus on Iraq

In January 2002, President Bush described Iraq as a regime that sponsored terrorism and that sought to develop **weapons of mass destruction.** In October, Congress authorized Bush to use armed force against Iraq on the grounds that Iraq was seeking to develop weapons of mass destruction and was supporting al Qaeda. (Both of these allegations later proved to be untrue.)

In September, President Bush enunciated a doctrine under which the United States was prepared to strike "preemptively" at Iraq. A **preemptive war** occurs when a nation goes to war against another nation because it believes that an attack from that nation is imminent. When President Bush did go to war against Iraq, though, it was not a preemptive war but a **preventive war**—a war to prevent the possibility that Iraq could attack the United States in the future. International law offers no support for this type of war.

Bush's Iraq policies were bolstered by the philosophy of **neoconservatism** held by many of his advisers. The neoconservatives were moral idealists who supported the use of economic and military power to bring democracy and human rights to other countries. They argued that by occupying Iraq and turning it into a democracy, we could create a positive example for the rest of the Middle East.

BACKGROUND TO INVASION—THE FIRST GULF WAR Back in 1990, Iraqi dictator Saddam Hussein had invaded neighboring Kuwait. Hussein's invasion was a spectacular violation of international law. The United Nations threatened Hussein with sanctions if he did not withdraw his troops. When he failed to do so, U.S.-led coalition forces attacked. Iraqi troops soon withdrew from Kuwait, and the first Gulf War ended. The coalition stopped short of sending troops to Baghdad to unseat Hussein.

The cease-fire that ended the conflict required Iraq to submit to inspections for chemical, biological, and nuclear weapons. In 1998, however, Hussein ceased to cooperate with the inspections. During 2002, the Bush administration sought a resolution from the United Nations on the use of military force in Iraq, but China, France, and Russia blocked the resolution. In March 2003, President Bush gave Saddam Hussein an ultimatum: leave Iraq or face war. Hussein was defiant.

THE SECOND GULF WAR BEGINS On March 20, 2003, U.S. and British forces entered Iraq. President Bush secured the support of several other nations, but most of the world opposed the attack. U.S. forces advanced rapidly, and Iraqi military units crumbled. With the fall of the regime, massive looting and disorder broke out across the country, and coalition troops were unable to restore order immediately. Saddam Hussein was not captured until December 2003. He was convicted of crimes against humanity and executed in 2006.

THE INSURGENCY   It soon became clear that many Iraqis opposed the occupation. Opposition was strongest among members of the Sunni branch of Islam, who had been Hussein's staunchest supporters. Iraqi rebels used terrorist tactics to kill occupation forces and Iraqis cooperating with the Americans. Between May 2003 and March 2004, casualty rates for American soldiers averaged more than fifty per month.

In 2005, Iraqi voters chose a new government in the first free elections for half a century. The winning parties represented Shiite Muslims, a sect that formed a majority of Iraq's population, and the Kurds, a minority ethnic group. The Shiites and Kurds had been severely repressed under Saddam Hussein.

The Sunni insurgent groups included al Qaeda in Iraq, which was organized after the U.S. invasion. Al Qaeda attacked not only U.S. and Iraqi government forces but also Shiite civilians, whom it considered apostates (religious traitors). Shiite radicals responded with attacks on Sunnis, and Iraq appeared to be drifting toward interethnic civil war. In reaction to seemingly endless violence, American voters began to turn against the war, and in the 2006 elections they handed Congress over to the Democrats.

Instead of withdrawing U.S. troops in response, however, the Bush administration increased troop levels in 2007 in a program known as the "surge." Under General David Petraeus, American forces for the first time began to employ time-tested counterinsurgency tactics based on protecting the security of ordinary civilians. The tactics were surprisingly successful.

Large numbers of Sunnis, who also had been terrorized by al Qaeda, turned against the insurgency and allied with the Americans.

WITHDRAWAL   With the insurgency fatally undermined, Iraq was finally on the path to long-term stability. In 2008, Iraqi prime minister Nouri al-Maliki and President Bush set a withdrawal target for the end of 2011. In February 2009, President Barack Obama announced that U.S. combat forces would leave Iraq by the end of August 2010, and the rest of the troops would be out by the end of 2011. In fact, combat forces departed in mid-August 2010, slightly ahead of schedule.

Again, Afghanistan

The war in Iraq tended to draw the Bush administration's attention away from Afghanistan, which was never completely at peace even after the Taliban were ousted from Kabul, the capital. In 2003, NATO took responsibility for coalition military operations in the relatively peaceful central and northern parts of Afghanistan. The hope was that with NATO in charge, European nations would be more willing to supply troops to assist the overstretched Americans. In 2004, Hamid Karzai became the first democratically elected president of Afghanistan, and in 2005, Afghans elected a parliament. By 2006, however, the Taliban had regrouped and were waging a war of insurgency against the new government. The United States remained responsible for the southern areas of the country, in which most of the fighting took place, although in 2006, NATO began to move some forces into the south.

A problem for the coalition forces was that the Taliban were able to take shelter on the far side of the Afghan-Pakistani border, in Pakistan's Federally Administered Tribal Areas. These districts are largely free from central government control. For several years, the United States complained that the government of Pakistan was not doing enough to keep the Taliban out of the Tribal Areas. In 2009, Taliban forces began to take complete control of districts in the Tribal Areas and in adjacent districts of the Northwest Frontier Province. Facing a direct challenge to Pakistan's sovereignty, the Pakistani military began to engage the Taliban forces in what soon became a major struggle.

These Iraqi soldiers march during Army Day celebrations in Baghdad. The Multi-National Force (mainly U.S. troops) handed over control of all parts of the country in late 2010.

AP PHOTO/KARIM KADIM

Palestine Liberation Organization (PLO) An organization formed in 1964 to represent the Palestinian people. The PLO has a long history of terrorism but for some years has functioned primarily as a political party.

Barack Obama had opposed the war in Iraq when it was first launched, but he had always supported the U.S. entry into Afghanistan. In February 2009, Obama ordered 17,000 additional troops into the country. In October, the Obama administration launched a major review of its Afghanistan policy. The resulting discussions were intense. It was not known publicly just how heated they became until 2010, when reporter Bob Woodward published an account of the debate.[4] In the end, President Obama ordered an additional 30,000 troops to Afghanistan but pledged to start withdrawing U.S. forces by July 2011. In June 2010, Obama relieved General Stanley McChrystal from command in Afghanistan for insubordination and replaced him with General Petraeus.

President Obama looks on as Israeli prime minister Benjamin Netanyahu shakes hands with Mahmoud Abbas, president of the Palestinian Authority in 2009. The United States has been heavily involved in helping Israel and the Palestinians reach a solution to their ongoing conflict. Why would the United States choose to become involved in other countries' political problems?

LO4 *The Israeli–Palestinian Conflict*

The long-running conflict between Israel and its Arab neighbors has poisoned the atmosphere in the Middle East for more than half a century. Some experts have argued that resolving this conflict is key to solving additional problems, such as terrorism. Others doubt that a resolution would really have that effect. Regardless, the conflict has caused enough bloodshed and heartbreak over the years to deserve attention on its own merits. American presidents dating back at least to Richard Nixon (1969–1974) have attempted to persuade the parties to reach a settlement. Barack Obama is only the latest American leader to address the problem.

The Arab-Israeli Wars

For many years after Israel was founded in 1948, the neighboring Arab states did not accept its legitimacy as a nation. The result was a series of wars between Israel and neighboring states, including Egypt, Jordan,

and Syria, waged in 1948, 1956, 1967, and 1973. Following the 1948 Arab-Israeli War, a large number of Palestinians—Arab residents of the Holy Land, known as Palestine until 1948—were forced into exile, adding to Arab grievances. The failure of the Arab states in the 1967 war led to additional Palestinian refugees and the rise of the **Palestine Liberation Organization (PLO)**, a nonstate body committed to armed struggle against Israel. In the late 1960s and early 1970s, Palestinian groups launched a wave of terrorist attacks against Israeli targets around the world.

In the 1973 Yom Kippur War, Egyptian armies acquitted themselves well, although Israel successfully repelled the attack. Egyptian president Anwar el Sadat was able to employ the resulting popular support to launch a major peace initiative. He traveled to Israel in 1977 and addressed the Israeli parliament, a major turning point. U.S. president Jimmy Carter (1977–1981) then sponsored intensive negotiations. Egypt and Israel signed a peace treaty in 1979 that marked the end to an era of major wars between Israel and other states. Lower-level conflicts continued, however. On several occasions, Israel launched attacks against nonstate militias in Lebanon in response to incursions across the Israeli-Lebanon border. Israel and Jordan eventually signed a peace treaty in

1994, but no peace treaty between Israel and Syria has yet been negotiated, and the conflict between Israel and the Palestinians has remained.

The Israeli-Palestinian Dispute

Resolving the Israeli-Palestinian dispute has always presented more difficulties than obtaining peace between Israel and neighbors such as Egypt. One problem is that the hostilities between the two parties run deeper. On the Palestinian side, not only had many families lost their homes after the 1948 war, but after the 1967 war, the West Bank of the Jordan River and the Gaza Strip fell under Israeli control. The Palestinians living in these areas became an occupied people.

On the Israeli side, the sheer viciousness of the Palestinian terrorist attacks—which frequently resulted in the deaths of civilians, including children—made negotiations with those responsible hard to imagine. A further complication was the series of Israeli settlements on the West Bank and the Gaza Strip, which the Palestinians considered their own. Settlers living on the West Bank had an obvious interest in opposing any peace deal that required them to move.

Despite the difficulties, the international community, including the United States, was in agreement on several principles for settling the conflict. Lands seized by Israel in the 1967 war should be granted to the Palestinians, who could organize their own independent nation-state there. In turn, the Palestinians would have to not only recognize Israel's right to exist, but also take concrete steps to guarantee Israel's security. The international consensus did not address some important issues. These included what compensation, if any, should go to Palestinians who had lost homes in what was now Israel. A second issue is whether Israel could adjust its pre-1967 borders to incorporate some of the Israeli settlement areas, plus part or all of eastern Jerusalem, which had been under Arab control before 1967.

Oslo Accords The first agreement signed between Israel and the PLO; led to the establishment of the Palestinian Authority in the occupied territories.

Negotiations

A long-running uprising in the occupied territories, known as the *Intifada*, broke out in 1987 and helped ensure that the world would not forget the Palestinians. Under the leadership of U.S. president George H. W. Bush, plus Russia and Spain, talks between Israel, Arab nations, and non-PLO Palestinians commenced in Madrid in 1991. In 1993, Israel and the PLO met officially for the first time in Oslo, Norway. The resulting **Oslo Accords** were signed in Washington under the eye of President Bill Clinton. A major result was the establishment of a Palestinian Authority, under Israeli control, on the West Bank and the Gaza Strip.

NEGOTIATIONS COLLAPSE Further attempts to reach a settlement in 2000 at Camp David in Maryland collapsed in acrimony. After the failure of these talks, a second Intifada led to Israeli military incursions into the West Bank and the almost complete collapse of the Palestinian Authority's control over its people. Israeli prime minister Ariel Sharon, concluding that he had no credible peace partner, carried out a plan to unilaterally withdraw from the Gaza Strip in 2005 and also to build an enormous security fence between Israel and the West Bank. The fence came under strong international criticism because it incorporated parts of the West Bank into Israel.

In 2007, Gaza was taken over by Hamas, a radical Islamist party that refuses to recognize Israel. After the imposition of an Israeli blockade, Hamas launched missile attacks on Israel, which in turn briefly occupied the strip in December 2008. The West Bank remained under the control of the PLO-led Palestinian Authority, and so the Palestinians, now politically divided, were in an even worse bargaining position than before. Nevertheless, President Obama sought in 2009 to restart peace talks and appointed a special representative for the region.

TOWARD NEW TALKS Developments in 2010 included an attempt in May by Turkish activists to "run" an Israeli blockade of Gaza with a flotilla of six ships. Israeli commandos seized the ships, but resistance by activists led to the death of nine passengers. The incident drew international attention to the blockade and criticisms of the Israeli ban on many ordinary consumer items. In June, Israel substantially eased the terms of the blockade.

"The purpose of foreign policy IS NOT TO PROVIDE AN OUTLET FOR OUR OWN SENTIMENTS OF HOPE OR INDIGNATION; it is to shape real events in a real world."

~ JOHN F. KENNEDY ~
THIRTY-FIFTH PRESIDENT
OF THE UNITED STATES
1961–1963

On the West Bank, the Palestinian Authority succeeded in reestablishing itself as an effective government, and the territory entered a period of relative stability and economic growth. The subsequent self-confidence—plus pressure from America and several Arab states—helped bring the West Bank Palestinians back to the bargaining table in September. Confidence between the parties was fragile, however, and the possibility that the talks might break down was constant.

LO5 *Weapons Proliferation in an Unstable World*

Although foreign policy in recent years has focused most visibly on Iraq and Afghanistan, the U.S. government has also had to deal with other threats to U.S. and global security. The Cold War may be over, but the threat of nuclear warfare—which formed the backdrop of foreign policy during the Cold War—has by no means disappeared. The existence of nuclear weapons in Russia and in other countries around the world continues to challenge U.S. foreign policymakers. Concerns about nuclear proliferation mounted in 1998 when India and Pakistan detonated nuclear devices within a few weeks of each other—events that took U.S. intelligence agencies by surprise. Increasingly, American officials have focused on the threat of an attack by a rogue nation or a terrorist group that possesses weapons of mass destruction. Of most concern today are recent developments in North Korea and Iran.

North Korea's Nuclear Program

North Korea signed the Treaty on the Non-Proliferation of Nuclear Weapons in 1985 and submitted to weapons inspections by the International Atomic Energy Agency (IAEA) in 1992. Throughout the 1990s, however, there were discrepancies between North Korean declarations and IAEA inspection findings. In 2002, North Korea expelled the IAEA inspectors.

OPENING NEGOTIATIONS The administration of George W. Bush had been reluctant to engage in diplomatic relations with North Korea. Bush insisted that any talks with North Korea must also include all of North Korea's neighbors—China, Japan, Russia, and South Korea. In 2003, North Korea finally agreed to such talks.

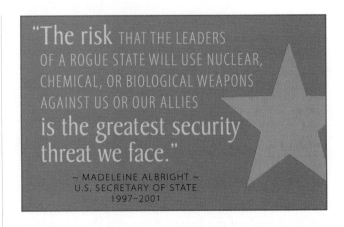

"**The risk** THAT THE LEADERS OF A ROGUE STATE WILL USE NUCLEAR, CHEMICAL, OR BIOLOGICAL WEAPONS AGAINST US OR OUR ALLIES is the greatest security threat we face."

~ MADELEINE ALBRIGHT ~
U.S. SECRETARY OF STATE
1997–2001

Since that time, it has proved quite difficult to keep North Korea at the bargaining table—its representatives have stormed out of the talks repeatedly, for the most trivial reasons. China is the one power with substantial economic leverage over North Korea, and typically, Chinese leaders have been the ones to lead the North Koreans back to the table.

Tensions heightened in October 2006, when North Korea conducted its first nuclear test. Nevertheless, the Bush administration continued to participate with North Korea's neighbors in multilateral negotiations. In the spring of 2007, North Korea agreed that it would begin to dismantle its nuclear facilities and would allow UN inspectors into the country. In return, the other nations agreed to provide various kinds of aid, and the United States would begin to discuss normalization of relations with North Korea. By mid-2007, North Korea had shut down one of its nuclear reactors and had admitted a permanent UN inspection team into the country.

A PSYCHOLOGIST SAYS KIM JONG IL'S NUKES ARE REALLY A DESPERATE CRY FOR HELP.

© 2009 HARLEY SCHWADRON

NEGOTIATIONS COLLAPSE In April 2009, North Korea tested a long-range missile under the guise of attempting to launch a satellite. The UN Security Council unanimously condemned the test. This demonstrated that the Chinese, who have a permanent Security Council seat, were annoyed as well. North Korea then pulled out of the six-party talks and expelled all nuclear inspectors from the country. In May 2009, North Korea tested another nuclear device, to universal disapproval.

In March 2010, tensions rose again after the sinking of a South Korean naval ship, the *Cheonan*, with the loss of forty-six lives. An investigation revealed in May that the sinking was due to a North Korean torpedo. North Korea's aggressive behavior may have been linked to the attempt by its leader, Kim Jong Il, to name a successor in case of his death. The future leader of North Korea is to be Kim Jong Eun, who is Kim Jong Il's third son. Kim Jong Il himself was the son of North Korea's first Communist dictator. North Korea, therefore, is unique in that it is effectively a Communist monarchy.

Iran: An Emerging Nuclear Threat?

For some time, Western intelligence agencies have believed that Iran is attempting to join the ranks of nuclear powers. Investigators for the International Atomic Energy Agency have reported that Iran has initiated a uranium enrichment program for nuclear weapons. U.S. intelligence reports have also found evidence that Iran is working on a missile delivery system for nuclear warheads. Iran has made considerable progress in many aspects of its nuclear program, although Iranian leaders have publicly stated that they have no intention of using their nuclear program for destructive purposes and claim that they are seeking only to develop nuclear energy plants.

Like North Korea, Iran has been openly hostile to the United States. Iran has implemented an extensive terrorism campaign in hopes of undermining U.S. influence in the Middle East. Many analysts have also tied Iran to Iraqi insurgency efforts against American occupation forces. Dealing with a nuclear-equipped Iran would strain already tense relations. Considering Iran's ties to terrorist groups, U.S. national security at home and foreign policy efforts abroad could be significantly endangered.

EUROPE TAKES THE LEAD During the George W. Bush administration, Britain, France, and Germany took the lead in diplomatic efforts to encourage Iran to abandon its nuclear program and engaged in talks with that country. The United Nations has imposed sanctions on Iran in an attempt to curb its nuclear ambitions. The United States has threatened to impose its own sanctions to isolate Iran from the community of nations. Past attempts to strengthen UN sanctions, however, have been frustrated by the opposition of China and Russia.

AMERICA JOINS THE TALKS After a hiatus of over a year, talks with Iran concerning its nuclear program resumed in Geneva on October 1, 2009. Britain, China, France, Germany, Russia, and the United States were at the table. In early discussions, Iran agreed to allow international inspectors access to its facilities. Some observers are hopeful about the talks, but others see them as a way for the Iranians to play for time as they develop their nuclear capabilities. If the Iranians do develop nuclear weapons, what can the United States do about it? We examine that question in this chapter's *Join the Debate* feature on the following page.

LO6 China— The Next Superpower?

Following former president Richard Nixon's historic visit to China in 1972, American diplomatic and economic relations with the Chinese gradually improved. Diplomacy with China focused on cultivating a more pro-Western disposition in the former isolationist nation. In 1989, however, when the Chinese

AP PHOTO/OFFICE OF THE SUPREME LEADER

Ayatollah Ali Khamenei is Iran's Supreme Leader— he is the spiritual head of that country. He refused to support those Iranians who contested the flawed reelection of that country's president, Mahmoud Ahmadinejad, in 2009. By fall, many protesters remained in jail and several had been sentenced to death. Why does the United States continue to be concerned about events in Iran?

Can We Tolerate a Nuclear Iran?

On November 4, 1979, militant students in Tehran, Iran, seized the U.S. embassy and took fifty-two American citizens hostage. The crisis lasted 444 days. Ever since, Iran and the United States have been at odds with each other. In the years that followed, the rest of the world discovered that Iran was engaged in a covert nuclear program. It was enriching uranium that could be used in the fabrication of a nuclear bomb. In spite of numerous UN resolutions, Iran is still producing uranium, and at a faster speed. The existence of a second uranium enrichment plant was made public in the fall of 2009. Simultaneously, Iran has been developing missiles that eventually could be capable of carrying a nuclear payload.

We Must Prevent a Nuclear-Armed Iran at All Costs

Repeatedly, the president of Iran, Mahmoud Ahmadinejad, has called for the complete destruction of Israel. Presumably, if he is serious, when Iran has the bomb, it will be used on Israel. Thus, a nuclear Iran carries with it the possibility of a nuclear holocaust. There would be retaliation, and the conflict could lead to massive destruction in the Middle East and elsewhere.

Currently, Iran is the largest state sponsor of terrorism. What if Iran itself does not use the bomb, but rather provides nuclear weapons to a terrorist group? There are many such groups that would have no scruples about killing millions of innocent civilians.

Finally, if Iran obtains a nuclear weapon, oil-rich countries in the Middle East may feel obligated to do so, too. There could be a dangerous arms race on yet another part of this fragile planet. We must stop Iran's production of uranium now. If all else fails, that means bombing Iran's nuclear facilities.

Belligerent Talk Doesn't Mean We Should Go to War

The fact that Ahmadinejad says Israel should not exist does not necessarily mean much. Such crazy talk is mostly for domestic consumption—to strengthen the regime's political position at home by emphasizing Islamic grievances. Further, Ahmadinejad doesn't actually control Iran's military. Supreme Leader Ayatollah Ali Khamenei does.

The United States has two thousand nuclear weapons. We tolerate nuclear weapons in the hands of the Chinese, Indians, Israelis, North Koreans, Pakistanis, and Russians. North Korea is run by a megalomaniac dictator and is arguably a more dangerous supporter of terrorist groups than Iran. So why should Iran be singled out?

Rather than start a war with Iran, if we are worried about Israel's safety, we can do two things. First, we can extend our nuclear deterrence umbrella to that country. Iran will know that if it strikes Israel, the United States will retaliate. Second, we can help Israel build up its missile defenses. In that way, it can effectively defend itself against Iranian missiles as well as deter their use.

For Critical Analysis *If the United States bombed Iran's uranium enrichment sites, what might be the consequences?*

---

government brutally crushed a pro-democracy student movement, killing many students and protesters while imprisoning others, Chinese-American relations experienced a distinct chill.

Chinese-American Trade Relations

During the Clinton administration, American relations with China began to improve once again. The rapid growth of the Chinese economy, and increasingly close trade ties between the United States and China, helped bring about a policy of diplomatic outreach. Many Americans protested, however, when the U.S. government extended **normal trade relations (NTR) status** to China on a year-to-year basis. Labor groups objected because they feared that American workers would lose jobs that could be performed at lower wages in Chinese factories. Human rights organizations denounced the Chinese government's well-documented mistreatment of its people. Despite this heavy opposition, Congress granted China permanent NTR status in 2000 and endorsed China's application to the World Trade Organization in 2001.

normal trade relations (NTR) status A trade status granted through an international treaty by which each member nation must treat other members at least as well as it treats the country that receives its most favorable treatment. This status was formerly known as *most-favored-nation status.*

OUR GOVERNMENT FACES A TROUBLED ECONOMY

Should We Fight China's Cheap Imports?

In the 1960s and 1970s, there was much concern that low-cost imports from Japan were destroying our manufacturing sector, especially the automobile industry. For a time, "Made in Japan" almost became a swearword. Fast-forward to the 2010s, and replace *Japan* with *China*. Some politicians—on both the political left and the right—argue today that China is flooding the U.S. market with its goods and thereby preventing the U.S. economy from enjoying a vigorous recovery from the Great Recession.

The Data Seem to Prove a Point

By the summer of 2010, the U.S. international trade deficit—exports minus imports—was running at more than $50 billion a month. In other words, American consumers are buying more from abroad than foreigners are buying from the United States. China, in contrast, is recording monthly trade surpluses of around $30 billion. That means that China is selling to the rest of the world $30 billion more than its residents are importing. Much of that surplus is coming from the United States. As Chinese goods pile up in America, U.S. dollars pile up in China in the form of treasuries held by the Chinese central bank.

We Buy So Many Chinese Goods Because They Are Cheaper

American consumers are not fools. If they have a choice between goods of equal quality at different prices,

they will purchase the ones that are less expensive. For the moment, those goods are frequently from China (as mentioned above, they used to be from Japan). Why are Chinese goods so inexpensive? One obvious reason, of course, is that Chinese workers earn much less than American workers. Another important reason, though, is that the Chinese government maintains a fixed exchange rate between our dollar and the Chinese currency, called the *renminbi* and denominated in *yuan*. When China deliberately keeps the value of its currency low relative to the dollar, its exports become cheaper and its imports more expensive.

A Threat from Congress and the President

Not surprisingly, many members of Congress—and the Obama administration—have demanded that China allow its currency to become more valuable relative to the dollar. Some would like to see the value of the Chinese currency rise by at least 10 to 20 percent. In that way, Chinese imports would no longer be so inexpensive, and we would stop buying so many Chinese goods.

The U.S. Congress does have a weapon if it really wants to reduce China's trade with the United States. It can impose taxes, called *tariffs*, on anything that we buy from China. In so doing, Chinese goods would be more expensive to Americans. Americans would buy fewer of them and buy more domestically produced goods instead. The last time the world saw a major trade war of this type was during the Great Depression, however, and trade restrictions made that economic collapse much worse than it already was.

You Be the Judge Who benefits and who loses from inexpensive Chinese imports?

A Future Challenger to American Dominance

Many U.S. observers have warned that China is destined to challenge American global supremacy. With one of the fastest-growing economies in the world, along with a population of 1.3 billion, China's gross domestic product (GDP) could surpass that of the United States by 2039. China's GDP is nearly ten times greater than

it was in 1978, when China implemented reforms to make the economy more market oriented. The United States already runs a multibillion-dollar trade deficit with China and could be vulnerable if Chinese economic growth continues at its present pace. How much of a problem do China's cheap exports really pose for the United States? We look at that question in this chapter's feature *Our Government Faces a Troubled Economy* above.

Diplomatic relations between China and the United States have been uneven. China offered its full support of the U.S. war on terrorism following the September 11 attacks, even providing intelligence about terrorist activities. The Chinese did not support the American invasion of Iraq in 2003, however. Although China has not shown ambitions to acquire more territory or become militarily aggressive, it has expressed a desire to take control of the island of Taiwan. China considers Taiwan, a former Chinese province, to be a legal part of China. In practice, however, since 1949 the island has functioned as if it were an independent nation. The United States has historically supported a free and separate Taiwan and has reiterated that any reunion of China and Taiwan must come about by peaceful means. More recently, relations between China and several Western nations have become strained due to criticisms by these nations of Chinese behavior in Tibet. While supposedly autonomous, Tibet is under tight Chinese control.

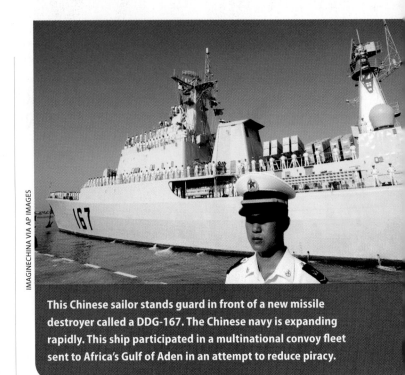

IMAGINECHINA VIA AP IMAGES

This Chinese sailor stands guard in front of a new missile destroyer called a DDG-167. The Chinese navy is expanding rapidly. This ship participated in a multinational convoy fleet sent to Africa's Gulf of Aden in an attempt to reduce piracy.

AMERICA AT ODDS *Foreign Policy*

In 1947, Republican senator Arthur Vandenberg of Michigan announced: "Politics stops at the water's edge." By this, Vandenberg, formerly a fierce isolationist, meant that Republicans and Democrats should cooperate in dealing with such foreign policy issues as the Cold War with the Soviet Union. Bipartisanship was never complete even in Vandenberg's day, however, and it is much less common today. True, the two major parties are more likely to cooperate over a foreign policy issue than over domestic policy. Nevertheless, Americans are at odds over many foreign policy issues, and that is reflected in Congress. The following are a few of these issues:

- In foreign policy, is it best to ally with other nations whenever possible—or should America carefully guard its ability to act alone?

- Should the president take complete charge of the foreign policy process, including the use of armed force—or should the president collaborate closely with Congress?

- Should the war on terrorism be the central focus of U.S. foreign policy—or should we devote equal energy to managing our relations with rising powers such as China?

- Is President Obama's plan to withdraw forces from Afghanistan in July 2011 a wise method of putting pressure on the Afghan government—or a recipe for failure in that country?

- In attempting to promote peace between Israelis and Palestinians, should the United States put most of its pressure on the Palestinians—or should it also pressure the Israelis to, for example, suspend the construction of new Jewish settlements on the West Bank?

Take Action

Many Americans of all political persuasions are taking action to help "support the troops" now fighting in Afghanistan. For example, a number of groups are working to help improve the lives of soldiers who have returned from the war. For ideas on what you can do to help, you can contact a veterans' group in your area or visit the Web sites of veterans' groups. For ideas, check out the Web site **www.troopssupport.com**, which lists more than a hundred organizations seeking to assist our soldiers. These groups represent a wide variety of outlooks and activities. A particular favorite is the Fisher House Foundation at **www. fisherhouse.org**, which provides housing for family members of hospitalized soldiers.

- You can find news about international events at an interesting Web site sponsored by the Peterson Institute for International Economics at **www.iie.com**. You can also get access to the group's working papers at this site.

- To learn more about national security policy and defense issues, you can go to the U.S. Department of Defense's site at **www.defense.gov**. For information on the U.S. Department of State and its activities, go to **www.state.gov**

- One of the best resources on the Web for learning about foreign countries is the *World Factbook* of the CIA. You can find it at **www.cia.gov/library/publications/the-world-factbook**

- The Global Legal Information Network (GLIN) provides a database of national laws from countries around the world via the Web server of the U.S. Library of Congress. The site consists of more than 54,000 records of legislation enacted from 1976 to the present. To access this site, go to **www.glin.gov**

- The World Bank's home page offers a wealth of information on international development, research studies containing economic data on various countries, and the like. Go to **www.worldbank.org**

- The Washburn University School of Law offers, among other things, extensive information on international affairs, including United Nations materials. To access this site, go to **www.washlaw.edu**

Access CourseMate to review and expand on this chapter through quizzes, flashcards, learning objectives, interactive timelines, a crossword puzzle, audio summaries, video, critical-thinking activities, simulations, and more.

{ Speak Up! }

We want to know – share your thoughts about this edition of GOVT online, anytime!

We're listening: **4ltrpress.cengage.com/politicalscience**

THE DECLARATION OF INDEPENDENCE

IN CONGRESS, JULY 4, 1776

A Declaration by the Representatives of the United States of America, in General Congress assembled. When in the Course of human Events, it becomes necessary for one People to dissolve the Political Bands which have connected them with another, and to assume among the Powers of the Earth, the separate and equal Station to which the Laws of Nature and of Nature's God entitle them, a decent Respect to the Opinions of Mankind requires that they should declare the causes which impel them to the Separation.

We hold these Truths to be self-evident, that all Men are created equal, that they are endowed by their Creator with certain unalienable Rights, that among these are Life, Liberty, and the Pursuit of Happiness—That to secure these Rights, Governments are instituted among Men, deriving their just Powers from the Consent of the Governed, that whenever any Form of Government becomes destructive of these Ends, it is the Right of the People to alter or to abolish it, and to institute new Government, laying its Foundation on such Principles, and organizing its Powers in such Forms, as to them shall seem most likely to effect their Safety and Happiness. Prudence, indeed, will dictate that Governments long established should not be changed for light and transient Causes; and accordingly all Experience hath shewn, that Mankind are more disposed to suffer, while Evils are sufferable, than to right themselves by abolishing the Forms to which they are accustomed. But when a long Train of Abuses and Usurpations, pursuing invariably the same Object, evinces a Design to reduce them under absolute Despotism, it is their Right, it is their Duty, to throw off such Government, and to provide new Guards for their future Security. Such has been the patient Sufferance of these Colonies; and such is now the Necessity which constrains them to alter their former Systems of Government. The History of the present King of Great-Britain is a History of repeated Injuries and Usurpations, all having

in direct Object the Establishment of an absolute Tyranny over these States. To prove this, let Facts be submitted to a candid World.

He has refused his Assent to Laws, the most wholesome and necessary for the public Good.

He has forbidden his Governors to pass Laws of immediate and pressing Importance, unless suspended in their Operation till his Assent should be obtained; and when so suspended, he has utterly neglected to attend to them.

He has refused to pass other Laws for the Accommodation of large Districts of People, unless those People would relinquish the Right of Representation in the Legislature, a Right inestimable to them, and formidable to Tyrants only.

He has called together Legislative Bodies at Places unusual, uncomfortable, and distant from the Depository of their Public Records, for the sole Purpose of fatiguing them into Compliance with his Measures.

He has dissolved Representative Houses repeatedly, for opposing with manly Firmness his Invasions on the Rights of the People.

He has refused for a long Time, after such Dissolutions, to cause others to be elected; whereby the Legislative Powers, incapable of Annihilation, have returned to the People at large for their exercise; the State remaining in the mean time exposed to all the Dangers of Invasion from without, and Convulsions within.

He has endeavoured to prevent the Population of these States; for that Purpose obstructing the Laws for Naturalization of Foreigners; refusing to pass others to encourage their Migrations hither, and raising the Conditions of new Appropriations of Lands.

He has obstructed the Administration of Justice, by refusing his Assent to Laws for establishing Judiciary Powers.

He has made Judges dependent on his Will alone, for the Tenure of their offices, and the Amount and payment of their Salaries.

He has erected a Multitude of new Offices, and sent hither Swarms of Officers to harrass our People, and eat out their Substance.

He has kept among us, in Times of Peace, Standing Armies, without the consent of our Legislatures.

He has affected to render the Military independent of, and superior to the Civil Power.

He has combined with others to subject us to a Jurisdiction foreign to our Constitution, and unacknowledged by our Laws; giving his Assent to their Acts of pretended Legislation:

For quartering large Bodies of Armed Troops among us:

For protecting them, by a mock Trial, from Punishment for any Murders which they should commit on the Inhabitants of these States:

For cutting off our Trade with all Parts of the World:

For imposing Taxes on us without our Consent:

For depriving us, in many cases, of the Benefits of Trial by Jury:

For transporting us beyond Seas to be tried for pretended Offences:

For abolishing the free System of English Laws in a neighbouring Province, establishing therein an arbitrary Government, and enlarging its Boundaries, so as to render it at once an Example and fit Instrument for introducing the same absolute Rule into these Colonies:

For taking away our Charters, abolishing our most valuable Laws, and altering fundamentally the Forms of our Governments:

For suspending our own Legislatures, and declaring themselves invested with Power to legislate for us in all Cases whatsoever.

He has abdicated Government here, by declaring us out of his Protection and waging War against us.

He has plundered our Seas, ravaged our Coasts, burnt our towns, and destroyed the Lives of our People.

He is, at this Time, transporting large Armies of foreign Mercenaries to compleat the works of Death, Desolation, and Tyranny, already begun with circumstances of Cruelty and Perfidy, scarcely paralleled in the most barbarous Ages, and totally unworthy the Head of a civilized Nation.

He has constrained our fellow Citizens taken Captive on the high Seas to bear Arms against their Country, to become the Executioners of their Friends and Brethren, or to fall themselves by their Hands.

He has excited domestic Insurrections amongst us, and has endeavoured to bring on the Inhabitants of our Frontiers, the merciless Indian Savages, whose known Rule of Warfare, is an undistinguished Destruction, of all Ages, Sexes and Conditions.

In every state of these Oppressions we have Petitioned for Redress in the most humble Terms: Our repeated Petitions have been answered only by repeated Injury. A Prince, whose Character is thus marked by every act which may define a Tyrant, is unfit to be the Ruler of a free People.

Nor have we been wanting in Attentions to our British Brethren. We have warned them from Time to Time of Attempts by their Legislature to extend an unwarrantable Jurisdiction over us. We have reminded them of the Circumstances of our Emigration and Settlement here. We have appealed to their native Justice and Magnanimity, and we have conjured them by the Ties of our common Kindred to disavow these Usurpations, which, would inevitably interrupt our Connections and Correspondence. They too have been deaf to the Voice of Justice and of Consanguinity. We must, therefore, acquiesce in the Necessity, which denounces our Separation, and hold them, as we hold the rest of Mankind, Enemies in War, in Peace, Friends.

We, therefore, the Representatives of the UNITED STATES OF AMERICA, in General Congress Assembled, appealing to the Supreme Judge of the World for the Rectitude of our Intentions, do, in the Name, and by the Authority of the good People of these Colonies, solemnly Publish and Declare, That these United Colonies are, and of Right ought to be, Free and Independent States; that they are absolved from all Allegiance to the British Crown, and that all political Connection between them and the State of Great-Britain, is and ought to be totally dissolved; and that as Free and Independent States, they have full Power to levy War, conclude Peace, contract Alliances, establish Commerce, and to do all other Acts and Things which Independent States may of right do. And for the support of this declaration, with a firm Reliance on the Protection of divine Providence, we mutually pledge to each other our lives, our Fortunes, and our sacred Honor.

THE CONSTITUTION OF THE UNITED STATES

PREAMBLE

We the People of the United States, in Order to form a more perfect Union, establish Justice, insure domestic Tranquility, provide for the common defence, promote the general Welfare, and secure the Blessings of Liberty to ourselves and our Posterity, do ordain and establish this Constitution for the United States of America.

ARTICLE I

SECTION 1. All legislative Powers herein granted shall be vested in a Congress of the United States, which shall consist of a Senate and House of Representatives.

SECTION 2. The House of Representatives shall be composed of Members chosen every second Year by the People of the several States, and the Electors in each State shall have the Qualifications requisite for Electors of the most numerous Branch of the State Legislature.

No Person shall be a Representative who shall not have attained to the Age of twenty five Years, and been seven Years a Citizen of the United States, and who shall not, when elected, be an Inhabitant of that State in which he shall be chosen.

Representatives and direct Taxes shall be apportioned among the several States which may be included within this Union, according to their respective Numbers, which shall be determined by adding to the whole Number of free Persons, including those bound to Service for a Term of Years, and excluding Indians not taxed, three fifths of all other Persons. The actual Enumeration shall be made within three Years after the first Meeting of the Congress of the United States, and within every subsequent Term of ten Years, in such Manner as they shall by Law direct. The Number of Representatives shall not exceed one for every thirty Thousand, but each State shall have at Least one Representative; and until such enumeration shall be made, the State of New Hampshire shall be entitled to chuse three, Massachusetts eight, Rhode Island and Providence Plantations one, Connecticut five, New York six, New Jersey four, Pennsylvania eight, Delaware one, Maryland six, Virginia ten, North Carolina five, South Carolina five, and Georgia three.

When vacancies happen in the Representation from any State, the Executive Authority thereof shall issue Writs of Election to fill such Vacancies.

The House of Representatives shall chuse their Speaker and other Officers; and shall have the sole Power of Impeachment.

SECTION 3. The Senate of the United States shall be composed of two Senators from each State, chosen by the Legislature thereof, for six Years; and each Senator shall have one Vote.

Immediately after they shall be assembled in Consequence of the first Election, they shall be divided as equally as may be into three Classes. The Seats of the Senators of the first Class shall be vacated at the Expiration of the second Year, of the second Class at the Expiration of the fourth Year, and of the third Class at the Expiration of the sixth Year, so that one third may be chosen every second Year; and if Vacancies happen by Resignation, or otherwise, during the Recess of the Legislature of any State, the Executive thereof may make temporary Appointments until the next Meeting of the Legislature, which shall then fill such Vacancies.

No Person shall be a Senator who shall not have attained to the Age of thirty Years, and been nine Years a Citizen of the United States, and who shall not, when elected, be an Inhabitant of that State for which he shall be chosen.

The Vice President of the United States shall be President of the Senate, but shall have no Vote, unless they be equally divided.

The Senate shall chuse their other Officers, and also a President pro tempore, in the Absence of the Vice President, or when he shall exercise the Office of President of the United States.

The Senate shall have the sole Power to try all Impeachments. When sitting for that Purpose, they shall be on Oath or Affirmation. When the President of the United States is tried, the Chief Justice shall preside: And no Person shall be convicted without the Concurrence of two thirds of the Members present.

Judgment in Cases of Impeachment shall not extend further than to removal from Office, and disqualification to hold and enjoy any Office of honor, Trust, or Profit under the United States: but the Party convicted shall nevertheless be liable and subject to Indictment, Trial, Judgment, and Punishment, according to Law.

SECTION 4.   The Times, Places and Manner of holding Elections for Senators and Representatives, shall be prescribed in each State by the Legislature thereof; but the Congress may at any time by Law make or alter such Regulations, except as to the Places of chusing Senators.

The Congress shall assemble at least once in every Year, and such Meeting shall be on the first Monday in December, unless they shall by Law appoint a different Day.

SECTION 5.   Each House shall be the Judge of the Elections, Returns, and Qualifications of its own Members, and a Majority of each shall constitute a Quorum to do Business; but a smaller Number may adjourn from day to day, and may be authorized to compel the Attendance of absent Members, in such Manner, and under such Penalties as each House may provide.

Each House may determine the Rules of its Proceedings, punish its Members for disorderly Behavior, and, with the Concurrence of two thirds, expel a Member.

Each House shall keep a Journal of its Proceedings, and from time to time publish the same, excepting such Parts as may in their Judgment require Secrecy; and the Yeas and Nays of the Members of either House on any question shall, at the Desire of one fifth of those Present, be entered on the Journal.

Neither House, during the Session of Congress, shall, without the Consent of the other, adjourn for more than three days, nor to any other Place than that in which the two Houses shall be sitting.

SECTION 6.   The Senators and Representatives shall receive a Compensation for their Services, to be ascertained by Law, and paid out of the Treasury of the United States. They shall in all Cases, except Treason, Felony and Breach of the Peace, be privileged from Arrest during their Attendance at the Session of their respective Houses, and in going to and returning from the same; and for any Speech or Debate in either House, they shall not be questioned in any other Place.

No Senator or Representative shall, during the Time for which he was elected, be appointed to any civil Office under the Authority of the United States, which shall have been created, or the Emoluments whereof shall have been increased during such time; and no Person holding any Office under the United States, shall be a Member of either House during his Continuance in Office.

SECTION 7.   All Bills for raising Revenue shall originate in the House of Representatives; but the Senate may propose or concur with Amendments as on other Bills.

Every Bill which shall have passed the House of Representatives and the Senate, shall, before it become a Law, be presented to the President of the United States; If he approve he shall sign it, but if not he shall return it, with his Objections to the House in which it shall have originated, who shall enter the Objections at large on their Journal, and proceed to reconsider it. If after such Reconsideration two thirds of that House shall agree to pass the Bill, it shall be sent together with the Objections, to the other House, by which it shall likewise be reconsidered, and if approved by two thirds of that House, it shall become a Law. But in all such Cases the Votes of both Houses shall be determined by Yeas and Nays, and the Names of the Persons voting for and against the Bill shall be entered on the Journal of each House respectively. If any Bill shall not be returned by the President within ten Days (Sundays excepted) after it shall have been presented to him, the Same shall be a Law, in like Manner as if he had signed it, unless the Congress by their Adjournment prevent its Return in which Case it shall not be a Law.

Every Order, Resolution, or Vote, to which the Concurrence of the Senate and House of Representatives may be necessary (except on a question of Adjournment) shall be presented to the President of the United States; and before the Same shall take Effect, shall be approved by him, or being disapproved by him, shall be repassed by two thirds of the Senate and House of Representatives, according to the Rules and Limitations prescribed in the Case of a Bill.

SECTION 8.   The Congress shall have Power To lay and collect Taxes, Duties, Imposts and Excises, to pay the Debts and provide for the common Defence and general Welfare of the United States; but all Duties, Imposts and Excises shall be uniform throughout the United States;

To borrow Money on the credit of the United States;

To regulate Commerce with foreign Nations, and among the several States, and with the Indian Tribes;

To establish an uniform Rule of Naturalization, and uniform Laws on the subject of Bankruptcies throughout the United States;

To coin Money, regulate the Value thereof, and of foreign Coin, and fix the Standard of Weights and Measures;

To provide for the Punishment of counterfeiting the Securities and current Coin of the United States;

To establish Post Offices and post Roads;

To promote the Progress of Science and useful Arts, by securing for limited Times to Authors and Inventors the exclusive Right to their respective Writings and Discoveries;

To constitute Tribunals inferior to the supreme Court;

To define and punish Piracies and Felonies committed on the high Seas, and Offenses against the Law of Nations;

To declare War, grant Letters of Marque and Reprisal, and make Rules concerning Captures on Land and Water;

To raise and support Armies, but no Appropriation of Money to that Use shall be for a longer Term than two Years;

To provide and maintain a Navy;

To make Rules for the Government and Regulation of the land and naval Forces;

To provide for calling forth the Militia to execute the Laws of the Union, suppress Insurrections and repel Invasions;

To provide for organizing, arming, and disciplining, the Militia, and for governing such Part of them as may be employed in the Service of the United States, reserving to the States respectively, the Appointment of the Officers, and the Authority of training the Militia according to the discipline prescribed by Congress;

To exercise exclusive Legislation in all Cases whatsoever, over such District (not exceeding ten Miles square) as may, by Cession of particular States, and the Acceptance of Congress, become the Seat of the Government of the United States, and to exercise like Authority over all Places purchased by the Consent of the Legislature of the State in which the Same shall be, for the Erection of Forts, Magazines, Arsenals, dock-Yards, and other needful Buildings;—And

To make all Laws which shall be necessary and proper for carrying into Execution the foregoing Powers, and all other Powers vested by this Constitution in the Government of the United States, or in any Department or Officer thereof.

SECTION 9. The Migration or Importation of such Persons as any of the States now existing shall think proper to admit, shall not be prohibited by the Congress prior to the Year one thousand eight hundred and eight, but a Tax or duty may be imposed on such Importation, not exceeding ten dollars for each Person.

The privilege of the Writ of Habeas Corpus shall not be suspended, unless when in Cases of Rebellion or Invasion the public Safety may require it.

No Bill of Attainder or ex post facto Law shall be passed.

No Capitation, or other direct, Tax shall be laid, unless in Proportion to the Census or Enumeration herein before directed to be taken.

No Tax or Duty shall be laid on Articles exported from any State.

No Preference shall be given by any Regulation of Commerce or Revenue to the Ports of one State over those of another: nor shall Vessels bound to, or from, one State be obliged to enter, clear, or pay Duties in another.

No Money shall be drawn from the Treasury, but in Consequence of Appropriations made by Law; and a regular Statement and Account of the Receipts and Expenditures of all public Money shall be published from time to time.

No Title of Nobility shall be granted by the United States: And no Person holding any Office of Profit or Trust under them, shall, without the Consent of the Congress, accept of any present, Emolument, Office, or Title, of any kind whatever, from any King, Prince, or foreign State.

SECTION 10. No State shall enter into any Treaty, Alliance, or Confederation; grant Letters of Marque and Reprisal; coin Money; emit Bills of Credit; make any Thing but gold and silver Coin a Tender in Payment of Debts; pass any Bill of Attainder, ex post facto Law, or Law impairing the Obligation of Contracts, or grant any Title of Nobility.

No State shall, without the Consent of the Congress, lay any Imposts or Duties on Imports or Exports, except what may be absolutely necessary for executing its inspection Laws: and the net Produce of all Duties and Imposts, laid by any State on Imports or Exports, shall be for the Use of the Treasury of the United States; and all such Laws shall be subject to the Revision and Controul of the Congress.

No State shall, without the Consent of Congress, lay any Duty of Tonnage, keep Troops, or Ships of War in time of Peace, enter into any Agreement or Compact with another State, or with a foreign Power, or engage in War, unless actually invaded, or in such imminent Danger as will not admit of delay.

ARTICLE II

SECTION 1. The executive Power shall be vested in a President of the United States of America. He shall hold his Office during the Term of four Years, and, together with the Vice President, chosen for the same Term, be elected, as follows:

Each State shall appoint, in such Manner as the Legislature thereof may direct, a Number of Electors, equal to the whole Number of Senators and Representatives to which the State may be entitled in the Congress; but no Senator or Representative, or Person holding an Office of Trust or Profit under the United States, shall be appointed an Elector.

The Electors shall meet in their respective States, and vote by Ballot for two Persons, of whom one at least shall not be an Inhabitant of the same State with themselves. And they shall make a List of all the Persons voted for, and of the Number of Votes for each; which List they shall sign and certify, and transmit sealed to the Seat of the Government of the United States, directed to the President of the Senate. The President of the Senate shall, in the Presence of the Senate and House of Representatives, open all the Certificates, and the Votes shall then be counted. The Person having the greatest Number of Votes shall be the President, if such Number be a Majority of the whole Number of Electors appointed; and if there be more than one who have such Majority, and have an equal Number of Votes, then the House of Representatives shall immediately chuse by Ballot one of them for President; and if no Person have a Majority, then from the five highest on the List the said House shall in like Manner chuse the President. But in chusing the President, the Votes shall be taken by States, the Representation from each State having one Vote; A quorum for this Purpose shall consist of a Member or Members from two thirds of the States, and a Majority of all the States shall be necessary to a Choice. In every Case, after the Choice of the President, the Person having the greater Number of Votes of the Electors shall be the Vice President. But if there should remain two or more who have equal Votes, the Senate shall chuse from them by Ballot the Vice President.

The Congress may determine the Time of chusing the Electors, and the Day on which they shall give their Votes; which Day shall be the same throughout the United States.

No person except a natural born Citizen, or a Citizen of the United States, at the time of the Adoption of this Constitution, shall be eligible to the Office of President; neither shall any Person be eligible to that Office who shall not have attained to the Age of thirty five Years, and been fourteen Years a Resident within the United States.

In Case of the Removal of the President from Office, or of his Death, Resignation or Inability to discharge the Powers and Duties of the said Office, the same shall devolve on the Vice President, and the Congress may by Law provide for the Case of Removal, Death, Resignation or Inability, both of the President and Vice President, declaring what Officer shall then act as President, and such Officer shall act accordingly, until the Disability be removed, or a President shall be elected.

The President shall, at stated Times, receive for his Services, a Compensation, which shall neither be increased nor diminished during the Period for which he shall have been elected, and he shall not receive within that Period any other Emolument from the United States, or any of them.

Before he enter on the Execution of his Office, he shall take the following Oath or Affirmation: "I do solemnly swear (or affirm) that I will faithfully execute the Office of President of the United States, and will to the best of my Ability, preserve, protect and defend the Constitution of the United States."

SECTION 2. The President shall be Commander in Chief of the Army and Navy of the United States, and of the Militia of the several States, when called into the actual Service of the United States; he may require the Opinion, in writing, of the principal Officer in each of the executive Departments, upon any Subject relating to the Duties of their respective Offices, and he shall have Power to grant Reprieves and Pardons for Offenses against the United States, except in Cases of Impeachment.

He shall have Power, by and with the Advice and Consent of the Senate to make Treaties, provided two thirds of the Senators present concur; and he shall nominate, and by and with the Advice and Consent of the Senate, shall appoint Ambassadors, other public Ministers and Consuls, Judges of the supreme Court, and all other Officers of the United States, whose Appointments are not herein otherwise provided for, and which shall be established by Law; but the Congress may by Law vest the Appointment of such inferior Officers, as they think proper, in the President alone, in the Courts of Law, or in the Heads of Departments.

The President shall have Power to fill up all Vacancies that may happen during the Recess of the Senate, by granting Commissions which shall expire at the End of their next Session.

SECTION 3. He shall from time to time give to the Congress Information of the State of the Union, and recommend to their Consideration such Measures as he shall judge necessary and expedient; he may, on extraordinary Occasions, convene both Houses, or either of them, and in Case of Disagreement between them, with Respect to the Time of Adjournment, he may adjourn them to such Time as he shall think proper; he shall receive Ambassadors and other public Ministers; he shall take Care that the Laws be faithfully executed, and shall Commission all the Officers of the United States.

SECTION 4. The President, Vice President and all civil Officers of the United States, shall be removed from Office on Impeachment for, and Conviction of, Treason, Bribery, or other high Crimes and Misdemeanors.

ARTICLE III

SECTION 1. The judicial Power of the United States, shall be vested in one supreme Court, and in such inferior Courts as the Congress may from time to time ordain and establish. The Judges, both of the supreme and inferior Courts, shall hold their Offices during good Behaviour, and shall, at stated Times, receive for their Services a Compensation, which shall not be diminished during their Continuance in Office.

SECTION 2. The judicial Power shall extend to all Cases, in Law and Equity, arising under this Constitution, the Laws of the United States, and Treaties made, or which shall be made, under their Authority;—to all Cases affecting Ambassadors, other public Ministers and Consuls;—to all Cases of admiralty and maritime Jurisdiction;—to Controversies to which the United States shall be a Party;—to Controversies between two or more States;—between a State and Citizens of another State;—between Citizens of different States;—between Citizens of the same State claiming Lands under Grants of different States, and between a State, or the Citizens thereof, and foreign States, Citizens or Subjects.

In all Cases affecting Ambassadors, other public Ministers and Consuls, and those in which a State shall be a Party, the supreme Court shall have original Jurisdiction. In all the other Cases before mentioned, the supreme Court shall have appellate Jurisdiction, both as to Law and Fact, with such Exceptions, and under such Regulations as the Congress shall make.

The Trial of all Crimes, except in Cases of Impeachment, shall be by Jury; and such Trial shall be held in the State where the said Crimes shall have been committed; but when not committed within any State, the Trial shall be at such Place or Places as the Congress may by Law have directed.

SECTION 3. Treason against the United States, shall consist only in levying War against them, or, in adhering to their Enemies, giving them Aid and Comfort. No Person shall be convicted of Treason unless on the Testimony of two Witnesses to the same overt Act, or on Confession in open Court.

The Congress shall have Power to declare the Punishment of Treason, but no Attainder of Treason shall work Corruption of Blood, or Forfeiture except during the Life of the Person attainted.

ARTICLE IV

SECTION 1. Full Faith and Credit shall be given in each State to the public Acts, Records, and judicial Proceedings of every other State. And the Congress may by general Laws prescribe the Manner in which such Acts, Records and Proceedings shall be proved, and the Effect thereof.

SECTION 2. The Citizens of each State shall be entitled to all Privileges and Immunities of Citizens in the several States.

A Person charged in any State with Treason, Felony, or other Crime, who shall flee from Justice, and be found in another State, shall on Demand of the executive Authority of the State from which he fled, be delivered up, to be removed to the State having Jurisdiction of the Crime.

No Person held to Service or Labour in one State, under the Laws thereof, escaping into another, shall, in Consequence of any Law or Regulation therein, be discharged from such Service or Labour, but shall be delivered up on Claim of the Party to whom such Service or Labour may be due.

SECTION 3. New States may be admitted by the Congress into this Union; but no new State shall be formed or erected within the Jurisdiction of any other

State; nor any State be formed by the Junction of two or more States, or Parts of States, without the Consent of the Legislatures of the States concerned as well as of the Congress.

The Congress shall have Power to dispose of and make all needful Rules and Regulations respecting the Territory or other Property belonging to the United States; and nothing in this Constitution shall be so construed as to Prejudice any Claims of the United States, or of any particular State.

SECTION 4.   The United States shall guarantee to every State in this Union a Republican Form of Government, and shall protect each of them against Invasion; and on Application of the Legislature, or of the Executive (when the Legislature cannot be convened) against domestic Violence.

ARTICLE V

The Congress, whenever two thirds of both Houses shall deem it necessary, shall propose Amendments to this Constitution, or, on the Application of the Legislatures of two thirds of the several States, shall call a Convention for proposing Amendments, which, in either Case, shall be valid to all Intents and Purposes, as part of this Constitution, when ratified by the Legislatures of three fourths of the several States, or by Conventions in three fourths thereof, as the one or the other Mode of Ratification may be proposed by the Congress; Provided that no Amendment which may be made prior to the Year One thousand eight hundred and eight shall in any Manner affect the first and fourth Clauses in the Ninth Section of the first Article; and that no State, without its Consent, shall be deprived of its equal Suffrage in the Senate.

ARTICLE VI

All Debts contracted and Engagements entered into, before the Adoption of this Constitution shall be as valid against the United States under this Constitution, as under the Confederation.

This Constitution, and the Laws of the United States which shall be made in Pursuance thereof; and all Treaties made, or which shall be made, under the Authority of the United States, shall be the supreme Law of the Land; and the Judges in every State shall be bound thereby, any Thing in the Constitution or Laws of any State to the Contrary notwithstanding.

The Senators and Representatives before mentioned, and the Members of the several State Legislatures, and all executive and judicial Officers, both of the United States and of the several States, shall be bound by Oath or Affirmation, to support this Constitution; but no religious Test shall ever be required as a Qualification to any Office or public Trust under the United States.

ARTICLE VII

The Ratification of the Conventions of nine States shall be sufficient for the Establishment of this Constitution between the States so ratifying the Same.

AMENDMENT I [1791]

Congress shall make no law respecting an establishment of religion, or prohibiting the free exercise thereof; or abridging the freedom of speech, or of the press; or the right of the people peaceably to assemble, and to petition the Government for a redress of grievances.

AMENDMENT II [1791]

A well regulated Militia, being necessary to the security of a free State, the right of the people to keep and bear Arms, shall not be infringed.

AMENDMENT III [1791]

No Soldier shall, in time of peace be quartered in any house, without the consent of the Owner, nor in time of war, but in a manner to be prescribed by law.

AMENDMENT IV [1791]

The right of the people to be secure in their persons, houses, papers, and effects, against unreasonable searches and seizures, shall not be violated, and no Warrants shall issue, but upon probable cause, supported by Oath or affirmation, and particularly describing the place to be searched, and the persons or things to be seized.

AMENDMENT V [1791]

No person shall be held to answer for a capital, or otherwise infamous crime, unless on a presentment or indictment of a Grand Jury, except in cases arising in the land or naval forces, or in the Militia, when in actual service in time of War or public danger; nor shall any person be subject for the same offense to be twice put in jeopardy of life or limb; nor shall be compelled in any criminal case to be a witness against himself, nor be deprived of life, liberty, or property, without due process of law; nor shall private property be taken for public use, without just compensation.

AMENDMENT VI [1791]

In all criminal prosecutions, the accused shall enjoy the right to a speedy and public trial, by an impartial jury of the State and district wherein the crime shall have been committed, which district shall have been previously ascertained by law, and to be informed of the nature and cause of the accusation; to be confronted with the witnesses against him; to have compulsory process for obtaining witnesses in his favor, and to have the Assistance of Counsel for his defence.

AMENDMENT VII [1791]

In Suits at common law, where the value in controversy shall exceed twenty dollars, the right of trial by jury shall be preserved, and no fact tried by a jury, shall be otherwise re-examined in any Court of the United States, than according to the rules of the common law.

AMENDMENT VIII [1791]

Excessive bail shall not be required, nor excessive fines imposed, nor cruel and unusual punishments inflicted.

AMENDMENT IX [1791]

The enumeration in the Constitution, of certain rights, shall not be construed to deny or disparage others retained by the people.

AMENDMENT X [1791]

The powers not delegated to the United States by the Constitution, nor prohibited by it to the States, are reserved to the States respectively, or to the people.

AMENDMENT XI [1798]

The Judicial power of the United States shall not be construed to extend to any suit in law or equity, commenced or prosecuted against one of the United States by Citizens of another State, or by Citizens or Subjects of any Foreign State.

AMENDMENT XII [1804]

The Electors shall meet in their respective states, and vote by ballot for President and Vice-President, one of whom, at least, shall not be an inhabitant of the same state with themselves; they shall name in their ballots the person voted for as President, and in distinct ballots the person voted for as Vice-President, and they shall make distinct lists of all persons voted for as President, and of all persons voted for as Vice-President, and of the number of votes for each, which lists they shall sign and certify, and transmit sealed to the seat of the government of the United States, directed to the President of the Senate;—The President of the Senate shall, in the presence of the Senate and House of Representatives, open all the certificates and the votes shall then be counted;—The person having the greatest number of votes for President, shall be the President, if such number be a majority of the whole number of Electors appointed; and if no person have such majority, then from the persons having the highest numbers not exceeding three on the list of those voted for as President, the House of Representatives shall choose immediately, by ballot, the President. But in choosing the President, the votes shall be taken by states, the representation from each state having one vote; a quorum for this purpose shall consist of a member or members from two-thirds of the states, and a majority of all states shall be necessary to a choice. And if the House of Representatives shall not choose a President whenever the right of choice shall devolve upon them, before the fourth day of March next following, then the Vice-President shall act as President, as in the case of the death or other constitutional disability of the President.—The person having the greatest number of votes as Vice-President, shall be the Vice-President, if such number be a majority of the whole number of Electors appointed, and if no person have a majority, then from the two highest numbers on the list, the Senate shall choose the Vice-President; a quorum for the purpose shall consist of two-thirds of the whole number of Senators, and a majority of the whole number shall be necessary to a choice. But no person constitutionally ineligible to the office of President shall be eligible to that of Vice-President of the United States.

AMENDMENT XIII [1865]

SECTION 1. Neither slavery nor involuntary servitude, except as a punishment for crime whereof the party shall have been duly convicted, shall exist within the United States, or any place subject to their jurisdiction.

SECTION 2. Congress shall have power to enforce this article by appropriate legislation.

AMENDMENT XIV [1868]

SECTION 1. All persons born or naturalized in the United States, and subject to the jurisdiction thereof, are citizens of the United States and of the State wherein they reside. No State shall make or enforce any law which shall abridge the privileges or immunities of citizens of the United States; nor shall any State deprive any person of life, liberty, or property, without due process of law; nor deny to any person within its jurisdiction the equal protection of the laws.

SECTION 2. Representatives shall be apportioned among the several States according to their respective numbers, counting the whole number of persons in each State, excluding Indians not taxed. But when the right to vote at any election for the choice of electors for President and Vice President of the United States, Representatives in Congress, the Executive and Judicial officers of a State, or the members of the Legislature thereof, is denied to any of the male inhabitants of such State, being twenty-one years of age, and citizens of the United States, or in any way abridged, except for participation in rebellion, or other crime, the basis of representation therein shall be reduced in the proportion which the number of such male citizens shall bear to the whole number of male citizens twenty-one years of age in such State.

SECTION 3. No person shall be a Senator or Representative in Congress, or elector of President and Vice President, or hold any office, civil or military, under the United States, or under any State, who having previously taken an oath, as a member of Congress, or as an officer of the United States, or as a member of any State legislature, or as an executive or judicial officer of any State, to support the Constitution of the United States, shall have engaged in insurrection or rebellion against the same, or given aid or comfort to the enemies thereof. But Congress may by a vote of two-thirds of each House, remove such disability.

SECTION 4. The validity of the public debt of the United States, authorized by law, including debts incurred for payment of pensions and bounties for services in suppressing insurrection or rebellion, shall not be questioned. But neither the United States nor any State shall assume or pay any debt or obligation incurred in aid of insurrection or rebellion against the United States, or any claim for the loss or emancipation of any slave; but all such debts, obligations and claims shall be held illegal and void.

SECTION 5. The Congress shall have power to enforce, by appropriate legislation, the provisions of this article.

AMENDMENT XV [1870]

SECTION 1. The right of citizens of the United States to vote shall not be denied or abridged by the United States or by any State on account of race, color, or previous condition of servitude.

SECTION 2. The Congress shall have power to enforce this article by appropriate legislation.

AMENDMENT XVI [1913]

The Congress shall have power to lay and collect taxes on incomes, from whatever source derived, without apportionment among the several States, and without regard to any census or enumeration.

AMENDMENT XVII [1913]

SECTION 1. The Senate of the United States shall be composed of two Senators from each State, elected by the people thereof, for six years; and each Senator shall have one vote. The electors in each State shall have the qualifications requisite for electors of the most numerous branch of the State legislatures.

SECTION 2. When vacancies happen in the representation of any State in the Senate, the executive authority of such State shall issue writs of election to fill such vacancies: Provided, That the legislature of any State may empower the executive thereof to make temporary appointments until the people fill the vacancies by election as the legislature may direct.

SECTION 3. This amendment shall not be so construed as to affect the election or term of any Senator chosen before it becomes valid as part of the Constitution.

AMENDMENT XVIII [1919]

SECTION 1. After one year from the ratification of this article the manufacture, sale, or transportation of intoxicating liquors within, the importation thereof into, or the exportation thereof from the United States and all territory subject to the jurisdiction thereof for beverage purposes is hereby prohibited.

SECTION 2. The Congress and the several States shall have concurrent power to enforce this article by appropriate legislation.

SECTION 3. This article shall be inoperative unless it shall have been ratified as an amendment to the Constitution by the legislatures of the several States, as provided in the Constitution, within seven years from the date of the submission hereof to the States by the Congress.

AMENDMENT XIX [1920]

SECTION 1. The right of citizens of the United States to vote shall not be denied or abridged by the United States or by any State on account of sex.

SECTION 2. Congress shall have power to enforce this article by appropriate legislation.

AMENDMENT XX [1933]

SECTION 1. The terms of the President and Vice President shall end at noon on the 20th day of January, and the terms of Senators and Representatives at noon on the 3d day of January, of the years in which such terms would have ended if this article had not been ratified; and the terms of their successors shall then begin.

SECTION 2. The Congress shall assemble at least once in every year, and such meeting shall begin at noon on the 3d day of January, unless they shall by law appoint a different day.

SECTION 3. If, at the time fixed for the beginning of the term of the President, the President elect shall have died, the Vice President elect shall become President. If the President shall not have been chosen before the time fixed for the beginning of his term, or if the President elect shall have failed to qualify, then the Vice President elect shall act as President until a President shall have qualified; and the Congress may by law provide for the case wherein neither a President elect nor a Vice President elect shall have qualified, declaring who shall then act as President, or the manner in which one who is to act shall be selected, and such person shall act accordingly until a President or Vice President shall have qualified.

SECTION 4. The Congress may by law provide for the case of the death of any of the persons from whom the House of Representatives may choose a President whenever the right of choice shall have devolved upon them, and for the case of the death of any of the persons from whom the Senate may choose a Vice President whenever the right of choice shall have devolved upon them.

SECTION 5. Sections 1 and 2 shall take effect on the 15th day of October following the ratification of this article.

SECTION 6. This article shall be inoperative unless it shall have been ratified as an amendment to the Constitution by the legislatures of three-fourths of the several States within seven years from the date of its submission.

AMENDMENT XXI [1933]

SECTION 1. The eighteenth article of amendment to the Constitution of the United States is hereby repealed.

SECTION 2. The transportation or importation into any State, Territory, or possession of the United States for delivery or use therein of intoxicating liquors, in violation of the laws thereof, is hereby prohibited.

SECTION 3. This article shall be inoperative unless it shall have been ratified as an amendment to the Constitution by conventions in the several States, as provided in the Constitution, within seven years from the date of the submission hereof to the States by the Congress.

AMENDMENT XXII [1951]

SECTION 1. No person shall be elected to the office of the President more than twice, and no person who has held the office of President, or acted as President, for more than two years of a term to which some other person was elected President shall be elected to the office of President more than once. But this Article shall not apply to any person holding the office of President when this Article was proposed by the Congress, and shall not prevent any person who may be holding the office of President, or acting as President, during the term within which this Article becomes operative from holding the office of President or acting as President during the remainder of such term.

SECTION 2. This article shall be inoperative unless it shall have been ratified as an amendment to the Constitution by the legislatures of three-fourths of the several States within seven years from the date of its submission to the States by the Congress.

AMENDMENT XXIII [1961]

SECTION 1. The District constituting the seat of Government of the United States shall appoint in such manner as the Congress may direct:

A number of electors of President and Vice President equal to the whole number of Senators and Representatives in Congress to which the District would be entitled if it were a State, but in no event more than the least populous state; they shall be in addition to those appointed by the states, but they shall be considered, for the purposes of the election of President and Vice President, to be electors appointed by a state; and they shall meet in the District and perform such duties as provided by the twelfth article of amendment.

SECTION 2. The Congress shall have power to enforce this article by appropriate legislation.

AMENDMENT XXIV [1964]

SECTION 1. The right of citizens of the United States to vote in any primary or other election for President or Vice President, for electors for President or Vice President, or for Senator or Representative in Congress, shall not be denied or abridged by the United States, or any State by reason of failure to pay any poll tax or other tax.

SECTION 2. The Congress shall have power to enforce this article by appropriate legislation.

AMENDMENT XXV [1967]

SECTION 1. In case of the removal of the President from office or of his death or resignation, the Vice President shall become President.

SECTION 2. Whenever there is a vacancy in the office of the Vice President, the President shall nominate a Vice President who shall take office upon confirmation by a majority vote of both Houses of Congress.

SECTION 3. Whenever the President transmits to the President pro tempore of the Senate and the Speaker of the House of Representatives his written declaration that he is unable to discharge the powers and duties of his office, and until he transmits to them a written declaration to the contrary, such powers and duties shall be discharged by the Vice President as Acting President.

SECTION 4. Whenever the Vice President and a majority of either the principal officers of the executive departments or of such other body as Congress may by law provide, transmit to the President pro tempore of the Senate and the Speaker of the House of Representatives their written declaration that the President is unable to discharge the powers and duties of his office, the Vice President shall immediately assume the powers and duties of the office as Acting President.

Thereafter, when the President transmits to the President pro tempore of the Senate and the Speaker of the House of Representatives his written declaration that no inability exists, he shall resume the powers and duties of his office unless the Vice President and a majority of either the principal officers of the executive department or of such other body as Congress may by law provide, transmit within four days to the President pro tempore of the Senate and the Speaker of the House of Representatives their written declaration that the President is unable to discharge the powers and duties of his office. Thereupon Congress shall decide the issue, assembling within forty-eight hours for that purpose if not in session. If the Congress, within twenty-one days after receipt of the latter written declaration, or, if Congress is not in session, within twenty-one days after Congress is required to assemble, determines by two-thirds vote of both Houses that the President is unable to discharge the powers and duties of his office, the Vice President shall continue to discharge the same as Acting President; otherwise, the President shall resume the powers and duties of his office.

AMENDMENT XXVI [1971]

SECTION 1. The right of citizens of the United States, who are eighteen years of age or older, to vote shall not be denied or abridged by the United States or by any State on account of age.

SECTION 2. The Congress shall have power to enforce this article by appropriate legislation.

AMENDMENT XXVII [1992]

No law, varying the compensation for the services of the Senators and Representatives, shall take effect, until an election of Representatives shall have intervened.

SUPREME COURT JUSTICES SINCE 1900

Chief Justices

Name	Years of Service	State App'd from	Appointing President	Age App'd	Political Affiliation	Educational Background*
Fuller, Melville Weston	1888–1910	Illinois	Cleveland	55	Democrat	Bowdoin College; studied at Harvard Law School
White, Edward Douglass	1910–1921	Louisiana	Taft	65	Democrat	Mount St. Mary's College; Georgetown College (now University)
Taft, William Howard	1921–1930	Connecticut	Harding	64	Republican	Yale; Cincinnati Law School
Hughes, Charles Evans	1930–1941	New York	Hoover	68	Republican	Colgate University; Brown; Columbia Law School
Stone, Harlan Fiske	1941–1946	New York	Roosevelt, F.	69	Republican	Amherst College; Columbia
Vinson, Frederick Moore	1946–1953	Kentucky	Truman	56	Democrat	Centre College
Warren, Earl	1953–1969	California	Eisenhower	62	Republican	University of California, Berkeley
Burger, Warren Earl	1969–1986	Virginia	Nixon	62	Republican	University of Minnesota; St. Paul College of Law (Mitchell College)
Rehnquist, William Hubbs	1986–2005	Virginia	Reagan	62	Republican	Stanford; Harvard; Stanford University Law School
Roberts, John G., Jr.	2005–present	District of Columbia	G. W. Bush	50	Republican	Harvard; Harvard Law School

*Source: Educational background information derived from Elder Witt, *Guide to the U.S. Supreme Court*, 2d ed. (Washington, D.C.: Congressional Quarterly Press, Inc., 1990). Reprinted with the permission of the publisher.

Associate Justices

Name	Years of Service	State App'd from	Appointing President	Age App'd	Political Affiliation	Educational Background*
Harlan, John Marshall	1877–1911	Kentucky	Hayes	61	Republican	Centre College; studied law at Transylvania University
Gray, Horace	1882–1902	Massachusetts	Arthur	54	Republican	Harvard College; Harvard Law School
Brewer, David Josiah	1890–1910	Kansas	Harrison	53	Republican	Wesleyan University; Yale; Albany Law School
Brown, Henry Billings	1891–1906	Michigan	Harrison	55	Republican	Yale; studied at Yale Law School and Harvard Law School
Shiras, George, Jr.	1892–1903	Pennsylvania	Harrison	61	Republican	Ohio University; Yale; studied law at Yale and privately
White, Edward Douglass	1894–1910	Louisiana	Cleveland	49	Democrat	Mount St. Mary's College; Georgetown College (now University)
Peckham, Rufus Wheeler	1896–1909	New York	Cleveland	58	Democrat	Read law in father's firm

Name	Years of Service	State App'd from	Appointing President	Age App'd	Political Affiliation	Educational Background*
McKenna, Joseph	1898–1925	California	McKinley	55	Republican	Benicia Collegiate Institute, Law Dept.
Holmes, Oliver Wendell, Jr.	1902–1932	Massachusetts	Roosevelt, T.	61	Republican	Harvard College; studied law at Harvard Law School
Day, William Rufus	1903–1922	Ohio	Roosevelt, T.	54	Republican	University of Michigan; University of Michigan Law School
Moody, William Henry	1906–1910	Massachusetts	Roosevelt, T.	53	Republican	Harvard; Harvard Law School
Lurton, Horace Harmon	1910–1914	Tennessee	Taft	66	Democrat	University of Chicago; Cumberland Law School
Hughes, Charles Evans	1910–1916	New York	Taft	48	Republican	Colgate University; Brown University; Columbia Law School
Van Devanter, Willis	1911–1937	Wyoming	Taft	52	Republican	Indiana Asbury University; University of Cincinnati Law School
Lamar, Joseph Rucker	1911–1916	Georgia	Taft	54	Democrat	University of Georgia; Bethany College; Washington and Lee University
Pitney, Mahlon	1912–1922	New Jersey	Taft	54	Republican	College of New Jersey (Princeton); read law under father
McReynolds, James Clark	1914–1941	Tennessee	Wilson	52	Democrat	Vanderbilt University; University of Virginia
Brandeis, Louis Dembitz	1916–1939	Massachusetts	Wilson	60	Democrat	Harvard Law School
Clarke, John Hessin	1916–1922	Ohio	Wilson	59	Democrat	Western Reserve University; read law under father
Sutherland, George	1922–1938	Utah	Harding	60	Republican	Brigham Young Academy; one year at University of Michigan Law School
Butler, Pierce	1923–1939	Minnesota	Harding	57	Democrat	Carleton College
Sanford, Edward Terry	1923–1930	Tennessee	Harding	58	Republican	University of Tennessee; Harvard; Harvard Law School
Stone, Harlan Fiske	1925–1941	New York	Coolidge	53	Republican	Amherst College; Columbia University Law School
Roberts, Owen Josephus	1930–1945	Pennsylvania	Hoover	55	Republican	University of Pennsylvania; University of Pennsylvania Law School
Cardozo, Benjamin Nathan	1932–1938	New York	Hoover	62	Democrat	Columbia University; two years at Columbia Law School
Black, Hugo Lafayette	1937–1971	Alabama	Roosevelt, F.	51	Democrat	Birmingham Medical College; University of Alabama Law School
Reed, Stanley Forman	1938–1957	Kentucky	Roosevelt, F.	54	Democrat	Kentucky Wesleyan University; Foreman Yale; Columbia University
Frankfurter, Felix	1939–1962	Massachusetts	Roosevelt, F.	57	Independent	College of the City of New York; Harvard Law School
Douglas, William Orville	1939–1975	Connecticut	Roosevelt, F.	41	Democrat	Whitman College; Columbia University Law School
Murphy, Frank	1940–1949	Michigan	Roosevelt, F.	50	Democrat	University of Michigan; Lincoln's Inn, London; Trinity College
Byrnes, James Francis	1941–1942	South Carolina	Roosevelt, F.	62	Democrat	Read law privately

Name	Years of Service	State App'd from	Appointing President	Age App'd	Political Affiliation	Educational Background*
Jackson, Robert Houghwout	1941–1954	New York	Roosevelt, F.	49	Democrat	Albany Law School
Rutledge, Wiley Blount	1943–1949	Iowa	Roosevelt, F.	49	Democrat	University of Wisconsin; University of Colorado
Burton, Harold Hitz	1945–1958	Ohio	Truman	57	Republican	Bowdoin College; Harvard University Law School
Clark, Thomas Campbell	1949–1967	Texas	Truman	50	Democrat	University of Texas
Minton, Sherman	1949–1956	Indiana	Truman	59	Democrat	Indiana University College of Law; Yale Law School
Harlan, John Marshall	1955–1971	New York	Eisenhower	56	Republican	Princeton; Oxford University; New York Law School
Brennan, William J., Jr.	1956–1990	New Jersey	Eisenhower	50	Democrat	University of Pennsylvania; Harvard Law School
Whittaker, Charles Evans	1957–1962	Missouri	Eisenhower	56	Republican	University of Kansas City Law School
Stewart, Potter	1958–1981	Ohio	Eisenhower	43	Republican	Yale; Yale Law School
White, Byron Raymond	1962–1993	Colorado	Kennedy	45	Democrat	University of Colorado; Oxford University; Yale Law School
Goldberg, Arthur Joseph	1962–1965	Illinois	Kennedy	54	Democrat	Northwestern University
Fortas, Abe	1965–1969	Tennessee	Johnson, L.	55	Democrat	Southwestern College; Yale Law School
Marshall, Thurgood	1967–1991	New York	Johnson, L.	59	Democrat	Lincoln University; Howard University Law School
Blackmun, Harry A.	1970–1994	Minnesota	Nixon	62	Republican	Harvard; Harvard Law School
Powell, Lewis F., Jr.	1972–1987	Virginia	Nixon	65	Democrat	Washington and Lee University; Harvard Law School
Rehnquist, William H.	1972–1986	Arizona	Nixon	48	Republican	Stanford; Harvard; Stanford University Law School
Stevens, John Paul	1975–present	Illinois	Ford	55	Republican	University of Colorado; Northwestern University Law School
O'Connor, Sandra Day	1981–2006	Arizona	Reagan	51	Republican	Stanford; Stanford University Law School
Scalia, Antonin	1986–present	Virginia	Reagan	50	Republican	Georgetown University; Harvard Law School
Kennedy, Anthony M.	1988–present	California	Reagan	52	Republican	Stanford; London School of Economics; Harvard Law School
Souter, David Hackett	1990–present	New Hampshire	Bush, G. H. W.	51	Republican	Harvard; Oxford University
Thomas, Clarence	1991–present	District of Columbia	Bush, G. H. W.	43	Republican	Holy Cross College; Yale Law Columbia School
Ginsburg, Ruth Bader	1993–present	District of Columbia	Clinton	60	Democrat	Cornell University; Columbia Law School
Breyer, Stephen G.	1994–present	Massachusetts	Clinton	55	Democrat	Stanford; Oxford University; Harvard Law School
Alito, Samuel Anthony, Jr.	2006–present	New Jersey	G. W. Bush	55	Republican	Princeton University; Yale Law School
Sotomayor, Sonia	2009–present	New York	Obama	55	Democrat	Princeton University; Yale Law School
Kagan, Elena	2010–present	District of Columbia	Obama	50	Democrat	Princeton and Oxford Universities; Harvard Law School

Appendix D

PARTY CONTROL OF CONGRESS SINCE 1900

Congress	Years	President	Majority Party in House	Majority Party in Senate
57th	1901–1903	T. Roosevelt	Republican	Republican
58th	1903–1905	T. Roosevelt	Republican	Republican
59th	1905–1907	T. Roosevelt	Republican	Republican
60th	1907–1909	T. Roosevelt	Republican	Republican
61st	1909–1911	Taft	Republican	Republican
62d	1911–1913	Taft	Democratic	Republican
63d	1913–1915	Wilson	Democratic	Democratic
64th	1915–1917	Wilson	Democratic	Democratic
65th	1917–1919	Wilson	Democratic	Democratic
66th	1919–1921	Wilson	Republican	Republican
67th	1921–1923	Harding	Republican	Republican
68th	1923–1925	Coolidge	Republican	Republican
69th	1925–1927	Coolidge	Republican	Republican
70th	1927–1929	Coolidge	Republican	Republican
71st	1929–1931	Hoover	Republican	Republican
72d	1931–1933	Hoover	Democratic	Republican
73d	1933–1935	F. Roosevelt	Democratic	Democratic
74th	1935–1937	F. Roosevelt	Democratic	Democratic
75th	1937–1939	F. Roosevelt	Democratic	Democratic
76th	1939–1941	F. Roosevelt	Democratic	Democratic
77th	1941–1943	F. Roosevelt	Democratic	Democratic
78th	1943–1945	F. Roosevelt	Democratic	Democratic
79th	1945–1947	Truman	Democratic	Democratic
80th	1947–1949	Truman	Republican	Democratic
81st	1949–1951	Truman	Democratic	Democratic
82d	1951–1953	Truman	Democratic	Democratic
83d	1953–1955	Eisenhower	Republican	Republican
84th	1955–1957	Eisenhower	Democratic	Democratic
85th	1957–1959	Eisenhower	Democratic	Democratic
86th	1959–1961	Eisenhower	Democratic	Democratic
87th	1961–1963	Kennedy	Democratic	Democratic
88th	1963–1965	Kennedy/Johnson	Democratic	Democratic
89th	1965–1967	Johnson	Democratic	Democratic
90th	1967–1969	Johnson	Democratic	Democratic
91st	1969–1971	Nixon	Democratic	Democratic
92d	1971–1973	Nixon	Democratic	Democratic
93d	1973–1975	Nixon/Ford	Democratic	Democratic
94th	1975–1977	Ford	Democratic	Democratic
95th	1977–1979	Carter	Democratic	Democratic
96th	1979–1981	Carter	Democratic	Democratic
97th	1981–1983	Reagan	Democratic	Republican
98th	1983–1985	Reagan	Democratic	Republican
99th	1985–1987	Reagan	Democratic	Republican
100th	1987–1989	Reagan	Democratic	Democratic
101st	1989–1991	G. H. W. Bush	Democratic	Democratic
102d	1991–1993	G. H. W. Bush	Democratic	Democratic
103d	1993–1995	Clinton	Democratic	Democratic
104th	1995–1997	Clinton	Republican	Republican
105th	1997–1999	Clinton	Republican	Republican
106th	1999–2001	Clinton	Republican	Republican
107th	2001–2003	G. W. Bush	Republican	Democratic
108th	2003–2005	G. W. Bush	Republican	Republican
109th	2005–2007	G. W. Bush	Republican	Republican
110th	2007–2009	G. W. Bush	Democratic	Democratic
111th	2009–2011	Obama	Democratic	Democratic
112th	2011–2013	Obama	Republican	Democratic

INFORMATION ON U.S. PRESIDENTS

	Term of Service	Age at Inauguration	Party Affiliation	College or University	Occupation or Profession
1. George Washington	1789–1797	57	None		Planter
2. John Adams	1797–1801	61	Federalist	Harvard	Lawyer
3. Thomas Jefferson	1801–1809	57	Democratic-Republican	William and Mary	Planter, Lawyer
4. James Madison	1809–1817	57	Democratic-Republican	Princeton	Lawyer
5. James Monroe	1817–1825	58	Democratic-Republican	William and Mary	Lawyer
6. John Quincy Adams	1825–1829	57	Democratic-Republican	Harvard	Lawyer
7. Andrew Jackson	1829–1837	61	Democrat		Lawyer
8. Martin Van Buren	1837–1841	54	Democrat		Lawyer
9. William H. Harrison	1841	68	Whig	Hampden-Sydney	Soldier
10. John Tyler	1841–1845	51	Whig	William and Mary	Lawyer
11. James K. Polk	1845–1849	49	Democrat	U. of N. Carolina	Lawyer
12. Zachary Taylor	1849–1850	64	Whig		Soldier
13. Millard Fillmore	1850–1853	50	Whig		Lawyer
14. Franklin Pierce	1853–1857	48	Democrat	Bowdoin	Lawyer
15. James Buchanan	1857–1861	65	Democrat	Dickinson	Lawyer
16. Abraham Lincoln	1861–1865	52	Republican		Lawyer
17. Andrew Johnson	1865–1869	56	National Union†		Tailor
18. Ulysses S. Grant	1869–1877	46	Republican	U.S. Mil. Academy	Soldier
19. Rutherford B. Hayes	1877–1881	54	Republican	Kenyon	Lawyer
20. James A. Garfield	1881	49	Republican	Williams	Lawyer
21. Chester A. Arthur	1881–1885	51	Republican	Union	Lawyer
22. Grover Cleveland	1885–1889	47	Democrat		Lawyer
23. Benjamin Harrison	1889–1893	55	Republican	Miami	Lawyer
24. Grover Cleveland	1893–1897	55	Democrat		Lawyer
25. William McKinley	1897–1901	54	Republican	Allegheny College	Lawyer
26. Theodore Roosevelt	1901–1909	42	Republican	Harvard	Author
27. William H. Taft	1909–1913	51	Republican	Yale	Lawyer
28. Woodrow Wilson	1913–1921	56	Democrat	Princeton	Educator
29. Warren G. Harding	1921–1923	55	Republican		Editor
30. Calvin Coolidge	1923–1929	51	Republican	Amherst	Lawyer
31. Herbert C. Hoover	1929–1933	54	Republican	Stanford	Engineer
32. Franklin D. Roosevelt	1933–1945	51	Democrat	Harvard	Lawyer
33. Harry S Truman	1945–1953	60	Democrat		Businessman
34. Dwight D. Eisenhower	1953–1961	62	Republican	U.S. Mil. Academy	Soldier
35. John F. Kennedy	1961–1963	43	Democrat	Harvard	Author
36. Lyndon B. Johnson	1963–1969	55	Democrat	Southwest Texas State	Teacher
37. Richard M. Nixon	1969–1974	56	Republican	Whittier	Lawyer
38. Gerald R. Ford‡	1974–1977	61	Republican	Michigan	Lawyer
39. James E. Carter, Jr.	1977–1981	52	Democrat	U.S. Naval Academy	Businessman
40. Ronald W. Reagan	1981–1989	69	Republican	Eureka College	Actor
41. George H. W. Bush	1989–1993	64	Republican	Yale	Businessman
42. William J. Clinton	1993–2001	46	Democrat	Georgetown	Lawyer
43. George W. Bush	2001–2009	54	Republican	Yale	Businessman
44. Barack Obama	2009–	47	Democrat	Columbia	Lawyer

*Church preference; never joined any church.

†The National Union Party consisted of Republicans and War Democrats. Johnson was a Democrat.

**Inaugurated Dec. 6, 1973, to replace Agnew, who resigned Oct. 10, 1973.

‡Inaugurated Aug. 9, 1974, to replace Nixon, who resigned that same day.

§Inaugurated Dec. 19, 1974, to replace Ford, who became president Aug. 9, 1974.

Religion	Born	Died	Age at Death	Vice President	
1. Episcopalian	Feb. 22, 1732	Dec. 14, 1799	67	John Adams	(1789–1797)
2. Unitarian	Oct. 30, 1735	July 4, 1826	90	Thomas Jefferson	(1797–1801)
3. Unitarian*	Apr. 13, 1743	July 4, 1826	83	Aaron Burr	(1801–1805)
				George Clinton	(1805–1809)
4. Episcopalian	Mar. 16, 1751	June 28, 1836	85	George Clinton	(1809–1812)
				Elbridge Gerry	(1813–1814)
5. Episcopalian	Apr. 28, 1758	July 4, 1831	73	Daniel D. Tompkins	(1817–1825)
6. Unitarian	July 11, 1767	Feb. 23, 1848	80	John C. Calhoun	(1825–1829)
7. Presbyterian	Mar. 15, 1767	June 8, 1845	78	John C. Calhoun	(1829–1832)
				Martin Van Buren	(1833–1837)
8. Dutch Reformed	Dec. 5, 1782	July 24, 1862	79	Richard M. Johnson	(1837–1841)
9. Episcopalian	Feb. 9, 1773	Apr. 4, 1841	68	John Tyler	(1841)
10. Episcopalian	Mar. 29, 1790	Jan. 18, 1862	71		
11. Methodist	Nov. 2, 1795	June 15, 1849	53	George M. Dallas	(1845–1849)
12. Episcopalian	Nov. 24, 1784	July 9, 1850	65	Millard Fillmore	(1849–1850)
13. Unitarian	Jan. 7, 1800	Mar. 8, 1874	74		
14. Episcopalian	Nov. 23, 1804	Oct. 8, 1869	64	William R. King	(1853)
15. Presbyterian	Apr. 23, 1791	June 1, 1868	77	John C. Breckinridge	(1857–1861)
16. Presbyterian*	Feb. 12, 1809	Apr. 15, 1865	56	Hannibal Hamlin	(1861–1865)
				Andrew Johnson	(1865)
17. Methodist*	Dec. 29, 1808	July 31, 1875	66		
18. Methodist	Apr. 27, 1822	July 23, 1885	63	Schuyler Colfax	(1869–1873)
				Henry Wilson	(1873–1875)
19. Methodist*	Oct. 4, 1822	Jan. 17, 1893	70	William A. Wheeler	(1877–1881)
20. Disciples of Christ	Nov. 19, 1831	Sept. 19, 1881	49	Chester A. Arthur	(1881)
21. Episcopalian	Oct. 5, 1829	Nov. 18, 1886	57		
22. Presbyterian	Mar. 18, 1837	June 24, 1908	71	Thomas A. Hendricks	(1885)
23. Presbyterian	Aug. 20, 1833	Mar. 13, 1901	67	Levi P. Morton	(1889–1893)
24. Presbyterian	Mar. 18, 1837	June 24, 1908	71	Adlai E. Stevenson	(1893–1897)
25. Methodist	Jan. 29, 1843	Sept. 14, 1901	58	Garret A. Hobart	(1897–1899)
				Theodore Roosevelt	(1901)
26. Dutch Reformed	Oct. 27, 1858	Jan. 6, 1919	60	Charles W. Fairbanks	(1905–1909)
27. Unitarian	Sept. 15, 1857	Mar. 8, 1930	72	James S. Sherman	(1909–1912)
28. Presbyterian	Dec. 29, 1856	Feb. 3, 1924	67	Thomas R. Marshall	(1913–1921)
29. Baptist	Nov. 2, 1865	Aug. 2, 1923	57	Calvin Coolidge	(1921–1923)
30. Congregationalist	July 4, 1872	Jan. 5, 1933	60	Charles G. Dawes	(1925–1929)
31. Friend (Quaker)	Aug. 10, 1874	Oct. 20, 1964	90	Charles Curtis	(1929–1933)
32. Episcopalian	Jan. 30, 1882	Apr. 12, 1945	63	John N. Garner	(1933–1941)
				Henry A. Wallace	(1941–1945)
				Harry S Truman	(1945)
33. Baptist	May 8, 1884	Dec. 26, 1972	88	Alben W. Barkley	(1949–1953)
34. Presbyterian	Oct. 14, 1890	Mar. 28, 1969	78	Richard M. Nixon	(1953–1961)
35. Roman Catholic	May 29, 1917	Nov. 22, 1963	46	Lyndon B. Johnson	(1961–1963)
36. Disciples of Christ	Aug. 27, 1908	Jan. 22, 1973	64	Hubert H. Humphrey	(1965–1969)
37. Friend (Quaker)	Jan. 9, 1913	Apr. 22, 1994	81	Spiro T. Agnew	(1969–1973)
				Gerald R. Ford**	(1973–1974)
38. Episcopalian	July 14, 1913	Dec. 26, 2006	93	Nelson A. Rockefeller§	(1974–1977)
39. Baptist	Oct. 1, 1924			Walter F. Mondale	(1977–1981)
40. Disciples of Christ	Feb. 6, 1911	June 5, 2004	93	George H. W. Bush	(1981–1989)
41. Episcopalian	June 12, 1924			J. Danforth Quayle	(1989–1993)
42. Baptist	Aug. 19, 1946			Albert A. Gore	(1993–2001)
43. Methodist	July 6, 1946			Dick Cheney	(2001–2009)
44. United Church of Christ	August 4, 1961			Joe Biden	(2009–)

FEDERALIST PAPERS NO. 10 AND NO. 51

The founders completed drafting the U.S. Constitution in 1787. It was then submitted to the thirteen states for ratification, and a major debate ensued. As you read in Chapter 2, on the one side of this debate were the Federalists, who urged that the new Constitution be adopted. On the other side of the debate were the Anti-Federalists, who argued against ratification.

During the course of this debate, three men well known for their Federalist views—Alexander Hamilton, James Madison, and John Jay—wrote a series of essays in which they argued for immediate ratifcation of the Constitution. The essays appeared in the New York City Independent Journal *in October 1787, just a little over a month after the Constitutional Convention adjourned. Later, Hamilton arranged to have the essays collected and published in book form. The articles filled two volumes, both of which were published by May 1788. The essays are often referred to collectively as the* Federalist Papers.

Scholars disagree as to whether the Federalist Papers *had a significant impact on the decision of the states to ratify the Constitution. Nonetheless, many of the essays are masterpieces of political reasoning and have left a lasting imprint on American politics and government. Above all, the* Federalist Papers *shed an important light on what the founders intended when they drafted various constitutional provisions.*

Here we present just two of these essays, Federalist Paper No. 10 *and* Federalist Paper No. 51. *Each essay was written by James Madison, who referred to himself as "Publius." We have annotated each document to clarify the meaning of particular passages. The annotations are set in italics to distinguish them from the original text of the documents.*

#10

Federalist Paper No. 10 is a classic document that is often referred to by teachers of American government. Authored by James Madison, it sets forth Madison's views on factions in politics. The essay was written, in large part, to counter the arguments put forth by the Anti-Federalists that small factions might take control of the government, thus destroying the representative nature of the republican form of government established by the Constitution. The essay opens with a discussion of the "dangerous vice" of factions and the importance of devising a form of government in which this vice will be controlled.

Among the numerous advantages promised by a well-constructed Union, none deserves to be more accurately developed than its tendency to break and control the violence of faction. The friend of popular governments never finds himself so much alarmed for their character and fate as when he contemplates their propensity to this dangerous vice. He will not fail, therefore, to set a due value on any plan which, without violating the principles to which he is attached, provides a proper cure for it. The instability, injustice, and confusion introduced into the public councils have, in truth, been the mortal diseases under which popular governments have everywhere perished, as they continue to be the favorite and fruitful topics from which the adversaries to liberty derive their most specious declamations. The valuable improvements made by the American constitutions on the popular models, both ancient and modern, cannot certainly be too much admired; but it would be an unwarrantable partiality to contend that they have as effectually obviated the danger on this side, as was wished and expected. Complaints are everywhere heard from our most considerate and virtuous citizens, equally the friends of public and private faith and of public and personal liberty, that our governments are too unstable, that the public good is disregarded in the conflicts of rival parties, and that measures are too often decided, not according to the rules of justice and the rights of the minor party, but by the superior force of an interested and overbearing majority. However anxiously we may wish that these complaints had no foundation, the evidence of known facts will not permit us to deny that they are in some degree true. It will be found, indeed, on a candid review of our situation, that some of the distresses under which we labor have been erroneously charged on the operation of our governments; but it will be found, at the same time, that other causes will not alone account for many of our heaviest misfortunes; and, particularly, for that prevailing and increasing distrust of public engagements and alarm for private rights which are echoed from one end of the continent to the other. These must be chiefly, if not wholly, effects of the unsteadiness and injustice with which a factious spirit has tainted our public administration.

In the following paragraph, Madison clarifies for his readers his understanding of what the term faction *means.*

By a faction I understand a number of citizens, whether amounting to a majority or minority of the whole, who are united and actuated by some common impulse of passion, or of interest, adverse to the rights of other citizens, or the permanent and aggregate interests of the community.

In the following passages, Madison looks at the two methods of curing the "mischiefs of factions." One of these methods is removing the causes of faction. The other is to control the effects of factions.

There are two methods of curing the mischiefs of faction: the one, by removing its causes; the other, by controlling its effects.

There are again two methods of removing the causes of faction: the one, by destroying the liberty which is essential to its existence; the other, by giving to every citizen the same opinions, the same passions, and the same interests.

It could never be more truly said than of the first remedy that it was worse than the disease. Liberty is to faction what air is to fire, an aliment without which it instantly expires. But it could not be a less folly to abolish liberty, which is essential to political life, because it nourishes faction than it would be to wish the annihilation of air, which is essential to animal life, because it imparts to fire its destructive agency.

The second expedient is as impracticable as the first would be unwise. As long as the reason of man continues fallible, and his is at liberty to exercise it, different opinions will be formed. As long as the connection subsists between his reason and his self-love, his opinions and his passions will have a reciprocal influence on each other; and the former will be objects to which the latter will attach themselves. The diversity in the faculties of men, from which the rights of property originate, is not less an insuperable obstacle to a uniformity of interests.

The protection of these faculties is the first object of government. From the protection of different and unequal faculties of acquiring property, the possession of different degrees and kinds of property immediately results; and from the influence of these on the sentiments and views of the respective proprietors ensues a division of the society into different interests and parties.

The latent causes of faction are thus sown in the nature of man; and we see them everywhere brought into different degrees of activity, according to the different circumstances of civil society. A zeal for different opinions concerning religion, concerning government, and many other points, as well of speculation as of practice; an attachment to different leaders ambitiously contending for pre-eminence and power; or to persons of other descriptions whose fortunes have been interesting to the human passions, have, in turn, divided mankind into parties, inflamed them with mutual animosity, and rendered them much more disposed to vex and oppress each other than to co-operate for their common good. So strong is this propensity of mankind to fall into mutual animosities that where no substantial occasion presents itself the most frivolous and fanciful distinctions have been sufficient to kindle their unfriendly passions and excite their most violent conflicts. But the most common and durable source of factions has been the various and unequal distribution of property. Those who hold and those who are without property have ever formed distinct interests in society. Those who are creditors, and those who are debtors, fall under a like discrimination. A landed interest, a manufacturing interest, a mercantile interest, a moneyed interest, with many lesser interests, grow up of necessity in civilized nations, and divide them into different classes, actuated by different sentiments and views. The regulation of these various and interfering interests forms the principal task of modern legislation and involves the spirit of party and faction in the necessary and ordinary operations of government.

No man is allowed to be a judge in his own cause, because his interest would certainly bias his judgment, and, not improbably, corrupt his integrity. With equal, nay with greater reason, a body of men are unfit to be both judges and parties at the same time; yet what are many of the most important acts of legislation but so many judicial determinations, not indeed concerning the rights of single persons, but concerning the rights of large bodies of citizens? And what are the different classes of legislators but advocates and parties to the causes which they determine? Is a law proposed concerning private debts? It is a question to which the creditors are parties on one side and the debtors on the other. Justice ought to hold the balance between them. Yet the parties are, and must be, themselves the judges; and the most numerous party, or in other words, the most powerful faction must be expected to prevail. Shall domestic manufacturers be encouraged, and in what degree, by restrictions on foreign manufacturers? Are questions which would be differently decided by the landed and the manufacturing classes, and probably by neither with a sole regard to justice and the public good. The apportionment of taxes on the various descriptions of property is an act which seems to require the most exact impartiality; yet there is, perhaps, no legislative act in which greater opportunity and temptation are given to a predominant party to trample on the rules of justice. Every shilling with which they overburden the inferior number is a shilling saved to their own pockets.

It is in vain to say that enlightened statesmen will be able to adjust these clashing interests and render them all subservient to the public good. Enlightened statesmen will not always be at the helm. Nor, in many cases, can such an adjustment be made at all without taking into view indirect and remote considerations, which will rarely prevail over the immediate interest which one party may find in disregarding the rights of another or the good of the whole.

The inference to which we are brought is that the causes of faction cannot be removed and that relief is only to be sought in the means of controlling its effects.

In the preceding passages, Madison has explored the causes of factions and has concluded that they cannot "be removed" without removing liberty itself, which is one of the causes, or altering human nature. He now turns to a discussion of how the effects of factions might be controlled.

If a faction consists of less than a majority, relief is supplied by the republican principle, which enables the majority to defeat its sinister views by regular vote. It may clog the administration, it may convulse the society; but it will be unable to execute and mask its violence under the forms of the Constitution. When a majority is included in a faction, the form of popular government, on the other hand, enables it to sacrifice to its ruling passion or interest both the public good and the rights of other citizens. To secure the public good and private rights against the danger of such a faction, and at the same time to preserve the spirit and the form of popular government, is then the great object to which our inquiries are directed. Let me add that it is the great desideratum by which alone this form of government

can be rescued from the opprobrium under which it has so long labored and be recommended to the esteem and adoption of mankind.

According to Madison, one way of controlling the effects of factions is to make sure that the majority is not able to act in "concert," or jointly, to "carry into effect schemes of oppression."

By what means is this object attainable? Evidently by one of two only. Either the existence of the same passion or interest in a majority at the same time must be prevented, or the majority, having such coexistent passion or interest, must be rendered, by their number and local situation, unable to concert and carry into effect schemes of oppression. If the impulse and the opportunity be suffered to coincide, we well know that neither moral nor religious motives can be relied on as an adequate control. They are not found to be such on the injustice and violence of individuals, and lose their efficacy in proportion to the number combined together, that is, in proportion as their efficacy becomes needful.

From this view of the subject it may be concluded that a pure democracy, by which I mean a society consisting of a small number of citizens, who assemble and administer the government in person, can admit of no cure for the mischiefs of faction. A common passion or interest will, in almost every case, be felt by a majority of the whole; a communication and concert results from the form of government itself; and there is nothing to check the inducements to sacrifice the weaker party or an obnoxious individual. Hence it is that such democracies have ever been spectacles of turbulence and contention; have ever been found incompatible with personal security or the rights of property; and have in general been as short in their lives as they have been violent in their deaths. Theoretic politicians, who have patronized this species of government, have erroneously supposed that by reducing mankind to a perfect equality in their political rights, they would at the same time be perfectly equalized and assimilated in their possessions, their opinions, and their passions.

In the following six paragraphs, Madison sets forth some of the reasons why a republican form of government promises a "cure" for the mischiefs of factions. He begins by clarifying the difference between a republic and a democracy. He then describes how in a large republic, the elected representatives of the people will be large enough in number to guard against factions— the "cabals," or concerted actions, of "a few." On the one hand, representatives will not be so removed from their local districts as to be unacquainted with their constituents' needs. On the other hand, they will not be "unduly attached" to local interests and unfit to understand "great and national objects." Madison concludes that the Constitution "forms a happy combination in this respect."

A republic, by which I mean a government in which the scheme of representation takes place, opens a different prospect and promises the cure for which we are seeking. Let us examine the points in which it varies from pure democracy, and we shall comprehend both the nature of the cure and the efficacy which it must derive from the Union.

The two great points of difference between a democracy and a republic are: first, the delegation of the government, in the latter, to a small number of citizens elected by the rest; secondly, the greater number of citizens and greater sphere of country over which the latter may be extended.

The effect of the first difference is, on the one hand, to refine and enlarge the public views by passing them through the medium of a chosen body of citizens, whose wisdom may best discern the true interest of their country and whose patriotism and love of justice will be least likely to sacrifice it to temporary or partial considerations. Under such a regulation it may well happen that the public voice, pronounced by the representatives of the people, will be more consonant to the public good than if pronounced by the people themselves, convened for the purpose. On the other hand, the effect may be inverted. Men of factious tempers, of local prejudices, or of sinister designs, may, by intrigue, by corruption, or by other means, first obtain the suffrages, and then betray the interests of the people. The question resulting is, whether small or extensive republics are most favorable to the election of proper guardians of the public weal; and it is clearly decided in favor of the latter by two obvious considerations.

In the first place it is to be remarked that however small the republic may be the representatives must be raised to a certain number in order to guard against the cabals of a few; and that however large it may be they must be limited to a certain number in order to guard against the confusion of a multitude. Hence, the number of representatives in the two cases not being in proportion to that of the constituents, and being proportionally greatest in the small republic, it follows that if the proportion of fit characters be not less in the large than in the small republic, the former will present a greater option, and consequently a greater probability of a fit choice.

In the next place, as each representative will be chosen by a greater number of citizens in the large than in the small republic, it will be more difficult for unworthy candidates to practice with success the vicious arts by which elections are too often carried; and the suffrages of the people being more free, will be more likely to center on men who possess the most attractive merit and the most diffusive and established characters.

It must be confessed that in this, as in most other cases, there is a mean, on both sides of which inconveniencies will be found to lie. By enlarging too much the number of electors, you render the representative too little acquainted with all their local circumstances and lesser interests; as by reducing it too much, you render him unduly attached to these, and too little fit to comprehend and pursue great and national objects. The federal Constitution forms a happy combination in this respect; the great and aggregate interests being referred to the national, the local and particular to the State legislatures.

In the remaining passages of this essay, Madison looks at another "point of difference" between a republic and a democracy. Specifically, a republic can encompass a larger territory and a greater number of citizens than a democracy can. This fact, too, argues Madison, will help to control the influence of factions because the interests that draw people together to act in concert are typically at the local level and would be unlikely to affect or dominate the national government. As Madison states, "The influence of factious leaders may kindle a flame within their particular States but will be unable to spread a general conflagration through the other States." Generally, in a large republic, there will be numerous factions, and no particular faction will be able to "pervade the whole body of the Union."

The other point of difference is the greater number of citizens and extent of territory which may be brought within the compass of republican than of democratic government; and it is this circumstance principally which renders factious combinations less to be dreaded in the former than in the latter. The smaller the society, the fewer probably will be the distinct parties and interests composing it; the fewer the distinct parties and interests, the more frequently will a majority be found of the same party; and the smaller the number of individuals composing a majority, and the smaller the compass within which they are placed, the more easily will they concert and execute their plans of oppression. Extend the sphere and you take in a greater variety of parties and interests; you make it less probable that a majority of the whole will have a common motive to invade the rights of other citizens; or if such a common motive exists, it will be more difficult for all who feel it to discover their own strength and to act in unison with each other. Besides other impediments, it may be remarked that, where there is a consciousness of unjust or dishonorable purposes, communication is always checked by distrust in proportion to the number whose concurrence is necessary.

Hence, it clearly appears that the same advantage which a republic has over a democracy in controlling the effects of faction is enjoyed by a large over a small republic—is enjoyed by the Union over the States composing it. Does this advantage consist in the substitution of representatives whose enlightened views and virtuous sentiments render them superior to local prejudices and to schemes of injustice? It will not be denied that the representation of the Union will be most likely to possess these requisite endowments. Does it consist in the greater security afforded by a greater variety of parties, against the event of any one party being able to outnumber and oppress the rest? In an equal degree does the increased variety of parties comprised within the Union increase this security. Does it, in fine, consist in the greater obstacles opposed to the concert and accomplishment of the secret wishes of an unjust and interested majority? Here again the extent of the Union gives it the most palpable advantage.

The influence of factious leaders may kindle a flame within their particular States but will be unable to spread a general conflagration through the other States. A religious sect may degenerate into a political faction in a part of the Confederacy; but the variety of sects dispersed over the entire face of it must secure the national councils against any danger from that source. A rage for paper money, for an abolition of debts, for an equal division of property, or for any other improper or wicked project, will be less apt to pervade the whole body of the Union than a particular member of it, in the same proportion as such a malady is more likely to taint a particular county or district than an entire State.

In the extent and proper structure of the Union, therefore, we behold a republican remedy for the diseases most incident to republican government. And according to the degree of pleasure and pride we feel in being republicans ought to be our zeal in cherishing the spirit and supporting the character of federalists.

Publius
(James Madison)

#51

Federalist Paper No. 51, *which was also authored by James Madison, is one of the classics in American political theory. Recall from Chapter 2 that a major concern of the founders was to create a relatively strong national government but one that would not be capable of tyrannizing over the populace. In the following essay, Madison sets forth the theory of "checks and balances." He explains that the new Constitution, by dividing the national government into three branches (executive, legislative, and judicial), offers protection against tyranny.*

To what expedient, then, shall we finally resort, for maintaining in practice the necessary partition of power among the several departments as laid down in the Constitution? The only answer that can be given is that as all these exterior provisions are found to be inadequate the defect must be supplied, by so contriving the interior structure of the government as that its several constituent parts may, by their mutual relations, be the means of keeping each other in their proper places. Without presuming to undertake a full development of this important idea I will hazard a few general observations which may perhaps place it in a clearer light, and enable us to form a more correct judgment of the principles and structure of the government planned by the convention.

In the following two paragraphs, Madison explains that to ensure that the powers of government are genuinely separated, it is important that each of the three branches of government (executive, legislative, and judicial) should have a "will of its own." Among other things, this means that persons in one branch should not depend on persons in another branch for the "emoluments annexed to their offices" (pay, perks, and privileges). If they did, then the branches would not be truly independent of one another.

In order to lay a due foundation for that separate and distinct exercise of the different powers of government, which to a certain extent is admitted on all hands to be essential to the preservation of liberty, it is evident that each department should have a will of its own; and consequently should be so constituted that the members of each should have as little agency as possible in the appointment of the members of the others. Were this principle rigorously adhered to, it would require that all the appointments for the supreme executive, legislative, and judiciary magistracies should be drawn from the same fountain of authority, the people, through channels having no communication whatever with one another. Perhaps such a plan of constructing the several departments would be less difficult in practice than it may in contemplation appear. Some difficulties, however, and some additional expense would attend the execution of it. Some deviations, therefore, from the principle must be admitted. In the constitution of the judiciary department in particular, it might be inexpedient to insist rigorously on the principle: first, because peculiar qualifications being essential in the members, the primary consideration ought to be to select that mode of choice which best secures these qualifications; second, because the permanent tenure by which the appointments are held in that department must soon destroy all sense of dependence on the authority conferring them.

It is equally evident that the members of each department should be as little dependent as possible on those of the others for the emoluments annexed to their offices. Were the executive magistrate, or the judges, not independent of the legislature in this particular, their independence in every other would be merely nominal.

One of the striking qualities of the theory of checks and balances as posited by Madison is that it assumes that persons are not angels but driven by personal interests and motives. In the following two paragraphs, which are among the most widely quoted of Madison's writings, he stresses that the division of the government into three branches helps to check personal ambitions. Personal ambitions will naturally arise, but they will be linked to the constitutional powers of each branch. In effect, they will help to keep the three branches separate and thus serve the public interest.

But the great security against a gradual concentration of the several powers in the same department consists in giving to those who administer each department the necessary constitutional means and personal motives to resist encroachments of the others. The provision for defense must in this, as in all other cases, be made commensurate to the danger of attack. Ambition must be made to counteract ambition. The interest of the man must be connected with the constitutional rights of the place. It may be a reflection on human nature that such devices should be necessary to control the abuses of government. But what is government itself but the greatest of all reflections on human nature? If men were angels, no government would be necessary. If angels were to govern men, neither external nor internal controls on government would be necessary. In framing a government which is to be administered by men over men, the great difficulty lies in this: you must first enable the government to control the governed; and in the next place oblige it to control itself. A dependence on the people is, no doubt, the primary control on the government; but experience has taught mankind the necessity of auxiliary precautions.

This policy of supplying, by opposite and rival interests, the defect of better motives, might be traced through the whole system of human affairs, private as well as public. We see it particularly displayed in all the subordinate distributions of power, where the constant aim is to divide and arrange the several offices in such a manner as that each may be a check on the other—that the private interest of every individual may be a sentinel over the public rights. These inventions of prudence cannot be less requisite in the distribution of the supreme powers of the State.

In the next two paragraphs, Madison first points out that the "legislative authority necessarily predominates" in a republican form of government. The "remedy" for this lack of balance with the other branches of government is to divide the legislative branch into two chambers with "different modes of election and different principles of action."

But it is not possible to give to each department an equal power of self-defense. In republican government, the legislative authority necessarily predominates. The remedy for this inconveniency is to divide the legislature into different branches; and to render them, by different modes of election and different principles of action, as little connected with each other as the nature of their common functions and their common dependence on the society will admit. It may even be necessary to guard against dangerous encroachments by still further precautions. As the weight of the legislative authority requires that it should be thus divided, the weakness of the executive may require, on the other hand, that it should be fortified. An absolute negative on the legislature appears, at first view, to be the natural defense with which the executive magistrate should be armed. But perhaps it would be neither altogether safe nor alone sufficient. On ordinary occasions it might not be exerted with the requisite firmness, and on extraordinary occasions it might be perfidiously abused. May not this defect of an absolute negative be supplied by some qualified connection between this weaker department and the weaker branch of the stronger department, by which the latter may be led to support the constitutional rights of the former, without being too much detached from the rights of its own department?

If the principles on which these observations are founded be just, as I persuade myself they are, and they be applied as a criterion to the several State constitutions, and to the federal Constitution, it will be found that if the latter does not perfectly correspond with them, the former are infinitely less able to bear such a test.

In the remaining passages of this essay, Madison discusses the importance of the division of government powers between the states and the national government.

This division of powers, by providing additional checks and balances, offers a "double security" against tyranny.

There are, moreover, two considerations particularly applicable to the federal system of America, which place that system in a very interesting point of view.

First. In a single republic, all the power surrendered by the people is submitted to the administration of a single government; and the usurpations are guarded against by a division of the government into distinct and separate departments. In the compound republic of America, the power surrendered by the people is first divided between two distinct governments, and then the portion allotted to each subdivided among distinct and separate departments. Hence a double security arises to the rights of the people. The different governments will control each other, at the same time that each will be controlled by itself.

Second. It is of great importance in a republic not only to guard the society against the oppression of its rulers, but to guard one part of the society against the injustice of the other part. Different interests necessarily exist in different classes of citizens. If a majority be united by a common interest, the rights of the minority will be insecure. There are but two methods of providing against this evil: the one by creating a will in the community independent of the majority—that is, of the society itself; the other, by comprehending in the society so many separate descriptions of citizens as will render an unjust combination of a majority of the whole very improbable, if not impracticable. The first method prevails in all governments possessing an hereditary or self-appointed authority. This, at best, is but a precarious security; because a power independent of the society may as well espouse the unjust views of the major as the rightful interests of the minor party, and may possibly be turned against both parties. The second method will be exemplified in the federal republic of the United States. Whilst all authority in it will be derived from and dependent on the society, the society itself will be broken into so many parts, interests and classes of citizens, that the rights of individuals, or of the minority, will be in little danger from interested combinations of the majority. In a free government the security for civil rights must be the same as that for religious rights. It consists in the one case in the multiplicity of interests, and in the other in the multiplicity of sects. The degree of security in both cases will depend on the number of interests and sects; and this may be presumed to depend on the extent of country and number of people comprehended under the same government. This view of the subject must particularly recommend a proper federal system to all the sincere and considerate friends of republican government, since it shows that in exact proportion as the territory of the Union may be formed into more circumscribed Confederacies, or States, oppressive combinations of a majority will be facilitated; the best security, under the republican forms, for the rights of every class of citizen, will be diminished; and consequently the stability and independence of some member of the government, the only other security, must be proportionally increased. Justice is the end of government. It is the end of civil society. It ever has been and ever will be pursued until it be obtained, or until liberty be lost in the pursuit. In a society under the forms of which the stronger faction can readily unite and oppress the weaker, anarchy may as truly be said to reign as in a state of nature, where the weaker individual is not secured against the violence of the stronger; and as, in the latter state, even the stronger individuals are prompted, by the uncertainty of their condition, to submit to a government which may protect the weak as well as themselves; so, in the former state, will the more powerful factions or parties be gradually induced, by a like motive, to wish for a government which will protect all parties, the weaker as well as the more powerful. It can be little doubted that if the State of Rhode Island was separated from the Confederacy and left to itself, the insecurity of rights under the popular form of government within such narrow limits would be displayed by such reiterated oppressions of factious majorities that some power altogether independent of the people would soon be called for by the voice of the very factions whose misrule had proved the necessity of it. In the extended republic of the United States, and among the great variety of interests, parties, and sects which it embraces, a coalition of a majority of the whole society could seldom take place on any other principles than those of justice and the general good; whilst there being thus less danger to a minor from the will of a major party, there must be less pretext, also, to provide for the security of the former, by introducing into the government a will not dependent on the latter, or, in other words, a will independent of the society itself. It is no less certain than it is important, notwithstanding the contrary opinions which have been entertained, that the larger the society, provided it lie within a practicable sphere, the more duly capable it will be of self-government. And happily for the *republican cause,* the practicable sphere may be carried to a very great extent by a judicious modification and mixture of the *federal principle.*

Publius
(James Madison)

Appendix G

HOW TO READ CASE CITATIONS AND FIND COURT DECISIONS

Many important court cases are discussed in references in endnotes throughout this book. Court decisions are recorded and published. When a court case is mentioned, the notation that is used to refer to, or to cite, the case denotes where the published decision can be found.

State courts of appeals decisions are usually published in two places, the state reports of that particular state and the more widely used *National Reporter System* published by West Group. Some states no longer publish their own reports. The *National Reporter System* divides the states into the following geographic areas: Atlantic (A. or A.2d, where *2d* refers to *Second Series*), South Eastern (S.E. or S.E.2d), South Western (S.W., S.W.2d, or S.W.3d), North Western (N.W. or N.W.2d), North Eastern (N.E. or N.E.2d), Southern (So. or So.2d), and Pacific (P., P.2d, or P.3d).

Federal trial court decisions are published unofficially in West's *Federal Supplement* (F.Supp. or F.Supp.2d), and opinions from the circuit courts of appeals are reported unofficially in West's *Federal Reporter* (F., F.2d, or F.3d). Opinions from the United States Supreme Court are reported in the *United States Reports* (U.S.), the *Lawyers' Edition of the Supreme Court Reports* (L.Ed.), West's *Supreme Court Reporter* (S.Ct.), and other publications. The *United States Reports* is the official publication of United States Supreme Court decisions. It is published by the federal government. Many early decisions are missing from these volumes. The citations of the early volumes of the *U.S. Reports* include the names of the actual reporters, such as Dallas, Cranch, or Wheaton. *McCulloch v.*

Maryland, for example, is cited as 17 U.S. (4 Wheat.) 316. Only after 1874 did the present citation system, in which cases are cited based solely on their volume and page numbers in the *United States Reports*, come into being. The *Lawyers' Edition of the Supreme Court Reports* is an unofficial and more complete edition of Supreme Court decisions. West's *Supreme Court Reporter* is an unofficial edition of decisions dating from October 1882. These volumes contain headnotes and numerous brief editorial statements of the law involved in the case.

State courts of appeals decisions are cited by giving the name of the case; the volume, name, and page number of the state's official report (if the state publishes its own reports); the volume, unit, and page number of the *National Reporter;* and the volume, name, and page number of any other selected reporter. Federal court citations are also listed by giving the name of the case and the volume, name, and page number of the reports. In addition to the citation, this textbook lists the year of the decision in parentheses. Consider, for example, the case *United States v. Curtiss-Wright Export Co.,* 299 U.S. 304 (1936). The Supreme Court's decision of this case may be found in volume 299 of the *United States Reports* on page 304. The case was decided in 1936.

Today, many courts, including the United States Supreme Court, publish their opinions online. This makes it much easier for students to find and read cases, or summaries of cases, that have significant consequences for American government and politics. To access cases via the Internet, use the URLs given in the *Politics on the Web* section at the end of Chapter 14.

Notes

Chapter 1

1. Harold Lasswell, *Politics: Who Gets What, When, and How* (New York: McGraw-Hill, 1936).
2. Charles Lewis, *The Buying of Congress* (New York: Avon Books, 1998), p. 346.
3. As quoted in Paul M. Angle and Earl Schenck Miers, *The Living Lincoln* (New York: Barnes & Noble, 1992), p. 155.
4. Martin J. Wade and William F. Russell, *The Short Constitution* (Iowa City: American Citizen Publishing, 1920), p. 38.
5. John W. Dean, *Conservatives without Conscience* (New York: Penguin, 2007), p. 11.
6. John Halpin and Karl Agne, *State of American Political Ideology, 2009: A National Study of Political Values and Beliefs* (Washington, D.C.: Center for American Progress, 2009).

Chapter 2

1. *U.S. v. Miller,* 307 U.S. 174 (1939), *District of Columbia v. Heller,* 128 S.Ct. 2783 (2008), and *McDonald v. Chicago,* 561 U.S. ___ (2010).
2. The first *European* settlement in today's United States was St. Augustine, Florida (a city that still exists), which was founded on September 8, 1565, by the Spaniard Pedro Menéndez de Ávilés.
3. Archaeologists recently discovered the remains of a colony at Popham Beach, on the southern coast of what is now Maine, that was established at the same time as the colony at Jamestown. The Popham colony disbanded after thirteen months, however, when the leader, after learning that he had inherited property back home, returned—with the other colonists—to England.
4. John Camp, *Out of the Wilderness: The Emergence of an American Identity in Colonial New England* (Middleton, Conn.: Wesleyan University Press, 1990).
5. Jon Butler, *Becoming America: The Revolution before 1776* (Cambridge, Mass.: Harvard University Press, 2000).
6. Ironically, the colonists were in fact protesting a tax reduction. The British government believed that if tea were cheaper, Americans would be more willing to drink it, even though it was still taxed. The Americans viewed the tax reduction as an attempt to trick them into accepting the principle of taxation. If the tea had been expensive, it would have been easy to organize a boycott. Because the tea was cheap, the protesters destroyed it so that no one would be tempted to buy it. (Also, many of the protesters were in the business of smuggling tea, and they would have been put out of business by the cheap competition.)
7. Paul S. Boyer *et al., The Enduring Vision: A History of the American People* (Lexington, Mass.: D. C. Heath, 1996).
8. Much of the colonists' fury over British policies was directed personally at King George III, who had ascended the British throne in 1760 at the age of twenty-two, rather than at Britain or British rule *per se.* If you look at the Declaration of Independence in Appendix A, you will note that much of that document focuses on what "He" (George III) has or has not done. George III's lack of political experience, his personality, and his temperament all combined to lend instability to the British government at this crucial point in history.
9. *The Political Writings of Thomas Paine,* Vol. 1 (Boston: J. P. Mendum Investigator Office, 1870), p. 46.
10. The equivalent in today's publishing world would be a book that sells between 9 million and 11 million copies in its first year of publication.
11. As quoted in Winthrop D. Jordan *et al., The United States,* 6th ed. (Englewood Cliffs, N.J.: Prentice Hall, 1987).
12. Some scholars feel that Locke's influence on the colonists, including Thomas Jefferson, has been exaggerated. For example, Jay Fliegelman states that Jefferson's fascination with the ideas of Homer, Ossian, and Patrick Henry "is of greater significance than his indebtedness to Locke." Jay Fliegelman, *Declaring Independence: Jefferson, Natural Language, and the Culture of Performance* (Stanford, Calif.: Stanford University Press, 1993).
13. Well before the Articles were ratified, many of them had, in fact, already been implemented. The Second Continental Congress and the thirteen states conducted American military, economic, and political affairs according to the standards and form specified later in the Articles of Confederation. See Robert W. Hoffert, *A Politics of Tensions: The Articles of Confederation and American Political Ideas* (Niwot, Colo.: University Press of Colorado, 1992).
14. Shays' Rebellion was not merely a small group of poor farmers. The participants and their supporters represented whole communities, including some of the wealthiest and most influential families of Massachusetts. Leonard L. Richards, *Shays' Rebellion: The American Revolution's Final Battle* (Philadelphia: University of Pennsylvania Press, 2003).
15. Madison was much more "republican" in his views—that is, less of a centralist—than Hamilton. See Lance Banning, *The Sacred Fire of Liberty: James Madison and the Founding of the Federal Republic* (Ithaca, N.Y.: Cornell University Press, 1995).
16. The State House was later named Independence Hall. The East Room was the same room in which the Declaration of Independence had been signed eleven years earlier.
17. Charles A. Beard, *An Economic Interpretation of the Constitution of the United States* (New York: Macmillan, 1913; New York: Free Press, 1986).
18. Morris was partly of French descent, which is why his first name may seem unusual. Note, however, that naming one's child *Gouverneur* was not common at the time in any language, including French.
19. Quoted in J. J. Spengler, "Malthusianism in Late Eighteenth-Century America," *American Economic Review* 25 (1935), p. 705.
20. For further detail on Wood's depiction of the founders' views, see Gordon S. Wood, *Revolutionary Characters: What Made the Founders Different* (New York: Penguin Press, 2006).
21. Some scholarship suggests that the *Federalist Papers* did not play a significant role in bringing about the ratification of the Constitution. Nonetheless, the papers have lasting value as an authoritative explanation of the Constitution.
22. The papers written by the Anti-Federalists are online (see the *Politics on the Web* section at the end of Chapter 2 for the Web URL). For essays on the positions, arranged in topical order, of both the Federalists and the Anti-Federalists in the ratification debate, see John P. Kaminski and Richard Leffler, *Federalists and Antifederalists: The Debate over the Ratification of the Constitution,* 2d ed. (Madison, Wis.: Madison House, 1998).
23. The concept of the separation of powers generally is credited to the French political philosopher Montesquieu (1689–1755), who included it in his monumental two-volume work entitled *The Spirit of the Laws,* published in 1748.
24. The Constitution does not explicitly mention the power of judicial review, but the delegates at the Constitutional Convention probably assumed that the courts would have this power. Indeed, Alexander Hamilton, in *Federalist Paper* No. 78, explicitly outlined the concept of judicial review. In any event, whether the founders intended for the courts to exercise this power is a moot point, because in an 1803 decision, *Marbury v. Madison,* the Supreme Court successfully claimed this power for the courts—see Chapter 14.
25. Eventually, Supreme Court decisions led to legislative reforms relating to apportionment. The amendment concerning compensation of members of Congress became the Twenty-seventh Amendment to the Constitution when it was ratified 203 years later, in 1992.
26. The Twenty-first Amendment repealed the Eighteenth Amendment, which had prohibited the manufacture or sale of alcoholic beverages nationwide (Prohibition). Special conventions were necessary because prohibitionist forces controlled too many state legislatures for the standard ratification method to work.

Chapter 3

1. The federal models used by the German and Canadian governments provide interesting comparisons with the U.S. system. See Arthur B. Gunlicks, *Laender and German Federalism* (Manchester, England: Manchester University Press, 2003); and Jennifer Smith, *Federalism* (Vancouver: University of British Columbia Press, 2004).
2. Text of an address by the president to the National Conference of State Legislatures, Atlanta, Georgia (Washington, D.C.: The White House, Office of the Press Secretary, July 30, 1981).
3. An excellent illustration of this principle was President Dwight Eisenhower's disciplining of Arkansas governor Orval Faubus when Faubus refused to allow a Little Rock high school to be desegregated in 1957. Eisenhower federalized the National Guard to enforce the court-ordered desegregation of the school.
4. 5 U.S. 137 (1803).
5. 17 U.S. 316 (1819).
6. 22 U.S. 1 (1824).
7. As quoted in Gavin Wright, *The Political Economy of the Cotton South: Households, Markets, and Wealth in the Nineteenth Century* (New York: W. W. Norton & Co., 1978), p. 147.
8. *Hammer v. Dagenhart,* 247 U.S. 251 (1918). This decision was overruled in *United States v. Darby,* 312 U.S. 100 (1941).
9. *Wickard v. Filburn,* 317 U.S. 111 (1942).
10. *McLain v. Real Estate Board of New Orleans, Inc.,* 444 U.S. 232 (1980).
11. 514 U.S. 549 (1995).
12. *Printz v. United States,* 521 U.S. 898 (1997).
13. *United States v. Morrison,* 529 U.S. 598 (2000).
14. 549 U.S. 497 (2007).
15. See George P. Fletcher, "The Indefinable Concept of Terrorism," *Journal of International Criminal Justice,* November 2006, pp. 894–911.

Chapter 4

1. 32 U.S. 243 (1833).
2. 330 U.S. 1 (1947).
3. 370 U.S. 421 (1962).
4. 449 U.S. 39 (1980).
5. *Wallace v. Jaffree*, 472 U.S. 38 (1985).
6. See, for example, *Brown v. Gwinnett County School District*, 112 F.3d 1464 (1997).
7. *Santa Fe Independent School District v. Doe*, 530 U.S. 290 (2000).
8. 393 U.S. 97 (1968).
9. *Edwards v. Aguillard*, 482 U.S. 578 (1987).
10. 403 U.S. 602 (1971).
11. *Mitchell v. Helms*, 530 U.S. 793 (2000).
12. *Zelman v. Simmons-Harris*, 536 U.S. 639 (2002).
13. Holmes v. Bush (Fla.Cir.Ct. 2002). For details about this case, see David Royse, "Judge Rules School Voucher Law Violates Florida Constitution," *USA Today*, August 6, 2002, p. 7D.
14. 98 U.S. 145 (1878).
15. *Christian Legal Society v. Martinez*, 561 U.S. ___ (2010).
16. For more information on this case, see Bill Miller, "Firefighters Win Ruling in D.C. Grooming Dispute," *The Washington Post*, June 23, 2001, p. B01.
17. *Schenck v. United States*, 249 U.S. 47 (1919).
18. 341 U.S. 494 (1951).
19. *Brandenburg v. Ohio*, 395 U.S. 444 (1969).
20. *Liquormart v. Rhode Island*, 517 U.S. 484 (1996).
21. 413 U.S. 15 (1973).
22. *Reno v. American Civil Liberties Union*, 521 U.S. 844 (1997).
23. *Ashcroft v. American Civil Liberties Union*, 542 U.S. 656 (2004). The district court, located in Philadelphia, made its second ruling on the case in 2007. On July 22, 2008, the U.S. Court of Appeals for the Third Circuit upheld the decision in *American Civil Liberties Union v. Mukasey*, 534 F.3d 181 (3d Cir. 2008).
24. *United States v. American Library Association*, 539 U.S. 194 (2003).
25. *Morse v. Frederick*, 551 U.S. 393.
26. See, for example, *Doe v. University of Michigan*, 721 F.Supp. 852 (1989).
27. "Meeting Minutes of the Wesleyan Student Assembly Meeting, 2002–2003," October 2, 2002, p. 10.
28. 249 U.S. 47 (1919).
29. 268 U.S. 652 (1925).
30. 484 U.S. 260 (1988).
31. Brandeis made this statement in a dissenting opinion in *Olmstead v. United States*, 277 U.S. 438 (1928).
32. 381 U.S. 479 (1965).
33. The state of South Carolina challenged the constitutionality of this act, claiming that the law violated states' rights under the Tenth Amendment. The Supreme Court, however, held that Congress had the authority, under its commerce power, to pass the act because drivers' personal information had become articles of interstate commerce. *Reno v. Condon*, 528 U.S. 141 (2000).
34. 410 U.S. 113 (1973). Jane Roe was not the real name of the woman in this case. It is a common legal pseudonym used to protect a party's privacy.
35. See, for example, the Supreme Court's decision in *Lambert v. Wicklund*, 520 U.S. 1169 (1997). The Court held that a Montana law requiring a minor to notify one of her parents before getting an abortion was constitutional.
36. *Schenck v. ProChoice Network*, 519 U.S. 357 (1997); and *Hill v. Colorado*, 530 U.S. 703 (2000).
37. *Stenberg v. Carhart*, 530 U.S. 914 (2000).
38. *Gonzales v. Carhart*, 127 S.Ct. 1610 (2007).
39. *Washington v. Glucksberg*, 521 U.S. 702 (1997).
40. *Gonzales v. Oregon*, 546 U.S. 243 (2006).
41. 372 U.S. 335 (1963).
42. *Mapp v. Ohio*, 367 U.S. 643 (1961).
43. 384 U.S. 436 (1966). In 1968, Congress passed legislation including a provision that reinstated the previous rule that statements made by defendants can be used against them as long as the statements were made voluntarily. This provision was never enforced, however, and only in 1999 did a court try to enforce it. The case ultimately came before the Supreme Court, which held that the *Miranda* rights were based on the Constitution and thus could not be overruled by legislative act. See *Dickerson v. United States*, 530 U.S. 428 (2000).
44. *Moran v. Burbine*, 475 U.S. 412 (1986).
45. *Arizona v. Fulminante*, 499 U.S. 279 (1991).
46. *Davis v. United States*, 512 U.S. 452 (1994).
47. Thomas P. Sullivan, *Police Experiences with Recording Custodial Interrogations* (Chicago: Northwestern University School of Law Center on Wrongful Convictions, Summer 2004), p. 4.
48. This example is drawn from Brenda Koehler, "Respond Locally to National Issues," in *50 Ways to Love Your Country* (Maui, Hawaii: Inner Ocean Publishing, 2004), pp. 110–111.

Chapter 5

1. *Michael M. v. Superior Court*, 450 U.S. 464 (1981).
2. See, for example, *Craig v. Boren*, 429 U.S. 190 (1976).
3. *Orr v. Orr*, 440 U.S. 268 (1979).
4. *Mississippi University for Women v. Hogan*, 458 U.S. 718 (1982).
5. 518 U.S. 515 (1996).
6. 163 U.S. 537 (1896).
7. 347 U.S. 483 (1954).
8. 349 U.S. 294 (1955).
9. *Swann v. Charlotte-Mecklenburg Board of Education*, 402 U.S. 1 (1971).
10. *Keyes v. School District No. 1*, 413 U.S. 189 (1973).
11. *Milliken v. Bradley*, 418 U.S. 717 (1974).
12. *Riddick v. School Board of City of Norfolk*, 627 F.Supp. 814 (E.D.Va. 1984).
13. Emily Bazelon, "The Next Kind of Integration," *The New York Times Magazine*, July 20, 2008.
14. *Oncale v. Sundowner Offshore Services*, 523 U.S. 75 (1998).
15. *Faragher v. City of Boca Raton*, 524 U.S. 775 (1998).
16. The Supreme Court upheld these actions in *Hirabayashi v. United States*, 320 U.S. 81 (1943); and *Korematsu v. United States*, 323 U.S. 214 (1944).
17. Historians in the early and mid-twentieth century gave much smaller figures for the pre-Columbian population—as low as 14 million people for the entire New World. Today, 40 million is considered a conservative estimate, and an estimate of 100 million has much support among demographers. If 100 million is correct, the epidemics that followed the arrival of the Europeans killed one out of every five people alive in the world at that time. See Charles C. Mann, *1491* (New York: Vintage, 2006).
18. The 1890 siege was the subject of Dee Brown's best-selling book *Bury My Heart at Wounded Knee* (New York: Holt, Rinehart & Winston, 1971).
19. *County of Oneida, New York v. Oneida Indian Nation*, 470 U.S. 226 (1985).
20. *Sutton v. United Airlines*, 527 U.S. 471 (1999); and *Toyota v. Williams*, 534 U.S. 184 (2002).
21. *Board of Trustees of the University of Alabama v. Garrett*, 531 U.S. 356 (2001).
22. 539 U.S. 558 (2003).
23. 517 U.S. 620 (1996).
24. 438 U.S. 265 (1978).
25. 515 U.S. 200 (1995).
26. 84 F.3d 720 (5th Cir. 1996).
27. 539 U.S. 244 (2003).
28. 539 U.S. 306 (2003).
29. 551 U.S. 701 (2007).

Chapter 6

1. David Bicknell Truman, *The Governmental Process: Political Interests and Public Opinion*, 2d rev. ed. (New York: Alfred A. Knopf, 1971). This work is a classic of political science.
2. Robert H. Salisbury, *Interests and Institutions: Substance and Structure in American Politics* (Pittsburgh: University of Pittsburgh Press, 1992).
3. *Democracy in America*, Vol. 1, ed. Phillip Bradley (New York: Knopf, 1980), p. 191.
4. Mancur Olson, *The Logic of Collective Action: Public Goods and the Theory of Groups*, rev. ed. (Cambridge, Mass.: Harvard University Press, 1971).
5. Pronounced ah-*mee*-kus *kure*-ee-eye.
6. Fred McChesney, *Money for Nothing: Politicians, Rent Extraction and Political Extortion* (Cambridge, Mass.: Harvard University Press, 1997).
7. The Agricultural Adjustment Act of 1933 (declared unconstitutional) was replaced by the 1937 Agricultural Adjustment Act, which later was changed and amended several times.
8. 545 U.S. 913 (2005).
9. *United States v. Harriss*, 347 U.S. 612 (1954).

Chapter 7

1. Letter to Francis Hopkinson written from Paris while Jefferson was minister to France, as cited in John P. Foley, ed., *The Jeffersonian Cyclopedia* (New York: Russell & Russell, 1967), p. 677.
2. The U.S. Senate presents the text of the address at www.access.gpo.gov/congress/senate/farewell/sd106-21.pdf.
3. The association of red with the Republicans and blue with the Democrats is barely a decade old. The terms *red* and *blue* are derived from the colors used by the major television networks to show the states carried by the Republican and Democratic presidential candidates. This use of colors deliberately reverses a traditional pattern. In most European countries, the right-of-center party uses blue, while the left-of-center party employs red. The use of red originated in the socialist movement, from which most European left-of-center parties descend. From time to time, Republicans have accused Democrats of socialism. U.S. television networks thus assigned red to the Republicans precisely so that the networks would not appear to be endorsing that accusation.
4. By August 2010, the cost of the stimulus package was reestimated as $814 billion.
5. For an interesting discussion of the pros and cons of patronage from a constitutional perspective, see the majority opinion versus the dissent in the Supreme Court case *Board of County Commissioners v. Umbehr*, 518 U.S. 668 (1996).
6. Thomas Nast, the cartoonist who drew these images, was a Republican. "Copperhead" was a derisive term for northern Democrats who sympathized with the South during the Civil War, and in the first cartoon Nash condemned Democratic newspapers for abusing Edwin Stanton, Lincoln's secretary of war, following Stanton's death. The elephant in the second cartoon referred to the large size of the Republican vote in the North. Nash depicted the elephant as stampeded into a pit by a jackass dressed in a lion skin. This referred to the *New York Herald*, a Democratic newspaper, which made accusations against Republican president Ulysses S. Grant that caused Republicans to panic.
7. The term *third party*, although inaccurate (because sometimes there have been fourth parties, fifth parties, and even more), is commonly used to refer to a minor party.

8. Today, twelve states have multimember districts for their state houses, and a handful also have multimember districts for their state senates.

Chapter 8

1. Doris A. Graber, *Mass Media and American Politics,* 7th ed. (Washington, D.C.: CQ Press, 2005).
2. Jimmy Carter, *Palestine: Peace Not Apartheid* (New York: Simon & Schuster, 2007).
3. John M. Benson, "When Is an Opinion Really an Opinion?" *Public Perspective,* September/October 2001, pp. 40–41.
4. As quoted in Karl G. Feld, "When Push Comes to Shove: A Polling Industry Call to Arms," *Public Perspective,* September/October 2001, p. 38.
5. Pew Research Center for the People and the Press, survey conducted September 21–October 4, 2006, and reported in "Who Votes, Who Doesn't, and Why," released October 28, 2006.
6. *Guinn v. United States,* 238 U.S. 347 (1915).
7. *Smith v. Allwright,* 321 U.S. 649 (1944).
8. The argument about the vote-eligible population was first made by Michael P. McDonald and Samuel L. Popkin, "The Myth of the Vanishing Voter," *American Political Science Review,* Vol. 95, No. 4 (December 2001), p. 963.
9. As quoted in Owen Ullman, "Why Voter Apathy Will Make a Strong Showing," *BusinessWeek,* November 4, 1996.
10. Thomas E. Mann and Norman J. Ornstein, *The Broken Branch: How Congress Is Failing America and How to Get It Back on Track* (New York: Oxford University Press, 2006), p. 277.

Chapter 9

1. Today, there are 100 senators in the Senate and 435 members of the House of Representatives. In addition, the District of Columbia has 3 electoral votes, as provided for by the Twenty-third Amendment to the Constitution.
2. This group includes those who support the National Popular Vote movement, a proposed interstate compact that would cast the electoral votes of each participating state for the candidate who won the national popular vote. The compact would go into effect if participating states controlled a majority of the votes in the electoral college.
3. These states award one electoral vote to the candidate who wins the popular vote in a congressional district and an additional two electoral votes to the winner of the statewide popular vote. Other states have considered similar plans.
4. The Maryland legislature would probably have to vote to accept the return of the District, because under the Constitution, state boundaries cannot be altered without state consent.
5. The word *caucus* apparently was first used in the name of a men's club, the Caucus Club of colonial Boston, sometime between 1755 and 1765. (Many early political and government meetings took place in pubs.) We have no certain knowledge of the origin of the word, but it may be from an Algonquin term meaning "elder" or from the Latin name of a drinking vessel.
6. Today, the Democratic and Republican caucuses in the House and Senate (the Republicans now use the term *conference* instead of caucus) choose each party's congressional leadership and sometimes discuss legislation and legislative strategy.
7. Due to the customs of the time, none of the candidates could admit that he had made a personal decision to run. All claimed to have entered the race in response to popular demand.
8. Parties cannot use their freedom-of-association rights to practice racial discrimination in state-sponsored elections: *Smith v. Allwright,* 321 U.S. 649 (1944). When racial discrimination is not involved, the parties have regularly won freedom-of-association suits against state governments. Examples are *Tashjian v. Republican Party of Connecticut,* 479 U.S. 208 (1986), and *California Democratic Party v. Jones,* 530 U.S. 567 (2000).
9. In Washington, the state government holds presidential primaries for both parties. The Democratic Party, however, ignores the Democratic primary and chooses its national convention delegates through a caucus/convention system. In 1984, following a dispute with the state of Michigan over primary rules, the state Democratic Party organized a presidential primary election that was run completely by party volunteers. In 2008, after a similar dispute with its state, the Virginia Republican Party chose its candidate for the U.S. Senate at its state party convention instead of through the Virginia primary elections.
10. The case was *California Democratic Party v. Jones,* cited in footnote 8.
11. *Washington State Grange v. Washington State Republican Party et al.,* 552 U.S. 442 (2008).
12. Christopher Rhoads, "Candidates Try New Web Tactics in Battle to Tap Fresh Supporters," *The Wall Street Journal,* October 30, 2008, p. 16.
13. This act is sometimes referred to as the Federal Election Campaign Act of 1972 because it became effective in that year. The official date of the act, however, is 1971.
14. 424 U.S. 1 (1976).
15. This figure is from the Center for Responsive Politics.
16. *Colorado Republican Federal Campaign Committee v. Federal Election Commission,* 518 U.S. 604 (1996).
17. Quoted in George Will, "The First Amendment on Trial," *The Washington Post,* December 1, 2002, p. B7.
18. 540 U.S. 93 (2003).
19. 551 U.S. 449 (2007).

20. 558 U.S. 50 (2010).
21. *Bush v. Gore,* 531 U.S. 98 (2000).

Chapter 10

1. *Mutual Film Corporation v. Industrial Commission of Ohio,* 236 U.S. 230 (1915).
2. *Joseph Burstyn, Inc. v. Wilson,* 343 U.S. 495 (1952).
3. *Reno v. American Civil Liberties Union,* 521 U.S. 844 (1997).
4. *United States v. Playboy Entertainment Group,* 529 U.S. 803 (2000).
5. Bernard Cohen, *The Press and Foreign Policy* (Princeton, N.J.: Princeton University Press, 1963), p. 81.
6. Interestingly, in the 2000 campaigns, a Texas group supporting George W. Bush's candidacy paid for a remake of the "daisy" commercial, but the target in the new ad was Al Gore.
7. As quoted in Michael Grunwald, "The Year of Playing Dirtier," *The Washington Post,* October 27, 2006, p. A1.
8. John G. Geer, *In Defense of Negativity: Attack Ads in Presidential Campaigns* (Chicago: University of Chicago Press, 2006).
9. The commission's action was upheld by a federal court. See *Perot v. Federal Election Commission,* 97 F.3d 553 (D.C.Cir. 1996).
10. For more details on how political candidates manage news coverage, see Doris A. Graber, *Mass Media and American Politics,* 7th ed. (Washington, D.C.: CQ Press, 2005).
11. For suggestions on how to dissect spin and detect when language is steering one toward a conclusion, see Brooks Jackson and Kathleen Hall Jamieson, *unSpun: Finding Facts in a World of Disinformation* (New York: Random House, 2007).
12. *Red Lion Broadcasting Co. v. FCC,* 395 U.S. 367 (1969).
13. Kathleen Hall Jamieson, *Everything You Think You Know about Politics . . . and Why You're Wrong* (New York: Basic Books, 2000), pp. 187–195.
14. Debra Reddin van Tuyll and Hubert P. van Tuyll, "Political Partisanship," in William David Sloan and Jenn Burleson Mackay, eds., *Media Bias: Finding It, Fixing It* (Jefferson, N.C.: McFarland, 2007), pp. 35–49.
15. Jamieson, *Everything You Think You Know about Politics,* pp. xiii–xiv.
16. Pew Research Center for the People and the Press and the Project for Excellence in Journalism, *The State of the News Media 2007: An Annual Report on American Journalism.*
17. The term *podcasting* is used for this type of information delivery because initially podcasts were downloaded onto Apple's iPods.

Chapter 11

1. These states are Alaska, Delaware, Montana, North Dakota, South Dakota, Vermont, and Wyoming.
2. 369 U.S. 186 (1962).
3. 376 U.S. 1 (1964).
4. See, for example, *Davis v. Bandemer,* 478 U.S. 109 (1986).
5. The plan was controversial because it was not implemented in response to the 2000 census. Rather, it was a "midterm" redistricting—held between censuses—that overturned what had been the postcensus redistricting plan in Texas.
6. *Amicus curiae* brief filed by the American Civil Liberties Union (ACLU) in support of the appellants in *Easley v. Cromartie,* 532 U.S. 234 (2001).
7. See, for example, *Shaw v. Reno,* 509 U.S. 630 (1993); *Miller v. Johnson,* 515 U.S. 900 (1995); *Shaw v. Hunt,* 517 U.S. 899 (1996); and *Bush v. Vera,* 517 U.S. 952 (1996).
8. *Easley v. Cromartie,* 532 U.S. 234 (2001).
9. *Powell v. McCormack,* 395 U.S. 486 (1969).
10. Some observers maintain that another reason Congress *can* stay in session longer is the invention of air-conditioning. Until the advent of air-conditioning, no member of Congress wanted to stay in session during the hot and sticky late spring, summer, and early fall months.
11. *U.S. Term Limits, Inc. v. Thornton,* 514 U.S. 779 (1995).
12. A term used by Woodrow Wilson in *Congressional Government* (New York: Meridian Books, 1956 [first published in 1885]).

Chapter 12

1. Lyndon B. Johnson, *The Vantage Point: Perspectives of the Presidency, 1963–1969* (New York: Henry Holt & Co., 1971).
2. Versailles, located about twenty miles from Paris, is the name of the palace built by King Louis XIV of France. It served as the royal palace until 1793 and was then converted into a national historical museum, which it remains today. The preliminary treaty ending the American Revolution was signed by the United States and Britain at Versailles in 1783.
3. *Ex parte Grossman,* 267 U.S. 87 (1925).
4. *Clinton v. City of New York,* 524 U.S. 417 (1998).
5. As cited in Lewis D. Eigen and Jonathan P. Siegel, *The Macmillan Dictionary of Political Quotations* (New York: Macmillan, 1993), p. 565.
6. The Constitution does not grant the president explicit power to remove from office officials who are not performing satisfactorily or who do not agree with the president. In 1926, however, the Supreme Court prevented Congress from interfering with the president's ability to fire those executive-branch officials

whom he had appointed with Senate approval. See *Myers v. United States*, 272 U.S. 52 (1926).

7. Ironically, Lincoln believed that the actions of the president ought to be strictly limited when war powers were not concerned. He therefore left most domestic issues that did not involve the war entirely to Congress. In doing so, Lincoln was true to the ideas of his former party, the Whigs. That party advocated a limited role for the presidency in reaction to the sweeping assumption of authority by President Andrew Jackson, their great opponent. See David Donald's classic essay "Abraham Lincoln: Whig in the White House," in *Lincoln Reconsidered: Essays on the Civil War Era*, 3d ed. (New York: Vintage, 2001), pp. 133–147.

8. Richard E. Neustadt, *Presidential Power: The Politics of Leadership* (New York: John Wiley, 1960), p. 10.

9. As quoted in Richard M. Pious, *The American Presidency* (New York: Basic Books, 1979), pp. 51–52.

10. A phrase coined by Samuel Kernell in *Going Public: New Strategies of Presidential Leadership*, 2d ed. (Washington, D.C.: Congressional Quarterly Press, 1992).

11. Congress used its power to declare war in the War of 1812, the Mexican War (1846–1848), the Spanish-American War (1898), and World War I (U.S. involvement lasted from 1916 until 1918) and on six different occasions during World War II (U.S. involvement lasted from 1941 until 1945).

12. Actually, the Republicans had some difficulty controlling the Senate during Bush's first term. After the 2000 elections, the Senate was split 50–50 and the Republicans gained control only when Vice President Dick Cheney cast a tie-breaking vote. Four months later, Senator Jim Jeffords of Vermont left the Republicans to caucus with the Democrats, granting that party control of the chamber. In the 2002 elections, however, the Republicans picked up two net seats and regained control of the Senate, 51–49.

13. As quoted in Thomas E. Cronin, *The State of the Presidency*, 2d ed. (Boston: Little, Brown, 1980), p. 11.

Chapter 13

1. This definition follows the classic model of bureaucracy put forth by German sociologist Max Weber. See Max Weber, *Theory of Social and Economic Organization*, ed. Talcott Parsons (New York: Oxford University Press, 1974).

2. It should be noted that although the president is technically the head of the bureaucracy, the president cannot always control the bureaucracy—as you will read later in this chapter.

3. For an insightful analysis of the policymaking process in Washington, D.C., and the role played by various groups in the process, see Morton H. Halperin and Priscilla A. Clapp, with Arnold Kanter, *Bureaucratic Politics and Foreign Policy*, 2d ed. (Washington, D.C.: The Brookings Institution, 2006). Although the focus of the book is on foreign policy, the analysis applies in many ways to the general policymaking process.

4. Colleen W. Cook, *CRS Report for Congress: Mexico's Drug Cartels* (Washington, D.C.: Congressional Research Service, 2008).

Chapter 14

1. *Boumediene v. Bush*, 128 S.Ct. 2229 (2008).
2. 347 U.S. 483 (1954).
3. See *Plessy v. Ferguson*, 163 U.S. 537 (1896).
4. 539 U.S. 558 (2003).
5. 478 U.S. 186 (1986).
6. Although a state's highest court is often referred to as the state supreme court, there are exceptions. In the New York court system, for example, the supreme court is a trial court, and the highest court is called the New York Court of Appeals.

7. Between 1790 and 1891, Congress allowed the Supreme Court almost no discretion over which cases to decide. After 1925, in almost 95 percent of appealed cases the Court could choose whether to hear arguments and issue an opinion. Beginning in October 1988, mandatory review was virtually eliminated.

8. *Citizens United v. Federal Election Commission*, 558 U.S. 50 (2010).
9. *McDonald v. Chicago*, 561 U.S. ___ (2010).
10. *Graham v. Florida*, 560 U.S. ___ (2010).
11. 347 U.S. 483 (1954).
12. 84 F.3d 720 (5th Cir. 1996).
13. *Grutter v. Bollinger*, 539 U.S. 306 (2003); and *Gratz v. Bollinger*, 539 U.S. 244 (2003).
14. *Parents Involved in Community Schools v. Seattle School District No. 1*, 127 S.Ct. 2738 (2007).
15. 5 U.S. 137 (1803). The Supreme Court had considered the constitutionality of an act of Congress in *Hylton v. United States*, 3 U.S. 171 (1796), in which Congress's power to levy certain taxes was challenged. That particular act was ruled constitutional, rather than unconstitutional, however, so this first federal exercise of judicial review was not clearly recognized as such. Also, during the decade before the adoption of the federal Constitution, courts in at least eight states had exercised the power of judicial review.
16. For an analysis of the Roberts Court's first term by a Georgetown University law professor, see Jonathan Turley, "The Roberts Court: Seeing Is Believing," *USA Today*, July 6, 2006, p. 11A.
17. Erwin Chemerinsky, "Roberts and Kennedy Were Most Often in the Supreme Court Majority in Term 2009," *California Bar Journal*, August 2010.
18. Antonin Scalia, *A Matter of Interpretation* (Ewing, N.J.: Princeton University Press, 1997).
19. Letter by Thomas Jefferson to William C. Jarvis, 1820, in Andrew A. Lipscomb and Albert Ellery Bergh, *The Writings of Thomas Jefferson*, Memorial Edition (Washington, D.C.: Thomas Jefferson Memorial Association of the United States, 1904).
20. As quoted in Carl Hulse and David D. Kirkpatrick, "DeLay Says Federal Judiciary Has 'Run Amok,' Adding Congress Is Partly to Blame," *The New York Times*, April 8, 2005, p. 5.

Chapter 15

1. Stan Dorn, *Uninsured and Dying Because of It: Updating the Institute of Medicine Analysis on the Impact of Uninsurance on Mortality* (Washington, D.C.: Urban Institute, 2008).
2. An alternative possibility would be to change the Senate rules so that sixty votes would no longer be necessary to pass legislation. Changing the rules, however, could easily prove more difficult than assembling sixty votes.
3. John Kerry and Teresa Heinz Kerry, *This Moment on Earth: Today's New Environmentalists and Their Vision for the Future* (New York: PublicAffairs, 2007).

Chapter 16

1. David L. Rousseau, *Identifying Threats and Threatening Identities: The Social Construction of Realism and Liberalism* (Palo Alto, Calif.: Stanford University Press, 2006), p. 154.
2. *Public Papers of the Presidents of the United States: Harry S. Truman, 1947* (Washington, D.C.: U.S. Government Printing Office, 1963), pp. 176–180.
3. The containment policy was outlined by George F. Kennan, the chief of the policy-planning staff for the Department of State at that time, in an article that appeared in *Foreign Affairs*, July 1947, p. 575. The author's name was given as "X."
4. Bob Woodward, *Obama's Wars* (New York: Simon & Schuster, 2010).

Glossary

A

Action-reaction syndrome For every government action, there will be a reaction by the public. The government then takes a further action to counter the public's reaction—and the cycle begins again.

Adjudicate To render a judicial decision. In regard to administrative law, the process in which an administrative law judge hears and decides issues that arise when an agency charges a person or firm with violating a law or regulation enforced by the agency.

Administrative law The body of law created by administrative agencies (in the form of rules, regulations, orders, and decisions) in order to carry out their duties and responsibilities.

Affirmative action A policy calling for the establishment of programs that give special consideration, in jobs and college admissions, to members of groups that have been discriminated against in the past.

Agenda setting Getting an issue on the political agenda to be addressed by Congress; part of the first stage of the policymaking process.

Agents of political socialization People and institutions that influence the political views of others.

Anti-Federalists A political group that opposed the adoption of the Constitution because of the document's centralist tendencies and because it did not include a bill of rights.

Appellate court A court having appellate jurisdiction. An appellate court normally does not hear evidence or testimony but reviews the transcript of the trial court's proceedings, other records relating to the case, and attorneys' arguments as to why the trial court's decision should or should not stand.

Apportionment The distribution of House seats among the states on the basis of their respective populations.

Appropriation A part of the congressional budgeting process that involves determining how many dollars will be spent in a given year on a particular set of government activities.

Articles of Confederation The nation's first national constitution, which established a national form of government following the American Revolution. The Articles provided for a confederal form of government in which the central government had few powers.

Australian ballot A secret ballot that is prepared, distributed, and counted by government officials at public expense; used by all states in the United States since 1888.

Authority The ability to legitimately exercise power, such as the power to make and enforce laws.

Authorization A part of the congressional budgeting process that involves the creation of the legal basis for government programs.

Autocracy A form of government in which the power and authority of the government are in the hands of a single person.

B

Biased sample A poll sample that does not accurately represent the population.

Bicameral legislature A legislature made up of two chambers, or parts. The United States has a bicameral legislature, composed of the House of Representatives and the Senate.

Bill of attainder A legislative act that inflicts punishment on particular persons or groups without granting them the right to a trial.

Bill of Rights The first ten amendments to the U.S. Constitution. They list the freedoms—such as the freedoms of speech, press, and religion—that a citizen enjoys and that cannot be infringed on by the government.

Block grant A federal grant given to a state for a broad area, such as criminal justice or mental-health programs.

Blue Dog Coalition A caucus that unites most of the moderate-to-conservative Democrats in the House of Representatives.

Bureaucracy A large, complex, hierarchically structured administrative organization that carries out specific functions.

Bureaucrat An individual who works in a bureaucracy. As generally used, the term refers to a government employee.

Busing The transportation of public school students by bus to schools physically outside their neighborhoods to eliminate school segregation based on residential patterns.

C

Cabinet An advisory group selected by the president to assist with decision making. Traditionally, the cabinet has consisted of the heads of the executive departments and other officers whom the president may choose to appoint.

Campaign strategy The comprehensive plan developed by a candidate and his or her advisers for winning an election. The strategy includes the candidate's position on issues, slogan, advertising plan, press events, personal appearances, and other aspects of the campaign.

Cap-and-trade A method of restricting the production of a harmful substance. A cap is set on the volume of production, and permits to produce the substance can then be traded on the open market.

Capitalism An economic system based on the private ownership of wealth-producing property, free markets, and freedom of contract. The privately owned corporation is the preeminent capitalist institution.

Case law The rules of law announced in court decisions. Case law includes the aggregate of reported cases that interpret judicial precedents, statutes, regulations, and constitutional provisions.

Categorical grant A federal grant targeted for a specific purpose as defined by federal law.

Caucus A meeting held to choose political candidates or delegates.

Checks and balances A major principle of American government in which each of the three branches is given the means to check (to restrain or balance) the actions of the others.

Chief diplomat The role of the president of the United States in recognizing and interacting with foreign governments.

Chief executive The head of the executive branch of government; in the United States, the president.

Chief of staff The person who directs the operations of the White House Office and who advises the president on important matters.

Citizen journalism The collection, analysis, and dissemination of information online by independent journalists, scholars, politicians, and the general citizenry.

Civil disobedience The deliberate and public act of refusing to obey laws thought to be unjust.

Civil law The branch of law that spells out the duties that individuals in society owe to other persons or to their governments, excluding the duty not to commit crimes.

Civil liberties Individual rights protected by the Constitution against the powers of the government.

Civil rights The rights of all Americans to equal treatment under the law, as provided for by the Fourteenth Amendment to the Constitution.

Civil rights movement The movement in the 1950s and 1960s, by minorities and concerned whites, to end racial segregation.

Civil service Nonmilitary government employees.

Closed primary A primary in which only party members can vote to choose that party's candidates.

Cloture A method of ending debate in the Senate and bringing the matter under consideration to a vote by the entire chamber.

Coalition An alliance of individuals or groups with a variety of interests and opinions who join together to support all or part of a political party's platform. Also, an alliance of nations formed to undertake a foreign policy action, particularly a military action. A coalition is often a temporary alliance that dissolves after the action is concluded.

Cold War The war of words, warnings, and ideologies between the Soviet Union and the United States that lasted from the late 1940s through the early 1990s.

Colonial empire A group of dependent nations that are under the rule of a single imperial power.

Commander in chief The supreme commander of a nation's military force.

Commerce clause The clause in Article I, Section 8, of the Constitution that gives Congress the power to regulate interstate commerce (commerce involving more than one state).

Commercial speech Advertising statements that describe products. Commercial speech receives less protection under the First Amendment than ordinary speech.

Common law The body of law developed from judicial decisions in English and U.S. courts, not attributable to a legislature.

Competitive federalism A model of federalism devised by Thomas R. Dye in which state and local governments compete for businesses and citizens, who in effect "vote with their feet" by moving to jurisdictions that offer a competitive advantage.

Concurrent powers Powers held by both the federal and the state governments in a federal system.

Concurring opinion A statement written by a judge or justice who agrees (concurs) with the court's decision, but for reasons different from those in the majority opinion.

Confederal system A league of independent sovereign states, joined together by a central government that has only limited powers over them.

Confederation A league of independent states that are united only for the purpose of achieving common goals.

Conference In regard to the Supreme Court, a private meeting of the justices in which they present their arguments concerning a case under consideration.

Conference committee A temporary committee that is formed when the two chambers of Congress pass differing versions of the same bill. The conference committee, which consists of members from both the House and the Senate, works out a compromise form of the bill.

Conference report A report submitted by a congressional conference committee after it has drafted a single version of a bill.

Congressional Budget Office (CBO) An agency established by Congress to evaluate the impact of proposed legislation on the federal budget.

Congressional district The geographic area that is served by one member in the House of Representatives.

Conservatism A set of beliefs that include a limited role for the national government in helping individuals and in the economic affairs of the nation, support for traditional values and lifestyles, and a cautious response to change.

Constitutional Convention The convention (meeting) of delegates from the states that was held in Philadelphia in 1787 for the purpose of amending the Articles of Confederation. In fact, the delegates wrote a new constitution (the U.S. Constitution) that established a federal form of government to replace the governmental system that had been created by the Articles of Confederation.

Constitutional law Law based on the U.S. Constitution and the constitutions of the various states.

Containment A U.S. policy designed to contain the spread of communism by offering military and economic aid to threatened nations.

Continuing resolution A temporary resolution passed by Congress when an appropriations bill has not been passed by the beginning of the new fiscal year.

Cooperative federalism The theory that the states and the federal government should cooperate in solving problems.

Corporate Average Fuel Economy (CAFE) standards A set of federal standards under which each manufacturer must meet a miles-per-gallon benchmark averaged across all cars or trucks that it sells.

Credentials Committee A committee of each national political party that evaluates the claims of national party convention delegates to be the legitimate representatives of their states.

Criminal law The branch of law that defines and governs actions that constitute crimes. Generally, criminal law has to do with wrongful actions committed against society for which society demands redress.

Cuban missile crisis A nuclear stand-off that occurred in 1962 when the United States learned that the Soviet Union had placed nuclear warheads in Cuba, ninety miles off the U.S. coast. The crisis was defused diplomatically, but it is generally considered the closest the two Cold War superpowers came to a nuclear confrontation.

D

De facto **segregation** Racial segregation that occurs not as a result of deliberate intentions but because of past social and economic conditions and residential patterns.

De jure **segregation** Racial segregation that occurs because of laws or decisions by government agencies.

Dealignment Among voters, a growing detachment from both major political parties.

Delegate A person selected to represent the people of one geographic area at a party convention.

Democracy A system of government in which the people have ultimate political authority. The word is derived from the Greek demos ("the people") and kratia ("rule").

Détente French word meaning a "relaxation of tensions." Détente characterized the relationship between the United States and the Soviet Union in the 1970s, as the two Cold War rivals attempted to pursue cooperative dealings and arms control.

Deterrence A policy of building up military strength for the purpose of discouraging (deterring) military attacks by other nations; the policy of "building weapons for peace" that supported the arms race between the United States and the Soviet Union during the Cold War.

Devolution The surrender or transfer of powers to local authorities by a central government.

Dictatorship A form of government in which absolute power is exercised by a single person who usually has obtained his or her power by the use of force.

Diplomat A person who represents one country in dealing with representatives of another country.

Direct democracy A system of government in which political decisions are made by the people themselves rather than by elected representatives. This form of government was practiced in some areas of ancient Greece.

Direct primary An election held within each of the two major parties—Democratic and Republican— to choose the party's candidates for the general election. Voters choose the candidate directly, rather than through delegates.

Direct technique Any method used by an interest group to interact with government officials directly to further the group's goals.

Dissenting opinion A statement written by a judge or justice who disagrees with the majority opinion.

Diversity of citizenship A basis for federal court jurisdiction over a lawsuit that arises when (1) the parties in the lawsuit live in different states or when one of the parties is a foreign government or a foreign citizen, and (2) the amount in controversy is more than $75,000.

Divine right theory The theory that a monarch's right to rule was derived directly from God rather than from the consent of the people.

Division of powers A basic principle of federalism established by the U.S. Constitution, by which powers are divided between the federal and state governments.

Domestic policy Public policy concerning issues within a national unit, such as national policy concerning health care or the economy.

Double jeopardy The prosecution of a person twice for the same criminal offense; prohibited by the Fifth Amendment in all but a few circumstances.

Dual federalism A system of government in which the federal and the state governments maintain diverse but sovereign powers.

Due process clause The constitutional guarantee, set out in the Fifth and Fourteenth Amendments, that the government will not illegally or arbitrarily deprive a person of life, liberty, or property.

Due process of law The requirement that the government use fair, reasonable, and standard procedures whenever it takes any legal action against an individual; required by the Fifth and Fourteenth Amendments.

E

Easy-money policy A monetary policy that involves stimulating the economy by expanding the rate of growth of the money supply. An easy-money policy supposedly will lead to lower interest rates and induce consumers to spend more and producers to invest more.

Economic policy All actions taken by the national government to smooth out the ups and downs in the nation's level of business activity.

Elector A member of the electoral college.

Electoral college The group of electors who are selected by the voters in each state to elect officially the president and vice president. The number of electors in each state is equal to the number of that state's representatives in both chambers of Congress.

Electorate All of the citizens eligible to vote in a given election.

Electronic media Communication channels that involve electronic transmissions, such as radio, television, and the Internet.

Enabling legislation A law enacted by a legislature to establish an administrative agency. Enabling legislation normally specifies the name, purpose, composition, and powers of the agency being created.

Entitlement program A government program (such as Social Security) that allows, or entitles, a certain class of people (such as elderly persons) to receive special benefits. Entitlement programs operate under open-ended budget authorizations that, in effect, place no limits on how much can be spent.

Equal protection clause Section 1 of the Fourteenth Amendment, which states that no state shall "deny to any person within its jurisdiction the equal protection of the laws."

Equality A concept that holds, at a minimum, that all people are entitled to equal protection under the law.

Establishment clause The section of the First Amendment that prohibits Congress from passing laws "respecting an establishment of religion." Issues concerning the establishment clause often center on prayer in public schools, the teaching of fundamentalist theories of creation, and government aid to parochial schools.

Ex post facto **law** A criminal law that punishes individuals for committing an act that was legal when the act was committed.

Exclusionary rule A criminal procedural rule requiring that any illegally obtained evidence not be admissible in court.

Executive agreement A binding international agreement, or pact, that is made between the president and another head of state and that does not require Senate approval.

Executive Office of the President (EOP) A group of staff agencies that assist the president in carrying out major duties. Franklin D. Roosevelt established the EOP in 1939 to cope with the increased responsibilities brought on by the Great Depression.

Executive order A presidential order to carry out a policy or policies described in a law passed by Congress.

Executive privilege An inherent executive power claimed by presidents to withhold information from, or to refuse to appear before, Congress or the courts. The president can also accord the privilege to other executive officials.

Expressed powers Constitutional or statutory powers that are expressly provided for by the Constitution.

F

Faction A group of persons forming a cohesive minority.

Federal mandate A requirement in federal legislation that forces states and municipalities to comply with certain rules. If the federal government does not provide funds to the states to cover the costs of compliance, the mandate is referred to as an *unfunded* mandate.

Federal Open Market Committee (FOMC) The most important body within the Federal Reserve System. The FOMC decides how monetary policy should be carried out by the Federal Reserve.

Federal question A question that pertains to the U.S. Constitution, acts of Congress, or treaties. A federal question provides a basis for federal court jurisdiction.

Federal system A form of government that provides for a division of powers between a central government and several regional governments. In the United States, the division of powers between the national government and the states is established by the Constitution.

Federalism A system of shared sovereignty between two levels of government—one national and one subnational—occupying the same geographic region.

Federalists A political group, led by Alexander Hamilton and John Adams, that supported the adoption of the Constitution and the creation of a federal form of government.

Feminism The belief in full political, economic, and social equality for women.

Filibustering The Senate tradition of unlimited debate undertaken for the purpose of preventing action on a bill.

First budget resolution A budget resolution, which is supposed to be passed in May, that sets overall revenue goals and spending targets for the next fiscal year, which begins on October 1.

First Continental Congress A gathering of delegates from twelve of the thirteen colonies, held in 1774 to protest the Coercive Acts.

Fiscal federalism The allocation of taxes collected by one level of government (typically the national government) to another level (typically state or local governments).

Fiscal policy The use of changes in government expenditures and taxes to alter national economic variables.

Fiscal year A twelve-month period that is established for bookkeeping or accounting purposes. The government's fiscal year runs from October 1 through September 30.

Foreign policy A systematic and general plan that guides a country's attitudes and actions toward the rest of the world. Foreign policy includes all of the economic, military, commercial, and diplomatic positions and actions that a nation takes in its relationships with other countries.

Free exercise clause The provision of the First Amendment stating that the government cannot pass laws "prohibiting the free exercise" of religion. Free exercise issues often concern religious practices that conflict with established laws.

Free rider problem The difficulty that exists when individuals can enjoy the outcome of an interest group's efforts without having to contribute, such as by becoming members of the group.

Fundamental right A basic right of all Americans, such as First Amendment rights. Any law or action that prevents some group of persons from exercising a fundamental right is subject to the "strict-scrutiny" standard, under which the law or action must be necessary to promote a compelling state interest and must be narrowly tailored to meet that interest.

G

Gender gap The difference between the percentage of votes cast for a particular candidate by women and the percentage of votes cast for the same candidate by men.

General election A regularly scheduled election to choose the U.S. president, vice president, and senators and representatives in Congress. General elections are held in even-numbered years on the Tuesday after the first Monday in November.

Gerrymandering The drawing of a legislative district's boundaries in such a way as to maximize the influence of a certain group or political party.

Glass ceiling An invisible but real discriminatory barrier that prevents women and minorities from rising to top positions of power or responsibility.

Global warming An increase in the average temperature of the Earth's surface over the last half century and its projected continuation.

Government The individuals and institutions that make society's rules and that also possess the power and authority to enforce those rules.

Government corporation An agency of the government that is run as a business enterprise. Such agencies engage in primarily commercial activities, produce revenues, and require greater flexibility than that permitted in most government agencies.

Grandfather clause A clause in a state law that had the effect of restricting the franchise (voting rights) to those whose ancestors had voted before the 1860s; one of the techniques used in the South to prevent African Americans from exercising their right to vote.

Great Compromise A plan for a bicameral legislature in which one chamber would be based on population and the other chamber would represent each state equally. The plan, also known as the Connecticut Compromise, resolved the small-state/large-state controversy.

Greenhouse gas A gas that, when released into the atmosphere, traps the sun's heat and slows its release into outer space. Carbon dioxide (CO_2) is a major example.

H

Head of state The person who serves as the ceremonial head of a country's government and represents that country to the rest of the world.

I

Ideologue An individual who holds very strong political opinions.

Ideology Generally, a system of political ideas that are rooted in religious or philosophical beliefs concerning human nature, society, and government.

Implied powers The powers of the federal government that are implied by the expressed powers in the Constitution, particularly in Article I, Section 8.

Independent executive agency A federal agency that is not located within a cabinet department.

Independent expenditure An expenditure for activities that are independent from (not coordinated with) those of a political candidate or a political party.

Independent regulatory agency A federal organization that is responsible for creating and implementing rules that regulate private activity and protect the public interest in a particular sector of the economy.

Indirect technique Any method used by interest groups to influence government officials through third parties, such as voters.

Individual mandate In the context of health-care reform, a requirement that all persons obtain health-care insurance from one source or another. Those failing to do so would pay a penalty.

Inherent powers The powers of the national government that, although not always expressly granted by the Constitution, are necessary to ensure the nation's integrity and survival as a political unit. Inherent powers include the power to make treaties and the power to wage war or make peace.

Institution An ongoing organization that performs certain functions for society.

Instructed delegate A representative who deliberately mirrors the views of the majority of his or her constituents.

Interest group An organized group of individuals sharing common objectives who actively attempt to influence policymakers.

Interstate commerce Trade that involves more than one state.

Interventionism Direct involvement by one country in another country's affairs.

Iron curtain A phrase coined by Winston Churchill to describe the political boundaries between the democratic countries in Western Europe and the Soviet-controlled Communist countries in Eastern Europe.

Iron triangle A three-way alliance among legislators, bureaucrats, and interest groups to make or preserve policies that benefit their respective interests.

Isolationism A political policy of noninvolvement in world affairs.

Issue ad A political advertisement that focuses on a particular issue. Issue ads can be used to support or attack a candidate.

Issue networks Groups of individuals or organizations—which consist of legislators and legislative staff members, interest group leaders, bureaucrats, the media, scholars, and other experts—that support particular policy positions on a given issue.

J

Judicial review The power of the courts to decide on the constitutionality of legislative enactments and of actions taken by the executive branch.

Judiciary The courts; one of the three branches of government in the United States.

Jurisdiction The authority of a court to hear and decide a particular case.

Justiciable controversy A controversy that is not hypothetical or academic but real and substantial; a requirement that must be satisfied before a court will hear a case. *Justiciable* is pronounced jus-*tish*-a-bul.

K

Keynesian economics An economic theory proposed by British economist John Maynard Keynes that is typically associated with the use of fiscal policy to alter national economic variables.

Kitchen cabinet The name given to a president's unofficial advisers. The term was coined during Andrew Jackson's presidency.

L

Labor force All of the people over the age of sixteen who are working or actively looking for jobs.

Legislative rule An administrative agency rule that carries the same weight as a statute enacted by a legislature.

Lemon test A three-part test enunciated by the Supreme Court in the 1971 case of *Lemon v. Kurtzman* to determine whether government aid to parochial schools is constitutional. To be constitutional, the aid must (1) be for a clearly secular purpose; (2) in its primary effect, neither advance nor inhibit religion; and (3) avoid an "excessive government entanglement with religion." The Lemon test has also been used in other types of cases involving the establishment clause.

Libel A published report of a falsehood that tends to injure a person's reputation or character.

Liberalism A set of political beliefs that include the advocacy of active government, including government intervention to improve the welfare of individuals and to protect civil rights.

Liberty The freedom of individuals to believe, act, and express themselves as they choose so long as doing so does not infringe on the rights of other individuals in the society.

Limited government A form of government based on the principle that the powers of government should be clearly limited either through a written document or through wide public understanding; characterized by institutional checks to ensure that government serves public rather than private interests.

Literacy test A test given to voters to ensure that they could read and write and thus evaluate political information; a technique used in many southern states to restrict African American participation in elections.

Lobbying All of the attempts by organizations or by individuals to influence the passage, defeat, or contents of legislation or to influence the administrative decisions of government.

Lobbyist An individual who handles a particular interest group's lobbying efforts.

Loophole A legitimate way of evading a certain legal requirement.

M

Madisonian Model The model of government devised by James Madison, in which the powers of the government are separated into three branches: executive, legislative, and judicial.

Majority leader The party leader elected by the majority party in the House or in the Senate.

Majority party The political party that has more members in the legislature than the opposing party.

Malapportionment A condition in which the voting power of citizens in one district is greater than the voting power of citizens in another district.

Managed news coverage News coverage that is manipulated (managed) by a campaign manager or political consultant to gain media exposure for a political candidate.

Markup session A meeting held by a congressional committee or subcommittee to approve, amend, or redraft a bill.

Marshall Plan A plan providing for U.S. economic assistance to European nations following World War II to help those nations recover from the war; the plan was named after George C. Marshall, secretary of state from 1947 to 1949.

Mass media Communication channels, such as newspapers and radio and television broadcasts, through which people can communicate to large audiences.

Material incentive Practical benefits from joining an interest group, such as discounts, subscriptions, or group insurance.

Mayflower Compact A document drawn up by Pilgrim leaders in 1620 on the ship *Mayflower*. The document stated that laws were to be made for the general good of the people.

Media Newspapers, magazines, television, radio, the Internet, and any other printed or electronic means of communication.

Medicaid A joint federal-state program that provides health-care services for low-income persons.

Medicare A federal government program that pays for health-care insurance for Americans aged sixty-five years or over.

Minority leader The party leader elected by the minority party in the House or in the Senate.

Minority party The political party that has fewer members in the legislature than the opposing party.

Minority-majority district A district in which minority groups make up a majority of the population.

Miranda warnings A series of statements informing criminal suspects, on their arrest, of their constitutional rights, such as the right to remain silent and the right to counsel; required by the Supreme Court's 1966 decision in *Miranda v. Arizona*.

Moderate A person whose views fall in the middle of the political spectrum.

Monarchy A form of autocracy in which a king, queen, emperor, empress, tsar, or tsarina is the highest authority in the government; monarchs usually obtain their power through inheritance.

Monetary policy Actions taken by the Federal Reserve Board to change the amount of money in circulation so as to affect interest rates, credit markets, the rate of inflation, the rate of economic growth, and the rate of unemployment.

Monroe Doctrine A U.S. policy, announced in 1823 by President James Monroe, that the United States would not tolerate foreign intervention in the Western Hemisphere, and in return, the United States would stay out of European affairs.

Moral idealism In foreign policy, the belief that the most important goal is to do what is right. Moral idealists think that it is possible for nations to cooperate as part of a rule-based community.

Mutually assured destruction (MAD) A phrase referring to the assumption, on which the policy of deterrence was based, that if the forces of two nations are equally capable of destroying each other, neither nation will take a chance on war.

N

National convention The meeting held by each major party every four years to select presidential and vice-presidential candidates, write a party platform, and conduct other party business.

National health insurance A program, found in many of the world's economically advanced nations, under which the central government provides basic health-care insurance coverage to everyone in the country. Some wealthy nations, such as the Netherlands and Switzerland, provide universal coverage through private insurance companies instead.

National party chairperson An individual who serves as a political party's administrative head at the national level and directs the work of the party's national committee.

National party committee The political party leaders who direct party business during the four years between the national party conventions, organize the next national convention, and plan how to obtain a party victory in the next presidential elections.

National Security Council (NSC) A council that advises the president on domestic and foreign matters concerning the safety and defense of the nation; established in 1947.

Natural rights Rights that are not bestowed by governments but are inherent within every man, woman, and child by virtue of the fact that he or she is a human being.

Necessary and proper clause Article I, Section 8, Clause 18, of the Constitution, which gives Congress the power to make all laws "necessary and proper" for the federal government to carry out its responsibilities; also called the *elastic clause.*

Negative political advertising Political advertising undertaken for the purpose of discrediting an opposing candidate in the eyes of the voters. Attack ads are one form of negative political advertising.

Neoconservatism A philosophy of foreign policy based on moral idealism. Neoconservatives support the use of economic and military power to bring democracy and human rights to other countries.

Neutral competency The application of technical skills to jobs without regard to political issues.

Neutrality A position of not being aligned with either side in a dispute or conflict, such as a war.

New Deal A program ushered in by the Roosevelt administration in 1933 in an attempt to bring the United States out of the Great Depression. The New Deal included many government-spending and public assistance programs, in addition to thousands of regulations governing economic activity.

New federalism A plan to limit the federal government's role in regulating state governments and to give the states increased power to decide how they should spend government revenues.

Nominating convention An official meeting of a political party to choose its candidates. Nominating conventions at the state and local levels also select delegates to represent the citizens of their geographic areas at a higher-level party convention.

Normal trade relations (NTR) status A trade status granted through an international treaty by which each member nation must treat other members at least as well as it treats the country that receives its most favorable treatment. This status was formerly known as *most-favored-nation status.*

O

Obscenity Indecency or offensiveness in speech, expression, behavior, or appearance. Whether specific expressions or acts constitute obscenity normally is determined by community standards.

Office of Management and Budget (OMB) An agency in the Executive Office of the President that assists the president in preparing and supervising the administration of the federal budget.

Office-block ballot A ballot (also called the Massachusetts ballot) that lists together all of the candidates for each office.

"One person, one vote" rule A rule, or principle, requiring that congressional districts have equal populations so that one person's vote counts as much as another's vote.

Open primary A primary in which voters can vote for a party's candidates regardless of whether they belong to the party.

Opinion A written statement by a court expressing the reasons for its decision in a case.

Oral argument A spoken agrument presented to a judge in person by an attorney on behalf of her or his client.

Oslo Accords The first agreement signed between Israel and the PLO; led to the establishment of the Palestinian Authority in the occupied territories.

P

Palestine Liberation Organization (PLO) An organization formed in 1964 to represent the Palestinian people. The PLO has a long history of terrorism but for some years has functioned primarily as a political party.

Parliament The name of the national legislative body in countries governed by a parliamentary system, such as Britain and Canada.

Partisan politics Political actions or decisions that benefit a particular party.

Party activist A party member who helps to organize and oversee party functions and planning during and between campaigns.

Party identifier A person who identifies himself or herself as being a member of a particular political party.

Party platform The document drawn up by each party at its national convention that outlines the policies and positions of the party.

Party ticket A list of a political party's candidates for various offices. In national elections, the party ticket consists of the presidential and vice-presidential candidates.

Party-column ballot A ballot (also called the Indiana ballot) that lists all of a party's candidates under the party label. Voters can vote for all of a party's candidates for local, state, and national offices by making a single "X" or pulling a single lever.

Patronage A system of rewarding the party faithful and workers with government jobs or contracts; giving government jobs to individuals belonging to the winning political party.

Peer group Associates, often close in age to one another; may include friends, classmates, co-workers, club members, or religious group members. Peer group influence is a significant factor in the political socialization process.

Personal attack ad A negative political advertisement that attacks the character of an opposing candidate.

Picket-fence federalism A model of federalism in which specific policies and programs are administered by all levels of government—national, state, and local.

Pluralist theory A theory that views politics as a contest among various interest groups—at all levels of government—to gain benefits for their members.

Pocket veto A special type of veto power used by the chief executive after the legislature has adjourned. Bills that are not signed die after a specified period of time.

Podcasting The distribution of audio or video files to a personal computer or a mobile device, such as an ipod.

Police powers The powers of a government body that enable it to create laws for the protection of the health, morals, safety, and welfare of the people. In the United States, most police powers are reserved to the states.

Policymaking process The procedures involved in getting an issue on the political agenda; formulating, adopting, and implementing a policy with regard to the issue; and then evaluating the results of the policy.

Political action committee (PAC) A committee that is established by a corporation, labor union, or special interest group to raise funds and make contributions on the establishing organization's behalf.

Political advertising Advertising undertaken by or on behalf of a political candidate to familiarize voters with the candidate and his or her views on campaign issues; also advertising for or against policy issues.

Political consultant A professional political adviser who, for a fee, works on an area of a candidate's campaign. Political consultants include campaign managers, pollsters, media advisers, and "get out the vote" organizers.

Political culture The set of ideas, values, and attitudes about government and the political process held by a community or a nation.

Political party A group of individuals who organize to win elections, operate the government, and determine policy.

Political realism In foreign policy, the belief that nations are inevitably selfish, and that we should seek to protect our national security regardless of moral arguments.

Political socialization The learning process through which most people acquire their political attitudes, opinions, beliefs, and knowledge.

Politics The process of resolving conflicts over how society should use its scarce resources and who should receive various benefits, such as public health care and public higher education. According to Harold Lasswell, politics is the process of determining "who gets what, when, and how" in a society.

Poll tax A fee of several dollars that had to be paid before a person could vote; a device used in some southern states to prevent African Americans from voting.

Poll watcher A representative from one of the political parties who is allowed to monitor a polling place to make sure that the election is run fairly and to avoid fraud.

Power The ability to influence the behavior of others, usually through the use of force, persuasion, or rewards.

Precedent A court decision that furnishes an example or authority for deciding subsequent cases involving identical or similar facts and legal issues.

Precinct A political district within a city, such as a block or a neighborhood, or a rural portion of a county; the smallest voting district at the local level.

Preemption A doctrine rooted in the supremacy clause of the Constitution that provides that national laws or regulations governing a certain area take precedence over conflicting state laws or regulations governing that same area.

Preemptive war A war launched by a nation to prevent an imminent attack by another nation.

Press secretary A member of the White House staff who holds news conferences for reporters and makes public statements for the president.

Preventive war A war launched by a nation to prevent the possibility that another nation might attack at some point in the future; not supported by international law.

Primary A preliminary election held for the purpose of choosing a party's final candidate.

Primary election An election in which voters choose the candidates of their party, who will then run in the general election.

Primary source of law A source of law that establishes the law. Primary sources of law include constitutions, statutes, administrative agency rules and regulations, and decisions rendered by the courts.

Print media Communication channels that consist of printed materials, such as newspapers and magazines.

Privatization The transfer of the task of providing services traditionally provided by government to the private sector.

Probable cause Cause for believing that there is a substantial likelihood that a person has committed or is about to commit a crime.

Progressivism An alternative, more popular term for the set of political beliefs also known as liberalism.

Public debt The total amount of money that the national government owes as a result of borrowing; also called the *national debt*.

Public opinion The views of the citizenry about politics, public issues, and public policies; a complex collection of opinions held by many people on issues in the public arena.

Public opinion poll A numerical survey of the public's opinion on a particular topic at a particular moment.

Public option In the context of health-care reform, a government-sponsored health-care insurance program that would compete with private insurance companies.

Public services Essential services that individuals cannot provide for themselves, such as building and maintaining roads, providing welfare programs, operating public schools, and preserving national parks.

Public-interest group An interest group formed for the purpose of working for the "public good." Examples of public-interest groups are the American Civil Liberties Union and Common Cause.

Purposive incentive A reason to join an interest group—satisfaction resulting from working for a cause in which one believes.

Push poll A campaign tactic used to feed false or misleading information to potential voters, under the guise of taking an opinion poll, with the intent to "push" voters away from one candidate and toward another.

Q

Quota system A policy under which a specific number of jobs, promotions, or other types of placements, such as university admissions, must be given to members of selected groups.

R

Radical left Persons on the extreme left side of the political spectrum, who would like major changes in the political order, usually to promote egalitarianism (human equality).

Radical right Persons on the extreme right side of the political spectrum. The radical right includes reactionaries (who would like to return to the values and social systems of some previous era) and libertarians (who believe in no regulation of the economy or individual behavior).

Random sample In the context of opinion polling, a sample in which each person within the entire population being polled has an equal chance of being chosen.

Rating system A system by which a particular interest group evaluates (rates) the performance of legislators based on how often the legislators have voted with the group's position on particular issues.

Rational basis test A test (also known as the "ordinary-scrutiny" standard) used by the Supreme Court to decide whether a discriminatory law violates the equal protection clause of the Constitution. Few laws evaluated under this test are found invalid.

Realignment A process in which the popular support for and relative strength of the parties shift and the parties are reestablished with different coalitions of supporters.

Reconciliation A special kind of legislation not subject to filibuster in the Senate. A reconciliation act must deal only with financial matters.

Renewable energy Energy from technologies that do not rely on extracted resources, such as oil and coal, that can run out.

Representative democracy A form of democracy in which the will of the majority is expressed through smaller groups of individuals elected by the people to act as their representatives.

Republic Essentially, a representative democracy in which there is no king or queen and the people are sovereign.

Reverse discrimination Discrimination against those who have no minority status.

Right-to-work laws Laws that ban unions from collecting dues or other fees from workers that they represent but who have not actually joined the union.

Rule of law A basic principle of government that requires those who govern to act in accordance with established law.

Rulemaking The process undertaken by an administrative agency when formally proposing, evaluating, and adopting a new regulation.

Rules Committee A standing committee in the House of Representatives that provides special rules governing how particular bills will be considered and debated by the House. The Rules Committee normally proposes time limits on debate for any bill.

S

Sample In the context of opinion polling, a group of people selected to represent the population being studied.

Sampling error In the context of opinion polling, the difference between what the sample results show and what the true results would have been had everybody in the relevant population been interviewed.

School voucher An educational certificate, provided by the government, that allows a student to use public funds to pay for a private or a public school chosen by the student or his or her parents.

Secession The act of formally withdrawing from membership in an alliance; the withdrawal of a state from the federal Union.

Second budget resolution A budget resolution, which is supposed to be passed in September, that sets "binding" limits on taxes and spending for the next fiscal year.

Second Continental Congress The congress of the colonies that met in 1775 to assume the powers of a central government and to establish an army.

Seditious speech Speech that urges resistance to lawful authority or that advocates the overthrowing of a government.

Self-incrimination Providing damaging information or testimony against oneself in court.

Senatorial courtesy A practice that allows a senator of the president's party to veto the president's nominee to a federal court judgeship within the senator's state.

Separate-but-equal doctrine A Supreme Court doctrine holding that the equal protection clause of the Fourteenth Amendment did not forbid racial segregation as long as the facilities for blacks were equal to those for whites. The doctrine was overturned in the *Brown v. Board of Education of Topeka* decision of 1954.

Separation of powers The principle of dividing governmental powers among the executive, the legislative, and the judicial branches of government.

Sexual harassment Unwanted physical contact, verbal conduct, or abuse of a sexual nature that interferes with a recipient's job performance, creates a hostile environment, or carries with it an implicit or explicit threat of adverse employment consequences.

Shays' Rebellion A rebellion of angry farmers in western Massachusetts in 1786, led by former Revolutionary War captain Daniel Shays. This rebellion and other similar uprisings in the New England states emphasized the need for a true national government.

Signing statement A written statement, appended to a bill at the time the president signs it into law, indicating how the president interprets that legislation.

Sit-in A tactic of nonviolent civil disobedience. Demonstrators enter a business, college building, or other public place and remain seated until they are forcibly removed or until their demands are met. The tactic was used successfully in the civil rights movement and in other protest movements in the United States.

Slander The public utterance (speaking) of a statement that holds a person up for contempt, ridicule, or hatred.

Social conflict Disagreements among people in a society over what the society's priorities should be when distributing scarce resources.

Social contract A voluntary agreement among individuals to create a government and to give that government adequate power to secure the mutual protection and welfare of all individuals.

Soft money Campaign contributions not regulated by federal law, such as some contributions that are made to political parties instead of to particular candidates.

Solid South A term used to describe the tendency of the southern states to vote Democratic after the Civil War.

Solidarity Mutual sympathy among the members of a particular group.

Solidary incentive A reason to join an interest group—pleasure in associating with like-minded individuals.

Sound bite A televised comment, lasting for only a few seconds, that captures a thought or a perspective and has an immediate impact on the viewers.

Soviet bloc The group of Eastern European nations that fell under the control of the Soviet Union following World War II.

Speaker of the House The presiding officer in the House of Representatives. The Speaker has traditionally been a longtime member of the majority party and is often the most powerful and influential member of the House.

Special election An election that is held at the state or local level when the voters must decide an issue before the next general election or when vacancies occur by reason of death or resignation.

Spin A reporter's slant on, or interpretation of, a particular event or action.

Spin doctor A political candidate's press adviser, who tries to convince reporters to give a story or event concerning the candidate a particular "spin" (interpretation, or slant).

Standing committee A permanent committee in Congress that deals with legislation concerning a particular area, such as agriculture or foreign relations.

Standing to sue The requirement that an individual must have a sufficient stake in a controversy before he or she can bring a lawsuit. The party bringing the suit must demonstrate that he or she has either been harmed or been threatened with a harm.

Stare decisis A common law doctrine under which judges normally are obligated to follow the precedents established by prior court decisions. Pronounced *ster*-ay dih-*si*-sis.

State Children's Health Insurance Program (SCHIP) A joint federal-state program that provides health-care insurance for low-income children.

Statutory law The body of law enacted by legislatures (as opposed to constitutional law, administrative law, or case law).

Straw poll A nonscientific poll; a poll in which there is no way to ensure that the opinions expressed are representative of the larger population.

Subcommittee A division of a larger committee that deals with a particular part of the committee's policy area. Most standing committees have several subcommittees.

Suffrage The right to vote; the franchise.

Supremacy clause Article VI, Clause 2, of the Constitution, which makes the Constitution and federal laws superior to all conflicting state and local laws.

Suspect classification A classification, such as race, that provides the basis for a discriminatory law. Any law based on a suspect classification is subject to strict scrutiny by the courts—meaning that the law must be justified by a compelling state interest.

Symbolic speech The expression of beliefs, opinions, or ideas through forms other than speech or print; speech involving actions and other nonverbal expressions.

T

Third party In the United States, any party other than one of the two major parties (Republican and Democratic).

Three-fifths compromise A compromise reached during the Constitutional Convention by which three-fifths of all slaves were to be counted for purposes of representation in the House of Representatives.

Trade organization An association formed by members of a particular industry, such as the oil industry or the trucking industry, to develop common standards and goals for the industry. Trade organizations, as interest groups, lobby government for legislation or regulations that specifically benefit their groups.

Treaty A formal agreement between the governments of two or more countries.

Trial court A court in which trials are held and testimony taken.

Trustee A representative who tries to serve the broad interests of the entire society and not just the narrow interests of his or her constituents.

Two-party system A political system in which two strong and established parties compete for political offices.

Tyranny The arbitrary or unrestrained exercise of power by an oppressive individual or government.

U

Unicameral legislature A legislature with only one chamber.

Unitary system A centralized governmental system in which local or subdivisional governments exercise only those powers given to them by the central government.

V

Veto A Latin word meaning "I forbid"; the refusal by an official, such as the president of the United States or a state governor, to sign a bill into law.

Veto power A constitutional power that enables the chief executive (president or governor) to reject legislation and return it to the legislature with reasons for the rejection. This prevents or at least delays the bill from becoming law.

Vital center The center of the political spectrum; those who hold moderate political views. The center is vital because without it, it may be difficult, if not impossible, to reach the compromises that are necessary to a political system's continuity.

Vote-eligible population The number of people who are actually eligible to vote in an American election.

Voting-age population The number of people residing in the United States who are at least eighteen years old.

W

Ward A local unit of a political party's organization, consisting of a division or district within a city.

Watergate scandal A scandal involving an illegal break-in at the Democratic National Committee offices in 1972 by members of President Nixon's reelection campaign staff. Before Congress could vote to impeach Nixon for his participation in covering up the break-in, Nixon resigned from the presidency.

Weapons of mass destruction Chemical, biological, or nuclear weapons that can inflict massive casualties.

Whip A member of Congress who assists the majority or minority leader in the House or in the Senate in managing the party's legislative preferences.

Whistleblower In the context of government employment, someone who "blows the whistle" (reports to authorities) on gross governmental inefficiency, illegal action, or other wrongdoing.

White House Office The personal office of the president. White House Office personnel handle the president's political needs and manage the media.

White primary A primary election in which African Americans were prohibited from voting. The practice was banned by the Supreme Court in 1944.

Winner-take-all system A system in which the candidate who receives the most votes wins. In contrast, proportional systems allocate votes to multiple winners.

Writ of *certiorari* An order from a higher court asking a lower court for the record of a case. *Certiorari* is pronounced sur-shee-uh-*rah*-ree.

Writ of *habeas corpus* An order that requires an official to bring a specified prisoner into court and explain to the judge why the person is being held in prison.

Index

slavery issues, 33, 34, 36
three-fifths compromise, 33
Virginia Plan, 31–32
Constitutional law, 306
Constitutional monarchy, 7
Constitution of United States. *See also* Bill of Rights
amending
methods of proposing amendments, 44
ratifying amendment, 44
Amendments
First, 42, 74–85
Second, 22, 42
Third, 42, 85
Fourth, 42, 85, 97
Fifth, 42, 85, 89
Sixth, 42, 89
Seventh, 42
Eighth, 42, 43, 89
Ninth, 42, 85
Tenth, 42, 54, 66–67, 306
Thirteenth, 54, 97
Fourteenth, 54, 73–74, 95–96, 109, 113
Fifteenth, 54, 97, 174, 176
Sixteenth, 244
Seventeenth, 236
Nineteenth, 54, 102, 175, 176
Twenty-second, 237
Twenty-fourth, 54
Twenty-fifth, 276
Twenty-sixth, 54, 175, 176
Article I, 37, 39
Section 4, 236
Section 7, 262
Section 8, 52, 53, 57
Section 9, 53, 72
Section 10, 54
Article II, 37, 39, 258, 262
Section 1, 256–257
Section 2, 53, 247, 312, 347
Article III, 37, 39, 311, 312
Section 2, 308, 311
Article V, 43
Article VI, Clause 2, 55
Article of Confederation as first draft for, 29–30
bill of attainder, 72–73
civil liberties, 11
commerce clause, 38, 57, 61
congressional representation of Washington, D.C., 192
constitutional law, 306
division of powers, 53–55
drafting of, 31–35
due process clause of, 73–74
establishment of Supreme Court, 34
ex post facto law, 73
federal system and, 50
full faith and credit clause, 54
health care reform and, 63
impeachment, 34
interstate relations, 54–55
necessary and proper clause, 53, 56–57
original intent vs. modernism, 320–321
presidential powers, 34, 262–264
principles of government
Bill of Rights, 41
checks and balances, 39, 41
federalism, 38–39
limited government, 37
popular sovereignty, 37
separation of powers, 39
ratification of, 35–37, 142
slavery and, 33, 34, 36
supremacy clause, 55, 57, 61
writ of *habeas corpus*, 72

Constitutions, state, 29
Consumer Federation for America, 127
Consumer interest groups, 129
Consumer Product Safety Act, 282
Consumer Product Safety Commission, 280, 282
Consumer Reports, 129
Consumer Union, 129
Containment, 351
Continental Congress, 26–27
Continuing resolutions, 251
Contracts, 13
Conventions
national, 198
nominating, 193–194
Cook, Charlie, 173
Cooper, Anderson, 213
Cooperative federalism, 60–61
Corporate Average Fuel Economy (CAFE), 334
Corporations, government, 289–291
Coughlin, Edward, 220
Coughlin, Patrick, 81
Counsel, right to, 89
Counties, number of, in U.S., 51
Couric, Katie, 211
Courts
appellate, 310–311
assessing role of, 321–322
court procedure, 309
district courts, 309–310
federal court system, 309–312
ideology and, 317–321
impact of court decisions, 315–316
judicial review, 39, 56
jurisdiction, 307–308
origins and sources of American law, 304–309
as policymakers, 315–317
power of judicial review, 316
standing to sue, 308–309
trial, 308
U.S. Supreme Court, 311–312
Courts of appeal, 310–311
appointments to, 314
Creationism, 77
Credentials Committee, 198
Criminal defendants, rights of, 89
Criminal law, 307
Cronkite, Walter, 211
Cross-cutting requirements, 66
Cruel and unusual punishment, 42, 89
death penalty as, 43
Cuba
Cuban missile crisis, 352
Spanish-American War and, 350
Cuban Americans, 105, 106
voting behavior, 183
Cuban missile crisis, 352
Culture, political, 11
Cuomo, Andrew, 194
Curiae regis (King's court), 304
Cyberspace. *See* Internet
Czechoslovakia, Soviet bloc, 350

D

Daily Show with Jon Stewart, The, 219
D.C. Voting Rights Act, 192
Dealignment, 147
Death penalty, as cruel and unusual punishment, 43
Debates, television, 218–219
Debt, public debt, 340–343
Declaration of Independence
equality and, 12

political culture and, 11
pursuit of happiness, 13
significance of, 28
slavery and, 36
Declaration of Sentiments, 101
De facto segregation, 98
Defense, Department of, 273
foreign policymaking and, 348
principle duties of, 286
Defense of Marriage Act (DOMA), 54–55
De Jonge v. Oregon, 74
De jure segregation, 98
DeLay, Tom, 234
Delegates
defined, 193
national convention, 198
to nominating convention, 193–194
unpledged, 195
Democracy. *See also* American democracy
American, 9–18
defined, 8
direct, 8
parliamentary democracy, 8
presidential democracy, 8
representative, 8
in Russia, 37, 38
Democratic National Committee, 126
Democratic Party
African American support for, 145, 183
beginning of, 143
Blue Dog Coalition, 332
business interest groups and, 126
Civil rights plank of platform in 1948 election, 145
control of Congress, 145–146, 231, 248, 271
current condition of, 146–148
dealignment, 147
devolution, 62
election of 2006, 146
Great Depression and, 145
growing partisanship, 147
health care proposal, 331–332
Hispanics identification with, 106
historical perspective of political parties, 142–146
liberals identify with, 16
national committees, 153
national conventions, 153, 154
party identification and voting behavior in 2008 election, 179, 180
Populist movement and, 145
realignment elections, 145–146
red state vs. blue state, 146
shifting political fortunes, 146–147
socioeconomic factors
age, 182
educational attainment, 180
gender and, 182
geographic region and, 183–184
moderates, 185
occupation and income level, 180, 182
religion and ethnicity, 183
Solid South, 183
stimulus package, partisan politics and, 148
symbol of, 156
tipping, 147–148
trouble for, 146–147
voter fraud claims, 177
Democratic Republicans, 143, 193
Demonstration techniques, of interest groups, 134
Dennis v. United States, 81
Depression. *See* Great Depression
Détente, 352
Deterrence, 352

action-reaction syndrome, 339–340
  defined, 66, 337
  federal tax system and, 338–340
  Great Recession and, 66
  Keynesian economics, 338
  simplifying tax system, 340
  tax loopholes, 340
Fiscal year, 250
501(c)4, 134, 204
527s, 133–134, 204
Food and Drug Administration (FDA)
  Avandia, 280
  lobbying and, 132
Ford, Gerald, 276
  legislative success of, 268
  pardon of Nixon, 263
Foreign policy, 345–364
  China and, 361–364
  defined, 347
  history of, 349–353
    Cold War, 350–353
    containment, 351
    Cuban missile crisis, 352
    interventionism, 350
    isolationism, 349–350
    Marshall Plan, 351
    Monroe Doctrine, 349–350
    neutrality, 350
    post-cold war, 353
    World Wars, 350
  Iran as emerging nuclear threat, 361, 362
  Israeli-Palestinian conflict, 358–360
  makers of, 347–349
  moral idealism, 347, 350
  North Korea's nuclear program,
    360–361
  Obama and U.S. image abroad, 167
  political realism, 347
  presidential power in, 269, 272
  war on terrorism, 353–358
  weapons proliferation in unstable
    world, 360–361
Foreign Relations Committee, 349
Fourteenth Amendment
  affirmative action, 113
  counting unauthorized immigrants for
    census, 94
  equal protection clause
    defined, 95
    intermediate scrutiny standard, 96
    ordinary scrutiny, 96
    original intention of, 97
    rational basis test, 96
    strict scrutiny standard, 96
  gender discrimination, 102
  incorporating Bill of Rights into, 73–74
  Native Americans, 109
  sodomy laws, 111
Fourth Amendment
  exclusionary rule, 89
  probable cause, 89
  right to privacy, 85
  text of, 42
  unreasonable search and seizure, 89
  warrants, 89
Fox News, 221
France
  Greece bailout, 354
  head of state and prime minister, 260
  improved image of U.S., 167
  national identity cards, 88
  Seven Years' War, 25
  as unitary system, 50
  World War II, 350
Franken, Al, 231
Franklin, Benjamin, 31
Freddie Mac (Federal Home Loan
  Mortgage Corporation), 289–291

Freedom(s)
  of assembly, 42
  of association, 195
  of expression, 79–84, 221
  individual, 10
  of petition, 42
  of the press, 42, 84–85, 211–212, 213
  of religion, 42, 74–79
  of speech, 42, 79–84
Freedom of Information Act (FOIA), 85,
  299
Free exercise clause, 74, 78–79
Free markets, 13
Free rider problem, 123
Free Soil Party, 158
Free Speech for People, 45
French and Indian War, 25
Freshwater economics, 148
Full faith and credit clause, 54
Fulton, Robert, 57
Fundamental Orders of Connecticut, 24
Fundamental rights, 73
  defined, 96
  strict scrutiny standard and, 96

G

Gallup, George, 169
Gallup Organization
  founding of, 169
  sampling by, 169
Gates, Robert M., 348
Gay Activist Alliance, 110
Gay Liberation Front, 110
Gay marriage, 54–55, 63
Gays
  changing attitude toward, 111
  changing legal landscape, 110–111
  civil rights of, 110–112
  "Don't ask, don't tell" policy, 112
  in military, 112, 172
  same-sex marriage, 54–55, 111–112
  student religious groups bar
    membership, 80
Geer, John, 218
Geithner, Tim, 249, 337
Gender
  intermediate-scrutiny standard, 96
  voting behavior and, 182
  wage discrimination, 103–104
Gender discrimination, 102
Gender gap, 182
General election, 189
General Electric, 216
General Services Administration
  formation of, 285, 288
  principle duties of, 290
Geographic region, voting behavior and,
  183–184
George III, King (England), 26, 27
Georgia, Russian attack on, 346
Germany, 50
  Berlin Wall, 352
  end of Cold War, 352
  Greece bailout, 354
  improved image of U.S., 167
  national identity cards, 88
  World War II, 350
Gerry, Elbridge, 234
Gerrymandering, 234
  racial, 234
Gibbons, Thomas, 57
Gibbons v. Ogden, 57, 61, 63
Gibbs, Robert, 274
Gideon v. Wainwright, 74, 89
Ginsburg, Ruth Bader, 103

Gitlow v. New York, 74, 84
Glass ceiling, 104
Global warming, 334–337
  cap-and-trade legislation, 336
  debate on, 335
  renewable energy and, 335
Going public strategy, 266
Goldberg, Arthur J., 43
Goldman Sachs, 125, 137
Goldwater, Barry, 194, 217–218
Gonzales, Alberto, 107, 288
Gorbachev, Mikhail, 352
Gore, Al
  election of 2000, 159
    closeness of election, 206
    exit polls, 170–172
    popular vote, 188
    voter fraud, 177
  as vice president, 276
Government
  access to, and interest groups, 124
  aristocracy, 8–9
  authority of, 4
  autocracy, 7
  cost of maintaining, 282–283
  defending nation and culture, 5
  defined, 4
  dictatorship, 7
  direct democracy, 8
  expanded government, under Obama,
    299–300
  limited, 9–10, 37
  monarchy, 7
  need for, 3
  organization of, 284–291
  plutocracy, 9
  power of, 4
  principles of, in Constitution
    Bill of Rights, 41
    checks and balances, 39, 41
    federalism, 38–39
    limited government, 37
    popular sovereignty, 37
    separation of powers, 39
  privatization, 298–299
  providing public service, 4–5
  representative, 10
  representative democracy, 8
  resolving conflicts, 4
  salary for workers, 293
  size of, 2
  in sunshine, 298
  theocracy, 9
  types of, 7–9
Government Accountability Office (GAO),
  296
Government corporations
  defined, 289
  list of selected, 291
Government interest groups, 131
Government Performance and Results Act,
  297
Government regulation. *See* Regulation/
  regulatory agencies
Graber, Doris A., 165
Grandfather clause, 175
Grand juries, 42
Grand jury, right to, 74
Granholm, Jennifer M., 257
Gratz v. Bollinger, 113–114
Great Britain. *See also* England; United
  Kingdom
  American independence from, 25–29
  coalition government in, 157
  Cold War and, 350–353
  Parliament, 10
  as parliamentary democracy, 8
  as representative democracy, 8

Nation-centered federalism, 61
Nation of Islam, 100
Native American Languages Act, 109
Native Americans
    assimilation of, 109
    civil rights of, 107–109
    compensation for past injustices, 109
    decline in population of, 108
    early policies toward, 109
    reservations, 109
    today, 109
Natural rights, 10
Nauru, 190
Navy, president of commander in chief, 259
Nazi Party, 17
NCLB. *See* No Child Left Behind Act
    (NCLB)
Near v. Minnesota, 74
Necessary and proper clause, 53, 56–57
Negative political advertising, 217–218
Nelson, Bill, 245
Neoconservatism, 356
Netanyahu, Benjamin, 358
Netroots groups, 226–227
Neustadt, Richard, 266
Neutral competency, 294
New Deal, 6, 14, 16, 60
New federalism
    defined, 61
    examples of, 62
    Supreme Court and, 62
New Jersey Plan, 32
News coverage
    bias in, 221–222
    candidates and, 219
    changing news culture, 223
    managed news coverage, 219
    news organizations online, 224
    podcasting news, 225
Newspapers
    compared to television news coverage,
        215
    future of, 210
    historical perspective on, 210
    online, 224
    usage of, by consumers, 215
New York Times, 210, 215, 222, 224
New York Times/CBS News poll, 172
Nichols, Terry, 355
Nigeria, 50
Nineteenth Amendment, 102, 175, 176
Ninth Amendment
    right to privacy, 85
    text of, 42
Nixon, Richard M., 135
    attorney general for, 288
    Cambodia invasion and, 270
    election of 1960
        television debates, 218
        use of television and, 199
    Ford's pardon of, 263
    legislative success of, 268
    resignation of, 247, 276
    rolling realignment, 145
    visit to China, 361
    War Powers Resolution, 270
    Watergate scandal, 272
No Child Left Behind Act (NCLB), 67, 155
Nominating convention, 193–194
Nomination process, 192–198
    insurgent candidates, 196
    party control over, 193–194
    party nominating conventions, 193–194
    presidential candidates, 196–198
    primary elections and loss of party
        control, 194–196
    self-nomination, 193
    write-in candidate, 193

Non-Proliferation of Nuclear Weapons,
    Treaty on, 360
Normal trade relations, 362
North American Free Trade Agreement
    (NAFTA), 155
North Atlantic Treaty, 351
North Atlantic Treaty Organization
    (NATO)
    forces in Afghanistan, 357
    formation of, 351
    troops in Afghanistan, 357
Northern Ireland, 354
North Korea
    nuclear cooperation treaty, 360–361
    nuclear program, 360–361
Northwest Ordinance, 29, 109
Nuclear Regulatory Commission, principal
    duties of, 291
Nuclear weapons
    arms race, 352
    Cuban missile crisis, 352
    détente and arms control, 352
    deterrence and, 352
    Iran as emerging threat, 361, 362
    mutually assured destruction (MAD),
        352
    nonproliferation treaties, 360–361
    North Korea's nuclear program, 360–361
    presidential powers in use of, 270

O

Obama, Barack, 64, 197, 206, 258, 261
    Afghanistan and, 358
    African American political participation
        and, 100
    age and voting behavior, 182
    antiterrorism policies of, 90
    appointments
        cabinet, 102, 107
        judicial, 103
        of women, 102, 103
    Bush tax cuts and, 244
    cabinet, 274
    choice of Biden as running mate, 275
    criticism of Bush use of signing
        statements, 268–269
    deficit spending to fight recession, 342
    effectiveness of, 255
    election of 2008
        David Axelrod, 199
        difficulties during, 227–228
        economy and, 164
        Internet fund-raising, 200
        national convention, 152, 154
        personal attack ads and, 217
        popular vote, 207
        red vs. blue states, 146
        use of Internet, 201
        voter perception of candidates,
            179–180
    Executive Office of the President, 274
    exit polls, 172
    expanding bureaucracy, 299–300
    federalism and, 63
    fuel efficiency standards, 334
    fund-raising, 226
    gays in military, 112
    health care reform
        constitutionality of, 63
        public opinion and, 171, 332–333
    illegal immigrants, 328
    image of U.S. abroad and, 167
    Iraq War and, 357
    legislation under, 244, 261, 266
    legislative success of, 266–267, 268
    lobbying and, 137–138

Middle East peace talks and, 358, 359
    Muslim myth of, 267
    offshore oil drilling, 336
    popular vote and, 194
    presidential debates, 219
    primaries, 198
    refusing federal funding for campaign,
        202
    renewable energy and, 335
    stimulus package, 6, 66, 342
        partisan politics and, 148
    Supreme court appointments, 314–315
    talk radio and fairness doctrine, 221
    use of Internet, 227–228
    vetoes by, 264
    withdrawal from Iraq, 357
Obscenity, 82–83
    in cyberspace, 83
    defined, 82
Occupation
    formation of political opinion and, 168
    voting behavior and, 180, 182
Occupational Safety and Health Act, 294
Occupational Safety and Health
    Administration (OSHA), 294
O'Connor, Sandra Day, 103, 115, 314, 319
Office-block ballot, 189
Office of Management and Budget (OMB),
    250, 273, 275
Office of National Drug Control Policy, 274
Office of Personnel Management (OPM),
    292
Office of Special Counsel, 296
Offshore drilling, 336
Ogden, Aaron, 57
Oklahoma City bombing, 355
Olbermann, Keith, 223
Olson, Mancur, 123
One person, one vote rule, 234
Open primary, 196
Operation TIPS, 87
Opinion leaders, 166
Opinions. *See also* Public opinion
    concurring, 312
    defined, 312
    dissenting, 312
    Supreme Court, 312
Oral argument, 312
Ordinances, 306–307
Ordinary-scrutiny standard, 96
O'Reilly, Bill, 221, 223
Organization of American States, 348
Original intent, modernism vs., 320–321
Orszag, Peter, 342
Oslo Accords, 359
Otis, James, Jr., 26
Oversight function of Congress, 246–249

P

Paine, Thomas, 27
Pakistan, 50
Palestinian Authority, 358, 359, 360
Palestinian Liberation Organization (PLO),
    358, 359
Palestinians, 354
    conflict with Israel, 358–360
    Israel Olympic athletes in Munich
        attacked by, 353
Palin, Sarah, 152, 154, 180, 275
Panama Canal Treaty, 263
Pan Am Flight 103 bombing, 353, 355
Pardon, 263
*Parents Involved in Community Schools v.
    Seattle School District No. 1*, 115
Parker v. Gladden, 74
Parks, Rosa, 98

Schenck, Charles T., 84
Schenck v. United States, 84
Schlesinger, Arthur, Jr., 184
Schools. *See also* Education
    affirmative action at colleges, 113–116
    African American challenges and, 101
    aid to parochial schools, 77–78
    busing, 98
    desegregation, 97–98
    evolution vs. creationism, 77
    formation of political opinion and, 165
    free speech for students, 83–84
    intelligent design, 77
    number of school districts, in U.S., 51
    prayer in, 76–77
    school voucher programs, 78, 298
Schumer, Charles, 203
Schwarzenegger, Arnold, 257
Search and seizure, 42, 89
Sebelius, Kathleen, 273
Secession, 58
Second Amendment
    debate over gun control, 22
    Supreme Court and right to bear arms, 4
    text of, 42
Second budget resolution, 251
Second Continental Congress, 27
Second Gulf War. *See* Iraq War
Secretary of state, 103
Securities and Exchange Commission
    (SEC), 127
    duties of, 291, 294
    establishment of, 289
Sedition Act, 81
Seditious speech, 81
Segregation
    Brown v Board of Education of Topeka,
        97–98
    on buses, 98–99
    de facto, 98
    de jure, 98
    school integration and busing, 98
    separate-but-equal doctrine, 97
Selection bias, 215, 222–223
Self-incrimination, 42, 89
Sellers, James L., 59
Semiclosed primary, 196
Semiopen primary, 196
Senate, United States. *See also* Congress
    African Americans in, 100
    budgeting process, 249–252
    campaign costs for, 201–202
    checks and balances and, 39, 41
    cloture, 241
    committees in, 240–241
    confirmation process, 247–249
    congressional districts, 233–234
    debate in, 241–242
    Democratic control of, 231
    differences between House and Senate,
        241–242
    filibustering, 241–242
    foreign policymaking and, 349
    gerrymandering, 234
    Great Compromise, 33
    health care and, 332–333
    impeachment power, 247
    investigative function, 246–247
    leadership in, 240
        majority and minority leaders, 240
        president pro tempore, 240
        vice president as president of, 240
    legislative process, 242–246
    malapportionment, 233–234
    one person, one vote rule, 234
    representation function of, 235–236
    requirements for, 236
    structure of, 232–236

supermajority to pass important
    legislation, 231
    term limits, 237–238
    terms of office for, 39, 41, 237
    three-fifths compromise, 33
Senatorial courtesy, 313
Separate-but-equal doctrine, 97, 306
Separation of powers
    defined, 39
    as principle of Constitution, 39
September 11, 2001 terrorist attacks, 353
    attack ads after, 217
    ban on torture, 268
    Bush's presidency changed by, 272
    federalism after, 63–64
    focus on Iraq, 356–357
    formation of public opinion, 167
    government's role in defending country
        since, 5
    Guantánamo prisoners and rights of,
        303, 329
    openness of government afterwards, 299
    personal privacy and national security
        since, 87
    planned and carried out by al Qaeda, 355
    U.S. response to, 356–358
    war on terrorism afterwards, 270
    War Powers Resolution, 270
Service Employees International Union
    (SEIU), 128, 138
Seventeenth Amendment, 236
Seventh Amendment, text of, 42
Seven Years' War, 25
Sexual harassment, 105
Sharon, Ariel, 359
Shays, Daniel, 30–31
Shays' Rebellion, 30–31
Sheridan, Philip, 59
Sherman, Roger, 32
Sherman, William T., 59
Shiite Muslims, 357
Sierra Club
    501(c)4 group, 134
    litigation used by, 134
    profile of, 122
Signing statements
    defined, 267
    by George W. Bush, 268
Singapore, 190
Single-issue interest groups, 131
Single-member district, 156
Sixteenth Amendment, 244
Sixth Amendment, 42, 89
Slander, 82
Slaves/slavery
    Civil War and, 58
    Constitutional Convention and, 33,
        34, 36
    Constitution of United States and, 33,
        34, 36
    Declaration of Independence, 36
    as presidential election issue, 144
    Republican Party and, 144
    three-fifths compromise, 33
Small Business Administration, 290, 299
Smith, Al, 258
Smith Act, 81
Social conflict, 3
Social conservatives, 16
Social contract, 10
Socialist, 17
Socialist Party, 158
Socialist Workers Party, 158
Social networking, as political force in
    Indonesia, 212
Social Security Administration (SSA), 290
Socioeconomic factors, voting behavior
    and, 180–185

Sodomy laws, 111, 306
Soft money, 133, 203
Solidarity, 151
Solidary incentive, 123
Solid South, 183
Solis, Hilda, 107
Somalia, 353
Sotomayor, Sonia, 103, 314
Sound bite, 215
Southern Christian Leadership Conference
    (SCLC), 99, 129
South Korea
    jury trials in, 305
    sinking of naval ship, 361
Sovereignty
    Articles of Confederation, 29
    popular, 37
Soviet bloc, 350
Soviet Union. *See also* Russia
    arms race and deterrence, 352
    breakup of, 346
    Cold War and, 350–353
    collapse of, 38
    Cuban missile crisis, 352
    détente and arms control, 352
    dissolution of, 352–353
    Soviet bloc, 350
    Strategic Arms Limitation Treaty
        (SALT I), 352
    World War II, 350
Spain
    Basque separatists terrorism in, 354–355
    constitutional monarchy in, 7
    Madrid commuter train bombing,
        354–355
    national identity cards, 88
    Spanish-American War and, 350
Spanish-American War, 350
Speaker of the House, 102, 238–239
    presidential succession and, 277
Speaker *pro tempore* of the House, 239
Special districts, number of, in U.S., 51
Special election, 189
Special interest groups. *See* Interest groups
Speech
    commercial, 81–82
    libel and slander, 82
    obscene, 82–83
    seditious, 81
    symbolic, 79
    unprotected, 82–83
Speech, freedom of, 42, 72, 79–84
    early restrictions on expression, 81
    government entities and, 71
    libel and slander, 82
    limited protection for commercial
        speech, 81–82
    obscenity, 82–83
    for students, 83–84
    symbolic speech, 79
    unprotected speech, 82–83
Spence, Gerry, 84
Spin, 219
Spin doctors, 219
Splinter party, 158
Stalin, Joseph, 7
Stamp Act, 26
Standing committees, 240–241
Standing to sue, 308–309
Stanton, Elizabeth Cady, 101
Stare decisis, 305, 322
State, Department of, 273
    foreign policymaking and, 348
    original size of, 282
    principle duties of, 286
State-centered federalism, 61
State Children's Health Insurance Program
    (SCHIP), 331

W

Wage discrimination, 103–104
Walker, Vaughn R., 318
Wallace, George, 158
Wallace, Henry, Progressive Party, 158
Wall Street Journal, 215
War
    Congressional power to declare, 269,
      270, 349
    preemptive, 356
    preventive, 356
War, Department of, original size of, 282
Ward, 153
War on terrorism. *See also* September 11,
    2001 terrorist attacks
    al Qaeda, 355–357
    ban on torture, 268
    Bush and, 356
    executive privilege claimed by Bush, 272
    federalism and, 63–64
    foreign terrorist networks, 355
    invasion of Iraq in 2003, 356
    local or regional, 354–355
    openness of government afterwards, 299
    Operation TIPS, 87
    presidential power and, 272
    state-sponsored, 355
    types of terrorism, 354–355
    U.S. response to 9/11, 356–358
War Powers Resolution, 270, 349
Warrants, 89
Warren, Earl, 97, 314, 317
Warren Court, 317
Washington, D.C., Congressional
    representation of, 192
Washington, George, 27, 30, 193, 272
    farewell address, 349
    powers of president under, 265
    president's role in foreign affairs and,
      269
    on slavery, 36
Washington Post, 210, 215, 224
Waterboarding, 90

Watergate scandal, 263, 272
Weapons of mass destruction
    defined, 356
    Iran as emerging threat, 361, 362
    Iraq and, 356
    media and fact checking prior to Iraq
      War, 213
    North Korea's nuclear program,
      360–361
Web. *See* Internet
Webb, Jim, 227
Webster, Daniel, 143
Welfare
    cooperative federalism and, 60–61
    reform, 155
    as devolution, 62
Welfare Reform Act, policy implementation,
    329
Wesberry v. Sanders, 233
West Germany, Berlin Wall, 352
West Wing, 219
Whig Party, 143–144
Whips, 239–240
Whistle-Blower Protection act, 296
Whistleblowers, 296–297
White House, 256
White House chief of staff, 273, 274
White House Office, 274
White primary, 175
Whitman, Meg, 194
Wilkow, Andrew, 220
Will and Grace, 219
William the Conqueror, 304
Wilson, Woodrow, 101, 145, 258, 264–265,
    272
    election of 1912, 159
    moral idealism and, 350
    neutrality policy, 350
    as progressive, 16
    Treaty of Versailles, 263
Wind power, 335
Winner-take-all system, 156, 191
Wolf v. Colorado, 74
Women
    civil rights of, 101–105

    feminist movement, 102
      World War I and, 101–102
    in federal office, 102–103
    feminist movement, 102
    glass ceiling, 104
    in politics today, 102–103
    rights of, in Afghanistan, 12
    sexual harassment, 105
    voting behavior and, 182
    voting rights, 101–102, 175
    wage discrimination, 103–104
    World War I and women's rights, 101–102
Wood, Gordon S., 36
Woodward, Bob, 358
Workplace
    religious practices in, 79
    sexual harassment, 105
    women in, 103–105
World Trade Center. *See also* September 11,
    2001 terrorist attacks
    terrorist attack on, in 2001, 353
World Trade Organization (WTO), China's
    membership in, 362
World War I
    neutrality policy, 350
    women's rights and, 101–102
World War II
    attack on Pearl Harbor, 350
    dropping atomic bomb, 270, 350
    formation of public opinion, 167
Wounded Knee, South Dakota, 109
Wright, Jeremiah, 227–228, 267
Write-in candidate, 193
Writ of *certiorari,* 311
Writ of *habeas corpus,* 72
Wyden, Ron, 203

Y

Yeltsin, Boris, 353
Yom Kippur War, 358
YouTube, 227